THE BOOK OF NRL LISTS

The Slattery Media Group Pty Ltd
1 Albert St, Richmond
Victoria, Australia, 3121

Text © Will Evans and Nick Tedeschi 2014
Design © The Slattery Media Group 2014
First published by The Slattery Media Group Pty Ltd 2014

All rights reserved. No part of this publication may be reproduced, stored in a retrieval system or transmitted in any form or by any means without the prior written permission of the copyright owner. Inquiries should be made to the publisher.

National Library of Australia Cataloguing-in-Publication entry
Author: Tedeschi, Nick, author.
Title: The book of NRL lists / Nick Tedeschi; Will Evans
ISBN: 9780992379124 (paperback)
Subjects: Rugby League football--Australia.
              Rugby League football players--Australia.
Dewey Number: 798.4010994

Group Publisher: Geoff Slattery
Editor: Bronwyn Wilkie
Creative Director: Kate Slattery
Design: Beck Haskins, Franky Demaria

Printed and bound in Australia by Griffin Press

To the best of our knowledge, the information in this guide was correct at the time of publication. The opinions are those of the authors.

Every effort has been made to verify the source of quoted material in the text. Inquiries should be made to the publisher.

slatterymedia.com

WILL EVANS & NICK TEDESCHI

THE BOOK OF
NRL
LISTS

slattery
MEDIA GROUP

visit *slatterymedia.com*

"To my beautiful fiancée Louise, who makes every day better. I couldn't have written this without your constant love and support. You are amazing."
– NICK TEDESCHI

"To Gramma and Grampa—equal No.1 in my list of absolute legends. Thank you for your many years of love and guidance, RIP."
– WILL EVANS

THE BOOK OF NRL LISTS

CONTENTS

FIRST GRADE REGULAR SEASON

Greatest regular season matches	9
Greatest comebacks	12
Biggest first grade upsets	14
Miracle finishes	17
Best individual performances	20

FINALS

Greatest finals matches	23
Greatest Grand Finals	26
Greatest playoff matches	29
Greatest finals comebacks	31
Best finals finishes	34
Best individual finals performances	36
Worst individual finals performances	38
Best Grand Final performances	41
Worst individual Grand Final performances	43
Unlucky to miss out on the Clive Churchill Medal	46
Greatest finals tries	47
Greatest Grand Final tries	50

REPRESENTATIVE MATCHES

Best Origin matches	53
Best Origin finishes	56
Greatest State of Origin tries	59
Best Test matches	61
Best Test finishes	64
Best Test tries	67

THE CLUBS

Adelaide Rams	70
Annandale	72
Balmain Tigers	73
Brisbane Broncos	81
Canberra Raiders	91
Canterbury-Bankstown Bulldogs	98
Cronulla Sharks	106
Cumberland	115
Eastern Suburbs/Sydney Roosters	117
Glebe	127
Gold Coast Giants/Seagulls/Chargers	129
Gold Coast Titans	136
Hunter Mariners	142

Illawarra Steelers	144
Manly-Warringah Sea Eagles/ Northern Eagles	152
Melbourne Storm	160
New Zealand Warriors	168
Newcastle	178
Newcastle Knights	179
Newtown	187
North Queensland Cowboys	195
North Sydney Bears	202
Parramatta Eels	211
Penrith Panthers	218
South Queensland Crushers	227
South Sydney Rabbitohs	229
St George Dragons	236
St George Illawarra Dragons	245
University	252
Western Reds	254
Western Suburbs Magpies	256
Wests Tigers	263
Club rivalries	271
12-month turnarounds for the better	274
12-month turnarounds for the worse	277
Late season rallies	280
Late season fade-outs	283
Remarkable one-week turnarounds	285
Greatest clubmen	287

THE PLAYERS

Best players	290
Best individual seasons	295
Greatest captains	297
Young captains	300
Best Indigenous players	302
Greatest families	304
Ageless stars	307
Prodigies	309
Best rookie seasons	312

Forward pack enforcers	315
Backline enforcers	317
Courageous performances	320
12-month turnarounds for the better	323
12-month turnarounds for the worse	326
Individual rivalries	330
Individual streaks	332
Ironmen	334
Textbook defenders	336
Late bloomers	338
Goalkickers	341
Goalkicking forwards	343
Left-footed goalkickers	345
Greatest field-goal exponents	347
Pointscoring feats	349
Tryscoring feats	351
Tryscoring droughts	353
Unlikely tryscoring champs	355
Speedsters	357
Premature retirements	359
Out of retirement	361
Shock exits	363
Unfulfilled potential	365
Entertainers	367
Enigmas	368
Maligned players	371
Unlikely heroes	374
Unique names	377
Smiths	379
Heart-throbs	381
Best hair	382
Beards	384
Moustaches	385
Redheads	388
Dally M Awards dominators	390
Best sevens players	393

THE POSITIONS

Greatest fullbacks	395
Greatest wingers	398
Greatest centres	401
Greatest five-eighths	404
Greatest halfbacks	407
Locks	410
Greatest second-rowers	413
Greatest props	416
Hookers	419
Greatest utilities	422
Greatest bench-warmers	425
Best positional switches	427

ALL SHAPES AND SIZES

Biggest players	430
Tallest players	432
Smallest players	434

SELECTIONS

Left-field first grade selections	437
One-game wonders—first grade	440
Grand final bolters	441
Origin bolters	444
One-game wonders—State of Origin	446
Best not to play Origin	448
International bolters	450
One-game wonders—Tests	452
Controversial international omissions	455
Best not to represent Australia	458
Snubbed after early representative rewards	460
Eligibility controversies	463

INJURIES

Injury-prone players	466
Worst injuries	469
Bizarre injuries	470

RECRUITMENT

Best recruits	475
Worst recruits	477
One-season stints	480
Successful mid-season transfers	483
Contract wrangles and backflips	485

THE BAD AND THE UGLY

Blunders	489
Bad boys	492
Off-field menaces	494
Violent matches	495
Longest suspensions	498
Biting incidents	500
Gouging incidents	502
Spitting incidents	505
Unlucky send-offs	507

CONVERTS

Best converts—Union to League	510
Worst converts—Union to League	513
Best converts—League to Union	515
Worst converts—League to Union	518
Rugby League and AFL	521
Rugby League and cricket	524
Rugby League and athletics	526
Rugby League and boxing	529
Rugby League and other sports	532

DEBUTS

Best first grade debuts	535
Unfortunate first grade debuts	537
Best Origin debuts	539
Worst Origin debuts	542
Best Test debuts	544
Worst Test debuts	545

THE BIG PLAYS

Greatest premiership tries	548
Greatest intercept tries	551
Golden point plays	553
Field goals	555
Conversions	557
Penalty goals	559
Costly errors	561
Worst missed goals	563

THE COACHES

Greatest coaches	566
Greatest coaching achievements	570
Coaching comebacks	572
Long coaching tenures	574
Short coaching tenures	577
Ill-fated ventures into coaching	579
Coaching blow-ups	582

REFEREES

Greatest referees	585
Worst refereeing performances	588
Biggest refereeing blunders	591
Referee handling	593

THE RULES

Best rule changes	596
Worst rule changes	599

AROUND THE WORLD

Britain's greatest players	601
New Zealand's greatest players	603
France's greatest players	606
Papua New Guinea's greatest players	609
Greatest Pacific Islands players	611
Best British imports	614
Worst British imports	616
Greatest Kiwi imports	618
Best Australian exports to Britain	621
Aussie flops in Britain	623
Average in Australia, brilliant in Britain	625
Greatest touring teams	628
Tour match upsets	631

RUGBY LEAGUE MISCELLANY

Bizarre matches	634
Incredible thrashings	636
Team streaks	638
Iconic grounds	640
Coincidences	642
Scandals	645
Rugby League and gambling	651
Rugby League and drugs	653
Rugby League jailbirds	656
Rugby league and politics	660
Rugby League and music	663
Rugby League and movies and television	665
Iconic fashion items	668

ABOUT THE AUTHORS ... 670
ACKNOWLEDGMENTS ... 671

Chapter 1

FIRST GRADE REGULAR SEASON

GREATEST REGULAR SEASON MATCHES

1. 2007: Sydney Roosters 31—New Zealand 31

The resurgent Sydney Roosters and the finals-bound New Zealand Warriors fought out a golden point draw that was heralded as one of the modern era's greatest matches late in 2007 at the SFS. The Warriors fought back from 0-16 down to lead 18-16 at halftime, and had charged to a 30-18 lead by the time their centre Simon Mannering was controversially sin-binned. The Roosters scored twice to level the scores while the Warriors were a man short before Braith Anasta nailed a 38-metre field goal to nudge the home side in front in the dying minutes. But the Warriors regained possession from a one-on-one strip and five-eighth Michael Witt landed an equalising one-pointer with 17 seconds on the clock. The frantic, thrilling golden point period failed to produce a scorer and the classic encounter fittingly finished 31-all.

2. 1926: Newtown 25—South Sydney 24

Newtown staged the first great comeback in premiership history in 1926. Down to 12 men after losing a player to injury and with no replacements allowed, Newtown trailed premiers Souths 18-0 in the late season SCG clash. But five tries—all converted by fullback Tommy Ellis—catapulted the Bluebags to a 25-21 advantage. The victory was not yet assured, however. A late try brought the Rabbitohs back to within a point, but captain Alf 'Smacker' Blair was unsuccessful with the conversion attempt and Newtown secured a celebrated victory 25-24.

3. 1985: Canterbury 20—Balmain 18

Defending premiers Canterbury and emerging force Balmain staged one of the great games of the 1980s at Leichhardt Oval. A 90-metre intercept try to Bulldogs winger Peter Mortimer—after a thrilling chase by the passer, Tigers halfback Scott Gale—was the highlight of a ferocious first half, but sharp goalkicking by Ross Conlon saw Balmain lead 12-10 at the break. Tries to Paul Langmack and Steve Mortimer set up a six-point advantage for Canterbury before Gale produced a breathtaking 60-metre individual try featuring a trademark kick and chase. The Bulldogs rebuffed a string of attacking forays by the exciting young Tigers to hang on for a two-point victory.

4. 1996: Sydney City 12—Brisbane 10

Heavyweights Brisbane and Sydney City marked Monday night football's return in 1996 with a gripping battle featuring some of the era's finest tries. Broncos youngsters Darren Lockyer and Robbie Ross scored superb four-pointers in the opening half, while a scintillating individual try to flamboyant Roosters winger Peter Jorgensen set up a 10-4 scoreline at halftime. The second half remained try-less until an equally sensational effort by Sydney City's other winger and fellow Rugby Union convert Darren Junee, who scored in the corner after a dazzling chip-and-chase. The game was destined for a draw until Brisbane prop Andrew Gee was penalised for an incorrect tap restart on his own 20-metre line in the final minute. Roosters sharpshooter Ivan Cleary slotted an easy penalty goal after fulltime to win an amazing encounter 12-10.

5. 2005: North Queensland 26—Manly 24

North Queensland's 26-24 defeat of Manly at Brookvale Oval late in 2005 was undoubtedly one of the most entertaining and topsy-turvy clashes of the NRL era. The Sea Eagles surged to an 18-6 halftime lead, but the visitors clawed back to trail by just two points before hitting the front with one of the great regular season tries. Winger Ty Williams accepted a pass deep in the Cowboys' in-goal area, raced out of danger, beat the challenge of Manly fullback Brett Stewart (who earlier scored a sizzling try of his own) and dotted down for a 108-metre special. A try and conversion to Sea Eagles winger Chris Hicks looked to have grabbed victory for the home side with two minutes remaining, but the Cowboys reclaimed the ball from a short kick-off and an Aaron Payne grubber to the Manly in-goal allowed Williams to collect his third try with only centimetres and seconds to spare.

6. 2002: Canterbury 22—Newcastle 21

A surging comeback from the Bulldogs in front of a parochial Newcastle crowd was capped by one of the most famous pressure kicks in premiership history. At the tail-end of a 17-match winning streak in 2002, the Bulldogs trailed an Andrew Johns-inspired Knights side 0-19 at halftime. Bulldogs five-eighth Braith Anasta sparked the revival—two of his kicks led to tries, while a superb long pass resulted in another. A no-try ruling against workhorse forward Steve Reardon with four minutes left appeared to cruel the Bulldogs' comeback with the score at 21-16. But when the Knights ran out of defenders in the final minute, Bulldogs fullback Luke Patten slid over in the corner to leave Hazem El Masri with an opportunity to win the match after the siren. Setting the ball up metres from a baying pro-Knights crowd and with a swirling breeze to contend with, 'El Magic' stepped up and curled a spine-tingling conversion through the posts to snatch a legendary victory.

7. 1976: Western Suburbs 17—South Sydney 13

Lidcombe Oval played host to one of the most memorable club clashes of the blood-and-thunder 1970s, with foundation rivals Wests and Souths producing a ferocious and enthralling duel early in '76. Graeme O'Grady and Geoff Foster scored for the Magpies, while Kiwi centre Bernie Lowther and barnstorming winger Terry Fahey kept the Rabbitohs in the hunt at 12-8 in arrears with time ticking down in the second stanza. Pugnacious Souths hooker George Piggins propelled his side into the lead with a famous individual try, powering past a posse of Wests defenders to score beside the posts inside the final few minutes. But the Magpies worked the ball downfield and Foster crossed for his second try, and the match-winner, in the dying stages to send the 17,425-strong crowd into a frenzy.

8. 1960: Balmain 19—St George 15

An improving Balmain side hosted four-time premiers St George at the halfway mark of the 1960 season—and pulled off a huge upset courtesy of captain Keith Barnes' mighty boot. Three unanswered tries saw the Tigers race to a shock 13-0 lead after 22 minutes, while they held a commanding 10-point advantage at the break. But two trademark individual tries to gun centre Reg Gasnier and a three-pointer to wily skipper Ken Kearney pegged the Saints—who were without several stars appearing for Sydney against France—back to 15-all. Barnes kicked a famous 58-yard penalty goal with four minutes remaining, however, and slotted another goal to seal the result, delighting the Leichhardt Oval throng.

9. 1990: Brisbane 22—Canberra 20

In what then shaped as a Grand Final preview, a sell-out Lang Park crowd witnessed a top-shelf clash between competition front-runners Brisbane and Canberra.

The Broncos raced out to an 18-2 lead after 22 minutes, with Kevin Walters integral, before the Raiders clawed back with three tries to lead 20-18 midway through the second half on the back of a titanic performance by captain Mal Meninga. But the home side rallied and snatched a 22-20 victory via a brilliant 50-metre try to rookie fullback Paul Hauff, giving Brisbane the outright premiership lead.

10. 2006: St George Illawarra 8—Parramatta 1

The Dragons and Eels played out one of the most bizarre and dramatic matches imaginable midway through 2006 in treacherous conditions at Kogarah Oval. The combatants waged an engrossing battle in the wet, with neither side able to land on the scoreboard. Just as the second scoreless draw in premiership history loomed, Parramatta five-eighth John Morris slotted a field goal—creating the first 1-0 scoreline in a match for 17 years. But Saints halfback and captain Ben Hornby drilled back-to-back field goals inside the final five minutes to snare a 2-1 lead. On the stroke of fulltime, Eels halfback Jeremy Smith stopped after feeding a scrum when he heard referee Sean Hampstead's whistle. But Hampstead was signalling time on, and Dragons centre Matt Cooper scooped up the loose ball for the match-sealing try. A frustrated Smith shoved Hampstead in the back and later received a four-week suspension for contrary conduct, adding a confounding postscript to a crazy night.

GREATEST COMEBACKS

1. 26 points—North Queensland v Penrith, 1998

North Queensland had achieved little in its infant years, making its comeback against the Panthers at Penrith Stadium all the more incredible. The Cowboys had won just 13 games in their first three seasons and recorded their most famous victory up to that point in Round 12 of the '98 season when coming back from a 0-26 halftime deficit to win 38-26. Sparked by a Noa Nadruku hat-trick and a double to Andrew Dunemann, the Cowboys were unstoppable in the second stanza. Both sides missed the 10-team playoffs.

2. 26 points—Penrith v New Zealand Warriors, 2009

New Zealand led 32-6 at Penrith Stadium against the Panthers after 53 minutes before the home side staged an extraordinary comeback to snatch a draw. Warriors centre Joel Moon had scored four tries and New Zealand seemed to have the two points in its grasp, but Shane Elford, Luke Walsh, Frank Puletua and Michael Jennings scored tries and Michael Gordon slotted a penalty in the dying moments to send the game to golden point. Neither team could break the deadlock and the two sides—who would both miss the finals—split the spoils.

3. 24 points—St George Illawarra v Manly, 2004
Fifth-placed St George Illawarra trailed 10-34 at Kogarah to third-last Manly in the second-last round of the 2004 season before staging a remarkable comeback. On a cold and wet day, Manly led 24-4 at the break and had a 24-point lead with just 23 minutes remaining before its defence capitulated and St George Illawarra ran in five unanswered tries. Nathan Blacklock scored a double, Matt Cooper brought the game to within four points with 13 minutes remaining and Mark Riddell converted a Justin Poore try 15 metres in from touch with two minutes on the clock to cap an incredible riposte.

4. 24 points—South Sydney v North Queensland, 2008
South Sydney and North Queensland both endured shocking 2008 seasons—but the Bunnies would at least have one of the great comebacks to reflect on fondly. Souths trailed 4-28 after 52 minutes in Townsville before three tries in less than 10 minutes brought the scores to 28-22 with 19 remaining. Luke Capewell then scored with six on the clock before an Issac Luke conversion from the sideline levelled the scores. Halfback Chris Sandow slotted the decisive field goal in the final minute to seal a memorable win.

5. 24 points—Wests Tigers v Newcastle, 2001
Second-year club Wests Tigers was anchored to the bottom of the ladder late in 2001 while Newcastle was on its way to premiership success, when the Tigers sprang one of the biggest comebacks in premiership history. Behind 0-24 after 26 minutes at Campbelltown, the Tigers fought their way back to win 36-32 against the Andrew Johns-less Knights. Ben Kennedy scored a hat-trick for Newcastle but it wasn't enough, with Joel Caine's haul of 16 points getting the Tigers home. Kevin McGuinness, in his comeback match from a drug suspension, scored the winning try with nine minutes remaining.

6. 23 points—Penrith v Wests Tigers, 2000
Penrith Stadium has been the scene of many great comebacks, and the come-from-behind bug struck again in 2000 when the Panthers overcame a 23-point deficit with just 27 minutes remaining to overrun premiership newcomers Wests Tigers. Wayne Pearce's Tigers led 31-8 before an inspired Panthers comeback saw them win 32-31. Shane Elford crossed out wide, Craig Gower darted over from dummy-half and Tony Puletua scored twice while Chris Hicks was perfect with the boot, nailing the winner from near the sideline with nine minutes to play.

7. 22 points—Parramatta v Penrith, 2010
Penrith led 22-0 at home against rivals Parramatta in 2010 before a blistering second-half performance from Jarryd Hayne spurred the Eels to a dramatic comeback win. Krisnan Inu and Jonathan Wright scored doubles, one of which was set up by Hayne, who also put Fuifui Moimoi over the line. The decisive moment was a spectacular solo try from Hayne, who caught a bomb on his own 10 metres, evaded four defenders and went the length of the field, putting the Eels eight in front as they went on to win 34-28.

8. 22 points—Melbourne v Cronulla, 2003
Cronulla jumped to a 22-0 lead against Melbourne at Shark Park in the opening round of the 2003 season, with Chris Anderson looking set to record an easy win against his former team. He would instead endure a heartbreaking loss and a defeat that would serve as a metaphor for the Sharks and Anderson for the rest of the year. Centre Steve Bell scored a hat-trick, Matt Geyer poached a double, and debutant Billy Slater crossed for his first career try in the epic 36-32 comeback win. Geyer's second proved the winner inside the last five minutes.

9. 22 points—Parramatta v Canberra, 1987
In the greatest comeback of the pre-NRL era, Parramatta overcame a 0-22 deficit against eventual Grand Finalists Canberra at Parramatta Stadium in Round 9, 1987. Mal Meninga, Matthew Corkery, Ivan Henjak and Peter Jackson all scored for the Raiders in the first half, but after a brilliant second half that saw Bob Lindner score a double and Neil Hunt, Don Price and Ken Wolffe all dot down, the Eels saluted 30-22.

10. 20 points—Manly v Penrith, 2005
Manly trailed 6-26 with just 28 minutes on the clock in its Round 12, 2005 clash with Penrith at Brookvale before a magical come-from-behind victory. The result made it four straight losses for Penrith, leaving its season in tatters after a title two years prior and a prelim spot the year before. Inspired by lock forward Ben Kennedy, Michael Witt scored a double and Scott Donald sealed the win in Manly's greatest-ever comeback.

BIGGEST FIRST GRADE UPSETS

1. Round 12, 2002: Brisbane 28—Wests Tigers 14
The 'Baby Broncos' defeat of Wests Tigers in '02 ranks as one of the most unbelievable boilovers of the modern era. Decimated by the absence of nine players on Origin duty (plus coach Wayne Bennett) and another six first-choice players on the injured list,

Brisbane was forced to pick a whopping six NRL debutants, while a further three had played less than three games. The Broncos, who were prepared by assistant Craig Bellamy, fielded five teenagers in a line-up with an average age of just 21. But the Shane Walker-captained side led 6-2 at halftime and powered away to a stirring 28-14 success at Campbelltown Stadium. The Broncos' first-timers included hooker Nathan Friend and gangly winger Scott Minto.

2. Round 14, 1958: Parramatta 19—St George 18
Although St George was missing several stars on Test duty, the two-time premiers were expected to extend their 12-match winning streak late in 1958, coming up against a Parramatta side that had recorded just one win all season and was on its way to the third of six straight wooden spoons. But the struggling Eels carved out a famous victory at Cumberland Oval, scoring three tries to the Saints' two and holding off a late fightback with a heroic defensive effort in the final 10 minutes.

3. Round 13, 1995: Western Reds 11—Manly 8
A whitewash loomed when premiership front-runners Manly travelled to Perth to take on the bottom-placed Western Reds midway through 1996. The Sea Eagles were on a nine-match winning streak while the ragtag Reds had lost their previous nine outings, but the form guide went out the window at a rain-swept WACA Ground. Manly led 8-4 at the break after Steve Menzies scored the only try of the first half, but a converted touchdown to big British centre Barrie-Jon Mather and a late field goal by unlikely stand-in captain Julian O'Neill sealed an 11-8 result.

4. Round 4, 1967: Penrith 24—St George 12
The most significant result of Penrith's inaugural '67 campaign came at the official opening of the club's home ground, with the Panthers rolling 11-time premiers St George 24-12. All-time greats Johnny Raper and Brian Clay scored tries for the Dragons, but the underdogs piled on four tries and winger Bob Landers slotted six goals to secure a spectacular win in front of 12,201 delirious fans at Penrith Park. It was one of just five wins for the Panthers as they finished second last, while St George eventually claimed yet another minor premiership.

5. Round 3, 1993: Parramatta 12—Brisbane 8
A crowd of 51,517 turned out for Brisbane's first match at new home ground ANZ Stadium early in 1993—the biggest attendance for a non-finals match since 1966—but unfancied Parramatta, second last the previous season, spoiled the defending premiers' party with a stunning 12-8 boilover. Broncos fullback Julian O'Neill scored the opening try, but a belated four-pointer in the 62nd minute to 19-year-old Eels centre Michael Buettner, who also slotted four crucial goals from as many attempts, sent the throng home unhappy.

6. Round 21, 1988: Western Suburbs 23—Manly 20

Last-placed Wests produced the shock result of '88, overturning a big deficit to roll defending champs Manly at Orana Park in the penultimate round. The Magpies trailed 8-20 at halftime, but muscled up in the second stanza and posted 15 unanswered points to secure a mighty win. Veteran lock Ian Schubert was the star, combining non-stop effort with five goals and a field goal, while unheralded players Wayne Simonds, Allan Fallah and Danny Peacock made outstanding contributions against a fourth-placed Sea Eagles outfit fielding seven internationals.

7. Round 14, 1922: University 7—North Sydney 6

Defending premiers North Sydney, one of the great club combinations of all time, was stunned by reigning wooden spooners University on the way to a second straight title in 1922. Norths had lost just two games all season to sit atop the ladder, but tries to legendary wingers Harold Horder and Cec Blinkhorn were not enough to get over the all-amateur University side. Jim Flattery scored the only try for the 'Students', while Hector Courtenay booted two goals in the momentous one-point victory.

8. Round 13, 1914: Annandale 16—Eastern Suburbs 14

Annandale achieved little success during its 11-season existence, winning just 25 of its 153 games from 1910 to 1920. But the 'Dales staged one of the great upsets of the premiership's formative years during their 1914 wooden-spoon season, downing three-time defending champs Eastern Suburbs 16-14 at Wentworth Park in the penultimate round. It was Annandale's only win of the season, while the staggering result saw the Tricolours slip to fourth place.

9. Round 20, 2012: Parramatta 16—Melbourne 10

Parramatta coach Stephen Kearney announced he would be quitting his post during the week leading up to the clash with competition leaders Melbourne, but the flailing Eels sent him out a winner with a remarkable 16-10 upset. Displaying defensive qualities that may have saved Kearney's job if they had been produced on a regular basis, the Eels led 10-6 at halftime and held on stoically before man-of-the-match Nathan Hindmarsh scored the match-winner in the 70th minute. Melbourne coach Craig Bellamy—Kearney's former mentor—labelled his side's effort as "pathetic", and Brad Arthur took the reins at Parramatta for the rest of the season.

10. Round 22, 1997: South Queensland 39—Western Suburbs 18

Western Suburbs headed into the final round of the '97 ARL premiership needing only a win to secure the last finals berth. Their opponents: the last-placed, financially stricken South Queensland Crushers, who were playing their final match before shutting their doors. But the Crushers produced the finest performance of their short history at Suncorp Stadium, romping away to a club-record 39-18 victory as young fullback Clinton Schifcofske racked up 18 points. With everything to play for and captain Paul Langmack making his 300th first grade appearance, the Magpies were dreadful; the humiliating loss left the club one point adrift of the playoffs and gifted a maiden finals appearance to the Gold Coast.

MIRACLE FINISHES

1. 2008: Brisbane 30—Parramatta 26
A seesawing 2008 clash between Brisbane and Parramatta at Suncorp Stadium appeared destined for extra-time at 26-all as the Broncos played the ball on halfway with only seconds remaining. A loose dummy-half pass prevented Darren Lockyer from having a long-range field-goal shot as the siren sounded, but the captain skirted the Eels' defence and chip-kicked towards the left-hand touchline. The ball sat up for young winger Denan Kemp, who scooted 30 metres to score in the corner as he was tackled by Joel Reddy and Eric Grothe, winning the match and equalling the club record of four tries in a match in the process.

2. 2012: Sydney Roosters 24—South Sydney 20
Archrivals Souths and Sydney Roosters produced two of the most stunning last-minute match-winners of all time in the same season, with each club stealing a miraculous victory over the other in 2012. In the opening round, the Roosters trailed 12-20 but clung to a sliver of hope when Jared Waerea-Hargreaves crashed over with two minutes and 20 seconds to go. From the restart, the Roosters spread the ball from their 30-metre line on the third tackle. Mitch Aubusson found space and passed inside on halfway to backrower Boyd Cordner, who kicked ahead. Roosters fullback Anthony Minichiello outpaced the cover to latch on to the ball and score with 20 seconds remaining.

3. 2012: South Sydney 24—Sydney Roosters 22
In a carbon copy of the opening-round match with the clubs' roles reversed towards the end of the 2012 season, Souths seemed headed for defeat when Mitchell Pearce scored with five minutes left to put the Roosters ahead 22-12. But Chris McQueen sent Nathan Merritt over to finish a 50-metre movement with less than two minutes on the clock, setting up another—even more unlikely—grandstand finish. The timepiece read 79:12 when the Roosters restarted, but Dave Taylor veered wide after accepting the kick-off and passed to McQueen, who strode up to halfway and linked

again with Merritt. The winger found Issac Luke, and the hooker flung the ball back for Adam Reynolds to scoop it up and dive over next to the posts, finishing a 95-metre match-winning try.

4. 2003: Brisbane 22—South Sydney 20
A rampaging performance by skipper Gorden Tallis saved Brisbane from an embarrassing early season loss to lowly Souths in 2003. Tallis had scored a powerful second-half try in an attempt to inspire his lacklustre teammates, but the Rabbitohs looked set to produce a major boilover when they led 20-12 in the final 10 minutes. Tallis intervened again, putting through a superb grubber kick that took a freakish bounce and resulted in a try to Michael De Vere. Souths held out a late Brisbane attacking raid and only had to ruck the ball out for the few remaining seconds to claim a famous two-point victory—but Tallis was intent on producing a trifecta of big plays. Reliable prop Paul Stringer carted the ball forward off his own line before Tallis wrenched it free in a one-on-one strip. Shaun Berrigan swung the ball wide for Brent Tate to score his second try in the corner and secure one of the NRL's great escapes, 22-20.

5. 2001: St George Illawarra 27—Wests Tigers 22
The Dragons trailed the Tigers by a point inside the final minute at Leichhardt Oval in 2001, when a cut-out pass found prolific winger Nathan Blacklock near the sideline with space in front of him and 75 metres to travel. Blacklock scorched over the halfway line, chipped over Tigers fullback Joel Caine and regathered to race away for a try—his third of the afternoon—regarded simultaneously as one of the finest individual tries and one of the greatest match-winning tries of all time.

6. 2006: Melbourne 16—Canterbury 12
Melbourne's 11-match winning streak at Olympic Park was in jeopardy when it trailed the Bulldogs 12-6 late in the second half of a mid-season encounter with its fellow contenders. But a superb pass from second-rower Ryan Hoffman sent Jake Webster over in the corner with a couple of minutes remaining. Cameron Smith's conversion attempt hit the post, however, leaving Melbourne two points adrift. In the final minute of play, Storm halfback Cooper Cronk put in a beautifully weighted cross-field kick from inside his own half that was picked up by a wide-ranging Hoffman on the first bounce. Despite the attention of Bulldogs Trent Cutler and Luke Patten, Hoffman again found Webster with a brilliant one-handed pass, and the Kiwi winger powered away for the match-winner in the shadows of fulltime.

7. 2010: New Zealand Warriors 20—Sydney Roosters 18
In rainy, freezing conditions at Christchurch's AMI Stadium, the Sydney Roosters led the Warriors 18-8 with five minutes to go, but a powerhouse try to Manu Vatuvei kept

the Warriors' hopes alive. Young winger Kevin Locke had already scored a memorable first-half double, and toed a Lance Hohaia grubber kick ahead from near halfway in the final minute of play. Displaying electrifying pace, Locke narrowly won the race to the ball ahead of Roosters speedster Phil Graham and planted the ball as his torso was simultaneously bent around the goalpost. Replays showed Locke had successfully scored the gutsy leveller, while James Maloney added the simple conversion after the siren to win a thrilling encounter 20-18. Locke's bravery cost him two weeks in the injury ward, but earned a place in club folklore.

8. 1998: Auckland 24—Melbourne 21
Brett Kimmorley appeared to wrap up a tense contest at Melbourne's Olympic Park with a field goal two minutes from fulltime, giving the home side a 21-18 advantage over Auckland. But on the last play of the game, the Warriors swung the ball from one sideline to the other before Stacey Jones launched a bomb after the siren sounded. Despite a horde of Storm players waiting at the kick's destination, the Warriors managed to bat the ball back, and centre Nigel Vagana fired it out for an unmarked Tony Tatupu to score. After an agonising wait for the video referee's decision as he dissected the myriad fumbles and rebounds in the movement, the try was awarded, handing victory to Auckland—a rare highlight in a dismal season for the club.

9. 2011: Penrith 23—Parramatta 22
Parramatta led Penrith 22-16 in the dying stages of captain Nathan Hindmarsh's 300th match, when Jarryd Hayne attempted to put in a clearing last-tackle kick for the Eels. The ball rebounded off a Panthers player and was cleaned up by Luke Burt, who took the tackle 10 metres out from his own line with 10 seconds remaining. But the referee ruled the ball had not been charged down and ordered a turnover, controversially calling time-off. The Panthers played the ball with two seconds on the clock, desperately flinging it from one sideline to the other and back again before it landed in Michael Jennings' hands. The quicksilver centre evaded several Eels defenders, then put in a grubber kick that was pounced on by Penrith fullback Lachlan Coote—20 seconds after the siren had sounded. Travis Burns' conversion locked up the scores and halfback Luke Walsh's field goal with four minutes of golden point left secured an extraordinary win for the Panthers.

10. 1999: Newcastle 22—St George Illawarra 20
The scorer of the most famous last-gasp try in Grand Final history reprised his match-winning role less than two years later in a dramatic Newcastle victory in 1999 at the SFS. St George Illawarra looked to have snatched a late victory in a seesawing Round 24 clash against the Knights when hooker Nathan Brown crossed for a try with three minutes on the clock. Trailing 18-20, the Knights recovered the

ball from a short kick-off. With only seconds remaining, centre Matthew Gidley slipped a brilliant trademark pass to winger Darren Albert, who tiptoed down the sideline to win the game 22-20. Albert scored the buzzer-beating try in the 22-16 Grand Final defeat of Manly at the same venue in 1997, which delivered Newcastle's first premiership.

BEST INDIVIDUAL PERFORMANCES

1. Dave Brown (Eastern Suburbs v Canterbury, 1935)
Eastern Suburbs champion Dave Brown was at the zenith of his marvellous career in 1935, and his finest performance came against new boys Canterbury. In a spectacular display, the bald-headed Eastern Suburbs centre racked up 45 points, a mark that still stands. Brown scored five tries and booted 15 goals in the 87-7 victory, which remains the second-largest win in premiership history.

2. Terry Campese (Canberra v Penrith, 2008)
Canberra five-eighth Terry Campese had an unforgettable day out in 2008 when he notched up 36 points in a 74-12 rout of the Panthers. Campese scored four tries and set up another three, booted 10 goals from 12 attempts, ran for 172 metres, busted the line three times, had three offloads and made 15 tackles to boot. Remarkably, his chance to equal Mal Meninga's post-war record for most points in a game was taken from him by captain Alan Tongue, who—blissfully unaware—gave the final conversion to halfback Marc Herbert.

3. Frank Burge (Glebe v University, 1920)
Great tryscoring forward Frank Burge set the premiership record for most tries in a single match in 1920, a mark that has not been approached nearly a century later. In a 41-0 thumping of University, Burge scored eight tries and booted four goals for good measure. A giant for his time, he ran rampant over the 'Students'.

4. Peter Sterling (Parramatta v St George, 1986)
The opening of Parramatta Stadium in 1986 paid witness to a masterly performance from brilliant halfback Peter Sterling, who led the Eels to a 36-6 thumping of '85 Grand Finalists St George. Sterling set up all four first-half tries, starting with a perfect short ball to Steve Sharp. A subsequent Stan Jurd try from a marvellous Sterling ball was followed by two four-pointers to winger Neil Hunt, the first coming from a Sterling break and the second from a bomb delivered by the No.7. He added to his

try-assist tally in the second half with a stab kick for Brian Jackson to score, while his general kicking game and control earned him a rare *Rugby League Week* rating of 10.

5. Andrew Johns (Newcastle v Melbourne, 2005)

The incomparable Andrew Johns turned in many brilliant performances, but none at premiership level more dominant than his match-winning display against Melbourne in 2005. In a 37-18 win, Johns scored one try and had a hand in the other five while kicking six goals and landing a field goal. The last-placed Knights desperately needed a brilliant showing from Johns and got just that when he scored under the posts after three minutes. A banana kick set up the Knights' second and a short ball their third before he potted a long-range one-pointer on halftime. The second half was no different, with Johns scintillating in an effort rated 10/10 by *Rugby League Week*.

6. Jarryd Hayne (Parramatta v New Zealand Warriors, 2009)

Few players have set the League alight like Jarryd Hayne in the back half of 2009, when the Eels fullback steamed home to win the Dally M Medal and take Parramatta to the Grand Final almost single-handedly. His finest showing came in Round 23 against the Warriors, where his brilliance inspired Parramatta to a 40-4 win. Hayne had a hand in all seven tries, with his most spectacular moment coming when he chipped for himself, collected the ball on the full, drew in numerous defenders and put Eric Grothe over in the corner. A weaving 70-metre run that sent Matt Keating in was not far behind.

7. Brett Kimmorley (Cronulla v Newcastle, 2002)

Brett Kimmorley's rivalry with Andrew Johns was at its peak in the early 2000s, and while Johns often got the upper hand it was Kimmorley who reigned supreme in the Round 22 clash of 2002 between the Sharks and Knights. 'Noddy' scored two tries and kicked 10 goals for a club-record 28 points in the 64-14 demolition at Shark Park. Kimmorley had four try assists to go with his double while he played a role in the five remaining tries, silencing his critics, who were plentiful in his first year with the Sharks.

8. Andrew Johns (Newcastle v Canberra, 2006)

Andrew Johns typically filled up when he took on Canberra and it was no exception in 2006 when he scored two tries and went home with 30 points in a 70-32 thrashing of the Raiders at Bruce Stadium. In a masterly display, Johns set up eight tries to go with his two solo efforts. His own tries came from a grubber kick and a dummy-and-run, while his eight assists came from the boot both long and short, the pass both long and short and one beautiful blindside move. Johns was unstoppable in the game that tallied the most points in premiership history.

9. Dally Messenger (Eastern Suburbs v South Sydney, 1911)

The game's first star, Dally Messenger, often saved his finest performances for rep games, but his showing against South Sydney at the back end of 1911 was one of total dominance. Messenger scored 20 of Easts' 23 points, with two tries and seven goals. It was reported after the match that "Dally Messenger beat 13 inferior men", such was the forcefulness of his display.

10. Terry Lamb (Canterbury v Western Suburbs, 1987)

Dazzling Canterbury five-eighth Terry Lamb was a one-man band in the Bulldogs' Round 4 match against Western Suburbs in 1987, scoring all 26 points for Canterbury in the 26-16 win over the Magpies at Belmore Sports Ground. The greatest back-up player in premiership history, Lamb was on hand to support his teammates in all four of his tries, while his kicking game in general play and for goal was near perfect. Lamb's monopoly on the scoresheet broke the premiership record for scoring all of a team's points, previously held by Les Johns with 19.

Chapter 2

FINALS

GREATEST FINALS MATCHES

1. 2010: Sydney Roosters 19—Wests Tigers 15
The 2010 qualifying final between the Roosters and the Tigers became the first post-season match to go into golden point, but contained a season's worth of excitement in regulation time. Tigers backrower Gareth Ellis was denied a try three times by the video referee in the first 10 minutes, but Benji Marshall laid on tries for Lote Tuqiri and Beau Ryan, centre Blake Ayshford scored a 70-metre intercept try and Robbie Farah kicked a field goal to give the third-placed side a 15-2 lead midway through the second half. Dally M medallist Todd Carney created two brilliant tries to cut the deficit to one point, however, and a rare scrum win against the feed inside the final minute was followed by a frantic passing sequence that resulted in Braith Anasta kicking an incredible after-the-siren field goal. Roosters centre Shaun Kenny-Dowall won the match in the 100th minute with a long-range intercept try, ending a hectic and at times brutal encounter.

2. 1998: Canterbury 32—Parramatta 20
Parramatta seemed destined for its first Grand Final in 12 years after building an 18-2 lead against a battle-weary Canterbury side in the preliminary final. But the

courageous Bulldogs scored three brilliant tries inside the final 11 minutes and winger Daryl Halligan kicked two sideline conversions to level the scores. A 50-metre field-goal attempt by Craig Polla-Mounter scraped under the crossbar as the fulltime siren sounded, but the Canterbury halfback slotted two one-pointers and scored his second try in extra-time to get his side home 32-20 over the shell-shocked Eels, capping the most famous comeback in finals history.

3. 1956: Balmain 36—South Sydney 33
Archrivals Balmain and Souths produced a 13-try classic in the '56 preliminary final. The game opened up after Rabbitohs prop Jim Richards and Tigers counterpart Jack Moon were sent off late in the first half. Balmain edged ahead 16-15 one minute into the second stanza and skipped to a 12-point lead with a quarter of the match to go, but defending champs Souths refused to give in before coming up just short. Lock Les 'Chicka' Cowie scored four tries for the vanquished Rabbitohs—who outscored their opponents seven tries to six—while Tigers centre Kevin Mosman bagged a hat-trick and fullback Keith Barnes kicked nine vital goals. The match remained the highest-scoring finals encounter in premiership history until 2003.

4. 1991: Canberra 34—Manly 26
Injury-ravaged heavyweights Canberra and Manly produced a modern-day epic in the 1991 minor semi. The Raiders gained the early ascendancy with a try to Gary Belcher and a first-half double to backrow workhorse Gary Coyne, but the Sea Eagles—who lost halfback Geoff Toovey to an eye injury in the opening minutes—kept pace through the attacking mastery of Cliff Lyons and Kevin Iro. The defending premiers appeared to have the match wrapped up at 28-14 following Mark Bell's runaway try and Coyne's third touchdown before a courageous Manly sliced the deficit to two points with a sensational Owen Cunningham try and Iro's second four-pointer. Coyne's fourth try from a quick tap sealed the result for Canberra in a match where neither side deserved to go home empty.

5. 1994: Canterbury 19—Canberra 18
The feverishly anticipated '94 major semi clash between minor premiers Canterbury and title favourites Canberra lived up to its heavyweight billing. The Bulldogs scored after just 90 seconds before the rivals traded tries for the remainder of the half to set up a 14-12 lead in favour of the blue-and-whites. Canterbury held a six-point advantage for most of the second stanza after a Steven Hughes try, but with time ticking into the final 45 seconds, Raiders backrower David Furner busted the line to send interchange forward David Westley under the posts and force extra-time. Both sides struggled to find the decisive score during the frantic added 20 minutes, until Bulldogs winger Jason Williams produced an audacious step to race 50 metres up the sideline on a

kick-return. Fellow Kiwi flanker Daryl Halligan slotted the match-winning field goal from close range two plays later with two and a half minutes on the clock, booking a Grand Final berth for the Bulldogs.

6. 2008: Melbourne 16—Brisbane 14

Archrivals Melbourne and Brisbane were placed on a high-stakes collision course during the 2008 finals after minor premiers Storm were upset in week one by the eighth-placed Warriors, while the Broncos were under siege following a sexual-assault allegation levelled at three of their representative stars. But in front of a bumper Suncorp Stadium crowd, Brisbane showed no signs of its torrid build-up, powering to a 12-0 halftime lead after brilliant team tries to wingers Darius Boyd and Denan Kemp. Tempers frayed when Storm duo Cameron Smith and Jeremy Smith were pinged for an ugly grapple tackle on Sam Thaiday (which eventually saw the captain suspended for the Grand Final), while Melbourne forward Jeff Lima was sin-binned soon after. Boyd and Ben Hannant were denied match-sealing tries for Brisbane either side of a Billy Slater touchdown, leaving the Broncos clinging to a two-point lead in the dying minutes. But an error by Broncos forward Ashton Sims with 90 seconds on the clock provided the ruthless defending champs with their chance, and Greg Inglis crossed in the corner two plays later to steal a dramatic victory. Devastated Brisbane players lay strewn on the turf as captain Darren Lockyer let out an anguished scream, with the heartbreaking exit doubling as Wayne Bennett's last match in charge after 21 seasons with the club.

7. 1990: Penrith 30—Canberra 12

Long-suffering Penrith qualified for its maiden Grand Final with an extra-time upset of Canberra in the 1990 major semi. Panthers halfback genius Greg Alexander, criticised during his career for failing to step up in big games, combined brilliantly with teenage centre Brad Fittler to score in the first half and kicked a pressure penalty goal near the end of regulation time to send the match into an extra 20 minutes at 12-all. 'Brandy' scored a sneaky dummy-half try in extra-time before Fittler wrapped up a historic Grand Final berth by breaking the tiring Canberra defence to score. Alexander's haul of 22 points (from two tries and seven goals) was the highest individual tally in a finals match in 26 years.

8. 1967: Canterbury 12—St George 11

The unthinkable happened in 1967, the first year of the limited-tackle era—St George's world-record run of 11 premierships was broken by Canterbury in the preliminary final. The Berries, with former Saints hardman Kevin Ryan in charge as captain-coach, were competing in their first finals series in seven years, and twice came from behind to record one of the great September victories. The Dragons cruised to a 9-0 lead, but were reeled in and trailed 9-10 at halftime. Saints winger Dennis Preston kicked his fourth goal to snatch back the lead in the second half, but a towering penalty goal from Canterbury second-rower George Taylforth put his side in front 12-11 and the Berries desperately hung on to bring a remarkable era to a close.

9. 1984: Canterbury 14—Balmain 8
Balmain transformed from emerging force to genuine contender in 1985—finishing the regular season in second place—and defending premiers Canterbury required every scrap of their grit and guile to subdue the Tigers in the major preliminary semi. The Tigers led 6-0 at halftime courtesy of a try to brilliant Brit Garry Schofield, but the Bulldogs squared the ledger shortly after the break with a superb team try finished off by Terry Lamb. The Canterbury pivot nudged his side in front 8-6 with a 51st-minute penalty goal before Balmain and ex-Canterbury winger Ross Conlon sent the match into extra-time with a calmly taken penalty in the last minute of regulation time. But neither combatant was able to capitalise on myriad opportunities during a frenetic added period. The match seemed destined for a replay until a sensational long-range try to Andrew Farrar in the dying stages of extra-time sealed the result for Canterbury.

10. 1938: Canterbury 31—Balmain 24
Emphatic minor premier after losing just one match during the 1938 regular season, Canterbury-Bankstown was coasting to a comfortable victory over Balmain in the semi-final at the SCG. Canterbury piled on five tries in the first half—including a double to Frank McCormack—before Balmain finally posted its first three-pointer through centre Darcy Kearney just before halftime to trail 7-21. But the Frank Hyde-led Balmain side launched a valiant comeback in the second half; forwards George Watt and Jimmy Quealey crossed for tries before Hyde set up Kearney's second with five minutes remaining and Bill Johnson took his match tally to six goals. Canterbury's advantage had been shredded to 28-24, but the minor premiers extinguished brave Balmain's season when halfback Ted Anderson dotted down for his second try of the half.

GREATEST GRAND FINALS

1. 1989: Canberra 19—Balmain 14
Almost unanimously regarded as the greatest Grand Final ever played, Canberra's first premiership came after just the second period of extra-time in premiership decider history. In a match featuring more than 25 rep players, Balmain jumped to a

12-2 first-half lead and could taste its first premiership in 20 years when coach Warren Ryan took off star forwards Paul Sironen and Steve Roach with the Tigers clinging to a 14-8 lead. Inside the last 20 minutes, Mick Neil was ankle-tapped with the line wide open, Wayne Pearce spilled the ball in similar circumstances and a Benny Elias field goal ricocheted off the crossbar. As fate had it, John Ferguson crossed for Canberra in the final 90 seconds. Mal Meninga converted and the game went into 20 minutes of extra-time. The Raiders had all the momentum, with a Chris O'Sullivan drop goal and a rampaging Steve Jackson try setting Canberra up for its first title win.

2. 1997 (ARL): Newcastle 22—Manly 16
Manly was unbackable favourite in the 1997 ARL Grand Final and all seemed to be going to plan when the Sea Eagles went into the main break up 16-8 in what had been a physical encounter. The Knights held on desperately just after the break as Manly launched raid after raid, and after booting a penalty, equalled the scores through a Robbie O'Davis try with five minutes remaining. Newcastle had one last push for the win in the dying seconds and came up trumps. Rather than set for a drop goal, Immortal Andrew Johns darted down the blindside and found blond winger Darren Albert on his inside, and the Knights were premiers for the first time.

3. 1963: St George 8—Western Suburbs 3
In the most debated Grand Final in premiership history, Western Suburbs came as close as any team during St George's run of 11 straight titles to winning a decider. Wests had been beaten by the Saints in the two previous Grand Finals but were confident of turning the tables before word filtered through to prop Jack Gibson that referee Darcy Lawler had backed St George. In a quagmire, Wests lost the penalty count heavily while St George winger Johnny King scored the most controversial Grand Final try ever in the 8-3 result. Wests players maintain they were robbed, while the lasting image of the Grand Final was the famous 'Gladiators' photo of a mud-splattered Norm Provan and Arthur Summons.

4. 1967: South Sydney 12—Canterbury 10
Canterbury ended St George's run of 11 straight premierships with a thrilling 12-11 prelim final win that shocked the Rugby League world. The Berries could not end their 25-year title drought though, with a Bob McCarthy try bringing the premiership back to Souths. Rabbitohs prop John O'Neill scored the first try but Canterbury led 8-5 on the stroke of halftime before McCarthy ran the length of the field after intercepting a Kevin Brown pass. Bulldogs forward George Taylforth levelled the scores early in the second half but a scrum penalty with five minutes to go saw Eric Simms boot Souths to victory.

5. 1999: Melbourne 20—St George Illawarra 18

One of the most dramatic—and contentious—Grand Final finishes of all time came in 1999 when second-year team Melbourne capped a magnificent second-half comeback against raging favourites St George Illawarra with a penalty try. The Dragons led 14-0 after a super first half highlighted by Nathan Blacklock's magnificent bootlace pick-up-and-go try, but were run down by a gallant Storm outfit. The match reached a crescendo with four minutes remaining when Storm winger Craig Smith was felled by a high shot from Dragons opposite Jamie Ainscough when catching a bomb. Video referee Chris Ward awarded a penalty try, Matt Geyer slotted the conversion and Melbourne claimed its maiden premiership.

6. 1965: St George 12—South Sydney 8

Sydney was at fever pitch on Grand Final day in 1965, with St George chasing a record 10th consecutive premiership against the up-and-coming South Sydney team. An official crowd of 78,000 packed the SCG, but many more climbed the roof and other vantage points to see the decider. In what was captain-coach Norm Provan's final game, the Saints triumphed in a hard-fought affair. A 55-yard penalty from Souths' Bruce Longbottom got the scoring underway, but the Dragons raced to a six-point lead late in the second half when Johnny King scored and, despite a late Souths surge, held on to win 12-8.

7. 2004: Canterbury 16—Sydney Roosters 13

An underrated decider, the 2004 Grand Final was the culmination of a three-year feud between Canterbury and the Sydney Roosters after the Bulldogs had been kicked out of the 2002 premiership only to see the Tricolours lift the trophy. The Roosters dominated the first half and went into the break 13-6 up, but a Matt Utai try two minutes into the second half pegged the score back to 13-12, and 10 minutes later the Bulldogs hit the front 16-13. The Bulldogs held on grimly for 27 thrilling minutes, only securing the premiership after Andrew Ryan ankle-tapped a wide-open Michael Crocker in the final minute.

8. 1991: Penrith 19—Canberra 12

Penrith's inaugural premiership came in the club's 25th year and was celebrated long and hard at the foot of the mountains. Led, at least spiritually, by veteran hooker Royce Simmons, the Panthers triumphed 19-12 over a Canberra team chasing three straight premierships. In his final game, Simmons scored two tries (his only double), while Greg Alexander put the Panthers up with a spectacular 35-metre field goal in the dying minutes and the aggressive Mark Geyer redeemed himself for an earlier sin-binning with a bull charge to the try-line to set up Simmons' second. Alexander's sideline conversion sealed the thrilling match.

9. 1976: Manly 13—Parramatta 10
Parramatta's first Grand Final appearance after 30 seasons in the premiership ended in disappointment with a 13-10 loss to rivals Manly. The Eels scored first through Jim Porter, but it is his wing partner that is most remembered. With Manly holding a slender 11-10 lead with minutes remaining, Parramatta winger Neville Glover spilled a ball 10 metres out with the try-line beckoning. Bob Fulton, in what was his last match for the Sea Eagles, skippered the side to its third premiership in five years in a memorable decider.

10. 1946: Balmain 13—St George 12
A Grand Final was required in 1946 following Balmain's defeat of St George in the first semi 22-14. The Tigers, with the great Harry Bath in the backrow and speedsters Arthur Patton and Joe Jorgensen on the wings, went in strong favourites but only just held on for a famous 13-12 win. The Dragons scored four tries to three, but Test cricket great Ray Lindwall missed all four shots at goal and Balmain secured its ninth premiership. Jack Lindwall scored for the Saints with just minutes to go, but when his brother pushed the conversion wide, Balmain had victory in its grasp. The match ended in a hail of fists and fighting, with players and spectators brawling after the whistle.

GREATEST PLAYOFF MATCHES

1. 1943: Newtown 11—Balmain 10
In front of an astonishing crowd of 47,320 people at the SCG (breaking a 22-year premiership-attendance record), Newtown and Balmain squared off in a minor premiership playoff in what was possibly the match of the year. Tom Bourke scored a double for Balmain but it wasn't enough, with Bruce Ryan scoring a double for the Bluebags and champion centre Len Smith also crossing. The win gave Newtown a critical second chance that would be required on its way to its last premiership.

2. 1991: Western Suburbs 19—Canterbury 14
A controversial finish only added to the drama of the premiership's last-ever playoff in a cracking contest between Wests and Canterbury. In what was a grudge match following the defection of four Canterbury stars to Wests under ex-Bulldogs coach Warren Ryan, the Bulldogs and Magpies scored two tries each but an 11-point haul from Jason Taylor separated the two teams. Canterbury's English import Jonathan Davies was streaking away on the last play of the game when Bill Harrigan blew fulltime and the crowd ran on to Parramatta Stadium, infuriating Bulldogs players and fans alike.

3. 1985: Penrith 10—Manly 7
Penrith reached its first finals series after 18 miserable seasons in the premiership when it eliminated Manly 10-7 in a memorable playoff win. In wild scenes, Brad Izzard set up Brett Lobb for a try with a brilliant chip-and-chase in the first half, while Manly responded in the second stanza through Chris Close. Paul Vautin kicked an unlikely field goal but the accurate boot of Greg Aexander took the Panthers to the promised land for the first time.

4. 1947: Western Suburbs 10—St George 5
Led by skipper Eric Bennett, who played one of his finest games in the black and white, Western Suburbs reached the finals in 1947 after a thrilling playoff win over St George. With 13,552 fans watching at the Sports Ground, Bennett scored a try in a brilliant display that saw Wests win 10-5. Don Milton scored the other try for Wests, while Stan Root scored all of the points for the Saints.

5. 1945: Balmain 9—North Sydney 5
On the Victory Day holiday in 1945, Balmain and Norths scored a try each in their playoff for fourth at the SCG, but the boot of champion back Joe Jorgensen and a field goal to Bob Nielson proved the difference. Stan Ponchard scored for Balmain, while speedster Johnny Bliss crossed for Norths. Balmain would go on to defeat Newtown and only just go down in the final to Easts.

6. 1986: Balmain 14—North Sydney 7
North Sydney had made just one finals series in 20 years and would have to wait longer after Balmain won 14-7 at the SCG in a midweek playoff. Ben Elias kicked two drop goals for the Tigers, while Scott Gale scored the winner to save the day after Ross Conlon's errant form with the boot. Gale's try was magnificent: he chipped twice and then outsprinted his Norths opponents to land on the ball first.

7. 1975: Parramatta 18—Western Suburbs 13
In the first playoff of the top-five finals era, Parramatta had to take on Wests, with the winner to play Balmain after the three teams finished tied on 21 points. Wests would have advanced but had been deducted a point for an illegal replacement in an earlier match. Russell Mullins scored twice for Wests, but it wasn't enough to hold out an Eels team that posted four tries. Parramatta would go on to beat Balmain and then win its first final against Canterbury in an epic week for the club.

8. 1956: Western Suburbs 10—Newtown 5
Tied for fourth place, Wests and Newtown staged a classic playoff in front of 21,000 fans at Redfern Oval in 1956 with a finals berth on the line. Bill Carson and Ernie

Hills scored tries for the Magpies, while Kevin Considine crossed for Newtown. Wests would go on to be hammered by Souths in the minor semi four days later.

9. 1934: Western Suburbs 7—Eastern Suburbs 2
With Easts and Wests tied at the top of the ladder with 24 points apiece, the League staged a playoff for the minor premiership. Over 20,000 turned up at the Sports Ground to see Wests win 7-2. Les Mead scored the only try of the clash that put Wests in the box seat for their second premiership.

10. 1990: Balmain 12—Newcastle 4
In what was Newcastle's first taste of post-season action, and in what would become Balmain's last post-season win as a stand-alone club, the Tigers downed the Knights 12-4. Steve O'Brien and Wayne Pearce scored for Balmain in front of 19,714 at Parramatta Stadium, while Newcastle was held try-less in a physical affair.

GREATEST FINALS COMEBACKS

1. 1998: Canterbury 32—Parramatta 20
Canterbury staged the most famous finals comeback of all time against Parramatta in 1998 during an incredible sudden-death charge. The Eels stormed to an 18-2 lead in the preliminary final on the back of the ball-playing class of former Bulldogs pair Jim Dymock and Jason Smith, and held on to that 16-point advantage with a shade over 10 minutes on the timepiece. But five-eighth Craig Polla-Mounter's try, followed by a sizzling half-field effort from Rod Silva in the 74th minute, saw Canterbury claw back to 12-18. Silva then delivered the pass for Kiwi centre Willie Talau to cross in the corner with three minutes remaining, and Daryl Halligan landed one of the great goals from touch to level the scores. A 48-metre field-goal attempt by Polla-Mounter after the siren—following a bizarre play on fulltime by Eels winger Paul Carige—fell just under the bar, but the Bulldogs dominated extra-time to advance to the Grand Final 32-20.

2. 2006: Brisbane 37—Canterbury 20
The Bulldogs had one hand on a berth in the '06 decider when they led Brisbane 20-6 at halftime of the preliminary final before a brilliant kick return by Broncos fullback Justin Hodges resulted in a length-of-the-field try to hooker Shaun Berrigan and launched a staggering fightback. With skipper Darren Lockyer in irresistible touch, the Broncos piled on another five unanswered tries and a field goal in a 31-0 second-half shut-out—on the way to an incredible 37-20 win—to advance to the Grand Final.

3. 1984: South Sydney 22—Manly 18

South Sydney trailed raging-hot favourites Manly 0-14 after just 15 minutes of the 1984 minor preliminary semi-final, following tries to Test three-quarters Kerry Boustead and Chris Close. But the aggressive Rabbitohs unleashed an aerial barrage to orchestrate one of premiership football's most celebrated comebacks, with two tries to Bill Hardy and another to captain Ziggy Niszczot all coming from bombs. Five-eighth Neil Baker added five goals in a rapturous 22-18 Souths victory.

4. 1997: Newcastle 28—Parramatta 20

Playing in their first finals match in 11 seasons, the Parramatta Eels shot out to an 18-0 lead over Newcastle in even time. But in a remarkable match with a casualty ward bursting at the seams, the Knights clawed back to trail by just two points at halftime courtesy of an Adam MacDougall double and a try to Adam Muir. A penalty goal seven minutes after the break edged the Eels out to 20-16, but they were unable to hold on–tries to Andrew Johns, who fatefully injured his ribs in scoring, and Brett Grogan saw Newcastle home 28-20. It remains the biggest comeback in finals history.

5. 2000: Sydney Roosters 26—Newcastle 20

An Andrew Johns masterclass propelled Newcastle to a commanding 16-2 halftime lead over the Sydney Roosters in the 2000 preliminary final showdown, but a Brad Fittler-led revival sank the shell-shocked Knights. A freakish try to Luke Phillips, a Fittler intercept try from a Johns pass, and a long-range touchdown finished off by Ryan Cross—all in the space of five minutes—gave the Roosters a shock four-point advantage with 23 minutes to play. Centre Shannon Hegarty extended the lead, while Timana Tahu's try with eight minutes on the clock was not enough for the Knights, who exited with a gut-wrenching 26-20 loss eerily reminiscent of their finals collapse against the Roosters two years earlier.

6. 2013: Manly 32—South Sydney 20

The gritty Manly Sea Eagles defied a gruelling finals campaign to extend Souths' much-publicised 42-year Grand Final wait, courtesy of a stunning preliminary final comeback during the 2013 post-season. Tries to John Sutton and Nathan Merritt opened up a 14-0 Rabbitohs lead at better than a point a minute, while resolute goal-line defence maintained an eight-point halftime advantage. But the Sea Eagles posted the first four tries of the second half as they terrorised Souths' left side—with David Williams' miracle put-down in the corner the highlight—to lead by 18 points with just eight minutes left. A late disallowed try to George Burgess confirmed the crestfallen Bunnies' fate, while Manly's gallant 32-20 win sealed the club's fourth Grand Final appearance in seven seasons.

7. 1998: Canterbury 28—Newcastle 16

Given their heroics a week later in the preliminary final against Parramatta, the Bulldogs' extraordinary comeback and subsequent extra-time win over Newcastle during the '98 post-season has been somewhat forgotten. An Andrew Johns-inspired Knights outfit led 16-0 after half an hour at the SFS, but a converted Glen Hughes try and three penalty goals by Daryl Halligan dragged Canterbury back into the contest. The score remained 16-10 for an age before the 'Dogs ran the ball on the last tackle in the 70th minute and halfback Corey Hughes finished off a 50-metre movement to level the scores. In the dramatic closing stages, Canterbury forward Tony Grimaldi lost the ball over the line just before the siren sounded to consign the match to extra-time. But the Bulldogs had too much gas in the tank for the weary Knights and scored two tries in the added period to prevail 28-16. It was Newcastle's second finals loss after holding a big first-half lead in the space of a week.

8. 2011: New Zealand Warriors 22—Wests Tigers 20

Thumped 40-10 by Brisbane in the qualifying final, the Warriors were headed for a straight-sets exit when they trailed the highly rated Wests Tigers 6-18 at halftime of the sudden-death semi-final a week later. But tries to Feleti Mateo and Lance Hohaia during an absorbing second stanza reeled the deficit back to two points before a freakish Krisnan Inu touchdown from a Shaun Johnson cross-field kick two minutes from time snatched a euphoric 22-20 victory for the Warriors.

9. 1998: Sydney City 26—Newcastle 15

Newcastle opened up a big lead over the Roosters in week two of the '98 finals before crumbling spectacularly. With sibling halves pairing Andrew and Matthew Johns mesmerising the Sydney City defence, the Knights posted three tries to build a 15-0 halftime scoreline in front of a baying Marathon Stadium crowd. But the home fans watched on in stunned disbelief as the Roosters ran in six unanswered tries in the second half. Ivan Cleary's radar was off target (one goal from six attempts), but it mattered little as Matt Sing and Brad Fittler ran riot, propelling the Roosters to an amazing 26-15 victory and a preliminary final berth.

10. 1974: Western Suburbs 23—Manly 20

Wests overturned a significant halftime deficit to bundle two-time premiers Manly out of the 1974 finals in a minor semi classic. The Sea Eagles, who were overwhelming favourites, dominated the opening 40 minutes to lead 15-4 at the break, but the Magpies surged back with three unanswered tries and a swag of goals to John Dorahy to take a 23-15 advantage heading into the final quarter. Bob Fulton pegged the deficit back to three points with eight minutes on the clock, but Wests hung on for a momentous victory.

BEST FINALS FINISHES

1. 1998 Preliminary Final: Canterbury 32—Parramatta 20
Parramatta held an 18-2 lead with just 11 minutes remaining when Canterbury steamed back into the match through tries to Craig Polla-Mounter, Rod Silva and Willie Talau. With three minutes remaining, reliable goalkicker Daryl Halligan slotted the equaliser from the sideline to send the dramatic clash into extra-time, but not before a 48-metre field-goal attempt from Polla-Mounter fell just under the crossbar. With all the momentum, Canterbury romped home 32-20 following a series of errors from Parramatta winger Paul Carige to cap an incredible preliminary final.

2. 2010 Qualifying Final: Sydney Roosters 19—Wests Tigers 15
In the longest premiership game played in the NRL era, the Sydney Roosters overcame a 2-15 second-half deficit to win one of the most sensational games ever played. The Roosters powered home, with tries to Braith Anasta and Mitchell Pearce bringing the Tricolours to within one. It seemed like Robbie Farah's earlier one-pointer would prove critical, however, until the Roosters produced one of the great field goals. After shockingly winning a scrum against the head and then throwing the ball wildy, Anasta became the hero, landing a field goal as time expired 35 metres out, just 10 metres in from touch. Extra-time followed and it took another 20 minutes of play before Roosters centre Shaun Kenny-Dowall plucked a wonderful intercept and ran 80 metres to end a gripping finals encounter.

3. 1969 Preliminary Final: Balmain 15—Manly 14
Balmain enjoyed a dramatic—and successful—run through the 1969 finals series, with its win over Manly in the preliminary final an absolute classic. The match was locked at 12-all with six minutes left when Manly fullback Bob Batty put the Sea Eagles in front with a booming penalty goal. They had one foot in the Grand Final with two minutes remaining before Tigers five-eighth Dave Bolton set himself for an equalising field goal. Bolton fumbled a pass backwards, stunting the Sea Eagles' defence. Fullback Bob Smithies scooped up the ball and flung it out to winger George Reubner, who put an in-and-away on opposite Danny Gough before crashing through Batty for the winning try.

4. 1933 Second Semi: St George 13—Eastern Suburbs 10
St George and Easts played out the most thrilling final of the 1930s in a dramatic second semi in 1933. St George led 7-2 at halftime after a try to Bernie Martin.

Easts responded via Max Nixon, the Saints went up 10-5 through Bill Killiby, and soon after the Tricolours once again levelled the scores with a Jim Morrison try. Then came one of the most dramatic finales in finals history. The scores were locked at 10-all when the fulltime bell rang. Saints centre Norm Tipping attempted a field goal that pushed wide and the match was seemingly headed to a replay. Unbeknown to the Eastern Suburbs players though, Dragons winger Jack Rutherford charged through and grounded the ball. Referee Bill Fry awarded the try despite the protests of Easts players, sending the Saints into the premiership decider with Newtown.

5. 1910 Final: Newtown 4—South Sydney 4
Newtown's first premiership was secured in the competition's third year with a famous kick from winger Charles 'Boxer' Russell. Needing only a draw after securing the minor premiership, the Bluebags trailed 2-4 against a 12-man South Sydney with the bell set to ring any moment. Then Rabbitohs fullback Howard Hallett hit a long, clearing kick that was marked by centre Albert Hawkes some 45 metres out, close to the touchline. Russell stepped in and drilled the premiership's most famous pressure goal, winning Newtown its first title.

6. 1963 Major Semi: Western Suburbs 10—St George 8
The closest Western Suburbs came to ending St George's incredible run of 11 straight titles was in 1963, with a dramatic major semi win and a controversial Grand Final loss. Their major semi win was one for the ages. The Saints led the gripping battle 8-7 inside the final minute and were holding the ball when the Magpies forced an error. Noel Kelly split the Dragons defence before finding centre Bob McGuiness, who linked with Kevin Smythe to cross for the winner.

7. 2008 Second Semi: Melbourne 16—Brisbane 14
The Melbourne Storm delivered a heartbreaking last-minute loss to rivals Brisbane in 2008 in an absorbing finale to a sensational semi. Brisbane led 12-0 at halftime, and a penalty 10 minutes from time pushed their lead to 14-6 after Michael Crocker had scored early in the half for the Storm. Billy Slater claimed a Cooper Cronk bomb minutes after the penalty to give the Storm some shot, but it wasn't until a critical Ashton Sims error in the dying moments that Melbourne managed to hit the front for the first time. Sims spilt the ball on a simple hit-up in his own 20, and a few plays later Greg Inglis crossed in the corner to seal a stunning victory for the Storm.

8. 1967 Preliminary Final: Canterbury 12—St George 11
St George's run of 11 straight premierships came to an end in a dramatic and compelling preliminary final loss to Canterbury. Captain-coached by ex-Dragon Kevin Ryan, the Berries shocked the Rugby League world with a 12-11 win. The Saints opened

9-0, but the loss of Graeme Langlands to injury seemed to spur Canterbury's belief. Tries to Ross Kidd and Barry Reynolds saw the Berries hit the front 10-9 on halftime. A penalty goal after 54 minutes restored order with the Saints up 11-10, but George Taylforth gave the Berries back the lead six minutes later with a goal on halfway 10 metres in from touch. The desperate Berries held out attacking raid after attacking raid from Reg Gasnier and Billy Smith to end St George's record title run.

9. 2011 Second Semi: Brisbane 13—St George Illawarra 12
In what would be his final club game, Darren Lockyer finished a hero in an exhilarating extra-time finals win, kicking the winning drop goal with a fractured cheekbone. Lockyer's Broncos led 12-6 with 10 minutes to go before a collision with teammate Gerard Beale left the star pivot with serious facial injuries. The Dragons equalised with three minutes to play through a try to Adam Cuthbertson, but Lockyer played the conqueror, landing a spectacular field goal in the second minute of golden point. While the Broncos advanced, Lockyer didn't, succumbing to his injury and missing the preliminary final loss to Manly.

10. 1983 Minor Semi: St George 17—Balmain 14
A dramatic extra-time clash, the opening final of the 1983 series was a thrilling affair not decided until the final two minutes of extra-time. Balmain led 14-6 at halftime after tries to Steve Martin and Mark Lawson, but a Richie Jones try early in the second stanza followed by a late penalty goal from Steve Gearin left the scores tied 14-all when the fulltime siren rang. The Saints and Tigers fought out a brutal extra-time until two minutes remaining, when Gearin landed another difficult penalty following a strip penalty on David Brooks. Michael O'Connor kicked a field goal at the end of extra-time to secure the 17-14 victory.

BEST INDIVIDUAL FINALS PERFORMANCES

1. Dick Dunn—Eastern Suburbs v Balmain, 1945
Unwanted by Easts after the club's disappointing 1944 campaign, goalkicking lock Dunn fought back the following season and was a key figure in their charge to the minor premiership. In the '45 premiership final (mandatory Grand Finals were still almost a decade away) Dunn produced one of the most famous individual performances of all time, scoring three of Easts' four tries and landing five crucial goals as the Tricolours outlasted Balmain 22-19 to take out the title.

2. Greg Alexander—Penrith v Canberra, 1990
'Brandy' Alexander buried reservations over his big-match temperament once and for all with a commanding individual display to propel Penrith into its first Grand Final. The major semi against Canberra was locked 12-all at fulltime, but the Panthers prevailed 30-12 after extra-time thanks to the wizardry of their halfback, who scored two tries and kicked seven goals for a 22-point haul. Alexander combined brilliantly with Brad Fittler to score in the first half and dived over from dummy-half for his second during the added period before laying on a try for Fittler to seal the result.

3. Darren Lockyer—Brisbane v Canterbury, 2006
Several players contributed immensely to the Broncos' comeback from a 14-point halftime deficit to down the Bulldogs 37-20 in the 2006 preliminary final, but none was better than talismanic skipper Lockyer. The cool-headed five-eighth finished off a thrilling 60-metre movement he started, had a major hand in three other tries, and kicked a field goal in Brisbane's 31-0 second-half shutout.

4. Anthony Mundine—St George Illawarra v Cronulla, 1999
St George Illawarra trailed minor premiers Cronulla 0-8 at halftime of the preliminary final in their first season as a joint venture. But gifted five-eighth Mundine swung the match with a second-half performance of rare virtuosity. He put the Dragons on the board with a fiercely determined close-range try in the 44th minute, and 10 minutes later outleaped Sharks fullback David Peachey to claim a Nathan Brown kick, pushing his side out to 12-8 in front. Mundine then handled twice brilliantly to set up teenage fullback Luke Patten's try before sealing the 24-8 boilover with a sizzling 30-metre sprint to the corner inside the final five minutes, completing a breathtaking second-half hat-trick and sending the Dragons into the Grand Final.

5. Francis Meli—New Zealand Warriors v Canterbury, 2003
Meli was a blockbusting but error-prone winger in the Warriors' exhilarating line-up of the early 2000s. The 23-year-old powerhouse was the main beneficiary of the Auckland-based club's stunning 48-22 thrashing of raging-hot favourites the Bulldogs on the 2003 qualifying final weekend, finding his way to the try-line a finals-record five times. It was just the sixth haul of five tries in a first grade match since 1977, and it remains a Warriors club record.

6. Jarryd Hayne—Parramatta v St George Illawarra, 2009
Hayne carried the Eels to the finals with an amazing sequence of individual displays that saw him carry off the Dally M Medal. The fullback was equally influential in Parramatta's qualifying final upset of minor premiers St George Illawarra, hoisting a bomb for his side's first try and making a long break in the lead-up to their second to

craft a 12-8 halftime lead. Hayne was faultless at the back as the Eels clung to their advantage before beating a horde of Dragons defenders on his way to one of the great finals tries, sealing the 25-12 win with three minutes to go.

7. Andrew Johns—Newcastle v Canterbury, 1998

Few players have deserved to be on a losing side less than the mercurial 'Joey' Johns when his depleted Newcastle outfit was run down by Canterbury during the '98 finals. The inspirational halfback set up all three tries as the Knights opened up a 16-0 lead, and was outstanding in all facets of play until the final whistle—but he could not prevent a Bulldogs comeback and an eventual 28-16 extra-time loss.

8. Brett Hodgson—Wests Tigers v North Queensland, 2005

Lightweight fullback Hodgson broke Graeme Langlands' 41-year-old finals record by racking up 30 points in the Tigers' 50-6 qualifying final demolition of North Queensland in 2005. Hodgson scored three tries—including two half-field efforts—and kicked nine goals from nine attempts, and went on to score a premiership-record 58 points across the entire finals campaign.

9. Graeme Langlands—St George v Parramatta, 1964

The 23-year-old fullback 'Changa' was the glittering star of St George's 42-0 major semi-final destruction of Parramatta in 1964. Langlands raced over for three tries and landed nine goals from 12 attempts for a finals-record 27 points—a mark that would still stand today if not for the increase in value of tries from three to four points.

10. Les Cowie—South Sydney v Balmain, 1956

Former Test lock Cowie was one of the great forward try-scorers of the code's first half-century, but had never scored more than two tries in a match for Souths until the '56 preliminary final in the twilight of his career. The 31-year-old scored a finals-record four tries in the high-scoring classic against Balmain, but it was not enough to prevent a 36-33 Tigers victory.

WORST INDIVIDUAL FINALS PERFORMANCES

1. Paul Carige—Parramatta v Canterbury, 1998

Parramatta winger Paul Carige was a rising talent in the 1998 season when a late game meltdown that mirrored Parramatta's preliminary final collapse saw his career prematurely ended. The Eels led 18-2 with 11 minutes remaining when the Bulldogs launched a stirring comeback to level the scores with three minutes to play.

Carige's nightmare soon started with a dead-ball line shocker and a chip from his own try-line as time expired that was centimetres from leading to a decisive Craig Polla-Mounter field goal. It just got worse in extra-time, with Carige dropping the ball, missing tackles and catching the ball over the sideline. He never played premiership football again, driven from the game by a rabid Eels fanbase who never forgave his shocker.

2. Steve Mavin—South Sydney v Canberra, 1987
South Sydney three-quarter Steve Mavin had spent nearly his entire first season in the centres before shifting to the wing in the final round. In just his third game on the flank in the '87 minor semi against the Raiders, Mavin made three critical errors early in the match, letting in three tries before being hooked by coach George Piggins. Mavin played another five seasons of first grade, renowned for his swan-dive tries.

3. Daryl Halligan—North Sydney v Penrith, 1991
Winger Daryl Halligan went on to become the premiership's greatest-ever point-scorer (since surpassed) and perhaps the finest kicker the game has known, but a shocker with the boot in his debut season cost the luckless North Sydney dearly. Despite the Bears scoring three tries to Penrith's two in the major semi, Halligan's wayward one-from-five was the difference in the 16-14 loss. The sharpshooter missed three from in front of the sticks in a forgettable day for the Kiwi.

4. Jason Bulgarelli—Canberra v New Zealand Warriors, 2003
Canberra centre Jason Bulgarelli was in only his 10th first grade game with the Raiders when he played the match he is most remembered for. In what would be just a 27-game top-grade career, Bulgarelli's blunder in the elimination final with the Warriors has lasted the longest in the memory of the Raiders faithful. With the scores tied at 16-all, Bulgarelli spilled a Mark McLinden grubber in what would have been a certain Raiders try. Soon after, Stacey Jones kicked the winning field goal for the Warriors.

5. Ashton Sims—Brisbane v Melbourne, 2008
Bustling forward Ashton Sims endured the nightmare of every footballer in 2008 when a simple error cost his side victory. The Broncos led 14-12 with just minutes remaining against red-hot favourites Melbourne, when Sims spilled the ball carting it out from his own line. A few plays later Greg Inglis crossed out wide and the Storm was into its third decider, while Sims was left to rue his costly error.

6. Tony Williams—Manly v Melbourne, 2012
Giant backrower Tony Williams had a forgettable farewell game for Manly before shifting to Canterbury in a horror 40-12 preliminary final loss to the Storm. Williams dropped the ball cold in the fourth minute to set up the Storm's first try. Minutes later

he lumbered at marker, with Billy Slater taking advantage and scoring Melbourne's second. Late in the game Williams attempted a shoulder charge right on his own line that allowed another Melbourne try. It was an inglorious farewell that Williams carried over to Canterbury in 2013.

7. Dale Copley—Brisbane v Manly, 2011
Brisbane winger Dale Copley was looking for a hole in which to hide after a dismal showing cost the Broncos their first Grand Final appearance in five years and a fitting farewell for Darren Lockyer. Copley accidentally knocked the ball out of teammate Jack Reed's hands, denying the Broncos a certain try, before spilling a pass from Reed on his own line a minute later to gift Manly a four-pointer. Some poor judgment in defence left the young winger to face the wrath of the Broncos fans.

8. Manu Vatuvei—New Zealand Warriors v Brisbane, 2011
Returning from an injured arm in the opening round of the 2011 finals series, Manu Vatuvei turned in a shocker in a 40-10 thrashing at the hands of Brisbane. Vatuvei almost allowed the first Broncos try when he was slow to react to a grubber, and he spilled numerous balls. A slew of dismal defensive reads meant not even a try could save an ordinary night for big Manu.

9. Anthony Mundine—St George v Canterbury, 1995
A prodigious talent who made his top-grade debut in 1993 as an 18-year-old, Anthony Mundine was a brilliant talent prone to controversial statements and wildly inconsistent performances. One of his most famous howlers came in the opening round of the 1995 finals series, when his team the Dragons had all the running early but couldn't put points on the board. Mundine spilled a ball over the line, trying a flamboyant pick-up rather than a simple dive, and generally struggled as the Bulldogs ground out a 12-8 win on their way to the premiership.

10. Aaron Raper—Cronulla v Manly, 1995
Hooker Aaron Raper enjoyed a successful final season with the Sharks in 1995, representing Australia and having his finest year with Cronulla. His finals showing against Manly, however, left many fans calling for his head. In one of the great finals clangers, Raper capped off a poor personal game and a blown 20-8 lead by being out of position and colliding with a teammate attempting to catch a bomb that led to Manly's winning try.

BEST GRAND FINAL PERFORMANCES

1. Clive Churchill—South Sydney, 1954
Clive Churchill was the standard-bearer for Rugby League greatness for many years and his performance in the 1954 Grand Final win over Newtown showed how special he was. Churchill simply dominated the Bluebags in the 23-15 win, setting up three of the Rabbitohs' five tries. Just 11 minutes in, he returned a kick and then put into space winger Ian Moir, who only had to beat fullback Gordon Clifford to score. With just 12 minutes to play, the Bunnies led 12-10 when Churchill took full control of the game, laying on two tries to Les 'Chicka' Cowie. The first came from a set piece in Souths' own half, where a smart inside ball put Cowie into a hole he took full advantage of. The next came when Churchill made a long, swerving run and broke through the Newtown defence before stumbling. He then popped a miracle ball to Cowie, who steamed over for the sealer.

2. Allan Langer—Brisbane, 1992
Star Broncos halfback Allan Langer lapped up the pressure of Brisbane's first Grand Final with a devastating performance that crushed St George's hopes. Langer scored the opening try after a nice step put prop Gavin Allen through a hole and Langer was there to collect Allen's offload and scoot over. He scored the Broncos' next try early in the second half with a smart dummy-half run. A Langer bust set up Alan Cann's first try, and a quick shift on his own line led to Steve Renouf's length-of-the-field special. Langer was rightly awarded the Clive Churchill Medal for a wonderful performance in the Broncos' first title win.

3. Bob Fulton—Manly, 1973
Bob Fulton's willingness to play football—and his ability to thrive—among the sea of violence that surrounded him was critical to Manly winning its second premiership in 1973. In a brutal Grand Final marred by continued brawling and thuggery, Fulton scored both of Manly's tries in the 10-7 win. His first left six Cronulla players grasping at air, and his second also came about because of his speed when he took a lob pass from Graham Eadie to place the ball down just inside the corner post.

4. Graeme Langlands—St George, 1964
St George great Graeme Langlands was a big-game player of the finest order and almost single-handedly kept the Saints' premiership streak alive with his performance against Balmain in the 1964 Grand Final. Langlands was magnificent all game,

setting up the only try of the decider and kicking four goals in the 11-6 victory. The aforementioned try came just after halftime, when a finely balanced Langlands, his toes right on the sideline, plucked a penalty kick for touch from well beyond the sideline before taking off on a diagonal run that split the Tigers and set up Johnny King to cross. Two pressure penalties late in the game gave the Saints the requisite space to make it nine straight titles.

5. Norm Provan—St George, 1957

Norm 'Sticks' Provan played in 10 of St George's famous run of 11 straight premierships, captain-coaching four. He was a regular Grand Final star but possibly his best performance came in the 1957 decider. In a 31-9 thumping of Manly, Provan dominated the match. He was involved in nearly everything, with a typically wholehearted display. The second-rower opened up Manly late with some devastating running, his ball-playing was sublime, and his defence was as fierce as ever, leaving Manly players strewn across the turf after one of his greatest all-round showings.

6. Dave Bolton—Balmain, 1969

Great English and Balmain five-eighth Dave Bolton had the game of his career in the shock 1969 Grand Final win over South Sydney. Bolton orchestrated the victory for a Tigers team that looked well outclassed on paper against a Rabbitohs team that had won the previous two deciders. Bolton opened the scoring with a clever drop goal and his kicking game kept the Tigers on top from the outset. His clever blindside play with skipper Peter Provan put Terry Parker away before the centre popped a ball to replacement winger Sid Williams to score the only try of the match. Another late field goal capped what was a sublime showing for the Brit.

7. Arthur Beetson—Eastern Suburbs, 1974

Great ball-playing prop Arthur Beetson was unstoppable in the 1974 Grand Final, with the young Canterbury side unable to halt his thumping runs and dangerous offloads. Beetson scored a first-half try after being put in a hole by Russell Fairfax and spent the remainder of the game terrorising the Berries. He set up the second try by giving a miraculous pass to Ron Coote, who hit a flying Mark Harris. A player whose skills defied his size, Beetson used all his assets in the 19-4 decimation of Canterbury in the '74 decider.

8. Andrew Johns—Newcastle, 2001

Team of the Century halfback and Newcastle skipper Andrew Johns had a hand in everything in the 2001 Grand Final upset of Parramatta. Along with lock Ben Kennedy, Johns willed the Knights home, and was the key man in the first-half onslaught that finished the Eels. Johns had the ball on a string with both the boot and hand, while he defended as stoutly and with as much impact as any halfback has. Johns has humbly said that Kennedy's performance had more of an impact, but he was a fine choice as Clive Churchill Medal winner.

9. Graham Eadie—Manly, 1978
One of the most consistent players of his era, Manly fullback Graham Eadie regularly shone on Grand Final day—but it is his performance in the 1978 Grand Final replay that stands above all others. Eadie dominated Cronulla in the 16-0 victory, scoring a magnificent try, kicking three goals and landing a drop goal to tally 10 of the Sea Eagles' points. 'Wombat' also played a hand in both of Russel Gartner's tries, including throwing the final pass for his first. Eadie stood tall as the best player on the paddock in Manly's fourth premiership win of the decade.

10. Gorden Tallis—Brisbane, 1998
Aggressive forward Gorden Tallis lived up to his 'Raging Bull' moniker in the 1998 Grand Final domination of Canterbury with a rollicking performance. Tallis took control of the game like few forwards ever have, setting the tone with his fearsome tackling and aggressive running. He burst over for a try from dummy-half, but it was his non-stop aggression that saw him awarded the Clive Churchill Medal.

WORST INDIVIDUAL GRAND FINAL PERFORMANCES

1. Graeme Langlands—St George, 1975
St George captain-coach Graeme 'Changa' Langlands' terrible performance in the record 38-0 Grand Final loss to Easts was exacerbated by his decision to wear a conspicuous, now-infamous pair of white boots as part of a sponsorship deal. A misdirected painkilling injection on his injured groin removed all feeling from his right leg and consigned the future Immortal to the role of passenger, unable to finish off a gilt-edged scoring opportunity during a close-fought first half. Following his ill-fated decision to continue after halftime, fullback Langlands could do little to halt the waves of Roosters attack as they ran in seven tries in the second stanza. For all of Easts' brilliance, the '75 decider will forever be known as "The Day of the White Boots".

2. Anthony Mundine—St George Illawarra, 1999
The Dragons' mercurial five-eighth Anthony Mundine single-handedly thrust the joint venture into the '99 decider with a mesmerising hat-trick in the preliminary final upset of Cronulla. But his trademark influence and spark were sorely missing in

the Grand Final against Melbourne. In a botched effort that could potentially have given the Saints a 20-2 lead, he bombed a certain try 10 minutes into the second half, losing the ball in the tackle of Storm winger Craig Smith as he reached out to plant it over the line. Mundine was powerless to stop the ensuing Melbourne comeback as the Dragons went down 18-20 courtesy of a late penalty try.

3. David Williams—Manly, 2013

One of the heroes of Manly's preliminary final defeat of Souths after scoring a crucial and miraculous second-half try, cult figure David Williams turned in a lamentable performance in the Grand Final loss to the Roosters. The 'Wolfman' failed to contest a cross-field kick during the first half, allowing opposing winger Daniel Tupou to climb high and score the Roosters' first try. With the Sea Eagles up by 10 points during the second half, he inexplicably let another bomb bounce, forcing his side back for a line dropout that led to Aidan Guerra's try. A dropped ball, with a chance to score in the corner beckoning, capped a horror night for the popular winger.

4. Neville Glover—Parramatta, 1976

Parramatta winger Neville Glover was responsible for the most infamous handling error in Grand Final history, putting down a regulation pass from his centre John Moran with the try-line wide open and the Eels down by one point during the second half. Although there was plenty of time remaining and it is unfair to blame Parramatta's 13-10 loss to Manly solely on Glover, he did let another pass from Ed Sulkowicz slip through his fingers while the Eels were hot on attack inside the final 10 minutes. Glover represented Australia against New Zealand two years later and scored two tries on Test debut, but his name will forever be associated with his unfortunate fumble at the SCG.

5. Scott Wilson—Canterbury, 1994

Rocks or diamonds fullback Scott Wilson's display in the '94 Grand Final against Canberra epitomised the Bulldogs' disastrous afternoon. He was far from the only subpar performer in Canterbury's 36-12 loss, but he spilled three bombs, was left grasping at air after being easily stepped by Raiders winger Ken Nagas, who raced away to score, and was unable to stop Laurie Daley's 40-metre run to the corner for another Canberra touchdown. Wilson was hooked after 32 minutes and replaced by Matthew Ryan.

6. Jonathan Wright—Canterbury, 2012

It was hard to fault the overall effort and performance of the Canterbury side in its 2012 Grand Final loss, with the clinical excellence of Melbourne forming the basis of a hard-fought 14-4 result. But winger Jonathan Wright was one Bulldog who had a particularly unhappy afternoon, making four handling errors in a horrendous display that saw him lumped with the lowest score in virtually every post-match player ratings list.

7. Billy Wilson—St George, 1962

Veteran Saints hardman Billy Wilson's long playing association with the club came to a disappointing conclusion in the '62 decider against Wests, while also putting his teammates under immense pressure. With the match evenly poised at 7-4 in favour of the Dragons, the enforcer was sent off for decking Magpies forward Jim Cody, an act of revenge after Cody had allegedly taken out Saints skipper Norm Provan earlier. St George was forced to battle on with 12 men as Wests narrowed the gap to one point, but the Dragons eventually secured their seventh straight title with a tense 9-6 win.

8. Kevin Yow Yeh—Balmain, 1966

Thursday Islander Kevin Yow Yeh, who ventured to Sydney with Redcliffe teammate Arthur Beetson in '66, was a brilliant but erratic three-quarter talent. Unfortunately, it was the latter quality that shone through in that season's Grand Final, with a slew of handling errors by the Balmain centre contributing to a convincing 23-4 loss to St George.

9. Krisnan Inu—New Zealand Warriors, 2011

The notoriously enigmatic Krisnan Inu produced some inspired pieces of play and several horrifying mistakes in the 2011 Grand Final, ultimately finishing on the debit side of the ledger in the Warriors' 24-10 loss to Manly. He made a stunning 40-metre break from a kick return in the second half, but lost the ball at the end of it before two minutes later making a meal of a grubber to the Warriors' in-goal that went within millimetres of gifting the Sea Eagles a try. Inu's mixed bag contained a total of three handling errors for a Warriors side that was desperately searching for continuity and momentum.

10. Frank Facer—North Sydney, 1943

Norths' Frank Facer battled an ankle injury in the lead-up to the 1943 Grand Final showdown with Newtown, and was eventually picked to play by the club's selectors against medical advice. Clearly hampered by the injury, the limping tough hooker was ineffective for the duration of the match and the Bluebags coasted to a crushing 34-7 victory. Facer later oversaw St George's record run of 11 premierships as a shrewd club secretary.

UNLUCKY TO MISS OUT ON THE CLIVE CHURCHILL MEDAL

1. Cooper Cronk—Melbourne, 2009
Melbourne halfback Cooper Cronk was a victim of selectors' blindness in 2009 when overlooked for the Churchill Medal in favour of perennial Australian custodian Billy Slater. Cronk set up two tries and booted Melbourne to victory over Parramatta with an outstanding in-play kicking game. Slater said in the postscript: "I don't deserve to wear it … Cooper Cronk deserved it."

2. Darren Lockyer—Brisbane, 2006
Brisbane's inspirational captain Darren Lockyer was desperately unlucky not to add a second Clive Churchill Medal to his list of accolades in 2006 when he was snubbed for teammate Shaun Berrigan in the Broncos' 15-8 win over Melbourne. Lockyer set up Brisbane's first try, played a key hand in the second and slotted the match-sealing field goal in a tremendous Grand Final display.

3. James Maloney—Sydney Roosters, 2013
The Roosters' best player in their 2013 Grand Final win, Maloney was stiff to miss out on the best-afield nod when Australian selectors plumped for Manly No.7 Daly Cherry-Evans. The Sea Eagles half was excellent but Maloney's poise and penetration in the second half were central to the Roosters' comeback, and he was perfect with the boot.

4. Ben Kennedy—Newcastle, 2001
Even champion halfback Andrew Johns admits that he "robbed" Ben Kennedy of the Clive Churchill Medal in 2001. Kennedy scored a try and set the tone with fearless running and intense defence. It was one of the most inspiring forward performances of the NRL era.

5. Greg Alexander—Penrith, 1991
Greg Alexander played a match-winning hand in Penrith's first premiership success but was scuttled for Clive Churchill honours when Bradley Clyde was awarded his second Clive Churchill in a losing side. Alexander's most important plays came off the boot: a 40-metre field goal put Penrith ahead 13-12 with seven minutes to play, while his sideline conversion wrapped up the Panthers' inaugural title.

6. Jason Nightingale—St George Illawarra, 2010
As is often the case in the decider, no single player dominated the 2010 Grand Final

so there was no clear-cut choice for the Clive Churchill Medal. But Jason Nightingale can consider himself unlucky not to become the first outside back to win the honour after a scintillating two-try effort that was quality from siren to siren.

7. Brad Fittler—Sydney Roosters, 2002
Craig Fitzgibbon was awarded the Clive Churchill Medal in 2002, but Brad Fittler's performance is the one that fans remember. A courageous Fittler got off the turf after being smacked high by Warrior Richard Villisanti, and turned in a masterly performance to lift himself and his team after the cheap shot.

8. Tonie Carroll—Brisbane, 1998
Renowned defensive protector Tonie Carroll put in an attacking performance of a lifetime in 1998 and was unlucky to be overlooked for Gorden Tallis in the Clive Churchill Medal stakes. Carroll finished a magnificent try and was involved in everything in a super showing by the tough Bronco lock.

9. Luke Phillips—Sydney Roosters, 2000
In a courageous Roosters performance against a superior Broncos team in 2000, Luke Phillips personified the effort of the Tricolours. Phillips was peppered all day and came up trumps on every occasion. The Roosters went down just 14-6 and there was no player who gave more than Phillips, who almost single-handedly prevented a blowout defeat.

10. Scott Gourley—St George, 1992
The Dragons were well and truly thumped in the 1992 decider, losing 28-8 to Brisbane, but Saints second-rower Scott Gourley was debatably best afield. He was relentless with his ball-carrying, offloading at will. A beautiful popped pass set up Ricky Walford's try, and he crossed himself in the dying minutes.

GREATEST FINALS TRIES

1. Shaun Berrigan—Brisbane, 2006
Brisbane trailed the Bulldogs 6-20 at halftime in the 2006 preliminary final showdown, but a length-of-the-field try four minutes after the break set a stunning comeback in motion. The Broncos' stand-in fullback, Justin Hodges, collected a long kick on his own try-line, got around two Bulldogs chasers and strode into open territory. He linked with Shaun Berrigan on Brisbane's 40-metre line, and the hooker

got rid of one defender before acrobatically planting the ball in the corner despite the desperate cover tackle of Willie Mason. The Broncos rode that momentum to pull off a remarkable 37-20 victory.

2. Eric Grothe—Parramatta, 1983

Eric Grothe scored perhaps the most barnstorming individual try in the game's history in the major preliminary semi against Canterbury. The wing giant took an offload from Steve Ella and headed in-field, fending and bumping off five Bulldogs defenders before crashing over in the tackle of Steve Mortimer at the end of a spectacular 60-metre run.

3. Andrew Farrar—Canterbury, 1985

A gruelling semi-final between defending champs Canterbury and upstarts Balmain was locked 8-all at fulltime, and appeared destined for a Tuesday replay after the first 19 minutes of extra-time failed to produce a scorer. But rookie fullback Michael Potter chanced his arm on the Bulldogs' 30-metre line and sent centre Andrew Farrar through a gap. Farrar brushed off Ross Conlon, outlasted the chase of John Davidson and took on Test fullback Garry Jack to plunge over in the corner for the match-winner.

4. Rod Silva—Canterbury, 1998

With Canterbury 6-18 down in the 74th minute of the preliminary final against Parramatta, backrower Robert Relf popped a sublime offload to a flying Rod Silva despite the attention of three Eels. The fullback dived over in the corner after a blistering 40-metre run, putting the Bulldogs' phenomenal comeback into overdrive. Canterbury eventually prevailed 32-20 after 20 minutes of extra-time.

5. Lewis Brown—New Zealand Warriors, 2011

The halftime score of 14-12 in favour of the Warriors over Melbourne in the 2011 preliminary final remained unchanged with four minutes of the pulsating second stanza remaining. But rookie halfback Shaun Johnson determined the Warriors' shock Grand Final berth, receiving the ball 20 metres out in front of the Storm's posts and displaying deceptive footwork, blistering speed and sleight of hand on a mesmerising cross-field jaunt. Johnson offloaded for Lewis Brown to dive over out wide, while James Maloney's sideline conversion confirmed a 20-12 boilover.

6. David Williams—Manly, 2013

Manly had fought back from 0-14 down to lead Souths 18-14 in the 2013 preliminary final before winger David Williams' unbelievable touchdown with 19 minutes remaining virtually sealed a Grand Final berth. Sea Eagles halfback Daly Cherry-Evans split the Rabbitohs' defence and fired a pass 10 metres out to Williams, who dragged the ball in from behind him and turned a moment before Greg Inglis arrived to bump him. The 'Wolfman' miraculously managed to stay in the field of play and kept his bearings to plant the ball in the corner for a freakish try.

7. Graeme Langlands—St George, 1968
Perennial powerhouse St George lost the 1968 preliminary final to Souths 20-8, but a sparkling try finished off by Graeme Langlands during the second half provided the Dragons with a glimmer of hope. Johnny Raper and Phil Hawthorne shifted the ball along the Saints' quarter-line before fullback Dennis Preston sliced through the Rabbitohs' defence. After a brilliant weaving 50-metre run, Preston floated a pass for Ken Maddison. Maddison flicked the ball out the back on Souths' quarter-line for Langlands, who scorched past two cover defenders to plant it in the corner.

8. Frank Stokes—Manly, 1991
A piece of trademark sleight of hand from Cliff Lyons released powerhouse centre Kevin Iro into space during the first half of Manly's epic 1991 minor semi loss to Canberra. The big Kiwi brushed off Raiders fullback Gary Belcher, then offloaded inside as he was swamped by the cover tackle of Mal Meninga, with nuggety Sea Eagles winger Frank Stokes backing up to finish off a 60-metre special.

9. Eric Grothe—Parramatta, 1982
A year before his famous finals try against Canterbury, Eric Grothe scored another scintillating SCG touchdown in the 1982 preliminary final defeat of Easts. The Eels swung the ball wide deep inside their own quarter to find Grothe, who produced three powerful fends to get rid of Roosters defenders on a scorching 90-metre run to the try-line.

10. Tony Iro—Manly, 1990
Manly's dazzling attacking armoury helped subdue Balmain in the minor preliminary semi in 1990, most notably in a breathtaking 80-metre movement finished off by giant Kiwi winger Tony Iro. Five-eighth wizard Cliff Lyons drifted across the Tigers' defensive line and feigned a long ball before popping a short pass over the top for a flying Michael O'Connor. The captain raced into Balmain's half before producing a brilliant move to get around Garry Jack. The fullback came at O'Connor again and reeled him in, but O'Connor unloaded for Iro, who crashed over in the tackle of Test teammate Gary Freeman.

GREATEST GRAND FINAL TRIES

1. Steve Gearin—Canterbury, 1980

An incredible try that capped Canterbury's first premiership win in 38 years, Steve Gearin's flyer in the 1980 decider against Eastern Suburbs rates as the greatest in Grand Final history. Inside their own half, Canterbury shifted the ball to its left with international Greg Brentnall steaming on to a Graeme Hughes short ball. Brentnall burst through the Easts' defence before launching a towering bomb 40 metres from the Roosters' line. Canterbury winger Steve Gearin came flying through and outjumped the shocked Eastern Suburbs defenders before diving over to score a magical try.

2. Ted Goodwin—St George, 1977

One of League's most flamboyant players during the 1970s, 'Lord' Ted Goodwin scored one of the great Grand Final tries in the drawn 1977 decider. Playing fullback, Goodwin collected a pass from a standing Rod Reddy near halfway and charged on to the ball and through the Parramatta defence. With only lanky Eels custodian Phil Mann between Goodwin and the try-line, the Dragons No.1 chipped. Goodwin and Mann chased desperately and an exaggerated lunge from Goodwin saw the Dragons score. Goodwin knocked himself out in the play but became a Grand Final legend because of its brilliance.

3. Johnny King—St George, 1964

Grand Final tryscoring great Johnny King finished it, but it was Graeme Langlands' lead-up work that made King's try in the 1964 decider win over Balmain so incredible. The only try of the 11-6 match, it showcased the emerging brilliance of fullback Langlands. Ten minutes into the second half, the Keith Barnes-captained Balmain led 4-2 when Tigers prop Bob Boland sent a thumping kick downfield for touch after receiving a penalty. Langlands, his toes millimetres from the line, leaned over and showed amazing balance to field the kick on his fingertips. He then put the ball under the wing and made a long, loping diagonal run. He burst through the Balmain line and found centre Billy Smith, who in turn put King over in the corner for a truly amazing try.

4. Darren Albert—Newcastle, 1997

Manly and Newcastle seemed destined for extra-time in the incredible 1997 Grand Final with the scores locked at 16-apiece well inside the final minute. The Knights were on the attack but seemingly setting for a field goal when future Immortal Andrew

Johns, at dummy-half, darted down the blindside in what was the final play of the game. Johns then cut back in, stood in an attempted tackle and found a flying Darren Albert charging on to it. Albert scooted through untouched to give the Knights their first premiership in the most dramatic of circumstances.

5. Pat Richards—Wests Tigers, 2005
It is perhaps the most mythologised and without question the most replayed Grand Final try of all. *That* try. The Benji flick. Pat Richards' forgotten fend. The 2005 Grand Final was all square at 6-apiece late in the first half when some Benji Marshall brilliance broke the game wide open. Inside their own 10, pinned in the corner, Wests Tigers fullback Brett Hodgson collected a kick from North Queensland star Johnathan Thurston and linked up with young five-eighth Marshall. Marshall put the after-burners on and sliced through the staggered Cowboys chase. With Matt Bowen coming across in cover, Marshall called Richards inside and threw a perfect flick pass that hit Richards on the chest. The Tigers winger then palmed off the covering Rod Jensen with a monster fend to dive over in the corner and set in motion a stunning Tigers Grand Final win.

6. Bob Fulton—Manly, 1973
The 1973 Grand Final was a bloodbath, an 80-minute opera of violence and thuggery. The dashing brilliance of Manly star Bob Fulton, one of the few players prepared to play football rather than resort to the vicious tactics of the majority, proved the difference in the clash with the Sharks. Fulton scored a double, with his first magnificent. Taking a flick pass from skipper Fred Jones, he scooted through four Sharks defenders, leaving them grasping at air, as he put Manly in front and well on its way to back-to-back Grand Final victories.

7. Nathan Blacklock—St George Illawarra, 1999
The most recent player to lead the premiership tryscoring tally for three straight years, Nathan Blacklock knew how to score like few others. He used both his unrivalled speed and an innate sense of timing to perfection in the 1999 Grand Final against Melbourne when he scored a scintillating try after collecting a Brett Kimmorley chip on his bootlaces 32 metres from his own line at full pace. He hit the ball so hard he emerged in a flash through the other side of the defence before sprinting away to score under the posts. The try gave the Dragons a 14-0 lead, but they were overrun by a gallant Melbourne 20-18 in the second half.

8. Brett Kenny—Parramatta, 1981
Parramatta five-eighth Brett Kenny incredibly scored three straight Grand Final doubles from 1981 to 1983, but without question his best was his second in the 1981 decider

that sealed the result against Newtown. A freakish talent, Kenny collected a deflected grubber 35 metres out from the Jets' line and tiptoed the sideline as he attempted to regain his balance. He then took off and, when confronted by Newtown fullback Phil Sigsworth, sold an incredible dummy and sprinted to the corner untouched.

9. Bob McCarthy—South Sydney, 1967
One of South Sydney's most beloved tries, Souths forward Bob McCarthy's intercept in the 1967 decider proved the difference in the Grand Final win over Canterbury. On the attack, the Berries shifted the ball right with hooker Col Brown attempting a long looping pass for centre Johnny Greaves. The pacy backrower McCarthy steamed on to it and ran the length of the field to give South Sydney a 5-2 lead on the stroke of halftime. Canterbury fought back to lead, but an Eric Simms penalty goal four minutes from time gave Souths a 12-10 premiership victory, their first in 12 seasons.

10. Steve Jackson—Canberra, 1989
Little-known Canberra prop Steve Jackson etched his name into Rugby League folklore with his barnstorming try at the end of extra-time in the 1989 decider. In just his 16th game, the bullocking front-rower charged on to a Mal Meninga pass 20 metres from the Tigers' line and pinned the ears back, stepping past Shaun Edwards and through the desperate tackle of Garry Jack, fending off Mick Neil and charging straight over the last-ditch efforts of Gary Freeman, Steve O'Brien and Kevin Hardwick to secure the Raiders' first premiership.

Chapter 3

REPRESENTATIVE MATCHES

BEST ORIGIN MATCHES

1. Game 2, 1991—Lewis and Geyer collide

One of the most fiery Origin clashes ever played, the second game of the 1991 series was a gripping affair from beginning to end. With the rain teeming down at the SFS, the game exploded on the stroke of halftime with NSW leading 8-6. An unnecessary high shot from Blues firebrand Mark Geyer on Queensland rake Steve Walters set the game alight and the two teams went to halftime with Wally Lewis and Geyer being separated by referee David Manson. More fireworks ensued in the second stanza, but Queensland looked set to wrap the series up when Dale Shearer sliced through to give the Maroons a 12-8 lead with just five minutes remaining and rain still pouring down. Mark McGaw quickly answered for NSW, however, before Michael O'Connor landed a pressure sideline conversion to keep the series alive 14-12.

2. Game 1, 1994—That's not a try, it's a miracle

The opening game of the 1994 Origin series is remembered for perhaps the competition's most iconic moment: Mark Coyne's match-winning try. NSW held the upper hand after a sensational Brad Mackay try set up by a sublime Brad Fittler chip that was collected by skipper Laurie Daley, who linked up with an unmarked

Mackay. Willie Carne brought the scores back to 12-10 with five minutes on the clock, and then, with a minute to play, the miracle. The Maroons went 60 metres, using the width of the field, with Coyne playing the ball to Meninga, who swept it to Langer, who put Carne away, who threw a one-hander to Renouf. The centre linked with Hancock, who passed to Darren Smith, who offloaded to Langer. Langer hit Meninga, who gave the ball to Coyne cutting back in. The Dragons centre burrowed his way over, giving Queensland its most famous win 16-12.

3. Game 3, 2012—Cronk keeps the streak alive

The deciding game of the 2012 series at Suncorp Stadium was an absolute classic. In what was Petero Civoniceva's farewell game at the ripe age of 36, Maroons halfback Cooper Cronk broke one of the tightest series ever played Queensland's way when he landed a 41-metre field goal with just seven minutes remaining. Queensland led 16-8 at the break, but Todd Carney levelled the scores 20-apiece with a pressure sideline conversion with 10 minutes left in the contest. Cronk's incredible drop goal proved the difference, though, giving Queensland seven straight series wins.

4. Game I, 1998—Carroll crashes over

Following three years of division caused by the Super League War, the game reunited in 1998 and the first match was an absolute belter. In a clash that saw the lead change five times and Queensland eventually win 24-23, debutant Tonie Carroll proved the hero for the Maroons. It seemed NSW had secured victory when Steve Menzies scored a try with five minutes to go, but Andrew Johns' missed conversion kept the game alive. The decisive play came from Kevin Walters, who kicked early in the set downfield. Ben Ikin won the chase, and three plays later Walters popped a short ball to Carroll, who crashed over next to the posts with 45 seconds remaining. Darren Lockyer slotted the goal and the Maroons had pulled a remarkable victory from the fire.

5. Game I, 1987—NSW sparkles

In the most remarkable finish in the first decade of State of Origin, NSW stunned a disbelieving Lang Park crowd when an incredible Mark McGaw try gave the Blues a remarkable win. NSW led 16-6 before the Maroons rallied, with Wally Lewis orchestrating tries to Dale Shearer and Tonie Currie that levelled the scores with just five minutes to play. Inside the last minute, the Blues found an overlap with Andrew Ettingshausen and McGaw combining to get close to the Maroons' line. McGaw's pass was deflected by Currie before a scramble in the Maroons' in-goal ensued, with McGaw and Peter Jackson grappling. 'Sparkles' McGaw got the ball down just a blade of grass before the dead-ball line. Referee Mick Stone awarded the try, leaving Wayne Bennett's Maroons in utter shock.

6. Game 2, 1989—Courageous Maroons survive

In what was unquestionably the most courageous Origin showing of all, an injury-ravaged Queensland desperately held off NSW. In front of a packed and baying SFS crowd, scores were locked at 6-apiece when the teams went for oranges, but it was the Blues holding the cards after Allan Langer was carted off with a broken ankle and Mal Meninga suffered a fractured eye socket. A busted elbow forced Paul Vautin off at halftime, and soon after the break Michael Hancock succumbed to a shoulder injury. Workhorse backrower Bob Lindner, who had played much of the match with a broken leg, could take no more in the final 15 minutes and the Maroons had just 12 men. The Blues kept coming, but the Maroons held firm for an awe-inspiring 16-12 win highlighted by Wally Lewis's iconic solo try.

7. Game 1, 2004—Golden Timmins

A stunning Shaun Timmins field goal gave NSW a remarkable victory in State of Origin's first golden point game. It was a low-scoring affair, with Queensland leading 4-0 at halftime after a Scott Prince dummy-half try. A Timmins touchdown levelled the scores and Craig Fitzgibbon's conversion put the Blues in front before Brent Tate finished off more Prince handiwork for Queensland to lock up the scores at 8-all. But it took just over two minutes of Origin's first instalment of golden point for Timmins to belt one of the competition's finest field goals. Timmins—in what was his second-ever field goal—kicked the ball 37 metres to cap a stunning game.

8. Game 3, 2006—Blues collapse

Queensland's incredible series streak started in dire circumstances for NSW. With 10 minutes to go, the Blues were leading 14-4 and seemed to have the 2006 series in their grasp. However, the Maroons clawed their way back into it with a beautiful Johnathan Thurston step putting Brent Tate away, the star centre racing 60 metres to score. Darren Lockyer then proved the hero by swooping on a loose Brett Hodgson pass deep in Blues territory and fending off Luke Bailey to score a memorable match-winner and kick off the Maroons' historic winning streak.

9. Game 3, 2002—A draw does it

Just the second draw in Origin history, the 2002 decider saw the game finish with scores level but Queensland retaining the shield. The match was filled with plenty of memorable moments: Gorden Tallis rag-dolling Brett Hodgson over the sideline; Shane Webcke's steamrolling try; video referee Chris Ward's contentious no-try decision against Darren Lockyer; and, of course, Dane Carlaw's open-field try that levelled the scores 18-apiece with 50 seconds remaining and gave the Maroons a series-saving draw.

10. Game 2, 1992—Alf's field goal

Allan Langer was known for many skills, but booting field goals was not one of them—that is, until the second game of the 1992 series at Lang Park. Queensland debutant Billy Moore scored the only try of the match—an 11-man Maroons team at one stage holding the Blues out after two players were sin-binned—while Rod Wishart's two penalty goals left the scores locked 4-all at the break. A desperate second stanza failed to see the deadlock broken until the final minute, when Langer potted a well-timed 18-metre one-pointer to give ecstatic Queensland a 5-4 victory.

BEST ORIGIN FINISHES

1. Game 1, 1994—Mark Coyne's miracle try

Behind 4-12 after struggling to keep pace with the Blues all night at the SFS, Queensland clung to a glimmer of hope when winger Willie Carne finished off a hot-potato try with five minutes to go, reducing the deficit to two points. The underdogs then concocted arguably the greatest match-winning try in the code's history in the dying stages. Starting on their own 40-metre line, the Maroons swept the ball from one sideline to the other and back again, passing it through 10 sets of hands before replacement back Mark Coyne stepped the NSW cover defence and reached out to score in the corner. Queensland had escaped with a 16-12 victory for the ages, one sure to haunt Blues players and supporters for eternity.

2. Game 3, 2002—Carlaw's charge

After the video referee had mystifyingly denied Queensland fullback Darren Lockyer a series-sealing touchdown, NSW snatched an 18-14 lead with five minutes of the 2002 decider to go courtesy of a Jason Moodie try. But as the clock ticked over into the 80th minute, veteran halfback Allan Langer—playing his 34th and final Origin match—shifted the ball to hard-running backrower Dane Carlaw on the Blues' 40-metre line. Carlaw fended off Moodie and strode into open territory before brushing off fullback Brett Hodgson to plunge over for a dramatic try out wide, stunning the Sydney crowd. Lote Tuqiri's missed conversion after the bell was academic—as the current holders Queensland retained the shield with the 18-all draw.

3. Game 1, 1998—Kevvie's big gamble

Queensland trailed by five points with less than two minutes of the '98 series opener remaining when, coming off their own line, Maroons five-eighth Kevin Walters produced one of the great all-or-nothing plays, booting the ball downfield. Ben Ikin won a desperate chase to the ball on halfway, and Queensland worked the ball into NSW's quarter over the next two rucks. A slick interchange of short passing stretched the Blues and saw Walters send debutant Tonie Carroll over near the posts with 45 seconds on the clock. Another first-gamer, fullback Darren Lockyer, slotted the pressure conversion after the siren to clinch an extraordinary 24-23 SFS triumph. The loss brought back harrowing memories for the seven NSW players who had endured a last-minute loss at the same venue in the corresponding match four years earlier.

4. Game I, 1987—McGaw's mad scramble

NSW debutant Mark McGaw scored the match-winning try after a crazy sequence inside the final 90 seconds of the '87 series opener at Lang Park. With the scores locked 16-all, Blues halves Peter Sterling and Brett Kenny combined to create an overlap on Queensland's 40-metre line. Kenny linked with Andrew Ettingshausen, who put clubmate McGaw away down the sideline. McGaw's return pass to 'ET' was desperately knocked down by Tony Currie before the ball ricocheted off Peter Jackson's boot back into the in-goal. McGaw and Jackson grappled in a frantic chase, and the Blues centre planted his hand on the ball just inside the dead-ball line. Referee Mick Stone pointed to the spot, to the disbelief of the Maroons players—but replays showed he had made the correct call and NSW went one-up.

5. Game 2, 1991—O'Connor's goal of a lifetime

Queensland led 12-8 near the end of the explosive second Origin clash of 1991, played in a Sydney downpour. But NSW trudged into the Maroons' quarter on the back of a series of daring offloads before Ricky Stuart's long speculative pass found centre Mark McGaw, who angled between three defenders to slide over in the corner. Michael O'Connor, who had missed a conversion from a similar position to draw the series opener and was dropped before injuries gave him a reprieve, curled the conversion through from the right touchline to edge the Blues in front with two and a half minutes remaining. Seldom remembered, however, are the frantic final stages after NSW fumbled the kick-off. Des Hasler narrowly beat Willie Carne to a Langer kick in the Blues' in-goal, while NSW was forced to rebuff more pressure after the subsequent line dropout with 50 seconds left. The home side hung on for a dramatic 14-12 win to level the series.

6. Game I, 2006—Finch's match-winner

An 11th-hour, fourth-choice inclusion as NSW halfback for the 2006 series opener, Brett Finch would prove the match-winner in the dying stages. Queensland had fought back from a 0-14 deficit to level at 16-all after Johnathan Thurston's 77th-minute sideline conversion of Steve Bell's try. But Finch stepped up with 90 seconds on the clock and drilled a 35-metre field goal down the middle, thereby becoming an unlikely Origin hero with the No.20 on his back.

7. Game 2, 1993—Big Mal's bad decision
One of the finest Origin matches on record finished with one of the great missed opportunities. NSW led 16-12 inside the final 90 seconds of a topsy-turvy SFS encounter when the Maroons desperately began to fling the ball around 10 metres out from their own line. Skipper Mal Meninga put lock Bob Lindner into space on the flank and backed up to take a return offload before speeding away from Blues forwards Paul Sironen and Glenn Lazarus, and bumping off fullback Tim Brasher on halfway. Meninga charged down the right-hand sideline and only had the cover defence of Laurie Daley to beat, but he propped and passed to cumbersome forward Mark Hohn instead of taking the NSW captain on, and the move broke down. The Blues' heart-stopping win sealed a second straight series triumph.

8. Game 2, 1992—Alfie's deadlock-breaker
A try to Queensland's debutant lock Billy Moore and two penalty goals to NSW winger Rod Wishart was the sum total of the scoring in the first 78 minutes on a rainy night at Lang Park in '92. However, after a Queensland scrum win, diminutive halfback Allan Langer broke the deadlock with a little over 60 seconds to go when he drifted behind a screen and snapped a field goal from just inside the Blues' 20-metre line. The Maroons claimed the Blues' desperate short kick-off and squared the series via the 5-4 result.

9. Game 1, 2005—Bowen's golden point intercept
A phenomenal series opener at Suncorp saw Queensland storm out to a 19-0 lead before NSW scored four unanswered second-half tries to snatch a one-point advantage. The Maroons' debutant halfback Johnathan Thurston forced the match into golden point with a wobbly field goal from close range just over two minutes from fulltime. In the fourth minute of extra-time, Blues No.7 Brett Kimmorley sealed his place in intercept infamy when he fired a cut-out pass in the direction of his centre Matt Cooper. The ball was plucked out of the air by Maroons interchange Matt Bowen, who raced 40 metres for the match-winning try.

10. Game 1, 2004—Timmins' towering field goal
History was made when the tense Sydney series opener in 2004 became the first Origin match to go into golden point after the scores were locked at 8-all at fulltime. The match-winning play came from an unlikely source, with makeshift five-eighth Shaun Timmins hammering over a magnificent 37-metre field goal in the third minute of added time.

GREATEST STATE OF ORIGIN TRIES

1. Mark Coyne—Queensland, Game 1, 1994
Queensland's "miracle" try started and ended with Mark Coyne in arguably the most memorable moment in Origin history. Inside the final minute and with the Maroons trailing 10-12, Coyne played the ball on his own 40 and it was collected from dummy-half by Mal Meninga, who swung it to Allan Langer, who fired it to Kevin Walters, who in turn hit Willie Carne. Carne straightened the attack before throwing an overhead basketball pass over Rod Wishart to Steve Renouf. The headgear-wearing centre took off down the left sideline for 20 metres before flipping the ball back inside to winger Mick Hancock, who got away an incredible pass to Darren Smith after being smashed by Andrew Ettingshausen. Smith hit a charging Langer, who found Meninga as a desperate David Gillespie held on. Meninga headed towards the corner before passing to Coyne, who then ducked inside through the tackle of Brad Fittler and under the last-ditch attempt of Ricky Stuart for an incredible match-winner. "That's not a try, that's a miracle!" screamed caller Ray Warren.

2. Billy Slater—Queensland, Game 2, 2004
One of the greatest individual tries ever scored, Billy Slater's chip-and-chase beauty in the second game of the 2004 series was sheer magic. In just his second Origin, Slater steamed on to a Darren Lockyer grubber inside Queensland's own half. He veered right before chipping left over Anthony Minichiello's head and outsprinting Blues winger Luke Lewis to scoop the ball up on the try-line and dive over. Slater spiked the ball in celebration—he'd just put the Maroons on top in what would be a series-levelling 22-18 victory.

3. Matt Gidley—New South Wales, Game 3, 2000
NSW centre Matt Gidley scored a double on debut in the Blues' 56-16 rout of Queensland in 2000, including arguably the greatest try in the state's history. Gidley finished an incredible movement that started with a scrum 40 metres out on the right edge that went wide to the left and came back to the right corner through 11 sets of hands before Gidley dived over. Andrew Johns made the initial break and then switched play with his second touch as the Blues desperately flung the ball to the right. Johns then touched the ball for a third time, throwing the final pass to Gidley in a spectacular four-pointer.

4. Greg Dowling—Queensland, Game 2, 1984

Maroons prop Greg Dowling scored one of the unlikeliest tries in State of Origin history on a rain-sodden SCG. Camped 10 metres out from the NSW try-line, Wally Lewis put up a chip towards the Blues' posts. Garry Jack and Peter Tunks turned to collect the kick but it clunked into the crossbar and bounced back towards Dowling, who took a fingertip catch off his bootlaces in the pouring rain before sliding over.

5. Jarryd Hayne—New South Wales, Game 1, 2007

A prodigious 19-year-old debutant in the opening game of the 2007 season, NSW winger Jarryd Hayne put his amazing skill set on display just before halftime when he scored a jaw-dropping try. Queensland centre Brent Tate put in a grubber on halfway, but it was trapped by Hayne. With no momentum and facing his own try-line, Hayne picked up the ball and pushed off Justin Hodges before tiptoeing down the sideline. He then grubbered past the Queensland cover and won the race to finish an incredible try.

6. Tonie Carroll—Queensland, Game 1, 1998

Maroons enforcer Tonie Carroll scored just one try in his lengthy State of Origin career, but it could not have been more important. NSW seemed to have the opening game of the '98 series—Carroll's debut match—in its keeping with a 23-18 lead and less than two minutes to play. Stuck on their own 10-metre line, Maroons pivot Kevin Walters kicked on the first tackle for a flying Ben Ikin, who won the race for the ball some 45 metres out from the try-line. The Maroons kept driving and three tackles later they were just 10 metres away. Jason Smith put a jink on and landed outside his opposite, hitting brother Darren, who threw a deft ball to Kevin Walters, whose pass to a charging Carroll was equally sublime. Carroll crashed over near the sticks, with Darren Lockyer's after-the-bell conversion wrapping up a famous 24-23 victory.

7. Mark McGaw—New South Wales, Game 1, 1987

Mark McGaw's magnificent winner on debut in the opening game of the 1987 series was perhaps the most thrilling moment NSW fans enjoyed during the Queensland-dominated 1980s. The scores were locked at 16-all with less than two minutes to play when McGaw flashed on to an Andrew Ettingshausen pass down the right edge. McGaw raced 20 metres before tossing the ball back inside to 'ET', who became tangled up with Queenslander Peter Jackson. The ball was knocked down by Tony Currie before hitting Jackson's foot and rolling into Queensland's in-goal. In a desperate chase, McGaw outpaced Jackson and grounded the ball just inside the dead-ball line to settle a famous victory.

8. Wally Lewis—Queensland, Game 2, 1989
A try that came to personify Wally Lewis's brilliance and determination, the Queensland skipper's solo effort in the second game of the '89 series was something special. Queensland half Michael Hagan collected a spilt NSW ball 30 metres out from the Blues line and quickly scooped it to Lewis, who went on a fierce angled run to the corner. He sliced between Chris Mortimer and the lunging Laurie Daley before fending off fullback Garry Jack and crashing over out wide. Lewis pumped his fists in celebration of a spectacular individual try.

9. Adam Mogg—Queensland, Game 3, 2006
A left-field selection from Canberra for the final two games of the 2006 series, Adam Mogg would became the hero of Queensland's series win after scoring a double in game two and then capping off his fairytale call-up with a magnificent try in the decider. With the game scoreless after 10 minutes, Maroons half Johnathan Thurston bombed for the corner. Mogg came flying through and leapt over Eric Grothe Jr to pluck the ball, but appeared to be pushed into touch before sending it to ground. However, after an indelible act of acrobatics, Mogg had somehow managed to plant the ball before landing over the touch in-goal line, his entire body out.

10. Israel Folau—Queensland, Game 3, 2008
Melbourne winger Israel Folau had a magnificent first season with Queensland in 2008, scoring in each match of the 2-1 series victory. Folau's best was unquestionably his flying effort in the Stadium Australia decider. Following a Johnathan Thurston bomb to the corner, Folau climbed above opposite Anthony Quinn, his knees reaching Quinn's head, to pull down the ball before grounding it, upside down, with one hand.

BEST TEST MATCHES

1. 1990: Australia 14—Great Britain 10
Great Britain's 19-12 series-opening upset at Wembley put immense pressure on the 1990 Kangaroos as they headed to Old Trafford for the next Test. In the second half of an absorbing encounter, a spectacular team try finished off by Cliff Lyons saw Australia holding a tenuous 10-6 lead before Great Britain replacement back Paul Loughlin intercepted a pass by Kangaroos halfback Ricky Stuart and raced 50 metres to level the scores. But with the clock deep into injury time and the Kangaroos hemmed inside their half, Stuart produced the ultimate redemption play when he dummied and broke into the clear on his own quarter-line, scampering 70 metres before the Great

Britain defence converged. Mal Meninga loomed in support to take a short ball from Stuart and crash over for the unforgettable match-winner.

2. 1950: Australia 5—Great Britain 2

The Ashes-deciding third Test between Australia and the 1950 Lions was played on an SCG quagmire, with 40 tonnes of river sand spread on the pitch to alleviate the deluge that had transformed the famed venue into a swimming pool. Skippers Clive Churchill and Ernest Ward traded penalty goals for a 2-all halftime scoreline before St George winger Ron Roberts etched his name into Rugby League folklore with 14 minutes of the series remaining. The conditions limited free-flowing attack, but Australia pieced together a sweeping backline movement and 19-year-old centre Keith Middleton drew winger Jack Hilton to put Roberts in the clear. The tall flanker powered 40 yards to the Sheridan Stand corner to score the most famous try in the Australian game's history. The hosts defended their 5-2 lead grimly to break Great Britain's three-decade-long stranglehold on the Ashes in potentially the greatest moment in Australia's 104-year Rugby League narrative.

3. 2013: New Zealand 20—England 18

New Zealand and England produced possibly the greatest World Cup match ever at Wembley as the 2013 tournament reached the championship stages. The hosts struck the first blow when Sam Burgess laid on a try for Sean O'Loughlin, but tries to Kiwi wing wunderkind Roger Tuivasa-Sheck—the first from a freakish pass by Dean Whare—either side of the break pushed the Cup holders out to a 14-8 lead. New Zealand's grip on the world-champions tag appeared to be slipping when England centre Kallum Watkins sliced through to score before Burgess powered over with 13 minutes to go. Trailing by four, the Kiwis were unable to convert several gilt-edged chances, but a hot-stepping try to halfback wizard Shaun Johnson levelled the scores inside the final 20 seconds. Johnson booted the pressure conversion from close range to propel the Kiwis into the final.

4. 2006: Australia 16—New Zealand 12

The Kangaroos gained revenge for their shock loss to the Kiwis a year earlier with a nail-biting victory in the 2006 Tri-Nations final in Sydney. Australia took a 10-6 lead into the break after both sides scored a first-half try, but New Zealand drew level when imposing centre Iosia Soliola crashed over. Opposing halfbacks Johnathan Thurston and Stacey Jones traded penalty goals in a tense closing half-hour, and the final became the first golden point Test when field-goal attempts by the brilliant No.7s went astray. Thurston was denied a match-winning try by the video referee in extra-time, but after 87 pulsating minutes the Kangaroos' linchpin made a break and sent skipper Darren Lockyer away to reassert their international supremacy with a score under the posts—Australia's first try in 76 minutes.

5. 1962: Australia 18—Great Britain 17

The dead-rubber third Test at the SCG in '62 produced one of the most thrilling and eventful encounters in Ashes history. Mike Sullivan was sent off for throwing a punch at opposing winger Ken Irvine, while Derek Turner was marched along with Australian prop Dud Beattie. Needing to leave the field due to a dislocated shoulder, Beattie famously goaded Turner into fighting him, and the pair were despatched by referee Darcy Lawler. Despite being down to 11 men, Great Britain led 17-11 inside the final quarter, but Irvine kept Australia in touch with a penalty goal before flashing over in the corner for his second try (from a dubious pass by Wests forward Bill Carson) in the dying minutes. In an oft-recounted yarn, the legendary winger—only a stopgap goalkicking option—landed the touchline conversion after Lawler suggested adjusting the positioning of the ball, snatching an epic 18-17 victory on fulltime.

6. 1995: Australia 30—New Zealand 20

Australia had one hand on a place in the 1995 World Cup final when it led New Zealand 20-6 after 50 minutes of the semi. Steve Menzies had just scored a spectacular 70-metre try—his second for the day and Australia's fourth unanswered touchdown—but the Kiwis, with just three penalty goals to show for their toil, launched an astonishing comeback in the final quarter. Richie Barnett and Tony Iro scored stunning tries to reduce the deficit to four points before a barnstorming try in the corner from Kevin Iro levelled the scores with two minutes on the clock. Matthew Ridge's sideline conversion and a long-range left-footed field goal both shaded the upright, and the match headed into extra-time. But New Zealand's brave riposte was doused by brilliant tries to Terry Hill and Brad Fittler in the added period, getting the relieved green-and-golds home after 100 incredible minutes.

7. 1974: Australia 22—Great Britain 18

Despite his side's win in the series opener, Australian captain-coach Graeme Langlands was controversially dropped as fullback for the second Test of the '74 Ashes. He was reinstated for the deciding third Test after the green-and-golds were upset in the return clash, and the match would prove to be a personal triumph for the great 'Changa'. Great Britain led 11-10 at halftime, but Langlands scored a brilliant try in the second half and kicked Australia to a 17-16 lead with a penalty goal. Ron Coote's try—converted by Langlands—sealed a 22-18 victory over the gallant underdogs and retained the Ashes. The skipper passed 100 points in Ashes Tests during the match and was chaired from the field by his teammates with the adoring SCG crowd chanting, "Changa! Changa!"

8. 2010: New Zealand 16—Australia 12

Australia and New Zealand were locked at 6-all at halftime of the tense 2010 Four Nations final in Brisbane, but the hosts gained a crucial advantage when Paul Gallen and Greg Bird combined to send Billy Slater away for a try. The Kiwis hung in grimly, however, before a glorious Benji Marshall grubber produced a try for winger Jason Nightingale. Marshall's conversion cannoned off the upright to leave New Zealand two points in arrears, but the skipper conjured a miraculous long-range try after running the ball on the last with less than two minutes remaining. Halfback Nathan Fien dotted down after a helter-skelter 70-metre movement, providing the shell-shocked Kangaroos with a sickening sense of déjà vu from their boilover loss to the Kiwis at the same venue in the '08 World Cup final.

9. 1955: France 29—Australia 28
The flamboyant 'Les Chanticleers' recovered from a double-figure deficit to level the 1955 series in the second Test at the 'Gabba in Brisbane. Trailing 16-28 during the second half, France produced some brilliant attacking football to run in three unanswered tries and take a shock one-point lead. A long-range penalty goal attempt 90 seconds before fulltime by second-rower Brian Davies was off-target and sealed a phenomenal comeback for the tourists, who went on to win their second straight series on Australian soil with another upset in the decider.

10. 1992: Australia 10—Great Britain 6
A Rugby League international record crowd of 73,361 packed London's Wembley Stadium for the gripping 1992 World Cup final between bitter Anglo-Australian rivals. The hosts led 6-4 at halftime courtesy of three penalty goals to halfback Deryck Fox. Australian skipper Mal Meninga landed two first-half penalties, the second after a vicious elbow from British hooker Martin Dermott that fractured five-eighth Brad Fittler's cheekbone. Fittler courageously battled on and played brilliantly, but the crucial moment came deep into the second half when Brisbane pivot Kevin Walters (who was injected from the bench) fired a beautiful pass for debutant centre Steve Renouf to sprint 20 metres and score in the corner. Meninga's sideline conversion made it 10-6—a lead Australia doggedly defended until fulltime to retain the Cup.

BEST TEST FINISHES

1. 1930 Ashes: Australia 0—England 0
One of the most famous Ashes matches ever played, the deciding Test of the 1929-30 series is still remembered for the most controversial call in Anglo-Australian Rugby League history. The match—played in freezing conditions at Swinton—was locked at 0-all with time close to expiring when Australia won a scrum 30 metres out from the England line. Halfback Joe 'Chimpy' Busch darted for the corner and crashed

over with England lock Fred Butters on his back. Referee Bob Robinson was about to award a try that would have given Australia the Ashes and the crowd was pouring out on to the field when, amidst the chaos, touch judge Albert Webster declared Busch had taken out the corner post. The final score was left at 0-0, with Robinson famously declaring, "Fair try Australia, but I am overruled."

2. 1950 Ashes: Australia 5—Great Britain 2

Australia regained the Ashes after 30 years in one of the most thrilling finishes in Test history. On a quagmire of an SCG, scores were locked at 2-all after captains Clive Churchill and Ernest Ward had traded penalties. And then, with 14 minutes to go, Ron Roberts scored debatably the most famous try in Australian Rugby League history. The lanky St George winger—who, remarkably, played just three years in the premiership—finished a marvellous backline move that saw Mick Crocker fire a pass from dummy-half to Keith Holman, who passed it on to Frank Stanmore, who linked with Doug McRitchie, who hit Keith Middleton, who found Roberts wide open. In deep mud, Roberts sprinted 40 metres with Australia riding him to the line to give the hosts a 5-2 lead. They defended stoutly for the remainder before the crowd stormed the field in jubilation to celebrate one of Australia's most important wins.

3. 2006 Tri Nations Final: Australia 16—New Zealand 12

Australia, who had not lost a major tournament since the 1972 World Cup but had dropped the 2005 Tri Nations to New Zealand, had a fight on its hands in 2006 against a gallant Kiwi team. Australia had built a 12-10 lead before a penalty goal to Stacey Jones with 10 minutes remaining levelled the scores. With 20 seconds to go, Australia appeared to have snatched victory after giant forward Willie Mason made a bust and kicked ahead with Johnathan Thurston diving on it, only to have the video ref rule no try for a Greg Inglis knock-on. Australia would not be denied in extra-time, though. In the seventh minute of golden point, Thurston fooled Kiwi Frank Pritchard with a dummy and sprinted 50 metres before linking with skipper Darren Lockyer, who outlasted the cover to plant the ball under the posts and break Kiwi hearts.

4. 1972 World Cup Final: Great Britain 10—Australia 10

The 1972 World Cup final was played in front of just 4500 fans, with the French seemingly not interested in the tournament, which was a classic battle between old foes Australia and Great Britain. The game featured an incredible length-of-the-field try from Great Britain speedster Clive Sullivan, and a phenomenal diving try from Graeme Langlands that was inexplicably disallowed. It was also an incredibly dramatic finish, with a try from Britain's Mike Stephenson levelling the scores at 10-all with just under seven minutes to go. A draw was good enough for the Brits and they defended stoutly, but Australia had plenty of chances to win late. Bob Fulton missed three field goals and Ray Branighan skewed a penalty attempt that saw the match go to extra-time. Britain missed a penalty in the added period but it didn't matter and they were crowned champions of the world.

5. 2010 Four Nations Final: New Zealand 16—Australia 12

The 2010 Four Nations final was a tight tussle from beginning to end, with the Kiwis and Kangaroos locked 6-all at the break and the latter holding a slender 12-10 advantage with less than two minutes to play. Stuck deep in the Kiwis' own half on the last tackle, New Zealand skipper Benji Marshall opted to run the ball. He fired a cut-out ball to Shaun Kenny-Dowall, who penetrated the Aussie line and found Jason Nightingale, who tiptoed along the sideline before throwing a one-arm overhead hook pass inside that went at least 3 metres forward. Marshall collected the bouncing ball but was pulled down a metre from the try-line. However, he managed to pop the ball to half Nathan Fien, who crashed over amid wild celebrations from a Kiwi team that had defeated Australia in the final of the World Cup and then the Four Nations in the space of two years.

6. 1977 World Cup Final: Australia 13—Great Britain 12

Great Britain looked set to claim the World Cup crown in 1977 in a gritty and determined performance in Sydney before the grand finale saw the cards fall Australia's way. Great Britain led late in the match before Parramatta halfback John Kolc proved the hero. In what would be his only Test appearance, the livewire halfback crossed in the dying stages to give Australia a 13-12 lead. Britain seemed to have pinched victory late but a controversial decision not to play advantage robbed the visitors and saw Australia claim its fifth World Cup.

7. 1990 Ashes: Australia 14—Great Britain 10

After two undefeated tours of Great Britain, Australia was shocked to lose the 1990 Ashes opener 19-12. Fear set in when Britain played a superb game in the second Test at Old Trafford. A fine Great Britain side that contained the likes of Ellery Hanley, Garry Schofield and Martin Offiah had the scores locked at 10-all deep into injury time, but Ricky Stuart busted the defence on his own line and ran 80 metres to link with skipper Mal Meninga, who dived over among three British players for a thrilling match-winner.

8. 2003 Ashes: Australia 22—Great Britain 18

The 2003 Ashes Series was one of the closest on record, with all three Tests decided by less than a converted try, but it was the series opener that stood out for its incredible finish. Great Britain led 18-14 with 10 minutes to play courtesy of a Brian Carney try and a magnificent Paul Deacon sideline conversion after the lead had switched numerous times in an enthralling match. Britain was clinging to victory before a Craig Wing bust from halfway and a turned ball inside to Darren Lockyer got Australia to a 20-18 lead that was capped by a consolation penalty goal.

9. 1924 Ashes: Great Britain 5—Australia 3
England secured the 1924 Ashes in the Second Test at the SCG with a thrilling 5-3 victory. Queensland winger Cecil Aynsley had given Australia a 3-0 lead that they clung grimly to until the very death. England captain and star Jonty Parkin toed the ball 15 metres to score in the final minute, and Clive Sullivan's conversion gave Great Britain a rousing 5-3 win.

10. 1955 Test Series: France 29—Australia 28
The dazzling French side that toured in 1955 set Australia alight, with the great Jean Dop the star of the series. Australia had beaten France 20-8 in the first Test at the SCG but 'Les Chanticleers' triumphed in the return clash in Brisbane. Australia led 28-16 late in the match before some exhilarating attacking football saw France eradicate the 12-point deficit in six minutes. Australian backrower Brian Davies could have won the game on fulltime with a 48-metre shot from the right of the sticks, but pushed it wide.

BEST TEST TRIES

1. Cliff Lyons—Australia v Great Britain, 1990
Australia's back-from-the-dead victory over Great Britain at Old Trafford featured another of the most spectacular Test tries ever scored prior to Mal Meninga's match-winner. The Kangaroos kept the ball alive from one sideline to the other and back again on the hosts' 40-metre line before Meninga's brilliant basketball pass—the 12th pass of the movement—put Andrew Ettingshausen into space down the right touchline. Confronted by the cover defence, Ettingshausen put in a perfect centring chip-kick that sat up for Cliff Lyons—who had handled twice earlier in the sequence—to crash over.

2. Brent Tate—Australia v New Zealand, 2005
Brent Tate scored a scintillating 90-metre individual try to spark a Kangaroos comeback in the 2005 Tri-Nations opener. With Australia trailing 0-18 during the first half, Tate received a pass from Anthony Minichiello 10 metres out from his own line. He scythed through the Kiwis' kick-chase line and produced another devastating step to get around Frank Pritchard. Tate's thrilling run to the corner featured powerful fends to get rid of Roy Asotasi and Brent Webb, but the centre's heroics were ultimately not enough and the Kiwis prevailed 38-28.

3. Nathan Fien—New Zealand v Australia, 2010
Benji Marshall spearheaded the Kiwis' stunning 2010 Four Nations final upset of Australia and crafted an unbelievable match-winning try inside the final two minutes. The skipper received the ball on the last tackle 35 metres out from his own line and skipped to the outside before firing a brilliant long ball to put Shaun Kenny-Dowall into space. The centre drew Lote Tuqiri to release winger Jason Nightingale on a tiptoeing run down the right touchline. Nightingale flung a (dubiously forward) one-handed speculator on the Kangaroos' 20-metre line. The ball was touched in flight by Darren Lockyer and regathered by Marshall, who headed towards the posts and threw the ball over his head as he was tackled by Cooper Cronk. Halfback Nathan Fien collected the loose ball to score behind the posts and steal an incredible 16-12 win in front of a Kiwi-heavy Suncorp Stadium crowd.

4. Mal Meninga—Australia v Great Britain, 1990
Trailing 0-1 in the Ashes series, and with the scores locked at 10-all deep into injury time, Australia conjured the most famous late match-winner in Test history in the second clash at Old Trafford. The Kangaroos kept the ball alive inside their own quarter before Ricky Stuart—who had earlier thrown an infamous intercept pass to loosen Australia's grip on the Ashes—dummied his way through the defensive line. The halfback scurried 70 metres before positioning captain Mal Meninga, who shouldered defenders out of his way to dive over for a miraculous 14-10 escape.

5. Hec Gee—Australia v England, 1932
Australia's courageous 'Battle of Brisbane' victory in the second Test of the 1932 Ashes series was sealed by a famous long-range try. Hampered by an ankle injury suffered earlier in the match, brilliant five-eighth Eric Weissel collected a ball dropped by England on Australia's quarter-line and raced 70 metres before being pulled down by the cover defence. The ball rolled loose and was picked up by halfback Hec Gee to score his second try and confirm a 15-6 triumph. In light of his injury, 'Weissel's Run' became part of the fabric of Ashes folklore.

6. Ron Roberts—Australia v Great Britain, 1950
St George winger Ron Roberts scored Australia's most famous Test try on an SCG swamp in 1950 to secure the Ashes for the first time in 30 years. The gruelling, mud-caked third Test decider against the touring Lions was locked at 2-all midway through the second half when Australia produced a sparkling backline movement that defied the conditions. Halves Keith Holman and Frank Stanmore combined before Doug McRitchie passed to his centre partner Keith Middleton. The 19-year-old Middleton fed tall powerhouse Roberts, who had had an unhappy day with his hands but gloved the ball when it mattered and streaked 40 metres to

score in the right-hand corner. The green-and-golds clung to the 5-2 lead to clinch the most treasured victory in their history.

7. Brian Carlson—Australia v Great Britain, 1959
A new superstar and a brilliant veteran combined for a magnificent 90-metre try in Australia's 18-12 loss in the Ashes decider at Wigan on the 1959-60 Kangaroo Tour. The green-and-golds swept the ball along the backline deep inside their own territory before 20-year-old centre Reg Gasnier scorched into open spaces. Confronted by the Great Britain cover defence on the quarter-line, Gasnier dummied past the fullback to send winger Brian Carlson over untouched. The casual genius Carlson stepped his way past a Great Britain defender in the in-goal to bring the ball around behind the posts.

8. Jonathan Davies—Great Britain v Australia, 1994
Great Britain was on the ropes in the first Ashes Test at Wembley in '94 after captain and halfback Shaun Edwards was sent off for a reckless high tackle on Bradley Clyde during the first half. But a brilliant individual try by Welsh wizard Jonathan Davies spearheaded a gutsy 8-4 win for the 12-man hosts. Receiving the ball on halfway from Dennis Betts, Davies got on the outside of Clyde and sped into open territory before the fullback—two days shy of his 32nd birthday—showed an incredible turn of pace to get around the Kangaroos' greyhound No.1 Brett Mullins and score in the corner just before halftime.

9. Steve Renouf—Australia v New Zealand, 1998
At the end of '98, Australia produced a dazzling try just six minutes into the third Test against New Zealand at Auckland's North Harbour Stadium. Lock Jason Smith chip-kicked ahead for his brother, centre Darren, who linked with Allan Langer. The mercurial halfback kicked ahead towards the vacant left corner and the ball sat up for winger Tim Brasher, who produced a brilliant airborne offload on the inside for centre Steve Renouf to finish a spectacular four-pointer that set the tone for an emphatic 36-16 win.

10. Frank Drake—Australia v Great Britain, 1962
Brisbane Souths' Frank Drake created history by becoming the first Australian fullback to score a try in an Ashes Test, finishing off a spectacular movement in the third match of the '62 series at the SCG. Captain and halfback Arthur Summons broke the line before sending powerhouse winger Eddie Lumsden into space down the right flank. Lumsden kicked in-field for John Raper, but former Balmain custodian Drake—who replaced ex-clubmate Keith Barnes for the dead-rubber encounter—displayed blinding speed to catch the ball on the full just short of the line and dot down near the posts. Australia eventually secured a famous last-gasp 18-17 victory.

Chapter 4

THE CLUBS

ADELAIDE RAMS—GREATEST PLAYERS (1997-98)

1. Kerrod Walters—41 games (1997-98)
A two-time Grand Final winner, 1990 Kangaroo and Queensland Origin hooker Kerrod Walters became Adelaide's highest-profile acquisition after a mass player cleanout at Brisbane. But the veteran rake was consistently the Rams' best player, featuring in all but one of their 42 premiership matches—including 34 as captain.

2. Dean Schifilliti—35 games (1997-98)
With Walters occupying his preferred No.9 spot, fellow stalwart Dean Schifilliti played 35 games for the Rams at hooker, lock, five-eighth, halfback and as an interchange, while also skippering the club in one match in each of the 1997 and '98 seasons.

3. Alan Cann—33 games (1997-98)
Nuggety second-row strongman Alan Cann was another member of the Broncos' purge at the end of 1996—just months after he made his only Origin appearance. The '92 Grand Final hero was an outstanding servant for Adelaide; after an injury-interrupted Super League season, he missed just three games in 1998.

4. Tony Iro—20 games (1998)
Dynamic second-rower and New Zealand Test veteran Tony Iro made a sizable impact in his sole season at Adelaide, playing 20 of the club's 24 NRL games. Iro played in five Tests for the Kiwis against Australia and Great Britain during his stay with the Rams.

5. Kevin Campion—14 games (1997)
Kevin Campion played 14 of the Rams' 18 Super League premiership games at prop and second-row, and was their only Tri-Series representative, featuring in two matches for Queensland. Campion left for Brisbane and Grand Final success in 1998.

6. Luke Williamson—29 games (1997-98)
Brisbane-born Luke Williamson was one of the Super League season's standout rookies, debuting as an 18-year-old and proving a fine goalkicker during 12 appearances at centre and five-eighth. He added starts at wing and lock to his repertoire in 1998 as one of the doomed club's best players.

7. Graham Appo—14 games (1998)
Utility wback Graham Appo set several club records in a remarkable half-season stint at Adelaide after being dumped by Canberra for disciplinary reasons. Appo's three tries and 24 points against Gold Coast were Rams match records (he equalled the latter a week later), while his tally of 12 tries and 116 points set new season marks and left him ranked as the top try-scorer and point-scorer in the club's short history.

8. Noel Goldthorpe—22 games (1998)
Former Wests, St George and Hunter halfback Noel Goldthorpe provided much-needed stability and class in the No.7 jumper throughout 1998—playing all but two of Adelaide's 24 games—after three players were tried with little success during the Rams' inaugural season. Goldthorpe also captained the Rams in six games during the first half of '98, but was replaced following coach Rod Reddy's axing.

9. Mark Corvo—36 games (1997-98)
A fringe player at Canberra, powerful prop Mark Corvo was a consistent contributor for the battling Rams, missing just six of the club's Super League and NRL premiership matches. Corvo returned to the Raiders after the Rams folded and had a season at Brisbane in 2001.

10. Andrew Hick—35 games (1997-98)
Strong no-frills front-rower Andrew Hick, a veteran of six seasons at Cronulla and Wests, featured in 35 of Adelaide's 42 premiership matches. Hick received few plaudits from outside the club, but was one of the Rams' steadier and more reliable performers.

ANNANDALE—GREATEST PLAYERS (1910-20)

1. Ray Norman—46 games (1910-13)
The most able of the famous Norman brothers—all four of whom played together in 1910, on one of only two occasions this has occurred in premiership history—Ray Norman was an outstanding centre/five-eighth who would go on to play two Tests for Australia after leaving the 'Dales. Norman played four seasons with Annandale, topping the pointscoring list with 84 in the club's first four years in the competition. He toured with NSW in 1912 and played on until 1921 with Eastern Suburbs and South Sydney. Norman coached Easts and Manly after retiring.

2. Bob Stuart—16 games (1911-12)
Annandale's first and only international, Bob Stuart defected to Rugby League in 1911 after playing for the Wallabies the year before. He played two tour matches with the 1911-12 Kangaroos, becoming Australia's 17th dual international. A mobile forward, he spent six seasons with Annandale, playing 45 games and scoring 27 points.

3. Rex Norman—56 games (1910-14)
The youngest of the Norman brothers, talented pivot Rex Norman played in Annandale's first five seasons, topping the club's tryscoring tally in 1913 and '14. He played another eight seasons with Eastern Suburbs and South Sydney and toured with the 1921-22 Kangaroos, where he played 21 games but did not appear in a Test.

4. Wal Palmer—54 games (1912, 1914-17)
A highly respected hooker, Wal Palmer represented NSW twice in 1915 while at Annandale. Originally at Western Suburbs, where he debuted in 1910, he moved to the 'Dales in 1912 and stayed for five seasons before returning to Wests and then spending two years with Newtown. Palmer scored two tries and kicked 11 goals in his time with Annandale.

5. Bill Haddock—80 games (1910-13, 1916-17, 1919-20)
Versatile forward Bill Haddock's two stints with the 'Dales saw him finishing as the club's most-capped player, with 80 appearances. He toured New Zealand with NSW in 1912 and scored 11 tries in his long Annandale career. Upon the 'Dales' demise, he played three seasons for equally ill-fated club Glebe.

6. Ted Burdett—28 games (1911, 1913-14, 1919)

An established top-grader with Newtown during the first two years of the premiership, Ted Burdett joined the 'Dales in their inaugural season of 1910 and became the club's first representative player when he was selected for NSW in 1911. The versatile forward played with Annandale until 1914, returning to Newtown before a final year with the 'Dales in 1919.

7. Jack Bain—61 games (1915-20)

Annandale's all-time leading try-scorer, the centre/winger crossed the stripe 16 times in his six-season career with Annandale. Jack Bain topped the 'Dales' tryscoring tally in the 1916 and '17 campaigns, scoring one of just two all-time Annandale hat-tricks in the latter season in a 14-9 loss to Easts.

8. William Doyle—27 games (1914-16)

One of Annandale's great point-scorers, William Doyle holds the record for most points in a season with 46 in 1916 (two tries, 20 goals) and most points in a match, scoring 12 against Norths in '15 (six goals). His 83 career points is just one behind record-scorer Ray Norman, who scored 84 in only three years at the club (1910-13).

9. Roy Norman—27 games (1910-12)

Along with brothers Ray, Rex and Bernard, Roy Norman was part of the only set of four brothers (until the Burgess boys at Souths in 2013) to play together in a first grade match. His 15 career tries with the 'Dales ranks second, while his 55 points ranks third—feats he achieved in just 31 games before shifting to Glebe and then South Sydney.

10. Lyall Wall—9 games (1913)

Lyall Wall scored a double and three goals against Western Suburbs in the second-last round of the 1913 season to set the record at 12 for most points in a single game (equalled in 1915 by William Doyle). Wall spent just the '13 season with Annandale, playing also for Balmain (1912, 1913-19), Western Suburbs (1920) and St George (1921). He played for NSW in 1919.

BALMAIN TIGERS—GREATEST PLAYERS (1908-99)

1. Charles 'Chook' Fraser—190 games (1910-26)

A pint-sized centre, five-eighth or fullback, Charles 'Chook' Fraser was a giant of the game in its formative years. Arguably the most important figure in the history of the club, Fraser played 17 years for the Watersiders, winning six premierships. The youngest player to represent Australia for nearly a century, he toured with the 1911-12 and 1921-22 Kangaroos, captaining Australia in all three Tests on the latter trio. Fraser scored 492 points for Balmain during an outstanding career and skippered the team to its 1924 triumph. He was named in the ARL's 100 Greatest Players and is a member of the Rugby League Hall of Fame.

2. Arthur 'Pony' Halloway—106 games (1909-11, 1915-20)
One of the game's great halfbacks and widely considered the finest coach of the first half-century of the code, Arthur 'Pony' Halloway enjoyed two stints with Balmain with the second netting five premierships under his stewardship. A tourist with the 1908-09 and 1911-12 Kangaroos, Halloway was front and centre in all of the Watersiders' five premiership triumphs that decade. He was named in the ARL's 100 Greatest Players in 2008 and holds the record for the most premiership medallions with, 11 won as a player and a coach.

3. Keith Barnes—194 games (1955-68)
An outstanding fullback in an era of champion custodians, Keith Barnes enjoyed a wonderful career with the Tigers despite never winning a premiership. One of the great goalkickers in premiership history, Barnes at one time held the premiership pointscoring record with 1519 points. His Test career spanned a decade despite competing with fullbacks like Les Johns, Ken Thornett and Graeme Langlands. After a stellar career that lasted 14 seasons, during which he won innumerable games for the Tigers with his accurate kicking, Barnes retired a year before Balmain's only premiership triumph in its last 50 years as a standalone club. He was named Player of the Year in 1963.

4. Wayne Pearce—192 games (1980-90)
A footballer ahead of his time, local junior Wayne Pearce became the archetype for the modern athlete with his healthy living and commitment to fitness and diet. One of the finest lock forwards in Rugby League history—recognised by his naming in three top 100 players of all time lists—Pearce represented NSW 15 times and Australia on 18 occasions, and served the Tigers with distinction for a decade. The lasting image of both the '88 and '89 decider defeats was captain Pearce in tears after the match. He toured with the '82 Kangaroos, playing all five Tests, but controversially missed the '86 tour after failing a fitness test. Pearce was awarded the Rothmans Medal in 1985 and was twice named Dally M Lock of the Year. *Going Home (Theme of the Local Hero)* by Mark Knopfler played at Leichhardt Oval when Pearce completed his lap of honour after his final home game in 1990 after a knee injury forced his retirement.

5. Jim Craig—49 games (1915-21)

A Balmain junior, Jimmy Craig won five premierships with the Watersiders during the club's first great era. One of the most versatile players the game has ever known, Craig could play any position in the backline and even played lock and hooker at times. An evasive runner and classy playmaker, he starred in the great Balmain sides of the 1910s before moving to Queensland and helping the Maroons dominate the 1920s. Craig was selected for the 1921-22 Kangaroo Tour and was named in the ARL's 100 Greatest Players and in the QRL Team of the Century.

6. Paul Sironen—246 games (1986-98)

A monstrous second-rower who made an immediate impact, Paul Sironen won the Dally M Rookie of the Year in his debut season and went on to forge a stellar career at club, state and Test level. A three-time Kangaroo tourist and a starter in both the '88 and '92 World Cup finals, Sironen's best was often saved for rep football. He played in both the '88 and '89 deciders for Balmain, though, and was close to the Tigers' best in the latter, scoring a memorable try. He was named in the second-row in David Middleton's 25-year team. Sironen is the Tigers' most-capped player and captained the club for several seasons at the end of his career.

7. Ben Elias—234 games (1982-94)

A niggly and classy rake who was the first choice NSW hooker for the better part of a decade, Benny Elias toured twice with the Kangaroos while suffering Grand Final defeats in both 1988 and '89. A fiery type who refused to take a backward step, Elias was outstanding in both decider defeats. The playmaking dummy-half scored a try in '88, and could have sealed victory in the '89 Grand Final had his attempt at a field goal not ricocheted off the crossbar. A three-time Dally M Hooker of the Year, Elias was named *Rugby League Week*'s Player of the Year in 1988. Elias played five Tests and assumed the NSW captaincy in 1990.

8. Tom Bourke—147 games (1939-48)

A Balmain great who featured in six premiership deciders with the Tigers, Tom Bourke was a talented centre-cum-lock. He scored twice in Balmain's 1939 premiership final win and played in the '44 triumph before captaining the club to the '46 and '47 titles, kicking the Tigers to victory in the former. His rep career was stymied by World War II, but Bourke was widely regarded as one of the most outstanding centres of the 1940s.

9. Steve Roach—185 games (1982-92)

A blockbusting and aggressive front-rower who often found himself on the wrong side of officials, Steve Roach was a regular in the representative arena for much of his career and a key component of Balmain's rise to premiership contention in the late 1980s. Roach played 17 Origins and 19 Tests, travelling on the 1986 and 1990 Kangaroo Tours. He was excellent in the 1989 Grand Final after missing the '88 decider through suspension, but a subbing decision left him stranded helplessly on the sideline when Canberra defeated the Tigers 19-14 in extra-time. Roach won three Dally M Prop of the Year gongs, and was named in the CRL Team of the Century and in the 100 Greatest Players in 2008.

10. Arthur Patton—117 games (1937-48)
Scoring a club-record 95 tries in 117 games for the Tigers, Arthur Patton was one of the game's top wingers throughout Balmain's glory era of the 1940s. He played in all three of the Tigers' title wins during the decade, and broke the club record for most tries in a match, with five. A broken leg kept him out of the '45 final loss, but he courageously played the second half of the 13-12 final win against St George with the same injury, in what was his final match.

11. Harry Bath—30 games (1946-47)
Known as 'The Old Fox' and considered by many to be the greatest player not to represent Australia, Harry Bath spent just two seasons with Balmain but won a premiership in both before forging a spectacular career in England. He joined Balmain from Queensland after the war, and his ball-playing and go-forward were central to the club's successes in both seasons. Bath played for NSW in '46 while at Balmain, but injury ruled him out of Australian consideration against the famed 'Indomitables'.

12. Joe Jorgensen—95 games (1944-53)
An outstanding goalkicking centre, Joe Jorgensen emerged during Balmain's golden era of the 1940s to become Australia's first post-war Test skipper. With 734 points for Balmain, he is third on the list of the Tigers' all-time leading scorers. Jorgensen played in the '44 Grand Final win but his finest hour came in the '47 decider, when he returned from a stint in the bush to score all 13 of the Tigers' points in their victory over Canterbury. He topped the premiership's pointscoring in 1950.

13. Arthur Beetson—74 games (1966-70)
An Immortal and widely regarded as one of the great forwards Australian Rugby League has seen, Arthur Beetson's time at Balmain was rocky and controversial. An immense talent who played for Australia during his first year in the premiership, Beetson was widely criticised for his weight and poor training ethic. Though he was occasionally brilliant at the Tigers, he was dogged by controversy and famously missed the 1969 Grand Final through suspension. Beetson left Balmain at the end of the 1970 season and went on to greater achievements at Eastern Suburbs.

14. Dave Bolton—78 games (1965-70)
An outstanding British half who toured with the Lions in 1958 and '62, Dave Bolton was the Tigers' best in their last Grand Final win in 1969. After joining the team in 1965, Bolton led the way for Balmain to become the first club side to defeat Britain in 1966. His shining moment came in the '69 decider where his fine organisation and outstanding kicking game, which netted two field goals, drove the Tigers to the greatest of all Grand Final upsets.

15. Pat Devery—38 games (1944-47)
A sensational five-eighth who played four seasons with Balmain before leaving to undertake an outstanding career in England in the great exodus of 1947, Pat Devery starred in three premierships and a finals loss and represented NSW and Australia. He topped the premiership scoring in '47 before departing for the UK, where he went on to become one of Huddersfield's finest players.

16. Garry Jack—242 games (1982-92, 1995)
Garry Jack was rated the best fullback in Australia from 1984 to 1988 and won the Golden Boot award in 1986. The three-time Dally M Fullback of the Year represented NSW 17 times and Australia on 21 occasions, including the 1986 Kangaroo Tour and the 1988 World Cup final. Jack played in the '88 and '89 deciders for the Tigers and is the club's second most-capped player.

17. Tim Brasher—185 games (1989-97)
A schoolboy phenom who played in the '89 Grand Final defeat as an 18-year-old, fullback/centre Tim Brasher went on to enjoy a long and decorated representative career with NSW and Australia. Brasher was the premiership's equal top try-scorer in 1992 and Australia's fullback in the 1995 World Cup final. In 2003 he was named as a reserve in Balmain's greatest team.

18. Peter Provan—155 games (1961-69)
The brother of St George legend Norm, Peter Provan carved his own bit of Rugby League history when he captained Balmain to their last premiership, the great upset of 1969 against South Sydney. Provan played a single Test and in two losing deciders, but the classy lock became a Tigers icon and was chaired from the SCG after his final game, the '69 Grand Final.

19. Bobby Lulham—85 games (1947-53)
A blistering winger with an outstanding step, Bobby Lulham scored an incredible 85 tries in 85 games before his career was curtailed by a poisoning scandal that gripped Sydney. Lulham scored an incredible 28 tries in his debut season and won a premiership that year before touring with the 1948-49 Kangaroos. He played three Tests.

20. Larry Corowa—98 games (1978-83)
A scintillating winger known as 'The Black Flash', Larry Corowa had a brilliant debut season with the club, scoring 24 tries and winning selection on the end-of-season Kangaroo Tour. He made his Test debut in 1979, scoring a try against Great Britain. The fastest player in the game during the late 1970s—beating the reigning Stawell Gift champion in a race at Wentworth Park—Corowa's career was curtailed by injuries and defensive woes come the 1980s.

BALMAIN TIGERS—GREATEST COACHES (1908-99)

1. Arthur 'Pony' Halloway—70 games (1916-20)
Arguably the top pre-war coach and the mentor with the most premiership successes, Arthur Halloway got his start as captain-coach of Balmain, where he guided the great team of the 1910s to four titles in his five seasons at the helm. Halloway took over the reigning premiers in 1916 and steered them to back-to-back titles in 1916-17 and 1919-20. He coached four teams after his playing days ended but never returned to Balmain. His 78.6 per cent strike rate remains the best in Balmain history.

2. Norm 'Latchem' Robinson—143 games (1930, 1944-47, 1954-56)
A giant at Balmain who had an association with the club for more than six decades as a player, coach and administrator, Norm 'Latchem' Robinson led the side to three premierships and two decider defeats during his eight years as a head coach. After an unsuccessful stint as captain-coach in 1930, he won three titles in four years as the fast and talented Balmain side of the 1940s reached its potential under his stewardship. He returned in 1954 and took the club to the Grand Final in 1956—a loss to St George in the first of the Dragons' 11 straight Grand Final wins.

3. Bill Kelly—120 games (1914-15, 1938-43)
An outstanding centre who became known as 'The Prince of Coaches' after guiding Balmain to a premiership on the back of an undefeated season in 1915, Bill Kelly returned to the club two decades later to add more silverware to the trophy cabinet. A New Zealander who represented his adopted country of Australia, Kelly helped set up the great Balmain dynasty of the 1910s and helped build the fine side of the 1940s. The Watersiders won a premiership in 1939 and made the finals in five of his six seasons before he left for stints at St George and Canterbury.

4. Warren Ryan—76 games (1988-90)

The coach of the 1980s lost nothing in his move to Balmain after successful stints at Newtown and Canterbury, taking the Tigers to Grand Finals in his first two seasons. Warren Ryan harnessed a quality Balmain side that had played finals footy in four of the previous five years, and took them to the '88 decider against his former club Canterbury. The Bulldogs won 24-12 and more heartache was to follow in '89 when the Tigers lost in extra-time to Canberra, where Ryan's use of the bench was widely criticised. After securing a finals berth in 1990, he left for Western Suburbs.

5. Athol Smith—60 games (1948-50)

A tough Balmain forward who won premierships with the Watersiders in 1939 and '44, Athol Smith led the club to three finals series in his three years as coach. Getting the head job in 1948, Smith's side lost the Grand Final challenge to Wests in his first year and the final to St George in his second. After a semis exit in 1950, Smith was replaced by Jim Duckworth and the Tigers failed to make the finals for five straight years.

BALMAIN TIGERS—BEST DAYS (1908-99)

1. September 20, 1969: An upset for the ages

In what is considered the greatest Grand Final upset in the history of the premiership, a plucky Balmain defeated great rivals South Sydney 11-2. Led by brilliant English five-eighth Dave Bolton and inspired by skipper Peter Provan, the Tigers shocked a Souths team that won two titles either side of the defeat. Reserve Sid Williams scored the only try of the decider, but it is rookie coach Leo Nosworthy who is credited with the 'lay down' tactics that won Balmain the Grand Final.

2. August 21, 1915: Unbeaten

Balmain claimed its first premiership and recorded the first undefeated season in premiership history with a 7-4 win over hated rivals Souths. The Rabbitohs led 4-2 at halftime but a George Robinson try took the Watersiders to victory in a famous clash at the Agricultural Ground. Balmain won 12 and drew two in a stellar season with a team that included 'Chook' Fraser, 'Pony' Halloway, Jimmy Craig and Bill Kelly.

3. July 28, 1917: Three in a row

Balmain made it three premierships in a row with a runaway title victory. The Watersiders lost just one game all season and finished eight points clear of Souths in second place. Jack Robinson scored 14 tries for Balmain that season but it was their defence that won them the title, conceding just 61 points in 14 games.

4. September 2, 1939: Souths smashed

In a total decimation of loathed rivals South Sydney, Balmain won its sixth premiership and its first in 15 years with a 33-4 demolition of the Rabbitohs. Balmain led 7-2 at halftime but a double to Tom Bourke and tries to Frank Hyde, Jack Redman, Jim Quealey, Dawson Buckley and Athol Smith saw the score blow out in the second stanza.

5. September 14, 1946: Balmain hang on

In a brutal and tight premiership decider, Balmain hung on to defeat St George 13-12 for its eighth premiership. The Saints scored four tries to three, but the boot of Tom Bourke got the Watersiders home. A brawl erupted after the final whistle but it didn't dampen the Tigers' spirits after a gritty win.

BALMAIN TIGERS—WORST DAYS (1908-99)

1. August 29, 1999: The end of days

Balmain played its final match as a standalone club two weeks after members voted to merge with Western Suburbs. The Tigers lost 42-14 to Canberra at Bruce Stadium. Wayne Pearce was coach and Darren Senter captain, with Senter and Laloa Milford the club's last try-scorers. Two weeks earlier the club had played its last home game, a 20-10 win over Parramatta at Leichhardt Oval.

2. September 19, 1909: South Sydney screw-job

Appalled by the decision of the League to stage the 1909 premiership final as a preliminary game to a Kangaroos-Wallabies feature, Balmain and South Sydney agreed not to play the match. Balmain held up its end of the bargain but Souths showed up, kicked off, regathered, scored and were awarded the premiership on forfeit.

3. September 24, 1989: So close

Balmain appeared to have its first premiership in 20 years in its grasp at halftime in the '89 decider, leading 12-2 in a dominating performance against the Canberra Raiders. The game seemed so in hand that coach Warren Ryan subbed off his two best forwards, Steve Roach and Paul Sironen, and replaced them with defensive specialists. A John Ferguson try in the dying minutes levelled the scores, and Canberra ran over the top of Balmain in extra-time in what was the greatest Grand Final ever.

4. September 11, 1988: Flattened
In one of the most controversial Grand Finals in history, Canterbury downed Balmain 24-12. The Tigers had made an extraordinary run from fifth spot to play in the decider, but midway through the first half star centre Ellery Hanley was knocked out from a late shot by Canterbury star Terry Lamb and the Tigers never recovered.

5. March 31, 1974: Wooden spoon pain
Five years after its last triumph, Balmain claimed just its second wooden spoon. The season kicked off with the club's worst-ever loss, a 62-5 smashing at the hands of Western Suburbs at Lidcombe where the Magpies ran in 14 tries. The Tigers won just four matches all season as the club reached its lowest ebb.

BRISBANE BRONCOS—GREATEST PLAYERS (1988-2013)

1. Darren Lockyer—355 games (1995-2011)
As a fullback, Darren Lockyer won three Grand Finals and captained Australia and Queensland to stunning successes, establishing himself as one of the all-time great No.1s. He switched to five-eighth in 2004 for the benefit of his club—and went on to become one of the code's best-ever pivots. Lockyer skippered the Broncos to a stirring title triumph in a remarkable 2006 season that saw him collect his second Golden Boot award. His phenomenal career ended with records for most appearances in first grade, Origin and Tests, and he also racked up unprecedented marks for Tests as captain and Test tries for Australia. Lockyer was named Brisbane's Player of the Year in 2002-03 and '11, won six Dally M positional gongs and has scored the most points (1195) and second-most tries (123) in the club's history. Brilliant in every facet of attacking play, Lockyer was a peerless clutch performer and a cool-headed leader; he is the benchmark to which every future Broncos linchpin and captain will be compared.

2. Allan Langer—258 games (1988-99, 2002)
Perhaps the dominant player of the 1990s, Allan Langer skippered Brisbane to its first four Grand Final triumphs. The Broncos regularly rode the diminutive Langer's match-turning brilliance in becoming Rugby League's premier club. Elusive, quick off the mark, and possessing a glittering array of kicking and passing attributes, Langer was at times an unstoppable attacking force. He endured disappointments on consecutive Kangaroo Tours, but represented Australia 24 times and played a then record 34 Origins across 16 seasons to be named halfback in Queensland's Team

of the Century. He was named Brisbane's Player of the Year five times and won a Rothmans Medal (1992) and a Dally M Medal (1996). The only halfback to score a century of first grade tries, Langer's comeback for Brisbane as a 35-year-old in 2002—following a famously successful Origin return the previous season—only enhanced his status as one of the game's greatest and most unique players.

3. Shane Webcke—254 games (1995-2006)

Shane Webcke is regarded by most as the greatest front-rower of the NRL era, and was Brisbane's engine-room cornerstone of four premiership victories after succeeding Glenn Lazarus as the club's No.1 prop. A ferocious proposition with or without the ball, Webcke's determination, commitment and courage were exemplified by his fighting through serious injuries to lead the charge for the Broncos. The veteran of 25 Tests for Australia and 21 consecutive Origins for Queensland played fewer than 20 games for Brisbane just once in his last 10 seasons—another pointer to his remarkable durability. Dally M Prop of the Year from 2000 to 2002, Webcke was named Brisbane's Player of the Year in 2001 and '03. Winning the 2006 Grand Final in his last match was a fitting exit for a tremendous clubman and all-round ornament to the game.

4. Kevin Walters—242 games (1990-2001)

Arriving from Canberra after playing in the '89 Grand Final, Kevin Walters formed a devastating combination with his twin brother, Kerrod, and halfback Allan Langer. The wily, durable five-eighth was one of just two players to feature in the Broncos' first five premiership triumphs—including captaining the club to NRL glory in 2000 after Langer's departure. Regularly a scapegoat following Queensland's losses after he succeeded Wally Lewis, and stuck behind the likes of Laurie Daley and Brad Fittler for the Australian five-eighth role, Walters nevertheless managed 20 Origin appearances, 11 Test caps and two Kangaroo Tours.

5. Petero Civoniceva—235 games (1998-2007, 2012)

Big, raw-boned prop Petero Civoniceva was an engine-room warhorse for the Broncos and a much-admired ambassador for Rugby League. He celebrated a debut-season Grand Final victory in 1998 before missing the 2000 Grand Final success through injury. But Civoniceva was an indefatigable forward-pack presence thereafter, starring in the Broncos' '06 premiership triumph and setting new records for most Test (45) and Origin (33) appearances by a forward, establishing himself as one of the game's greatest-ever front-rowers in the process. Civoniceva reluctantly left at the end of 2007 over a contract squabble, but returned to the Broncos for a swansong season after four years at Penrith. He was named Brisbane's Player of the Year in 2004 and '06-07.

6. Steve Renouf—183 games (1989-99)

A breathtaking attacking force in the centres, Steve Renouf scored a phenomenal 142 tries in 183 games for the Broncos. The headgeared flyer possessed unbelievable acceleration, great footwork, a unique swerve and a whip-crack of a fend, but also matured into a fine defensive player. The co-owner of club records for tries in a match (four, on five occasions) and a season (23), Renouf averaged more than 16 tries a year from 1991 to 1998. He played in Brisbane's first four premiership wins, scoring a famous long-range try in the '92 Grand Final and crossing for a hat-trick as man-of-the-match in the '97 Super League decider. Although he didn't produce his best in 11 Origins, Renouf scored 11 tries in 10 Tests and starred on the '94 Kangaroo Tour.

7. Gorden Tallis—160 games (1997-2004)

One of the great modern-day forwards, former St George wrecking ball Gorden Tallis spent eight seasons with the Broncos after sitting out the '96 season at the height of the Super League War. He was an intimidating game-changer with or without the ball and featured in Grand Final victories in three of his first four seasons in Brisbane. The veteran of 13 Tests (one as captain) and 17 Origins (seven as captain) skippered the club from 2001 to 2004 and continued to be an inspirational enforcer despite a career-threatening neck injury suffered in '01. He retired with 49 tries for the Broncos.

8. Wendell Sailor—189 games (1993-2001)

Flamboyant and extroverted but most of all a devastating presence on the flank, Wendell Sailor was regarded as the game's No.1 winger from 1995 until his defection to Rugby Union at the end of 2001. He crossed for 110 tries in 189 games for the Broncos, including a career-high total of 18 in three of his last four seasons at the club. A three-time Grand Final winner at Brisbane—and the club's Player of the Year in its 2000 premiership season—Sailor scored 17 tries in 16 Tests for Australia and represented Queensland with distinction in 14 Origin matches. Sailor returned from Union and a two-year recreational drug suspension to finish his career in great form for St George Illawarra under his former Broncos mentor, Wayne Bennett.

9. Michael Hancock—274 games (1988-2000)

Blockbusting winger Michael Hancock was the last of the Broncos originals to leave the club, posting 120 tries in a then record total of 274 games for the club, while he was one of only two players to feature in Brisbane's first five premiership triumphs. Twice told during the second half of the '90s his services were no longer required, Hancock stayed on to fight for a first grade spot, and playing in the Broncos' 1997-98 and 2000 Grand Final victories were just reward for his tenacity. Hancock played 14 Origins and 14 Tests, and toured twice with the Kangaroos.

10. Corey Parker—277 games (2001-13)

Goalkicking lock Corey Parker made his NRL debut in 2001, played a handful of Origin matches in '04-05 and featured prominently in the Broncos' '06 premiership success. But he truly established himself as one of the game's elite forwards in his second decade of first grade. Parker was named *Rugby League Week*'s Player of the Year in 2011 and '13, earning a Queensland recall and a Test debut in the former season; he remained an automatic rep selection two years later at the age of 31. A tremendous workhorse and dynamic in attack, Parker has developed into a leader: the 2009 and '13 club Player of the Year was installed as co-captain ahead of the 2014 season. Parker is poised to become just the second Bronco to play 300 games and the third to post 1000 points.

11. Kerrod Walters—182 games (1988-96, 2000)

Kerrod Walters displaced veteran hooker Greg Conescu in the Brisbane, Queensland and Australian line-ups, winning Dally M Hooker of the Year in 1989-90 and starring on the Origin and Test stages in those seasons. Although he was usurped at rep level by his older brother Steve, Walters was integral to the Broncos' 1992-93 premiership triumphs and won the club's Player of the Year award in '92. A brilliant attacker out of dummy-half, he rates among his era's finest hookers but joined Adelaide after a huge player purge in response to the Broncos' subpar '96 campaign.

12. Glenn Lazarus—118 games (1992-97)

Also a revered figure at Canberra and Melbourne, Glenn Lazarus was regarded as the missing piece of the Broncos' premiership puzzle, with the club claiming its first two titles in the peerless front-rower's first two seasons in Brisbane. Mobile, skilful and tough, Lazarus played 11 of his 21 Tests and 11 of his 19 Origins as a Bronco, but a serious knee injury robbed him of a third Grand Final win in 1997 ahead of his move to become the Storm's inaugural skipper.

13. Justin Hodges—156 games (2000-01, 2005-13)

Intermittently regarded as the game's best centre, Justin Hodges has been a marquee performer for Brisbane when not sidelined by persistent injuries. He left the club as a teenager in acrimonious circumstances, but returned after a three-year stint with the Roosters and was sensational at fullback in the Broncos' '06 premiership win. Hodges extended his representative tallies to 13 Test and 18 Origin appearances—figures that would certainly have been much higher if not for a luckless run with injuries. An often tempestuous character on and off the field, Hodges matured into a club leader and was named co-captain with Corey Parker ahead of the 2014 season.

14. Tonie Carroll—218 games (1996-2000, 2003-09)
Tonie Carroll arrived on the first grade scene as a hard-running three-quarter, but gained greater acclaim as a powerful lock and one of the code's most punishing defenders. He played in the 1997-98, 2000 and 2006 Grand Final victories, returning to the club in 2003 after a two-season stint with Leeds. The Christchurch-born torpedo controversially represented New Zealand at the 2000 World Cup before adding seven Test caps for Australia to his 18 Origin appearances for Queensland.

15. Sam Thaiday—189 games (2003-13)
The dynamic Sam Thaiday developed from a burly impact player into a tough, hardworking forward leader, breaking through for Queensland and Australian debuts during the Broncos' 2006 premiership season. The Broncos' '08 Player of the Year was routinely one of their most consistent players and popular clubmen. Dally M Second-rower of the Year in 2010-11, Thaiday's subsequent two-season stint as captain brought little success and saw the club sink to perhaps its lowest ebb, but he remained an automatic rep selection and had extended his record to 23 Tests and 20 Origins by the end of 2013.

16. Brad Thorn—200 games (1994-2000, 2005-07)
Roundly acclaimed for his cross-code exploits in becoming an All Blacks great on top of a host of representative honours in Australian Rugby League, towering forward Brad Thorn was a remarkably durable performer for the Broncos and featured in four Grand Final victories. He was a strong ball-runner and a bruising defender who played three Tests for Australia and made 11 Origin appearances for Queensland. Thorn returned impressively from his first Rugby Union stint to win an Origin recall, star in the Broncos' '06 title triumph and bring up 200 games for the club before embarking on another success-laden tenure in the 15-a-side game.

17. Karmichael Hunt—125 games (2004-09)
Karmichael Hunt was a courageous and brilliant all-round fullback for six seasons with the Broncos before his shock switch to the AFL. Mature beyond his years, Auckland-born Hunt made his NRL debut in 2004 aged 17 and was named Dally M Rookie of the Year before breaking into the Queensland and Australian sides while still a teenager. He played on the wing in the '06 Grand Final after returning from injury, but resumed in the No.1 the following season and cemented a legacy as one of the decade's best custodians. Hunt enjoyed a wonderful combination with five-eighth Darren Lockyer as a second receiver, and finished with 11 Test and 10 Origin appearances as a fullback or bench utility.

18. Wally Lewis—46 games (1988-90)
Immortal Wally Lewis's three seasons with the Broncos provided some of the extreme lowlights of his glittering career, but the incomparable five-eighth put the club on the map and was undoubtedly the dominant player of the late 1980s. Lewis scored 15 tries and was named Dally M Five-eighth of the Year in the Broncos' inaugural 1988 campaign. He was stripped of the captaincy at the end of '89 and virtually forced out of the club a year later after an injury-riddled season, but he still played eight Tests and eight Origins for the Broncos—all as skipper. Despite the glaring disappointments, 'The King' remains an iconic figure at the club.

19. Andrew Gee—255 games (1989-99, 2002-03)
Bullish prop/second-rower Andrew Gee became one of the most highly respected players in the Broncos' history. A tough no-frills forward, Gee later introduced deft touches into his game and became a leader for the club, for which he featured in the 1992-93 and 1997-98 Grand Final successes. The Broncos' Player of the Year in '98, he left the club at the end of '99, but returned from Super League to finish his career with Brisbane as a 33-year-old. Gee toured Papua New Guinea with the Australian side in 1991 (no Tests) and did not get the chance to play for his country again, but represented Queensland 17 times in an Origin career spanning 14 seasons.

20. Shaun Berrigan—186 games (1999-2007)
One of the most versatile players of all time, Berrigan filled several roles in magnificent style for the Broncos. Among his finest achievements for the club were coming off the bench in the 2000 Grand Final win, starring in the halves from 2001 to 2003, scoring 19 tries as a centre in '05, and winning the Clive Churchill Medal as a hooker in '06. Berrigan's 14 Test and 15 Origin outings were shared between starts at centre, five-eighth and halfback, and as an interchange utility.

BRISBANE BRONCOS—GREATEST COACHES (1988-2013)

1. Wayne Bennett—539 games (1988-2008)
Wayne Bennett's legacy as potentially the greatest coach in Rugby League history was cultivated at the Broncos. He guided the club from its inception for 21 seasons and 539 games—both all-time records—and six premiership victories from as many Grand Final appearances. Regarded as a father figure by the vast majority of his players, Bennett nurtured a culture that saw the Broncos become the code's pacesetters on and off the field. He was not afraid to make the tough calls, bucking

public opinion to do what he believed needed to be done for the club to move forward. Bennett's controversial decision to strip the seemingly untouchable Wally Lewis of the captaincy and eventually move him on from the club, as well as his extensive roster and staff cleanouts in 1996 and 2005, ultimately delivered titles. The Broncos lost more games than they won in just one season of his unprecedented tenure, joining St George Illawarra in 2009 after winning an astounding 63.7 per cent of his games with Brisbane.

2. Anthony Griffin—76 games (2011-13)

Highly regarded from a term as Craig Bellamy's assistant at Melbourne and as Brisbane's NYC mentor, Anthony Griffin was pitched into the Broncos' first grade role just over a fortnight out from the commencement of the 2011 NRL season. He enjoyed an outstanding start to his tenure, lauded for his Bennett-like qualities as the Broncos finished third and reached the preliminary final. Brisbane's start to life without Darren Lockyer was seamless—it won seven of its first eight games in 2012—but quickly came undone for Griffin and the club. The Broncos faded late in the year to scrape into eighth spot and were easily eliminated in week one of the finals, while the club had its worst-ever season in 2013, winning just 10 games and finishing 13th. Griffin's position was under intense scrutiny as former greats came out of the woodwork to lambaste the Broncos' decline, but the coach was given a reprieve ahead of 2014 and received the public backing of club management.

3. Ivan Henjak—51 games (2009-10)

A long-time reserve grade and assistant coach under Wayne Bennett at the Broncos, Henjak was given the arduous task of filling the master mentor's shoes in 2009. After a solid start, the knives were out for Henjak when a club-record 56-0 loss to Canberra saw the Broncos slide to 10th. But they came home with a wet sail, winning seven straight games before being bundled out in the preliminary final. Injuries did not help Henjak's cause in 2010—Justin Hodges missed the entire season and Darren Lockyer was rubbed out just as a late charge was beginning to materialise—but becoming the first Broncos coach to miss the finals in 19 years was an undesirable tag to wear. Amid reports of an unfavourable assessment of the coach by the playing group, Henjak was sensationally dumped less than three weeks out from the start of the 2011 season.

BRISBANE BRONCOS—BEST DAYS (1988-2013)

1. September 27, 1992—Premiership hijacked to Queensland
The international-laden Broncos entered the premiership in 1988 immediately burdened with sky-high expectations, but missed the finals in three of their first four seasons. However, coach Wayne Bennett's strength in his convictions, the brilliance of Allan Langer, the Walters twins and Steve Renouf, and the astute recruitment of forwards Glenn Lazarus and Trevor Gillmeister bore fruit in '92. The Broncos were runaway minor premiers and duly despatched Illawarra in the major semi to qualify for their maiden Grand Final before producing one of the most dominant performances of all time to rout St George 28-8 in the decider. Captain Langer and nuggety second-rower Alan Cann bagged doubles, while Renouf iced the result with a length-of-the-field try, sparking wild celebrations as the premiership trophy headed north of Sydney for the first time.

2. October 1, 2006—Sixth Grand Final the sweetest of them all
The Broncos became renowned for their late season fade-outs during the first half of the 2000s, and were headed for a similarly meek exit in '06 before embarking on a stirring revival in the latter rounds and staging a phenomenal preliminary final comeback to sink the Bulldogs. Brisbane entered the Grand Final as underdogs for the first time against minor premiers Melbourne, but the guile of captain Darren Lockyer and a committed all-round team performance set the platform for a tense 15-8 victory, sending retiring club legend Shane Webcke out a winner.

3. September 27, 1998—Best of the best
Stung by claims they had only won half a premiership by taking out the 1997 Super League title, the Broncos set about proving they were the best team in the land by winning the inaugural NRL competition. Brisbane's path to the minor premiership included an emphatic 26-6 away defeat of ARL champs Newcastle, while they swamped Melbourne and the Roosters in the finals on their way to the decider. Trailing Canterbury 10-12 at the break in the Grand Final, the Broncos' overwhelming class—including backline guns Langer, Walters, Lockyer, Renouf and Sailor, and engine-room trumps Tallis, Webcke and Carroll—ultimately told with a 28-point second-half shutout. Langer became the first skipper to hoist the NRL trophy following Brisbane's emphatic 38-12 victory.

4. September 17, 2011—Locky's courageous last act at Suncorp
The Broncos were overwhelming favourites to dispose of St George Illawarra in week two of the 2011 finals and led throughout, but couldn't land the killer blow. The 48,474-strong Brisbane crowd held its collective breath when skipper Darren Lockyer, making his final appearance at the ground, was left dazed after colliding with airborne Broncos fullback Gerard Beale, while the Dragons scored late to send the match into golden point. Lockyer played on with a fractured cheekbone, and in just the second minute of extra-time snapped a brilliant field goal under immense pressure to see the Broncos home 13-12. He was mobbed by teammates as the crowd went berserk—a spine-tingling moment that would turn out to be Lockyer's last in a Brisbane jumper when he was eventually forced to withdraw from the preliminary final.

5. March 6, 1988—Astonishing premiership debut
Fielding six Test players and a further two Origin reps in their starting line-up meant the Broncos were under pressure to perform from day one—and they lived up to expectations in spectacular fashion in their premiership debut in the opening round of 1988 at Lang Park. Brisbane obliterated defending premiers the Manly Sea Eagles (who contained seven Test stars themselves) to the tune of 44-10. Broncos captain Wally Lewis was at his masterly best, scoring two tries, while unheralded ex-Roosters lock Terry Matterson notched 24 points, a club record that stood for 14 years. The Broncos won their first six games before fading to miss the finals.

BRISBANE BRONCOS—WORST DAYS (1988-2013)

1. April 28, 1999—'Alfie' quits
The Broncos began their defence of the inaugural NRL premiership in disastrous fashion, losing their first five games in 1999 with several superstars battling to find form. In an unprecedented act by coach Wayne Bennett, captain and perpetual linchpin Allan Langer was benched during a jammy draw with North Queensland. The brilliant halfback, who had played for Australia just two days before the Cowboys clash, announced his immediate retirement the following Wednesday in a tearful press conference, citing his loss of enthusiasm for the game. The Broncos rallied to reach the finals, while Langer made an admirable comeback with the club in 2002.

2. September 20, 2008—Semi-final heartbreaker ends Bennett's tenure
Following a qualifying final victory over the Roosters, the Broncos were rocked by a police investigation into sexual assault allegations levelled at rep stars Karmichael

Hunt, Sam Thaiday and Darius Boyd ahead of their semi-final showdown with defending champs Melbourne Storm, who had been shock week-one losers to the Warriors. With the off-field crisis, coach Wayne Bennett's impending departure and the 50,466-strong Suncorp Stadium lifting the atmosphere to fever pitch, the archrivals staged one of the most absorbing and dramatic finals matches of all time. Underdogs Brisbane led throughout and held a two-point advantage in the dying minutes, but match-sealing tries to Boyd and Ben Hannant were denied by the video referee. An error by Ashton Sims then gifted the Storm possession deep in Broncos territory, and Greg Inglis dived over out wide with 30 seconds remaining to snatch a 16-14 win. Most Broncos lay slumped on the turf, while captain Darren Lockyer's anguished screaming remains one of the most poignant post-match scenes in recent memory.

3. August 1, 2009—Capital punishment
Life after Wayne Bennett must have seemed like a dark and scary place for the Broncos following their Round 21 trip to Canberra in 2009. The Raiders, languishing in 14th spot, subjected the visitors to a 10-try, 56-0 drubbing—a club-record defeat and Brisbane's seventh in eight games. After being given a bath by the media and supporters in the days that followed, the Ivan Henjak-coached Broncos won their next seven matches to reach the preliminary final stage.

4. September 21, 2011—Lockyer pulls out of preliminary final
Following Darren Lockyer's heroic golden point field goal in the semi-final eclipse of St George Illawarra, attention turned to the retiring skipper's race against the clock to be declared fit for the preliminary final showdown with Manly. He had surgery to insert three titanium plates into his fractured cheekbone, and each passing day seemed to deliver a different theory on the likelihood of his availability. Lockyer took a helicopter flight to Sydney two days before the game to protect the injury from the air pressure of commercial aeroplane travel, but made the agonising decision to pull out the following day. The gallant but rudderless young Broncos went down 26-14 to the Sea Eagles, ending Lockyer's glittering career with the club.

5. September 10, 1994—Three-peat quest halted by Bears
Two-time premiers Brisbane had struggled for consistency throughout 1994, failing to win more than two games in row during the first 17 rounds. But the star-studded glamour club built some nice momentum heading into the finals and emphatically despatched Manly in the opening week of the post-season. The September specialists met long-suffering Norths in the minor semi and started overwhelming favourites. Despite falling 10 points behind, the Broncos levelled at 14-all early in the second half and were dominating field position and possession,

but could not land the go-ahead score. A field goal by Bears halfback Jason Taylor with six minutes remaining consigned the frustrated Broncos to a 15-14 defeat, ending their premiership reign.

CANBERRA RAIDERS—GREATEST PLAYERS (1982-2013)

1. Mal Meninga—167 games (1986-1994)
Considered by many to be next in line for Immortal status, colossal centre Mal Meninga helped transform the Raiders from a struggling club to the game's standard-bearer. Despite battling injury with a series of broken arms, Meninga played in all five of Canberra's Grand Finals, famously sending the '89 decider into extra-time with a late conversion and then scoring a runaway intercept try in the '94 Grand Final, his farewell match and third premiership as captain. Meninga won the Golden Boot award in 1989 and the *Rugby League Week* Player of the Year award in 1990, and retired as Queensland's most-capped player and the only man to go on four Kangaroo Tours. Meninga spent five years as Raiders coach but had more success as the man in charge of Queensland during their record Origin run. A grandstand at Canberra Stadium is named in his honour.

2. Laurie Daley—246 games (1987-2000)
The last remaining vestige of Canberra's glory era when he retired, Laurie Daley won three premierships with Canberra before guiding both NSW and Australia as captain. A cheeky centre when the Raiders won their first title in 1989, Daley went on to become one of the top five-eighths of the 1990s, where he played 23 Origins for NSW and 21 Tests for Australia, missing the opportunity to play more due to the Super League War. A five-time Canberra Player of the Year, Daley won the Dally M Medal in 1995 and the Dally M Five-eighth of the Year in both '95 and '96. A statue of Daley outside Canberra Stadium was unveiled in 2001.

3. Ricky Stuart—205 games (1988-98)
A naturally brilliant halfback who harnessed an outstanding kicking game over the course of his decorated playing career, Ricky Stuart played a key hand in all three of the club's premierships. Stuart's kicking and passing expertise were central to Canberra's first title, and he won the Clive Churchill Medal in the 1990 success, also taking home the Dally M Halfback of the Year award. His finest year was unquestionably 1993, when he won the Rothmans Medal-Dally M double, but a broken leg picked up in the second-last game of the year—a 68-0 thrashing of Parramatta—ended his season and

Canberra's hopes. Stuart steered the NSW team for five seasons (winning four series) and played nine Tests for Australia on two Kangaroo Tours. He was appointed coach of the Raiders in 2014.

4. Brad Clyde—180 games (1988-98)

A textbook lock forward whose early ascension was stymied by a series of injuries, Brad Clyde is the only player in premiership history to win two Clive Churchill Medals and one of just three players to win one on a losing team. In just his second year, 1989, he won the first of two Dally M Lock of the Year gongs as well as the aforementioned Churchill, while he also made his NSW and Australian debuts that season. Clyde would play 12 Origins and 19 Tests but his rep career was stalled by injury and the Super League War. The tireless, dynamic backrower won four Players' Player gongs while at the Raiders.

5. Steve Walters—229 games (1986-96)

Regarded as possibly the greatest hooker the game had known upon his retirement, Steve Walters featured in all five of Canberra's Grand Final appearances and was a central figure in elevating the club during its glory era. The three-time Dally M Hooker of the Year and '93 *Rugby League Week* Player of the Year ousted brother Kerrod as the game's best hooker in 1991 and spent four years as Queensland's and Australia's first-choice rake. Walters was the Raiders' Player of the Year in 1991 and was named one of Rugby League's 100 Greatest Players in 2008.

6. Gary Belcher—149 games (1986-93)

The finest custodian in the game in the late 1980s and early 1990s, Gary Belcher was a Queensland and Australian regular and the Dally M Fullback of the Year three times between 1987 and 1990. Belcher won club Player of the Year gongs in his first two years at the Raiders and made his Australian debut in 1988, ousting Garry Jack permanently the following season. One of the best kick returners in the game and a brilliant attacking No.1, Belcher topped the premiership's pointscoring in '88 and won Grand Finals in the ensuing two years, but injuries took their toll in 1991-92 and he quit a year later.

7. Jason Croker—319 games (1991-2006)

Canberra's most durable and flexible player, Jason Croker's club-record 318 appearances came at every position bar halfback and hooker. The Raiders' leading all-time try-scorer with 120 four-pointers, Croker began his career as an outside back before a mid-career move into the forwards, but was also a regular five-eighth fill-in. He played five Origins and five Tests and was named Dally M Lock of the Year and Canberra Player of the Year in 2000. A tough character, he finished the final 20 minutes of one game with a torn ACL.

8. Ruben Wiki—225 games (1993-2004)

New Zealand's most-capped international, hardman Ruben Wiki started out as a rough-and-rugged centre before forging a career as one of the toughest and most respected props in the game. Canberra's Player of the Year in 2002 and 2003, Wiki stamped his mark for the Raiders with a superb display in the '94 premiership win, and maintained a standard of being one of the most feared players in the League throughout his career.

9. David Furner—200 games (1992-2000)

Canberra's all-time leading point-scorer, goalkicking backrower David Furner was a skilful ball-player capable of winning a match for his team. A Clive Churchill Medal-winning performance in the '94 decider won him a spot on the Kangaroo Tour that year and he played eight Origins over the last five years of his career. He went on to coach the Raiders for five seasons.

10. Glenn Lazarus—93 games (1987-91)

Widely regarded as one of the greatest prop forwards of all time, Glenn 'The Brick with Eyes' Lazarus featured in three Grand Finals during his five-year stint with Canberra. A mobile, hulking type with the ability to offload from anywhere, Lazarus started his decorated representative career while playing with the Raiders. Salary cap issues eventually forced his move to Brisbane in 1992.

11. Brett Mullins—184 games (1990-2000)

A scintillating fullback who is one of just two Canberra Raiders to top the 100-try mark, Brett Mullins at his best was an out-and-out superstar but too often was below his top due to injury and form lapses. The 1994 Dally M Fullback of the Year scored an incredible 11 tries in three weeks that year, winning a Grand Final and debuting for NSW and Australia the same season, but he never again reached those peaks as a failing body and discipline issues took hold.

12. Clinton Schifcofske—139 games (2001-06)

Canberra's second-greatest point-scorer with 1052, Clinton Schifcofske was an outstanding fullback who won the Dally M Fullback of the Year in 2006, his final season before he switched to Rugby Union. After stints with the Crushers and Eels, Schifcofske came into his own at Canberra, representing Queensland twice, winning Player of the Year Honours in 2001 and '04 and captaining the club.

13. John Ferguson—95 games (1986-90)

The reigning Dally M Winger of the Year when he joined Canberra in 1986, John 'Chicka' Ferguson added another Dally M positional gong in 1988 and lifted the Raiders to their first premiership with his heroics in the 1989 Grand Final. A dashing and elusive winger, Ferguson topped the premiership with 20 tries in '88, scored in Canberra's first two Grand Final wins, and was a NSW regular across 1988-89.

14. Alan Tongue—220 games (2000-11)
One of Canberra's most popular players throughout the early part of the century, the red-headed Alan Tongue was not as popular with representative selectors, who persistently overlooked the tenacious defensive lock. Tongue won Canberra's Player of the Year gong in 2006 and was awarded the Dally M Lock and Captain of the Year awards in 2008.

15. Chris O'Sullivan—203 games (1982-92)
One of the Raiders' finest players during their formative years, Chris O'Sullivan won the club's Player of the Year award in 1984 and '85 before featuring in the club's first three Grand Finals. A shifty five-eighth who was a dogged defender, O'Sullivan famously put the Raiders in front 15-14 in the extra-time period of the '89 decider with a well-struck field goal.

16. Noa Nadruku—92 games (1993-97)
An absolute sensation during his five seasons with the Raiders, Fijian Rugby Union convert Noa Nadruku scored 76 tries in just 92 matches with the club. He was named the Dally M Winger of the Year in 1993 and '96, topping the premiership's tryscoring table in both years and setting a new club record for the most tries in a season in '93 with 22. A blistering speedster, Nadruku was sacked by the club over an off-field incident in 1998.

17. Ken Nagas—143 games (1992-2002)
A crackerjack of a winger/fullback, Ken Nagas rated among the best wingers in the game during the early part of his career, which was highlighted by two tries in the 1994 Grand Final thrashing of Canterbury. Nagas represented NSW twice in '94 and featured heavily in Super League rep matches, but a host of injuries saw his form taper off over his final years and he retired at just 29.

18. Joel Monaghan—129 games (2001-04, 2008-10)
A sizable outside back with a shock of red hair, Joel Monaghan had two stints with the Raiders but left in embarrassment after an off-field prank gone wrong. Monaghan won the 2008 Mal Meninga Medal in his first season back with the club after a stint with the Roosters, playing his first of three Origins and all five of his Tests that year. His 69 tries is equal sixth on the all-time Raiders list.

19. Gary Coyne—160 games (1986-92)
An underrated second-rower from Queensland, Gary Coyne was an Origin staple during his last four years in Canberra, while he also played two Tests for Australia

in 1991. Coyne famously scored four tries in the Raiders' epic 34-26 minor semi win against Manly in 1991 in one of the great Canberra performances. The two-time premiership winner was twice named the club's most consistent player.

20. Josh Dugan—70 games (2009-13)
A long-striding fullback with outstanding skills, Josh Dugan left the club in contentious circumstances but remains one of the best local juniors the club has produced. Dugan won the Mal Meninga Medal in his first season and debuted for NSW while at Canberra in 2011.

CANBERRA RAIDERS—GREATEST COACHES (1982-2013)

1. Tim Sheens—218 games (1988-96)
Unquestionably the greatest Canberra coach of all, Tim Sheens was in charge for the club's three premierships, four of its five Grand Finals and its only minor premiership. Joining the Raiders in 1988 as a replacement for Wayne Bennett, Sheens made the finals in eight of his nine years in Canberra. In his second season, the Raiders became the first non-Sydney side to win the premiership. He followed this up with a second title a year later and a third in 1994. Sheens won Coach of the Year in 1990 and had a strike rate of 67.6 per cent in the capital. He was touted for a return to the Raiders in 2014 but was eventually overlooked for Ricky Stuart.

2. Wayne Bennett—28 games (1987)
Wayne Bennett lasted just one year in Canberra but the future coach of the Team of the Century achieved instantaneous success with the Raiders, guiding the club to third on the ladder and its first Grand Final as co-coach with Don Furner. Bennett left in 1988 to become Brisbane's inaugural coach but only after great consternation, as the Raiders had a long-term deal with him.

3. Matthew Elliott—125 games (2002-06)
Mal Meninga's replacement in 2002, Matthew Elliott led the Raiders to four finals series in his five-season stint in Canberra before he left to sign with Penrith, where he failed to find the same success. A little-known hardworking backrower as a player with St George, Elliott guided the Raiders to their best post-Sheens finish in 2003, a 16-8 record at the end of the regular season. Despite making four finals series, Elliott failed to win a single post-season match with Canberra.

4. Don Furner—152 games (1982-87)
Canberra's inaugural coach Don Furner has a record that does not stack up relative to other Raiders mentors, but his work in building the fledgling club into a Grand Final side within six years deserves recognition. The former Roosters coach became the face of the Raiders during the 1980s and did such a fine job he won appointment as Australia's coach, guiding the unbeaten 1986 Kangaroos while still with Canberra. Furner was Canberra co-coach in the club's first Grand Final.

5. Mal Meninga—131 games (1997-2001)
Raiders great Mal Meninga was appointed coach three seasons after his retirement following the departure of Tim Sheens, and he took the club to the finals in three of his five seasons in charge. Despite a win rate of 54.2 per cent, Canberra's standing fell dramatically after the Sheens era, and after a fourth-last finish in 2001, Meninga was replaced by Matt Elliott.

CANBERRA RAIDERS—BEST DAYS (1982-2013)

1. September 24, 1989: A premiership for the ages
In what is widely regarded as the greatest Grand Final ever played, Canberra won its first premiership in the most dramatic of circumstances. Trailing 2-14, a try to Gary Belcher and one on the stroke of fulltime to John Ferguson saw the Raiders send the decider to extra-time for just the second time in Grand Final history. A Chris O'Sullivan field goal and a blockbusting Steve Jackson try later, the Raiders became the first team outside Sydney to win the title, saluting 19-14.

2. September 25, 1994: Mal leaves in style
Canberra finished the 1994 regular season with eight straight wins—six of them by 18-plus—and entered the finals series as hot favourites to send champion skipper Mal Meninga out in style. But a major semi loss to Canterbury saw Canberra reach the Grand Final the hard way. The Raiders avenged that defeat, though, with a 36-12 dismantling of the Bulldogs. Late inclusion Paul Osborne started the rout and Canberra was never in trouble, Mal Meninga finishing his career with an intercept try.

3. September 23, 1990: Back-to-back
The Raiders backed up their inaugural premiership triumph with a second title a year later, beating Penrith 18-14. Minor premiers Canberra led 12-0 through tries to John Ferguson and Laurie Daley and sealed the win late with a try to winger Matthew

Wood following a spirited Panthers fightback. After a masterly game, halfback Ricky Stuart was awarded the Clive Churchill Medal.

4. April 18, 1982: A win at last
The Raiders were lambasted in their first season for being wildly uncompetitive when they lost their first seven games by an average of 23.5 points. After a 54-3 hammering by the great Eels team, the Raiders bounced back with their first win, sneaking home with a 12-11 success at Seiffert Oval against Newtown. The Jets scored three tries to the Raiders' two, but Steve O'Callaghan's boot proved the difference.

5. April 15, 1990: Magnificent Mal
In one of the most destructive individual performances ever, Mal Meninga scored a post-war record 38 points in a 66-4 demolition of Eastern Suburbs. Meninga scored five tries and kicked nine from 12 in the beat-down of the Roosters. John Ferguson also scored three tries in front of an adoring home crowd.

CANBERRA RAIDERS—WORST DAYS (1982-2013)

1. September 17, 2010: Croker choker
Canberra's first finals win in more than a decade sparked high hopes of an unlikely title run. Awaiting the winner of a home final against the Wests Tigers was St George Illawarra, a team that has struggled to beat Canberra for nearly the entirety of its existence. The Raiders fought back to 26-24 against the Tigers, but after Jarrod Croker missed a late penalty from nearly in front and a shattered Terry Campese knee, the Raiders were left to rue what might have been.

2. September 22, 1991: Grand Final defeat
Accustomed to success after two straight Grand Final triumphs, the Raiders were ill prepared for the shock of the 1991 decider, when a Penrith team of destiny stood tall against the Canberra juggernaut. Penrith won its first premiership 19-12, securing a late victory after the Raiders had dominated most of the game.

3. August 4, 2013: Home horrors
It was the second-biggest home loss in premiership history when the Raiders were humiliated by the Melbourne Storm 68-4 on a stunning Sunday afternoon at Canberra Stadium. The Storm ran 12 tries by the hapless Raiders, who turned in a pathetic effort. It was a significant embarrassment that saw coach David Furner fired just weeks later.

4. September 20, 2003: Crash and burn
In their best season since 1995, the Raiders finished fourth on the ladder and were eyeing a return to Grand Final football. It wasn't to be. After being well beaten by Melbourne a week earlier, the Raiders blew a 10-0 lead to go down 17-16 to the Warriors. With the scores locked at 16-all, Raiders centre Jason Bulgarelli fumbled a certain try before Stacey Jones slotted the winning field goal in the final five minutes.

5. March 7, 1999: The end of an era
Canberra's era of domination seemingly came to an end after the 1998 season when salary cap dramas forced club legends Brad Clyde and Ricky Stuart out of the club, leaving just Laurie Daley from the glory days. Raiders fans were desperately sad in the opening round of the '99 season when Stuart and Clyde were wearing the blue and white of Canterbury.

CANTERBURY-BANKSTOWN BULLDOGS— GREATEST PLAYERS (1935-2013)

1. Terry Lamb—262 games (1984-96)
The greatest Bulldog of them all, champion five-eighth and local junior Terry Lamb featured in three premiership wins and was named in the ARL's 100 Greatest Players in 2008. After spending four seasons with Western Suburbs, the one-time appearances record holder returned to the Bulldogs in 1984 and made an immediate impact, winning the Rothmans Medal and his second of six Dally M Five-eighth of the Year awards for the club and playing in the Grand Final win over Parramatta. He missed the decider win a year later, but toured with the Kangaroos in 1986 and became the only player to turn out in every match on a tour. Lamb was outstanding in the Bulldogs' 1988 Grand Final win (in which he controversially knocked out Ellery Hanley) and became captain of the club a year later. Although he didn't play Origin or Test match football post-1990, Lamb was the central figure of Canterbury's resurgence under Chris Anderson in the early '90s. No player had the instinctive sense of being in the right place at the right time more than Lamb, and few players had his drive to win. He was a tough defender, a sharp ball-player and a very good kicker. He won the Dally M Five-eighth of the Year from '91 to '93 and was arguably the best player on the field in the 1995 Grand Final success. Lamb was sent out a victor in the '95 title win but came back in '96 after the Super League War had torn the club apart. Lamb won six club Player of the Year gongs and was named captain of the club's 70-year anniversary team.

2. Steve Mortimer—272 games (1977-88)

A magnificent halfback who could turn a game in a single play, Steve Mortimer ranks as one of League's finest-ever No.7s. Part of a famous footballing family that saw him win premierships with brothers Peter and Chris, Mortimer was a prodigious talent. He turned in a mighty performance for the beaten Bulldogs side in the 1979 decider and captained the club to Grand Final wins in 1984 and '85. In the latter season, he captained NSW to the state's first Origin series win. A fine cover defender with a brilliant short-kicking game, Mortimer was lethal from anywhere on the park, but a broken arm meant he played just a cursory role in the '88 Grand Final win, his final game for the club. Mortimer was named in the 70-year anniversary team in 2004.

3. Les Johns—103 games (1963-71)

Perhaps the most gifted Canterbury player ever, fullback Les Johns achieved greatness despite having a wretched run with injuries that eventually forced his premature retirement. In an era of outstanding fullbacks such as Graeme Langlands, Keith Barnes and Ken Thornett, Newcastle product Johns played 14 Tests, the first in his debut season with the Berries. While he had many fine games for Canterbury, his best came in defeat with an inspirational performance in the 1967 Grand Final loss to Souths that nearly lifted the Berries to victory. A great support player, Johns had tremendous vision and seemed to see the game unfold before him. Knee injuries forced his retirement at just 29.

4. Chris Anderson—230 games (1971-84)

A brilliant winger who scored 94 tries in a decorated career with Canterbury, Chris Anderson became one of the club's favourite sons as a premiership-winning player and coach in a career that spanned nearly three decades. Anderson played in three Grand Finals for Canterbury, including the 1980 drought-breaking triumph in which he scored a magnificent try. He played 11 Tests for Australia and scored State of Origin's first hat-trick in 1983. He was named on the wing in the 70-year anniversary team and coached Canterbury from 1990 to 1997.

5. Eddie Burns—212 games (1935-50)

Part of Canterbury's fabled 'Three Musketeers' front-row triumvirate with Henry Porter and Roy Kirkaldy that is regarded as the greatest ever, forthright prop Eddie Burns was the anchor during the formative years of the Berries. Tough and hardheaded, Burns also had a penchant for scoring tries, crossing for 65 from his debut as a teenager through to his retirement 15 years later. Burns played in both the '38 and '42 premiership triumphs and the 1939 City Cup win, and went on to coach the club in the 1960s. He is a member of the Bulldogs Ring of Champions and was named in the 70-year anniversary team.

6. Steve Price—222 games (1994-2004)

Steve Price was the Bulldogs skipper from 2002 to 2004 and one of Canterbury's finest leaders, winning the Dally M Captain of the Year twice. Few would have imagined that the weedy youngster from Queensland who scored a decisive try in the '95 Grand Final would become one of the great prop forwards. That, however, is exactly what Price did, becoming just the third prop to win the *Rugby League Week* Player of the Year award in 2003 and winning Bulldogs Player of the Year that season. Had injury not robbed him of his final game at the club, Price would have been the only player to step out in all four Canterbury Grand Finals in the last decade of the 1900s and the first of the 2000s.

7. Hazem El Masri—317 games (1996-2009)

Rugby League's greatest all-time point-scorer, Hazem El Masri was not only an incredible goalkicker but also a fine try-scorer who crossed for 159 tries in his time at the club. No player has donned the blue and white more often than El Masri, who is potentially the Bulldogs' most popular player. Often maligned for his height and supposed lack of speed, El Masri did represent Australia and NSW but not nearly as often as he deserved. Amazingly, El Masri, who was the top point-scorer in the NRL in six seasons (including a premiership record 342 in 2004) and retired with 2418 points to his name, was not Canterbury's first-choice kicker during his first five seasons.

8. Roy Kirkaldy—147 games (1938-48)

Dubbed 'The Prince of Hookers', Roy Kirkaldy ranks as one of Canterbury's great rakes and one of the finest ball-winners in history. With bookends Eddie Burns and Henry Porter, Kirkaldy was a member of an outstanding front-row that led Canterbury to premierships in 1938 and '42. Only World War II stopped Kirkaldy representing Australia. He shifted to Canterbury from the Newcastle competition at 28 but played 11 years with the Berries, showing remarkable durability. Kirkaldy was named on the bench in the 70-year anniversary team.

9. Greg Brentnall—108 games (1977-83)

A brilliant fullback from Wagga who grew up playing both Australian Rules and Rugby League, Greg Brentnall was one of the most naturally gifted players ever to wear the blue and white. Safe in defence, Brentnall was sizzling in attack. His most famous moment came in the 1980 Grand Final, when his running bomb for Steve Gearin set up the finest try ever seen in a decider. Brentnall won the Rothmans Medal in 1982 and was the Dally M Fullback of the Year in 1981-82. He toured with the '82 Kangaroos before a series of injuries forced him to retire at just 26.

10. Kevin Ryan—52 games (1967-69)

A punishing defender who played most of his career with the great St George team that won 11 straight premierships, Kevin Ryan made Canterbury relevant again when signing on as captain-coach in '67 after the club had made the finals in just one of the previous 19 seasons. The dual international orchestrated the downfall of his former club in one of the code's most famous preliminary finals. Though he spent just three years with the Berries, Ryan was named as a starting prop in the 70-year anniversary team.

11. Henry Porter—142 games (1936-48)

A member of the lauded 'Three Musketeers' front row with Eddie Burns and Roy Kirkaldy, Henry Porter was a grizzled, burly prop forward who thrived in the toughness of the era. Porter starred in the 1938 and '42 premiership wins and captained the Berries to their 8-7 Grand Final loss in 1947, but missed the 1940 decider through suspension. Porter represented both NSW and Queensland and captained the Bulldogs on 59 occasions. He was named in the 70-year anniversary team and is a member of the Bulldogs' Ring of Honour.

12. Ron Bailey—79 games (1941-46)

A brilliant centre who became Canterbury's first Test captain in 1946, Ron Bailey's entire time at the Berries was as captain-coach of the club. He skippered Canterbury to the 1942 premiership and the 1946 decider loss to Balmain before quitting the club to return to the Newcastle competition. A tough and strong three-quarter, Bailey was named in the club's 70-year anniversary team.

13. John Greaves—112 games (1964-72)

Joining Canterbury in 1964 after two seasons with St George for an opportunity to lock down a first grade spot, bustling centre Johnny Greaves became one of the top players in his position of the late 1960s and early 1970s. Rated by Reg Gasnier as the best centre partner he played with, Greaves represented Australia 12 times, touring with the 1967-68 Kangaroos and the '68 World Cup team. Greaves played in the famous preliminary final that eliminated the Saints after 11 straight premierships and skippered the club for his final two seasons. He was named in the 70-year anniversary team and is in the club's Ring of Honour.

14. Andrew Ryan—218 games (2003-11)

A deft backrower with sharp skills and a heart for a heavy workload, Andrew Ryan was a rock at Canterbury during a tumultuous time for the club. In his first game as skipper of the Bulldogs, the '04 Grand Final, he lifted the premiership trophy, and led the club from that clash until his retirement after the 2011 season. For much of his time at the Bulldogs, Ryan was a representative staple with NSW and Australia. He was named the Bulldogs' best in the premiership season of 2004 as well as 2008.

15. George Peponis—131 games (1974-82)
Dr George Peponis became the first local junior to represent Australia while still playing for Canterbury, and led the team that broke a 38-year premiership drought with Grand Final success in 1980. A fantastic hooker, Peponis rose to the mantle of Australian captain, succeeding Bob Fulton in 1979. A tough but intelligent rake, Peponis was renowned for his smart dummy-half running. He went on to become chairman of the club and was named in the 70-year anniversary team.

16. Edgar Newham—72 games (1938-45, 1948)
A sensational winger from Cowra who signed with Canterbury in 1938, flyer Edgar Newham won premierships with the club in 1938 and '42. His five tries in a clash with Balmain to decide the '42 minor premiership remains a Bulldogs record. Although his representative career was stymied by World War II, he became Australia's oldest debutant when playing twice in 1946. Newham scored 55 tries in his 72 games with Canterbury.

17. Steve Folkes—245 games (1978-91)
A workaholic backrower who would go on to coach the club for 11 seasons after his retirement, Steve Folkes was a relentless competitor, representing the 'Dogs of War' ethos as well as any player from the great 1980s era. A thorough professional, Folkes started in six Grand Finals for Canterbury from 1979 to 1988, winning four titles with the club. He played nine Origins and toured with the 1986 Kangaroos, and was named in the 70-year anniversary team that was unveiled in 2004.

18. Jason Hetherington—118 games (1994-2000)
Dally M Hooker of the Year in 1998, Jason Hetherington was a fine player on both sides of the ball. A hearty defender and a creative ball-player, Hetherington deserved the Australian and Queensland jerseys he won late in his career. One of the top hookers of his generation and critical to Canterbury making it to three deciders, Hetherington embodied the Bulldog spirit. His retirement coincided with a dramatic fall from grace for the much-lauded club.

19. Frank Sponberg—110 games (1935-44)
An outstanding lock over Canterbury's first decade, Frank Sponberg returned from Western Suburbs when the Berries were formed to play a central role in the club's first two premierships in 1938 and '42. Sponberg was named at lock in the 70-year anniversary team and has been inducted into the Bulldogs Ring of Champions.

20. Darren Britt—168 games (1994-2001)
A big-framed prop from Orange, Darren Britt joined Canterbury from Western Suburbs in 1994 and enjoyed eight successful seasons at the club that saw him play in three Grand Finals, represent Australia and become Canterbury captain. Only Terry Lamb and Andrew Ryan have captained the Bulldogs on more occasions.

CANTERBURY-BANKSTOWN BULLDOGS— GREATEST COACHES (1935-2013)

1. Chris Anderson—187 games (1990-97)
One of the game's great wingers, Chris Anderson rebuilt a Canterbury side in desperate need of repair to win a premiership amid the most difficult circumstances imaginable. 'Opes', son-in-law of club patriarch Peter Moore, was named as Phil Gould's successor. After three fair seasons that included a controversial playoff loss, Canterbury won back-to-back minor premierships in 1993-94, losing the Grand Final to Canberra in the latter season. Anderson's Bulldogs atoned a year later with a famous premiership triumph against Manly, one of the biggest Grand Final upsets in history. It came in a season when Anderson held the side together as the Super League War erupted and threatened to tear the club apart. After disappointing years in 1996-97, Anderson departed to become Melbourne's inaugural coach.

2. Warren Ryan—106 games (1984-87)
A controversial figure, Warren Ryan took Canterbury to three Grand Finals during his four seasons at Belmore, but ostracised a club great and left amid a feud with powerbroker Peter Moore. Having achieved success at Newtown, Ryan was eyed by Canterbury as Ted Glossop's replacement and had instant success, shedding 'The Entertainers' style and implementing a grinding defensive strategy that became known as 'Wazza-Ball' and led to premierships in 1984 and '85 and a Grand Final defeat in 1986. The abrasive Ryan quit after the '87 season to take up the post at Balmain.

3. Jim Craig—13 games (1938)
An Australian representative and named one of the 100 greatest Australian Rugby League players in 2008, 'Mr Versatile' Jim Craig lost only one game in charge of the Berries in what was his only premiership season as a non-playing coach. Just three seasons after the debacle of its 1935 debut year, Craig moulded Canterbury into a premiership-winning outfit, ending the run of the great Eastern Suburbs team of the era.

4. Ted Glossop—151 games (1978-83)

A genial and popular mentor, Ted Glossop arrived at Canterbury in 1978 as Malcolm Clift's replacement and brought in 'The Entertainers' era with his ability to harness the great attacking talent at the club. The Bulldogs returned to the finals in his first season and suffered a close loss to St George in the decider in his second. A year later, Glossop had his premiership, ending a 38-year title drought for the club with a famous win over Eastern Suburbs. The club made the finals just once in the next three years, however, and Glossop resigned after the 1983 season.

5. Steve Folkes—289 games (1998-2008)

Canterbury's longest-serving coach, Steve Folkes won a premiership and took Canterbury to two Grand Finals but also presided over the team's first wooden spoon in more than four decades and was in charge during one of its most tumultuous periods. A club great as a player and son-in-law of Bulldogs supremo Peter Moore, Folkes was appointed in 1998 and took Canterbury to an unlikely Grand Final berth after a ninth-place finish. He eventually won his first—and only—premiership in 2004, two seasons after the Bulldogs were thrown out of the NRL for salary cap breaches. Folkes led the Bulldogs to the finals in seven of his 11 seasons and had a strike rate above 56 per cent, but left after they finished last in '08.

CANTERBURY-BANKSTOWN BULLDOGS—BEST DAYS (1935-2013)

1. September 27, 1980: The drought is over

After winning two premierships in its first eight seasons, Canterbury endured a 38-year drought between drinks. The rains came in 1980 when, after losing deciders in 1947, '67, '74 and '79, Canterbury overcame minor premiers Eastern Suburbs in a major upset in the Grand Final. The Bulldogs won 18-4 with Steve Gearin's famous try from a Greg Brentnall bomb—long regarded as the greatest Grand Final try ever—the highlight.

2. September 3, 1938: The first premiership

In just its fourth season in the premiership, Canterbury ended the seemingly unstoppable run of Eastern Suburbs to win its first title. The Berries had suffered record defeats that still stand in their debut year, but led by their great front-row of Eddie Burns, Henry Porter and Roy Kirkaldy, they defeated the Tricolours in the final 19-6. Joe Gartner scored twice in the historic win.

3. September 9, 1967: Dragon slayers

St George had won 11 straight premierships and seemed destined for a 12th in 1967 when ex-St George forward Kevin Ryan led the Berries to a historic 12-11 win in the preliminary final, ending the Saints' record run. St George led 9-0, but tries to Ross Kidd and Barry Reynolds—and three goals from nine attempts by goalkicking forward George Taylforth—saw Canterbury home.

4. September 20, 1998: A comeback for the ages

Without question the most famous finals comeback, Canterbury overcame a 2-18 deficit with 11 minutes remaining against archrivals Parramatta in the 1998 preliminary final to book a spot in the decider. The Bulldogs scored three tries and Daryl Halligan slotted the equaliser from the sideline to leave the score locked at the end of regulation time—but only after a 50-metre Craig Polla-Mounter field goal missed by millimetres. The Bulldogs ran away in extra-time, winning 32-20.

5. October 3, 2004: Redemption

Two years after famously being booted out of the 2002 premiership for salary-cap rorting, Canterbury was crowned NRL premier. Forced to play without skipper Steve Price, who had been injured in the preliminary final win over Penrith, the Bulldogs overcame a seven-point halftime deficit to win 16-13 over the Sydney Roosters. A desperate Andrew Ryan ankle-tap on Michael Crocker in the final minute secured the redemptive title.

CANTERBURY-BANKSTOWN BULLDOGS—WORST DAYS (1935-2013)

1. August 23, 2002: Salary cap shock

In one of the most dramatic days in League history, NRL CEO David Gallop announced that Canterbury had been stripped of 37 points and fined $500,000 for rorting the salary cap. The club had won 17 games straight and was poised for the minor premiership when Gallop dropped the bombshell following a *Sydney Morning Herald* investigation.

2. May 11, 1935: Record thrashing

In just its fifth competition match Canterbury endured the worst defeat in premiership history, losing by the incredible score of 91-6 to St George at Earl Park. The score came in the era of three-point tries. The Saints scored 19 tries and Les Griffin scored

36 points in the humiliation. A week later, the Berries were hammered 87-7 by Eastern Suburbs—the second-biggest thrashing in premiership history.

3. February 22, 2004: Coffs Harbour
The NRL and Canterbury-Bankstown were thrown into controversy when a 20-year-old woman accused a number of unidentified Bulldogs of gang rape. No player was ever charged, but chief executive Steve Mortimer stepped aside over the incident and football manager Garry Hughes was sacked. The club lost a substantial sum in sponsorship dollars and the Bulldogs brand was tarnished almost beyond repair.

4. July 25, 2008: Sonny walks
Canterbury was enduring a difficult 2008 season when star backrower Sonny Bill Williams boarded a plan for France, walking out on the club in the first year of a five-year deal. With the club stuck at second last and devastated by injury, Williams' shock announcement that he was moving to Rugby Union was a devastating blow. The Bulldogs won a financial settlement and Williams was barred for five years, but Canterbury collected the wooden spoon.

5. May 21, 1995: Betrayal
The Super League War tore much of the game apart and the Canterbury club was not exempt. After signing with Super League and sticking with the Bulldogs, the club's four highest-paid players—Dean Pay, Jim Dymock, Jarrod McCracken and Jason Smith—defected to the ARL and Parramatta. The quartet took the club to court. McCracken never played for Canterbury again while Smith was briefly dropped to reserve grade in what turned out to be a premiership season for the club.

CRONULLA SHARKS—GREATEST PLAYERS

1. Steve Rogers—202 games (1973-82, 1985)
One of the all-time great centres, Steve Rogers became a Cronulla Sharks icon in a decorated career that began when he was an 18-year-old rookie playing in the club's maiden Grand Final appearance in '73. He made the first of three Kangaroo Tours that year and went on to play 24 Tests for Australia. The 1975 Rothmans medallist captained the Sharks in the drawn '78 Grand Final and agonising replay loss to Manly. Exclusively a centre at rep level, the skilful and defensively outstanding 'Sludge' was also a fine five-eighth and won the 1981 Dally M Medal while playing lock. He went to St George in an ultimately unsuccessful search for a premiership in 1983-84, but his

Cronulla homecoming was wrecked by a broken jaw courtesy of an infamous tackle by Canterbury hardman Mark Bugden in the opening round of '85. His 1253 points is still a Cronulla record, while only two players have passed his mark of 82 tries. Rogers sadly passed away in 2006, but was named Cronulla's Clubman of the Century by the Men of League and as a reserve in the NSW Team of the Century two years later.

2. Andrew Ettingshausen—328 games (1983-2000)

A durable tryscoring machine who later became a fine captain, Andrew Ettingshausen stuck with the Sharks through some lean times and was a leader of the club's 1990s resurgence. He debuted as a schoolboy in '83 and retired 17 years later as the first player to make 300 appearances for one club. He scored 165 tries for Cronulla (second in premiership history at the time), including a club-record five in a match on two occasions. Primarily a centre—winning Dally M positional gongs in '94 and '96—he featured extensively at fullback and wing at rep level. 'ET' was the Sharks' Player of the Year in 1990 and '94, and the top try-scorer on Kangaroo Tours in each of those years. He scored 14 tries in 25 Tests and played a then record 27 Origin matches for NSW from 1987 to 1998. A wonderful defensive centre to complement his obvious attacking class, Ettingshausen captained the Sharks from 1995 to 2000—including a Grand Final appearance in the '97 Super League season.

3. Paul Gallen—232 games (2001-13)

Something of a late bloomer who battled a reputation as an on-field grub for several years, Paul Gallen developed into arguably the game's best forward and an inspirational leader for Cronulla and NSW. The aggressive lock debuted for the Blues in 2006 and won the first of four club Player of the Year awards the following season. Gallen broke into the Australian side in '08 and was a permanent fixture thereafter, making his 30th Test appearance in the 2013 World Cup final. A tremendous captain for NSW since 2011, Gallen began his second stint as Sharks skipper that season, leading the club to the finals in 2012-13 and helping to negotiate the ASADA scandal. Gallen was named *Rugby League Week*'s Player of the Year in 2010, and has won the Dally M Lock of the Year award, the RLIF Lock of the Year award and the Harry Sunderland Medal twice each.

4. Gavin Miller—180 games (1980-83, 1986-92)

Brilliant ball-playing backrower Gavin Miller was at the heart of Cronulla's rise in the late 1980s. After struggling to find his niche as a five-eighth or centre early in his career, Miller captained the Sharks in '83 as a second-rower. But it was a two-year stint dominating the British competition with Hull KR that ignited his career; he returned to the Shire in '86 and won a swag of awards as the Sharks collected the minor premiership in '88 and reached the finals again in '89. Miller was the 1988-89

Dally M medallist and won the Rothmans Medal and *Rugby League Week*'s Player of the Year award in the latter season. He played two Tests for Australia in '88 (including the World Cup final) and captained NSW to a 3-0 series loss in '89 in his first Origin appearances in six years. Boasting peerless sleight of hand and a remarkable capacity for absorbing punishment, Miller's career wound down over the next three seasons as Cronulla slumped to also-ran status. He was named as one of three club 'Immortals' along with Steve Rogers and Andrew Ettingshausen in 2006.

5. Greg Pierce—210 games (1969-80)

Moustachioed backrower Greg Pierce became Cronulla's first Australian Test player and captain after being graded by the club in its early years. He featured in the Sharks' Grand Final debut in '73, but incurred a suspension during the '78 finals to miss the chance to skipper the club in its second decider. Pierce toured with the 1973 Kangaroos, played in World Series/Cup wins in '75 and '77, and captained Australia in a Test against New Zealand in '78. The vice-captain of the 1978 Kangaroos, Pierce became the first player to bring up 200 appearances for Cronulla before hanging up his boots. He coached the club to the finals in 1981 during a two-year stint with the clipboard.

6. David Peachey—232 games (1994-2005)

Long-striding fullback David Peachey was an outstanding attacking presence for Cronulla, playing in four preliminary finals and a Super League Grand Final during the longest period of sustained success in the club's history. Unlucky in the rep selection stakes—he played one Test for Super League Australia and one Origin for NSW—Peachey was one of his era's best No.1s, winning two Dally M Fullback of the Year awards along with three club Player of the Year honours. He scored 110 tries for the Sharks (including a club-record 19 in 1999) and captained the side to back-to-back preliminary finals in 2001-02, winning the Dally M Captain of the Year gong in '01.

7. Dane Sorensen—216 games (1977-83, 1985-89)

A tough prop from a famous Kiwi Rugby League family, Dane Sorenson played a then club-record number of games during two stints with Cronulla. He missed the '78 Grand Final through suspension, but was the cornerstone of the Sharks' pack for the ensuing decade. Also a handy goalkicker, Sorensen made 13 of his 18 Test appearances for New Zealand while at Cronulla.

8. Tommy Bishop—60 games (1969-73)

A veteran of 15 Tests for Great Britain, wily halfback Tommy Bishop joined the struggling young Sharks in 1969 and took over the captain-coach position the following season. The aggressive No.7 was named *Rugby League Week*'s Player of the Year in '70 and gradually turned the Sharks into a premiership contender, guiding his young charges to the 1973 Grand Final. Never afraid to push Rugby League's boundaries of violence, Bishop was one of the players most responsible for the decider—a 10-7 loss to Manly—that is regarded as the most brutal of all time. He was unable to come to terms with the club for '74 but returned for a one-season stint as coach in 1980.

9. Mat Rogers—123 games (1995-2001)
Wiry winger Mat Rogers—son of Cronulla legend Steve—was an elusive try-scorer and valuable goalkicker, with his totals of 75 tries and 1112 points fourth and second in Sharks history respectively. Mat played five Origins in 1999-2000, and scored a whopping 168 points in just 11 Tests from 1998 to 2000. The 1995 Dally M Rookie of the Year finished second in the premiership's pointscoring race on two occasions, including a then club-record 212 points (and a career-best 18 tries) in 2000. Rogers quit at the end of 2001 to embark on a successful Rugby Union stint.

10. Brett Kimmorley—140 games (2002-08)
A controversial arrival in 2002 after virtually taking the No.7 jumper from reigning Dally M medallist Preston Campbell, Brett Kimmorley recovered from a rocky start to quickly settle as the club's linchpin and leader. He set new Cronulla records for most points in a match (28) and season (251) in his first year, guiding the Sharks to a preliminary final and winning their Player of the Year gong. He captained the club from 2003 to 2007, and despite Paul Gallen taking over as skipper in '08, spearheaded the Sharks' top-four surge that year before joining Canterbury. Kimmorley represented Australia in 10 Tests and NSW in three Origins while at Cronulla.

11. Mark McGaw—159 games (1984-92)
Dynamic centre Mark McGaw emerged in the mid-1980s and formed a devastating backline combination with fellow local junior Andrew Ettingshausen. The pair debuted for NSW together in 1987, the first of McGaw's 13 appearances in a memorable Blues career that included two match-winning tries. He played four Tests and toured with the 1990 Kangaroos, but the 1988-89 finals star's career waned in the early 1990s. Subsequent stints with Penrith and Souths produced few highlights, but he was named as a reserve in Cronulla's Dream Team in 2006.

12. Mitch Healey—223 games (1989-2000)
Behind only Andrew Ettingshausen on the club's all-time appearances list by the time he retired, five-eighth Mitch Healey was a wonderful servant for Cronulla. The Sharks' 1993 Player of the Year formed an excellent halves combination with Paul Green as the club surged up the ladder in the mid-1990s, featuring in the '97 Super League decider, then switched to halfback after Green left and steered his team to the

minor premiership in '99. Possessing one of the best kicking games in the premiership, the underrated Healey was incredibly durable, playing at least 20 games per season from 1992 to 2000.

13. Danny Lee—212 games (1988-98)
Regularly at the forefront of top tacklers lists and most underrated players polls, durable prop Danny Lee was an outstanding Cronulla clubman. He was the club's Player of the Year in 1992 and '95, collecting Dally M Prop of the Year honours in the latter season. Lee featured in the club's 1988-89 finals campaigns and was a key member of the effervescent young Sharks' rise to contender status in the second half of the 1990s, playing in the '97 Super League Grand Final. Rep rewards arrived late in his career—he played for Country Origin in '96 and Super League NSW the following season. Lee was picked to tour Great Britain with Super League Australia but did not play a match.

14. Paul Green—95 games (1994-98)
Bubbly halfback Paul Green arrived from Brisbane Easts with John Lang in 1994 and was the key player in the Sharks' rise to heavyweight status in subsequent seasons. He won the Rothmans Medal in '95 as Cronulla finished in the top four, and spearheaded the club's drive to the preliminary final the following season with a string of outstanding post-season performances. Green represented the Super League Queensland and Australian sides in '97 as the Sharks reached the Grand Final, but his final season at the club was wrecked by injury.

15. Kurt Sorensen—132 games (1979-83, 1985)
Fearsome second-rower/prop Kurt Sorensen joined his older brother Dane at Cronulla in 1979 after sitting out a season to beat an international transfer ban in place in New Zealand at the time. He acted as an enforcer for the Sharks for five seasons—robust in attack and defence—before an ill-fated one-year stay at Easts. Sorensen returned to Cronulla for a year before a decorated stint in England to end his career. He played 11 of his 28 Tests for the Kiwis while at Cronulla, including upsets of Australia in 1983 and '85.

16. Jason Stevens—167 games (1997-2005)
Former St George prop Jason Stevens was a pack anchor in nine seasons at neighbouring Cronulla. After playing for Super League Australia and helping the Sharks to the rebel competition's Grand Final in his first season, Stevens became established as one of the NRL's most prominent front-rowers, representing NSW in eight Origins and Australia in 14 Tests from 1999 to 2004. Stevens regularly fell foul of the judiciary, but featured in three subsequent preliminary finals for the Sharks and was named in the club's Dream Team in 2006.

17. Ken Maddison—77 games (1972-75)

A two-time Grand Final centre with St George, Ken Maddison earned the greatest individual honours of his career as a formidable second-rower in four seasons at Cronulla. He won the Rothmans Medal in 1973 before starring as the Sharks reached their first Grand Final that season. Maddison toured with the Kangaroos at the end of the year, playing four of the five Tests and scoring two tries in the Ashes decider win.

18. Ron Turner—92 games (1970-75)

Gunnedah product Ron Turner spent six seasons as Cronulla's hooker, featuring in the historic 1973 Grand Final. He played three matches of Australia's 1970 World Cup campaign—including the victory over England in a brutal final—to become the club's first international, while he was recalled four years later to play in the famous Ashes decider success at the SCG. Turner was named at hooker in Cronulla's Dream Team in 2006.

19. David Hatch—188 games (1979-90)

Rugged and hardworking backrower David Hatch was a tremendous clubman and captain for Cronulla, racking up a total of 188 games that was behind only club legends Rogers, Pierce and Dane Sorensen at the time. Hatch was named Dally M Captain of the Year in 1985 and '88—the latter after leading the Sharks to their maiden minor premiership. Rep honours largely eluded the unassuming Hatch, but he toured Papua New Guinea with the President's XIII in 1985.

20. Dan Stains—135 games (1987-94)

A robust forward versatile enough to feature extensively at second-row, prop and hooker, Toowoomba product Dan Stains was a key member of the Sharks' pack that powered the club to the 1988-89 finals. He played four Origins for Queensland and toured New Zealand with the Australian side in 1989, although he did not play any Tests. Stains captained Cronulla from 1992 to 1994.

CRONULLA SHARKS—GREATEST COACHES

1. John Lang—206 games (1994-2001)

A successful coach in the Brisbane premiership, former Test hooker John Lang transformed Cronulla into a premiership contender after arriving in 1994. Following a respectable seventh in his first season in charge, Lang's exciting young squad broke a six-year finals drought in 1995 by finishing fourth, and reached the preliminary final a year later. The Sharks lost the '97 Super League Grand Final to Brisbane and were upset at the preliminary final stage by St George Illawarra after claiming the minor premiership in '99. Lang left Cronulla after a fourth-placed finish and another preliminary final defeat in 2001. The longest-serving coach in the Sharks' history, Lang recorded an outstanding 61.4 win percentage and steered the club to six finals series in eight seasons.

2. Norm Provan—51 games (1978-79)

St George legend Norm Provan controversially replaced Ted Glossop as Cronulla coach following the Sharks' improved 1977 campaign, but justified the decision with a successful two-season tenure in the Shire. Provan guided the Sharks to a second-placed regular season finish in '78 before his injury- and suspension-hit squad was agonisingly defeated by Manly in the Grand Final replay. He stepped down after another admirable campaign the following season—third spot on the ladder before back-to-back finals losses. Provan's 62.7 per cent win rate is a record for a Cronulla coach.

3. Tommy Bishop—114 games (1970-73, 1980)

Former Great Britain halfback Tommy Bishop arrived at Cronulla in 1969 and assumed the captain-coach role the following season. The young Sharks side thrived under his tutelage, achieving respectable mid-table finishes in Bishop's first three seasons in charge before reaching its maiden finals series in 1973. The second-placed Sharks subsequently went down 10-7 to Manly in what is regarded as the most violent Grand Final of all time, but Bishop left the club after he was unable to come to terms for the '74 season. Following a disastrous one-season stay as North Sydney coach in 1979, he took over from Norm Provan at Cronulla in 1980, but the Sharks slipped to a disappointing ninth.

4. Allan Fitzgibbon—92 games (1988-91)

Illawarra's foundation coach, Allan Fitzgibbon, succeeded Jack Gibson at Cronulla in 1988 and captured the minor premiership in his first year with 16 regular season wins. But consecutive finals losses ultimately tagged the season as a lost opportunity for the club. The Sharks reached the top five again in '89, but were swiftly eliminated by Canberra. Fitzgibbon's last two seasons garnered back-to-back 10th-place finishes.

5. Shane Flanagan—80 games (2010-13)

Long-serving assistant coach Shane Flanagan took the reins at struggling Cronulla after Ricky Stuart quit midway through 2010, and gradually moulded his squad into a competitive unit through savvy recruiting and tactical nous. After finishing 13th in 2011, the Sharks surged to their first finals series in five years the following season. Flanagan was in the gun as the ASADA investigation bore down on the club at the beginning of 2013, focusing on an alleged illegal supplements program run at Cronulla two years earlier. He was stood down for the opening two rounds of the season but was cleared to return and guided the tight-knit side to the second week of the finals—a remarkable achievement under the circumstances. The highly rated mentor's future became clouded again at the end of the year, however, when he was banned for 12 months by the NRL for his role in the supplements scandal.

CRONULLA SHARKS—BEST DAYS

1. August 25, 1973: Shutout of 'Big Brother' on finals debut
Cronulla reached its maiden finals series in second place in 1973 under the shrewd captain-coaching of British halfback Tommy Bishop. Drawn to play neighbour and perennial powerhouse St George in their maiden post-season assignment, the Sharks thumped the Graeme Langlands-led Dragons 18-0 at the SCG. Bishop and Ken Maddison scored tries, while rookie centre Steve Rogers landed six goals as Cronulla started its march to the Grand Final.

2. September 16, 1978: Sharks edge out minor premiers to reach Grand Final
After downing Manly in the opening week of the '78 finals series, Cronulla qualified for its second Grand Final with a hard-fought 14-10 win over minor premiers Western Suburbs in the major semi. Captain Greg Pierce and winger Steve Edmonds scored fortuitous three-pointers as the Sharks held their opponents try-less to advance to the decider and earn a week off.

3. September 13, 1997: Cronulla outlasts Canberra for GF spot
Cronulla recovered from a 34-2 major semi drubbing at the hands of Brisbane to grind out a gripping 10-4 preliminary final victory over star-studded Canberra at Shark Park during the 1997 Super League post-season. Despite the presence of Daley, Stuart, Clyde and Mullins, the Raiders were held to just one try as the Sharks held on after leading 10-0 at halftime, booking a spot in the rebel premiership's Grand Final.

4. September 14, 1996: Sharks sink Brisbane
The exciting young Cronulla team qualified for the club's first preliminary final appearance in eight years with a momentous upset of glamour side Brisbane at the SFS in 1996. Veteran captain Andrew Ettingshausen scored from a bomb before David Peachey raced 50 metres for a try to give the Sharks an early 12-0 lead. Kiwi winger Richie Barnett scored a spectacular try from a Paul Green cross-field kick in the second half, and the underdogs held off the international-laden Broncos 22-16.

5. August 11, 2002: 'Noddy' leads thrashing of premiers

Following a rocky start with the club in 2002, star halfback recruit Brett Kimmorley settled into the role of Cronulla linchpin—culminating in one of the most dominant individual performances of the decade against defending champs Newcastle. Kimmorley, lining up against great rival and the NRL's best player Andrew Johns, scored a club-record 28 points in the Sharks' resounding 64-14 win over the Knights in Round 22, earning a rare 10/10 rating from *Rugby League Week*. Wing speedster Matthew Rieck bagged a hat-trick, while David Peachey and Paul Mellor crossed for doubles in the remarkable rout.

CRONULLA SHARKS—WORST DAYS

1. March 8, 2013: Coach stood down as ASADA probe grips club

The Australian Sports Anti-Doping Authority investigation that gripped Australian sport in February 2013 shone a harsh spotlight on the Cronulla Sharks, focusing on a supplements regimen run by the club during 2011. Highly regarded coach Shane Flanagan was stood down by the club just days out from the commencement of the 2013 NRL season, clouding the Sharks' immediate and long-term future. Flanagan was reinstated after two games and the gutsy Cronulla side reached the finals, but at the end of the year the coach was banned for 12 months by the NRL for his role in the supplements scandal.

2. September 19, 1978: Shorthanded Sharks whitewashed in GF replay

The Sharks were the first team through to the 1978 Grand Final after knocking off minor premiers Wests, but the decider showdown against battle-hardened Manly ended at 11-all. No provisions for extra-time were allowed, and the impending departure of the Kangaroo Tour squad dictated that the Grand Final replay be scheduled for the following Tuesday. Cronulla took the field in the replay minus a host of injured stars and suspended Test forwards Greg Pierce and Dane Sorensen, and crashed to a 16-0 defeat to the Graham Eadie-inspired Sea Eagles.

3. September 19, 1999: Minor premiers' preliminary final choke
Cronulla secured the second minor premiership in the club's history in 1999 and crushed defending champs Brisbane in the qualifying final, but the Sharks' best opportunity to break their premiership drought in the last three decades came undone in a woeful second-half performance in the preliminary final. Leading St George Illawarra 8-2 at halftime, Cronulla capitulated against the Anthony Mundine-sparked Dragons, suffering a soul-destroying 24-8 defeat.

4. March 16, 1985: Returning legend Rogers' comeback lasts one game
Along with the arrival of Jack Gibson as coach, Cronulla's greatest player Steve Rogers returning to the club in 1985 after two seasons at St George raised hopes of a revival in the Shire. But 'Sludge's' comeback was cut short in the opening round when his jaw was shattered by a high tackle from Canterbury forward Mark Bugden. Rogers did not play for the Sharks again, while another comeback later in the year with English club Widnes was foiled by a broken leg.

5. August 23, 2003: Record defeat at Parramatta Stadium
After three preliminary final appearances in the previous four seasons, Cronulla's disastrous 2003 campaign culminated in a humiliating 74-4 defeated to fellow also-rans Parramatta in Round 24. The Eels ran in 14 tries—including five to centre Jamie Lyon—and Sharks skipper David Peachey was sent off for dissent. The margin and winning score were the third biggest in premiership history after Canterbury's 1935 losses to St George and Easts.

CUMBERLAND—GREATEST PLAYERS (1908)

1. Harry Bloomfield—8 games (1908)
The club's greatest player, fullback Harry Bloomfield played in all eight of Cumberland's matches, finishing as the club's highest point-scorer with 19 (one try, eight goals). His finest hour came against rivals Western Suburbs when he scored 11 of Cumberland's 14 points in its 14-6 victory. Bloomfield kicked two first-half goals to give Cumberland a 4-2 lead, and then scored an intercept and regather try late to seal the team's only win. Bloomfield was rewarded with two NSW guernseys. He finished his career with Wests in 1909.

2. Ted Bellamy—5 games (1908)

The only Cumberland player to score two tries, winger Ted Bellamy crossed in the 22-7 loss to Glebe (in which he scored all seven points with a goal and a field goal to go with his try) and the 26-5 loss to Easts two weeks later. He also kicked three goals in the 16-6 loss to Newtown. Bellamy finished his career with Western Suburbs in 1909.

3. A. Harris—6 games (1908)

Along with Bloomfield, second-rower Harris was one of just two representative players from Cumberland. He played in NSW's second interstate match against Queensland at the Royal Agricultural Ground.

4. Albert Halling—8 games (1908)

Among just five players to pull on the blue and gold in all eight games of Cumberland's only season, Albert Halling was a respected centre. He played for Western Suburbs in the two seasons after Cumberland's omission from the premiership.

5. Syd Jarvis—8 games (1908)

One of just five men to play in all eight of Cumberland's matches, Syd Jarvis was a hooker who moved to Western Suburbs following the demise of Cumberland, playing first grade in 1910.

6. Thomas Lalor—8 games (1908)

One of five players to represent Cumberland in all eight of their premiership matches, Thomas Lalor was a front-rower.

7. F. O'Grady—8 games (1908)

O'Grady was a wing three-quarter, and one of just five players to turn out for Cumberland in all eight of the club's games in its sole season.

8. George Cribb—4 games (1908)

The only other player to score a try outside of Bloomfield and Bellamy, halfback Cribb scored the try that put Cumberland in front of Western Suburbs in the club's only win.

9. Robert Casey—7 games (1908)

A front-rower, Casey played in Cumberland's first match, a 23-2 loss to South Sydney at the Royal Agricultural Ground.

10. Paddy Boland—1 game (1908)

A prop forward for North Sydney, the club allowed Boland to play for Cumberland against it when Cumberland was short of players. Norths won 45-0 in what would be Cumberland's last game. Boland played until 1916 with Norths before finishing with two years at Wests.

THE CLUBS

EASTERN SUBURBS/SYDNEY ROOSTERS— GREATEST PLAYERS (1908-2013)

1. Dave Brown—94 games (1930-36, 1939-41)
Named captain of Eastern Suburbs' Team of the Century in 2000, Brown was the undisputed star of the Tricolours' premiership-winning juggernaut of the mid-1930s and rates as arguably the greatest pointscoring phenomenon of all time. The devastating centre scored 93 tries and 661 points in just 94 games for Easts, including the then premiership record for points in a season (244) and still-standing marks for tries in a season (38) and points in a match (45)—all achieved in an extraordinary 15-game 1935 season. He was captain of the '36 title win and coached an Easts premiership in 1940 (he was injured and unable to play in the finals) after returning from Leeds. He smashed all manner of records on the 1933-34 Kangaroo Tour and became Easts' third Test captain in '35. Brown's overwhelming class defies description, while the sheer weight of his career numbers garnered him the nickname 'The Bradman of League'.

2. Dally Messenger—48 games (1908-13)
Australian Rugby League's first superstar, Herbert Henry 'Dally' Messenger made the Eastern Suburbs club his home during six seasons in which his brilliance helped shape the fledgling code. Messenger was extraordinarily gifted, with his feats—scoring tries, setting them up, goalkicking and potting scarcely believable drop goals—passing into the game's early lore. An insatiable point-scorer at representative level on the 1908-09 Kangaroo Tour and for NSW in interstate football, Messenger captain-coached Easts to three straight premierships from 1911 to 1913. He racked up 148 points during 1911—the most scored in the competition's first 14 seasons—but his mastery could not be conveyed in mere numbers. Dubbed 'The Master', Messenger's legacy continues to loom large over Rugby League—he was named Easts' greatest-ever clubman by the Men of League and as a reserve in the Australian Team of the Century in 2008.

3. Brad Fittler—217 games (1996-2004)
The 23-year-old 'Freddy' was already the Australian Test captain and established as one of Penrith's all-time greats when he joined the Roosters at the height of the Super League War, but the five-eighth/lock went on to establish an even bigger legacy at Bondi. Fittler led the club to the finals in all nine of his seasons there, captaining the Roosters to four Grand Finals in his last five years (including a long-awaited premiership in 2002), and became just the third player to bring up 200 appearances

in the Tricolours. An inspirational match-winner and one of the best ball-players of his generation, the robust Fittler's 91 tries for the Roosters is fourth in club history. A giant of the modern era.

4. Arthur Beetson—131 games (1971-78)

Immortal forward Arthur Beetson confirmed his standing as one of the greatest forwards of all time during eight seasons at Easts, overcoming a reputation for ill-discipline and laziness that had haunted him at Balmain. After helping the Roosters to the '72 Grand Final, Beetson was installed as captain by Jack Gibson two years later. The leadership elevated his performances to another level. A peerless ball-player, remarkably mobile and punishing in defence, Beetson guided the Tricolours to emphatic premiership wins in 1974-75 and captain-coached the club in 1977-78. 'Big Artie' made 22 of his 28 Test appearances (including eight as captain) from the club. One of the code's best-loved characters, the Indigenous legend was named as a prop in Australia's Team of the Century in 2008.

5. Sid 'Sandy' Pearce—157 games (1908-21)

A pioneering great, incredibly durable at club and rep level, and arguably the finest hooker of the pre-World War II era, Sid 'Sandy' Pearce featured in the first 14 premiership seasons—including Easts' 1911-13 title triumphs. Pearce represented Australia 14 times in a Test career spanning a record 14 calendar years and encompassing the 1908-09 and 1921-22 Kangaroo Tours. Dubbed 'The Prince of Hookers', Pearce was a tough and unyielding rake, and still holds records as the oldest player in Eastern Suburbs and Australian Test history. He was named NSW Team of the Century hooker and as one of the ARL's 100 Greatest Players in 2008, and finished well inside the Top 50 of similar lists named by *Rugby League Week* (1992) and *The Daily Telegraph* (2000).

6. Ray Stehr—174 games (1929-46)

The youngest player in premiership history when he debuted for Easts at just 16 in 1929, Stehr enjoyed a long and decorated career at club and representative level. The brutal front-rower waged many famous battles with his English counterparts on consecutive Kangaroo Tours and in the '36 home Ashes series among 11 Test appearances, while he represented NSW in 30 interstate matches. The enforcer of the Tricolours' incredible 1935-37 premiership treble, Stehr captained the club to further titles in 1940 and '45. He was also a player-coach in 1939, '41 and '46, and a non-playing coach in '49. Stehr, whose club appearances record stood for more than 50 years, was named in Easts' Team of the Century in 2000 and as one of Australia's 100 Greatest Players in '08.

7. Ron Coote—109 games (1972-78)

Ron Coote was already an NRL great when he joined Easts in 1972, a veteran of six Grand Finals with Souths and an automatic Test selection in the backrow. The brilliant lock added several chapters to his enormous legacy with the Tricolours. He skippered the club to the Grand Final in his first season, and although he relinquished the captaincy to Arthur Beetson two seasons later, he was integral to the Roosters' emphatic 1974-75 premiership triumphs, racking up double-figure try tallies in each campaign. After sitting out several years of representative football, Coote played in the '74 Ashes series and '75 World Series at home to boost his Test tally to 23 matches. He became the second player to make 100 appearances for two clubs and was named as a second-rower in Easts' and the ARL's Teams of the Century in 2000 and 2008 respectively.

8. Sid 'Joe' Pearce—147 games (1929-42)

The son of legendary hooker 'Sandy' Pearce, Sid 'Joe' Pearce carved out his own enduring legacy for Eastern Suburbs and Australia as a magnificent second-rower in a career as long and decorated as his father's. He was part of Easts' dominant backrow triumvirate as the club swept to three straight premierships from 1935 to 1937, and savoured another title success in 1940. Pearce made his Test debut in 1932 and toured with the 1933-34 Kangaroos after captaining Easts to the '33 finals, but a broken leg against New Zealand prevented him from playing in Britain on a second tour; he finished with 13 Test appearances and 31 games for NSW to his name. Among Australia's 100 Greatest Players announced in 2008, 'Joe' Pearce was a listed inside the Top 50 in similar honour rolls in 1992 and 2000.

9. Andy Norval—106 games (1934-41)

A versatile, fast and tough-tackling lock, Andy Norval was a genuine star in one of great club sides, winning premierships with Easts in 1935-37 and 1940. He was one of the era's most respected players among his peers and scored 42 tries in the Tricolours. Kept out of the Australian Test side by the great Wally Prigg, Norval displayed his remarkable utility value on the 1937-38 Kangaroo Tour by playing three Tests against England and France on the wing, scoring a try in each match. World War II curtailed his rep career thereafter, but he was named at lock in Easts' Team of the Century in 2000 and as one of Australia's 100 Greatest Players in 2008.

10. Ernie Norman—101 games (1931-39)

The pivot in Easts' incomparable title-winning side of the mid-1930s, centre/five-eighth Ernie Norman was one of the decade's standout players. He broke into the Australia Test side in 1932—a year after his first grade debut—and although he missed the 1933-34 Kangaroo Tour due to injury, he made the trip four years later, stepping out of Wests five-eighth Vic Hey's shadow and finishing with 12 Test appearances. Norman formed a brilliant scrumbase combination with No.7 Viv Thicknesse at club and representative level, and was honoured as one of Australia's 100 Greatest Players in 2008.

11. Les Cubitt—89 games (1913-22)

A brilliant attacking centre/five-eighth in a decade with Easts, Les Cubitt scored 62 tries in 89 games for the club. Cubitt was Glebe's pivot in their 1911 final loss to Easts, but joined the Tricolours two years later and contributed to their third straight premiership success. World War I curbed his international aspirations, but he made up for lost time by scoring an outrageous 24 tries in just eight games on Australia's 1919 tour of New Zealand—including five touchdowns in the four Test matches. Named one of Australia's 100 Greatest Players more than eight decades after he retired, Cubitt captained the 1921-22 Kangaroos to Britain, although his trip was severely hampered by injury.

12. Anthony Minichiello—275 games (2000-13)

A veteran of six Grand Finals for the club, Anthony Minichiello's crowning achievement in an admirable career was captaining the Sydney Roosters to a stunning premiership triumph as a 33-year-old in 2013. He played on the wing in the Tricolours' '02 Grand Final victory before switching to fullback and becoming a representative star, featuring in three straight NSW series wins and 18 consecutive Tests for Australia. Mincihiello was awarded the Golden Boot in 2005. The subsequent four seasons of his career were savaged by injuries, but he fought back courageously to break the Roosters' career tryscoring record (122 at the end of 2013) and become the second player in club history to play 250 games. An explosive ball-runner and busy at both ends of the field, Minichiello combines outstanding clubmanship with a reputation as one of the code's nice guys.

13. Jack Beaton—38 games (1934-38)

Supremely talented fullback or centre Jack Beaton became a giant of Eastern Suburbs' history in just five seasons with the club. He made his NSW debut and played in Easts' final loss to Wests in his 1934 rookie season before starring during the club's 1935-37 premiership seasons. A fine goalkicker, Beaton featured at fullback in the 1936 home Ashes series and in the centres on the 1937-38 Kangaroo Tour—on which he top-scored with 124 points—to finish his career with 10 Test appearances. He retired at the tender age of 24 to pursue other career interests, but his impact is reflected in his naming as a reserve in Easts' Team of the Century and as one of the ARL's 100 Greatest Players.

14. Viv Thicknesse—75 games (1932-37)

As the champion halfback of Easts' premiership-winning outfit of the 1930s, perhaps the most tangible mark of Viv Thicknesse's standing in the club's history is his naming in its Team of the Century in 2000 ahead of Kevin Hastings and Arthur 'Pony' Holloway. Thicknesse possessed a peerless passing game and was the focal point of the Tricolours' vast attacking arsenal. He toured with the 1933-34 Kangaroos, played seven Tests for Australia and represented NSW in 11 interstate matches before retiring after Easts' third straight title in 1937. Thicknesse was named as one of Australia's 100 Greatest Players during the 2008 Centenary celebrations.

15. Dan Frawley—70 games (1908-15)
Pioneering winger Dan Frawley featured in the first eight seasons of the premiership, scoring 54 tries in just 70 games for Eastern Suburbs as one of the stars of the code's formative years. A strong contributor to the Tricolours' hat-trick of premierships from 1911 to 1913, Frawley was a member of the 1908-09 and '11-12 Kangaroo Tour squads, standing out with his tryscoring feats on both trips. Frawley finished with seven Test appearances, and scored six tries in just three interstate games for NSW. He was named as one of Australia's 100 Greatest Players in 2008.

16. Harry Pierce—137 games (1934-44)
A backrow stalwart for more than a decade with Easts, Harry Pierce was one of the most prolific tryscoring forwards in the game, bagging 59 in 137 games for the club. The former St George backrower was a key component of the Tricolours' 1935-37 premiership hat-trick and scored two tries in their victory over Canterbury in the 1940 final, taking his tally to 16 for the season—second in the competition. Pierce toured with the 1937-38 Kangaroos and played all five Tests against England and France at hooker before World War II cut short his international career.

17. Kevin Hastings—228 games (1976-87)
Widely regarded as one of the unluckiest players to miss out on selection for Australia during his career, Kevin 'Horrie' Hastings established a reputation as one of the great Roosters clubmen and most consistent halfbacks of the 1970s and '80s. The moustachioed No.7 was at his peak in the early 1980s, winning the *Rugby League Week* Player of the Year award and finishing second in the Dally M Medal in three straight seasons from 1980 to 1982, but he was a shock omission from the '82 Kangaroo Tour squad. A dogged competitor, Hastings—Easts' halfback in the 1980 Grand Final loss to Canterbury—became the first player in the club's history to make 200 first grade appearances.

18. Jack Watkins—112 games (1913-26)
Jack 'Bluey' Watkins was a superb cover-defending lock in a career with Easts spanning 14 seasons. He debuted during the club's 1913 premiership season before making his Test debut against the touring England side the following season. The Tricolours mainstay played all four Tests of Australia's 1919 tour of New Zealand and

toured with the 1921-22 Kangaroos, featuring in two Tests against England. Watkins starred in Easts' 1923 title triumph and captained the club in his 1926 farewell season, guiding it to the finals. He was named as one of *Rugby League Week*'s 100 Greatest Players in 1992.

19. Craig Fitzgibbon—228 games (2000-09)

Craig Fitzgibbon was an indefatigable second-rower and an outstanding goalkicker, becoming the highest point-scorer in Roosters history (1454) and the highest pointscoring forward of all time (1690, including stints with the Steelers and Dragons). He played in four Grand Finals for the club, winning the Clive Churchill Medal in the 2002 premiership success. The chrome-domed workhorse represented Australia in 18 Tests and NSW in 11 Origins from 2002 to 2008, and was a four-time winner of the Roosters' Player of the Year. Gravitating towards the front-row later in his career, Fitzgibbon skippered the Roosters in 72 games from 2005 to 2009, and equalled Kevin Hastings with the second-most appearances in club history in his last game.

20. Luke Ricketson—301 games (1991-2005)

Teenage backline debutant Luke Ricketson developed into one of the game's hardest-working backrowers and the longest-serving player in Roosters history. Ricketson featured in 24 finals matches in nine straight post-season campaigns, including three Grand Finals and a premiership in 2002, but a suspension cruelly ruled him out of the '04 decider. A latecomer to the representative scene, Ricketson played 10 Origins for NSW from 1999 to 2003 before breaking into the Australian side as a 30-year-old in '03 and making five Test appearances. He captained the Roosters during his 2005 farewell season and passed the hallowed 300-game mark for the Tricolours—just the third player in history to bring up the triple century for one club.

EASTERN SUBURBS/SYDNEY ROOSTERS— GREATEST COACHES

1. Jack Gibson—119 games (1967-68, 1974-76)

Legendary mentor Jack Gibson began his first grade coaching career at Eastern Suburbs and won his first premierships with the club. He took Easts, who famously finished winless in 1966, to the finals in 1967-68 before embarking on fruitful stints with St George and Newtown. Gibson returned to the Roosters in 1974 and moulded one of the great club combinations of all time, winning consecutive Grand Finals in '74-75—the club's first titles in 29 years. He departed after a fifth-place finish in 1976, but his achievements ensured he retained a hallowed place in Easts' history. After winning three premierships with Parramatta, Gibson returned to Bondi in a football manager role during the early 1990s.

2. Arthur Halloway—154 games (1930-31, 1933-38, 1945, 1947)

One of the great halfbacks of Rugby League's formative years—including winning titles with Easts in 1912-13—Arthur 'Pony' Halloway rates as the most successful coach of all time in terms of premierships. The captain-coach of Balmain's 1910s dynasty, he returned to Easts in 1930 and guided the club to either first or second on the ladder in his first four seasons. He was at the helm for the Tricolours' 1935-37 premiership hat-trick, stepping down after his side went down to Canterbury in the 1938 final before reprising his role in 1945 and winning another premiership—his fourth with Easts and eighth overall. Halloway's final season with Easts garnered a disappointing eighth-place finish but did little to diminish his enormous legacy at the club, where his 154 games as coach is a record.

3. Bob Fulton—100 games (1979-82)

After two years at Easts as a player, future Immortal centre/five-eighth Bob Fulton succeeded Arthur Beetson as captain-coach in 1979. Injury forced his playing retirement early in the season, but he remained as coach for four seasons. After a subpar eighth in '79, 'Bozo' guided the Roosters to consecutive minor premierships in 1980-81, including a Grand Final loss to Canterbury in '80. Fulton departed after another preliminary final appearance in 1982 and joined Manly, where he achieved belated premiership success during two lengthy stints.

4. Phil Gould—125 games (1994-99)

After seven years in the doldrums for the club, dual premiership-winning coach Phil Gould returned the Roosters to contender status. He took over for the last round of 1994 after quitting Penrith, and led the Tricolours to the cusp of the finals in '95. Luring several ARL-loyal stars to the club the following season, master motivator Gould ensured the Roosters were there when the whips were cracking from 1996 to 1999. Sydney City finished in the top four in 1996 and '99, but were bundled out in the second week of the finals both years, and reached the preliminary final stage in 1997-98. Gould departed at the end of 1999 and, despite returning to representative coaching, has resisted the temptation to take on a first grade role since. His 61.6 win percentage is behind only Trent Robinson, Jack Gibson and 'Pony' Halloway in the club's history.

5. Arthur Beetson—152 games (1977-78, 1985-88, 1994)

The captain of Jack Gibson's 1974-75 premiership-winning juggernaut, peerless ball-playing forward Arthur Beetson took on the captain-coach duties in 1977 after Gibson departed. The Roosters reached the preliminary final in '77 before sliding to sixth the following season, after which Beetson linked with Parramatta. He coached Queensland to four straight seasons of Origin glory from 1981 to 1984 before returning to Sydney as Easts' head coach in '85. Following mid-table finishes in 1985-86, he led the Roosters to a second-place regular season finish and a preliminary final in '87, but stepped down after a dismal 12th the following year. After a difficult stint at Cronulla, Beetson filled in at Easts in a caretaker role for the last eight rounds of 1994. He remains the second-longest-serving coach in Roosters history.

EASTERN SUBURBS/SYDNEY ROOSTERS—BEST DAYS

1. September 20, 1975: Easts' greatness confirmed in record GF romp

Defending champs Easts were runaway minor premiers in 1975 after piecing together an all-time-record 19-match winning streak. Despite a major semi hiccup against St George, the Roosters were confirmed as one of the greatest club combinations in history after destroying the Dragons 38-0 in the Grand Final two weeks later. The Jack Gibson-coached Tricolours led just 5-0 at the break, but ran seven second-half tries past the Saints and their hobbled, white-boots-wearing skipper Graeme Langlands. Centre John Brass and halfback Johnny Mayes bagged doubles, while skipper Arthur Beetson and teenage fullback sensation Ian Schubert also crossed in the unprecedented decider rout.

2. September 16, 1911: Maiden premiership success

Eastern Suburbs secured its first title in the NSWRL's fourth season by twice defeating minor premiers Glebe. The Tricolours had overcome archrivals Souths in a playoff for second before downing Glebe 22-9. The 'Dirty Reds' exercised their right of challenge as minor premiers, but fell to Easts in a tight final. Second-rower Charlie Lees scored Easts' only try 13 minutes from fulltime, with superstar captain Dally Messenger's conversion edging them one point in front. Messenger added a field goal to seal an 11-8 triumph before being carried shoulder-high from the Royal Agricultural Ground by his elated teammates.

3. September 12, 1936: Unbeaten Tricolours go back-to-back

Easts swept to their first title in 12 years in 1935, incurring just one loss. But the club bettered that effort the following season by going through 15 matches undefeated—including an emphatic 32-12 victory over Balmain in the premiership final. Coached by the sage 'Pony' Halloway and skippered by incomparable centre Dave Brown, the Tricolours' all-time great line-up—featuring six players who would be named among Australia's 100 Greatest in 2008—swamped the black-and-golds with six second-half tries after leading just 8-6 at the break.

4. October 6, 2013: Roosters complete transition from also-rans to premiers

After a dismal 13th-place finish in 2012, the Sydney Roosters installed largely unheralded 36-year-old Trent Robinson as coach and took a punt on high-profile signings Sonny Bill Williams, Michael Jennings and James Maloney. The Roosters surged to the minor premiership on the back of aggressive, resolute defence and a remarkable attacking arsenal before defeating Manly in the Grand Final to secure the club's 13th title. The gritty Roosters trailed 8-18 early in the second half, but stormed home on the back of the aforementioned recruits' brilliance to win a pulsating decider 26-18. The Tricolours' rags-to-riches premiership success was mirrored in the myriad personal comebacks within the squad—several players had endured form slumps, excessive criticism or off-field tumult before responding with career-best campaigns.

5. October 6, 2002: 'Freddy' leads Roosters to drought-breaking triumph

Perennial contenders since Brad Fittler had joined the club in 1996, the Roosters approached their '02 campaign on the back of 26 seasons without a premiership. They struggled for consistency during Ricky Stuart's rookie season as coach, but clicked into gear in the latter rounds and headed into the Grand Final on an eight-match winning streak. Falling behind 6-8 to the Warriors early in the second half of the decider, the Roosters were fired up by a heavy hit of questionable legality on Fittler by Richard Villasanti. With his head swathed in bandages, the captain was instrumental as the Roosters romped to a 30-8 victory with four unanswered tries. Six of the Roosters' Grand Final squad earned Test debuts for Australia within a year.

EASTERN SUBURBS/SYDNEY ROOSTERS—WORST DAYS

1. August 13, 1966: Easts lose every game

A 33-2 defeat to Western Suburbs in the final round of 1966 was Easts' 18th in succession, consigning the Tricolours to the unwanted distinction of being the first club in 20 years to lose every game in a season. No team has failed to win a game in the 47 premiership seasons since Easts' disastrous campaign under British coach Bert Holcroft.

2. September 27, 1980: Minor premiers insipid in Grand Final loss

After two years on the outside of the finals looking in, Eastern Suburbs pipped Canterbury for the minor premiership in 1980. The Bob Fulton-coached Roosters fell 13-7 to the Bulldogs in the major semi, but approached the Grand Final in imperious form after thrashing Wests 41-5 in the preliminary final. But Easts produced one of the most listless displays seen by any team in a decider, crashing 18-4 to Canterbury in a dour season finale and letting a premiership chance fall by the wayside.

3. April 15, 1990: Biggest-ever loss at Bruce

Eastern Suburbs started the 1990 season with two wins and two losses, but the club's campaign crumbled after a shattering 66-4 away loss to Canberra in Round 5. Despite fielding four Test or Origin players in their pack, the Roosters were woefully inept in defence as the Raiders piled on 12 tries, with Mal Meninga racking up 38 points on his own. The club-record defeat sparked a 10-match winless streak, after which coach Russell Fairfax was sent packing.

4. September 6, 2009: Final-round loss attracts wooden spoon, betting investigation

A season marred by dreadful on-field results and a series of lamentable off-field incidents came to a suitably calamitous conclusion in the final round of '09. A win over fellow stragglers North Queensland would have been enough to avoid the wooden spoon, and the Roosters started as slight favourites. The Brad Fittler-coached Roosters led 16-0 during the first half, but a spate of handling errors allowed the Cowboys back into the match and the Tricolours eventually went down 32-16. A pre-game betting plunge on the Cowboys to win by more than 12 points sparked rumours of a sting, but a subsequent investigation revealed nothing untoward by Roosters players. Nevertheless, the club finished the season with its first wooden spoon since the winless 1966 campaign.

5. September 19, 1998: Roosters savaged by Broncos in preliminary final

Sydney City's bid for the club's first Grand Final appearance in 18 years turned into a nightmare on the open expanses of Brisbane's ANZ Stadium when it crashed to a 46-18 preliminary final defeat at the hands of the Broncos. The Phil Gould-coached Roosters had fallen 12 points behind by halftime before the star-studded Broncos put them to the sword to open up a 40-6 lead during a disastrous second-half display by the Roosters. Captain and chief playmaker Brad Fittler carried a painful rib injury into the match and was ineffective despite scoring an intercept try, while his charges displayed glaring ineptitude in defence.

GLEBE—GREATEST PLAYERS (1908-29)

1. Frank Burge—138 games (1911-26)
Frank 'Chunky' Burge's legacy towers over the history of the Glebe club. Debuting as a 16-year-old, he set virtually every club record on offer, including most games (138), tries (137) and points (509). Burge scored eight tries in a match against University in 1920—an all-time mark that still stands—and set early premiership records for points in a match (32) and tries in a season (24). A fast, unstoppable powerhouse at lock, second-row or prop, Burge rates in the top echelon of pre-World War II players. He played 13 Tests for Australia from 1914 to 1922, and scored a phenomenal 33 tries in 23 games on the 1921-22 Kangaroo Tour. Decades ahead of his time in regards to professionalism and dedication to fitness, Burge was named as a reserve in the ARL Team of the Century and at prop in the NSW Team of the Century.

2. Chris McKivat—54 games (1910-14)
Dual international Chris McKivat carved out a five-season tenure in Rugby League's early years that still sees him regarded as one of Australia's greatest halfbacks and captains. He switched to the professional code at the end of 1909 and played two Tests against the touring England side the following season. After steering Glebe to the 1911 final—a narrow loss to Easts—the 32-year-old McKivat skippered the Kangaroos to Britain and a historic series win over England. He stayed with the 'Dirty Reds' until 1914 before coaching North Sydney to premiership glory in 1921-22.

3. Bert Gray—99 games (1912-27)
Small by forwards' standards, Bert Gray was a highly regarded prop, second-rower or lock and a tremendous clubman, with his first grade career at Glebe spanning 16 seasons. He played six interstate matches for NSW from 1913 to 1920 and broke into the Australian side in 1920, playing all three Tests of the home series against England. Gray toured with the 1921-22 Kangaroos, making one further Test appearance, and featured in Glebe's premiership final loss to Norths in '22.

4. Jack Hickey—51 games (1910, 1912-15)
Star Rugby Union centre Jack Hickey was part of the second wave of Wallaby defectors in 1909, joining the likes of fellow convert Chris McKivat at Glebe. He partnered Dally Messenger in the centres in two Tests of the 1910 home series against England before spending the following season at Balmain. Hickey

returned to Glebe in 1912 and played another four seasons for the club, bringing up 50 appearances and finishing with 14 tries and 29 goals.

5. Alex Burdon—18 games (1908-10)
Although it was somewhat falsely mythicised that Wallaby rep Burdon's treatment from the Rugby Union after breaking his arm led directly to the formation of the new professional code, the prominent forward was nonetheless a key figure in Rugby League's early years. Glebe's foundation captain, Burdon toured with the pioneering Kangaroos at the end of 1908 and captained Australia in the third Test against England. He retired at the age of 31 after three seasons with Glebe.

6. Alby Burge—60 games (1911-12, 1914-19)
Alby 'Son' Burge, arguably the most prominent of club legend Frank's three brothers, was a former Wallaby and spent the 1910 season at Souths. He represented NSW and captained Glebe to the premiership final in his first season at the club, and skippered the 'Dirty Reds' for much of the next decade. A goalkicking forward, Burge scored 206 points in 60 games before hanging up the boots in 1919.

7. Bill Benson—94 games (1917-24)
Long-serving Glebe halfback Bill 'Binghi' Benson played in the club's loss to Norths in the 1922 premiership final, and scored 20 tries in 94 first grade games for the 'Dirty Reds'. He represented NSW in five interstate matches—playing opposite legendary halfbacks 'Pony' Halloway and Duncan Thompson—from 1921 to 1924, and captained a 'Rest of Australia' combination against the Kangaroos in '24.

8. Tom Leggo—87 games (1913-19)
Three-quarter Tom Leggo started his career at Newtown in 1912 but joined Glebe the following season and racked up 41 tries in seven years with the club—second only to Frank Burge. He represented NSW in two matches at centre in 1913, with his career-high tallies of 11 tries in 1915 and '16 including a hat-trick against Annandale and a four-try haul against Norths in consecutive weeks in 1915.

9. Jack Toohey—67 games (1917-28)
Winger Jack Toohey's first grade career with Glebe spanned 12 seasons and netted 31 tries—including a team-high 18 in 1922 as the 'Dirty Reds' reached the premiership final. He crossed for three hat-tricks in that watershed season. Toohey represented NSW three times from 1923 to 1926, memorably scoring 18 points (two tries, six goals) in a 30-17 win in '26, just the Blues' second victory in 12 interstate matches. A handy goalkicker, Toohey tallied 177 points in his long career with Glebe.

10. Charlie Ogle—57 games (1917-22)
The most potent try-scorer in Glebe's history after Frank Burge, flying winger Ogle scored 40 tries in just 57 games during six seasons with the club. He scored a try and a goal in his only interstate appearance for NSW, a 24-10 win in 1919, and notched a four-try haul against Newtown among a career-high 12 tries in 1920. Ogle crossed 11 times in 1922 and played his last game for the club in the premiership final loss to Norths.

GOLD COAST GIANTS/SEAGULLS/CHARGERS— GREATEST PLAYERS (1988-98)

1. Wally Lewis—34 games (1991-92)
'The King' arrived at the Gold Coast under inauspicious circumstances, virtually forced out of Brisbane. But the 31-year-old legend captained Queensland to a thrilling series victory and played one last Test for Australia in his first season with the Seagulls, and will likely go down as the last captain-coach in premiership history, taking on both roles for his farewell '92 season. Fittingly, Lewis scored the winning try in his last game as the wooden-spoon Seagulls upset defending champs Penrith.

2. Jamie Goddard—86 games (1992-98)
Feisty hooker Goddard made a record number of appearances for the Gold Coast and finished second on the club's all-time try-scorers list with 23. Debuting in 1992, he didn't cement a first grade spot until four years later, but was a key member of the Chargers' historic first finals campaign in '97 and played four Origin matches for Queensland in '97-98. He was the club's last captain, joining Norths after the Gold Coast folded.

3. Wayne Bartrim—77 games (1991-94)
A dynamic goalkicking hooker or lock, Wayne Bartrim was one of the few players to thrive in the struggling Gold Coast side. In a breakout '94 season, he set club records for most points in a match (20), most points in a season (124) and most tries in a season (10), of which only the latter was broken. His 224 career points are the second-most by a Gold Coast player. Bartrim joined St George in 1995, becoming an Origin and Test player at the beginning of a long tenure in the Red V.

4. Brett Horsnell—82 games (1989-94)
Former Australian Schoolboys captain Brett Horsnell was tipped for big things after emerging as a robust young player at the Gold Coast, capable of lining up at

centre, five-eighth or lock. He was a mainstay for the Seagulls during some bleak seasons, but was recruited by the fledgling South Queensland Crushers in 1995. Horsnell was the co-holder of the club's appearance record until it was broken by Jamie Goddard in '98.

5. Jeremy Schloss—51 games (1994-97)
Hardworking lock Jeremy Schloss used his consistent performances for the Chargers as a springboard to Queensland Origin honours. After cementing a permanent first grade spot in '96, he came off the bench in all three matches of the Maroons' '97 campaign. Schloss was superb as the Gold Coast qualified for the ARL finals that season, scoring seven tries in 19 games, but linked with Souths the following season.

6. Craig Coleman—44 games (1994-95)
South Sydney great Craig Coleman returned to the Australian premiership with the struggling Seagulls after a stint with English club Salford. 'Tugger', who was 31 when he linked with the Gold Coast, played all 44 games of the Seagulls' 1994-95 campaigns and was captain in every one of them. The cagey veteran was a rare shining light for a side that perennially finished near the foot of the ladder.

7. Danny Peacock—67 games (1991-95)
Fullback Danny Peacock is the top try-scorer in the Gold Coast's history with 28, racing over for half of them in 1995 to set a club record. His hat-trick against Penrith was another unprecedented achievement for a Gold Coast player, but the mark was eclipsed by Shane Russell two years later. The long-striding custodian finished his career with a disappointing season for South Queensland in '96.

8. Peter Gill—67 games (1992-95)
Ball-playing lock/five-eighth Peter Gill joined the club from St George and gave tremendous service to a Gold Coast side short on genuine class. Injury wrecked Gill's first season back in his home state, but the veteran missed just five games from 1993 to 1995 and spearheaded several rare victories before embarking on a fine stint with the London Broncos.

9. Wes Patten—43 games (1997-98)
Former Balmain livewire Wes Patten was the halves spearhead of the Gold Coast's only side to reach a finals series. Joining the club in 1997, the tiny No.7 played all 24 of the Chargers' games and scored a team-high 11 tries—including a hat-trick against South Queensland—and starred in both games of their spirited post-season campaign. Patten played 19 games during the Gold Coast's difficult 1998 season and was halfback in the club's last game.

10. Martin Bella—35 games (1996-97)
Origin and Test veteran Martin Bella was well past his best when he landed at the Gold Coast, playing his first game for the ramshackle Chargers just days before turning 32. But 'Munster' was a key performer in two seasons there, providing trademark no-nonsense front-row displays along with experience and guidance to the club's misfit playing group. Bella retired after the Chargers' historic and gallant '97 ARL finals campaign came to an end.

11. Chris Close—67 games (1988-91)
Veteran former Manly, Queensland and Australian centre Chris 'Choppy' Close was one of the fledgling Giants' highest-profile acquisitions for their 1988 entry. A try-scorer in the club's first match, Close soon moved into the pack and averaged 17 matches in his four seasons with the Gold Coast. He retired as a 32-year-old at the end of 1991 after spending the season playing alongside long-time representative teammate Wally Lewis.

12. Brendan Hurst—74 games (1994-97)
Goalkicking backrower Brendan Hurst set a modest club record with 285 career points, racking up three of the top four highest season totals in the Gold Coast's history. Hurst, who would not have looked out of place in a Queensland jumper during Origin's Super League-affected years, featured prominently in the Chargers' run to a maiden finals berth in '97 before joining the Roosters.

13. Adrian Vowles—38 games (1993-94)
Charleville product Adrian Vowles was the first player to make his first grade debut at the Gold Coast and go on to play State of Origin football. Clubman of the Year after missing just one game in his '93 rookie season, Vowles was chosen on the Queensland bench for his sole Origin appearance the following year. The centre/five-eighth, who predominantly played at lock later in his career, subsequently joined North Queensland for two seasons before becoming a Castleford legend.

14. Scott Sattler—54 games (1992-93, 1997-98)
The son of legendary Souths enforcer John Sattler, Scott Sattler's initial stint with the Gold Coast garnered just six appearances. But after similarly unsuccessful spells with Easts and South Queensland, the backrower returned to the Chargers in 1997 and played in 48 consecutive games—including the historic '97 finals campaign and the club's final match in '98. Sattler subsequently joined Penrith, representing Queensland and winning a premiership.

15. Billy Johnstone—61 games (1988-90)
Tough ex-Canterbury and St George hooker Billy Johnstone was the Gold Coast's first captain. The former premiership-winning rake missed just five games during the troubled club's first three seasons in existence, retiring at the end of 1990.

16. Clinton Mohr—82 games (1990-94)
A young BRL star with the Brothers club before embarking on a promising two-season stint with St George, fullback/winger Clinton Mohr returned to Queensland in 1990 with the Giants. He played 17 or more games in four of his five seasons at the Gold Coast to equal Brett Horsnell's then club record for appearances.

17. Andrew King—49 games (1995-98)
Talented fullback Andrew King was a mainstay in the Chargers' final two seasons, playing 21 games in each of the 1997 and '98 campaigns. Speedy, elusive and safe at the back, King was a vital component of the only Gold Coast side to reach a finals series in '97. After the club folded, King—older brother of future international three-quarter Matt—gave good service to Manly, the Northern Eagles and Souths.

18. Dale Shearer—33 games (1992-94)
The enigmatic, injury-prone Dale Shearer rarely produced his best in three seasons on the Gold Coast, but in terms of representative football he is unmatched in the club's chequered history. The versatile two-time Kangaroo tourist played five Origins for Queensland and three Tests for Australia during his time with the battling Seagulls.

19. Brent Todd—34 games (1992-93)
Rugged Kiwi prop Brent Todd—a four-time Grand Finalist with the Raiders—spent the twilight of his distinguished career at the Gold Coast, squeezed out of Canberra in the wake of the club's salary cap crisis. A steady influence for a Seagulls side that finished last in both of his seasons at the club, Todd played the last six of his 28 Tests for New Zealand in 1992-93—a record for a Gold Coast player.

20. Tony Durheim—78 games (1989-98)
Sturdy forward Tony Durheim was the Gold Coast's longest-serving player in terms of time, making his debut as a 21-year-old in 1989 and retiring after playing in the club's last match in 1998. 'Bull' Durheim sits fourth on the defunct club's all-time most appearances list.

GOLD COAST GIANTS/SEAGULLS/CHARGERS— GREATEST COACHES (1988-98)

1. Phil Economidis—70 games (1996-98)
Moustachioed coach Phil Economidis took over the renamed Chargers in unenviable circumstances in 1996, handed the reins of a ragtag squad in the wake of numerous coaching staff, administrative and ownership changes at the financially stricken club. After guiding the Gold Coast's reserve grade side to a preliminary final in '95, he arguably overachieved by leading the Chargers to five wins and an 18th-place finish the following season. He was named ARL Coach of the Year after taking the club to the only finals series in its history in 1997, winning a record 10 regular season games and eliminating Illawarra on finals debut. The '98 season garnered four wins in 24 games and the Chargers were axed at the end of the year, ending Economidis' first grade coaching career.

2. Bob McCarthy—66 games (1988-90)
South Sydney legend Bob McCarthy had enjoyed considerable coaching success on the Brisbane club and representative scenes, and was a popular choice to take on the head coach role for the fledgling Giants. He enjoyed just 15 wins in three seasons at the helm and struggled to get the best out of his high-profile recruits, but the club avoided the wooden spoon under McCarthy's tutelage and the seven wins and 13th-place finish in 1989 was the second best result in its 11-year history.

3. John Harvey—44 games (1994-95)
A highly rated, aggressive prop for Manly and Easts who should have represented Australia, John Harvey was pitched into the first grade coaching post at the Gold Coast in 1994 despite having little experience other than as a captain-coach in NSW country football. But the Seagulls managed to avoid a fourth straight wooden spoon under him, winning five games to finish second last. Harvey's charges won four games in '95 and finished 17th of 20 teams. He accepted a coaching director role at the end of that season and Graham Eadie took over as head coach, but the former Sea Eagles teammates both left the troubled club shortly afterwards. Harvey later coached Salford.

4. Wally Lewis—44 games (1992-93)
The Seagulls finished last in both of 'The King's' seasons in charge, but he holds the notable distinction of being the last fulltime captain-coach in premiership football, steering the club to a somewhat respectable six wins in '92. The following season

as non-playing coach was less enjoyable, garnering just one win and punctuated by ongoing clashes with the club's board, although Lewis did coach Queensland to a narrow series loss to NSW. He resigned at the end of 1993.

5. Malcolm Clift—22 games (1991)

Malcolm Clift guided Canterbury to the 1974 Grand Final (a 19-4 loss to Easts) during five seasons as coach before making a surprise return to the limelight as Bob McCarthy's replacement at the Gold Coast—14 years after his last premiership appointment. Despite the arrival of Wally Lewis as captain, Clift's season in charge was not a success, reaping just two wins and resulting in the Seagulls' maiden wooden spoon.

GOLD COAST GIANTS/SEAGULLS/CHARGERS— BEST DAYS (1988-98)

1. May 8, 1988—Maiden win comes against 'Big Brother'

The Giants waited 10 long weeks in their debut season to secure their first win—but they knew how to pick out the best victim. In the first Gold Coast-Brisbane derby, the Giants rolled the international-laden Broncos—who were running second on the ladder—in a 25-22 thriller. Centre Scott Mieni scored a double and old-stager Chris Close raced away for a memorable try in front of a delirious 13,423-strong home crowd, which remained a record attendance for Seagulls Stadium.

2. September 5, 1997—Chargers spring major upset on finals debut

The long-suffering Gold Coast club qualified for its first finals series in the 1997 ARL season. The Chargers grabbed the seventh and last-available spot, and drew sixth-placed Illawarra—to whom they had lost 28-6 in the final round—for their maiden post-season encounter. Rank outsiders, the Gold Coast raced to a shock 14-4 halftime lead and held off the Steelers to advance with a 25-14 victory at Parramatta Stadium.

3. March 18, 1994—Broncos boilover at Carrara

The Gold Coast was coming off three straight wooden spoons and Brisbane had secured back-to-back premierships when the clubs met for the south-east Queensland derby in Round 2 of 1994. But the Seagulls delighted the club-record 22,688-strong Friday night crowd at Carrara Stadium by pulling off a stunning 25-12 upset. Veterans Craig Coleman and Peter Gill were outstanding as the unfancied Gold Coast opened up a 14-0 lead midway through the second half and held on for the win. The result created history for the lowly Seagulls, who had secured a draw with Penrith in the opening round—they led the competition for the only time in their history, albeit for just 18 hours.

4. August 29, 1992—'The King' farewelled in style
The Seagulls had already confirmed a second straight wooden spoon heading into their final game of 1992 against defending champs Penrith, which doubled as the last-ever match in the hallowed career of captain-coach Wally Lewis. The Gold Coast trailed 6-8 during the second half at Seagulls Stadium, but 'The King' had one last piece of magic left. He grubbered close to the line in the 53rd minute, regathered the rolling ball and crashed over to score. The Seagulls hung on to win 12-8 and finish a difficult season on a high note.

5. August 23, 1997—Emphatic Manly defeat helps Gold Coast to first finals series
The Gold Coast's historic maiden finals berth was effectively achieved via a monumental upset of defending premiers and competition leaders Manly in the penultimate round of the 1997 ARL season. The Chargers kicked out to a 14-4 lead by halftime before outplaying the full-strength Sea Eagles—who fielded nine internationals in their starting line-up—in the second stanza to carve out a 25-10 victory in front of 15,872 fans at Carrara Stadium. The stunning result lifted the Chargers into seventh spot, which they hung on to despite a last-round loss to Illawarra to participate in their first finals series.

GOLD COAST GIANTS/SEAGULLS/CHARGERS— WORST DAYS (1988-98)

1. December 3, 1998: Fold Coast
After living on the breadline for the majority of its 11 tortured seasons, the Gold Coast club officially closed its doors in December 1998. The widely expected announcement came from chairman David Barnhill, who had taken over from the sacked Tom Bellew only a couple of months earlier. The Chargers had rejected a number of merger offers in the preceding two years, and the area would not have an NRL presence again until 2007.

2. August 29, 1995: Seagulls withdraw from the premiership
With the Super League War decimating crowd support and sending player payments through the roof, the Seagulls Leagues club withdrew its financial support of the Gold Coast outfit in August 1995. The Gold Coast officially withdrew from the premiership two days after its last regular season match.

3. January 26, 1996: Mad Muller sacks Harvey

The ARL accepted an offer from Gold Coast businessman Jeff Muller to buy a controlling interest in the club in December 1995, but within weeks it was clear the flamboyant Muller was going to be a destructive influence for the renamed 'Gladiators'. Multiple chief executives and coaching staff resigned, the players passed a vote of no-confidence in their new owner, and the debacle culminated in Muller sacking coaching director John Harvey after he refused to sign an agreement guaranteeing Muller's input in team selections. Following an equally bizarre sequence of events during February, the ARL ousted Muller and took over the running of the Gold Coast club, which they rebranded as the Chargers.

4. August 28, 1993: Record losing streak caps horror season

The Seagulls' 1993 season was an unrelenting mire of dreadful on-field results and ructions off the paddock, with coach Wally Lewis embroiled in a year-long battle with members of the club's board. The 24-10 loss to Easts at home in the final round of '93 was the Gold Coast's 16th in succession, breaking the club record set in 1991-92. It was the equal-seventh-longest losing streak in premiership history, and the worst since Newtown's 20-game run in 1977. Lewis resigned two weeks later.

5. April 4, 1992: Courageous win foiled by interchange bungle

The Gold Coast's 18-8 win over emerging heavyweight Illawarra early in 1992—the Seagulls' first victory since the previous May—was among the finest in the club's history. They ground out the result with 12 men after Kiwi Test prop Brent Todd was sent off in the opening minutes. But the elation turned to despair when the Seagulls' two competition points were stripped for breaching replacement rules—they had inadvertently used five interchange players.

GOLD COAST TITANS—GREATEST PLAYERS (2007-13)

1. Luke Bailey—132 games (2007-13)

A terrorising ball-runner who gave no quarter and asked none, former Dragons stalwart Luke Bailey was an ageless warrior who won three of the club's first five Paul Broughton Medals. Tough and uncompromising, the 2006 *Rugby League Week* Player of the Year ranked in the top handful of props in the game during his first half-decade at the club. The inaugural Titans co-captain, Bailey played a Test and four Origins from the Gold Coast and could have played more had he not retired early from representative duty.

2. Scott Prince—124 games (2007-12)

Named co-captain for the Titans' inaugural year, the Wests Tigers' 2005 Clive Churchill Medal winner was the club's captain—either solo or in a shared capacity—for the first six years of its existence. A compact halfback with sublime skills, Scott Prince enjoyed his best year in 2010 when winning Dally M Halfback of the Year honours and guiding the Titans to the preliminary final. Prince played two Tests and two Origins while at the Gold Coast, leaving in 2013 over a contract dispute.

3. Greg Bird—78 games (2010-13)

An established NSW and Australian backrower when he joined the Titans, Greg Bird needed to overcome off-field dramas after being forced out of Cronulla. He managed to do just that and became captain of the side in 2013, winning the Paul Broughton Medal that year. He reclaimed his Country, NSW and Australian jerseys in his first year at the club and has since played six Tests and 10 Origins. A tough, relentless competitor, Bird has an all-round game few could contemplate.

4. Anthony Laffranchi—102 games (2007-11)

Arguably the Titans' most underrated great, Anthony Laffranchi rose from solid first grader at the Wests Tigers to NSW and Origin star at the Gold Coast. The leading tryscoring forward in Titans history, Laffranchi was named the RLIF International Second-rower of the Year in 2008, the year he made his Origin and Test debuts, playing in the World Cup final for Australia. Laffranchi shared the inaugural Paul Broughton Medal in 2007 with Luke Bailey.

5. Nate Myles—41 games (2012-13)

One of just five players to represent Australia while at the Gold Coast, Nate Myles enjoyed a fantastic debut season after signing from the Roosters, winning the Dally M Second-rower and Dally M Rep Player of the Year awards to go with the Paul Broughton Medal. A ferocious defender who enjoys plenty of work, Myles was named Titans co-captain in 2013.

6. Ashley Harrison—107 games (2008-13)

A veteran journeyman who played for Brisbane, South Sydney and the Sydney Roosters before joining the Titans in 2008, Ashley Harrison played the best Rugby League of his career at the Gold Coast. A skilful lock with a strong thirst for work, he played 14 of his 15 Origins for Queensland while at the Titans. The courageous Harrison overcame a number of serious injuries to become the fourth-most-capped Titan.

7. Preston Campbell—103 games (2007-11)

The 2001 Dally M Medal winner while at Cronulla and premiership winner with Penrith, Preston Campbell became the face of the Titans after he became the first player to sign with the fledgling franchise. He was electric in 2008, winning the Paul Broughton Medal on the back of his dynamic work from fullback. A significant worker away from the paddock, Campbell won the 2008 Ken Stephen Medal and was instrumental in setting up the Indigenous v NRL All Stars game.

8. Mat Rogers—77 games (2007-11)
A dual international and son of Cronulla legend Steve, Mat Rogers became an inaugural Titan in 2007 after notable careers with Cronulla and the Wallabies Rugby Union outfit. Though he was 31, he was a contributor for four seasons at centre and five-eighth. The second-greatest scorer in club history, Rogers' most famous moment was a snapped field goal in the club's 11-10 win over the Dragons in 2010.

9. Nathan Friend—100 games (2007-11)
A tackling machine, diminutive hooker Nathan Friend was the heart and soul of the Titans through their first five seasons. The winner of the 2009 Paul Broughton Medal, Friend was the club's greatest tackler and most-capped player before he quit the club to play with the Warriors in 2012.

10. David Mead—89 games (2009-13)
One of the fastest men in Rugby League, Papua New Guinea international David Mead was locked in a race with fellow speedster Kevin Gordon for the club's top tryscoring record. Mead led the way after the 2013 season with 51, his most famous being a spectacular collect-and-score in the corner of Shark Park in 2012.

11. Luke Douglas—48 games (2012-13)
Rugby League's great ironman Luke Douglas has not missed a game since debuting in the opening round of the 2006 season. The workaholic prop was a surprise signing from Cronulla in 2012, a reliable centrepiece of the Gold Coast pack and a strong middle defender always willing to take the next hit.

12. Kevin Gordon—94 games (2009-13)
With 50 tries in his first five seasons at the club, Kevin Gordon became one of the Titans' most dangerous weapons. Capable of playing on the wing, in the centres or at fullback, the likable outside back was a threat from anywhere on the paddock. A consistent scorer, he has managed 10 tries in each of his four injury-free seasons.

13. Mark Minichiello—150 games (2007-13)
Brother of former Australian fullback Anthony, backrower Mark Minichiello made a career of running excellent angles and hitting the line with great speed. The Gold Coast's most-capped player, Minichiello was a City Origin rep for the first five seasons of his Titans career and represented Italy at the 2013 World Cup.

14. William Zillman—106 games (2009-13)
A speedy yet oft-injured fullback with the Raiders, William Zillman was a prize signing for the Titans in 2009. The third-greatest scorer in Gold Coast's history, Zillman has played every position in the Titans backline. He scored two tries in the Titans' only finals win.

15. Brad Meyers—75 games (2007-11)
A red-bearded monster, Brad Meyers was one of the Gold Coast's most underrated players. A former international with Brisbane, he joined the Titans as an inaugural member after a three-season stint with Bradford. He scored a try in the Titans' first final in 2009 and was a fan favourite throughout his five-year run on the Gold Coast.

16. Albert Kelly—21 games (2013)
A reclamation project when signing with the club in 2013 after being sacked by both Cronulla and Newcastle, Albert Kelly turned in one of the best individual seasons of any Titan, scoring 11 tries in 21 appearances. A livewire halfback, he formed a dangerous combination on the right edge with centre Jamal Idris.

17. Brett Delaney—63 games (2007-09)
A burly centre who was renowned for his toughness, Brett Delaney scored just 14 tries in 63 appearances but was a staple in the Titans' midfield for three seasons. After he was a City representative in 2008, a hamstring injury brought about a premature end to Delaney's Titans career, ensuring he never played a final with the club.

18. Luke O'Dwyer—102 games (2007-13)
An honest utility who was the Titans 'Mr Fix-It' across their first seven years, Luke O'Dwyer was no star but survived in the NRL on his work ethic and ability to plug any hole. He is one of just nine players to play 100 games for the Titans.

19. Matt Petersen—21 games (2007-08)
A popular cult figure at the Titans, 'Sideshow Bob' played just two years on the Gold Coast but proved himself a capable tryscoring winger. The former Cowboy and Eel played 21 games for the Titans, scoring 14 tries. He managed two hat-tricks before being released midway through 2008 to play with Wakefield in Super League.

20. Matt White—88 games (2009-13)
A no-nonsense prop forward and Luke Bailey doppelganger, Matt White has served primarily as a rotation forward and all-round workhorse. The former Knights big man joined the Titans in 2009 and was a consistent cornerstone who played in all four of the Titans' finals to 2014.

GOLD COAST TITANS—GREATEST COACHES (2007-13)

1. John Cartwright—172 games (2006-13)
The Titans' inaugural and only coach up until the 2014 season, Penrith premiership-winning backrower John Cartwright was an assistant under Ricky Stuart before joining the fledgling club. Two solid 10-14 seasons were followed by a very good run in 2009-10 where the club finished 16-8 and top four both years, reaching the preliminary final in the latter season. A collapse in 2011, however, saw the Gold Coast claim the wooden spoon. In Cartwright's first seven seasons at the Titans, the club made the playoffs twice.

GOLD COAST TITANS—BEST DAYS (2007-13)

1. September 10, 2010: First finals win
The high point of the Titans' first push for a premiership came in 2010, when a win against the New Zealand Warriors in the qualifying final pushed the club into its first preliminary final. In front of 27,026 fans at Skilled, William Zillman scored a double in a blistering 28-16 win. The Titans led 22-6 at the break and never let the Warriors back into the contest.

2. May 27, 2005: Readmission
It was announced on May 27, 2005 by NRL chief executive David Gallop that there would once again be Rugby League on the Gold Coast with the Titans admitted to the premiership for the 2007 season, nine years after the Chargers had last played. A new team was born.

3. March 26, 2007: Win No.1
After a close loss in the club's first-ever game against St George Illawarra, the Titans found their first win a week later when rolling Cronulla 18-16 in the club's first game at Carrara. Preston Campbell scored a try and kicked three-from-three in the thrilling first win.

4. May 26, 2013: A record win
The NSW country town of Mudgee was where the Titans recorded their biggest-ever beatdown, thumping a hapless Parramatta 42-4 in 2013. Kevin Gordon and Jamal

Idris scored doubles, Albert Kelly terrorised and Aidan Sezer kicked a perfect seven-from-seven in a record Gold Coast victory.

5. April 13, 2007: 'Big Brother' beaten
The Titans were given little chance in their first clash against 'Big Brother' Brisbane, but in an upset for the ages pulled off a memorable boilover. On the back of a Brett Delaney double, the Titans extended their 12-6 halftime lead to win 28-12 in front of a stunned Suncorp Stadium crowd. The Broncos would win 11 of the next 14 clashes but couldn't take away the memory of the Titans' historic win.

GOLD COAST TITANS—WORST DAYS (2007-13)

1. September 3, 2011: Playoff for the wooden spoon
The 2011 wooden spoon went down to the wire, with the Titans and Eels playing off for the dubious 'honour' in the final round. In an embarrassing effort on its home patch, the Gold Coast trailed 0-22 at the break and were finished off 32-12, in the process collecting the club's first wooden spoon.

2. September 18, 2009: Finals brutality
The Titans made it to the finals in just their third year but it would be a brutal series. After losing a high-scoring shootout to the Broncos, hopes were high for a good showing against Parramatta but the Titans were never in the contest, with the Eels rollicking home to a 27-2 win.

3. July 15, 2007: Capital caning
The Titans never had much luck in the nation's capital and it started off in horrific fashion with a record 56-10 loss in their first year of existence. The Raiders had an incredible 10 individual try-scorers in the embarrassing rout.

4. March 28, 2012: Financial crisis
The very existence of the club was thrown into question when it was revealed that the Titans owed $35 million and were on the brink of insolvency. The NRL helped but only after making significant governance changes. Owner Michael Searle took a backseat while chairman Paul Broughton resigned.

5. July 31, 2011: Streaking
The Titans finished July of the 2011 season with a sixth straight loss, a 50-20 hammering at the hands of the Newcastle Knights. The Titans conceded 197 points

during the six-game streak, a low point for the wooden-spoon-bound Gold Coast outfit. The Knights finished the contest with six second-half tries.

HUNTER MARINERS—GREATEST PLAYERS (1997)

1. Brett Kimmorley—10 games (1997)
A future star, halfback Brett Kimmorley debuted two seasons earlier with Newcastle but, unable to work ahead of Andrew Johns in the pecking order, he joined cross-town rivals Hunter during the Super League season of '97. He eventually surpassed club captain Noel Goldthorpe as the club's first-choice No.7 and became the only Mariner to represent the Super League Australia team against Great Britain. When he retired at the end of the 2010 season, he was the last ex-Mariner in the NRL.

2. Scott Hill—18 games (1997)
One of only two players to pull on the Mariners jersey in all 18 Super League games, five-eighth Scott Hill debuted with Canterbury the year prior but was sent to bolster the Mariners' stocks in '97. He scored a decisive try in Hunter's upset win over Wigan in the World Club Challenge. Hill did not represent as a Mariner but played five times for NSW and 12 Tests for Australia in a 200-game career, mostly spent at the Storm following the demise of Hunter.

3. Robbie Ross—16 games (1997)
A scintillating fullback whose career would sadly be cut short by injury, Newcastle junior Robbie Ross had debuted for the Knights in 1994 before a one-year stint with Brisbane in '96 after signing with Super League. Joining the Mariners in '97, he was among the competition's best custodians, playing off the bench in two of NSW's Tri-Series matches. Like the cream of Hunter's talent, he would move to Melbourne in 1998 and carve out a quality career with the Storm, graduating to Origin and Test honours.

4. Nick Zisti—17 games (1997)
The owner of nearly all of Hunter's pointscoring and tryscoring records, Nick Zisti was a bastion of consistency in Hunter's only season. A clever outside back, Zisti joined the Mariners after stints with South Sydney and St George. He was appointed goalkicker in the club's opening game and played 17 Super League matches, scoring a record 76 points. He led the tryscoring tally with nine, while his 14 points in the record win against the Cowboys was a record. The burly Zisti was outstanding

in the finals of the World Club Challenge tournament, scoring five tries in three games, including a double in the final loss to Brisbane.

5. Tim Maddison—16 games (1997)
A hard-headed forward, Tim Maddison joined the Mariners after spells with Newcastle and the Sydney City Roosters. He had a great season with Hunter, winning the club's Player of the Year and Players' Player awards after 16 Super League games. Maddison would have stints with Cronulla, North Queensland and Newcastle for a second time before retiring after the 2003 season.

6. Robbie McCormack—15 games (1997)
Already a State of Origin rep and nine-year Newcastle veteran after playing in the Knights' inaugural season, Robbie McCormack was a critical veteran presence when he signed on with Hunter. He assumed the captaincy from Noel Goldthorpe midway through the season and led the Mariners into their biggest game, the World Club Challenge final. He joined Wigan after his year with the Mariners.

7. Noel Goldthorpe—14 games (1997)
For Hunter's inaugural captain, halfback Noel Goldthorpe, 1997 was a rollercoaster of a season. He joined the club as a highly touted No.7 after stints with Western Suburbs and St George. His '97 season is best remembered for his 104th-minute field goal that sealed victory for NSW in the Tri-Series final against Queensland. A week later, however, he fell out of favour with coach Graham Murray, lost the captaincy and was dropped to the bench, where he would start just one more match in the red, blue and yellow.

8. Tony Iro—14 games (1997)
A 25-Test New Zealand star, Tony Iro was at the backend of his career after long spells with Manly and the Roosters when he joined brother Kevin at Hunter. He scored three tries in 14 Super League games and played in the World Club Challenge final before spending a year each with Adelaide and South Sydney.

9. Troy Stone—18 games (1997)
A no-nonsense front-rower, Troy Stone joined the Mariners after spells with Cronulla and St George. With Scott Hill, he was the only player to turn out in all 18 Super League games, along with the World Club Challenge final. Stone rounded out his premiership career with four seasons at Canterbury before a move to England.

10. John Carlaw—13 games (1997)
Journeyman try-scorer John Carlaw played for six clubs during his nomadic career but got his start under Graham Murray at the Hunter Mariners. The former Newcastle lower-grader scored a double in his top-grade debut in the Mariners' biggest win,

a 38-10 Round 4 drubbing of the Cowboys, and back-to-back doubles against the Warriors and Reds in Rounds 7 and 8. He finished his Mariners career with eight tries in 13 games, second on Hunter's tryscoring list.

ILLAWARRA STEELERS—GREATEST PLAYERS (1982-98)

1. Rod Wishart—154 games (1989-98)

Goalkicking winger Rod Wishart holds dominion over most categories in the Steelers' record books: most points (1092), most tries (68), most points in a season (176), and most points in a match (22—four times). Third on the club's all-time appearance register, the Gerringong product was also one of the finest in his position during the 1990s. Wishart was a reliable powerhouse on the flank, playing 15 Tests for Australia (scoring 126 points)—including a stellar '94 Kangaroo Tour—and becoming a NSW great in 22 appearances for the Blues, an Origin record for a winger. The Steelers' first home-grown international, the 1995-96 Player of the Year retired after coming off the bench in St George Illawarra's '99 Grand Final loss.

2. Paul McGregor—124 games (1991-98)

Dapto centre Paul McGregor did not make his first grade debut until the age of 23 in 1991, but he became one of the decade's dominant centres. Tall and powerful with great footwork and silky ball skills, he broke into the NSW side in '92 and was one of the Blues' finest in 14 matches in arguably their greatest era. McGregor was frequently cut down by injury (he played no more than 18 games in a first grade season), restricting him to just three Test appearances and prematurely ending his Kangaroo Tour in '94 after it appeared he was Mal Meninga's natural successor in the Australian side. Outstanding as the Steelers qualified for their maiden finals series in '92, McGregor captained the club in '97-98 and led the St George Illawarra joint venture to a debut-season Grand Final in '99.

3. Alan McIndoe—127 games (1983-88, 1991-93)

Hailing from Emerald in central Queensland, Alan McIndoe became the Steelers' first Australian representative and was an outstanding wingman during two stints with the club. After overcoming serious injury problems early in his first grade career, he was Illawarra's top try-scorer in the 1986-88 seasons. McIndoe played all three matches of Queensland's '88 Origin series whitewash and featured in Australia's victory over Rest of the World later that year. Following a fruitful two-year spell at Penrith, the flyer returned to Wollongong in 1991 and topped the premiership with a club-record

19 tries, including five in a match against Gold Coast—another unprecedented mark for a Steelers player. He scored two tries in Illawarra's finals debut upset of St George in '92, but the club captain was shown the door after he negotiated with other clubs as an agent for five-eighth Dale Fritz. McIndoe's club record of 65 career tries stood until Rod Wishart eclipsed it the Steelers' final season.

4. John Simon—120 games (1990-95)
John Simon debuted for Illawarra as a 17-year-old in 1990 and quickly became the linchpin of an exciting young side. Boasting deft playmaking ability, a brilliant kicking game and strong defence, the Indigenous halfback leapfrogged several more established No.7s to play for NSW in the 1992 series opener while still a teenager. He was the Steelers' Player of the Year in 1994 and finished fifth in the Rothmans Medal, but after representing Country Origin for the fourth straight year in '95, he was lured to the Sydney City Roosters. Simon was named at halfback in the Illawarra Steelers' greatest team in 2006.

5. Brett Rodwell—156 games (1989-97)
Classy centre Brett Rodwell made his first grade debut as an 18-year-old and racked up the second-most appearances (156) and third-most tries (60) in the Steelers' history. A dangerous ball-runner and distinctive in headgear, Rodwell formed one of the premiership's finest centre pairings with Paul McGregor. He represented Country Origin three times (including 1993 at fullback) and played his sole match for NSW in '95, scoring a try off the bench but suffering a season-ending knee injury—a shame, as he had scored nine tries in the opening 10 rounds for the Steelers. One of only three players to feature in Illawarra's 1992 and '97 finals campaigns, Rodwell joined Souths after the latter.

6. Brian Hetherington—144 games (1982-88)
An Illawarra representative from Dapto during the 1970s, Brian Hetherington returned to the region to become a foundation Steeler after spending four seasons at Newtown. The dependable centre became the Steelers' first Origin representative in 1984 and picked up the club's Player of the Year award that season; he played a further match for NSW in '86, featuring on the wing in the Blues' series-sealing game two win. The veteran was a regular captain later in his career, and remains fifth on the club's all-time appearances list after playing at least 18 games in each of his seven seasons in scarlet and white.

7. Ian Russell—115 games (1986-94)
Gifted lock Ian Russell was arguably the Steelers' most important player during their upward surge in the early 1990s. A brilliant ball-player and tough in defence, Russell

was the club's Player of the Year in 1990-91, finishing fourth and third respectively in the Rothmans Medal in those seasons. He was named Dally M Lock of the Year as the Steelers claimed a historic finals berth in '92, although a hamstring injury ruled him out of the post-season campaign. The remainder of the Indigenous playmaker's tenure at Illawarra was punctuated by injuries, while a stint as a high-profile acquisition for the fledgling Cowboys was a disaster. Russell took the lock spot in the Steelers' greatest team named in 2006.

8. Michael Bolt—168 games (1982-90)
Durable hooker Michael Bolt made a record number of first grade appearances for Illawarra, while he played a then premiership-record 187 consecutive games in all grades. The local junior, a foundation Steeler, was the club's Player of the Year in 1983 and '87—a rare constant during its difficult first decade. Bolt regularly filled in as skipper of the Steelers and was given the Ken Stephen Memorial Award for his contribution to Rugby League in 1990.

9. John Dorahy—73 games (1982-85)
The Steelers' undisputed—and perhaps only—superstar during their tough formative seasons, 'Joe Cool' was a Wollongong junior who found fame with Wests and Manly before returning home. The former Test fullback was Illawarra's inaugural skipper, featuring at centre or five-eighth in his first two seasons with the club before reverting to the No.1 jumper. He scored a then record 463 points for the Steelers, including 175 in 1983—a mark that stood for 12 years before Rod Wishart pipped it by a point. Dorahy was named as fullback and captain of the Steelers' greatest team in 2006.

10. Trent Barrett—45 games (1996-98)
Prodigiously talented Temora five-eighth Trent Barrett shaped as the Steelers' future until their merger with St George. An immediate sensation in first grade, the 19-year-old was called up to make his NSW debut in 1997 after just 12 appearances for his club. Barrett scored 12 tries that year, but bettered that the following season with 18 from 24 games—equalling the premiership record for a five-eighth. While his powerful running netted bucketloads of tries, his bullet-like passes and mature direction garnered just as much praise. He was an obvious choice as the Steelers' Player of the Year in their final season, and became the linchpin and later captain of the St George Illawarra joint venture, and a representative star. Despite his short tenure with the Steelers, he was named in the club's best-ever line-up in 2006.

11. Neil Piccinelli—145 games (1989-96)
Lanky second-rower Neil Piccinelli, a Helensburgh junior, was integral to Illawarra's arrival as a premiership force in the early 1990s. Clever with the ball in hand and a

superb defender, Piccinelli starred as the Steelers reached the '92 finals and was named Player of the Year after representing City Firsts during the club's disappointing '93 campaign. Piccinelli set a club record with 57 tackles in a 1991 match in an era when half-century tackle counts were uncommon, and was second on the Steelers' all-time appearances list when he left at the end of 1996 after signing a Super League contract. He was named in the Steelers' best-ever team in 2006.

12. Chris Walsh—77 games (1987-92)
Port Kembla product Chris Walsh debuted for St George in 1982—Illawarra's first season in the premiership—and represented NSW two years later, but returned to his home region in '87 and was a fine leader for the young Steelers. He was their Player of the Year in 1988-89, and captained the club to the Panasonic Cup final in '89 and a historic Toohey's Challenge Cup triumph in '92. Sadly, injuries restricted the hardy prop/second-rower to just nine first grade games in 1991-92 and he missed the Steelers' maiden finals campaign. He was named vice-captain of Illawarra's best-ever line-up in 2006.

13. Dean Schifilliti—102 games (1989-93)
North Queensland native Dean Schifilliti played 102 of a possible 113 games during his five seasons with the Steelers. Regarded as one of the best young hookers in the premiership, the creative and hardworking Schifilliti captained Illawarra to its maiden finals campaign in 1992 at the age of 24. He linked with Souths in '94 before becoming the Cowboys' inaugural captain a year later. Schifilliti was named at hooker ahead of stalwart Michael Bolt in Illawarra's greatest team in 2006.

14. John Cross—137 games (1991-97)
Energetic lock John Cross was an unwaveringly consistent workhorse who developed into a fine leader for the Steelers. The Port Kembla junior missed just eight games in seven seasons at Illawarra after making his debut as a 19-year-old, playing all 25 games of the club's watershed '92 campaign. Cross skippered the Steelers from 1994 to 1996 and represented Country Origin in '95. He departed for Penrith after playing in Illawarra's finals loss in 1997.

15. Brad Mackay—56 games (1996-98)
Former St George star Brad Mackay joined the Steelers after his new club, the Western Reds, aligned with Super League. The veteran of 17 Origins and 12 Tests was outstanding in three seasons in Wollongong as a backrower (and occasional five-eighth), taking out Player of the Year honours as the Steelers reached the 1997 ARL finals. Mackay donned the Red V again for the St George Illawarra joint venture and headed for England after the Dragons' '99 Grand Final loss. He was named as a reserve in the Steelers' greatest team in 2006.

16. Greg Mackey—105 games (1984-88)
Ex-Souths halfback Greg Mackey spent five seasons with the Steelers, playing at least 19 first grade games in each year he spent in the 'Gong. He was the highest-polling Illawarra player in the 1986 Rothmans Medal, and a valuable director of traffic in a team short on big-name talent. Predominantly a halfback or five-eighth, Mackey displayed his versatility in his last season with the Steelers by also making appearances at fullback, wing and centre. He went on to have a successful tenure in England with Hull and Warrington.

17. Shaun Timmins—86 games (1994-98)
A 17-year-old debutant in 1994, Shaun Timmins was one of the Steelers' most consistent and constructive players in their final four seasons—primarily in the centres, but also at five-eighth, lock and second-row. He missed just one match in the 1995-97 seasons and finished with 28 tries in 86 games for Illawarra. Timmins quickly earned his Test and Origin spurs from St George Illawarra, spending eight seasons with the joint venture. He ousted Brett Rodwell for a centre spot in the Steelers' greatest line-up named in 2006.

18. Craig Smith—49 games (1996-98)
Tough and aggressive Kiwi prop Craig Smith arrived at the Steelers from Souths in 1996 as an unheralded 25-year-old. But by the following season, he was established as the club's top front-rower and played all three matches of the 1997 Origin series for Queensland under the ultra-flexible eligibility rules of the Super League War era. Smith also played for Rest of the World against Australia that year before breaking into the New Zealand Test side at the end of '98. He captained the Steelers five times in their final season, but missed the opportunity to play in their last game due to a lengthy suspension—a common occurrence during his subsequent stint with St George Illawarra. Smith was named in the Steelers' greatest team in 2006.

19. Michael Carberry—88 games (1985-90)
Michael Carberry was a popular clubman for the Steelers after arriving from South Sydney in 1985. The second-rower was named Illawarra's Player of the Year after playing all 26 games in '86, while he showed his versatility three seasons later by featuring at prop and hooker. Carberry was named as a reserve in the Steelers' best-ever team in 2006.

20. Bob Lindner—20 games (1993)
A long-serving representative star who was tagged as a mercenary for his inability to settle at a club, Bob Lindner spent the last season of his decorated career in Australia with the Steelers. He produced arguably his best season at premiership level, playing

a career-high 20 games and winning the '93 Dally M Lock of the Year gong. Lindner starred in his Origin farewell for Queensland and became just the Steelers' third Australian representative when he featured in the Test series against New Zealand. Despite spending only one season at the club, he was named as a second-rower in Illawarra's 'Team of Steel' in 2006.

ILLAWARRA STEELERS—GREATEST COACHES (1982-98)

1. Graham Murray—95 games (1991-95)

After excelling in lower-grade and assistant posts with Penrith, Balmain and Illawarra, Graham Murray was belatedly given a first grade opportunity with the Steelers in 1991. He achieved almost instant success with the long-suffering club— an unprecedented eighth-place finish in his first season was followed by the club's first piece of silverware in the '92 pre-season Tooheys Challenge. Murray steered his charges to a maiden finals appearance in third spot that year—claiming Dally M Coach of the Year honours—but fell agonisingly short of a Grand Final appearance courtesy of a 4-0 loss to St George in the preliminary final. The Steelers won more games than they lost in each of the 1993 and 1994 seasons, but could not crack the final five. Murray was sacked for signing with Super League early in '95 but the genial mentor later coached the Sydney Roosters and North Queensland to Grand Finals. He was named coach of the greatest Illawarra team in 2006.

2. Allan Fitzgibbon—70 games (1982-83, 1995)

Former Balmain and NSW rep Allan Fitzgibbon was the Steelers' inaugural coach. With a limited roster at his disposal, he led the fledgling outfit to just 14 wins in their first two seasons, but managed to stave off the wooden spoon. Fitzgibbon, who took Cronulla to a minor premiership in 1988, returned to Illawarra early in '95 when Graham Murray was sacked. After a dreadful mid-season run, Fitzgibbon's caretaker stint ended on a high with six wins in the final seven rounds as the Steelers finished 12th. Despite an unflattering 31.4 per cent win rate, he remains a popular figure in the Illawarra club's 18-season narrative.

3. Brian Smith—96 games (1984-87)

An Under-23s premiership winner with Souths, Brian Smith received his first shot at coaching big time with struggling Illawarra in 1984. In charge of a team boasting little in the way of top-class talent, Smith led the Steelers to 12 wins and a respectable ninth-place finish—the club's best result in its first eight seasons. But two wooden spoons followed in 1985-86 and Smith left after a marginally improved 11th in '88. The perennial coaching bridesmaid, Smith took St George, Parramatta and the Sydney Roosters to four Grand Finals in total from 1992 to 2010, losing them all.

4. Andrew Farrar—47 games (1997-98)

A former international from Canterbury who spent the last season of his distinguished playing career at Illawarra, Andrew Farrar progressed through the grades to take on the Steelers' first grade coaching role. His initial season in charge saw the club reach the finals for only the second time in its history—the seven-team ARL finals in '97—but ended via an upset loss to Gold Coast. The financially embattled Steelers won 11 and drew one of 24 games under Farrar in '98, finishing just outside finals reckoning. He was an assistant to David Waite as the St George Illawarra joint venture qualified for a debut-year Grand Final before taking over the head-coach position in 2000 and guiding the Dragons to the 2001-02 finals.

5. Ron Hilditch—44 games (1989-90)

Former Parramatta hardman Ron Hilditch was handed the tough task of moulding the lowly Steelers into a competitive unit, and despite famously taking the side to the Panasonic Cup final in 1989, his initial first grade season resulted in a paltry two wins and the wooden spoon. But with Hilditch bringing along a host of young local products who would form the nucleus of the side that contended for the title a couple of years later, the Steelers won half of their games in 1990 and finished ninth. Assistant Graham Murray took over the following season.

ILLAWARRA STEELERS—BEST DAYS (1982-98)

1. September 6, 1992: Steelers beat 'Big Brother' on finals debut

Illawarra made a stunning entry into finals football in 1992, upsetting traditional 'Big Brother' St George 18-16 in the major preliminary semi-final at the SFS. A double to veteran winger Alan McIndoe provided the Steelers with a 12-6 halftime lead before a superb Paul McGregor touchdown extended the advantage to 12 points. Two brilliant Dragons tries ensured a nervous finish, but the Steelers held on for a victory in their first-ever post-season encounter.

2. March 15, 1992: Pre-season silverware to start breakthrough season

The Steelers' watershed 1992 campaign began with success in the pre-season Challenge Cup—the club's first major competition victory. The scarlet-and-whites downed

Brisbane 4-2 in a try-less final at Dubbo, with two goals from Brett Docherty—a late replacement for Rod Wishart—enough to secure a tense, history-making victory.

3. August 21, 1992: Last-gasp victory confirms maiden finals series appearance

Illawarra sealed a top-five spot with a thrilling late win over fellow finals contenders Manly in the penultimate round of 1992. Trailing by four points in the dying minutes at Brookvale Oval, the Steelers levelled via a barnstorming try to Test winger Rod Wishart, who added the conversion from in front for a 10-8 victory. The result ensured the Steelers would play finals football for the first time in their 11-season history.

4. March 31, 1991: Illawarra's rise marked by Canterbury thrashing

The Steelers announced themselves as an emerging force with a 44-4 rout of Canterbury early in the 1991 season. Teenage fullback David Riolo scored two tries, while star wing Rod Wishart bagged a try and kicked eight goals for a then club-record 20-point haul as Illawarra thrilled the 11,021-strong Wollongong Showgrounds crowd. The Steelers remained in or around the top five for the ensuing three months, but ultimately faded to miss the finals.

5. June 7, 1989: Minnows gallant in midweek final loss

Illawarra finished with the wooden spoon after winning just two premiership matches in 1989, but the club won an army of admirers for its stirring performances in the midweek Panasonic Cup. In the Parramatta Stadium-hosted final, a Brisbane side containing seven internationals and another four Origin players skipped to a 16-0 lead before the unfancied Steelers reeled them in to trail by just two. The Broncos eventually won a thriller 22-20, but the Steelers were widely acclaimed for their performance and British import Andy Gregory was named man-of-the-match in a losing side.

ILLAWARRA STEELERS—WORST DAYS (1982-98)

1. September 20, 1992: Preliminary final anguish

The Steelers' plucky maiden finals campaign came to an agonising conclusion courtesy of a 4-0 loss to St George in an extraordinary preliminary final. Illawarra had pipped the Saints in the semi a fortnight earlier, but the club's shot at a Grand Final berth slipped by in a controversial contest—Brett Rodwell was denied two tries by questionable forward pass calls, while Alan McIndoe had a late leveller disallowed by the in-goal judge.

2. April 5, 1995: Coach sacked amid Super League upheaval
Illawarra sided with the ARL after the Super League War broke out on April Fool's Day 1995, and Steelers coach Graham Murray became the first high-profile casualty of the tumult that gripped the code when he was sacked for signing with the rebel organisation. Murray had led the club to unprecedented success only a couple of years earlier. Foundation coach Allan Fitzgibbon stepped into the breach, but the Steelers won just two of their next 11 games to tumble out of finals contention.

3. September 23, 1998: Cash-strapped Steelers forced to merge
Illawarra had intended to remain as a single entity in a rationalised NRL competition, but it became apparent the club would struggle to subsist on its own after the League outlined its survival criteria. Inflated player payments and BHP Steel's impending discontinuation of its long-running sponsorship of the club forced the Steelers' hand, and they entered merger talks with St George. Long-serving CEO Bob Millward announced the decision to wrap up the Illawarra Steelers after 18 seasons in favour of the premiership's first joint venture a month after the club's final game.

4. September 5, 1997: Steelers rolled by Gold Coast
The Steelers headed into their minor qualifying final date with post-season debutants Gold Coast in the 1997 ARL premiership as red-hot favourites. The scarlet-and-whites had whipped the ragtag Chargers 28-6 six days earlier in the final regular season round, but fell behind early in the elimination final at Parramatta Stadium and never recovered, slumping to a devastating 25-14 loss. It was to be Illawarra's second and last finals campaign as a single entity.

5. May 30, 1982: Harsh premiership realities grip Illawarra
Premiership newcomers Illawarra mustered three wins in the opening 13 rounds of its debut season, but the long, hard road to becoming competitive was put in stark perspective after a 55-5 drubbing at the hands of Parramatta at Belmore Oval. The Steelers conceded 11 tries in the romp, which remains the highest score conceded in their 18 seasons.

MANLY-WARRINGAH SEA EAGLES/NORTHERN EAGLES— GREATEST PLAYERS (1947-2013)

1. Bob Fulton—213 games (1966-76)
Recognised as one of Rugby League's Immortals in 1981, Bob Fulton ranks among the top handful of players ever to strap on a boot. A champion centre/five-eighth

from Wollongong, Fulton played in three premiership triumphs with the Sea Eagles before coaching two more. He was excellent in the '72 decider but was the star in '73, scoring two tries in the rough-and-tumble Grand Final. Deceptively fast with a fiery drive, Fulton captained Manly to the '76 Grand Final win. He enjoyed Test and state careers that lasted well over a decade, including the '73 and '78 Kangaroo Tours. Fulton was honoured in 2008 by being named in the ARL, NSW and CRL Teams of the Century.

2. Graham Eadie—237 games (1971-83)

A fabulous goalkicking fullback who possessed rare strength for a custodian, Graham Eadie played in Manly's first four premiership triumphs. Playing in seven Grand Finals in all for the club, Eadie at one stage held the premiership record for most points with a career tally of 1917 points. He booted two critical goals in the 10-7 '73 Grand Final triumph and five in the three-point win in '76 where he was Manly's best. Eadie was again the star in '78 with a try, three goals and a field goal in the Grand Final replay. He enjoyed a long rep career where he played 20 Tests and wore the blue of NSW for close to a decade. The 1974 Rothmans Medal winner was named in the ARL's 100 Greatest Players.

3. Roy Bull—177 games (1947-59)

A tough and pugnacious front-rower who was arguably the best prop in the game during the 1950s, Roy Bull was a Manly local junior who became the club's first international. Renowned for his bald head and imposing physique, Bull played 22 Tests for Australia and was named EE Christensen's Player of the Year in 1954 and NSW Player of the Year in 1955. Bull was named in the NSW Team of the Century and rated among the game's Top 100 players. While the raw-boned front-rower played in Manly's first three Grand Finals, he never won a title with the Sea Eagles.

4. Steve Menzies—349 games (1993-2008)

One of Manly's favourite sons, local junior Steve Menzies went on to become the second-greatest try-scorer in premiership history with 180 four-pointers. He was a brilliant edge runner who started his career running off Cliff Lyons' shoulder and finished with a try in his final game, the 2008 Grand Final triumph. Menzies—if Northern Eagles games are included—is Manly's most-capped player. He played in five deciders for the Sea Eagles, including the 1996 and 2008 titles. The champion backrower played 20 Origins for NSW over a 12-year period and 13 Tests for Australia. A four-time Dally M positional award winner, Menzies' longevity saw him retire as the equal-most-capped player in premiership history.

5. Max Krilich—215 games (1970-83)
Captain of the undefeated 'Invincibles' Kangaroo Tour in 1982, Max Krilich built a career as a tough, uncompromising hooker who skippered the Sea Eagles to their 1978 premiership triumph and was part of the club's '76 success. Initially stuck behind Fred Jones, Krilich emerged as Australia's leading rake on two Kangaroo Tours. Renowned for consistently playing at a high level, Krilich was named as Manly's hooker in its 2006 anniversary side.

6. Jamie Lyon (168 games, 2007-13)
The finest centre of the NRL era, Jamie Lyon's arrival at Manly signalled the return to success of the Sea Eagles. In his seven seasons with Manly, the club has reached four Grand Finals and won premierships in 2008 and 2011. A three-time Dally M Centre of the Year, Lyon has shunned rep football for most of his time with Manly but would have been a walk-up starter nearly every year. A blockbusting runner with an amazing ability to make the right call, Lyon has few weaknesses. He was appointed Sea Eagles skipper in 2010.

7. Geoff Toovey—286 games (1988-2001)
One of the toughest little men to play premiership football, Geoff Toovey forged a reputation as a reliable and dogged performer who always lifted when required. A shifty halfback-cum-hooker who was one of the shortest players of his era, Toovey skippered Manly to a premiership and captained both NSW and Australia. An inspirational leader, he was appointed Manly skipper at just 24 and won the Clive Churchill Medal in the '96 Grand Final triumph. He played 15 Origins and 13 Tests, with the highlight of his rep career being starting at halfback in the 1995 World Cup final win. Toovey was named the halfback in Manly's 60-year anniversary team.

8. Michael O'Connor—115 games (1987-92)
A dual international who signed with Manly from St George in 1987, Michael O'Connor made an immediate impact, assisting the club to the '87 premiership with 14 of Manly's 18 points in the decider. A supremely skilful three-quarter, O'Connor was a NSW and Australian regular for most of his Sea Eagles career, inspiring the Blues to victory on more than one occasion. He captained the Sea Eagles from 1990 to 1992 and was named in their 2006 anniversary side.

9. John O'Neill—51 games (1972-74)
A brute of a front-rower who won four premierships with South Sydney, John O'Neill won titles with Manly in his first two years at Brookvale after being poached from the Bunnies. Nicknamed 'Lurch' and respected as one of the toughest players in the game, O'Neill thrived in the brutal 1973 decider where he rated among Manly's best.

He made his international debut at Souths but went to the '72 World Cup and on the '73 Kangaroo Tour as a Sea Eagle. He was named in the ARL's 100 Greatest Players and at prop in Manly's 60-year team.

10. Malcolm Reilly—89 games (1971-75)

As fierce as he was skilful, British forward Malcolm Reilly was a loathed figure outside of Manly but beloved by the Sea Eagles faithful. A hardman of the old school, Reilly was willing to bend the laws of the game to gain an edge and was often suspended, but made such an impact that he was integral in guiding Manly to its first two titles. He was front and centre in the violence of the 1973 Grand Final, wreaking havoc until a kidney injury ensured he would not see out the match. Reilly was named lock in Manly's 60-year anniversary team.

11. Cliff Lyons—309 games (1986-99)

An outstanding ball-player with incredible longevity, Cliff Lyons played 309 games for Manly as one of the finest five-eighths of his generation, in an era that included Wally Lewis, Brett Kenny and Terry Lamb. The moustachioed Lyons moved to Manly following a year at Norths, and after debuting for NSW in his second year with the Sea Eagles led the club to the 1987 premiership, winning the Clive Churchill Medal. He would go on to play in the '96 premiership triumph and the '95 and '97 Grand Final losses, while he played six Origins and six Tests and toured with the 1990 Kangaroos. Lyons was named the Dally M Player of the Year in both 1990 and '94 and came second in 1995. He is the club's fifth-greatest try-scorer and was named on the bench in the Manly 60-year anniversary team. Lyons retired at the end of the '98 season but made a comeback in '99 as a saviour for the club, playing exceptionally well at the age of 37.

12. Des Hasler—256 games (1984-96)

Though he bookended his career with stints at Penrith and Western Suburbs, Des Hasler spent the vast majority of his career at Manly, where he became arguably the most successful utility player in Rugby League history. One of the most versatile players the code has known, Hasler was most at home in the halves but could play centre, hooker or lock. Sharp and incredibly fit, he made the most of his abilities to forge a career that saw him win two premierships and represent NSW 13 times and Australia in 12 Tests, touring with the 1986 and '90 Kangaroo Tours. Hasler was named on the bench in the 60-year anniversary team.

13. Terry Randall—208 games (1970-82)

A fierce and frenetic forward who played in all four of the Sea Eagles' premierships during the 1970s, Terry 'Igor' Randall was one of the most feared men in Rugby League during a physical era in the game. A local junior, he played in Australia's World Cup wins in 1975 and '77 and was named in the second-row in Manly's 60-year anniversary team.

14. Ben Kennedy—42 games (2005-06)
Ben Kennedy spent just two seasons at Manly after a successful career with Canberra and Newcastle, but was so influential he was named in its 60-year anniversary team in 2006. A relentless and forceful lock forward, he was the Dally M Lock of the Year and the club's best and fairest in both his seasons at the club, with Manly reaching the finals on each occasion—under his captaincy in the latter. Kennedy continued to play rep football during his time at the Sea Eagles.

15. Ken Irvine—58 games (1971-73)
The greatest try-scorer in premiership history, Ken Irvine spent the majority of his illustrious first grade tenure at North Sydney before a late career move to the Sea Eagles. One of the game's greats, Irvine played 25 times for NSW and 33 times for Australia but had retired from rep football before his move to Brookvale. In his three seasons with Manly, he scored 41 tries and starred in Grand Final wins in 1972 and '73. Irvine was named in the Australian Team of the Century, the NSW Team of the Century and in the ARL's 100 Greatest Players, and was included in the Sea Eagles' 2006 anniversary team.

16. Wally O'Connell—34 games (1950-52)
An Australian Test five-eighth when he was recruited from Eastern Suburbs, Wally O'Connell was one of Manly's best players during the club's infant years. Captain-coach for three years, O'Connell guided the Sea Eagles to their first Grand Final in 1951 and played Test match football while at the club. He was named five-eighth in Manly's 2006 anniversary team.

17. Ian Roberts—100 games (1990-95)
A punishing forward who played his best football at Manly, Ian Roberts was a regular for NSW and Australia during his six years with the Sea Eagles. Recruited from Souths, the statuesque Roberts made his Origin and Test debuts in his first year with Manly, playing all nine of his interstate matches and all 13 of his matches for Australia while with the Sea Eagles. Roberts won the Dally M Prop of the Year in 1993 and '94, running second in the overall count in '93. His last game for the club was the 1995 Grand Final loss to the Bulldogs.

18. Brett Stewart—178 games (2003-13)
An outstanding fullback talent who had a knack for finding the try-line like few others, Brett Stewart played a key role in Manly's 2008 and 2011 premierships. He was the club's second-leading try-scorer (and top 20 in premiership history) with 136 in 178 games to the start of 2014. Manly made four Grand Finals in the five years

Stewart was healthy between 2007 and 2013. An absolute flyer, he overcame two serious knee injuries and a sordid police matter to represent NSW and Australia in an era of great fullbacks. No player has scored more tries at Brookvale Oval.

19. Paul Vautin—204 games (1979-89)
Rugby League's court jester, who has starred in the media since retiring, Paul Vautin was an excellent lock forward and outstanding servant for Manly. The Sea Eagles' premiership captain in 1987, Vautin played in Grand Final losses in 1982 and '83. A gutsy player who always gave his all, he was a Queensland regular, playing 22 Origins and captaining his state twice, while playing 13 Tests. Vautin was named on the bench in the club's all-time team in 2006.

20. Ron Rowles—81 games (1950-54)
An outstanding goalkicking winger, Ron Rowles led the premiership in scoring in four of his five seasons in the Big League. Recruited from Wollongong, he just missed selection for the 1948-49 Kangaroos and played in the Sea Eagles' first Grand Final in 1951. Rowles remains the sixth-greatest scorer in Sea Eagles history with 842.

MANLY-WARRINGAH SEA EAGLES/NORTHERN EAGLES— GREATEST COACHES (1947-2013)

1. Bob Fulton—306 games (1983-88, 1993-99)
The Sea Eagles' longest-serving mentor, Bob Fulton, won two premierships as a coach after winning three with the club as a player. With a combined 524 games as both player and coach of Manly, Immortal Fulton is considered the club's greatest figure. After coaching Eastern Suburbs, he returned to Brookvale in 1983 and led the club to post-season football in each of his 12 full seasons. The Sea Eagles made the decider in his first year and then claimed a premiership in 1987, the team's first in nine years. Fulton left after the '88 season to take up national duties but, after four disappointing seasons under Alan Thompson and Graham Lowe, returned in 1993. Manly made three straight Grand Finals from 1995 to 1997, winning in '96 but losing the other two as heavy favourites. Fulton quit early in 1999 after opening with seven straight losses but maintains the second-best win percentage in Manly history.

2. Ron Willey—139 games (1962, 1970-74)
A talented goalkicking fullback whose playing career spanned 16 years and three clubs including Manly, Ron Willey guided the Sea Eagles to their first two premierships

and his strike rate of 69.8 per cent remains top in club history. After an unsuccessful stint as captain-coach in 1962, Willey returned to Manly in 1970 and steered the club through its first great period. After a losing Grand Final in his first year and a preliminary final defeat the season after, Manly won its first premiership in its 26th season in 1972 and backed it up with another a year later in a brutal decider against Cronulla. Willey left after semi-final elimination in 1974.

3. Des Hasler—207 games (2004-11)
An outstanding utility player who ran out for 289 first grade games—256 with Manly—Des Hasler successfully rebuilt the club after the Northern Eagles debacle. Missing the finals in his first season, the Sea Eagles made the playoffs for the next seven years under Hasler, winning premierships in 2008 and 2011 and losing the decider in 2007. Named the RLIF Coach of the Year in both 2008 and '11, Hasler controversially quit the Sea Eagles after the 2011 premiership triumph to coach Canterbury.

4. Frank Stanton—123 games (1975-79)
A fine back who spent nine seasons as a player with Manly and made a Kangaroo Tour, Frank Stanton rose through the ranks to coach the Sea Eagles to two premierships. Named reserve grade coach in 1971, he won a reserve grade premiership in 1973 before assuming first grade duties from Ron Willey in 1975. Under Stanton, Manly won premierships in 1976 and '78 and made the playoffs in '75 and '77. Appointed Australian coach in 1978, he left Manly when the club failed to make the finals for the first time in 12 years in 1979.

5. Ken Arthurson—98 games (1957-61)
The Godfather of Manly, Ken Arthurson, has been associated with the club since 1950 as a player, coach and administrator. More widely known as the boss of the League from 1983 to 1997, Arthurson spent five years in charge of the Sea Eagles' first grade team during St George's famous run of 11 straight titles. He led Manly to two Grand Finals (1957 and '59), the first as a 27-year-old, and the playoffs in 1958 and '61.

MANLY-WARRINGAH SEA EAGLES/NORTHERN EAGLES— BEST DAYS (1947-2013)

1. September 16, 1972: A premiership at last
After 25 years and five losing Grand Finals, Manly was finally crowned premier in 1972 when it beat Eastern Suburbs 19-14. The scores were locked at 4-all at the

break but tries to skipper Fred Jones and Ray Branighan secured the Sea Eagles' first premiership. Halfback Dennis Ward was awarded man-of-the-match.

2. October 5, 2008: Storm warning
In the biggest Grand Final win in premiership history, Manly defeated Melbourne 40-0. The Sea Eagles, who started as outsiders, led 8-0 at halftime before running riot in the second half. Michael Robertson scored a hat-trick and Steve Menzies crossed in his final game for Manly, where he equalled the premiership record for most games played (since surpassed). The win atoned for a defeat in the previous year's decider to Melbourne.

3. September 15, 1973: Guts and glory
In the most brutal Grand Final in premiership history, Manly out-bashed and outscored Cronulla 10-7. Bob Fulton scored a classy double but the match is remembered for the wild brawling and plentiful violence that broke out from the opening whistle. Among the carnage, the Sea Eagles held their nerve to go back-to-back.

4. September 19, 1978: Replay
Manly capped one of the great finals series charges when it won its fourth premiership in a replay against Cronulla. After an 11-all draw on the Saturday, the Sea Eagles thumped the Sharks 16-0 three days later. Champion fullback Graham Eadie scored a try, kicked three goals and added a drop goal in a man-of-the-match performance.

5. September 27, 1987: Eagles soar at SCG farewell
Manly claimed its fifth premiership and its first in nine seasons in the last Grand Final played at the SCG. The mercurial Cliff Lyons, who was awarded the Clive Churchill Medal, starred in the 18-8 win over Canberra. Lyons scored a try along with Michael O'Connor, who also booted a perfect five-from-five.

MANLY-WARRINGAH SEA EAGLES/NORTHERN EAGLES— WORST DAYS (1947-2013)

1. October 9, 1999: The merger
A proud club who had won six premierships across the previous three decades, Manly was devastated by a decision to merge with hated rivals North Sydney after the 1999 season, in which it missed the finals for the first time in seven years. The merger proved a disaster and Manly was back in business four seasons later, but there are few fond memories for Sea Eagles fans from the wretched year that was 1999.

2. September 28, 1997: A bitter defeat
For the third straight year, Manly went into the Grand Final heavy favourite against Newcastle. All seemed to be going well with a 16-10 lead and just five minutes to play, but a Robbie O'Davis try and a Darren Albert last-minute miracle turned Manly's dream into a nightmare. The Sea Eagles enjoyed the running for most of the game but could not put away a gallant Knights outfit.

3. September 19, 1970: Another bloody loss
Manly entered the 1970 Grand Final without a premiership win and with four Grand Final losses. It was again beaten, this time by a courageous South Sydney team led by the great John Sattler, who played on after having his jaw smashed. The Rabbitohs won 23-12 and the Sea Eagles were bridesmaids again.

4. September 23, 1951: Welcome to the Big League
Manly reached its first Grand Final in just its fifth year but proved no match for powerhouse South Sydney. Captain-coach Wally O'Connell didn't play and Johnny Graves ran in four tries in the 42-14 rout.

5. September 24, 1995: Unbelievable
Manly had lost just twice in 1995, dominating the competition. It went into the Grand Final heavy favourites against a Canterbury team that had snuck into the eight in sixth spot. However, the attacking powerhouse failed to score a try in the decider as Canterbury lifted to win 17-4 in one of the great Grand Final upsets.

MELBOURNE STORM—GREATEST PLAYERS (1998-2013)

1. Cameron Smith—261 games (2002-13)
The skipper who presided over one of the great dynasties of the modern era, Cameron Smith is the Storm's greatest player. He does it all: a huge defensive workload, sharp work out of dummy-half, goalkicking, in-play kicking, organising, leadership. Danny Buderus may have changed the role of the modern hooker but Smith took it to the next level. His commitment to the team ethos has ensured Melbourne has been the best defensive team in the competition for many years, while his will to win has garnered the Storm plenty of victories and three premierships. The 2007 Golden Boot winner has played at a high level since entering the League and deserves every honour that comes his way. Smith's importance to his team can be seen in the 2008 Grand Final: he was suspended for the match, and Melbourne lost 40-0. He won the 2006 Dally M Player of the Year, the 2006,

2008 and 2011-13 Dally M Hooker of the Year, the 2007 and 2011 Dally M Rep Player of the Year, and the Storm Player of the Year from 2005 to 2007 and 2011 to 2013.

2. Billy Slater—248 games (2003-13)

Billy Slater has revolutionised the fullback position and drawn comparisons to the great Clive Churchill. His scything runs, ability to leap in the air, sheer speed, instinctive ability to find the ball—Slater has it all. He won the Golden Boot in 2008 and was robbed of the Dally M that year after a suspension. He won the Dally M Medal in 2011, though, when he swept the pool for major awards. Slater was brilliant in the 2009 decider, winning the Churchill Medal, while his effort in 2007 was nearly as good. In 2005 he topped the NRL tryscoring list, and he has racked up an astonishing 158 tries in 248 games. Slater has donned the green and gold 24 times and the maroon of Queensland in 22 Origins. Throw in the Dally M Fullback of the Year in 2008 and 2011, the Dally M Rep Player of the Year in 2010 and the Storm Player of the Year in 2008 and 2009, and Slater is one of the most decorated players in the NRL.

3. Cooper Cronk—233 games (2004-13)

One of the most consistent halfbacks over the past decade, Cooper Cronk made his Test debut in 2007 and Origin debut three seasons later and has rarely been out of either side from '10 onwards. He has never had the sheer brilliance of a Thurston or the reputation of a Prince but he is one of the best halfbacks of the modern game. In his first season in the Storm No.7 jersey, Cronk won the Dally M Halfback of the Year and led the Storm to the Grand Final. In 2007, he was instrumental in the Melbourne premiership; in 2008, he skippered the team in the Grand Final; and in 2009, he should have been awarded the Churchill Medal. He won it in 2012 when he played a match-winning hand in Melbourne's fourth premiership, and claimed the Dally M Medal a year later. With an outstanding kick, a sharp pass and a fantastic understanding of Rugby League, Cronk has elevated himself to the game's elite.

4. Greg Inglis—118 games (2005-10)

One of the most gifted players of the modern game, Greg Inglis achieved plenty in six seasons at the Storm. At his best, he was the most unstoppable outside back in the NRL, a sheer force who combined electric speed, awesome strength and amazing athleticism. In 118 games for Melbourne he scored 78 tries, many of them needing to be seen to be believed. His abilities did not go unrecognised: Inglis won the Golden Boot in 2009, the Clive Churchill Medal in 2007, the Dally M Five-eighth of the Year in 2008 (when playing out of position) and the Dally M Rep Player of the Year in 2008 and 2009, along with two premierships, 13 caps for Queensland and 16 Australian jerseys while at the Storm. Melbourne won 70.94 per cent of games with Inglis in the team, more than any player who played 60 games for the club.

5. Brett Kimmorley—79 games (1998-2000)

The Melbourne Storm may not be around if it weren't for Brett Kimmorley. The Storm needed early success and 'Noddy' brought it. He played his best football at the club, at one stage disposing Andrew Johns from the mantle of top halfback in the game. In only the second year of the club's existence, Kimmorley had a sensational 1999, winning the Storm Player of the Year as well as the Churchill Medal after a sublime Grand Final performance. He followed that up by winning the Dally M Halfback of the Year and *Rugby League Week*'s Player of the Year in 2000. Kimmorley made his Origin and Test debuts while at the Storm and etched his name into club lore by being the leading figure in the '99 title victory. The measure of his contribution to the Storm came in 2001 and 2002 when they missed the finals for the only times in the club's history, the two years after 'Noddy' moved to Cronulla.

6. Robbie Kearns—169 games (1998-2005)

The greatest asset Robbie Kearns had was ticker. He was never the best prop forward in the game. He was never a dominating tackler or a brutal ball-runner. He just kept on coming though. For eight seasons, Kearns was the heart and soul of the Melbourne Storm, a gritty and tough player who squeezed every last ounce out of his body over 169 games. The reward was eight Origin jerseys and 20 Test matches but sadly, no premiership ring, as he missed the '99 Grand Final through injury. The Storm Player of the Year in 1998 and 2003, Kearns—club captain from 2000 to 2002—never left anything on the paddock.

7. Ryan Hoffman—221 games (2003-10, 2012-13)

A hardworking backrower, Ryan Hoffman is one of the cornerstones of Melbourne's dynasty. Hoffman has played in all five of the Storm's deciders since 2006, turning in a sensational effort in the 2012 victory with the opening try. His eight appearances for NSW and his five Test appearances are testament to what a contributor he has been for Melbourne, despite having to depart for a season at the height of the club's salary cap crisis.

8. Israel Folau—52 games (2007-08)

Israel Folau spent only two seasons at the Storm but they were arguably Melbourne's two most dominant, with the club winning 82.7 per cent of matches and reaching two Grand Finals while the big jumping three-quarter was at the club. Folau was an instant hit in 2007, winning the Dally M Rookie of the Year, topping the NRL tryscoring list and making his Test debut while also winning a premiership. He went on to win the Dally M Centre of the Year in 2008 before defecting to Brisbane. In only 52 games, Folau scored 36 tries for Melbourne. He played seven Tests and three Origins during his time at the club.

9. Dallas Johnson—157 games (2003-09)

No player has loved to tackle more than Dallas Johnson. He didn't give much with the ball in hand but he didn't need to as the backbone of Craig Bellamy's vaunted defence that drove the Storm to four straight deciders. 'DJ' played in all four Grand Finals and knocked up 12 Origin appearances and a Test while at the club. He won Dally M Lock of the Year honours in 2007.

10. Rodney Howe—106 games (1998-2004)

Two-time Storm Player of the Year (2000 and '02) Rodney Howe was one of the leaders in the Anderson era, a bullocking prop forward who could rip apart any defensive line. He played eight Origins and four Test matches while at Melbourne but copped a 22-week suspension for steroid use. He came back in 1999 to win a premiership, with his go-forward very important to that title win.

11. Matt Geyer—262 games (1998-2008)

Matt Geyer was never the fastest player, nor was he the strongest or the most skilful. But he was and is one of the Storm greats. In 11 seasons with Melbourne, Geyer played 262 games and scored 113 tries and 662 points. He was the only Storm player to play in both the 1999 and 2007 triumphs, and kicked the winning conversion in the 1999 victory. A true professional whose versatility was much valued by the Storm, three-game NSW rep Geyer will always be remembered as the little engine that could of the Storm. He holds the record for most games without ever playing a game for a Queensland, NSW, New Zealand or ACT club.

12. Scott Hill—177 games (1998-2006)

The ultra-skilful Scott Hill was a delight to watch, and at his best played like a young Jim Dymock with an amazing ability to pop an astonishing pass or throw a beautiful flat ball. He never won a title with the Storm (he was injured in '99) but rates among their most naturally gifted talents. Hill was excellent in the 2006 Grand Final loss to Brisbane, his last NRL game. The five-eighth/lock played 12 Tests and five Origins for NSW while at Melbourne.

13. Matt Orford—120 games (2001-05)

A tough and gritty half, Matt Orford led Melbourne through its toughest period and was a remarkably prolific try-scorer, getting over 52 times in 120 games. He left in 2006 and the Storm made four straight deciders in the four years after his exit, though to Orford's credit, he did win a title with Manly and play in two Grand Finals (both against Melbourne) as well as winning a Dally M Medal. The Storm Player of the Year in 2004, Orford scored a then record 877 points for the club.

14. Matt King—91 games (2003-07)
At his peak in 2006-07, it could be argued that Matt King was the best centre in the NRL. He was big, strong, fast and skilful with a taste for the try-line. Forced out by salary cap pressures, King left on a high with the 2007 title and 20 tries from 23 games in his last season, taking his career tally to 60 for the club. He played 10 Tests and nine Origins.

15. Stephen Kearney—139 games (1999-2004)
Stephen Kearney is a player to whom history has not given its proper due. The prototype of the modern-day backrower, he was a damaging fringe runner and a heavy-hitting defender with great ball skills. Kearney racked up 139 games for the Storm and added 18 Test jerseys while at the club, and starred in the '99 Grand Final. He had it all: strength, smarts and heart.

16. Glenn Lazarus—44 games (1998-99)
Glenn Lazarus spent only two seasons at Melbourne but was the inaugural skipper of the Storm and the man who led the club to its first title. He created history when leading the Storm to the '99 title, becoming the only player to win premierships for three different clubs after playing for Canberra in '89 and '90 and Brisbane in '92 and '93. One of the best prop forwards ever to play the game, the Storm certainly didn't get his best years but he undeniably had a major role in its early successes.

17. Robbie Ross—89 games (1998-2003)
In six injury-riddled seasons with the Storm, Robbie Ross was one of the most dangerous players of the pre-Bellamy era. An electric fullback when his knees held up, Ross played Origin and for Australia while at the Storm and scored 53 tries in only 89 games, including 20 in 25 games in an outstanding 1999. Sadly, he was forced to retire at 28 with a bulging disc in his back. The best was never seen of Ross, who could have been a true superstar had he not spent so much time on the trainer's table.

18. Tawera Nikau—53 games (1998-99)
Tawera Nikau spent only two seasons at Olympic Park but the uber-skilful lock was critical to the Storm's inaugural title in 1999 and made such an impact that the Richmond-side grandstand at Olympic Park was named after him. Unlucky not to have been awarded the Clive Churchill Medal for his Grand Final effort, Nikau sparked the Storm into a big second-half comeback.

19. Richard Swain—132 games (1998-2002)
The Storm has always built its team around a hardworking hooker, and before Cameron Smith there was Richard Swain, who led the NRL in tackles for four straight seasons from 1999 through 2003. While he didn't offer a lot in attack, he was the rock around

which the Storm's defence was built in the Anderson years. Swain won the Storm Player of the Year award in 2001 and scored a decisive try in the 1999 preliminary final win over Parramatta. He did not miss a game in his five years with Melbourne.

20. Marcus Bai—145 games (1998-2003)
A cult hero, Marcus Bai is a beloved figure in Melbourne—one of the most popular Rugby League heroes in an AFL town. Before Billy lit up Olympic Park, Bai did, scoring 70 tries in 144 games over six seasons on the right wing. He still had a "stand" named after him where many of the Storm's biggest diehards sat. Bai was named the 1998 Dally M Winger of the Year in the Storm's inaugural season and was named in the club's Team of the Decade.

MELBOURNE STORM—GREATEST COACHES (1998-2013)

1. Craig Bellamy—293 games (2003-13)
Considered by many to be the greatest coach of all time, Craig Bellamy joined the Storm in 2003 after rejecting overtures from the Wests Tigers. He has since led the club to five Grand Finals, three premierships and four minor premierships, with Melbourne missing the finals just once under his stewardship (when barred by the NRL in 2010). His strike rate of 67.6 per cent after the 2013 season sits behind only Norm Provan for coaches with 50-plus games' experience. He has been awarded the Dally M Coach of the Year gong three times. Arguably his greatest coaching performance came in 2010 when he led Melbourne to 14 wins despite the club having nothing but pride to play for.

2. Chris Anderson—89 games (1998-2001)
The premiership-winning Canterbury mentor was appointed Melbourne's inaugural coach three seasons after winning a title with the Bulldogs. An avid Super League supporter, Anderson became News Limited's first choice to head up its Melbourne franchise and the wily mentor achieved near-immediate success, guiding the Storm to an unlikely NRL title in just its second year. Appointed Australian coach in 1999, Anderson fell out with Storm powerbrokers in 2001 and quit seven games into the year to link with the Sharks in 2002.

3. Mark Murray—43 games (2001-02)
The former Eastern Suburbs and Queensland coach made a surprise return to the NRL in 2001, replacing Chris Anderson after Anderson fell afoul of club management.

Murray had little success with the Storm's only two missed finals appearances (aside from the salary cap-related miss in 2010) coming on his watch. The club went 9-9-1 under him in 2001, finishing ninth, before running 10th in 2002. Murray was ultimately replaced by Bellamy.

MELBOURNE STORM—BEST DAYS (1998-2013)

1. September 26, 1999: The inaugural premiership
In one of the most dramatic premiership deciders ever—in front of a world-record Rugby League crowd of 107,999—Melbourne won its first premiership in just its second season in a dramatic comeback against St George Illawarra. The Dragons led 14-0 at halftime but a penalty try to Craig Smith with four minutes remaining allowed Matt Geyer to kick the premiership-winning conversion from in front of the sticks. The Storm won 20-18 in a Grand Final for the ages.

2. September 30, 2012: Redemption
Two seasons after its lowest point—being thrown out of the premiership for rorting the salary cap—Melbourne achieved a measure of redemption by winning the 2012 Grand Final. The Storm were ruthless in a gritty defensive clash with Canterbury, triumphing 14-4. It was a typical Storm win, relying on heart, competitiveness and its unmatched defence. Cooper Cronk again showed what a big-game player he was with a deserved Clive Churchill Medal on the back of a superb kicking game that gave the Bulldogs nothing.

3. September 30, 2007: Birth of a dynasty
The first premiership win of the Craig Bellamy era in 2007 marked the first high-water mark of the great Melbourne Storm dynasty. Against a rising Manly team who would stand as the Storm's great enemy over the next half-decade, Melbourne built on a 10-4 halftime lead to win 34-8. Greg Inglis won the Clive Churchill Medal but a second-half tackle on Brett Stewart from Michael Crocker was the seminal moment of a physically brutal decider.

4. October 4, 2009—Title No.3
Craig Bellamy's Melbourne had established itself as a premiership powerhouse over the previous four years, the 2009 decider being the Storm's fourth straight. With the club having won just one of its previous three—and enduring a horrid record Grand Final defeat the year prior—the 2009 decider could have only one result.

A sublime game from Cooper Cronk guided the Storm to a 23-16 win over the red-hot Parramatta Eels, Melbourne's relentless professionalism reigning supreme.

5. March 3, 2000: The Storm quieten Mundine
Loud-mouthed St George Illawarra pivot Anthony Mundine was highly critical of the Storm in the lead-up to the Grand Final rematch early in the 2000 season, labelling Melbourne unworthy premiers. The club responded by obliterating a disgraceful Dragons outfit 70-10 in front of an adoring MCG crowd, with Tasesa Lavea posting 24 of the Storm's record tally of points.

MELBOURNE STORM—WORST DAYS (1998-2013)

1. April 22, 2010: Salary cap rorts exposed
The darkest day in Melbourne's history was the result of a ticking time bomb waiting to explode. It blew up all over the Storm—and Rugby League—on April 22, 2010 when NRL chief executive David Gallop announced that the club had been stripped of two premierships and three minor premierships, and would play the remainder of the 2010 season for zero premiership points. It rocked the game to its core and gutted the Storm and its brethren of stars.

2. October 5, 2008: Record rout
Despite the loss of Cameron Smith to a controversial suspension, the Storm entered the 2008 Grand Final against Manly as marginal favourites. The betting could not have been more wrong. Manly led 8-0 at halftime before a Michael Robertson hat-trick blew the scoreline out to a record 40-0, the largest Grand Final defeat in premiership history.

3. August 10, 2010: Farewell, GI
The most naturally gifted athlete ever to wear the purple of the Storm—and arguably play Rugby League—Greg Inglis was the highest-profile loss due to the salary cap indiscretions. Inglis, part of the fabled 'Big Four', announced he had signed with the Broncos on August 10. He eventually reneged on Brisbane to join South Sydney, but the player developed within the Storm system was gone forever.

4. June 4, 2000: 50 of the worst
Only four months after sticking it to the Saints and Anthony Mundine for calling the club unworthy premiers, Melbourne conceded 50 points in the return bout with the Dragons. In the Storm's equal worst loss of all-time, the Dragons won

50-4 at WIN Stadium, with Trent Barrett, Nathan Blacklock and Lee Hookey all running in doubles.

5. July 17, 2004: Danny's disgrace
Veteran forward Danny Williams' last act as a member of the Melbourne Storm was one of the club's lowest. Williams king-hit Wests Tigers forward Mark O'Neill and was subsequently suspended for 18 games; he left the club without another appearance in purple. Williams refused to apologise after the incident.

NEW ZEALAND WARRIORS—GREATEST PLAYERS (1995-2013)

1. Stacey Jones—261 games (1995-2005, 2009)
Just a shade behind the likes of Andrew Johns and Allan Langer in the pantheon of his era's finest halfbacks, 'The Little General' was a brilliant match-winner and one of the few Warriors to earn the universal respect of Australian critics during the club's tumultuous first decade. Jones was a teenage debutant during the Warriors' foundation season and secured the New Zealand No.7 for the first of 45 Test appearances later that year. The diminutive talisman skippered the Warriors to a maiden minor premiership and Grand Final—in which he scored a dazzling individual try—in 2002 to claim the Golden Boot award. A comeback in 2009 failed to deliver the desired results, but still featured familiar flashes of genius from arguably New Zealand's greatest-ever Rugby League product.

2. Simon Mannering—188 games (2005-13)
Tireless backrower Simon Mannering, a regular gap-filler in the centres at club and Test level, has based his game on unerring consistency in a notoriously fickle side. A three-time winner of the Warriors' Player of the Year gong, he assumed the club captaincy in 2010 aged just 23 and led his side to a Grand Final the following season. The unassuming Mannering is poised to become just the second player to bring up 200 first grade appearances for the Warriors. He had earned 34 Test caps for New Zealand by the end of the 2013 World Cup, in which he skippered the team for the first time.

3. Manu Vatuvei—171 games (2004-13)
Giant winger Manu Vatuvei rates among the NRL's most maligned figures—he is just as well known for his butter-fingered shockers as his blockbusting blinders—but has repeatedly risen above the detractors to become one of the game's most prolific

try-scorers. Boasting outstanding pace to complement his massive frame, Vatuvei is virtually unstoppable in full flight and is an attacking specialist in the air. His 118 tries include five hat-tricks, and he has topped the Warriors' tryscoring charts for seven straight seasons. Dally M Winger of the Year in 2008 and Warriors Player of the Year in 2010, Vatuvei's 24 Test appearances for New Zealand have netted 17 touchdowns. He featured heavily in the Kiwis' euphoric 2008 World Cup triumph.

4. Lance Hohaia—185 games (2002-11)
The diminutive 'Huntly Hurricane' proved his utility value time and again during a decade at the Warriors. Hohaia was a teenage rookie sensation at five-eighth in 2002, coming off the bench in that year's Grand Final and making his Test debut. Following an injury-plagued few seasons, he was a vital component of the Warriors' finals charges in 2008 and '10 from fullback, while also starring in New Zealand's World Cup final ('08) and Four Nations final ('10) upsets in the No.1 jumper at the end of those seasons. The 26-Test veteran signed off on his tenure at the Warriors as the club's Grand Final hooker in 2011.

5. Steve Price—91 games (2005-09)
Long-serving Bulldogs captain Steve Price joined the Warriors at the age of 30, but played some of the most inspiring football of his career during his five seasons in Auckland. The lion-hearted prop was magnificent in leading the club back to the finals in 2007 after a four-year absence, collecting the Dally M Captain and Prop of the Year awards (and a top-10 Dally M Medal finish) in the process. Price retained his Test and Origin spots despite relocating to the NRL outpost, representing Australia and Queensland 12 times each while at the Warriors before a foot injury he suffered in 2009 forced the 2006-07 club Player of the Year into premature retirement.

6. Shaun Johnson—62 games (2011-13)
A mind-boggling individual talent, Shaun Johnson will challenge Stacey Jones as the Warriors' greatest by the time he retires if he can introduce week-to-week consistency to his devastating kitbag. Boasting blinding pace, electric footwork and mesmerising ball skills, the halfback steered the Warriors to the Grand Final in his rookie season; Johnson's cross-field jaunt to lay on the match-sealing try in the club's preliminary final upset of Melbourne ranks as one of truly iconic moments in the club's history. Johnson, a 2012 Test debutant, is earmarked to become one of the NRL's elite superstars in coming years.

7. Brent Webb—103 games (2002-06)
Brent Webb arrived from Queensland in 2002 as an unheralded and somewhat erratic utility back, but developed into an attacking linchpin after cementing the Warriors'

fullback spot the following season. Brilliant in the club's run to the '03 preliminary final (including an 18-point haul in the qualifying final demolition of the Bulldogs), Webb was a shining light through subsequent lean seasons and was at the peak of his powers in 2006, finishing ninth in the Dally M Medal count—his last year in the NRL before being lured to Leeds. Cairns-born Webb fulfilled residential requirements to represent New Zealand in 17 Tests from 2004 to 2008, starring in the Kiwis' 2005 Tri-Nations final boilover against Australia.

8. Clinton Toopi—129 games (1999-2006)

Regarded by some as the world's best centre at one stage of his career, Clinton Toopi was an enigmatic but brilliant attacking presence in the Warriors' backline. Vital to the club qualifying for a maiden finals berth in 2001—his first full season in the NRL—Toopi scored 18 tries in the Warriors' charge to the Grand Final the following season, and followed that up with 17 touchdowns in their admirable 2003 campaign. Inconsistency marked the remainder of his tenure in Auckland, but two hat-tricks in rare wins over Australia among 22 Test appearances for the Kiwis marked Toopi as a special talent.

9. Ruben Wiki—87 games (2005-08)

Ruben Wiki controversially backed out of a contract to become a foundation Warrior in 1995 to remain at Canberra, but became one of the club's best-ever recruits following his belated arrival a decade later. The durable front-row hardman, who became the first player in history to make 50 Test appearances (in 2006), turned 32 prior to his club debut and was the Warriors' spiritual leader during his four seasons in Auckland. Wiki collected the club's Player of the Year award in 2005, and was central to the Warriors' top-four finish in 2007 and their memorable charge to the preliminary final in his farewell 2008 season.

10. Ali Lauitiiti—115 games (1998-2004)

Hyperbolically described as 'the Michael Jordan of Rugby League' by coach Mark Graham early in his career, Ali Lauitiiti was one of the NRL's most gifted attacking forwards. The tall, mobile ball-player was named Dally M Second-rower of the Year in 2002 and was a key figure in the Warriors' memorable charge to that year's Grand Final, winning the club's Player of the Year gong and briefly challenging Gorden Tallis' mantle as the code's best backrower. Lauitiiti regularly produced majestic passes and was capable of busting defences and finding his way to the try-line via a powerful running game. His shock departure from Auckland early in 2004 was a career low point, but he finished with 18 Test appearances after joining Leeds.

11. Ben Matulino—132 games (2008-13)
Hard-hitting forward Ben Matulino became the first NYC graduate to play 100 NRL games, but needed just 33 appearances for the Warriors to break into the New Zealand Test team as a 20-year-old. He came on to the first grade scene as a second-rower before gravitating towards the front-row, building a reputation as one of the competition's most punishing defenders but also boasting deft ball skills. The Warriors' 2012 Player of the Year, Matulino had played 19 Tests for the Kiwis by the end of the following season despite being just 24 years of age.

12. Logan Swann—195 games (1997-2003, 2007-08)
A New Zealand Test debutant in 1996 before even making his first grade debut, tall backrower Logan Swann cemented a permanent spot in the Warriors' pack the following season and racked up the second-most appearances in club history during two stints. Dynamic, durable and hardworking, Swann was a vital member of the Warriors' 2001-03 and 2007-08 finals sides. He made the last of 28 appearances for the Kiwis in 2004 during a three-season Super League stint.

13. Sam Rapira—151 games (2009-13)
Sam Rapira's maturity and toughness at the NRL's front-row coalface were immediately apparent when he was called up to make his Test debut less than two weeks after his 20th birthday with just 15 appearances for the Warriors to his name. Trademark straight and hard charges coupled with fearsome defence saw the 105kg Rapira develop into one of the competition's most respected props. He was the front-row conerstone of the Warriors' 2011 Grand Final charge, but injuries stymied his progress—and Test aspirations—the following season. He responded with a consistent 2013 campaign to bring up 150 games for the club.

14. Kevin Locke—87 games (2009-13)
Kevin Locke arrived as an exciting match-winner on the wing in 2009 before claiming the Warriors' fullback spot two years later and enjoying a spectacular campaign in the club's run to the Grand Final. A naturally gifted ball-player and elusive runner, his courageous last-line efforts belie his diminutive frame. Locke made his Test debut in 2011, and although he lost the spot during an inconsistent and injury-hampered 2012 season, he displaced Josh Hoffman at the 2013 World Cup. The arrival of Wigan and Great Britain superstar fullback Sam Tomkins in 2014 represents a new challenge for the incumbent Kiwi Test No.1.

15. Francis Meli—110 games (1999-2005)
Although inconsistent and prone to the occasional brain explosion, Francis Meli was a fearsome presence on the flank and responsible for some of the club's most remarkable

tryscoring achievements. Meli forged a permanent first grade spot in 2001, scoring 11 tries as the Warriors reached the finals for the first time, before featuring in their maiden Grand Final appearance a year later. But his lasting legacy was an all-time finals-record five tries in a qualifying final upset of the Bulldogs in 2003, giving him a club-record 23 tries for the season and securing Warriors Player of the Year honours. The 13-Test winger left for Super League club St Helens with 60 career tries for the Warriors to his name.

16. James Maloney—75 games (2010-12)
Tenacious Orange-born five-eighth James Maloney kick-started his career with a stellar stint at the Warriors. With only four NRL games for Melbourne to his name before he joined the Warriors in 2010, Maloney scored a club-record-equalling 28 points against Brisbane in just his third appearance for the Auckland-based club. He finished the year with 188 points before becoming just the second Warriors player to score 200 points in a season as a linchpin in their memorable run to the 2011 Grand Final. An outstanding hole-runner, clever playmaker and clutch goalkicker, Maloney's disappointing 2012 campaign mirrored that of the Warriors, but he underlined his ability by breaking into the NSW side and winning a premiership after joining the Sydney Roosters in 2013.

17. Micheal Luck—150 games (2006-12)
Former North Queensland backrower Micheal Luck developed into an invaluable workhorse in the Warriors' pack, playing at least 20 games in each of his first six seasons in Auckland. A standby player for Queensland during the 2007 Origin series, Luck was a tireless contributor on both sides of the ball and regularly captained the club during the 2008-10 seasons. He played in the 2011 Grand Final loss to Manly, and his injury-ravaged farewell campaign was a largely overlooked factor in the Warriors' woeful 2012 season. Lock was the club's Player of the Year in 2009.

18. Jacob Lillyman—100 games (2009-13)
Another ex-Cowboys engine-room stalwart, backrower Jacob Lillyman rejuvenated his career by joining the Warriors in 2009. He overcame serious injury to help the club to the 2010 finals, and regained a spot in the all-conquering Queensland Origin side the following season after being transformed into a prop by coach Ivan Cleary. He was a forward pack anchor of the Warriors' surge to the 2011 Grand Final and was desperately unlucky to miss out on Australia's squad for the subsequent Four Nations. The robust front-rower, who brought up 100 Warriors appearances in 2013, remains on the fringes of Maroons selection despite his veteran status.

19. Awen Guttenbeil—170 games (1996-2006)
The early years of Awen Guttenbeil's career were wracked with injury, restricting the talented forward to 31 games in his initial five seasons. But his ability to overcome

that luckless run coincided with the Warriors' first golden period, and he starred as the club qualified for the finals from 2001 to 2003—including a maiden Grand Final appearance in 2002. The intimidating, dynamic lock averaged 23 games per season from 2001 and retired second on the Warriors' all-time appearances list. An occasional captain of the club, Guttenbeil made nine Test appearances for New Zealand.

20. Stephen Kearney—79 games (1995-98)

Tough ball-playing second-rower Stephen Kearney returned from Wests in Sydney to become a foundation Auckland Warrior, and was an all-too-rare shining light during the club's largely dismal first four seasons. The Warriors' Player of the Year in 1996, Kearney made 19 of his 43 Test appearances while based in Auckland. But the ultra-talented forward butted heads with Warriors management and left to join Melbourne, where he won a Grand Final in 1999 and continued to star for his country.

NEW ZEALAND WARRIORS—GREATEST COACHES (1995-2013)

1. Ivan Cleary—154 games (2006-11)

The Warriors' 2002 Grand Final fullback, Ivan Cleary returned as coach after serving an impressive apprenticeship in the Roosters' lower grades. He arrived under difficult circumstance—the club had been docked four competition points in the '06 pre-season—but steered his new charges to 12 wins that would have been enough to qualify for the finals. Cleary took the Warriors to just their second top-four finish in '07, a preliminary final appearance in '08 and a Grand Final in '11, instilling a previously unseen defensive steel and stability in the notoriously flighty New Zealanders. His achievements with the Warriors saw him become regarded as one of the hottest coaching properties in the game, prompting Phil Gould to poach him on behalf of Penrith at the end of 2011—a departure the Warriors are yet to recover from.

2. Daniel Anderson—92 games (2001-04)

Highly rated Parramatta lower-grade coach Daniel Anderson guided the Warriors to unprecedented and long-awaited success in the early 2000s. A maiden finals appearance in his first season at the helm was followed by a Dally M Coach of the Year award, minor premiership and Grand Final appearance 12 months later, and a spirited run to the 2003 preliminary finals confirmed the Warriors' status as an NRL powerhouse. But it all unravelled for Anderson and the Warriors during '04, with the coach resigning halfway through a tumultuous season. Anderson, who coached the New Zealand Test side in 2003-04, enjoyed a 55.4 per cent win rate with the Warriors—a record for the club.

3. John Monie—60 games (1995-97)
Regarded as one of the world's best thanks to his glittering achievements at Parramatta and Wigan, John Monie provided the fledgling Warriors with the high-profile coach they needed to lure top-line talent to Auckland—and he delivered in spades, attracting Wigan stars Dean Bell, Dennis Betts, Andy Platt and Frano Botica to the club. Monie led the Warriors to 13 wins from 22 games in their inaugural season, but they were denied a finals spot by points stripped for an interchange bungle, which he took the blame for. A disappointing 11th followed in '96, and Monie departed halfway through the '97 Super League campaign following a disastrous start. Although his stint was considered a failure, his win percentage was only a fraction behind Daniel Anderson's.

4. Frank Endacott—33 games (1997-98)
Long-serving New Zealand Test coach (1994-2000) Frank Endacott guided the Warriors' reserve grade team to the 1996 Grand Final before taking the first grade reins from John Monie midway through the following season. His finest achievement in charge of the Warriors was taking them to the World Club Challenge semi-finals, where they were gallant in going down to all-conquering Brisbane. But the 1998 NRL campaign netted just nine wins and was mired in boardroom and ownership battles, while Endacott struggled to get the best out of the majority of his Kiwi Test stars. He was ousted by the new Graham Lowe-led consortium at the end of the year.

5. Matthew Elliott—24 games (2013)
A surprise choice as coach for 2013 after Warriors management had pledged a mentor of Bellamy-like status, Matthew Elliott's tenure began in atrocious fashion as his side slumped to eight losses in the first 10 rounds, culminating in a record defeat to his former club Penrith. But the animated coach managed to lead the Warriors on a spectacular mid-season run of seven wins in eight matches, knocking off finalists Newcastle, Manly, Sydney Roosters and Melbourne along the way. A slump late in the year saw the Warriors miss the top-eight spot that was apparently theirs for the taking, heaping the pressure on Elliott for 2014.

NEW ZEALAND WARRIORS—BEST DAYS (1995-2013)

1. September 24, 2011: Preliminary final upset of Melbourne
The Warriors' 20-12 triumph in Melbourne to advance to the 2011 Grand Final has already taken on mythical status in the club's two-decade narrative. Already regarded as a bogey side for the mighty Storm and always enjoying overwhelming crowd support in the Victorian capital, the Auckland-based club still started as rank outsiders but led 14-12 after a seesawing first half. Outstanding commitment in defence held the Storm scoreless during the gripping second stanza, while rookie halfback Shaun Johnson's mesmerising cross-field jaunt to set up Lewis Brown's 77th-minute match-winner has passed into finals folklore. James Maloney's booming sideline conversion of Brown's try sealed the Warriors' shock decider berth.

2. September 29, 2002: Victory over Sharks to earn maiden Grand Final berth
After the Bulldogs' salary cap penalty handed the 2002 minor premiership to the Warriors, the New Zealanders advanced to their first preliminary final by thumping Canberra in Auckland. Only Cronulla and a trip to Sydney stood between the Warriors and a historic Grand Final berth. The club's sponsors famously purchased 15,000 tickets and gave them away free to anyone who could show a New Zealand passport, providing the Warriors with overwhelming support among the 45,702-strong Stadium Australia throng. In a pulsating final, Motu Tony put the Warriors on the board first by spectacularly burgling the ball from Paul Mellor, while a brilliant individual effort by Clinton Toopi gave them a 10-4 lead. Brett Kimmorley hit back to level for the Sharks before a centimetre-perfect Stacey Jones grubber in the 75th minute saw centre John Carlaw plant the ball for a 16-10 lead and a history-making win.

3. September 16, 2011: Warriors advance with nail-biting semi-final win over Tigers
Pumped 40-10 by Brisbane in the qualifying final a week earlier, the Warriors were on course for a straight-sets finals exit when they trailed Wests Tigers 6-18 at halftime at the SFS. But the Warriors scored the only three tries of a frenetic second half, pegging the deficit back to two points with 15 minutes remaining before Shaun Johnson's fateful cross-field bomb at the 77-minute mark. Inscrutable centre Krisnan Inu batted the ball back, Tigers winger Lote Tuqiri was unable to handle it and it popped back into the prostrate Inu's hands. Inu reached out to score a remarkable match-winning try and send the Warriors into the preliminary final, 22-20.

4. September 14, 2008—Last-gasp qualifying final win in Melbourne creates history
Olympic Park was a graveyard for most visiting teams, but the Warriors had enjoyed disproportionate success at the all-conquering Storm's home ground. Nevertheless, the eighth-placed Warriors were expected to be easily despatched by the minor premiers in the first week of the '08 finals. Tries to Manu Vatuvei and Jerome Ropati saw the underdogs lead 14-8 soon after the break, but an Israel Folau try and Greg Inglis field goal edged the Storm in front, seemingly extinguishing the Warriors' gallant upset bid. With time running into the last couple of minutes, Ropati and Vatuvei combined brilliantly to send Michael Witt into the clear. After a bizarre and risky pre-try celebration, Witt dotted down in the corner just before the Storm cover defence arrived, and the Warriors snatched a famous 18-15 victory. It was the first time an eighth-placed team had beaten the minor premiers in a decade of the controversial McIntyre System.

5. September 13, 2003—Incredible qualifying final blitz of Bulldogs
Rated little chance of upsetting the third-placed Bulldogs at the Sydney Showgrounds, the enigmatic sixth-placed Warriors produced one of the most dazzling finals displays in premiership history. Powerhouse winger Francis Meli crossed for an all-time finals-record five tries, while Brent Webb racked up 18 points and the likes of Sione Faumiuna, Clinton Toopi and Motu Tony were at their unstoppable ad-lib, ball-promoting best. The Warriors led 16-4 at the break before powering to a 48-22 victory in the highest-scoring finals match in the code's history to that time.

NEW ZEALAND WARRIORS—WORST DAYS (1995-2013)

1. January 4, 2009: Sonny Fai tragedy leaves Warriors heartbroken
Sonny Fai was a dynamic centre/backrower on the cusp of stardom when he was caught in a rip at Te Henga (Bethells Beach) while trying to save his brother and cousins. Fai's body was never found; he was just 20 years old. The Warriors had been installed as one of the pre-season favourites for the 2009 NRL premiership, but the shattered squad struggled throughout the year in the wake of the tragedy. After winning their first two games, the Warriors failed to notch consecutive victories and eventually finished 14th with just seven wins.

2. May 18, 2013: Mauled by Panthers in record rout
A terrible start to Matthew Elliott's tenure as coach culminated in the most inept display in the Warriors' history against his former club the Panthers, who were

coached by ex-Warriors mentor Ivan Cleary. Awful in every facet of play—but especially defence and discipline—the Warriors were crushed 62-6, a club-record loss. Adding to the humiliation was Warriors discard Isaac John scoring a hat-trick of tries and their former finals hero Lewis Brown grabbing a double for the Panthers. Gun halfback Shaun Johnson was hooked by Elliott during the second half, while the sight of Warriors players apparently joking with their Penrith oppressors on the field post-match incensed fans and was jumped on by the media. The horrific loss was the catalyst for a remarkable, giant-killing mid-season form reversal.

3. April 20, 2004: Ali dropped, leaves Auckland

A watershed period that included three straight finals appearances and a Grand Final disintegrated in a matter of weeks at the beginning of 2004. Superstar second-rower Ali Lauitiiti was dropped from first grade by coach Daniel Anderson after six rounds because of poor form and attitude, and he left the Warriors for Leeds soon afterwards. Anderson lasted just six more weeks, resigning at the end of May. With Tony Kemp taking over, the Warriors eventually finished 14th with just six wins on the board, ending a disastrous year on a six-match losing streak.

4. May 6, 2000: Diabolical Warriors catch Dragons on the rebound

The Auckland Warriors headed to Wollongong confident of a win in Round 14 of the 2000 season—St George Illawarra had just been whipped 50-4 by lowly North Queensland. But the visitors became the unwitting victims of one of the most remarkable one-week turnarounds in history when they were crushed 54-0 by the rampant Dragons, a then club-record defeat for the Warriors and just the second time they had been held scoreless. The club was on the brink of collapse only months later when businessman Eric Watson swooped in and rescued it under the New Zealand Warriors banner.

5. March 26, 1995: Maiden win spoiled by interchange bungle

The Warriors recorded their initial first grade win in emphatic fashion, disposing of Western Suburbs to the tune of 46-12 in front of a 21,446-strong home crowd. Veteran Phil Blake scored four tries from fullback in the outstanding win. But Auckland's first premiership points were stripped following the revelation of an illegal fifth interchange player. Young prop Joe Vagana was erroneously put on late in the match as a blood-bin replacement for Willie Poching. Coach John Monie took full responsibility for the snafu, but the lost points cost the fledgling Warriors dearly—they eventually missed the top eight on points difference.

NEWCASTLE—GREATEST PLAYERS (1908-09)

1. Bill 'Jerry' Bailey—17 games (1908-09)
A founding father of Rugby League in the Newcastle district, winger Bill 'Jerry' Bailey was the most potent attacking star in the short history of the 'Rebels'. He top-scored with nine tries in both of the club's seasons in the premiership, and notched a record three tries in consecutive weeks against Glebe and Western Suburbs in 1909, adding two goals for 13 points—another club-best mark—against Wests. Bailey toured with the pioneering 1908-09 Kangaroos, scoring three tries in three minor games.

2. Stan Carpenter—19 games (1908-09)
Newcastle's leading point-scorer with 80 (38 in 1908 and a record 42 in 1909), Stan Carpenter represented NSW in one match at hooker in the 1908 foundation season and played for Australia against New Zealand Maori the following year. Carpenter missed just one game in the Rebels' two seasons and played lock in the club's last match—a semi-final loss to Souths.

3. Ernie Patfield—14 games (1908-09)
Integral to the formation of the Newcastle 'Rebels', halfback Ernie Patfield represented NSW in 1908 and played for Australia against New Zealand Maori in '09—although he and clubmate Stan Carpenter did not receive recognition as international representatives until 2004. Patfield, who was halfback in Newcastle's first-ever match, missed the club's semi-final loss to South Sydney in 1909.

4. Ted McGuinness—20 games (1908-09)
Fullback/winger Ted McGuinness holds the unique distinction of playing every game in the Newcastle club's two-season existence. He scored seven tries for the Rebels before representing NSW from Balmain in 1910 and embarking on further stints with Glebe and Annandale.

5. Pat Walsh—2 games (1908)
Three-Test Wallaby forward Pat Walsh switched codes during Rugby League's foundation 1908 season. He played just two games for Newcastle but his reputation saw him picked in the pioneering Kangaroo Tour squad. Walsh made 29 appearances on tour—encompassing all three Tests against England—and stayed on in Britain with Huddersfield.

6. Artie Coleman—16 games (1908-09)
Centre Artie Coleman crossed for 10 tries in his 16 appearances for Newcastle—second in club history to 'Jerry' Bailey. He featured in the Rebels' maiden game in 1908, scored two tries in their first-ever win against Cumberland and played in their semi-final loss to Souths in '09.

7. George Cox—17 games (1908-09)
George Cox missed just three games in Newcastle's two seasons in the premiership, crossing for five tries. He played on the wing in the club's first match in 1908 and at halfback in the Rebels' last match, the semi-final defeat at the hands of Souths in 1909.

8. R. Lawson—13 games (1908-09)
'Darkie' Lawson scored four tries in 13 first grade games for Newcastle, featuring at five-eighth in the club's maiden outing in 1908 and playing in the centres in the Rebels' semi-final exit to Souths in '09.

9. Les Carpenter—16 games (1908-09)
Les Carpenter played 16 of Newcastle's 20 games in 1908-09, featuring in the backrow alongside brother Stan in the club's last premiership match. He scored two tries and kicked eight goals for the Rebels.

10. Charlie Croft—12 games (1908-09)
Front-rower Charlie Croft played 12 games for Newcastle, crossing for four tries. He lined up at prop in the club's last match, the semi-final loss to Souths in 1909.

NEWCASTLE KNIGHTS—GREATEST PLAYERS (1988-2013)

1. Andrew Johns: 249 games (1993-2007)
The game's most recent Immortal, Andrew 'Joey' Johns could do things with a football that most simply could not. Blessed with an amazing kicking game, a sensational pass and a thorough understanding of the halfback role, Johns had a near-flawless game and he made the most of it with a manic drive to win. He was an outstanding goalkicker, retiring as the all-time leading point-scorer in the NRL, a genuine leader of men and a hard-hitting defender. On debut he scored 23 points in a sublime performance, and such was his standing that Newcastle struggled to win without him. Johns represented both New South Wales and Australia on 23 occasions and was the key figure in the Blues' amazing 2005 series win, making an incredible comeback in game two from a serious injury. Few players in the modern game have been as decorated, with Johns one of only

two players to win the Golden Boot twice. He won the Dally M Medal an unprecedented three times (1998, 1999 and 2002), won the Churchill Medal in 2001 after making the winning play in the 1997 Grand Final victory, and was four times Dally M Halfback of the Year. It was one of the great tragedies of modern Rugby League that a serious neck injury forced Johns to retire prematurely with 249 first grade games to his name.

2. Danny Buderus—258 games (1997-2008, 2012-13)

Perhaps the best indication of Buderus's quality as a player comes in the fact that the hooker won four Newcastle Player of the Year awards (1999, 2003, 2004 and 2006) compared to the two won by Andrew Johns. A Dally M Medal winner in his own right, receiving the coveted award in 2004, Buderus revolutionised the hooking role, carrying on the torch from Steve Walters. He was the undisputed top No.9 in the game for nearly a decade, playing 24 Test matches and 21 consecutive matches (15 as captain) for NSW. Sharp, creative and tough-as-nails, Buderus is deservedly remembered as one of the all-time great hookers. After being forced out by Brian Smith, he returned for a popular two-season run under Wayne Bennett to become the club's most-capped player.

3. Paul Harragon—169 games (1988-99)

Paul 'Chief' Harragon was Newcastle's first popular hero, a fearless prop forward who delighted in shedding blood for the region. He ranked with Glenn Lazarus as the top prop forward of the 1990s, and made 20 straight appearances for the Blues. Harragon also played 14 Test matches and became the club's first Australian skipper. He managed 169 matches for Newcastle and skippered the inaugural premiership-winning team but was cruelled by injury and illness often and forced to retire during the '99 season. Harragon was the man who kept Newcastle loyal during the Super League War, and he is as beloved as any Knight ever to pull on the jersey.

4. Ben Kennedy—86 games (2000-04)

Ben Kennedy came of age at Newcastle. He was as raw as veal at Canberra and he was a true leader at Manly, but at Newcastle he came into his own as a bull-like runner who could carry a team on his back. Kennedy played only five seasons and 86 games for the club but his class was such that he is revered as one of the great Knights. Newcastle would not have won the 2001 premiership if not for Kennedy and his blazing intensity. He played eight Origins and nine Tests as a Knight.

5. Kurt Gidley—207 games (2001-13)

An outstanding utility who is capable of playing anywhere in the backline along with hooker and backrow, Kurt Gidley has led from the front in the post-'Joey' era. The Newcastle Player of the Year in 2007, 2008 and 2011, he was appointed the

NSW Origin captain in 2009. A leader, talented ball-player and workhorse, Gidley was a NSW and Australian staple from 2007 when fit, and his 1102 points is second only to Andrew Johns for Newcastle.

6. Matthew Johns—176 games (1992-2000)
Destined always to play second fiddle to his brother Andrew, five-eighth Matthew Johns was a classy player in his own right. Not blessed with Andrew's natural skill-set, Matthew led more through grit and a deep understanding of the sport. Such was his popularity in Newcastle after nine seasons and 176 games that the city nearly erupted when he was forced out after the 2000 season. Johns, who booted the Knights into their first Grand Final with a famous field goal, played four Origin matches and eight Tests as a Knight and was named in Newcastle's Team of the Era in 2007 and in the club's Hall of Fame in 2012.

7. Robbie O'Davis—224 games (1992-2004)
Few players bled the blue and red more than Robbie O'Davis. He loved the club and would still be playing if Newcastle would have him. He knocked up 224 games on the wing and at fullback for Newcastle, playing in both Knights premierships. His finest performance came in the 1997 Grand Final when a sublime two-try effort saw him awarded the Clive Churchill Medal. Exciting and elusive, O'Davis represented Queensland 12 times and Australia on six occasions. He won the club Player of the Year award in '97.

8. Matt Gidley—222 games (1996-2006)
With his hallmark flick pass, Matt Gidley was a staple of an outstanding Knights backline for 11 seasons and 222 matches. He scored only 69 tries in his time at the club but was far more a distributor than a scorer, renowned for his intelligent line running and deft ball movement that no doubt came from his junior days when he was a five-eighth. Gidley played 17 Test matches and 11 Origin games while a Knight, and featured in the 2001 Grand Final win after missing the '97 triumph through injury.

9. Steve Simpson—217 games (1999-2010)
In his heyday, Steve Simpson was a skilled fringe runner and a hardworking defender who was a staple of both the NSW and Australian teams. A two-time Newcastle Player of the Year (2001, 2005), towards the backend of his career he added class to a Knights pack that was often lacking in it. A veteran of the 2001 premiership campaign, where he was the best player for the Knights throughout the season, Simpson was forced into a premature retirement due to chronic knee and ankle injuries.

10. Timana Tahu (124 games, 1999-2004 and 2012-13)
Newcastle's greatest try-scorer, with 91 in 124 appearances, Timana Tahu has enjoyed two spells at the club. In his first stint playing outside Matt Gidley at the turn of

the century, Tahu was a legitimate star. He debuted at 18 and scored in the Knights' Grand Final win in 2001. He returned to the club in 2012 and reclaimed the top try-scorer mantle but struggled as age and injury took their toll.

11. Akuila Uate—114 games (2008-13)
One of the fastest men in the NRL, Akuila Uate also became one of its most devastating attacking weapons, crossing for 85 tries after just 114 games. He scored at least 15 tries a season from 2010 to 2013 and seems destined to set a big standard as the club's all-time top try-scorer. The Dally M Winger of the Year from 2010 to 2012 and the RLPA Player of the Year in 2011, Uate had represented NSW and Australia five times to the beginning of the 2014 season and turned out for Fiji at consecutive World Cups.

12. Tony Butterfield—229 games (1988-2000)
A hard-running prop forward and the skipper for the 1999 and 2000 seasons, Tony Butterfield showed remarkable longevity for a big man, playing 229 games for the club. He seemed to get better with age, partnering Paul Harragon in the '97 decider and making his only Origin appearance in 1998. Butterfield was named Newcastle's Player of the Year in 1996.

13. Marc Glanville—188 games (1988-97)
A warhorse remembered for his high work-rate in defence, Marc Glanville played 188 games for the Knights over 10 seasons after joining the club in its inaugural season. He never received the accolades he deserved outside of the Knights but was well enough respected at the club, winning the Knights Player of the Year award in 1991 and 1993. Glanville retired after helping Newcastle to victory in the 1997 Grand Final.

14. Adam MacDougall—158 games (1997-2003, 2007-11)
One can only imagine how impressive the career of 'Mad Dog' would have been had it not been for constant injury, a drugs ban and a silly decision to leave Newcastle for South Sydney at the height of his career. In 158 games for the Knights over 12 seasons, MacDougall played in both Grand Final victories. He is second on the club's all-time leading try-scorer list with 87, and represented NSW and Australia during his first spell at Newcastle.

15. Michael Hagan—111 games (1989-93)
Michael Hagan's career was winding down come the 1990s and his blossoming coaching career was still a decade off, but he was captain of the first good Newcastle team in 1992. The classy five-eighth slotted a key field goal in Newcastle's 21-2 semi-final win over Wests—the club's first finals win—and he was named on the bench of Newcastle's all-time side and is a member of the Knights' Hall of Fame.

16. Mark Sargent—126 games (1989-95)

The 1989 joint Rothmans Medal winner probably played his best football prior to 1991, but Mark Sargent was still a force for Newcastle in its first finals run in 1992. The bustling, hard prop played Origin in 1990 and made his Test debut the same year, donning the green and gold five times as the club's first international. Sargent retired before Newcastle's glory days but laid the foundation for them through his toughness and grit.

17. Mark Hughes—162 games (1997-2005)

Mark 'Boozy' Hughes was probably the beneficiary of playing in a fine era of outstanding Newcastle backs, having a role in both premiership victories and representing NSW in all three matches in 2001. In nine seasons, the Knights won 59 per cent of all matches when Hughes played. The popular fullback/centre scored 66 tries in his career with Newcastle.

18. Robbie McCormack—154 games (1988-95)

An underrated centre-cum-hooker, Robbie McCormack was a foundation Knight who saw the club through its trying early days to play in its first two finals series. Sharp out of dummy-half and with a good pass, he played 154 matches for the Knights and got the call-up for NSW in 1992 and 1993, replacing Benny Elias on both occasions. McCormack was named the Knights Player of the Year in '92 and '94.

19. Bill Peden—191 games (1994-2002)

'Bustling' Billy Peden never got the credit he deserved but the hardworking backrower was a staple of the Newcastle team for a decade, playing 190 games for the club. Peden was one of only five Knights to play in both premiership sides, starting at hooker in 1997 and scoring two tries against Parramatta as the starting lock in the 2001 Grand Final.

20. Darren Albert—89 games (1996-2001)

A fair-haired winger who spent six seasons with the Knights, Darren Albert became a Newcastle hero when he scored the winning try in the 1997 Grand Final on the last play of the game. With scores locked at 16-all, Albert cut inside after Andrew Johns burst down the blind and crossed to secure the Knights' first title. With speed to burn, he scored 65 tries in 89 games and won his only NSW jersey in 1999 while at the club.

NEWCASTLE KNIGHTS—GREATEST COACHES (1988-2013)

1. Malcolm Reilly—98 games (1995-98)
A feared British hardman, Mal Reilly won two premierships with Manly as a player in the early 1970s and returned to Australia in 1995 to take the Knights' head coaching job after a long career that had included a seven-year stint as Great Britain coach. The forthright Reilly was an instant hit in the working-class city of Newcastle. He took the club to a preliminary final in his first season and the club's first premiership in his third, etching his name into city lore in the process. He returned to England after the '98 season for family reasons, leaving with the still-standing best strike rate in club history.

2. Michael Hagan—155 games (2001-06)
A fine playmaker who spent five seasons as a player with the Knights in their formative years, Michael Hagan won a premiership in his first season as Newcastle coach. Guiding a champion team that included Andrew Johns and Ben Kennedy, he became the first coach in 13 years to win a premiership at his first attempt. In his fourth year at the club, he was appointed Queensland coach. The Knights finished with the wooden spoon in 2005 but despite a finals finish in 2006, Hagan moved to Parramatta in 2007.

3. Warren Ryan—53 games (1999-2000)
The coach of the 1980s made a shock return to the coaching ranks in 1999 when he was named as Malcolm Reilly's replacement. Though Ryan made some oddball decisions—such as naming American Greg Smith in first grade—the Knights made consecutive finals campaigns under his tutelage. Ryan retired for good after a controversial preliminary final defeat in 2000.

4. Wayne Bennett—51 games (2012-13)
Queensland Team of the Century coach Wayne Bennett made a highly publicised move to Newcastle in 2012 and, after a disappointing initial year when the club missed the playoffs, achieved a preliminary final finish in 2013. Famously reserved, Bennett had pressure heaped on him immediately by owner Nathan Tinkler, who claimed the Knights would win four titles under the former Raiders, Broncos and Dragons mentor.

5. David Waite—76 games (1991-94)
The former Test winger replaced Allan McMahon at the Knights midway through 1991 and a year later took the team to its first finals campaign, where it was famously eliminated 3-2 by St George. Disappointing finishes of ninth and 10th in 1993-94 led to his sacking, to be replaced by Malcolm Reilly.

NEWCASTLE KNIGHTS—BEST DAYS (1988-2013)

1. September 28, 1997: Premiership glory
After the drama of the Super League War, in which the Newcastle Knights were central figures as ARL figureheads, there was no greater tonic than the club's first premiership. In one of the great Grand Final upsets, the Knights downed Manly 22-16. The game was decided in the final 30 seconds when Andrew Johns ran down the short side and threw back inside to a streaking Darren Albert, who scored one of the most famous Grand Final tries to send the city of Newcastle into party mode.

2. September 30, 2001: Another title
Parramatta entered the 2001 decider as massive favourites, but a Newcastle first-half blitz provided the Knights with their second title. Led by Ben Kennedy and Andrew Johns, they jumped to a 24-0 lead thanks to a double from Bill Peden and tries to Kennedy and Steve Simpson. Timana Tahu snuffed out any chance of a Parramatta comeback with a second-half sealer.

3. March 13, 1994: A champion is born
Young halfback Andrew Johns excited the Knights faithful with a brilliant starting debut, scoring 23 points against South Sydney. He would become one of the game's great players, named Team of the Century halfback in 2008 and an Immortal in 2012, and at one stage also was the game's top point-scorer.

4. March 13, 1988: Win No.1
Allan McMahon's Knights broke through for their first win in Round 2, 1988 when they downed Western Suburbs 20-16 at Orana Park with Brian Quinton and captain Sam Stewart scoring tries and Steve Fulmer scoring the late match-winner in the memorable victory. The club would enjoy its first home win a week later against Balmain.

5. February 11, 1991: Sevens heaven
The Knights won their first piece of silverware in 1991 when they claimed the Nissan Sevens at Parramatta. Newcastle pipped the Dragons 24-22 in the final, with Robbie McCormack, Jeff Doyle, John Schuster and Marc Glanville scoring tries and Ashley Gordon booting four goals. The Knights would also win the pre-season tournament in 1996.

NEWCASTLE KNIGHTS—WORST DAYS (1988-2013)

1. April 2, 2007: Farewell 'Joey'
Players of the quality of Andrew Johns are once-in-a-lifetime, so the Newcastle faithful knew nothing would be the same again when he hit the turf on a freezing Canberra Monday night against the Raiders. The Team of the Century halfback—on whom the Knights relied so heavily—injured his neck and then announced his retirement after doing further damage at training. The club did not win a final for seven years after Johns retired.

2. August 19, 2000: Rooster rampage
The Knights had one foot in the Grand Final in 2000 before an extraordinary Roosters comeback saw them eliminated in one of the most dramatic preliminary finals of all. Newcastle led 16-2 at the break but a meltdown in the second half saw the Roosters score three tries in five minutes to get away with a 26-20 victory.

3. September 12, 1998: Finals choke
Newcastle's defence of its ARL premiership seemed to be on track in 1998 when it led Canterbury 16-4 deep into the second half of the elimination final. Canterbury scored twice to equalise, though, and ran away with a 28-16 victory in extra-time, leaving the Knights stunned and shattered.

4. September 4, 2005: Wooden-spoon agony
A proud club like the Newcastle Knights never thought of themselves as wooden spooners—they had finished bottom four just twice before the 2005 season—but a horrid run of injuries and poor form saw the club finish last in 2005. A gallant 36-28 last-round loss to heavyweights St George Illawarra sealed the Knights' fate.

5. August 28, 1990: Playoff pain
In its third season Newcastle nearly found itself in its first finals series, but a lost playoff left the Knights waiting another two years for finals footy. They downed Balmain 16-14 in the last round to force a playoff, but the Tigers turned the tables two days later with a 12-4 win to knock the Knights out.

NEWTOWN—GREATEST PLAYERS (1908-83)

1. Frank Farrell—204 games (1938-51)
The most feared forward in the game in the 1940s, Frank 'Bumper' Farrell ruled the Sydney premiership scene with an iron fist. He captained Newtown to its last premiership in '43 and captain-coached the club from 1946 to 1951 in becoming the only Bluebags player to make over 200 first grade appearances. World War II restricted his Test representation to just four matches (1946 and '48) but he played 14 interstate matches for NSW. Although an ear-biting incident involving St George's Bill McRitchie in 1945 cast a shadow over Farrell's career (the Newtown prop was controversially exonerated), he rates as one of the era's dominant players and characters, and was named Newtown's Clubman of the Century by the Men of League in 2008.

2. Dick Poole—115 games (1950-58)
Dashing centre Dick Poole developed into a tremendous leader for club and country. During a breakout 1955 season, captain-coach Poole scored 16 tries in steering the club to the minor premiership and a second straight Grand Final appearance—an agonising 12-11 loss to Souths. He debuted for Australia against France that year and played in five of the six Tests on the 1956-57 Kangaroo Tour. In the crowning achievement of his career, Poole captain-coached Australia to a historic World Cup triumph in 1957. He scored 51 tries for the Bluebags before joining big-spending Wests.

3. Herb Narvo—48 games (1937, 1943-45, 1949)
Regarded as one of Australia's greatest second-row forwards, Herb Narvo was a late call-up for the injured Joe Pearce in the 1937-38 Kangaroo Tour squad after just one season with Newtown, playing four Tests abroad. He spent the next four seasons in Newcastle but returned to the Bluebags in 1943 and was outstanding in the club's Grand Final defeat of Norths that year. The renowned pugilist won the Australian heavyweight championship in 1945 as well as captaining NSW and helping Newtown to the finals. After captain-coaching St George to the '46 Grand Final, Narvo spent one last season at Newtown in 1949. He was named as one of Australia's 100 greatest players and in the NSW Country Team of the Century during the 2008 Centenary celebrations.

4. Viv Farnsworth—33 games (1910-14, 1919)
Named as one of the ARL's 100 Greatest Players in 2008, centre Viv Farnsworth was one half of the first set of brothers to represent Australia in Rugby League, with

five-eighth and Newtown teammate Bill. The Rugby Union convert top-scored for the Bluebags with 10 tries in his first season as the club claimed the 1910 premiership. He represented NSW in 1910 and toured with the 1911-12 Kangaroos, scoring two tries on Test debut at pivot before playing the remaining matches of the historic series win in the centres. After serving in World War I, Farnsworth returned to Newtown in 1919 and played in Australia's home series against England from Wests in 1920. The brilliant attacking three-quarter scored 23 tries in his 33 games for Newtown.

5. Charlie Russell—69 games (1910-15, 1919)

Former Rugby Union Test star Charlie 'Boxer' Russell, part of the second wave of Wallaby stars who switched to the professional code in 1909, holds a cherished place in Newtown's history. He played fullback in the first Anglo-Australian Test on home soil in 1910 before kicking two goals as the Bluebags' captain-coach to tie the final against Souths—Newtown was awarded the premiership on countback as minor premiers. Russell, predominantly a winger, toured with the 1911-12 Kangaroos, playing in two Tests against England.

6. Len Smith—74 games (1943-48)

Len Smith is chiefly remembered as the incumbent Australian captain-coach who was inexplicably left out of the 1948-49 Kangaroo Tour squad, ostensibly due to the hidden agenda of the national selectors. But the Rugby Union convert was a wonderful centre for Newtown, scoring a try in the club's Grand Final thrashing of Norths in his first season. He scored a career-high 14 tries and debuted for NSW in 1947 before being named captain-coach of Australia for the two home Tests against New Zealand in '48. Smith cut all ties with the code after his great selection injustice, but left behind a record of 43 tries in 74 games for Newtown.

7. Lionel Williamson—112 games (1969-74)

Innisfail winger Lionel Williamson came to Newtown a year after debuting for Australia. The powerful 11-Test flankman featured in the 1970 World Cup triumph and on the 1973 Kangaroo Tour while at the club, captaining Newtown to the preliminary final in '73. At the age of 30, Williamson was called into the Australian squad for the Ashes-deciding third Test in '74, and scored a try in the famous 22-18 win at the SCG. He left Newtown at the end of the year with 41 tries to his credit.

8. Keith Froome—72 games (1943, 1946-50)

Arguably the finest halfback of the 1940s, Keith Froome—a NSW debutant from Newcastle in 1941—scaled the heights of representative football while at Newtown. The goalkicking No.7 broke into the Australian Test side on the tour of New Zealand in 1948 and played a further four Tests on the Kangaroo Tour at the end of the year. Froome captain-coached Australia on its two-Test tour of New Zealand in 1949, but injury kept him out of the historic home Ashes series victory the following season. He featured in Newtown's 1946-47 and '50 finals campaigns, and scored 296 points for the Bluebags.

9. Paddy McCue—81 games (1910-16)

A four-Test Wallaby before switching codes as part of the widespread 1909 Rugby Union defections, Paddy McCue joined several former amateurs at Newtown and starred in the club's maiden premiership success in 1910. The mobile forward was named vice-captain for the 1911-12 Kangaroo Tour, playing 22 games in Britain—including all three Tests of Australia's historic series defeat of England. The Bluebags stalwart captained NSW to New Zealand in 1912 and '13 before making the last of his four Test appearances against the touring England side in 1914. McCue scored 33 tries in 81 games for Newtown.

10. Gordon Clifford—114 games (1951-58)

Gordon 'Punchy' Clifford is best remembered as an outstanding goalkicking fullback for Newtown and the player who succeeded Clive Churchill in the Australian Test side. He played in the Bluebags' 1954-55 Grand Final losses to Souths, landing six goals in the former and three goals and a field goal in the latter—but his long range penalty attempt late in the '55 decider was off-target and the Rabbitohs snuck home 12-11. Clifford debuted for Australia against New Zealand the following season and top-scored on the 1956-57 Kangaroo Tour with 94, playing in four of the six Tests. His eight-Test international career—which netted 24 goals—wrapped up after he played all three matches of the home series against the '58 Lions. Clifford left Newtown with a then club-record 919 points.

11. Brian Moore—173 games (1962-73)

One of the great clubmen in Newtown's history, Brian 'Chicka' Moore racked up the second-most appearances and tries for the Bluebags—173 and 90 respectively. The tall, balding centre was a reliable backline performer and played four interstate matches for NSW from 1963 to 1970. His crowning representative achievement was winning selection on the 1967-68 Kangaroo Tour, on which he featured in 11 games (no Tests) and top-scored with 10 tries. The popular Moore played finals football for Newtown in the first and last seasons of his admirable career.

12. Tony Brown—116 games (1956-64)

Clever five-eighth Tony Brown, a member of Newtown's Team of the Century squad, played 10 Tests for Australia encompassing the 1958 Ashes series against the touring Lions, the 1959-60 Kangaroo Tour and the 1960 World Cup. A veteran of nine matches for NSW from 1958 to 1962, Brown led the Bluebags to finals series in 1959 and '62 during six seasons as first grade captain.

13. Arthur Folwell—82 games (1928-37, 1940)

England-born hooker Arthur Folwell's first grade career at Newtown spanned 13 seasons, and he was among Australia's finest hookers of the 1930s. He made the first of six appearances for NSW in 1932 and was chosen in the following season's Kangaroo Tour squad, missing the Bluebags' '33 premiership success while abroad but playing in two Tests against England. The club stalwart retired for good after a brief comeback in 1940, before coaching Newtown to its last premiership in 1943. He was named in the club's Team of the Century.

14. Felix Ryan—125 games (1914-23)

Newtown Team of the Century second-rower Felix Ryan represented Australia in five Tests on tours of New Zealand (1919) and Britain (1921-22), and represented NSW in seven interstate matches from 1915 to 1923 during a decade-long first grade career with the Bluebags. The stalwart forward's total of 125 games stood as a club record for a decade.

15. Col Geelan—75 games (1948-54)

Col Geelan was a representative regular at centre or five-eighth during his seven seasons with Newtown. He debuted for Australia at centre against France in 1951, played three Tests against New Zealand at pivot in '52 (scoring a hat-trick in a heavy second Test loss) and featured in four Tests on the 1952-53 Kangaroo Tour. Geelan steered the Bluebags to the minor premiership in 1954 as captain-coach, although he was ruled out of the Grand Final with injury before joining Canterbury the following season.

16. Graham Wilson—128 games (1960-67)

Outstanding second-rower Graham Wilson debuted for NSW in 1961, his second season with Newtown, before touring New Zealand as a guest player with South Africa in 1963. He was subsequently selected in the 1963-64 Kangaroo Tour squad and played the only two Tests of his career against France. He made the last of five interstate appearances in '66 before joining Cronulla. Wilson ranks in the top 10 for appearances for Newtown and was named in the club's Team of the Century.

17. Ray Preston—113 games (1949-56)

As one of the most potent try-scorers in premiership history—109 in just 113 games for Newtown—Ray Preston must surely rank as one of the best wingers not to represent his state or country. The Newcastle product scored an astounding 34 tries, the second-highest season tally ever, as the Bluebags won the 1954 minor premiership and reached the Grand Final, and played in another decider for the club in '55. Preston, who scored four tries in a match on three occasions, finished his career at Parramatta.

18. Noel Mulligan—31 games (1945-48)

Port Kembla hooker Noel Mulligan became an outstanding lock for Newtown, making seven of his 10 Test appearances for Australia from the club. 'The Count' featured at hooker in the Bluebags' 1945 finals campaign before switching to the backrow and making his Test debut against the '46 Lions. He starred on the 1948-49 Kangaroo Tour and played against New Zealand in '49 while at Bowral before joining St George. Mulligan was named lock in Newtown's Team of the Century.

19. Paul Quinn—61 games (1964-67)

Gerringong prop Paul Quinn toured with the 1963-64 Kangaroos and joined Newtown upon his return. He made the last three of his seven Test appearances from the club, and also represented NSW in 1964-65 as a Bluebags star. Quinn captained Newtown to the 1966 finals series before returning to the South Coast at the end of the following season. He was named in the club's Team of the Century.

20. Jack Troy—34 games (1949-52)

Athletics star Jack Troy had a short but eventful stint at Newtown, scoring a phenomenal 37 tries in just 34 matches across four seasons. The flying winger scored four tries in three interstate appearances for NSW in 1950 to win a Test call-up and feature in the first and third Ashes encounters of Australia's historic series defeat of Great Britain. In between those matches, Troy scored six tries for the Bluebags against Easts—the last player to achieve this feat in first grade for any club. He led the premiership with 16 tries that season and bagged another 12 in 1951, but leg injuries forced his premature retirement after he joined Easts in 1953.

NEWTOWN—GREATEST COACHES (1908-83)

1. Arthur Fowell—48 games (1942-44)

A former club great and Test hooker, Arthur Folwell became Newtown's last premiership-winning coach. After he led the Bluebags to a disappointing seventh in 1942, they finished second on the ladder in '43 and crushed Norths 34-7 in the Grand Final. Newtown took out the minor premiership in 1944 but suffered back-to-back losses to Balmain in the final and Grand Final—Folwell's last games as a first grade coach.

2. Dick Poole—140 games (1955-58, 1966-68)
Outstanding centre Dick Poole captain-coached Newtown in his last four seasons with the club, including a minor premiership and Grand Final appearance—a heartbreaking loss to Souths—in 1955. The next three seasons included two fourth-place playoff losses and a dismal eighth-place finish, but Poole famously captain-coached Australia to a maiden World Cup triumph from the club in '57. He finished his career at Wests, but returned to Newtown as coach in 1966, taking the club to the finals. His coaching tenure finished with a wooden spoon two years later.

3. Charlie Russell—16 games (1933)
Effectively the captain-coach—and the match-winning hero—of Newtown's historic premiership success in 1910, Charlie 'Boxer' Russell returned to the club as coach for one season in 1933. Russell's term started with four straight losses, but the Bluebags won nine of their last 10 to take out the minor premiership. His charges defeated St George 18-5 in the final to secure the club's second title.

4. Frank Farrell—108 games (1946-51)
Front-row enforcer Frank 'Bumper' Farrell captained Newtown to its last premiership in 1943, and he took on the captain-coach role for the last six seasons of his career. The club reached the four-team finals series four times during his tenure at the helm, and won 60 of its 108 games under the colourful prop. Farrell is widely hailed as Newtown's greatest player.

5. Warren Ryan—97 games (1979-82)
Warren Ryan began a long and decorated first grade coaching career at Newtown in 1979. The Jets had collected three straight wooden spoons before 'Wok' arrived, but he gradually moulded a competitive unit and guided the club to a second-place regular season finish in 1981 and the subsequent Grand Final, a valiant 20-11 loss to Parramatta. Ryan left the financially embattled outfit after it finished seventh in 1982.

NEWTOWN—BEST DAYS (1908-83)

1. September 4, 1943: Newtown claims last premiership with Grand Final romp
Defeated by North Sydney in three matches during 1943—including the semi-final three weeks earlier—minor premiers Newtown atoned with one of the most emphatic Grand Final victories of all time. The Frank Farrell-led Bluebags stormed to a 34-7 triumph over Norths in front of an SCG record crowd of 60,922 (although many more

were in attendance after busting into the ground after 'house full' signs went up). It was to be last of the proud club's three premierships, and certainly one to savour after the performance in the decider.

2. September 17, 1910: 'Boxer' Russell kicks Bluebags to first title
Newtown became just the second club to win the premiership in the NSWRL competition's third season, securing the 1910 title on countback after a try-less drawn final against Souths. The defending champs led 4-2 in the dying stages before Newtown centre Albert Hawkes called "mark" near halfway after catching a Souths kick. The rules of the game's early days allowed a team to take a shot at goal from a mark, and Bluebags skipper Charles 'Boxer' Russell stepped up to land the long-range pressure kick. The match ended in a draw and Newtown was declared premiers after finishing one point clear of Souths at the top of the regular season competition table. Russell's goal is regarded as one of the greatest in premiership history.

3. September 9, 1933: Premiership No.2
Newtown battled through the 1920s and the early part of the 1930s with little success, but secured its second title in a watershed 1933 campaign. The Bluebags finished one point clear of Souths and Easts to claim the minor premiership before downing the Rabbitohs in the semi-final. They fell behind 0-5 to St George in the first half of the final, but surged to a convincing 18-5 victory to win the competition for the first time in 23 years under the coaching of inaugural premiership-winning captain 'Boxer' Russell.

4. September 4, 1973: Gibson takes battlers to preliminary final
After several seasons in the doldrums, Newtown snapped a seven-year finals drought in 1973 under incoming coach Jack Gibson. The Bluebags drew their minor semi showdown with St George 12-all before returning to the SCG two days later and prevailing 8-5 in the replay. Steve Hansard's second-half try proved to be the decisive moment of the hard-fought encounter, which secured a preliminary final berth—the club's best effort since losing the 1955 Grand Final.

5. September 19, 1981: Jets into the Grand Final
Newtown had wallowed in the lower reaches of the premiership ladder throughout the second half of the 1970s but earned one last shot at glory in a stunning 1981 campaign. With millionaire businessman John Singleton turning the club's fortunes around off the field, the Jets had recruited Tom Raudonikis a year earlier, and the Test halfback led them to second spot at the end of the regular season. Newtown charged into its first Grand Final in 26 years via a 15-5 upset of minor premiers Easts in the preliminary final, holding the Roosters scoreless in the second half after the sides were

locked 5-all at the break. John Ferguson, Ray Blacklock and Phil Gould scored tries for the victorious Jets, who were gallant in going down 20-11 to Parramatta in the decider a week later.

NEWTOWN—WORST DAYS (1908-83)

1. September 26, 1983: Newtown gets the chop
Crippled by debt, subpar facilities and dwindling on-field fortunes, Newtown—along with Western Suburbs—was axed from the NSWRL premiership just two years after playing in a Grand Final. The Magpies were later given a reprieve, but it was the end of the line for fellow foundation club Newtown at the elite level. The Jets were the first club to exit the competition since University in 1937.

2. September 9, 1944: Newtown accused of throwing final
Minor premier Newtown, shooting for a second straight title, was embroiled in controversy after its 16-19 loss to Balmain in the final. Rumours the Bluebags had 'dogged it' to secure the extra revenue of playing the challenge Grand Final a week later clouded the aftermath of the match, while betting on the final indicated Balmain's upset win was widely anticipated. The NSWRL cleared both clubs' players of anything untoward, and the Tigers went on to win the Grand Final rematch 12-8.

3. September 17, 1955: Minor premiers pipped in the Grand Final
For the second year running, Newtown took out the minor premiership only to lose the Grand Final to South Sydney. The Bluebags led 11-7 heading into the final minutes of the decider, but the Rabbitohs hit the front via a dramatic late try to halfback Col Donohoe. Newtown fullback Gordon Clifford had a chance to win the premiership in the dying moments, but his long-range penalty goal attempt was off target. Souths had won a string of sudden-death matches with late comebacks to complete the 'Miracle of '55' at Newtown's expense.

4. May 16, 1976: Humiliated by Manly on the way to wooden spoon
After two seasons of steady decline, Newtown collected three straight wooden spoons from 1976. The club's plunge to whipping-boy status was highlighted by a crushing defeat at Henson Park at the hands of Manly, with Newtown conceding 12 tries in going down 57-6 to the eventual premiers. It was the second-biggest loss in the club's history, and beat the record for its worst defeat at home by 15 points. The Clarrie Jeffries-coached side won just one of its remaining 13 games.

5. June 20, 1948: Smith left out of Kangaroo Tour squad

Incumbent Australian Test captain-coach Len Smith's omission from the 1948-49 Kangaroo Tour squad rates as the most controversial and deplorable selection debacle in the code's history. In a move apparently motivated by a selector's own designs on the coaching role, brilliant centre Smith—an obvious choice to lead the squad—was left out altogether. His naming as NSW Player of the Year emphasised the farce, and he retired abruptly at the end of the season and shunned all connection with the game thereafter. Newtown missed the finals for the first time in seven years in 1949 in the wake of the departure of one of their greatest players.

NORTH QUEENSLAND COWBOYS—GREATEST PLAYERS (1995-2013)

1. Johnathan Thurston—190 games (2005-13)

One of the most decorated players of the NRL era, Johnathan Thurston has won nearly everything there is to win in Rugby League and holds most of the Cowboys' records. He was named Dally M Player of the Year in 2005 and 2007, winning the *Rugby League Week* Player of the Year award with clubmate Matt Bowen in the latter season, and was the 2011 Golden Boot winner. He won Dally M positional gongs in 2005, 2007, 2009, 2012 and 2013 and was named in the RLIF Team of the Year in 2009 and 2012. He has made 27 Origin appearances in succession and played 30 Tests as a Cowboy, twice winning club Player of the Year honours. 'JT' has spearheaded five of the Cowboys' six finals series and is the club's all-time leading point-scorer. The champion half is one of the all-time greats.

2. Matt Bowen—270 games (2001-13)

Arguably the most popular Cowboy of all time, Cairns product Matt Bowen is the club's most-capped player, its top try-scorer with 129 four-pointers and one of just four Cowboys to win a Dally M positional gong. Fleet-footed with a huge heart, Bowen has outplayed his size to represent Queensland 10 times and Australia once, while being named *Rugby League Week*'s Player of the Year in 2007. The 2007 Paul Bowman medallist, Bowen scored 22 tries that season, the most ever by a Cowboy in a single year.

3. Paul Bowman—203 games (1995-2007)

A club legend, rugged defensive centre Paul Bowman was the only foundation Cowboy to play in the club's first Grand Final. With 12 Origin appearances for Queensland, he was one of the most respected centres in the game in the early part of the 2000s. The Player of the Year award, which he won twice, is now named in Bowman's honour.

4. Matt Scott—163 games (2004-13)

A tough, old-school prop from Longreach, Matt Scott made his Origin debut after less than 20 top-grade games and established himself among the top echelon of props in 2009 when he returned to the Origin arena and a year later, when he became an Australian rep. Appointed co-captain in 2011, Scott won the Dally M Prop of the Year and the RLIF Prop of the Year that season. He was named Cowboys Player of the Year in 2010 and 2013.

5. Matt Sing—104 games (2002-06)

A great finisher and outstanding all-round winger, Matt Sing scored 73 tries in just five seasons with the Cowboys, with 13-plus in his four full seasons with the club. Player of the Year in 2002, Sing played eight Origins and 10 Tests for Australia while at North Queensland, and scored a try in its only Grand Final appearance.

6. James Tamou—100 games (2009-13)

A big-framed forward with the feet of a dancer, James Tamou debuted with North Queensland in 2009 but really made his mark in 2011 when he became one of the top metre-eaters in the game. He was selected for NSW and Australia in 2012 and has played five Origins and nine Tests, including the 2013 World Cup final. With Matt Scott, he has forged one of the great club front-row combinations.

7. Luke O'Donnell—117 games (2004-10)

A hot-head and one of the most suspended players of the NRL era, Luke O'Donnell became a NSW and Australian representative during a fine tenure with the Cowboys. Aggressive and fiery, he nonetheless played a total of 19 games for City, NSW and Australia during his time in Townsville. He won the 2004 and 2009 Player of the Year gongs and a place in the hearts of the faithful as one of the team's great enforcers.

8. Aaron Payne—219 games (2002-12)

The second-most-capped Cowboy of all time, hooker Aaron Payne was a staple in the Cowboys side for a decade, often deputising for Johnathan Thurston as skipper. Smart and tough, he was a reliable middle defender who was named North Queensland's Player of the Year in 2006 and 2008.

9. Dallas Johnson—65 games (2011-13)

One of the most courageous players ever to lace a boot, Dallas Johnson added steel and toughness to a Cowboys team in desperate need of these qualities during his three-year stint at the club. During his time there, the team made the finals for three straight years for the first time. A tireless tackler, Johnson owns the Cowboys records for most tackles in a game (64) and most in a season (1006).

10. Ashley Graham (161 games, 2006-13)

A proficient finishing winger, Ashley Graham scored 84 tries for the Cowboys, including four seasons of 10-plus. His 21 in 2012 was second in the NRL and is the second most of all time in a season for the Cowboys. He was named the Cowboys' Player of the Year in 2011. Graham retired after the 2013 season following a bad run with injury.

11. Ty Williams—151 games (2002-10)

The second-greatest try-scorer in Cowboys history, Ty Williams scored 85 tries in a nine-year career with the club. That career started with a bang when he scored 58 tries in 91 games across his first four seasons. He played all three Origins in 2005 before injuries and form issues saw his output decline. Williams retired after the 2010 season.

12. Brent Tate—55 games (2011-13)

Decorated centre Brent Tate joined the Cowboys in 2011 and, despite not debuting until late in the season following a serious knee injury, he has been a standout. Tate was recalled to the Queensland team in 2012 and held his spot in 2013, winning back an Australian jersey in the latter season. A true professional, he brought a defensive toughness to the Cowboys that saw them make the finals in his first three years at the club.

13. Paul Rauhihi—72 games (2003-05)

It came as no surprise that North Queensland's rise to finals football for the first time coincided with the arrival of hard-headed prop Paul Rauhihi from the successful Canterbury team. Rauhihi was named the club's Player of the Year in his first season and a year later was awarded the Dally M Prop of the Year. His last game with the Cowboys was a strong showing in the 2005 Grand Final.

14. Willie Tonga—60 games (2009-11)

A premiership winner with Canterbury, skilful centre Willie Tonga joined the Cowboys in 2009 after losing all form with the Bulldogs. He enjoyed a return to his best in Townsville, playing six Origins and five Tests. His 34 tries in 60 games sits eighth on the Cowboys list, and three of the four seasons in his career in which he scored 10-plus tries came at the club.

15. Carl Webb—115 games (2005-10)
An aggressive front-rower who had spent five seasons with the Broncos, Carl Webb enjoyed a renaissance at North Queensland, playing eight Origins and a Test as a Cowboy. A wrecking ball when on song, he was one of the most feared players in the game during the middle of the 2000s.

16. Travis Norton—58 games (2004-06)
A Grand Final player during a seven-year career with Canterbury and a Queensland regular during his final two seasons at Belmore, Travis Norton was a quality contributor for three years in Townsville. He represented the Maroons in 2004 and scored a try as the Cowboys' captain in the club's only Grand Final a year later.

17. Josh Hannay—150 games (1998-2006)
An honest centre who got the most out of his limited skill set, Josh Hannay is the second-greatest point-scorer and seventh-greatest try-scorer in North Queensland's history. He was originally a local junior, and the Cowboys attempted to play him as a 16-year-old before he eventually debuted two seasons later. He represented Queensland twice, played in the 2006 decider and holds club records for most points in a match (24) and most points in a season (230).

18. John Buttigieg—101 games (1996-2003)
A hulking prop forward during the Cowboys' formative years, John Buttigieg was a surprise selection for Queensland in 2001 and again played for the Maroons in 2002. Constantly battling injuries, he retired at just 26. He was voted the club's Players' Player in 1999.

19. Glenn Morrison—94 games (2000-04)
A gritty lock forward who won the Dally M Rookie of the Year award in 1996 when at Balmain, Glenn Morrison joined the Cowboys in 2000 following the demise of North Sydney. He was named the club Player of the Year in 2001 and represented Country three times.

20. Steve Southern—124 games (2004-10)
A bloodnut from Wollongong, Steve Southern found himself at Rugby League's most northern outpost during the club's strongest period. A tireless defender, he started in North Queensland's first seven finals, including the 2005 premiership decider.

NORTH QUEENSLAND COWBOYS—GREATEST COACHES (1995-2013)

1. Graham Murray—161 games (2002-08)
Arguably the greatest coach never to win a premiership, Graham Murray led North Queensland to its first finals campaign in 2004 and its first Grand Final a year later. Replacing Murray Hurst in 2002 after stints with Illawarra, Hunter and the Sydney Roosters, Murray's first six seasons resulted in the club's six best finishes to that date. The Cowboys snuck into the 2004 playoffs and shocked Canterbury before a close preliminary final loss to the Roosters. Murray's side went one better in 2005, losing the premiership decider to the Wests Tigers. The Cowboys made the preliminary final again in 2007 but became a lame duck in 2008, and the coach quit mid-season. Murray sadly died in 2013 at just 58.

2. Neil Henry—124 games (2009-13)
Considered one of the most talented young coaches in the game, Neil Henry was poached from Canberra in just his second year as a first grade coach. He inked a five-year deal and served out the full term of his contract despite finishes of 12th and 15th in his first two seasons. Finals showings in 2011-12 made him just the second North Queensland coach to see back-to-back playoffs. The Cowboys again played finals football in 2013 but only after they put a six-game winning streak on end following the announcement Henry would not have his deal extended. He was replaced by rookie Paul Green.

3. Tim Sheens—109 games (1997-2001)
After two dismal seasons in the premiership, the Cowboys believed they had struck gold when they lured three-time title-winning coach Tim Sheens to Townsville. It was a failed move. Under Sheens, the Cowboys won two wooden spoons and never finished higher than fifth from bottom in five full seasons. He had a win rate of just 29.4 per cent at North Queensland and 'stood down' 10 games into the 2001 season.

4. Graham Lowe—21 games (1996)
Appointed to replace inaugural coach Grant Bell (who went 2-20), former Manly coach Graham Lowe, who had enjoyed successful stints as a rep coach of New Zealand and Queensland, had only marginally more success. His Cowboys won just six games but it was enough to finish 17th and avoid the wooden spoon. Lowe stood aside for Tim Sheens after his solitary year.

5. Murray Hurst—18 games (2001-02)
The mid-season replacement for Tim Sheens in 2001 after the Cowboys started 2-8, Murray Hurst finished the year with just four wins from the last 15 games but was appointed senior coach for the 2002 season. He lasted just three games—losses of 36, 32 and 28 margins—before standing down and being replaced by Graham Murray.

NORTH QUEENSLAND COWBOYS—BEST DAYS (1995-2013)

1. September 25, 2005: Eel-ectric Cowboys
North Queensland booked a spot in its first Grand Final with a stunning upset of minor premiers Parramatta in the preliminary final. The Eels went in heavy favourites but were blown off the park in a 29-0 thrashing in Sydney. Johnathan Thurston turned in a masterly performance in what was his first season at the Cowboys.

2. September 11, 2004: Finals at last
It had taken a decade but North Queensland finally won its way into the finals in the 2004 season. The Cowboys didn't waste their opportunity, stunning Canterbury in the opening final 30-22. Matt Sing scored a hat-trick and Matt Bowen played a dominant game in what was the shock of the finals series.

3. September 18, 2004: 'Big Brother' beaten
A week after their first finals win, the Cowboys held off Brisbane 10-0 in a stunning final in Townsville. Nearly 25,000 fans crammed into Dairy Farmers to see David Myles score the only try of the game in an epic final, the first to be played outside of a state capital. It was the 17th time the two Queensland sides had played and the first time the Cowboys emerged victorious.

4. April 30, 1995: First win
North Queensland lost its first seven matches and would win just twice in its first year in the premiership, so its first victory eight rounds in was sweet. Having been beaten by 16-plus in five of their first seven, the Cowboys stunned the Steelers in Wollongong with a 14-10 victory. David Bouveng scored twice for the visitors.

5. September 7, 2013: Finals miracle
The Cowboys seemed destined to miss the finals in 2013, with coach Neil Henry informed he would not be re-signed for 2014. Upon hearing the news, the Cowboys rattled off six straight to collect an unlikely finals berth. They needed to win the last

game of the year to secure eighth place and did, thumping the Wests Tigers 50-22 in a match that doubled as Matt Bowen's home farewell.

NORTH QUEENSLAND COWBOYS—WORST DAYS (1995-2013)

1. October 2, 2005: So close, so far
North Queensland's first Grand Final appearance came in its 11th season but it was not to be. Betting had the Cowboys as only marginal outsiders and Matt Bowen opened the scoring for them, but some Benji Marshall magic spurred the Tigers to a famous 30-16 win, leaving Graham Murray's Cowboys devastated at the defeat. The club is still yet to win a premiership decider.

2. May 23, 2011: Sam Faust dies
The Rugby League world was saddened midway through 2011 when young tyro Sam Faust passed away after a battle with leukaemia. Faust, who played 23 top-grade games for the Cowboys as a backrower, was just 26.

3. September 26, 2004: Finals heartache
North Queensland shocked both Canterbury and Brisbane during its first finals campaign in 2004 but fell a win short of a maiden Grand Final, losing 19-16 to the Sydney Roosters in a dramatic preliminary final. The scores were locked at 16-all with five minutes remaining before the Chooks pulled away, despite being out-scored three tries to two.

4. September 14, 2013: Robbed
A year after being on the receiving end of some dubious decisions in a finals loss to Manly, the Cowboys endured more post-season hard luck against Cronulla. The Sharks scored a seventh-tackle try in a dramatic 22-20 result, leading to North Queensland coach Neil Henry claiming the NRL wanted an all-Sydney Grand Final.

5. August 27, 1995: Annus horribilis
North Queensland's horrible first season, which netted just two wins, came to an embarrassing end at Belmore Sports Ground when Canterbury, in what was supposed to be Terry Lamb's last game at the ground, piled on 13 tries in a 66-4 win. It was coach Grant Bell's last game in charge.

NORTH SYDNEY BEARS—GREATEST PLAYERS (1908-99)

1. Ken Irvine—176 games (1958-70)
ARL Team of the Century winger Ken Irvine was named North Sydney's greatest clubman by the Men of League—due recognition of his stunning record of 171 tries in 176 games in a team that largely struggled during his tenure. The flying winger scored at least 13 tries in each of his 11 full seasons in Bears colours, a testament to his durability as well as his devastating ability, and was a driving force in Norths' run to rare finals appearances in 1964-65. He made all of his 33 Test appearances (33 tries) for Australia—including three Kangaroo Tours—and 25 interstate appearances (28 tries) for NSW while at Norths. Irvine captained the Bears later in his career (infamously attempting to lead his team off the field in protest at Keith Page's refereeing in a 1970 match) before joining Manly and winning Grand Finals in the last two seasons of his glittering career.

2. Duncan Thompson—58 games (1916, 1920-23)
All-time great Queensland-born halfback Duncan Thompson played for North Sydney in 1916 before serving in World War I. He made his Test debut in 1919 and returned to the club the following season. Thompson was the architect of Norths' 1921-22 premiership triumphs, captaining the latter and directing their star-studded backline with expert precision. He played five Tests while at the club—encompassing the 1920 Ashes series success and the 1921-22 Kangaroo Tour—but left Sydney in protest at a controversial suspension meted out to him in 1923 on a kicking charge. Thompson, who further enhanced his reputation in Toowoomba, had a stand named after him at North Sydney Oval in 1929 and was chosen as the club's Team of the Century halfback in 2006.

3. Harold Horder—50 games (1920-23)
Incomparable winger Harold Horder—a South Sydney legend—spent four seasons of his phenomenal career with North Sydney, helping the club to unparalleled success. The dazzling Test star joined Norths in 1920—his ninth season of first grade—and scored 50 tries in four seasons, including four in a final-round victory over Wests that secured the club's maiden, first-past-the-post premiership victory in 1921 of which he was the captain. He scored 35 tries in 25 games on the subsequent Kangaroo Tour before racking up 17 touchdowns in Norths' 1922 premiership season. Horder returned to Souths two years later, and ousted long-time wing partner Cec Blinkhorn for a place in the North Sydney Team of the Century in 2006.

4. Cec Blinkhorn—93 games (1914-18, 1920-23)

One of the great wingers, Cec Blinkhorn was a productive try-scorer for several seasons for Norths before spending the 1919 season at Souths. He returned to Norths the following season along with fellow wing champion Harold Horder and was integral to the club's halcyon era of the early 1920s, setting club records for tries in a match (five in 1920) and a season (20 in 1922). Blinkhorn toured with the 1921-22 Kangaroos, scoring a record 39 tries in just 29 games. He scored two tries in Norths' 35-3 final win over Balmain to secure the '22 title, and his tally of 79 tries remained a club record until bettered by Ken Irvine. Blinkhorn returned to Souths for a season with Horder in 1924, making the last of his four Test appearances against Great Britain. While he was unlucky to miss out to Horder for a place in Norths' Team of the Century, he was named as one of Australia's 100 Greatest Players in 2008.

5. Brian Carlson—72 games (1957-62)

A supremely gifted backline superstar who rates alongside Australia's finest players of all time, Brian Carlson spent six sparkling seasons at North Sydney, scoring 31 tries and 515 points. Equally devastating at fullback, wing or centre, he was an automatic Test selection while playing in Newcastle and Wollongong before joining Norths in 1957. The club failed to reach the finals during his tenure but he was brilliant nonetheless, and made the last 15 (two as captain) of his 23 Test appearances while a Norths player—including starring roles in the 1957 World Cup success and on the 1959-60 Kangaroo Tour. Carlson was named at fullback in North Sydney's Team of the Century in 2006.

6. Greg Florimo—285 games (1986-98)

A strong-running centre or robust five-eighth who dabbled in the backrow, Greg Florimo became a North Sydney club legend in a 13-season first grade career, racking up a record 285 games for the Bears—the most appearances for one club in premiership history at the time. He made one appearance for NSW in 1988 before falling off the selectors' radar, but enjoyed a representative renaissance after a career-best '94 season for Norths. Florimo was selected in the Kangaroo Tour squad and played two Ashes Tests before playing all three matches for the Blues in '95 and featuring in two further Tests against New Zealand. The durable utility never played less than 18 games in a season, and played in all four of the Bears' agonising preliminary final defeats during the 1990s. A centre in North Sydney's Team of the Century named in 2006, he has since been at the forefront of the Central Coast Bears' push for inclusion in the NRL, as CEO.

7. Mark Graham—146 games (1981-88)

Adorned with the "world's best second-rower" tag for much of the 1980s, New Zealand Player of the Century Mark Graham was a devastating performer for a North Sydney side that largely struggled during his eight seasons with the club. The unwaveringly tough and skilful forward captained the Bears to their first finals series in 17 years in 1982 and was named Dally M Second-rower of the Year in 1982-83, skippering the Bears for the bulk of his time in Sydney. The long-serving Kiwi captain made 16 of his 29 Test appearances from Norths. He later coached in the club's lower grades, but his NRL head coach stint with the Auckland Warriors was a disaster. Graham claimed a second-row spot in Norths' Team of the Century named in 2006.

8. Herman Peters—101 games (1917-25)

Brilliant centre Herman Peters more than held his own in Norths' champion backline of the 1920s that is regarded as one of the best club combinations of all time. A star of the 1921-22 premiership successes, he was one of five Norths players to tour with the '21-22 Kangaroos—although he only played four matches abroad and was destined not to play a Test for Australia. A NSW rep in 1923, Peters scored a career-high 16 tries in just 16 games for Norths that year; he captained the club later in his career as one of the last remnants of its title-winning line-ups. He finished with 62 tries from 101 games, and was arguably the most notable absentee from North Sydney's Team of the Century in 2006.

9. Gary Larson—234 games (1987-99)

Gladstone forward Gary Larson was an invaluable workhorse in 13 seasons at North Sydney, racking up the second-most first grade appearances in the club's history. A tireless second-rower who regularly tallied astounding tackle counts, the blond-haired Larson gravitated towards the front-row later in his career. He played a then Origin record 24 consecutive matches for Queensland from 1991 to 1998 and, while he was an unlucky omission from '94 Kangaroo Tour squad, Larson played nine Tests for Australia during the Super League War years—including the '95 World Cup final victory at Wembley. Larson, a prop in Norths' Team of the Century, played in four preliminary finals for the Bears but was sent off in the '94 loss to Canberra.

10. Fred Griffiths—68 games (1963-66)

South African Rugby Union convert Fred Griffiths joined Norths in 1963 after a decorated stint with Wigan. The goalkicking fullback immediately assumed the captain-coach role and steered the club to finals appearances in 1964-65—Norths' first in a decade, and their last for 17 years. He topped the premiership's pointscoring in all four of his seasons with the Bears, including a then club-record total of 177 in 1965, and left to captain-coach in the country after tallying 590 points in red and black.

Griffiths also represented South Africa in its historic Test series against Australia in 1963 and captained Other Nationalities against Sydney Colts the following season.

11. David Fairleigh—193 games (1989-99)

A mobile, dynamic backrower in the Bradley Clyde mould, David Fairleigh was one of Norths' most regular representative players during their 1990s renaissance. Fifth on the Bears' all-time appearances register and with 37 tries to his credit, the Central Coast junior featured in the club's 1994-98 finals campaigns, claiming the Rothmans Medal in 1994 and finishing second to teammate Jason Taylor in '96. He represented NSW in 10 Origins from 1991 to 1997, toured with the '94 Kangaroos and played five Tests for Australia. He was named alongside Mark Graham in the second-row in Norths' Team of the Century. A long-serving NRL assistant coach, Fairleigh has been touted as the proposed Central Coast Bears franchise's foundation coach.

12. Jason Taylor—147 games (1994-99)

Former Wests halfback Jason Taylor was Norths' halfback and linchpin in 147 consecutive games—136 of them as captain. Although his running and defensive capabilities were below those of his elite No.7 rivals, Taylor was an outstanding ball-player and director of play with a superb all-round kicking game. He ranks as one of the great goalkickers of all time, and chalked up the only four season totals above 200 points in Norths' history among a club-record 1274 career points. Taylor led the Bears to preliminary finals in 1994 and '96-97, and won the last Rothmans Medal in 1996. Representative opportunities were scarce for Taylor, but the '93 NSW Origin rep played for City twice while at Norths.

13. Billy Moore—211 games (1989-99)

Hardworking inspirational lock Billy Moore chalked up the third-most appearances in North Sydney's history. Underlining his durability by playing 20 games or more in every season from 1992 to 1998, Moore also represented Queensland in 17 straight matches during that period as one of the decade's most iconic Origin performers. He made four Test appearances during the Super League War years. Moore scored 34 tries for the club and appeared in all four of the Bears' preliminary finals losses during the '90s. He was named as a reserve in Norths' Team of the Century in 2006.

14. Don McKinnon—183 games (1977-88)

Steeped in North Sydney tradition as the son of long-serving player, coach and president Harry McKinnon, Don was an intimidating prop in 12 seasons of first grade with the club. He was the engine-room cornerstone of the Bears' first finals appearance in 17 years in 1982, represented NSW in one Origin and toured with the 'Invincibles' Kangaroos squad at the end of the year, making his sole Test appearance against Papua

New Guinea. His total of 183 games was third in club history at the time, but his one-season, six-game stint with Manly in 1988 at the end of his career is mostly remembered for his urinating on Lang Park during the Broncos' first-ever game.

15. Norm Strong—210 games (1949-62)
Norm Strong is widely regarded as one of the great clubmen of premiership football, and his mark of 210 first grade games stood as a North Sydney record for more than three decades after his retirement. The consistent, hardworking hooker was part of Norths' 1952-54 finals campaigns, including the side that lost the '52 final to South Sydney. The likes of Kevin Schubert, Ken Kearney and Noel Kelly thwarted Strong's representative aspirations, but he was nevertheless a highly valued part of the Bears' set-up, repealing his decision to retire at the end of 1960 to spend two more seasons with the club.

16. Peter Diversi—63 games (1952-55)
A tough, mobile lock renowned for his punishing tackles and outstanding cover defence, Peter Diversi played seven interstate matches for NSW and five Tests for Australia during his four seasons at North Sydney. The Wollongong product was a key part of the Norths side that qualified for finals series in 1953-54, but left to captain-coach in the country in '56 before returning to Sydney with Manly. Diversi was named lock in Norths' Team of the Century in 2006.

17. Ross Warner—186 games (1963-74)
Ross Warner took over the hooker position from club stalwart Norm Strong, who was the only player in Norths' history Warner trailed on the club's appearances roster by the time he retired. The Tamworth product made three appearances for NSW early in his tenure with the Bears, and was a non-playing reserve for Australia against France in 1964. Warner's only finals appearances came in his first two seasons in Sydney, but he captained the club during the early 1970s. He ousted the likes of Strong and John Gray to be named hooker in the Bears' Team of the Century in 2006.

18. Sid Deane—35 games (1908, 1912-14, 1917, 1919)
Pioneering five-eighth or centre Sid Deane played for NSW against the fabled New Zealand 'All Golds' during the NSWRL's foundation 1908 season before touring with the original Kangaroos and playing in two Tests against England. He stayed on in Britain with Oldham but returned to Norths in 1912 and captained Australia in all three Tests of the home series against England in 1914. After two seasons with Hull, Deane came back for his third stint with Norths in 1917. He was named as a reserve in Norths' Team of the Century in 2006.

19. Jim Devereux—21 games (1908, 1910-13, 1922)

Jim Devereux played just 21 first grade games for North Sydney, but such is his status as a pioneering great that the centre was named in the club's Team of the Century in 2006. A foundation Norths player in 1908, Devereux played in three Tests against New Zealand before embarking on the inaugural Kangaroo Tour. He top-scored with 17 tries, including a hat-trick in the drawn first Test against England. Devereux spent successful stints with Hull either side of a 1910-13 term with North Sydney, and returned in his mid-30s to play three games in Norths' 1922 premiership success.

20. Billy Wilson—54 games (1963-67)

Hard-nut front-rower Billy Wilson played the last four seasons of the longest career in first grade history with North Sydney. The St George great played the last three of his 11 Tests for Australia in his first year at Norths, captaining his country against New Zealand before touring with the 1963-64 Kangaroos. A broken leg kept him out of the Bears' '64 finals campaign, but he was a key part of the side that reached the 1965 preliminary final. Taking on the role of non-playing coach in 1967, Wilson came out of retirement to play three games for his injury-riddled team, becoming the first player to appear in first grade at the age of 40 and the first whose career spanned 20 seasons. He was named as a prop in Norths' Team of the Century in 2006.

NORTH SYDNEY BEARS—GREATEST COACHES (1908-99)

1. Chris McKivat—25 games (1921-22)

One of the all-time great halfbacks and the 1911-12 Kangaroo Tour skipper, Chris McKivat coached one of the greatest club combinations of all time at North Sydney—the only premiership-winning sides in the club's history. Blessed with players such as Duncan Thompson, Harold Horder and Cec Blinkhorn, McKivat steered Norths to emphatic title successes in 1921-22, losing just four games in those two seasons. He later had a fruitless season in charge of Wests in 1928.

2. Peter Louis—161 games (1993-99)

After two Grand Final losses in charge of Parramatta's reserve grade outfit, Peter Louis joined Norths and guided their reserves to premierships in 1991-92. He succeeded Steve Martin as first grade coach in '93 and steered the Bears to a much-improved sixth in his first season before reaching the finals in the next five straight seasons. Louis endured preliminary final heartbreak in 1994 and '96-97 with the long-suffering club, and quit midway through the disastrous 1999 campaign—Norths' last before entering an ill-fated merger with Manly. The 1997 City Origin coach was in charge of Norths for 72 more games than the second-most prolific coach in the club's history, and achieved an impressive 59.6 per cent win rate in seven seasons at the helm.

3. Fred Griffiths—75 games (1963-66)
South African fullback Fred Griffiths spent four seasons at Norths as captain-coach following a charmed stint at Wigan. Griffiths, who was also the premiership's top point-scorer in his four seasons with the Bears, led the club to fifth in his first season and to their first finals series in a decade in 1964. Norths finished second in 1965—their highest ladder position since winning the '21-22 titles—and reached the preliminary final, their last for 26 years. Griffiths departed at the end of a disappointing '66 campaign with the most games as coach in Norths' history—a figure that was subsequently passed only by Noel Kelly and Peter Louis.

4. Ross McKinnon—58 games (1952-53, 1959)
Former Easts and Australian Test centre of the 1930s Ross McKinnon coached Canterbury with considerable success in 1946-47, and resurfaced with North Sydney in the early 1950s. He guided the club to consecutive fourth-placed finishes in 1952-53, Norths' best efforts since reaching their only Grand Final in 1943. They made it as far as the preliminary final in '52. McKinnon returned for a season in 1959, with Norths finishing just one win shy of a finals spot in fifth.

5. Ron Willey—72 games (1980-82)
Ex-Manly premiership-winning coach Ron Willey arrived at North Sydney in 1980 after a mixed three-season stint at Balmain. He inherited a Bears side who had just collected a wooden spoon, but led them on a three-year path of improvement—from six wins and 11th in '80, to nine wins and seventh in '81, and then finally 16 wins and third in '82. The 1982 tally smashed Norths' wins-in-a-season record by five games, and despite exiting with back-to-back finals losses, it was the club's best year since 1965. Willey was inexplicably sacked by the club secretary Ken McCaffery, a teammate of his on the 1952-53 Kangaroo Tour, at the end of the season due to his defence-oriented methods, and linked with Souths.

NORTH SYDNEY BEARS—BEST DAYS (1908-99)

1. June 18, 1921: Maiden premiership success
Norths had little to celebrate during the premiership's first 13 seasons—a fourth-place finish in the inaugural 1908 competition their best result. But when legendary

former Test captain Chris McKivat came on board as coach in 1921, the red-and-blacks charged through the shortened season undefeated. A 31-17 win over Wests in their last regular season match, with brilliant winger Harold Horder scoring four tries, confirmed Norths' first-past-the-post premiership success. Five of the club's stars were selected to go on the subsequent Kangaroo Tour.

2. September 6, 1922: Norths crush Glebe to go back-to-back
A deadlock for top spot on the ladder at the end of the 1922 regular season necessitated a final between North Sydney and Glebe to decide the premiership. Star-studded Norths were unstoppable at the SCG, running out emphatic 35-3 victors. Backline guns Harold Horder, Cec Blinkhorn and Frank Rule all bagged doubles, while Horder kicked seven goals for a 20-point haul. Their successful title defence sealed Norths' legacy as one of the greatest club combinations of all time.

3. September 1, 1991: Bears down bitter rivals to break finals drought
Norths qualified for their first finals series in nine years by finishing second in 1991, and won their first post-season match in 39 years by outlasting archrivals Manly 28-16 in the major preliminary semi-final. The match was on a knife's edge at 16-all midway through the second half, but the Bears—of whom only three players had appeared in a finals match previously—kicked away with tries to Billy Moore and David Hall. The win was particularly sweet in light of disparaging remarks made about Norths by prop Martin Bella, who had left the Bears to join Manly a year earlier.

4. September 3, 1994: Norths sink defending champs in minor semi
After a convincing first-up loss to Canberra in the 1994 finals, Norths went into their minor semi-final showdown with two-time premiers Brisbane as distinct underdogs. The Bears raced to a 14-4 lead during the first half, but the Broncos clawed back to level the scores just after halftime. An engrossing arm-wrestle ensued, with Norths absorbing countless waves of Brisbane attack before Bears captain Jason Taylor slotted a sweet 30-metre field goal with six minutes remaining. Taylor's one-pointer clinched a euphoric 15-14 win and a preliminary final date.

5. June 27, 1993: Miracle comeback at Belmore
The long-suffering Bears scored one of the most famous regular season victories in their history against Canterbury in 1993. They trailed the ladder-leading Bulldogs 0-17 after just 23 minutes, but clawed back with three unconverted tries to trail by just five points. Norths winger David Hall dived over for his second touchdown six minutes from fulltime, with referee Bill Harrigan awarding a potential eight-point try after Bulldogs halfback Craig Polla-Mounter dived on Hall late. Craig Makepeace

hooked the first conversion attempt wide—his fourth miss from as many attempts—but slotted the second from in front to seal the Bears' remarkable 18-17 escape.

NORTH SYDNEY BEARS—WORST DAYS (1908-99)

1. October 1, 1999: Bears forced into bed with the enemy
A proposed move to the Central Coast in '99 fell apart for Norths due to stadium construction delays, while their increasingly dire financial situation and the NRL's move to reduce the number of teams in the premiership to 14 at the end of the year backed the club into a corner. At the end of a season that saw long-serving coach Peter Louis dumped midyear and the Bears miss the finals for the first time in six years, North Sydney reluctantly entered into a merger with bitter neighbouring rivals Manly—the ill-fated Northern Eagles joint venture that dissolved in 2002. The Central Coast Bears have been on a crusade for admission to the NRL since '09.

2. September 4, 1943: Norths thumped in only Grand Final appearance
North Sydney contested just one Grand Final in its 92-season history—and was crushed 34-7. The Frank Hyde-captained red-and-blacks entered the '43 decider as favourites after downing minor premiers Newtown in the major semi, but were rocked by the unforeseen absence of star lock Harry Taylor, who had been whisked away on military duty. The Bluebags carved out an eight-tries-to-one victory over shell-shocked Norths in front of a then Grand Final record crowd of 60,922.

3. September 20, 1997: Cliff-hanger loss extends preliminary final Knight-mares
Norths sank to their fourth preliminary final defeat of the decade in an SFS heartbreaker against a patched-up Newcastle. The Bears fought back from 4-12 down to level the scores in the second half, but a Matthew Johns field goal put the Knights back in front and a try on fulltime sealed a devastating 17-12 loss for Norths. Halfback and captain Jason Taylor endured a horror day, spilling Andrew Johns kicks to gift the Knights two first-half tries and kicking just two goals from five attempts.

4. September 21, 1996: Bears choke one short of the decider
The Bears' best chance to reach a post-war Grand Final fell by the wayside in '96 thanks to an inexplicable second-half collapse in the preliminary final against seventh-placed St George. Norths, who finished the regular season third, trailed by just one point at halftime, but had no answer to Dragons five-eighth Anthony Mundine after the break and crashed to a 29-12 loss.

5. January 1, 1997: Bad News Bears

Norths officials went into damage control after one of the most unsavoury off-field incidents of the 1990s, involving skipper Jason Taylor and several Bears teammates at a New Year's Day ODI cricket match at the SCG. The players reportedly threw cups of urine over fellow patrons during a Mexican wave, with the shameful incident attracting more negative headlines for Rugby League while the game was reeling from the Super League split. Taylor was retained as Norths' captain despite public outrage over the players' antics.

PARRAMATTA EELS—GREATEST PLAYERS (1947-2013)

1. Peter Sterling—227 games (1978-92)

One of the most talented halfbacks ever to play the game, Peter Sterling was an astute thinker and skilful passer and kicker who thrived in an era of great halves. One of just two NSW players to win four Origin man-of-the-match awards, Sterling was the Eels' best in the 1986 Grand Final, winning the first-ever Churchill Medal. He won the Golden Boot in 1987 and has the unique distinction of winning two Rothmans Medals, two Dally M Medals and two *Rugby League Week* Player of the Year awards. A champion playmaker, the 18-Test veteran forged a prominent media career after injuries curtailed his playing career.

2. Mick Cronin—216 games (1977-86)

A tough goalkicking centre with a thirst for points, Mick Cronin is Parramatta's all-time leading scorer. A veteran of 33 Tests and 25 interstate matches, he held the record for most premiership points for over 15 years and maintains the record for most points in a calendar year. Cronin played in seven Grand Finals with Parramatta and went out a winner in 1986 with teammate Ray Price. He won back-to-back Rothmans Medals as well as three Dally M positional gongs.

3. Nathan Hindmarsh—330 games (1998-2012)

One of the finest defenders the game has known, Nathan Hindmarsh became the first player since stats were kept to make 10,000 tackles. A rock during some lean years for Parramatta, Hindmarsh won five positional Dally M gongs during an illustrious career that saw him also claim five Provan-Summons Medals as the most popular player in the code. He played 17 Origins and 23 Tests and set the standard for defenders during his outstanding career.

4. Ray Price—259 games (1976-86)

A dual international who added a level of professionalism to a Parramatta team in desperate need of it, Ray Price played in eight Grand Finals during his 11-year career, winning four. A bruising defender known as 'Mr Perpetual Motion' for his relentless competitiveness, Price was sent out a winner as captain of the '86 Grand Final triumph. He won the Rothmans Medal in 1979, the Dally M Medal in 1982, the *Rugby League Week* Player of the Year in '79 and '85 and the Dally M Lock of the Year for five straight years, while playing 22 Tests. A statue was erected outside Parramatta Stadium in the former NSW Origin skipper's honour.

5. Brett Kenny—265 games (1980-93)

A sublimely talented five-eighth, Brett Kenny was so brilliant during the early stages of his career that he ousted future Immortal Wally Lewis from the Australian No.6. Kenny played in all four of Parramatta's premierships, scoring doubles in three straight Grand Finals from 1981 to 1983. He was clearly the best player on the paddock in the latter two deciders. Kenny was awarded the Golden Boot in 1985 and was named among the Top 100 players in 2008. He played 17 Origins and 17 Tests and was the X-factor during Parramatta's great era of success.

6. Ken Thornett—129 games (1962-68, 1971)

A champion fullback who was adorned with the nickname 'The Mayor of Parramatta', Ken Thornett's abilities are shown in his 12 Tests in an era when the likes of Graeme Langlands, Les Johns and Keith Barnes were competing for the top No.1 job. A Rugby Union convert, Thornett was safe at the back and a super attacking player when chiming into the line. He was named the best player in the premiership in 1965 by revered journalist EE Christensen.

7. Brian Hambly—105 games (1961-67)

A hardened and tough forward who came into grade at South Sydney, Brian Hambly joined Parramatta in 1961 having already toured with the Kangaroos. He was a key player during the Eels' first finals series while he continued his rep career. Captain-coach in '67, he brought the curtain down on his own career by sacking himself from the team.

8. Eric Grothe—152 games (1979-89)

A blockbusting winger who devastated opponents with his hard running and sheer strength, Eric Grothe scored 78 tries for the Eels. Between 1982 and 1985 he crossed for 52 tries in 74 games, playing eight Tests and nine Origins. Injuries cruelled the latter part of his career but the image of 'Guru' skittling opponents was a highlight of the 1980s.

9. Steve Edge—118 games (1980-84)

An inspirational skipper who had already led St George to two titles, Steve Edge captained the great Parramatta teams to their first three premierships, selected ahead of the likes of Ray Price and Mick Cronin. A fine hooker, he played in the first Origin match and overcame a detached retina in 1984 to play in that season's Grand Final loss, which doubled as his final game.

10. Dick Thornett—160 games (1963-71)

A former Rugby Union international and the brother of fellow Eels legend Ken, Dick Thornett was a champion forward in his own right with Parramatta during the 1960s. He toured with the 1963-64 Kangaroos, scoring during the 'Swinton Massacre', and played 14 Tests. The ball-playing backrower jointly held the club record for most tries in a game for nearly four decades after scoring four against Canterbury in 1968.

11. Ron Lynch—194 games (1961-71)

A hard-running and reliable defensive lock, Ron Lynch played 12 Tests and 19 interstate matches while at Parramatta. Country tough, 'Thirsty' was appointed captain by Ken Kearney in 1963 and guided the Eels through their first period of success. They did not sustain their success under Lynch but he was consistently one of their best for a decade.

12. Bob O'Reilly—216 games (1967-75, 1980-82)

A tough, no-nonsense prop known as 'Bear', Bob O'Reilly had two stints with the Eels and contributed strongly in both spells. The ball-playing bookend played 16 Tests, including the 1970 World Cup final, during his first stint at Parramatta and in his second stanza played in the club's first premiership triumph, where he was arguably the best on ground against Newtown.

13. Steve Ella—157 games (1979-88)

Known as 'The Zip Zip Man', Steve Ella was one of the most entertaining and brilliant players of the 1980s. A stunning attacking master, Ella played in all four of the Eels' premiership triumphs and led the competition in tryscoring in 1985. With 94 tries and 552 career points, he sits third on both lists, and he was named Dally M Centre of the Year three times. Ella played seven Origins and four Tests.

14. Nathan Cayless—259 games (1997-2010)

Parramatta's youngest and longest-serving captain, Nathan Cayless was a workhorse prop who is rated among the finest leaders of the NRL era. Tough and uncompromising, he played 39 Tests for New Zealand and captained the Eels to the '01 and '09 deciders. The honest bookend famously nailed a field goal to send a clash with Newcastle to golden point in 2008, and he skippered the Eels in over 200 games.

15. Jarryd Hayne—155 games (2006-13)

One of the most gifted players the Eels have ever had, the enigmatic Jarryd Hayne struggled with consistency but at his best was a genuine match-winner. The Dally M Rookie of the Year in 2006, Hayne nearly always excelled at rep level but in a tough era for the Eels his sublime brilliance was only seen in glimpses. His finest hour came in 2009, when his magical form took the Eels to an unlikely Grand Final berth as well as the Dally M Medal.

16. Peter Wynn—171 games (1979-1990)

A sizable and rangy forward, Peter Wynn overcame a series of injuries early in his career to feature strongly throughout the club's glory era of the 1980s. He took part in just 22 games in the Eels' first three premiership seasons but played in the Grand Final victories in '82 and '83. Wynn debuted for NSW in 1984 and was awarded the Dally M Lock of the Year in 1985, also debuting for Australia that season. He came off the bench in the '86 premiership win.

17. Jim Dymock—112 games (1996-2000)

The reigning Clive Churchill medallist when he joined the Eels after a prolonged legal battle with his former club, Canterbury, Jim Dymock enjoyed five fruitful seasons at the Eels where the club reached three preliminary finals. Dymock placed third in the Dally M Medal count in his first year with the Eels and his six Origin caps came at Parramatta.

18. Luke Burt—264 games (1999-2012)

The club's greatest try-scorer with 124, popular winger Luke Burt also ranks second on the club's pointscoring list with 1793. His hauls of 28 points against the Panthers in 2002 and the Raiders in 2005 are equal club records. Also a capable fullback or centre, the reliable Burt holds the premiership record for points by a left-footed goalkicker.

19. Paul Taylor—157 games (1981-89)

A genuine utility who could play anywhere on the field, Paul Taylor featured in five Grand Finals for the Eels in his first six seasons of top-grade football, coming off the bench in the '81 triumph and starting at fullback in the other four deciders. Though he never received the rep honours some of his teammates did, Taylor was a reliable custodian during the club's glory era.

20. Jason Smith—89 games (1996-2000)

A silky-skilled five-eighth/lock, premiership winner Jason Smith was lured from Canterbury at the height of the Super League War in a play that saw the Bulldogs pursue legal action. Smith was an international and Queensland rep throughout his Parramatta career and won the Dally M Lock of the Year gong in 1999.

PARRAMATTA EELS—GREATEST COACHES (1947-2013)

1. Jack Gibson—84 games (1981-83)
Still a revered figure at Parramatta, Team of the Century coach Jack Gibson won three of Parramatta's four premierships in his three years at the club. Gibson provided the Eels' first title after the club had spent 35 seasons in the premiership, famously declaring "Ding, dong, the witch is dead" after the triumph. The Eels went on to win again in 1982 and '83 under Gibson, and Parramatta is the last team to win three consecutive premierships. Champion Eels such as Peter Sterling and Mick Cronin speak in hushed tones about Gibson's ability to motivate as well as his tactical acumen. As was the case throughout his career, he did not stay long and took a year off after the '83 title before coaching Cronulla.

2. John Monie—149 games (1984-89)
Jack Gibson's replacement in 1984, John Monie became the only other Parramatta coach to taste premiership success when he coached the Eels to the 1986 title in what was the last game for Mick Cronin and Ray Price. In Monie's first season, Parramatta reached its fourth straight Grand Final but was outgunned by Canterbury in a dour affair. The Eels missed the decider in 1985 before winning in '86. Three missed finals series from 1987 onwards saw Monie replaced by Mick Cronin; Monie went to Wigan and achieved tremendous success.

3. Brian Smith—243 games (1997-2006)
A unique character, Brian Smith pulled the Eels out of a decade-long rut when he took over in 1997. Though significantly improving the team, he failed to bring a long-awaited fifth title. Having made his bones with Illawarra and then St George, Smith's signing was considered a coup for the Eels after 10 years without a finals appearance, and it proved so when Parramatta made the playoffs in his first six years at the helm, winning the minor premiership and playing in the Grand Final in 2001. The Eels again won the minor title in 2005 under Smith's tutelage before losing in the preliminary final—the fourth prelim defeat Smith endured at Parra. He left midway through the 2006 season after it was announced Michael Hagan would coach the club in 2007.

4. Ken Kearney—59 games (1962-64)
A St George legend credited with adding the steel and professionalism to the Dragons that led to their great title run, Ken Kearney joined Parramatta in 1962 a year after leading the Saints to a sixth straight premiership as a result of the club's policy of only

using captain-coaches. After the Eels had achieved nine wooden spoons and zero finals appearances in 15 seasons, Kearney led them to their first three finals series in his three seasons at the club before he moved to Western Suburbs.

5. Terry Fearnley—101 games (1976-79)

The gruff Eastern Suburbs prop forward made his first and most successful foray into premiership coaching with Parramatta, where in his first two seasons he took the Eels to their first two Grand Finals, 30 seasons after the club had debuted in the big league. Fearnley replaced Norm Provan in 1976 and went within a Neville Glover catch of the club's first premiership; the Eels returned to the decider a year later but lost it in a replay. His last two seasons saw finals appearances and he would go on to coach NSW, Australia and three other premiership clubs.

PARRAMATTA EELS—BEST DAYS (1947-2013)

1. September 27, 1981: Ding, dong, the witch is dead

Led by new coach Jack Gibson, Parramatta put to bed a 35-year premiership drought to win its first title. The star-studded Eels rolled over the top of Newtown 20-11. Brett Kenny scored a double but hulking prop Bob O'Reilly was the Eels' best. After the victory, Gibson uttered the immortal words: "Ding, dong, the witch is dead". Fans later burned down home ground Cumberland Oval in their jubilation.

2. September 28, 1986: Farewell 'Crow' and 'Mr Perpetual Motion'

Grand Final day 1986 was the end of an era for Parramatta, the final stand of its glory era. In what was a memorable farewell for Eels champions Mick Cronin and Ray Price, the club won its fourth title in six years, defeating Canterbury 4-2 in a try-less epic. Cronin kicked both goals and Peter Sterling was awarded the inaugural Clive Churchill Medal.

3. August 18, 1962: Finals at last

After 15 seasons and 10 wooden spoons, the recruitment of Ken Kearney as coach and Rugby Union convert Ken Thornett as player led Parramatta to its first finals series. The Eels went on an undefeated streak of nine games—including a win over heavyweights St George—to book a spot in the finals. Despite losing in their last four games, they ran fourth. The next week, they were eliminated by Wests 6-0.

4. September 25, 2009: Back at the dance
The incredible form of Jarryd Hayne put Parramatta in an unlikely Grand Final showdown against Melbourne. The Eels won seven on the trot to sneak into eighth place and then rolled through St George Illawarra and Gold Coast to set up a preliminary final clash with rivals Canterbury. Over 74,000 attended the most anticipated final in years, with the Eels triumphing 22-12.

5. September 25, 1983: The last hat-trick
In Jack Gibson's final season in charge of Parramatta, the Eels become the last team to win three straight premierships with a rousing 18-6 win over rivals Manly. Brett Kenny scored his third consecutive Grand Final double and was best afield in a dominant win; his second try, two minutes after the break, gave Parramatta an unassailable 18-0 lead.

PARRAMATTA EELS—WORST DAYS (1947-2013)

1. September 18, 1976: Neville's blunder
Parramatta's first Grand Final came in its 30th season, but it would be a forgettable day for the Eels faithful who had waited so long. The clash was locked at seven apiece when oranges were called but a John Peard penalty miss cost Parramatta the halftime lead. The Eels hit the front 10-7 through a Geoff Gerard try, but the boot of Graham Eadie had Manly leading inside the final 10. Parramatta had its chance to reclaim the lead with five minutes to play when winger Neville Glover dropped the ball with the line wide open. Eadie hit another penalty and Manly was crowned premier.

2. September 20, 1998: Clutching defeat from the jaws of victory
In arguably the greatest finals choke in premiership history, Parramatta led hated rivals Canterbury 18-2 with just 11 minutes remaining and a Grand Final berth in its grasp. Canterbury rallied late, though, and a Daryl Halligan sideline conversion levelled the scores. Parramatta fullback Paul Carige, in what would be his last NRL game, had an epic meltdown in extra-time as the Bulldogs cruised to a 32-20 win.

3. September 30, 2001: The unthinkable
Parramatta dominated the 2001 regular season: after opening the year 3-3, the Eels lost just once for the remainder of the season and then waltzed into the Grand Final with finals wins of 56-12 against New Zealand and 24-16 over defending premiers Brisbane. Heavy favourites in the decider against Newcastle, the Eels were stunned by an early Knights onslaught and trailed 0-24 at the break. The final score was a respectable 30-24 but Parramatta fans are still shocked at the brutality of the defeat.

4. June 13, 1960: A diabolical low
For its first 14 seasons Parramatta had been diabolical, claiming 10 wooden spoons. The club's low point arguably came during 1959-60, though, when it lost a record 19 straight matches in what remains the sixth-longest losing streak of all time. The streak lasted 11 months and culminated in a 44-14 loss to St George.

5. September 8, 2013: Another spoon
Parramatta had won 12 wooden spoons in its history but rarely had it spent as much as when it collected its 13th. The Eels had signed coach Ricky Stuart to a big-money deal but he could only deliver a last-placed finish before ditching the club to switch to Canberra. The Eels, who had been through seven coaches in eight years, became the first team in a decade to claim back-to-back spoons.

PENRITH PANTHERS—GREATEST PLAYERS (1967-2013)

1. Greg Alexander—228 games (1984-94, 1997-99)
Supremely gifted halfback/fullback Greg Alexander is almost unanimously regarded as the greatest Panther. Maligned earlier in his career for failing to measure up in big games, he virtually carried the club's hopes on his shoulders for a decade. Penrith rode the attacking genius's brilliance to a maiden Grand Final in 1990, and he was even more dominant in the Panthers' '91 premiership-winning campaign after taking over the captaincy. On the losing side in each of his six Origin appearances for NSW, Alexander nevertheless experienced several highlights on two Kangaroo Tours and in six Test outings for Australia. Dally M Rookie of the Year in '84, Player of the Year in '85, and Halfback of the Year on three occasions, Alexander won the club's Player of the Year gong twice. The tragic death of his younger brother and teammate Ben rocked Alexander and led to a two-year stint in Auckland, but he returned to finish his career at the club he had lifted to such dizzying heights in his prime.

2. Brad Fittler—119 games (1989-95)
Local product Brad Fittler played at Penrith only until the age of 23, but packed in a plethora of achievements during his seven seasons with the Panthers. The prodigiously talented centre, five-eighth or lock played 15 Origins and 21 Tests from the club—both Penrith records—and toured twice with the Kangaroos. He scored Penrith's first-ever Grand Final try as an 18-year-old in 1990 and was magnificent a year later as the Panthers broke through for a maiden title. Dally M Centre of the Year in 1992-93 and Lock of the Year in 1994, Fittler was also named the Panthers'

best player in '93, but left Super League-aligned Penrith and went on to cement his status as an all-time great with the Sydney Roosters.

3. Craig Gower—238 games (1996-2007)
A dominant presence at halfback or hooker, Craig Gower was Penrith's key player for a decade. A Super League representative star as an 18-year-old, the playmaker was predominantly utilised in the No.9 early in his career, making his Origin and Test debuts as a dummy-half in 1999. He settled as the Panthers' halfback and captain in 2002, and although he was denied an almost certain Dally M Medal by an RLPA boycott the following season, leading his team to a Grand Final triumph was ample compensation. A four-time Penrith Player of the Year, Gower finished with 18 Test appearances for Australia. Lamentable off-field incidents chequered his career and cost him the club captaincy in 2006, but his status as one of the Panthers' best ever is unquestioned.

4. Royce Simmons—237 games (1980-91)
Durable hooker Royce Simmons became Penrith's first Australian representative and ranks as one of the club's best-loved characters. Lacking the zip of most modern hookers, he negated that with toughness and determination to play 10 Tests and 10 Origins during the mid-1980s. Penrith's Player of the Year on four occasions, Simmons captained the club from 1983 to 1990, culminating in the club's maiden Grand Final appearance. Although he was replaced as skipper and spent time in reserve grade the following season, the veteran rake enjoyed one of the great farewells by scoring two tries in the Panthers' euphoric 19-12 Grand Final defeat of Canberra in 1991.

5. John Cartwright—188 games (1985-96)
John Cartwright was Penrith's dominant forward as the club powered into the 1990-91 Grand Finals—a rugged ball-player capable of turning a match with a brilliant offload or stinging defence. The 1989 NSW debutant toured with the 1990 Kangaroos following the Panthers' maiden Grand Final appearance. Dally M Second-rower of the Year in 1991-92 and Penrith's Player of the Year in the latter season, Cartwright played the last of his seven Tests and eight Origins in '92. He was a tower of strength for Penrith during the difficult years that followed its premiership success, assuming the captaincy and providing excellent leadership to complement his tough play in tight.

6. Luke Lewis—208 games (2001-12)
Blacktown junior Luke Lewis scored 18 tries as a 19-year-old three-quarter in Penrith's 2003 premiership season, earning a Kangaroo Tour call-up in the process. Despite making his NSW debut the following season, Lewis's career subsequently plateaued as the Panthers skidded down the ladder. But the ultra-versatile performer

surged back on to the representative scene in 2009 as a backrower, eventually playing 12 Tests and 11 Origins before departing Penrith in acrimonious circumstances at the end of 2012. The club's Player of the Year in 2010, Lewis succeeded Petero Civoniceva as captain but was controversially replaced due to his representative commitments.

7. Ryan Girdler—204 games (1993-2004)

Ryan Girdler was one of the great goalkickers and a brilliant attacking centre, becoming the first player in history to notch 1500 points and 100 tries in first grade. After a breakout 1997 Super League season that included winning the club's Player of the Year award, Girdler forced his way into the NSW and Australian sides in 1999—a year in which he racked up career-high totals of 229 points and 18 tries. He went on a representative record-breaking rampage in 2000, and while injuries affected the remaining years of his career, his experience was a key component of the Panthers' 2003 title triumph.

8. Rhys Wesser—177 games (1998-2008)

'Rhys Lightning' was a devastating ball-runner from fullback, with his 113 tries the most by a Penrith player. The Indigenous flyer set another club record with 19 tries in 2002 before topping the NRL with 25 the following season—an all-time record for a fullback—as the Panthers' Player of the Year (an award he claimed again in '06) in their surge to an unlikely premiership. One of the modern era's genuine crowd-pleasers, Wesser was unlucky not to represent Australia, although he played for Queensland in four Origins.

9. Mark Geyer—135 games (1986-92, 1998-2000)

The most damaging forward in the game during his all-too-brief heyday, local junior Mark Geyer is one of Penrith's most iconic players. The intimidating, dynamic second-rower toured with the 1990 Kangaroos after helping the Panthers to their first Grand Final, and was integral to the club's premiership breakthrough the following season despite a hefty suspension for a notorious Origin display. Geyer's tenure at the club unravelled in 1992 after he failed a drug test; ultimately he left Penrith, but he returned six years later and rounded out his career with a handy three-year stint in Panthers colours.

10. Tony Puletua—211 games (1997-2008)

Destructive second-rower Tony Puletua was a valuable weapon and wonderful clubman for Penrith who also earned 22 Test caps for New Zealand. Puletua starred during the Panthers' 2003 premiership-winning campaign—just reward for sticking by the club through leaner times. The well-respected powerhouse left for Super League at the end of 2008 after racking up the fifth-most first grade appearances in Penrith's history.

11. Steve Carter—242 games (1988-2001)

Despite competing with the likes of Chris Mortimer, Brad Fittler and Brad Izzard for the five-eighth role early in his career, Steve Carter was a vital member of Penrith's side during the halcyon days of the early 1990s, wearing the No.6 in the Panthers' 1991 Grand Final triumph and claiming the club's Player of the Year award that season. A NSW representative in 1992, the niggly, gritty and creative Carter broke Penrith's appearances record and captained the club for several seasons late in his career.

12. Brad Izzard—206 games (1982-92)

Brad Izzard burst on to the scene in 1982 as a 20-year-old wonder-boy, becoming Penrith's first NSW Origin player during a remarkable rookie season. Further representative honours did not eventuate for the robust centre/five-eighth, and he was pegged as an enigma with a poor attitude to training, but the burly Izzard was outstanding in the Panthers' rise to heavyweight status. He starred in the No.6 as the club reached its first Grand Final in 1990 before scoring a vital try off the bench in the '91 decider triumph—the same year he made a return for the Blues after a nine-year absence.

13. Trent Waterhouse—186 games (2002-11)

Unheralded lock Trent Waterhouse rocketed to prominence as a member of Penrith's 2003 Grand Final-winning outfit, gaining selection for the subsequent Kangaroo Tour. He debuted for NSW the following season and had made nine Test appearances by the end of 2005 before he fell off the representative radar. Waterhouse rediscovered his best form in 2009, winning Test and Origin recalls and the club's Player of the Year award before heading off to Super League as a 30-year-old two years later.

14. Luke Priddis—162 games (2002-08)

Well-travelled hooker Luke Priddis enjoyed the greatest highlights of his career during a seven-season stay at Penrith, producing a masterly Churchill Medal-winning performance in the 2003 Grand Final victory and making his sole Test appearance for Australia two years later. Durable, creative and hardworking, Priddis rates as one of the most astute purchases in Panthers history. He shared the club's 2005 Player of the Year award with Craig Gower.

15. Preston Campbell—97 games (2002-06)

Former Cronulla Dally M Medal winner Preston Campbell resurrected his career in spectacular fashion at Penrith in 2003, scoring 13 tries and 164 points as a linchpin of its stirring title triumph. Extremely versatile, the courageous Campbell played exclusively in the halves during his four seasons with the Panthers, scoring 43 tries and creating many more with his speed and creative ball-playing before becoming a foundation Gold Coast Titan. Regularly overlooked by NSW selectors, Campbell made the first of three appearances for Country Origin in 2005.

16. Luke Rooney—140 games (2001-08)

Tall, fast and strong, winger Luke Rooney was a potent try-scorer in eight seasons of first grade for Penrith, scoring 17 tries during the club's 2003 premiership season—including a memorable double in the Grand Final. He scored six tries in six Tests in 2004-05, featuring in NSW's series victories in each of those seasons. His career stalled in ensuing seasons, but Rooney sent a reminder of his class with a four-try haul and a hat-trick late in 2008 before switching to Rugby Union.

17. Petero Civoniceva—74 games (2008-11)

Brisbane great Petero Civoniceva was 31 when he joined Penrith, but provided tremendous value during four seasons as Panthers captain. Dally M Prop of the Year and club Player of the Year in his first year at the foot of the mountains, Civoniceva played 15 Tests and 10 Origins while a Panther. His leadership was as important as his front-row play, and he guided the club to its first finals series in six years in 2010, helping the likes of Tim Grant and Sam McKendry develop into representative-quality props.

18. Michael Jennings—122 games (2007-12)

Dazzling centre Michael Jennings' tenure at Penrith was sullied by his repeated off-field indiscretions—which eventually led to his departure to the Sydney Roosters—but he remains one of the Panthers' finest attacking players and most prolific try-scorers. Penrith's Player of the Year in a stunning 2007 rookie year, Jennings was the club's top try-scorer in his first three seasons and made his Test and Origin debuts in 2009. He scored 71 tries in just 122 games for the Panthers.

19. Col van der Voort—119 games (1986-94)

Ill-timed injuries robbed luckless lock Col van der Voort of higher representative honours, but he remains one of the Penrith club's favourite sons. The tyro's form was a major factor in the Panthers' climb up the ladder in the late 1980s—he was named the club's Player of the Year in '89—and featured in their historic 1990-91 Grand Final appearances. A City Origin representative in 1991-92, van der Voort was forced to withdraw from the NSW side in the former season; injuries forced his retirement at the age of 29 in 1994.

20. Tim Sheens—177 games (1973-82)

Better known as one of the all-time great coaches, Tim Sheens was a skilful, rugged forward and a tremendous Penrith clubman. He established a club record of 258 games in all grades, including a then record 177 games in a decade of first grade. A rare constant during a tough period for the vastly underachieving Panthers, the 1974 Player of the Year regularly captained the side in the latter seasons of his career before coaching the club to a historic finals appearance in 1985.

PENRITH PANTHERS—GREATEST COACHES (1967-2013)

1. Phil Gould—109 games (1990-94)
Phil Gould began his first grade playing career with Penrith in 1976 and returned to the club as coach after falling out with the Bulldogs, whom he had steered to the 1988 premiership. A master motivator and brilliant strategist, 'Gus' harnessed the Panthers' raw array of talent and guided them to a maiden Grand Final appearance in his first season. A year later, the former laughing-stock of the competition had a minor premiership and its first title in the clubhouse—largely thanks to Gould's influence. His empire at the Panthers crumbled in '92 following Ben Alexander's tragic death and the turbulent departure of star forward Mark Geyer; the coach eventually left before the end of the '94 season, but he retains legendary status at the club and returned as general manager in 2011. Gould coached NSW to three straight series wins while he was at Penrith.

2. John Lang—126 games (2002-06)
Coaching veteran John Lang inherited a Penrith outfit that had just collected a wooden spoon, but delivered the club its second premiership after just two seasons in charge. With few genuine stars to work with initially, he moulded a squad predominantly made up of promising youngsters and largely unheralded players from rival clubs into a committed, exciting unit. After just seven wins and a 12th-place finish in his first season, Lang and the Panthers surged to a minor premiership and upset Grand Final triumph in 2003. They finished in the top four and reached the preliminary final in their title defence, but Lang departed at the end of 2006 after two disappointing campaigns.

3. Tim Sheens—98 games (1984-87)
Former Penrith stalwart forward Tim Sheens is the man credited with belatedly turning the Panthers into a competitive force after they spent their first 17 seasons as easybeats and high-priced flops. He led the Panthers to a record 12 wins and seventh-place finish at his first attempt, collecting Dally M Coach of the Year honours, and helped create history in 1985 when the club beat Manly in a fifth-place playoff to qualify for its first finals series. A late season slump saw the Panthers fade to eighth in '86, while a dreadful '87 campaign netted just six wins before Sheens left to create a dynasty at Canberra.

4. Royce Simmons—177 games (1994-2001)

Club legend Royce Simmons took over late in 1994 after his former coach, Phil Gould, quit the club. The popular knockabout, who had gained experience with Hull FC, became Penrith's longest-serving coach, beating Bob Boland's record by 67 games. The Panthers enjoyed little tangible success under Simmons, but he took a side that perennially had trouble recruiting top-line talent to finals appearances in 1997 and 2000. He was shown the door after the '01 wooden-spoon season, but later found success as an assistant to another former Penrith mentor, Tim Sheens, at the Wests Tigers.

5. Ron Willey—47 games (1988-89)

A double premiership-winning coach at Manly, hard-nosed Ron Willey was controversially handed the reins at Penrith over lower-grade coach Graham Murray, but helped establish the Panthers as premiership contenders for the first time in their history as he guided them to a then club-record 15 wins in a 1988 season that ended with a fifth-place playoff loss to Balmain. Penrith extended that mark under Willey in '89, winning 16 of 22 regular season games to land in second spot before exiting the finals via back-to-back losses. Despite the unprecedented results, Willey was dumped by the club after a series of contentious team selections during the Panthers' disappointing finals campaign.

PENRITH PANTHERS—BEST DAYS (1967-2013)

1. September 22, 1991: Premiership success at last

Penrith's long-awaited title breakthrough came in its 25th season courtesy of a gripping 19-12 Grand Final defeat of keen rivals Canberra. The minor premiers trailed by six at halftime but rallied in the second half to down the two-time champs. Retiring stalwart Royce Simmons scored the first and last tries of the match before promising to have a beer with everyone; Brad Izzard finished off superb play by Mark Geyer (who spent 10 minutes in the sin bin during the match) and Brad Fittler to level the scores; and skipper Greg Alexander nailed a long-range field goal and a sideline conversion in the latter stages to seal the result before hoisting the Winfield Cup trophy.

2. October 5, 2003: Panthers defy odds to claim second title

The unfancied Panthers—wooden spooners just two seasons earlier—surged to take out the minor premiership in 2003 but started the Grand Final against defending premiers the Sydney Roosters as rank outsiders. With the scores tied 6-all during the second half, lock Scott Sattler's try-saving cover tackle on runaway Roosters winger Todd Byrne changed the complexion of the contest and earned him a place in Grand Final folklore. Man-of-the-match Luke Priddis scored a try and set up another for Luke Rooney to propel the Panthers to an 18-6 upset.

3. September 9, 1990: Extra-time upset garners maiden Grand Final appearance
A week after notching their maiden finals win with an upset of Brisbane, the Panthers truly came of age with a sensational major semi defeat of defending and minor premiers Canberra at a wet SFS. The scores were locked at 12-all after 80 minutes, but Penrith romped home 30-12 in extra-time to book the first Grand Final berth in the club's history. Greg Alexander racked up 22 points from two tries—the first a mesmerising effort in conjunction with 18-year-old Brad Fittler—and seven goals, putting to rest long-held reservations over the halfback genius' big-match temperament.

4. September 3, 1985: Playoff victory confirms long-awaited finals series appearance
Penrith's first 18 seasons brought nothing in the way of success, but 1985 was a watershed for the long-suffering club. The Panthers finished the regular season equal fifth with Manly, forcing a midweek playoff for the last finals spot. In a gripping Tuesday-nighter at the SCG, they snatched a history-making 10-7 victory after Greg Alexander booted two pressure goals in extra-time. The club crashed back to reality with a 38-6 pummelling at the hands of Parramatta in the minor preliminary semi-final four days later, but had achieved a significant milestone by qualifying for its maiden finals series.

5. September 2, 1990: First finals victory courtesy of Broncos boilover
The Panthers became established as one of the strongest sides in the competition during the late 1980s, but their ordinary finals performances meant they had failed to completely shed the derisive 'Chocolate Soldiers' tag. They went into the major preliminary semi-final in 1990 against star-studded finals debutants Brisbane as underdogs, but pulled off a convincing 26-16 upset at the SFS for the club's maiden finals win. Brad Izzard played all over opposing five-eighth Kevin Walters to score a powerful double, while teenage centre Brad Fittler fired a brilliant long pass for winger Alan McIndoe to touch down in the momentous victory.

PENRITH PANTHERS—WORST DAYS (1967-2013)

1. June 21, 1992: Ben Alexander tragically killed
The euphoria of Penrith's maiden Grand Final triumph nine months earlier was shattered midway through the 1992 season when 20-year-old half/hooker Ben Alexander—a veteran of 36 first grade games and brother of captain Greg—was killed in a car accident after a celebration to present the players with their premiership blazers. The tragedy left the district heartbroken, and the club took several years to recover.

2. May 28, 1978: John Farragher left a quadriplegic
In one of the most harrowing incidents witnessed in a premiership match, a scrum collapsed during a clash between Penrith and Newtown at Henson Park, dislocating Panthers prop John Farragher's neck and damaging his spinal cord. Playing in his seventh game after joining the club from Gilgandra, the young forward was left a quadriplegic by the freak accident. The Rugby League community rallied around Farragher, whose courageous disposition in the face of his enormous setback has been an inspiration in the decades since. His son Jake played for Cronulla in the National Youth Competition in 2008.

3. July 18, 1994: Gould quits as coach
The Panthers' rapid decline in the wake of their 1991 premiership success culminated in coach Phil Gould quitting the club six weeks before the end of the '94 season. Gould, who had guided Penrith to unprecedented success, had been infamously banished from the sideline by referee Bill Harrigan during a heavy defeat to Cronulla a week earlier. He resigned a day after the 10th-placed Panthers' narrow win over the lowly Gold Coast, and subsequently linked with Eastern Suburbs. Former captain Royce Simmons stepped into a caretaker role and stayed on as coach for the following seven seasons.

4. July 29, 1973: Panthers concede record score against Manly
The Panthers were the whipping boys of the 1970s, and their on-field performances hit their lowest ebb late in the '73 season. Playing at home, Penrith was crushed 70-7 by defending premiers Manly. The Sea Eagles ran 14 tries past the hapless Panthers, who recorded the biggest first grade losing margin in 36 years and the third-most points conceded of all time. The club finished with its first wooden spoon after losing its remaining three games.

5. September 18, 2010: Watershed season ends with semi-final whimper
After a six-year finals drought, Penrith finished the 2010 regular season in second spot, but it was upset 24-22 at home by seventh-placed Canberra in the qualifying final before making a straight-sets exit from the playoffs via a 34-12 loss to the Sydney Roosters. Thwarted by a heavy injury toll, the Panthers did not land on the scoreboard until the final 20 minutes of the match and offered little resistance to the rampant Roosters. The club is yet to qualify for another finals series.

SOUTH QUEENSLAND CRUSHERS—GREATEST PLAYERS (1995-97)

1. Trevor Gillmeister—41 games (1995-96)
Veteran hitman Trevor Gillmeister scored the Crushers' first try, took over the captaincy in just their third match and missed only two of the club's games in 1995-96. He enjoyed the crowning achievements of a fantastic career while with the Crushers, leading Queensland to an improbable series clean sweep and making his Test debut for Australia at the age of 31 in 1995.

2. Craig Teevan—58 games (1995-97)
Miles ahead on the Crushers' all-time appearances register, hooker/half Craig Teevan missed just seven games during the club's three-year existence and was one of the previously unheralded heroes of Queensland's 1995 Origin series triumph. Teevan was installed as captain in 1997 following the retirement of Gillmeister.

3. Brett Horsnell—38 games (1995-96)
An outstanding prospect at the Gold Coast whose career never really kicked on, Brett Horsnell was a fine backrow servant during two seasons for the Crushers. A centre or five-eighth early in his career, Horsnell played all 22 games of the Crushers' debut campaign as a starting second-rower or lock before making 16 appearances the following season ahead of a move to Parramatta.

4. Grant Young—33 games (1995-96)
Grant Young was a massive, hard-hitting prop who used his consistent performances in the Crushers' first two seasons as a springboard to New Zealand Test selection. After playing in all but two of the Crushers' games in 1996, Young was a front-row starter in each of the Kiwis' five post-season Tests against Papua New Guinea and Great Britain. His career stalled after joining Super League-aligned Auckland in '97.

5. Mark Hohn—22 games (1995)
A Test debutant the previous season, long-serving Brisbane forward Mark Hohn played all 22 matches of the Crushers' debut campaign. The two-time Grand Final winner was one of the few members of Queensland's '95 Origin triumph with significant previous experience, coming off the bench in all three matches of the series boilover. Hohn, a Test player in '94, retired at the end of the season.

6. Terry Cook—25 games (1995-96)
Former Gold Coast centre/backrower Terry Cook played 18 games for the Crushers in 1995 and performed a handy role in the no-name Queensland side's series success that season, coming off the bench in all three games and earning a treasured niche in Origin folklore. The tall forward's '96 season garnered just seven first grade appearances.

7. Travis Norton—33 games (1995-96)
A future Queensland Origin rep and Cowboys Grand Final skipper, Travis Norton began his first grade career with the fledgling Crushers. The versatile and creative youngster, who debuted at the age of 18, made starts at five-eighth, centre, wing and fullback during his two seasons at South Queensland, but became better known as a ball-playing lock.

8. Clinton O'Brien—30 games (1996-97)
Front-row hardhead Clinton O'Brien, who joined the club after three years at Easts, was especially impressive during the Crushers' 1997 campaign, playing 17 first grade games. He won a call-up to the Queensland Origin side for two matches of that year's series and went on to win a premiership at Newcastle in 2001.

9. Jason Hudson—39 games (1996-97)
Jason Hudson played in all but four of the Crushers' games in the 1996-97 seasons to climb to third on the club's all-time appearances register. Mixing starts at centre, wing and five-eighth in '96, Hudson played exclusively on the flank the following season and led the Crushers with nine tries in 21 games. His 11 career tries is a Crushers record, albeit a modest one.

10. Clinton Schifcofske—23 games (1996-97)
Clinton Schifcofske overcame a suspension for returning a positive steroids test as a Crushers rookie to set records for most points in a career (108), season (94) and match (18)—the latter in the club's swansong, a stunning 39-18 upset of Western Suburbs in 1997. The elusive fullback/winger went on to represent Queensland and became one of the greatest point-scorers in premiership history.

SOUTH SYDNEY RABBITOHS—GREATEST PLAYERS (1908-2013)

1. Clive Churchill—157 games (1947-58)
Regarded by many as the greatest ever to play the game, Clive Churchill played his 12-year premiership career with Souths. The Team of the Century fullback, an Immortal and the man honoured in the Grand Final man-of-the-match medal, Churchill was a once-in-a-lifetime player. A daring fullback, he excelled at every facet of the game. He won five premierships with the Rabbitohs and played an incredible 99 straight representative games. In a career chock-full of highlights, the play that arguably summed up Churchill's equal-parts brilliance and toughness was his conversion from the sideline with a broken arm in 1955 that kept the Rabbitohs' unlikely premiership dream alive. His nickname, 'The Little Master', says it all.

2. Harold Horder—86 games (1912-19, 1924)
Known simply as 'The Wonder Winger', Harold Horder helped establish Rugby League as the most popular code in NSW during his career with his amazing deeds. A fabulous try-scorer who crossed for 102 in just 86 matches with the cardinal and myrtle, Horder signalled his brilliance on debut with a spectacular length-of-the-field try. His tryscoring potency was equally prevalent on the 1921-22 Kangaroo Tour and in interstate football; he crossed 11 times in 13 Tests. The champion winger won two titles with Souths (and another two with Norths) and was an unlucky omission from the ARL Team of the Century.

3. Ron Coote—148 games (1964-71)
A magnificent backrow forward who was known as 'The Prince of Locks', Ron Coote was equally effective in both attack and defence. A devastating runner and a master cover defender, Coote was a legitimate match-winner. He won four premierships with the Rabbitohs and was a regular in NSW and Australian teams. An ARL Hall of Fame inductee, Coote was the best player in the premiership in 1968-69, winning the EE Christensen-NSW Player of the Year doubles in both seasons. His departure to Easts in 1972 contributed significantly to Souths' steady decline.

4. John Sattler—195 games (1963-72)
Etched into the fabric of Rugby League through his courageous act of playing most of the 1970 Grand Final with a shattered jaw, John Sattler was central to the rise of South Sydney in the 1960s. He skippered the Bunnies to five Grand Finals, winning four premierships. Sattler rose to the position of Australian Test captain, with the firebrand's leadership style one of example rather than talk.

5. Howard Hallett—155 games (1909-24)
Rugby League's first superstar fullback, Howard Hallett rated among South Sydney's best during the club's infant days. Extremely durable, Hallett played 16 seasons, winning premierships in 1909, '14 and '18. Such was Hallett's stardom in the 1910s that he was awarded a silver belt to signify him as the champion player of the premiership. Hallett played six Tests for Australia before World War I stymied his rep ambitions.

6. George Treweek—118 games (1926-34)
One of the finest attacking second-rowers the game has known, George Treweek was South Sydney's star during the club's domination of the premiership during the 1920s and early 1930s. He played in six title wins in his first seven years with the club, winning plenty of clashes with his ability to find the try-line. Treweek played 22 times for NSW and seven times for Australia, and was named among the code's 100 greatest in 2008.

7. John O'Neill—150 games (1965-71, 1975)
A rugged front-row forward who won an astonishing six premierships and played in nine Grand Finals with Souths and Manly during his 11-year career, 'Lurch' was a devastating defender who punished like few before or since. O'Neill played 10 Tests for Australia and was posthumously named in the ARL's 100 greatest in 2008.

8. Bob McCarthy—211 games (1963-75, 1978)
The prototype of today's edge-running second-rower, Bob McCarthy was as unique as he was brilliant when he starred for South Sydney for the best part of 15 years. Burly and fast, McCarthy changed the way second-rowers played. He scored 100 tries for Souths, becoming just the second forward to achieve the feat in premiership history. McCarthy won three premierships with the club, scoring a memorable intercept try in the 1967 Grand Final, and played 15 Tests for Australia. He remained Souths' most-capped player at the end of 2013.

9. Eric Simms—206 games (1965-75)
Such an incredible kicker that the field goal was reduced in value from two points to one almost entirely because of his proficiency, Eric Simms remains one of South Sydney's favourite sons. The long-time pointscoring record holder after tallying 1841 in his career, Simms' boot was the difference for the Bunnies on many occasions. He slotted the winning goal in the 1967 decider four minutes from time, and his accuracy was central to triumphs in 1968 and '71. Simms was the leading point-scorer in the premiership from 1967 to 1970 (including a then premiership-record 265 in 1969) while his kicking ability was also on show for Australia on eight occasions: he booted 37 goals in the '68 and '70 World Cup wins.

10. Greg Inglis—60 games (2011-13)
A sensational athlete who landed at South Sydney after the Melbourne Storm salary-cap scandal, star fullback Greg Inglis was instrumental in ending South Sydney's horror run of over two decades with just a single finals appearance. He featured for Queensland and Australia throughout his time at Souths, winning the 2013 Dally M Fullback of the Year and scoring 34 tries in 60 outings in the red and green as the club reached back-to-back preliminary finals.

11. Benny Wearing—172 games (1921-33)
A fabulous tryscoring winger and one of the most popular players of the 1920s, Benny Wearing played only one Test but was rated by most as one of the finest players of the era. His 144 tries remained a club record for 80 years and he won seven premierships with Souths. In his only Test, Wearing scored two tries and 12 points; his constant snubbing is one of Rugby League's great mysteries. He scored 836 first grade points.

12. Billy Cann—75 games (1908-16)
A beautiful backrow forward in the game's infant days, Billy Cann shaped the role of the lock in the 13-man code. Creative yet tough, he was one of the finest players during Rugby League's early stages. Cann toured with the 1908-09 and '11-12 Kangaroos and played in South Sydney's premiership wins in 1909 and '14.

13. Jack Rayner—194 games (1946-57)
Relentless backrower Jack Rayner was held in such high esteem at South Sydney during his time with the Rabbitohs that he was preferred as club captain ahead of Test skipper Clive Churchill. No-nonsense, tough and as honest as the day is long, Rayner captain-coached the Rabbitohs to five premierships during his decorated career. he skippered Souths for 10 of his 12 years at the club and played five Tests for Australia.

14. Alf Blair—167 games (1917-30)
One of the stars of South Sydney's great team during the 1920s, Alf 'Smacker' Blair is one of the greatest captains and finest leaders the club has produced. A tough yet skilful and intelligent five-eighth—think Brian 'Poppa' Clay—Blair captained Souths to four premierships. He played a solitary Test in 1924.

15. Denis Pittard—120 games (1968-73)
A two-time Rothmans Medal winner in his six years with South Sydney, champion five-eighth Denis Pittard won three premierships with the Bunnies. A darting, running type, he was a key member of the great Souths team of the late 1960s and early 1970s. Pittard played five Tests for Australia and added two *Sun Herald* Best and Fairest awards in 1972-73 to follow his Rothmans Medal wins in 1969 and '71.

16. Bernie Purcell—173 games (1949-60)
One of the game's great goalkicking forwards, Bernie Purcell featured in five Grand Finals in his first seven seasons, winning four premierships. He played just one Test but it was a beauty, turning out in the famous 5-2 win in 1950 that brought the Ashes back to Australia for the first time in 30 years. The first forward to score 1000 points, Purcell booted the winning goal in the 1955 Grand Final to give the Bunnies a 12-11 win over Newtown.

17. Johnny Graves—77 games (1947-52)
A superstar winger recruited from Maitland after starring against the touring English side, John 'Whacka' Graves shone in South Sydney's premiership success during the early 1950s, scoring in three straight deciders. Among his 79 tries in just 77 games, he holds the record for most tries in a Grand Final, with four in the 1951 thumping of Manly. Graves is tied for the Souths record for most tries in a game with five, and holds the record for most points in a match by a Rabbitoh with 29.

18. Ian Moir—110 games (1952-58)
A scintillating speed merchant who scored an incredible 105 tries in just 110 outings for South Sydney, Ian Moir was rated as one of the game's premier outside backs in the 1950s. He scored a hat-trick in the 1953 Grand Final and also scored in both the '54 and '55 decider wins. Moir played 12 Tests for Australia, and his five tries against Parramatta in 1957 remains tied for the club record.

19. Bob Grant—135 games (1966-75)
An underrated halfback who played in four Grand Finals and won three titles with the Rabbitohs, Bob Grant's crowning hour came in the 1970 decider when he scored two tries in a match-winning hand. While he played just two Tests, he was an integral part of South Sydney's success in its last great glory era. He was named *Rugby League Week*'s Player of the Year in 1971.

20. Nathan Merritt—206 games (2002-03, 2006-13)
Poised to pass Benny Wearing's long-standing South Sydney tryscoring record, dashing winger Nathan Merritt could finish like few others. He topped South Sydney's tryscoring tally from 2006 to 2013 bar one season. While his rep career has been limited to one Origin appearance for NSW, only 13 players in the history of the game have scored more hat-tricks.

SOUTH SYDNEY RABBITOHS—GREATEST COACHES (1908-2013)

1. Charlie Lynch—165 games (1928-34, 1937-40)
One of the first great coaches, Charlie Lynch guided Souths to premierships in four of his first five seasons in charge. Joining the club in 1928, he learnt his craft under the great 'Ash' Hennessy and was an apostle of attacking football. With the likes of Benny Wearing at his disposal, it was the perfect fit. Souths won premierships in 1928-29 and 1931-32. After two semi-final exits, Lynch left at the end of the 1934 season but returned in 1937. Souths finished runners-up in 1939 but Lynch could not rediscover the magic that had been central to such a brilliant period a decade earlier.

2. Jack Rayner—162 games (1950-57)
South Sydney's captain-coach for eight years throughout its second great glory era, Jack Rayner was a tough and respected second-rower. He took over from Dave Watson in 1950 and the Rabbitohs won five premierships in six years, with Rayner, among others, believing Souths were robbed by referee George Bishop in the 1952 decider. Such was his standing as a leader that he was chosen ahead of Clive Churchill for leadership honours and as the coach of the 'South Sydney Dream Team' named in 2004. His strike rate of 70.4 per cent sits first among all Souths coaches with 50-plus games. After retiring in 1957, Rayner coached Parramatta for four seasons.

3. Clive Churchill—225 games (1958, 1967-75)
An Immortal considered by many as the greatest player Rugby League has known, Clive Churchill won four premierships as coach of the club for which he played so valiantly. Appointed captain-coach in 1958 as Jack Rayner's replacement, Churchill lasted just one year in the role after Souths missed the finals and a financial dispute with the club. He returned in 1967 and guided the Rabbitohs through their last great era, winning four titles in his first five seasons with a host of great players at his disposal. He resigned in 1975 after a 5-12 start that would eventually lead to the club's first wooden spoon since 1962.

4. Howard Hallett—30 games (1925-26)
One of South Sydney's first legitimate superstars, Howard Hallett took the coaching reins at the Rabbitohs in 1925 after a 15-year playing career. In his two seasons at the helm he lost just two games while winning two premierships. South Sydney's titles in 1925-26 started a glory era during which the club won seven titles in eight years. Hallett retired from the game after the '26 premiership triumph.

5. Arthur Hennessy—30 games (1908, 1918, 1946)
Considered one of the founding fathers of the game, Arthur 'Ash' Hennessy was Australia's first Test captain and the captain-coach of South Sydney in the first premiership season. His no-kicking policy was instrumental in Souths winning the first premiership, with their running style leading to the label 'The Pride of the League'. As a non-playing coach in 1918, he led Souths to their fourth premiership. He returned in 1946—an incredible 28 years after last coaching in the premiership—but the Rabbitohs finished with the wooden spoon.

SOUTH SYDNEY RABBITOHS—BEST DAYS (1908-2013)

1. September 17, 1955: A Redfern miracle
In one of the great comebacks in premiership history, South Sydney won its last 11 matches to go from last to first and win an unlikely fifth title in six years. In one game Clive Churchill kicked the winning goal from the sideline with a broken arm, while Souths won the Grand Final 12-11 over Newtown after trailing until the final six minutes.

2. September 19, 1970: Captain courageous
In what is widely regarded as the most courageous act on a Rugby League field ever, Souths captain John Sattler played most of the 1970 Grand Final with a shattered jaw to lead the club to its third win in four years. Souths beat Manly 23-12 and Sattler entered Rugby League lore for his heroics.

3. July 6, 2001: The Rabbitohs return
After being excluded from the competition for two years, the Rabbitohs won their appeal against the NRL in the Supreme Court and were readmitted to the premiership. Two marches of over 80,000 people led by George Piggins helped the Bunnies secure an unlikely win over the League.

4. September 14, 1929: Five straight
South Sydney became the first team to win five premierships in a row with a 30-10 win over Newtown. Alf Blair and Reg Williams both scored hat-tricks as the two-loss Rabbitohs routed the Bluebags. Blair's performance was regarded as the greatest of his long and illustrious career.

5. September 17, 1967: Bobby's intercept
Souths started their third glory era with a Grand Final win over Canterbury, the team that had eliminated St George after 11 straight premierships. A length-of-the-field Bob McCarthy intercept just before halftime turned the match in the Rabbitohs' favour, while an Eric Simms penalty goal with five minutes remaining handed them a gripping 12-10 win.

SOUTH SYDNEY RABBITOHS—WORST DAYS (1908-2013)

1. October 15, 1999: Cut
After 92 consecutive seasons in the premiership, South Sydney was axed from the competition by the NRL after failing to meet the League's controversial criteria for inclusion. After a two-year legal battle Souths won reinstatement, but not after a hefty dent to their finances and the loss of their entire roster.

2. September 20, 1952: Robbed
In one of the most controversial Grand Finals ever played, South Sydney lost to Western Suburbs 22-12 in the club's only decider defeat between 1950 and 1955. The Bunnies had a number of notable calls go against them, with captain-coach Jack Rayner claiming referee George Bishop had bet against the Rabbitohs.

3. September 20, 1969: Lay-down Tigers
In what is regarded as the greatest upset in premiership history, Balmain stunned Souths 11-2 in the 1969 Grand Final. Souths won two premierships apiece either side of the '69 Grand Final but could not beat a Balmain team who continually stopped Souths' momentum by feigning injury.

4. August 17, 1946: Winless
The most successful team in the premiership with 11 titles, Souths were forced to endure a winless season in 1946 as they claimed their second consecutive wooden spoon. They won just one game across 1945-46 and finished the latter year with a 19-7 defeat to hated rivals Easts.

5. August 26, 1990: The rot sets in
A year after winning the minor premiership and reaching the preliminary final, Souths won just two games in 1990 and claimed the wooden spoon. They were touched up 48-0 by Canberra in the final round. The rot had set in, with Souths unable to reach another finals series until 2007.

ST GEORGE DRAGONS—GREATEST PLAYERS (1921-99)

1. Johnny Raper—180 games (1959-69)
The Australian Team of the Century lock and one of the four original Immortals, Johnny Raper was arguably the finest player in the greatest club side in history. He joined the Dragons from Newtown in 1959, immediately establishing a reputation as a brilliant attacking player and peerless cover defender, and played in the last eight of the club's 11 straight Grand Final victories. Following Ian Walsh's retirement, Raper assumed the club captaincy in 1968 and captain-coached the Saints in his farewell '69 season, leading his beloved side to the finals both years. A celebrated larrikin and one of the code's best-loved characters, 'Chook's' glittering 39-Test career encompassed three Kangaroo Tours and a World Cup triumph as skipper. He was named St George's Clubman of the Century by the Men of League in 2008.

2. Reg Gasnier—125 games (1959-67)
Dubbed 'Puff, the Magic Dragon', Reg Gasnier is widely regarded as the greatest centre in the game's history, and is a legend among an all-star St George line-up. The Immortal 'Gaz' missed the Grand Final in his stellar 1959 rookie year, but starred in the ensuing six deciders before again being ruled out in '66. The premiership's top try-scorer in 1960 and '64, his outrageous career figures of 127 tries in 125 games are rarely discussed when summarising his greatness, such was the incomparably gifted three-quarter's all-round brilliance. He represented Australia in 39 Tests (crossing for 28 tries) and captained the last of his three Kangaroo Tours in 1967-68, where a leg injury prematurely ended his career at the age of 27. Gasnier was named in Australia's Team of the Century in 2008.

3. Graeme Langlands—227 games (1963-76)
Wollongong's Graeme 'Changa' Langlands was astutely recruited by St George in 1963, and after initially making his way as a centre, he became established as one of the code's greatest-ever fullbacks. A prolific point-scorer—his 1554 points is a Dragons club record—Langlands' attacking genius in the three-quarter line or from the back was legendary. He played in the last four of the Saints' world record streak of premierships and with Billy Smith was the last remnant of that unparalleled side, captaining the club to the 1971 Grand Final and captain-coaching it for the following five seasons. Langlands infamously led the Dragons to a record Grand Final defeat to Easts in 1975, wearing conspicuous white boots and producing the worst performance of his decorated career after a painkilling injection rendered him a passenger. Injury

forced his retirement early in '76 but the setbacks could not diminish his colossal legacy. He played 45 Tests for Australia—15 as captain—and led the 1973 Kangaroo Tour. Granted Immortal status in 1999 (it was rumoured he was close to being an original inductee), Langlands was named as a reserve in Australia's Team of the Century in 2008.

4. Norm Provan—256 games (1951-65)

Norm Provan's record of 10 straight Grand Final wins created an icon, and is unlikely ever to be matched. The towering second-rower's role in St George's world-record run cannot be understated. He starred in the 1956-61 deciders before captain-coaching the Dragons to four premierships from 1962 to 1965. A powerful defender and formidable ball-runner, 'Sticks' scored 64 tries in his club-record 256 games (a then premiership-appearances record) for the Saints. He played 18 Tests for Australia from 1954 to 1960, while proof his individual ability matched his extraordinary team achievements came in the form of his naming as a second-rower in the Australian Team of the Century in 2008. The famous 'Gladiators' photo of Provan and rival Wests captain Arthur Summons after the 1963 Grand Final was immortalised on the premiership trophy in 1982.

5. Ken Kearney—156 games (1952-61)

Few individuals had as big an impact on St George's record run of premierships as hooker Ken 'Killer' Kearney. The former Wallaby honed his craft in the professional code with English club Leeds before joining the Dragons in 1952 and playing the first of 31 consecutive Test matches for Australia. He toured twice with the Kangaroos, including in 1956-57 as captain-coach. Tough hooker Kearney captain-coached the Saints in 1954-55 before skippering them to Grand Final success in '56 (Norm Tipping was coach). He resumed in the captain-coach role in 1957 and led the club to five more premierships, although injury restricted him to the role of non-playing coach for the 1961 Grand Final, after which he retired as a player and coached Parramatta to its first finals series the following season. A giant of the code, Kearney was named as one of Australia's 100 greatest players in 2008.

6. Ian Walsh—94 games (1962-67)

In the top bracket of the code's greatest-ever hookers and captains, Test rake Ian Walsh joined St George in 1962 following Ken Kearney's retirement. 'Abdul' featured in four Grand Final victories, in 1962-63 and 1965-66 (he missed the '64 decider through injury)—the last as captain-coach. He made 17 of his 25 Test appearances while at the club, including 10 as captain, and embarked on his second Kangaroo Tour in 1963. The highly respected Walsh, a master of the fine art of hooker play in a tough era, retired after the Saints' streak ended in 1967 under his leadership. He was named in the Team of the 1960s in 2006 and the NSW Country Team of the Century in '08, and was a controversial omission from Australia's Team of the Century.

7. Billy Smith—234 games (1963-77)

A centre in St George's 1963-65 Grand Final wins, Billy Smith rates as one of the all-time great halfbacks, wearing the No.7 in the last of the Dragons' 11 straight premierships in '66. A rugged, tenacious linchpin and an attacking livewire, Smith played 26 Tests for Australia—all at halfback—from 1964 to 1970 and toured twice with the Kangaroos. Smith played in the Saints' 1971 and '75 Grand Final losses but was dropped to reserve grade in '77 as the club surged to its first premiership in 11 years. His 234 first grade games was second only to Norm Provan, while he played a record 296 games in all grades.

8. Brian Clay—183 games (1957-67)

Brian 'Poppa' Clay played in two Grand Final losses for Newtown before joining St George and winning eight deciders, equalling Norm Provan's premiership record of 10 Grand Final appearances. The former centre became a magnificent five-eighth for the Saints' unstoppable machine—a punishing tackler and a robust, skilful attacker. The bald-headed Clay played eight Tests (five at five-eighth, three at lock) from 1957 to 1960 and toured with the 1959-60 Kangaroos. Kept out of the 1962-63 Grand Finals by injury, he retired after the Saints' streak-ending preliminary final loss in '67, which was the popular clubman's 200th grade match. He was named as one of Australia's 100 greatest players in 2008.

9. Eddie Lumsden—158 games (1957-66)

Powerhouse winger Eddie Lumsden played in nine Grand Final triumphs for St George from 1957 to 1966 (he missed the '60 decider with injury) and scored a record eight tries, including a hat-trick in the '59 shutout of his former club, Manly. He scored 136 tries in a glittering decade with the Dragons, topping the premiership in 1958 and '62. Lumsden made 15 Test appearances and toured with the 1959-60 Kangaroos, while he scored 14 tries in 16 interstate appearances for NSW. A winger in Newcastle's Team of the Century, the Kurri Kurri product was named as one of Australia's 100 greatest players in 2008.

10. Johnny King—191 games (1960-71)

Dazzling winger Johnny King featured in the last seven of the Saints' world-record run of Grand Finals, and set a phenomenal record by scoring tries in six straight deciders (1960-65), including a double in the defeat of Easts in his 1960 rookie season. King is the greatest try-scorer in St George's history, with 143 in 191 games, and led the competition in 1961 and '65. He made a belated international debut in the

1966 Ashes series, but went on to score eight tries in 16 Tests and toured with the 1967-68 Kangaroos. King continued to be a consistent try-scorer in the seasons after the Dragons' halcyon era finished, and retired in 1971. Coach of Western Division's famous Amco Cup success in 1974 before spending two seasons in charge of Souths, he was named as one of Australia's 100 greatest players in 2008.

11. Kevin Ryan—106 games (1960-66)

Wallaby forward Kevin 'Kandos' Ryan switched codes with St George in 1960 and played in the last seven of the club's record sequence of Grand Final triumphs, but is equally remembered for being the man who masterminded the end of the Dragons' run as captain-coach of Canterbury in 1967. A prop with refined ball skills, he was best known as perhaps the most feared defender of all time as the hardman in the Saints' imposing pack. His international career was short—consisting of an injury-hampered 1963-64 Kangaroo Tour and just two Tests, against France on home soil in '64—but his status as one of the era's finest forwards is assured. Ryan guided the emerging young Canterbury outfit to a history-making preliminary final defeat of St George in '67 before losing the subsequent Grand Final to Souths; he retired in 1969.

12. Craig Young—234 games (1977-88)

The game's dominant prop in the late 1970s and early 1980s, Craig Young's 234 first grade appearances in the Red V was second only to Norm Provan. He featured in the premiership success of 'Bath's Babes' in his 1977 rookie season before captaining St George to its last Grand Final victory as a single entity in '79 at the tender age of 23. 'Albert' played 20 Tests, starred on two Kangaroo Tours, and was twice named Dally M Prop of the Year. He skippered the Dragons to a minor premiership and losing Grand Final appearance in 1985, but his two-season stint as coach immediately after his playing retirement was not a success.

13. Harry Bath—60 games (1957-59)

Tough, brilliant forward Harry Bath won two premierships with Balmain before carving out a magnificent tenure in Britain, but he had a monumental impact at the end of his career at St George. 'The Old Fox' won three Grand Finals in his three seasons at the club and scored 510 points in 60 games, including all-time season scoring records for a second-rower (225 in 1958) and prop (205 in 1959). He kicked a Grand Final record eight goals in the '57 defeat of Manly and was sent off in his last premiership game—the '59 Grand Final win over the Sea Eagles.

14. Bobby Bugden—135 games (1954-61)

Resourceful halfback Bobby Bugden played in the first six of St George's phenomenal run of premierships, scoring three Grand Final tries. In all he scored 60 tries for the club, including a career-high 16 in 1959 that helped him gain selection on that year's Kangaroo Tour. Bugden scored three tries on Test debut against France in Brisbane the following season in the first of his two Test appearances. The brilliant No.7 spent the last four seasons of his career at Parramatta, helping the Eels to their first four finals series.

15. Rod Reddy—204 games (1972-83)
The 'Rockhampton Rocket' was one of the game's most damaging backrowers of the 1970s and early 1980s, scoring 65 tries in 204 games for St George. He starred in the Dragons' 1977 and '79 premiership successes, with his heavy-handed display in the '77 Grand Final replay thrashing of Parramatta arguably the most memorable of his career. A ruthless defender and a powerhouse ball-running forward, Reddy played 17 Tests for Australia and toured with the 1978 and '82 Kangaroos.

16. Billy Wilson—174 games (1948-62)
Durable enforcer Billy Wilson started out as a centre/lock but developed into one of the game's most intimidating props during an association with the Saints that spanned 15 seasons. 'Captain Blood' played in six of the first seven of the club's record sequence of Grand Final wins, including the 1961 victory over Wests as skipper. He made the first of 11 Test appearances as a 32-year-old against New Zealand in 1959 before touring with the Kangaroos at the end of the year. Wilson was sent off in his final match—the '62 Grand Final win over the Magpies—before joining Norths.

17. Noel Pidding—104 games (1947-53)
Goalkicking fullback-cum-winger Noel Pidding scored two tries in St George's 1949 Grand Final victory over Souths, and 34 tries and 598 points in 104 games across seven seasons with the club. He scored 140 points in 19 Test appearances for Australia from 1948 to 1954 and top-scored on the 1952-53 Kangaroo Tour with a mammoth 228. He racked up a then club-record 200 points in 1951, and left the Saints after their loss to the Rabbitohs in the '53 premiership final.

18. Jack Lindwall—110 games (1938-49)
Centre/winger Jack Lindwall was among the premiership's most brilliant attacking players of the 1940s, scoring 110 tries in just 133 games for St George. The competition's top try-scorer in 1940, '42 and '46, Lindwall scored an incredible six tries in a match against Manly in 1947 and added nine goals for a colossal 36-point haul. Injury kept him out of the club's maiden Grand Final win in 1941, while he crossed in the Saints' 1942 and '46 Grand Final losses. World War II curbed his representative aspirations but he retains a treasured place in St George's history.

19. Elton Rasmussen—126 games (1962-68)

Mackay product Elton Rasmussen featured in the last five of St George's run of 11 Grand Final wins (1962-66) as a powerful second-row partner for Norm Provan. A 13-match Queensland rep, Rasmussen played in eight interstate matches for NSW while with the Saints and made half of his 18 Test appearances from the club. He also toured with the 1967-68 Kangaroos—his second trip after embarking on the 1959-60 tour. Rasmussen scored 21 tries and 49 goals in his 126 games in the Red V.

20. Mark Coyne—207 games (1989-98)

Mark Coyne, an outstanding all-round centre from Brisbane Brothers, became the eighth and last player to bring up 200 appearances for St George as a standalone entity. He played in three losing Grand Finals for the club in 1992-93 and '96—the latter as captain—and skippered the Dragons in their last five seasons. A veteran of 19 Origin matches for Queensland, Coyne was unlucky not to tour with the 1994 Kangaroos but made nine Test appearances during the Super League War years, including Australia's '95 World Cup triumph. The highly respected and consistent centre scored 56 tries for the standalone Saints before finishing his career with the St George Illawarra joint venture in 1999.

ST GEORGE DRAGONS—GREATEST COACHES (1921-99)

1. Ken Kearney—141 games (1954-55, 1957-61)

Ken 'Killer' Kearney's extraordinary 80.1 per cent win record as St George coach speaks for itself, but only partly explains how he helped mould the greatest club combination in Rugby League history. After an ideal 13-a-side tuition in Britain, the former Wallaby joined St George in 1952 and captain-coached the club to preliminary finals in 1954-55. He was replaced as coach by Norm Tipping in '56 due to his rocky relationship with referees and public criticism of club officials, as the Saints won the first of their 11 straight titles. But he resumed in the captain-coach role the following season and steered the club to five more Grand Final successes (encompassing an unbeaten season in '59), all but the last while featuring on the field as a tough, wily hooker. The ultra-professional Kearney set the standard for subsequent title-winning Dragons captain-coaches Norm Provan and Ian Walsh. He also captain-coached Australia against New Zealand in 1956 and on the '56-57 Kangaroo Tour, with his only two losses in nine Tests coming in the Ashes series.

2. Norm Provan—105 games (1962-65, 1968)

The towering, all-time great second-rower who played in 10 winning Grand Finals for St George, Norm Provan took over from the revered Ken Kearney as captain-coach of the club in 1962. The highly respected Provan guided the club to premierships in the dual role in the last four seasons of his playing career, providing outstanding leadership as a batch of new young superstars emerged in the St George line-up. Provan's Dragons rebuffed the ambitious challenges of Wests, Balmain and Souths to take their Grand Final winning streak into double figures. He returned as non-playing coach in 1968 and steered his beloved club to a preliminary final appearance. 'Sticks' later coached Parramatta and Cronulla with considerable success.

3. Harry Bath—118 games (1977-81)

Legendary forward Harry Bath won three Grand Finals at St George in the last three years of one of the great careers (1957-59), but 'The Old Fox' added to his enormous legacy at the club—and within the game in general—as a coach. After club stints with Balmain (including two Grand Final losses to the Saints) and Newtown, and 20 Tests in charge of Australia, Bath returned to St George as coach in 1977. Mixing toughness with youthful exuberance, 'Bath's Babes' swept to Grand Final triumphs in 1977 (in a historic replay) and '79. The Dragons reached the finals again in 1980, but Bath retired at the end of '81 following a disappointing eighth-place finish.

4. Frank Burge—74 games (1927-30, 1937)

St George endured an arduous introduction to premiership football in the 1920s, but when he arrived in 1927 Glebe legend Frank Burge immediately transformed the club into a title contender. Captain-coach Burge took the previous year's wooden spooners to a maiden finals series in second place before they went down to Souths in the final. Retiring as a player at the end of '27, he remained as coach and guided the Saints to second-place regular season finishes (and subsequent semi-final exits) in 1928-29, and a Grand Final loss to Wests in 1930. Following stints at Easts, Norths and Canterbury, Burge returned to St George in 1937 and achieved another second-place result in the shortened first-past-the-post premiership season.

5. Ian Walsh—45 games (1966-67)

Magnificent Test hooker Ian Walsh joined St George in 1962 and captain-coached the last of the club's sequence of 11 Grand Final victories in 1966. Australia's captain-coach against New Zealand in 1965, 'Abdul' assumed the dual role at club level the following season after Norm Provan retired. Following his Ashes success as captain-coach in '66, he led the Dragons to a comprehensive 23-4 Grand Final defeat of Balmain. The Saints claimed another minor premiership under Walsh's guidance in 1967, but their world-record run came to an end via consecutive finals losses to Souths and Canterbury. Walsh accepted the era-closing defeat with trademark grace before retiring. He later coached Parramatta to the finals in 1971.

ST GEORGE DRAGONS—BEST DAYS (1921-99)

1. September 18, 1965: Provan retires after a perfect 10
In front of a record SCG crowd of 78,056 (thousands more admissions went unrecorded amid chaotic scenes), St George won its 10th straight premiership via a gripping 12-8 defeat of a plucky young Souths outfit in the 1965 Grand Final. Dragons winger Johnny King posted a try for the sixth decider in succession, while Billy Smith also scored as the Saints held the Rabbitohs try-less. It was a triumphant exit for retiring second-row legend Norm Provan, who had played in all 10 Grand Final victories—the last four as captain-coach.

2. August 23, 1963: Saints prevail in 'Mudbath' Grand Final
St George faced arguably the toughest challenge of its 11-season reign in 1963. Despite finishing as minor premiers and conceding only 95 points at the extraordinary rate of just over five per game, the Saints' only two regular season losses had come against Wests, their opponents in the previous two Grand Finals. The Magpies prevailed again in the major semi, setting up a tantalising Grand Final showdown. With the SCG a sodden, muddy mess and a then record 69,860-strong crowd in attendance, the Dragons won an epic, highly controversial decider 8-3 after a disputed try awarded to Johnny King and an equally contentious no-try ruling against Wests' Peter Dimond. The Saints became the fourth and last club to win premierships in all three grades in the same season.

3. August 30, 1941: Premiership breakthrough
St George finished as runners-up three times in its first two decades before finally cracking it for a premiership in the club's 21st season. After finishing fourth in the 1941 regular season, the Saints trounced Balmain to advance to the final. Five-eighth Roy Hasson and winger Owen Campbell scored two tries apiece in a thrilling, open decider won 31-14 by captain-coach Neville Smith's relatively unheralded side against star-studded defending champs Eastern Suburbs.

4. August 15, 1959: Unbeaten season sealed with Grand Final shutout
Three-time premiers St George set new standards of excellence in 1959, securing a fourth straight title by going through the season unbeaten. The Dragons won 17 and

drew one of their 18 regular season matches before downing Wests to reach the Grand Final. The Saints romped home over Manly in the decider, with powerhouse winger Eddie Lumsden scoring three of their six tries in a comprehensive 20-0 triumph.

5. September 24, 1977: 'Bath's Babes' win historic replay

Coached by former forward great Harry Bath, the young St George side of '77 featured an aggressive, skilful pack and the brilliant Ted Goodwin at fullback. The club's decider showdown with minor premiers Parramatta finished in a historic 9-all draw, forcing the first Grand Final replay in history. But the Dragons dominated the Eels a week later and powered to a 22-0 shutout. The Saints' forwards, led by tyros Rod Reddy and Craig Young, battered their Parramatta counterparts into submission, while Goodwin kicked six goals and a field goal. 'Bath's Babes' claimed the club's first title since its run of 11 premierships from 1956 to 1966.

ST GEORGE DRAGONS—WORST DAYS (1921-99)

1. September 20, 1975: 'White boots' Grand Final

St George was the first side through to the '75 Grand Final after upsetting runaway minor premiers Easts in the major semi. But after trailing the Roosters just 0-5 at halftime of the decider, the Dragons capitulated to suffer the then biggest defeat in Grand Final history. Legendary captain-coach Graeme Langlands carried a leg injury into the game, and a misdirected painkilling injection during the break rendered the fullback a passenger for the second half as brilliant Easts ran in seven tries. Langlands' decision to wear white boots—which were extremely uncommon in those days—as part of a sponsorship deal only drew more attention to his plight as he turned in the worst performance of his glorious career. The 38-0 scoreline remained a Grand Final record for 33 years.

2. September 26, 1993: Saints freeze on the big stage

Trounced 28-8 by Brisbane in the 1992 Grand Final, St George approached the '93 decider rematch against the Broncos with far more confidence. The Saints had defeated the Broncos in the final regular season round and were the first side through to the Grand Final. But the match was a disaster from start to finish for the Dragons: powerful prop tyro Jason Stevens badly broke his thumb in the first tackle of the match, and coach Brian Smith's rattled troops inexplicably diverted away from their highly successful game plan. The error-riddled, try-less Saints were never in the hunt, and the 14-6 scoreline did not fully reflect the Broncos' level of domination.

3. August 26, 1944: Finals humiliation
Perennial finalists during the first half of the 1940s, St George's first successful period came to a shattering halt in the '44 semi-final against Newtown. The Bluebags inflicted the biggest finals defeat in premiership history on the Saints, racking up an extraordinary 55-7 scoreline by piling on 11 tries. It remained a club-record loss for 50 years, and the Saints missed the finals for the first time in seven years in 1945.

4. July 3, 1994: Record defeat confirms fall from grace
Runners-up in 1992-93, the Dragons' tumble down the ladder in '94 culminated in a club-record defeat to Manly. The Saints had broken a six-match losing streak a week before their trip to Brookvale, but were flogged 61-0 by the Sea Eagles, who raced over for 10 tries. The embarrassing result was 13 points worse than the club's previous biggest loss.

5. August 11, 1928: Earl Park riot
St George's clash with Balmain at its Earl Park base in 1928 ranks as one of the most infamous matches in Rugby League history. Saints forward Harry Flower was sent off, and star centre George Carstairs was kicked in the head by Balmain's Tony Russell in the dying minutes. A large contingent of the 9000-strong crowd stormed the field at fulltime in pursuit of Russell as the field descended into a brawling warzone, with police hopelessly outnumbered and struggling to maintain control.

ST GEORGE ILLAWARRA DRAGONS—GREATEST PLAYERS (1999-2013)

1. Mark Gasnier—175 games (2000-08, 2010-11)
The nephew of St George legend Reg, Mark Gasnier was destined for greatness after a fine debut season that saw him score five tries in eight games. A year later he made his Australian debut, scoring a try against Papua New Guinea. Representative honours would elude him for another three years but after debuting for NSW in 2004, he would be close to a staple in the team for the next half-decade while a recall to the Australian team was inevitable after a super 2005 season. He played 14 Tests across the next four years before controversially walking out on the Dragons to head to French Rugby Union in 2008. He returned midway through 2010 and scored a try in the club's breakthrough Grand Final triumph, retiring a year later to take up a media career. With 92 tries, the brilliant centre sits fourth on St George Illawarra's tryscoring list.

2. Matt Cooper—246 games (2000-13)
An outstanding defensive centre who posted 126 tries in a stellar 14-year career with St George Illawarra, Matt Cooper rated among the game's top three-quarters throughout much of his career. The club's greatest try-scorer, Cooper debuted for NSW and Australia in 2004, playing 17 Origins and seven Tests. While he is rated among the game's greatest-ever defensive centres, his hard running also won the Dragons many games.

3. Luke Bailey—119 games (2000-06)
A durable and forthright prop, Luke 'Bull' Bailey was regarded as one of the top handful of props in the game during his time at St George Illawarra. Though he made just four Test appearances, he represented NSW 11 times during his time at the Dragons. Bailey won the Dally M Prop of the Year award in 2005, the *Rugby League Week* Player of the Year in 2006 and the Dragons' top gong in '05. He left to join the inaugural Titans team in 2007.

4. Ben Creagh—227 games (2003-13)
A talented wide-running backrower who made a move to prop late in his tenure with the Dragons, Ben Creagh was a NSW player for much of his career. The sandy-haired Creagh was named St George Illawarra's Player of the Year in 2007, '09 and '10 and turned in an excellent performance in the 2010 premiership triumph. He was appointed captain in 2013 following the retirement of Ben Hornby.

5. Brett Morris—154 games (2006-13)
A wonderfully talented winger with speed to burn, Brett Morris (the son of Dragons legend Steve) became the third St George Illawarra player to score 100 tries for the club in 2013. Debuting for Australia in 2009 and NSW in 2010, Morris topped the NRL's tryscoring tally in 2009 and scored 20 tries in the Dragons' 2010 premiership season. He was awarded the club's top player award in 2012.

6. Ben Hornby—275 games (2000-12)
St George Illawarra's most-capped player and its inaugural premiership skipper, fullback-cum-halfback Ben Hornby is a revered figure at the Dragons. A talented Wollongong junior, he emerged to represent NSW on three occasions from 2004 to 2008 and played a single Test for Australia in 2006. The 2003 Player of the Year was a steady hand in the No.7 during the club's 2010 premiership season.

7. Trent Barrett—154 games (1999-2006)
One of the most highly rated five-eighths in the early days of the NRL era, Trent Barrett was a representative regular during his eight-year stint with St George Illawarra. After a disappointing showing in the '99 decider, he won the Dally M

Medal and Dragons Player of the Year award in 2000. A fine passer and superb hole-runner, the robust Barrett was often blamed for the Dragons' lack of finals success but his 15 Tests are testament to his outstanding skill set. He skippered the joint venture during his last five seasons there.

8. Shaun Timmins—124 games (1999-2006)
St George Illawarra's 2002 Player of the Year, Shaun Timmins overcame constant knee troubles to become one of the stars of the merged outfit after spending five years with the Steelers. After an impressive showing in the 1999 Grand Final, Timmins played the first of his nine Tests and became an Origin hero in 2004 with a match-winning field goal. He was named Dally M Lock of the Year in 2004 but played much of his career in the centres or at five-eighth.

9. Nathan Blacklock—114 games (1999-2004)
A tryscoring marvel, Nathan Blacklock was one of the most scintillating players in the game at the turn of the century. Scoring an incredible 100 tries in 114 games for St George Illawarra, Blacklock was named the Dally M Winger of the Year for three straight years (1999-2001) and topped the premiership's tryscoring in each of those seasons. His ankle-high pick-up-and-go try in the 1999 Grand Final was one highlight in a career filled with electric plays.

10. Dean Young—210 games (2003-12)
The heart and soul of St George Illawarra for much of his time in the top grade, Dean Young received much of the recognition his hard work deserved at the backend of his career. Debuting in 2003, the son of former Dragons title-winning captain Craig was a flexible hooker/backrower/half who loved the tough stuff. Young won a premiership with the Dragons in 2010, debuting for Australia that season and playing his sole Origin a year later. He was lauded for his courage in playing on through a series of serious injuries.

11. Jason Nightingale—159 games (2007-13)
An ultra-reliable winger, Jason Nightingale has held a wing spot down at the Dragons since 2007, debuting for New Zealand a year later. Arguably the best player on the field in the 2010 Grand Final after a magnificent two-try display, 18-Test veteran Nightingale was awarded the Dragons' Player of the Year gong in 2011 and had racked up 65 tries to the end of 2013.

12. Trent Merrin—94 games (2009-13)
A wonderfully talented and mobile forward, Trent Merrin emerged as a blockbusting front-rower in 2009 before adding work-rate and subtlety to his game as a lock forward. Merrin came off the bench in the Dragons' 2010 Grand Final win and played for NSW from 2011 to 2013; he was named the club's Player of the Year in 2013.

13. Jamie Soward—143 games (2007-13)
St George Illawarra's greatest point-scorer, Jamie Soward was the most popular player during the club's premiership run in 2010 but was ignominiously sacked three years later when his form nosedived. The diminutive five-eighth thrived under Wayne Bennett and played a winning hand in many games, including the 2010 preliminary final where he booted the decisive field goal. Soward won the Dally M Five-eighth of the Year gong in 2009 and played all three Origins in 2011 but was cut altogether midway through 2013.

14. Darius Boyd—70 games (2009-11)
A hired gun brought in by Wayne Bennett in 2009, Darius Boyd enjoyed three quality seasons at the Dragons. Playing a key hand in the run to the 2009 minor premiership, he won the Clive Churchill Medal in the 2010 triumph; in 2010 he was also named the best fullback in the NRL and the world.

15. Jeremy Smith—30 games (2009-10)
A winner nearly everywhere he went, journeyman forward Jeremy Smith spent just two seasons at the Dragons but helped lift the club from also-rans to premiers. In New Zealand Test stalwart Smith's two years, the Dragons won back-to-back minor premierships, claiming the title in 2010 before he left for Cronulla.

16. Lance Thompson—132 games (1999-2005)
A foundation St George Illawarra player who had spent four seasons with St George prior to the merger, red-headed workhorse Lance Thompson was a gritty type who never took a backward step. Representing City three times while at the joint venture, Thompson was often touted as an Origin prospect but was routinely overlooked. A member of the '99 Grand Final side, he left the club in acrimonious circumstances after the '05 preliminary final loss.

17. Jason Ryles—156 games (2000-08)
A hulking front-rower who emerged in 2000, Jason Ryles spent close to a decade at the Dragons, winning myriad representative honours along with three Dragons Player of the Year awards. Ryles played eight times for NSW and 15 Tests for Australia but remained a divisive figure with his penchant for giving away penalties. At his best, though, he was regarded as one of the top bookends in the game.

18. Beau Scott—119 games (2007-12)
A country-tough centre-cum-backrower, Beau Scott provided toughness and competitive zeal during the club's golden era under Wayne Bennett. Brought across from Cronulla, Scott rose to Origin representative status in 2010 and Australian honours a year later, while he started in the Dragons' 2010 title win. The hard-nosed backrower followed Bennett to Newcastle in 2013.

19. Michael Weyman—96 games (2009-13)
Recruited from Canberra as an injury-prone prop forward by Wayne Bennett, Weyman played his best football during the supercoach's tenure at the Dragons. A bruising runner, Weyman debuted for NSW in his first year with the club and made his sole appearance for Australia in 2010 before starting in the front-row in the Dragons' Grand Final win.

20. Mark Riddell—94 games (2001-04)
A cult hero during his four seasons at the Dragons, local junior Mark 'Piggy' Riddell was a charismatic goalkicking hooker most renowned for raising his right hand when moving in to attempt a place kick. In each of his four seasons with the Dragons, the robust and creative rake topped 100 points, with his 18-point effort and winning penalty goal in the 26-25 upset of Brisbane still lauded.

ST GEORGE ILLAWARRA DRAGONS—GREATEST COACHES (1999-2013)

1. Wayne Bennett—80 games (2009-11)
Wayne Bennett was named Queensland Team of the Century coach in 2008, and the six-time premiership winner's signature was hailed as a major coup when he was lured from the Broncos by the Dragons in 2009. It proved a masterstroke, with Bennett guiding St George Illawarra to back-to-back minor premierships in his first two years and their first-ever Grand Final win in 2010 (and St George's first in 31 years). His 65 per cent strike rate is the highest-ever among St George Illawarra coaches. The revered Bennett departed after the 2011 season—as he always said he would—to chase a premiership at Newcastle.

2. David Waite—48 games (1999-2000)
St George Illawarra's inaugural coach David Waite had coached St George for three seasons prior to taking charge of the merged club in 1999. He had guided St George to a Grand Final in 1996 and won Dally M Coach of the Year honours the same season. Waite took the joint venture to within a penalty try of Grand Final success in his first season, but stepped down late in the 2000 season after a 9-11 start.

3. Nathan Brown—151 games (2003-08)
The Dragons' longest-tenured coach, mentoring the club for six seasons and 151 games, Nathan Brown endured a torrid start. He found reasonable success but ultimately

could not lead a talented roster to the promised land of the Grand Final. Appointed in 2003 at the age of just 29, Brown initially succumbed to the pressure, infamously slapping captain Trent Barrett across the face during a dismal loss to Manly. Brown's Dragons missed the playoffs in his first year but he guided them to the finals in four of the next five, including back-to-back preliminary final losses in 2005-06. Brown was not re-signed for 2009 and departed for England, where he enjoyed success at Huddersfield and St Helens.

4. Andrew Farrar—60 games (2000-02)
A champion centre with Canterbury, Western Suburbs and Illawarra, Andrew Farrar was the Steelers' last standalone coach. Overlooked for the St George Illawarra job initially, Farrar was David Waite's assistant in 1999 and 2000 before taking over at the backend of the latter season. Farrar's teams made the finals in both 2001 and 2002 but he stood down after what many considered two underachieving years.

5. Steve Price—48 games (2012-13)
Appointed to succeed the great Wayne Bennett, Steve Price found little success during his first two seasons with the Dragons. He became the first (and to date, only) coach to lead the Dragons to consecutive non-finals appearances with ninth- and 14th-placed finishes. The latter season saw St George Illawarra score below 400 points for the first time in history.

ST GEORGE ILLAWARRA DRAGONS—BEST DAYS (1999-2013)

1. October 3, 2010: A premiership at last
The Dragons' long-awaited moment of glory came on an overcast Sunday in October 2010 when the club won its first premiership, thumping the Sydney Roosters 32-8. A scintillating two-try performance from Jason Nightingale and excellent showings from Jamie Soward, Darius Boyd and Dean Young secured Wayne Bennett's Dragons the title they had craved for so long.

2. April 1, 2008: Saviour secured
The most important signing in club history was made official on April 1, 2008 when it was revealed that 21-year Brisbane coach Wayne Bennett was leaving the Broncos for the Dragons. Locked in a battle with Canterbury for Bennett's signature, the Dragons won out. In three years, he won a premiership and two minor premierships for a club that had perennially underachieved.

3. September 4, 2009: Minor glory

Confidence was high when Wayne Bennett arrived at the Dragons but few would have anticipated the minor premiership in his first year. The club achieved that on the last Friday night of the season when the Dragons belted an under-strength Parramatta team 37-0 and fellow front-runner Canterbury was smacked 34-12 by the Wests Tigers at the same time.

4. August 19, 2004: Comeback for the ages

The Dragons recorded the third-biggest comeback in premiership history late in the 2004 season when overcoming a 10-34 deficit against Manly at Kogarah to win 36-34. The Dragons trailed by 24 with 23 minutes remaining, but a Justin Poore try out wide followed by a Mark Riddell conversion sealed the famous win.

5. September 19, 1999: Instant success

Viewed as a super-club upon the merger, St George Illawarra took a while to find its groove but reached the Grand Final in its first season after a preliminary final win against southern Sydney rivals Cronulla. The Sharks led 8-0 at halftime but were overrun by Anthony Mundine, who scored a hat-trick in the 24-8 victory that sent the Dragons to their first decider as a merged entity.

ST GEORGE ILLAWARRA DRAGONS—WORST DAYS (1999-2013)

1. September 26, 1999: Penalty try blues

St George Illawarra seemed destined for premiership glory in its inaugural season when it led Melbourne 14-0 at halftime in the Grand Final. The Dragons led 18-14 with just four minutes to play when Storm winger Craig Smith was left unconscious in the corner after collecting a bomb. Dragons winger Jamie Ainscough had hit him high and video referee Chris Ward awarded a penalty try. Matt Geyer slotted the goal from in front and the Dragons were left to rue the one that got away.

2. April 13, 2003: The slap heard around the game

Nathan Brown seemed ill prepared for the pressures of first grade coaching when he took the reins from Andrew Farrar in 2003. Still just 29—younger than some members of his team—the pressure finally told on Brown in Round 5 when Manly was running in a big score on the Dragons. Brown grabbed captain Trent Barrett on the sideline and slapped him across the face, embarrassing the skipper and the club in a true meltdown.

3. March 3, 2000: Revenge
St George Illawarra genuinely believed it was robbed of the 1999 Grand Final, and Anthony Mundine had few qualms in calling defending champs Melbourne pretenders. The Storm didn't take kindly to this and put an incredible points tally on the Dragons, winning 70-10 at the MCG. It was the greatest loss in Dragons history.

4. April 12, 2011: Farewell to the supercoach
Wayne Bennett transformed St George Illawarra in his three years at the club, guiding the Dragons to a premiership and two minor premierships in what was a spectacular reign. He announced early in the 2011 season that he would not remain at the Dragons, though, and despite the club's hopes of a turnaround, he confirmed on April 12 that he would be moving to the Knights.

5. September 24, 2005: Tiger tragedy
The Dragons were short-priced favourites to win it all in 2005 after winning their last seven regular season games and their opening final. Their hopes were dashed in an epic preliminary final by the Wests Tigers, who booked a spot in their first decider with a 20-12 boilover in front of a sold-out Sydney Football Stadium.

UNIVERSITY—GREATEST PLAYERS (1920-37)

1. Alby Lane—41 games (1924-28)
Halfback/five-eighth Alby 'Georgie' Lane holds a distinguished place in University's history as captain of the team that reached the 1926 final. He also skippered NSW that season, among eight appearances for his state from 1925 to 1928.

2. Ernest Ogg—116 games (1925-33)
The only player to top a century of first grade games for University, Ernest 'Sammy' Ogg also holds the record for most tries for the club (24). The hardy forward featured in the watershed 1926 season that saw University reach the premiership final, and represented City Firsts in 1929. Ogg was an occasional goalkicker and racked up 104 career points for the 'Students'.

3. Jim Craig—12 games (1922)
'Mr Versatile' was the biggest name the University club ever had on its books. The Balmain and Australian Test great joined the 'Students' as captain-coach in 1922 after returning from the Kangaroo Tour. Craig played 12 games and established a record

for points in a match, scoring 15 against his former club. He would surely have been University's first (and only) international but Australia did not play any matches that year. Craig left for a decorated stint in Queensland at the end of the season.

4. Frank O'Rourke—34 games (1924-27, 1934)

One of the few University players to regularly play representative football, three-quarter Frank O'Rourke made eight interstate appearances for NSW from 1925 to 1927. He featured in the club's historic appearance in the 1926 final before embarking on a fruitful stint with English club Leeds. O'Rourke returned to Australia and played for University again in 1934.

5. Hubert Finn—70 games (1920-26)

A player in University's foundation season, Hubert 'Butt' Finn represented NSW against New Zealand and played his last match for the club at fullback in the historic finals loss to Souths. His total of appearances is second in University's history; he later became the NSWRL's medical officer.

6. Ray Morris—5 games (1933)

Former Wests three-quarter Ray Morris played the last of his seven interstate matches for NSW after joining University in 1933, and was picked in the Kangaroo Tour squad that departed mid-season—the first player from the club to win national selection. Tragically, Morris developed an ear infection while en route to the northern hemisphere and died in Malta.

7. Clive Evatt—40 games (1922-25)

Hooker Clive Evatt featured in 40 of University's 47 matches during his five seasons with the club. He represented NSW in five interstate matches from 1922 to 1924—all losses—against the powerful Queensland side, but became better known as a barrister and politician, sitting as a member of the NSW Legislative Assembly for two decades.

8. Jim Flattery—45 games (1920-25)

A winger in University's first-ever game, Jim Flattery was the club's top try-scorer in its foundation season, with six. The talented three-quarter represented NSW in three matches in 1921-22, scoring four tries in one interstate match in '21 and another two touchdowns in his sole appearance the following season.

9. Ross McKinnon—18 games (1933-34)

Ross McKinnon began his first grade career with University in 1933, representing NSW at five-eighth in his first season. He joined Easts two years later and was a key part of the Tricolours' 1935-37 premiership-winning juggernaut while also representing Australia in eight Tests.

10. John McIntyre—39 games (1926-28)
John McIntyre racked up 176 points in three seasons with University—including a club-record 86 points in 1928. He featured at prop in the '26 final loss to Souths and represented City Firsts at lock in 1928, landing two goals in a one-point loss to Country.

WESTERN REDS—GREATEST PLAYERS (1995-97)

1. Julian O'Neill—26 games (1996-97)
One of Rugby League's most infamous players, former Bronco Julian O'Neill played just 26 games for the Reds and was sacked over disciplinary issues, but he was outstanding during his time at the club. The talented fullback/five-eighth made an immediate impact with the Reds, winning a Queensland Origin jersey. In 1997 he broke the Reds' record for most tries and points in a match with four and 26 respectively before he was chosen for Super League Australia in the Anzac Test. After being sacked, he played five more seasons with South Sydney and North Queensland.

2. Robbie Kearns—37 games (1996-97)
One of the Western Reds' finest signings, Robbie Kearns was poached as an established first grader from Cronulla in 1996 and was outstanding in his two years with the club. The hardworking front-rower played 37 games for the Reds, representing Super League Australia in 1997. He would go on to play eight Origins and 20 Tests while at the Melbourne Storm.

3. Rodney Howe—40 games (1995-97)
A hard-headed and thick-bodied bookend, Rodney Howe was one of three Western Reds players to represent Super League Australia while with the club. Debuting with his local club Newcastle and spending a season at Widnes, Howe established himself as one of the props of the future at the Reds, playing 40 games for the club. He represented Super League NSW and Australia in 1997 before a knee injury cut short his season. Howe would go on to have a decorated and controversial career with the Melbourne Storm for the next seven seasons.

4. Matt Fuller—59 games (1995-97)
An underrated hooker who had a taste for the tough stuff, Matt Fuller cycled through Canterbury, South Sydney, Wakefield Trinity and St George before landing in Perth. He was the top rake for his three-season spell, finishing as the Reds' most-capped player. His 10 tries in 1995 remarkably topped the club's

tryscoring tally and was the most by any Reds player in a season. He finished with one season at Western Suburbs upon the Reds' demise.

5. Chris Ryan—58 games (1995-97)
The Western Reds' greatest point-scorer and try-scorer, Chris Ryan tallied 21 tries and 210 points in 58 appearances. The goalkicking three-quarter spent three years with Manly before joining the Reds, and played the best football of his career in Perth. Ryan shifted to the London Broncos for a two-season stint after the Reds went under.

6. Matt Rodwell—57 games (1995-97)
A skilful half who had won Rookie of the Year honours when at Newcastle in 1992, Matt Rodwell joined the Reds in 1995 and played 57 games across the club's three seasons. His 14 tries ranks equal third in club history, and he was one of just six players to turn out for the Reds in both their first and last premiership matches.

7. Mark Geyer—33 games (1995-97)
Firebrand backrower Mark Geyer was one of the most controversial and feared figures in Rugby League in the 1990s and he certainly left his mark with the Reds, where he continued his role as an enforcer. It made him a fan favourite but earned the ire of the judiciary, with four suspensions in three years. Over three seasons he played just 33 games due to suspensions and injury but was the highest-profile Red during his time in Perth.

8. Scott Wilson—23 games (1996-97)
Scott Wilson's turbulent career saw him spend time with six premiership and two English clubs, but he had arguably his best run with the Western Reds, where he spent two seasons. The naturally gifted yet trouble-prone fullback/five-eighth scored seven tries in 23 appearances for the Reds and won selection for the NSW Tri-Series team against New Zealand.

9. Brad Mackay—21 games (1995)
The 1993 Clive Churchill Medal winner was one of the Reds' biggest recruits when he signed on for 1995 and captained the new franchise in their first game against his former club St George—a 28-16 win. After declaring his loyalty to the ARL—while the club defected to Super League—Mackay played for City and NSW but was part of a divided club because of his decision. He moved to Illawarra in 1996 and finished his 237-game career with St George Illawarra in 1999, coming off the bench in the losing Grand Final showing.

10. Peter Shiels—48 games (1995-97)
A handy utility forward who had spent a season each with Penrith and Western Suburbs before moving to Perth, Peter Shiels played all three seasons with the Reds, scoring four tries in 48 games. He spent three years with Newcastle after the Western Reds folded, and then moved to England.

WESTERN SUBURBS MAGPIES—GREATEST PLAYERS (1908-99)

1. Keith Holman—200 games (1949-61)
One of the greatest halfbacks to play the game, Keith 'Yappy' Holman played 200 games for Western Suburbs, becoming Australia's second-most-capped player and winning a host of awards in a spectacular career. Holman was an unquestioned star of the 1950s—perhaps the next best player of the decade after Churchill—who played 35 Tests, including the famous Ashes series win in 1950, two Kangaroo Tours and two World Cup campaigns. He missed the 1952 premiership triumph while on Kangaroos duty but put the Magpies in position to win the title after some magnificent early-season form. A legend of the code, Holman was named EE Christensen's Player of the Year three times and in the ARL's 100 greatest players.

2. Noel Kelly—111 games (1961-69)
Named at hooker in the ARL Team of the Century, Noel 'Ned' Kelly rates as one of the finest hooker-props to play the game. A Queenslander who joined the Magpies in 1961 as part of the club's spending spree to win a premiership, Kelly played in three losing Grand Finals. A no-nonsense customer, he regularly found himself on the wrong side of officials with his take-no-prisoners approach. Kelly played for Australia 28 times, making three Kangaroo Tours—the first front-rower to do so.

3. Frank McMillan—148 games (1921-24, 1926-35)
A revolutionary fullback who was one of the first custodians to join the front line in attack, Frank 'Skinny' McMillan starred in the club's first premiership win in 1930 and then captain-coached it to its second title in 1934. McMillan toured twice with the Kangaroos, captain-coaching the 1933-34 side. One of the game's finest attacking fullbacks, he was named in the Top 100 in 2008.

4. Kel O'Shea—111 games (1956-63)
Part of the great Western Suburbs teams of the late 1950s and early 1960s, Kel O'Shea was a decorated international second-rower and one of the finest running forwards to play the game. O'Shea played in Wests' four losing Grand Finals of the era and represented Australia 15 times. He was named in the Team of the 1950s and in the ARL's 100 Greatest Players in 2008.

5. Harry Wells—86 games (1956-61)
A robust, rollicking centre with a fine step and brutal fend, Harry 'Dealer' Wells joined Wests from Wollongong as an already-established international. He had a decorated career for Australia, touring twice with the Kangaroos and playing in three World Cups. Wells played in two deciders for the Magpies, captaining the side in '58. He was named in the Team of the 1950s and in the ARL's Top 100 players.

6. Arthur Summons—56 games (1960-64)
A Wallaby five-eighth when recruited by Wests in 1960 as part of the 'Millionaires' drive for a premiership, Arthur Summons took the Magpies to three Grand Finals in his five years at the club while he captain-coached the 1963-64 Kangaroos to Ashes success. A tough five-eighth/halfback with beautiful hands, he was immortalised after the 1963 Grand Final in the image with Norm Provan known as 'The Gladiators'.

7. Tom Raudonikis—201 games (1969-79)
A tenacious halfback who was as competitive as any player to pull on a boot, Tommy Raudonikis was a tough, dogged leader who always got the best out of himself and the players around him. 'Tom Terrific' won the 1972 Rothmans Medal and played 29 Tests for Australia. He represented NSW 22 times, skippering the team in the inaugural Origin match. An inspirational player, Raudonikis was named in the game's 100 greatest in 2008.

8. Tedda Courtney—161 games (1909, 1911-24)
One of the game's most durable players during the code's infant days, Tedda Courtney was a Rugby League giant who was revered as Wests' best player during the club's first 15 years. A hard-nosed and stocky prop, he played over 300 grade matches and lasted long enough to play with his son for the Magpies. Courtney made two Kangaroo Tours, including the 1911-12 Ashes series win, where he played in all three Tests.

9. Vic Hey—27 games (1933-35)
Widely considered the code's best five-eighth during the first 50 years of Rugby League, Vic Hey started his premiership career with Western Suburbs before shifting to England. A brilliant all-round player with a deft touch in attack and a hardness in defence, he played in the 1934 premiership success and starred on the 1933-34 Kangaroo Tour.

10. Peter Dimond—155 games (1958-67)

A powerful winger whose representative career spanned nearly his entire decade with Wests, Peter Dimond is the Magpies' greatest-ever try-scorer with 84. A powerful three-quarter built more like a forward than a winger, Dimond played in four losing Grand Finals for Wests during the club's 'Millionaires' era. He played 10 Tests from 1958 to 1966, scoring a double in the famous 'Swinton Massacre' on the 1963-64 Kangaroo Tour.

11. Jim Craig—32 games (1929-30)

Arguably the game's finest-ever utility, 'Mr Versatile' Jimmy Craig was the architect behind Western Suburbs' first premiership. Captain-coach of the inaugural title-winning side, he scored a try and kicked two goals in the 27-2 decider victory over St George. Craig's leadership transformed Western Suburbs from easybeats to premiers.

12. Herb Gilbert—54 games (1917-20)

A bruising, physical centre who moved to Wests after spells with Souths and Easts and in England, Herb Gilbert's stint with the Magpies saw him resume his state and Test career. He scored tries against New Zealand and England in Tests in 1919 and '20 respectively and was the club's leading try-scorer in 1920. Gilbert was named in the code's 100 greatest in 2008.

13. Arthur Clues—50 games (1943-46)

A tall and rangy second-row forward, Arthur Clues was outstanding in four years with the Magpies before he left for England in the great exodus of 1947, where he became one of Australia's greatest exports. Clues was revered for his creativity and ability to link with his backline. He was named as one of Australia's 100 greatest players in 2008.

14. Alan Ridley—64 games (1931-36)

A hulking winger with plenty of toe, Alan Ridley made two Kangaroo Tours and still holds a number of tryscoring records. He toured with the 1929-30 Kangaroos as a 19-year-old and four years later was the leading try-scorer on the '33-34 tour. Ridley scored two tries in Wests' second premiership win in 1934, and holds the club record for most tries in a match with six and most tries in a season with 18.

15. Jim Abercrombie—14 games (1908-13)

Western Suburbs' first great player and the club's first international, tireless goalkicking hooker/prop Jim Abercrombie toured with the First Kangaroos in 1908-09 and played in 31 matches on tour. He scored Wests' first points in their second-round 42-7 loss to Balmain with a penalty. Abercrombie was an inaugural inductee into Wests' hall of fame.

16. John Donnelly—148 games (1975-84)

Arguably Western Suburbs' most popular player, John 'Dallas' Donnelly was a fearless forward during the club's 'Fibros' era of the late 1970s and early 1980s. Always prepared to do anything to win, Donnelly was on the receiving end of some long suspensions but his attitude set the tone for an exciting era in Magpies history. He represented Australia four times. Donnelly sadly died in the surf outside Byron Bay in 1986, aged just 32.

17. Terry Lamb—88 games (1980-83)

Canterbury-Bankstown's greatest player, Terry Lamb made his top-grade debut with Western Suburbs in 1980 and spent four excellent seasons with the Magpies. Lamb crossed for 41 tries in 88 games for the club and won the Dally M Medal in his final season at Wests despite playing for a team that won the wooden spoon.

18. Bill Keato—119 games (1938-50)

Western Suburbs' greatest point-scorer, goalkicking fullback Bill Keato scored 776 points for the Magpies and led the premiership's scoring in 1947 and '49. The courageous Keato booted six goals in the 1950 Grand Final loss to South Sydney. Roy Masters said of Keato that he "won more matches for the Magpies than any other player".

19. Les Boyd—68 games (1976-79)

One of the most aggressive forwards to play the game, Les Boyd had the talent to play for NSW and Australia but was eventually rubbed out over two nasty and grubby incidents that have tarnished his reputation. Boyd toured with the '78 Kangaroos while at the Magpies but made a shock exit to Manly in 1980.

20. Andrew Leeds—114 games (1993-99)

The best Western Suburbs player during the difficult era of the 1990s, Andrew Leeds was a reliable custodian and fine goalkicker who scored 100-plus points in four straight seasons. A fine defender, he was a rock in the club's last days.

WESTERN SUBURBS MAGPIES—GREATEST COACHES (1908-99)

1. Jim Craig—65 games (1929-30, 1932, 1939)

Balmain great Jim Craig switched to Western Suburbs in 1929 and was immediately appointed captain-coach. In his first season, Wests made just their second finals series after 22 years in the premiership. In his second year at the helm, Craig led the Magpies to their first premiership, scoring a try and kicking two goals in the Grand Final challenge. He returned two seasons later as a non-playing coach and Wests again made the Grand Final challenge, losing to the great South Sydney outfit. He had one more season in 1939 that brought little success.

2. Roy Masters—94 games (1978-81)
One of the great motivators, ex-schoolteacher Roy Masters didn't coach Wests to a premiership or even a Grand Final but his place in establishing the great 'Fibros' legacy saw him named as the Magpies' Team of the Century coach in 2004. A true student of Rugby League psychology, Masters built an aggressive and fearless team that made three straight finals series, including preliminary final losses in 1978 (a year in which it also won the minor premiership) and '80. Masters left in 1982 when the club could not pay a number of his 'Fibro' charges.

3. Tom McMahon—20 games (1952)
One of the game's great referees, Tom McMahon jnr retired from officiating in 1951 and made the unusual career move to coaching. He was an instant success, guiding Western Suburbs to its fourth and final premiership in his only year in charge of the club. He retired after the controversial title triumph and never coached again.

4. Jeff Smith—59 games (1948, 1950-51)
In his first year in charge of Western Suburbs, new coach Jeff Smith guided Western Suburbs to its third premiership with an 8-5 defeat of Balmain. After Col Maxwell captain-coached the team in 1949, Smith returned for two seasons, finishing in the finals both years. His 64.4 per cent strike rate sits fourth all time among Wests coaches.

5. Jack Fitzgerald—80 games (1961-64)
A quality winger who played seven seasons with Wests, Jack Fitzgerald achieved greater renown as a coach, guiding the Magpies to three straight Grand Finals during St George's indomitable run of 11 straight titles. Taking the reins in 1961, Fitzgerald lost three consecutive deciders, the last the famous Darcy Lawler game that Wests still believe they were robbed of. After a disappointing '64 season, Fitzgerald stood down due to illness; he died in 1965 aged just 40.

WESTERN SUBURBS MAGPIES—BEST DAYS (1908-99)

1. October 4, 1930: Wests win
Led by the great Jim Craig, Western Suburbs ended South Sydney's run of five straight titles to claim its first premiership. St George scored first to go up 2-0 but an Alan Brady hat-trick among seven Wests tries saw the black-and-whites run out 27-2 winners in the competition's first official Grand Final. It was a fine send-off for champion Craig in what was his last match.

2. September 18, 1948: Hansen's heroics
In torrential rain at the Sydney Sports Ground, two-time defending premiers Balmain led Wests 5-3 with less than 15 minutes of the '48 Grand Final challenge remaining when bustling Wests second-rower Kevin Hansen made a 50-metre bust to score a controversial try. After the conversion, Wests held on grimly for an 8-5 win and their third premiership.

3. September 8, 1934: Western Suburbs reigns again
Guided by captain-coach Frank McMillan, Wests won their second premiership via a 15-12 final win over Eastern Suburbs. Heavy rain delayed the Grand Final a week before Alan Ridley's double helped the Magpies to victory. It was an incredible win against a rising Easts team that would win the next three premierships.

4. September 20, 1952: Souths stunned
In one of the most controversial Grand Finals ever played, Western Suburbs stunned a South Sydney team that won every other title between 1950 and '55, prevailing 22-12. Getting the rub of the green from referee George Bishop, Wests claimed their fourth and final premiership, scoring six tries to two.

5. August 20, 1978: Back on top
In a thrilling last-round victory, Western Suburbs defeated second-placed Cronulla 18-17 to win the club's fifth and final minor premiership. Steve Rogers booted seven goals for the Sharks but it wasn't enough after tries to Les Boyd, Graeme O'Grady and Don Moseley. Wests were eliminated from the finals in straight sets.

WESTERN SUBURBS MAGPIES—WORST DAYS (1908-99)

1. August 24, 1963: Darcy decides
In the most controversial and discussed Grand Final of them all, Western Suburbs lost the 1963 decider to powerhouse St George after rumours swirled that referee Darcy Lawler had backed the Saints heavily. Wests were on the receiving end of numerous controversial calls—including the famous Johnny King try after he was tackled—and maintain 50 years later that they were robbed.

2. September 26, 1983: Kicked out
After a disappointing 1983 season and under severe financial stresses, Western Suburbs was excluded from the 1984 season by the NSWRL. The Magpies took the League to court and succeeded in winning their way back into the premiership, but the incident had left a huge impact on the club's finances and it managed just one win in 1984.

3. August 29, 1999: A sad farewell
Western Suburbs endured a wretched farewell in 1999, its last season as a standalone club before merging with Balmain. Under Tommy Raudonikis, Wests won just four games and claimed the wooden spoon. They lost their last 12 matches, including a 60-16 hammering by Auckland at Campbelltown in their final match.

4. September 9, 1978: Silvertails supreme
Wests' hopes of returning to the Grand Final after 15 years were shattered by archrivals Manly in a 14-7 preliminary final loss. Under new coach Roy Masters, the Magpies had returned to the finals with the start of the 'Silvertails-Fibros War' occurring earlier that season. The Wests players were shattered at the defeat, and the club would never again play in a Grand Final.

5. June 27, 1982: Cooper goes ballistic
Western Suburbs backrower Bob Cooper was sent from the field and suspended for 15 months after a wild brawl that saw him shatter the jaw of Illawarra winger Lee Pomfret and injure two other Steelers. Judiciary chairman Jim Comans, in the process of trying to clean up the game, said, "Acts such as these must be obliterated from the game, and I'll begin by obliterating you."

WESTS TIGERS—GREATEST PLAYERS (2000-13)

1. Robbie Farah—203 games (2003-13)
A gritty, hardworking hooker boasting the playmaking class and kicking game the equal of the game's best halves—consequently wearing the No.7 14 times during his club-record total of appearances—Robbie Farah has been the most valuable and consistent contributor in the Tigers' history. The 2005 premiership season was his first full season of NRL football, but he swiftly established himself as one of the game's top rakes. He has captained the Tigers since 2009, was their Player of the Year in 2006-07 and is the third-highest try-scorer in club history with 52. A veteran of nine Tests for Australia and eight Origins for NSW (including one as skipper) from 2009 to 2013, Farah finished second in the Dally M Medal in 2007 and '10 and equal fourth in '09.

2. Benji Marshall—201 games (2003-13)
Although his form slump and exit from the code in 2013 tarnished his legacy somewhat, Benji Marshall put the Wests Tigers on the map and remains a club legend. His audacious '05 Grand Final flick pass is arguably the most iconic moment in the Tigers' history, but he provided a plethora of highlights in 11 seasons in the NRL. His unique arsenal of attacking talents was vital to the Tigers' sole premiership success and spearheaded top-four finishes in 2010-11—seasons in which Marshall finished fourth and second in the Dally M Medal. The veteran of 25 Tests for New Zealand (17 as captain) steered the Kiwis to World Cup ('08) and Four Nations ('10) glory, claiming the Golden Boot after the latter. He holds records for most tries (76) and points (1118) for the Tigers, and captained the club on 17 occasions in Robbie Farah's absence.

3. Brett Hodgson—102 games (2004-08)
Courageous lightweight fullback Brett Hodgson was a pointscoring machine and an incredibly valuable custodian for a Tigers side short on high-profile players. Named Fullback of the Year after coming fifth in the '05 Dally M Medal, he scored an all-time finals-record 30 points in the Tigers' thrashing of North Queensland and finished the premiership-winning season with a colossal 308 points (including 15 tries)—the second-highest tally ever. The elusive and skilful Hodgson assumed the Tigers' captaincy in 2006 and remained in the role until his departure to Super League at the end of 2008. The 2004-05 club Player of the Year (joint winner with Scott Prince in the latter season) scored 38 tries and 786 points in five seasons with the Tigers. He became just the club's second NSW Origin rep when he won a recall in '06.

4. Chris Heighington—201 games (2003-12)

The first player in the joint venture's history to play 200 first grade games, Chris Heighington initially forged a regular spot in 2005 and featured in the Tigers' Grand Final victory. The backrower was tireless in defence and a bustling runner, scoring 39 tries for the club. He was named the Tigers' Player of the Year after a breakthrough 2008 campaign. Unlucky not to represent NSW or Australia, Heighington turned out for Country Origin twice and played for England in the 2011 Four Nations. The club's decision to let the overwhelming crowd favourite go to Cronulla was met by howls of protest from supporters.

5. Scott Prince—73 games (2004-06)

Scott Prince provided the Tigers with the No.7 linchpin they needed to finally challenge for a finals spot and ultimately led the club to premiership glory. After debuting for Queensland in his first season, Prince spearheaded a number of crucial victories during '05 and formed a deadly combination with precocious five-eighth Benji Marshall. He took over as skipper mid-season and was named Dally M Captain of the Year and finished fourth in the Dally M Medal count before collecting the Clive Churchill Medal as best afield in the Tigers' Grand Final triumph. Joint Player of the Year with Brett Hodgson, Prince became the club's first Australian Test player during the subsequent Tri-Nations tournament, but his decision to sign on as a foundation Gold Coast Titan saw him lose the Tigers' captaincy for 2006.

6. Gareth Ellis—75 games (2009-12)

One of the great British imports, Test veteran Gareth Ellis was named the Tigers' Player of the Year in his first three seasons at the club. Big, mobile and aggressive, the backrower was integral to the Tigers' top-four finishes in 2010-11, while his injury-enforced absence for half of the '12 campaign contributed immensely to their subpar season performance. Castleford-born Ellis, named RLIF Second-rower of the Year in 2009-10, represented England in 11 Tests while a Tiger.

7. Chris Lawrence—132 games (2006-13)

The fourth of just five Australian internationals the Tigers have produced, hard-running centre Chris Lawrence has had a career that has been frequently interrupted by serious injuries. He made a memorable NRL debut as a 17-year-old in 2006 and scored 16 tries in 18 games the following season. Big and skilful enough to be utilised at lock or five-eighth, his performances in the Tigers' surge to top-four finishes in 2010-11 saw him play six Tests (scoring four tries) in those seasons' Four Nations tournaments. Lawrence, who surely would have represented NSW by now if not for untimely injuries, is the second-highest try-scorer in Wests Tigers history.

8. Liam Fulton—156 games (2003-08, 2010-13)
A valuable and popular clubman during 10 seasons of first grade—interrupted by one year at Huddersfield—Liam Fulton has been one of the Tigers' most consistent and versatile performers. Primarily a hardworking backrower, his skill set has seen him used as a stopgap five-eighth and hooker, while he remains an ideal bench option. He moved into fifth on the Tigers' appearance register in 2013 and was named the club's Player of the Year in a difficult season.

9. John Skandalis—186 games (2000-06, 2009-10)
One of the few Western Suburbs or Balmain survivors to spend a significant period of time with the merged entity, former Magpies enforcer John Skandalis chalked up a then record number of appearances for the Tigers. The veteran prop was the cornerstone of the Tigers' unfancied premiership-winning pack in 2005, playing 27 games. Player of the Year in 2002, Skandalis left for Super League at the end of '06 but returned to the Tigers for a farewell year in '09 before coming out of retirement for a late season stint in '10; he was 34 when he finally hung up the boots.

10. Keith Galloway—132 games (2006-13)
Towering red-headed cult hero Keith Galloway became the Tigers' fourth NSW Origin rep and fifth Australian Test player during a stellar 2011 campaign. The tough-nut prop's career has been regularly interrupted by injuries, but he has continually proved his worth to the club when on the paddock. A key member of the Tigers' 2010-11 finals outfits, Galloway featured in all five Tests of the Kangaroos' post-season schedule after the latter campaign and scored a rare try on debut against New Zealand.

11. Bryce Gibbs—155 games (2003-11)
A rugged, no-frills front-rower, Bryce Gibbs was one of six members of the Tigers' premiership-winning side to debut for the club in 2003. He became established in first grade the following season before scoring a memorable try in the '05 Grand Final victory. The four-time City Origin rep was controversially moved on to accommodate high-priced flop Adam Blair after becoming the sixth player to bring up 150 games for the Tigers, but he continued to thrive at Cronulla.

12. Dene Halatau—128 games (2003-09)
One of the most versatile players of the NRL era, Dene Halatau featured at lock, second-row, centre and hooker in seven seasons at the Wests Tigers. He wore the No.13 throughout the club's stunning 2005 finals campaign, scoring two tries in the preliminary final upset of St George Illawarra and playing his part in the Grand Final victory. Halatau made all 15 of his Test appearances for New Zealand—

predominantly at hooker—during his time as a Tiger. He signed on to rejoin the club in 2014 after four seasons with Canterbury.

13. Todd Payten—151 games (2004-11)
Journeyman Todd Payten built his reputation as a skilful prop, but the burly, mobile forward regularly played in the backrow for the Tigers. He joined the club in 2004 and scored a try off the bench in the '05 Grand Final triumph—his 10th season in first grade despite being only 26. Payten graduated into more of a leadership role with the Tigers as his career went on, captaining the side 10 times and featuring in the 2010 finals campaign.

14. Ben Galea—150 games (2000-07)
Ben Galea, a foundation player for the Wests Tigers, was something of an unsung hero for the joint venture. Player of the Year in 2001, the versatile Galea filled in at hooker early in '05 before Robbie Farah became established in the No.9, and reverted to the backrow to play an outstanding role in the club's premiership success. In 2007 he became just the second player to bring up 150 appearances for the Tigers.

15. Anthony Laffranchi—102 games (2001-06)
Part of the core group of Tiger cubs brought along by the club who eventually carried the joint venture to a premiership, forceful second-rower/prop Anthony Laffranchi was named the Tigers' Player of the Year in 2003. He played all but one of the club's 28 games in 2005 and scored a crucial try as a front-rower in the Grand Final. Laffranchi debuted for Country Origin in 2006—his last season with the Tigers—before achieving Origin and Test honours from the Gold Coast Titans.

16. Taniela Tuiaki—78 games (2006-09)
Bulldozing Auckland-born winger Taniela Tuiaki did not make his NRL debut until the age of 24, but he was a fearsome presence on the flank during four seasons for the Tigers before injury tragically ended his career. Tuiaki played four Tests for the Kiwis in 2007 and was named Dally M Winger of the Year in '09 after scoring a club-record 21 tries in just 22 games, but he was unable to make his way back from a shocking leg break suffered in the latter stages of that watershed season.

17. Aaron Woods—64 games (2011-13)
A big young prop with outstanding go-forward and refined ball skills, Aaron Woods displayed immediate promise during a superb 2011 rookie season. He was named the Tigers' Player of the Year and debuted for City Origin during their ultimately disappointing 2012 campaign, finishing just outside the top 10 in the Dally M Medal. Woods played two matches for NSW in 2013, becoming just the fifth player to represent the Blues from the club.

18. Beau Ryan—104 games (2007-12)

A larger-than-life character arguably better known for his comedic work on *The Footy Show* than for his playing, Beau Ryan provided excellent value to the Tigers as a winger, fullback or centre. He scored a career-high 13 tries in 2009 after bagging doubles in his last three games before starring in the Tigers' 2010-11 finals campaigns. The fourth-highest try-scorer in the joint venture's history with 46, Ryan was controversially shifted on by the club at the end of 2012; he joined several former Tigers teammates at Cronulla.

19. Mark O'Neill—121 games (2000-05)

Balmain stalwart (1994-99) Mark O'Neill was a mainstay of the Wests Tigers' pack during their first six seasons in existence. The industrious backrower was installed as captain at the start of 2005 but was replaced on a permanent basis by Scott Prince after a three-month injury stint. O'Neill kicked up a stink at the time but eventually accepted the decision and featured in the second-row as the Tigers surged to Grand Final success, after which he joined Leeds. In 2004, he became just the ninth player in premiership history to play 100 games for two different clubs.

20. Daniel Fitzhenry—137 games (2002-07, 2010)

Daniel Fitzhenry was remarkably versatile, featuring extensively at fullback, wing, centre and five-eighth while also making the occasional appearance as a fill-in hooker. Best known as a winger, he scored four tries in the Tigers' '05 finals campaign, including a vital four-pointer in the Grand Final. Fitzhenry crossed for 11 tries that season and racked up the same total again in '06. He held the Tigers' career tryscoring record for several seasons and returned for a farewell campaign in 2010 after two years with Hull KR.

WESTS TIGERS—GREATEST COACHES (2000-13)

1. Tim Sheens—259 games (2003-12)

Having established himself as a coaching giant with three premierships at Canberra, Tim Sheens endured a disastrous five-season stint with North Queensland but restored his reputation with the battling joint venture. In 2005 he guided an unheralded squad to its first finals appearance and won the Dally M Coach of the Year award—the third time he had collected the gong. The Tigers capitalised on late season momentum to surge to Grand Final glory, with old sage Sheens masterminding the victory. A few inconsistent seasons followed before a return to the finals in 2010-11, with the team finishing in the top four both years. An acrimonious split with the Tigers at the end of 2012 was an unbefitting way to end his decade-long tenure. Sheens has coached the Australian side since 2009 and led the nation to World Cup success in 2013.

2. Wayne Pearce—26 games (2000)

Club legend Wayne 'Junior' Pearce coached Balmain with little success from 1994 to 1999 before ousting Western Suburbs coach Tom Raudonikis for the Wests Tigers post. His gritty, aggressive squad packed with journeymen occupied a top-four spot for most of its debut season, but capitulated to lose eight of its last 10 games and miss the finals. Pearce, who stood down from the role at the end of the season, coached NSW to a record-breaking series clean sweep in 2000.

3. Terry Lamb—50 games (2001-02)

Canterbury legend Terry Lamb enjoyed outstanding results as a coach emerging through the Bulldogs' ranks, winning second-grade premierships in 1998 and 2000, but his two-season stint in charge of Wests Tigers was a nightmare. A drug suspension for stars Kevin McGuinness and Craig Field, John Hopoate's infamous contrary conduct suspension and sacking, and a feud with international centre Terry Hill conspired to make Lamb's term in charge a stressful one, while on the field the Tigers won a total of 16 games to finish 12th and 13th respectively. His contract was not renewed at the end of '02.

4. Michael Potter—24 games (2013)

Highly regarded for his Super League achievements with Catalans, St Helens and Bradford, Michael Potter beat an impressive field of coaching candidates to step into the Wests Tigers hot seat in 2013. The season threw up myriad challenges for him, including a horrific injury toll, Benji Marshall's dramatic loss of form and eventual defection to Rugby Union, and unsettling boardroom conflict. The Tigers won just seven games and finished second last.

WESTS TIGERS—BEST DAYS (2000-13)

1. October 2, 2005: Premiership success for joint venture

Wests Tigers became arguably the most unlikely premiers of the modern era in 2005, playing an exuberant brand of attacking football and confounding the critics with their unheralded, compact forward pack. The Tim Sheens-coached Tigers conceded the first try of the Grand Final but led North Queensland 12-6 at halftime on the back of Pat Richards' famous try—set up by a Benji Marshall break and audacious flick pass. Despite boasting no Australian Test reps and just two players who had attained Origin status, the Tigers ran away with the entertaining decider with a couple of late tries. Captain Scott Prince was awarded the Churchill Medal after his side's 30-16 triumph.

2. September 24, 2005: Tigers upset Dragons for maiden Grand Final berth

The Tigers' stunning charge through the 2005 finals continued with a 20-12 preliminary final upset of premiership favourites St George Illawarra. Benji Marshall set the tone by scoring the opening try—a dazzling individual effort from a scrum win. The Tigers led 16-6 at halftime and their high-energy performance ran the second-placed Dragons ragged. Kiwi international Dene Halatau's second try was enough to seal a euphoric 20-12 victory over the shattered Saints.

3. September 9, 2011: Tigers down premiers for club-record winning streak

Wests Tigers won their last eight regular season matches in 2011 to snare fourth spot, setting up a fascinating duel with joint-venture archrivals St George Illawarra in the first week of the finals. Trailing the defending champs 6-12 at the break, the Tigers atoned for their devastating preliminary final loss to the Dragons a year earlier by surging to a high-quality 21-12 victory in front of 45,361 fans at ANZ Stadium.

4. September 9, 2005: Spectacular finals debut

After qualifying for their maiden finals series in fourth spot via a late season charge, the Tigers lined up against the equally exciting North Queensland Cowboys in their first post-season assignment. But they looked anything but finals novices, building a 14-6 halftime lead before blitzing the Cowboys with six unanswered second-half tries. Brett Hodgson scored a finals-record 30 points (three tries, nine goals) and the 50-6 victory was the second biggest in finals history.

5. February 6, 2000: Wests Tigers draw with heavyweights in NRL entry

The unfancied Wests Tigers went within an ace of upsetting NRL superpowers Brisbane in their debut as a joint venture, snaring a 24-all draw in the opening round of the 2000 season at Campbelltown Stadium. The Tigers raced out to a shock 18-6 lead before the competition favourites rallied to take a six-point advantage. But fullback Joel Caine, a surprise Round 1 selection ahead of Matt Seers, scored his third try and nailed the sideline conversion to secure a premiership point for the newcomers.

WESTS TIGERS—WORST DAYS (2000-13)

1. September 16, 2011: Tigers title tilt ends with Warriors heartbreaker
Wests Tigers headed into their semi-final clash with the Warriors on a club-record nine-match winning streak, while their opponents had been embarrassed 40-10 by Brisbane in the qualifying final. The Tigers led 18-6 at the break and 20-12 with 15 minutes to go, but a freakish try to Warriors centre Krisnan Inu at the 77-minute mark sent the overwhelming favourites packing.

2. September 25, 2010: Soward field goal sinks Tigers
Riding the finals rollercoaster, the Tigers had endured golden point defeat at the hands of the Sydney Roosters before pipping Canberra in a heart-stopping semi-final. A massive 71,212-strong ANZ Stadium crowd turned out for the preliminary final showdown between the Tigers and minor premiers St George Illawarra, and the rivals produced an absolute nailbiter. The Tigers led 12-6 at halftime after four-pointers to Lote Tuqiri and Robert Lui, but the Dragons scored early in the second stanza to set up a long stalemate that was eventually broken by a Jamie Soward field goal in the 74th minute.

3. March 28, 2001: Tigers disgraced by star trio's indiscretions
The NRL and the Wests Tigers attracted worldwide notoriety in 2001 when volatile winger John Hopoate was sensationally revealed to have poked the backsides of several North Queensland players. The former Test player was banned for 12 weeks by the NRL judiciary on a contrary conduct charge on the same day that the Tigers handed Craig Field and Kevin McGuinness six-month suspensions for cocaine use. Hopoate and Field were eventually sacked by the club.

4. May 17, 2013: Benji benching beginning of the end
A shocking injury toll and the indifferent form of experienced stars such as linchpin Benji Marshall combined to provide Michael Potter with a horror introduction to NRL coaching in 2013. After a run of six straight losses, Potter took the drastic step of relegating Marshall to the interchange bench for the Round 10 clash with front-runners South Sydney. The controversial call had little effect, with the Rabbitohs pummelling the last-placed Tigers 54-10. Marshall was reinstated and the Tigers won four of their next five games, but the club great's form continued to waver and he signed with Rugby Union franchise the Auckland Blues before the end of the season amid torrents of criticism.

5. July 5, 2001: Melbourne inflict record defeat

Plagued by lengthy player suspensions and sackings for on- and off-field incidents, the Tigers battled through the remainder of 2001 under rookie coach Terry Lamb. The joint venture's performances plumbed new depths on a trip to Melbourne when they conceded 11 tries in a 64-0 flogging to a Storm side that did not even reach the finals. It was the fifth-biggest defeat in premiership history at the time, and the worst in 66 years. Remarkably, the Tigers won four of their next five games.

CLUB RIVALRIES

1. South Sydney-Sydney Roosters

The Souths-Roosters rivalry has lasted over 100 years and is built on geography and class. Souths portray themselves as working-class battlers while Eastern Suburbs are cast as the moneyed elites. The Roosters have long been aggrieved that their borders have been marginalised by Souths, while the Rabbitohs are perpetually upset at losing their players to the Roosters. Ron Coote, Arthur Hennessy, Craig Wing, Michael Cleary, Elwyn Waters and Terry Fahey are some of the greats who have crossed from Souths to Easts. The two clubs met in the first premiership final and have played in six deciders, winning three apiece. Incredibly, the only two remaining foundation clubs have not met in a finals match since 1938. They have met 207 times since 1908, with Souths winning 108 times and the Roosters 94, and five matches drawn, to the start of the 2014 season.

2. Canterbury-Parramatta

In a heated rivalry that started in the 1980s when the two clubs rose to prominence and fought it out for premiership top dog, Canterbury and Parramatta came to loathe each other in a deep and passionate way. The teams met three times during the finals in the 1970s, but it was in the 1980s, when they won eight premierships between them (four apiece), that the enmity began. It was as much a matter of style and culture as mutual respect, but by the time the Super League War rolled around, it was outright hatred. Parramatta lured four Super League-aligned Canterbury players to break their contracts, and won their services after a protracted legal battle. When the two teams met in the 1998 preliminary final, the Eels seemed to have finally wrested the upper hand when they led 18-2 with 11 minutes remaining, but Canterbury staged a miraculous comeback to shatter Eels hearts. Eleven years later the two met in front of the biggest finals crowd in premiership history for a rugged preliminary final, won by the Eels. The record stands at Canterbury 72, Parramatta 57 and five draws from 1947 to the end of 2013.

3. South Sydney–Balmain

Once one of Rugby League's most bitter rivalries, the South Sydney–Balmain feud can be traced to the day of the 1909 final. Both teams had agreed to refuse to play after the League scheduled the decider as a preliminary match to a Kangaroos–Wallabies clash. The Watersiders upheld their end but Souths did not, turning up, kicking off and scoring to win the game and the premiership via forfeit. For the next 90 years, Balmain supporters never forgave Souths. The teams met in four premiership deciders (excluding the forfeit) and Balmain remarkably won them all. It won deciders in 1916, 1924 and 1939 but most famously upset the Rabbitohs in 1969, when its lay-down tactics infuriated South Sydney but handed the Tigers their last premiership. Through the 1980s the feud got personal, with rival hookers Benny Elias and Mario Fenech reigniting the enmity between the two teams.

4. St George/St George Illawarra–Cronulla

This rivalry is a local derby located in the south of Sydney. Cronulla was born out of St George—a fact the Dragons have never let the Sharks forget—and entered the premiership on the back of St George's 11 straight titles, but has rarely sustained a period of dominance over 'Big Brother'. St George won the opening nine contests between the clubs despite the Sharks being filled by a host of former Dragons. The tide ebbed and flowed throughout the 1980s and '90s, but the greatest clash between the two outfits occurred a year after St George merged with Illawarra. Cronulla led the Dragons 8-0 in the preliminary final but an Anthony Mundine hat-trick scuppered the Sharks' Grand Final hopes. The two clubs continue to play out epic encounters with the venom still very much there.

5. Canterbury–Sydney Roosters

Starting with Eastern Suburbs decimating Canterbury 87-7 in the second-biggest defeat in premiership history, Canterbury and Eastern Suburbs have met in five premiership deciders in their near 80-year feud. The Berries downed the Tricolours 19-6 to claim their first premiership in 1938, while Easts rolled Canterbury 24-14 two years later. The sides met again in 1974 with Easts triumphant, but Canterbury turned the tables in 1980 to end a 42-year premiership drought. The rivalry really got hot in the early 2000s, though, when both teams were fighting for premiership dominance. The Roosters won the title after Canterbury was thrown out for salary cap breaches in 2002 and then eliminated the Bulldogs in the 2003 preliminary final, but the Bulldogs exacted revenge in a classic 2004 Grand Final, winning 16-13. The Roosters' insistence on luring outspoken Canterbury players such as Willie Mason, Braith Anasta, Nate Myles, Mark O'Meley and Sonny Bill Williams has only added fuel to a bitter feud.

6. Manly–North Sydney

In a rivalry based on geography, Manly and North Sydney eventually engaged in an unsuccessful merger that killed the Bears. Norths, whose last premiership came in 1922, held a slight edge after Manly's entry into the premiership, but when the 1970s rolled around, the Sea Eagles dominated. The feud escalated through the 1970s and '80s as Manly continued to poach players such as Ken Irvine, John Gray, Bruce Walker, Cliff Lyons and Don McKinnon. The brief merger between the two clubs from 2000 to 2002 proved fatal for the Bears, who were on the wrong side of politicking that saw the licence revert to Manly if the joint venture fell over.

7. Manly–Western Suburbs

A short but fierce rivalry manufactured almost alone by Western Suburbs coach Roy Masters, the 'Silvertails-Fibros' war is perhaps the most romanticised in Rugby League history. The feud began in earnest in a 1978 trial in Melbourne when the two clubs engaged in bloody warfare in what was meant to be a carnival of the codes. It set in motion a rivalry based on class: the well-to-do of the northern beaches versus the strugglers of the west. A savage brawl marked the next match, with hardmen Dallas Donnelly and Terry Randall swinging wildly and Eagles winger Stephen Knight sent off. The two sides met again in the preliminary final, with Manly triumphant over a devastated Wests. The hatred escalated at the end of the '79 season when Manly poached Wests stars Les Boyd, John Dorahy and Ray Brown, and the clubs waged several ferocious battles in ensuing seasons.

8. Melbourne–Manly

A modern rivalry born out of a battle for premiership superiority during the NRL era, Melbourne and Manly have been the two most successful sides since 2006. The Storm and the Sea Eagles won five premierships and played in two Grand Finals against each other, with one of the clubs featuring in every decider bar one from 2006 through 2013. The two met in the 2007 Grand Final, a brutal affair won 34-8 by Melbourne. A year later, the Sea Eagles walloped a Cameron Smith-less Storm 40-0. Subsequent finals matches in 2009 and 2012 saw Melbourne thrash Manly 40-12 on each occasion. Regular season battles were much more tense and boiled over in 2011 in what has become known as 'The Battle of Brookvale', when a vicious sideline brawl between Adam Blair and Glenn Stewart saw both served with lengthy suspensions.

9. Melbourne–Brisbane

Two teams who have held similar attitudes towards a Sydney-centric League, Melbourne and Brisbane's rivalry has been one-sided but played out predominantly during finals. Set up very much as a 'little Brisbane' with original powerbrokers John

Ribot and Chris Johns as well as skipper Glenn Lazarus, Melbourne also assumed the Broncos' 'us against them' mentality. The two teams met in every finals series from 2004 through 2009 with the Storm winning every encounter except the 2006 Grand Final, when a gritty Broncos side out-gutted the Storm 15-8. Brisbane famously had Melbourne beaten in the 2008 semi-final before an Ashton Sims error and a Greg Inglis try with just seconds remaining stole a memorable win for the Storm.

10. Parramatta-Penrith
In the battle of Sydney's west, Parramatta and Penrith have shown little care for each other since the Panthers entered in 1967. The Eels dominated for the first two decades and have held the upper hand more often than not. Parramatta thumped Penrith 38-6 in the latter's finals debut in 1985, while a 64-6 thrashing in the opening round of the 2002 season left the Panthers licking their wounds. Arguably the greatest clash between the two sides came in 2011, when Michael Jennings scored after the siren to send the derby to extra-time in a thriller won by the Panthers on the back of a Luke Walsh field goal.

12-MONTH TURNAROUNDS FOR THE BETTER

1. Eastern Suburbs—1966-67
Despite collecting two of the previous three wooden spoons, nothing could have prepared Easts for their disastrous 1966 campaign. The club lost all 18 of their regular season matches—the last time a first grade club has gone through a year winless. But the arrival of untried coach Jack Gibson turned Easts' fortunes around dramatically in '67. The season started in familiar fashion, with four losses and a draw to show from the opening five rounds, but Gibson guided his charges to 13 wins and another draw in their remaining 17 games to secure fourth spot. Making their first finals appearance in seven years, the Tricolours were eliminated 13-2 by Canterbury in the minor semi.

2. Sydney Roosters—2012-13
The Roosters' promising start to 2012 quickly came unstuck when they won just four games in the last 20 rounds to wind up in 13th spot. Veteran coach Brian Smith was dumped at the end of the dismal campaign, but under rookie mentor Trent Robinson, and with high-profile recruits Sonny Bill Williams, James Maloney and Michael Jennings each enjoying career-best seasons, the Tricolours claimed the minor premiership and surged to a stunning Grand Final triumph. The Roosters held their opponents scoreless a record six times while also developing into the

NRL's slickest attacking unit. No team in premiership history has come from a lower ladder position to win the following season's title.

3. Western Suburbs—1933-34
Wests remain the only team in premiership history to win the competition a year after finishing last. The Magpies' 1933 campaign fell apart following the Kangaroos' mid-season departure, which robbed the club of the services of Frank McMillan, Vic Hey, Les Mead, Alan Ridley and Cliff Pearce. They lost their last eight games to end up with the wooden spoon in the eight-team premiership. But with their stars back on deck in 1934, Wests rallied to win the club's second title, defeating Easts in a playoff for the minor premiership and again in a tight final.

4. Canterbury—2008-09
Perennial contenders the Bulldogs slumped to a disastrous wooden-spoon season in 2008, exacerbated by Willie Mason's off-season departure and Sonny Bill Williams' shock mid-season walkout. Steve Folkes' 11-season tenure as coach came to an unfortunate close after his side mustered just five wins. Long-serving assistant Kevin Moore took over in 2009 and a recruitment drive that netted Brett Kimmorley, Josh Morris and Broncos quartet Michael Ennis, Ben Hannant, David Stagg and Greg Eastwood paid enormous dividends. Morris, Ennis, Hannant and Stagg won Dally M positional gongs and Moore was named Coach of the Year and Andrew Ryan Captain of the Year after the Bulldogs finished second, with an early-season replacement bungle costing them the minor premiership. The Bulldogs' outstanding campaign finished courtesy of a 22-12 loss to Parramatta in a classic preliminary final.

5. Sydney Roosters—2009-10
After a top-four finish in 2008 the Roosters endured a horror '09 campaign, winning just five games and collecting the wooden spoon. Several alcohol-related incidents compounded the club's woes, including one that involved coach Brad Fittler, who was shown the door at the end of the season. But despite losing former rep forwards Craig Fitzgibbon, Mark O'Meley and Willie Mason, the Roosters returned to the finals under incoming coach Brian Smith and landed in sixth spot. Troubled Todd Carney claimed a spectacular Dally M Medal win after being thrown a lifeline by the club, while aggressive Kiwi prop Jared Waerea-Hargreaves was another important addition to the roster. The Roosters pipped Wests Tigers in an epic extra-time qualifying final before thumping Penrith and Gold Coast to become the first team in history to reach a Grand Final a year after coming last. The valiant Tricolours went down 32-8 to St George Illawarra in the decider after leading 8-6 at halftime.

6. Parramatta—1961-62

The Parramatta Eels were the undisputed whipping boys of the premiership in the late 1950s and early 1960s, collecting six straight wooden spoons from 1956 to 1961 and winning just 16 of 108 games. But with St George luminary Ken Kearney coming on board as coach and the Saints' former Test halfback Bobby Bugden and future Kangaroo fullback Ken Thornett arriving at the club, the Eels claimed a historic finals berth in 1962. The blue-and-golds embarked on a nine-match unbeaten run mid-season to eventually finish fourth. Their watershed campaign ended with a 6-0 minor semi loss to Wests.

7. St George—1926-27

St George's first six seasons in the premiership brought little success and culminated in a wooden spoon after they won just two of 16 games in 1926. But the arrival of veteran Glebe legend Frank Burge as captain-coach transformed the Saints into a competitive unit in 1927, when they won 12 and drew one of their 16 games to finish in second spot. The club's breakthrough season ended with a 20-11 finals loss to a South Sydney side in the midst of a dynasty.

8. Canterbury—1935-36

Canterbury-Bankstown's initiation to premiership football was as tough as they come. The club avoided a debut-season wooden spoon in 1935 after beating University twice, but was subjected to the two biggest defeats in the competition's history—91-6 to St George and 87-7 to Easts—early in the season and conceded in excess of 60 points twice in the last three rounds. But Frank Burge, St George's saviour nine years earlier, took over as Canterbury's coach in 1936 and led the fledgling club to the finals. Losing just three regular season games, Canterbury finished third before being eliminated in the semi-final by undefeated champs Easts.

9. Manly—1950-51

Manly endured a tough start to life in the premiership, finishing near the foot of the ladder in its first four seasons—including eighth of 10 teams in 1950 after winning just a third of its 18 games. But with captain-coach Wally O'Connell ably supported by the likes of Roy Bull, Ken Arthurson and prolific scorers Ron Rowles, Johnny Bliss and Gordon Willoughby, the club claimed second spot in a breakthrough 1951 campaign. Manly accounted for Wests and St George on its way to a Grand Final showdown with South Sydney, but with O'Connell sidelined by injury, the Rabbitohs ran away with the decider 42-14.

10. Warriors—2000-01

Mired in financial and management crises in 2000, the bumbling Auckland Warriors were on the brink of collapse. Results on the field were equally grim as the Mark Graham-coached outfit finished second last. But millionaire businessman Eric Watson bought the flailing outfit, effectively establishing a new club under the New Zealand Warriors banner. Parramatta lower-grade coach Daniel Anderson succeeded Graham while astute recruiting brought the likes of Ivan Cleary and Kevin Campion to Auckland, and the Warriors reached their maiden finals series in 2001 on the back of a late season surge. They were pumped 56-12 by minor premiers Parramatta on finals debut, but the club had turned a significant corner.

12-MONTH TURNAROUNDS FOR THE WORSE

1. South Sydney—1989-90

The Rabbitohs claimed their first minor premiership in 19 years in 1989, losing just three regular season games. Deflating back-to-back finals losses rendered the season a lost opportunity, but the club had every reason to expect to challenge again in '90 despite Ian Roberts' high-profile departure to Manly. But the season was a nightmare from start to finish: Souths won just two of their 22 games, ending the year on 13 straight losses. A recreational drugs scandal hit the club, with 10 players testing positive to illegal substances and young fullback Scott Wilson having his contract torn up. The club also sank into dire financial trouble, leading to star players Mario Fenech, Les Davidson, Phil Blake and standout rookie Terry Hill leaving Redfern at the end of the year along with coach George Piggins.

2. Western Suburbs—1952-53

After claiming the minor premiership and their fourth (and last) title via a controversial Grand Final defeat of South Sydney in 1952, Wests became the only champions in the competition's history to finish stone motherless last the following season. The Magpies won four of their first six games in a promising start to their title defence, but lost 11 of their last 12 to finish at the foot of the ladder and collect the wooden spoon just 12 months after a euphoric success.

3. Canterbury—2004-05

The Canterbury club boasted an unenviable record of ordinary title defences, having failed to qualify for the finals in 1943, 1981, 1989 and 1996 after winning the previous year's premiership. That woeful run continued after the Bulldogs' rousing Grand Final success in 2004 when they sank to a 12th-placed finish in '05 with six straight losses to end the season. Test forwards Willie Mason and Mark O'Meley were missing for the first half of the year, while season-ending injuries at regular intervals to Sonny Bill Williams, Willie Tonga, Luke Patten, Hazem El Masri and Brent Sherwin saw the Bulldogs' campaign disintegrate. The Sydney Roosters, minor premiers and beaten Grand Finalists in '04, and preliminary finalists Penrith slipped to ninth and 10th respectively in 2005.

4. Wests Tigers—2005-06

The effervescent Wests Tigers charged to a remarkable premiership triumph in 2005, becoming arguably the least-heralded champions in the code's history. But any prospect of the joint venture developing into a regular heavyweight of the NRL was washed away by a dismal title defence in '06. Halfback Scott Prince was stripped of the captaincy in the pre-season after he signed a contract to join Gold Coast for '07, while heroes of the previous season Benji Marshall, Brett Hodgson, Liam Fulton and Paul Whatuira all suffered season-ending injuries at various stages of the year. The Tigers won consecutive games just once all season and finished 11th.

5. Sydney Roosters and Cronulla—2008-09

After finishing in the top four in 2008, the Sydney Roosters and Cronulla had cause to approach the '09 NRL season with optimism. But the year was a resounding disaster for both sides. The Roosters had by the far the worst defence in the competition, while the Sharks were the weakest attacking outfit. They scraped together just five wins apiece, with the Tricolours collecting the wooden spoon due to an inferior for-and-against. Off-field turmoil also gripped both of the hapless clubs. Alcohol, drugs and sex scandals resulted in unwanted attention for the Sharks, while chief executive Tony Zappia resigned in shame after being accused of assaulting a female staff member. Not to be outdone, a string of alcohol-related atrocities peppered the Roosters' season—most notably the hotel capers of rep forward Nate Myles and coach Brad Fittler in separate incidents. Canberra and the Warriors finished 13th and 14th respectively after charging into the finals in '08.

6. Penrith, Canberra, North Sydney and Manly—1991-92

The 1992 season witnessed the dramatic decline of the previous year's finalists. Premiers Penrith finished ninth after its title defence was ripped apart by Ben Alexander's tragic death; beaten Grand Finalists and perennial heavyweights Canberra slipped to 12th after shedding several players in the wake of a salary cap breach and enduring injuries to several of its remaining stars; Norths finished 11th after reaching the preliminary final in '91, the club's best result in 26 years; and Manly dropped from second in the '91 regular season to eighth spot. The only club to reach the finals in both 1991 and '92 was Wests, who finished fifth in each season.

7. New Zealand Warriors—2011-12

The Warriors' stunning charge to the 2011 Grand Final—spearheaded by a clutch of exciting young talent—captured the imagination of the New Zealand sporting public, and expectations for the following season were sky-high despite coach Ivan Cleary's departure to Penrith. However, their 2012 campaign gradually unravelled under former Kiwi Test coach Brian McClennan. With the club hovering in finals contention midyear, back-to-back losses to Newcastle and Manly after holding 18-0 leads in both games—an unprecedented occurrence in premiership history—sparked a club-record eight-match losing streak to finish the season. McClennan quit with two rounds remaining and the Warriors eventually finished 14th.

8. Gold Coast—2010-11

In a few short years of existence, the Titans had become established as one of the NRL's strongest clubs, finishing in the top four in 2009-10. They reached the preliminary final stage for the first time in the latter season and headed into 2011 confident after retaining their entire first-choice squad. But their ageing roster caught up with the club dramatically, and the Titans won just six games to pick up the dreaded wooden spoon. Captain and linchpin Scott Prince's loss of form was a microcosm of the Titans' decline—the 2010 Dally M Halfback of the Year polled a paltry three votes (all from one game) in '11 and could not ignite his weary team.

9. St George—1993-94

Firmly established as heavyweights after second-place regular season finishes and Grand Final appearances in 1992-93, St George approached the '94 season determined to convert that consistency into the club's first premiership in 15 years. The progress of young stars Nathan Brown, Gorden Tallis and Jason Stevens buoyed those hopes, as did five wins in the opening six rounds. But the Dragons capitulated, winning just four further games to finish the year in 11th spot, nine competition points out of finals reckoning. For the first time in the club's proud history, St George did not contribute a player to the Kangaroo Tour squad.

10. Parramatta—1986-87

Parramatta's golden era garnered five Grand Final appearances and four premierships from 1981 to 1986, culminating in an epic 4-2 decider victory over archrivals Canterbury in '86 after the Eels had captured their first minor premiership in four years. But the retirement of club legends Mick Cronin and Ray Price had more of an impact than expected, despite the acquisition of Test lock Bob Lindner as Price's replacement: the

Eels began their title defence with three heavy losses and never recovered. A late season revival lifted Parramatta to a more respectable seventh and Peter Sterling was magnificent in claiming the Dally M-Rothmans Medal double, but the subpar campaign was the beginning of a wretched decade for the former superpower.

LATE SEASON RALLIES

1. South Sydney—1955
Since referred to as 'The Miracle of '55', Souths' sudden-death run to successfully defend the premiership holds a lofty place in the game's folklore. The Rabbitohs were languishing in eighth after 10 rounds with just three wins on the board, but rallied to win their final eight regular season matches. Their most famous victory came in the penultimate round against third-placed Manly, when Clive Churchill landed a last-minute goal from the sideline—despite breaking his arm earlier in the match—to secure a 9-7 result. Carrying on without their brilliant fullback, Souths snared fourth spot after defeating St George in the final round, before beating Manly and the Dragons again on their way to a Grand Final showdown with Newtown. The Bluebags led 11-7 late in the decider, but a try to halfback Col Donohoe and a pressure conversion by Bernie Purcell sealed the Rabbitohs' 11th straight win and their fourth title in five seasons.

2. Parramatta—2009
Daniel Anderson's tenure as Parramatta coach began turbulently—halfback Brett Finch left after just four weeks of the NRL season, Anderson's experiment with Jarryd Hayne at five-eighth failed, and the Eels found themselves in 14th with just five wins in the bank after 18 rounds. But on the back of Hayne's blistering Dally M Medal-winning form at fullback, Fuifui Moimoi's muscle, and an unheralded halves combination in Jeff Robson and rookie Daniel Mortimer, the Eels won seven straight to grab eighth spot. The blue-and-golds recovered from a last-round thrashing at the hands of St George Illawarra to roll the minor premier Dragons in the qualifying final before knocking off Gold Coast and the Bulldogs on their way to the Grand Final. The 23-16 decider loss to Melbourne could not detract from Parramatta's extraordinary charge.

3. Wests Tigers—2005

Boasting plenty of attacking flair but few representative-class players and only a small pack of forwards, Wests Tigers were not expected to challenge seriously for the NRL title in 2005. Despite stirring early-season wins over '04 Grand Finalists the Bulldogs and Sydney Roosters, Tim Sheens' Tigers sat in 12th with 10 weeks remaining after mustering just three wins in their previous 10 games. Then something clicked within the unfancied squad. Riding the brilliance of Benji Marshall, Scott Prince and Brett Hodgson, the Tigers won eight consecutive games to qualify for their maiden finals series in fourth spot. After routing North Queensland (50-6) and Brisbane (34-6), they upset title favourites St George Illawarra 20-12 in the preliminary final and secured the unlikeliest premiership triumph of the modern era with a memorable 30-16 defeat of the Cowboys in the Grand Final.

4. Brisbane—1999

The Broncos endured a catastrophic start to their NRL title defence in '99, winning just one of their first 10 games to languish in last place. Meanwhile, captain Allan Langer made a shock retirement announcement and the squad was further decimated by a raft of injury problems. But a new-look line-up turned the Broncos' season around dramatically as the premiers went on a spectacular 11-match winning streak. After stumbling momentarily in the latter rounds, they scored a gripping 14-12 win over heavyweights Canterbury in Round 26 to sneak into the top eight. Cronulla emphatically ended their season at the qualifying final stage, but the revival holds a cherished place in the Broncos' glittering history.

5. Balmain—1988

The Tigers were sitting in ninth spot on a congested table at the halfway mark of the 1988 season, struggling to build any consistency in their first season under Warren Ryan. But nine victories in 11 matches—including wins over fellow finals hopefuls Penrith and Brisbane in the last two rounds—pitched the Tigers into a share of fifth spot at the end of the premiership proper. Balmain thumped the Panthers 28-8 in a playoff for the last finals berth before upsetting Manly, Canberra and minor premiers Cronulla (conceding just three tries along the way) to reach the Grand Final. The black-and-golds' run ended via a spirited 24-12 loss to Canterbury in the decider—just their third defeat in 16 games.

6. Canberra—2012

The Raiders, who were renowned for starting the year slow and making a late charge for the finals, were sitting second-last at the halfway point of the 2012 season following a 40-0 drubbing at the hands of the Wests Tigers—their eighth loss in 12 matches. But with young stars Josh Dugan, Blake Ferguson, Josh McCrone, Reece Robinson,

Josh Papalii and Shaun Fensom on fire, the Green Machine won nine of its remaining 12 games—including its last five straight—to land in sixth spot. Canberra's run was highlighted by big wins over fellow top-eight sides Melbourne, Canterbury, Cronulla and Brisbane. The Raiders thumped the Sharks 34-16 at the qualifying final stage before crashing to a 22-point semi-final loss to Souths.

7. St George—1996
The Super League upheaval saw St George in disarray as the '96 season approached, with David Waite coming in late as a coaching replacement for Rod Reddy, who signed with the rebel outfit. The Dragons' results in the first half of the year reflected their difficult build-up, and they struggled in 13th after 12 rounds with only four wins. But on the back of a favourable draw the Saints suffered just one loss in the last 10 weeks of the regular season to snare seventh spot. A thrilling two-point win over Canberra in week one of the finals was followed by emphatic upsets of top-four sides Sydney City and Norths to claim an unlikely Grand Final berth. Manly halted St George's run in the decider, however, inflicting just the Dragons' second loss in over three months.

8. South Sydney—1968
Souths became premiers after St George's 11-year reign ended in 1967, but the Clive Churchill-coached side endured a difficult start to its title defence, lagging in seventh spot with nine rounds to go. The Rabbitohs rallied spectacularly, winning all of their remaining regular season matches to edge out Manly for the minor premiership. The Sea Eagles upset the Rabbitohs in the major semi, but bounced back to defeat St George in the preliminary final and sewed up the title with a tense 13-9 Grand Final victory over Manly—Souths' 11th win in 12 games.

9. Newcastle—2005
Contending with Andrew Johns' broken-jaw-enforced absence and injuries to a host of other key players, Newcastle lost its first 13 games in 2005—the worst start to a season by any team since Easts' winless 1966 campaign. But with Johns back on deck, the Knights jagged their first win in Round 16, and a few weeks later embarked on an inspiring six-match winning streak that included the scalps of finals-bound Parramatta, Melbourne, Manly and Cronulla, and defending champs the Bulldogs. A gallant last-round loss to second-placed St George Illawarra consigned the club to its first-ever wooden spoon, but the revival won the Knights an army of admirers. Johns came within a point of winning the Dally M Medal despite playing just 16 games, Newcastle broke the premiership record for most wins by a last-placed team, and some suggested the Knights should be granted a wildcard entry into the finals as arguably the NRL's form team at the end of the season.

10. New Zealand Warriors—2008
Like Canberra, the Warriors built a reputation as a team that took a while to get going before coming home strong to reach the finals. In 2007, they stormed from 13th at the halfway point of the competition to finish in the top four before a straight-sets finals exit. But the Auckland-based club arguably trumped that effort the following season, recovering from 14th on the ladder after 14 rounds. The Warriors walked the tightrope, winning eight of their last 10 matches—including upsets of heavyweights Melbourne, Brisbane and Cronulla—to scrape into eighth spot. They kept the dream run alive by becoming the first eighth-placed club to defeat the minor premiers under the McIntyre finals system courtesy of an incredible last-gasp win over the Storm, and thumped the Sydney Roosters 30-13 to reach the preliminary final, where they were halted 32-6 by Manly.

LATE SEASON FADE-OUTS

1. Wests Tigers—2000
The Wests Tigers joint venture's maiden campaign was exceeding expectations two-thirds of the way through the season—the gritty, aggressive amalgam of journeymen and battlers occupied a top-four spot from Round 5 until Round 17. But with a debut-year finals berth at their mercy, the Wayne Pearce-coached Tigers lost eight of their last 10 games to slip from second to an eventual 10th-place finish. They gave up a 23-point lead to lose to Penrith, and subsequent losses to also-rans St George Illawarra, North Queensland and the Bulldogs capped a spectacular tumble out of contention.

2. Brisbane—2003
Buffeted by a heavy injury toll, Brisbane's perennial post-Origin trough was deeper than ever in 2003. The Broncos held the competition lead after 17 rounds but could only muster one victory in the final 10 weeks of the regular season, and were forced to rely on other results to scrape into eighth. Without several representative stars for key periods of the run to the finals—headlined by Darren Lockyer and Gorden Tallis—the Broncos' horror stretch culminated in a plucky 28-18 qualifying final defeat to minor premiers Penrith, extending their club-record losing streak to eight games.

3. Gold Coast—2008
A second-season finals appearance was on the cards for the fledgling Gold Coast in 2008 when they headed the NRL table after Round 10. But captain and linchpin

Scott Prince suffered a broken arm in the State of Origin decider, sending the Titans spiralling out of the top eight. Fourth at the halfway mark of the season, they won just two further matches and averaged 31 points conceded to finish a dismal 13th. The club endured a similar collapse in its maiden season, losing nine of its last 11 games to slide from a top-four position to 12th.

4. South Sydney—1982
Battling South Sydney appeared on the cusp of a major resurgence after 14 rounds of 1982, dropping just three games to earn a share of the competition lead with eventual Grand Finalists Manly and Parramatta. But the Bill Anderson-coached Rabbitohs crumbled badly, winning just three (including a major upset of the Eels) and drawing one of their last 12 games to finish sixth, three competition points adrift of the finals. A season-ending injury to brilliant but luckless five-eighth Micheal Pattison proved critical in Souths' dramatic decline.

5. Brisbane—2005
Brisbane was sailing towards the minor premiership in 2005 on the back of a 10-match winning streak and held a six-point ladder lead at the end of Round 21 after adequately negotiating the Origin period. But losses in their last five matches—including an extraordinary late collapse against also-rans Penrith—saw the Broncos slip to third spot at the end of the regular season. Finals losses to Melbourne (24-18) and Wests Tigers (34-6) extended their losing run to seven matches, prompting a major cleanout of Wayne Bennett's coaching staff.

6. Manly—1980
After plundering archrivals Wests' playing ranks and luring Les Boyd, Ray Brown and John Dorahy to Brookvale, Manly was strongly favoured to return to the premiership penthouse in 1980 after a dismal title defence the previous season. The Sea Eagles sat alongside the Magpies at the top of the table after 13 rounds following a six-match winning streak. The bubble burst, however, as the heavyweights lost eight and drew two of their last 12 games—including defeats to lowly Norths, Balmain and Cronulla. The Sea Eagles landed in seventh, one point shy of a playoff for fifth spot.

7. Western Suburbs —1976
After a replacement bungle had cost them a spot in the 1975 finals, Wests appeared set to qualify for just their second post-season since the club's early 1960s heyday. The Magpies sat in outright second after 13 rounds of the '76 season, incurring just two losses, but a tally of just three wins in their last 10 games saw them tumble to a seventh-place finish—three points outside the finals—and brought Don Parish's five-season stint as coach to an end.

8. Newtown—1974

Looking to build on a fairytale 1973 campaign under coach Jack Gibson, Newtown was second on the ladder at the halfway mark of the '74 premiership under new mentor Clarrie Jeffries. The Jets managed only two wins and two draws from their last 12 matches, however, and slumped to seventh place—five competition points out of the finals race—while Gibson led Easts to their first title in 29 years. Newtown finished 10th the following season before collecting three consecutive wooden spoons.

9. North Sydney—1942

Wooden spooners the previous season, North Sydney lost just two games during the first half of its '42 campaign (both by one point, to contenders Canterbury and St George) and was hanging on to third place after nine of the 14 premiership rounds. But Norths lost their last seven games—a defeat to each of the other seven clubs in the competition—to drop to sixth, three wins adrift of the finals. They qualified for the only Grand Final in their history a year later.

10. Balmain—1966

The Harry Bath-coached Balmain Tigers threw down the gauntlet to 10-time premiers St George early in 1966, holding a five-point competition lead over the Saints after staying unbeaten for the first 11 rounds of the year. But defeats in their last five regular season games—four of them to sides that finished out of finals contention—left the Tigers in a hole despite their second-place finish. They were subsequently beaten by St George 10-2 in the major semi. An 8-5 preliminary final success over Manly was their first win in two months, but it delayed the inevitable as Keith Barnes' out-of-sorts Tigers were swamped 23-4 by the Dragons in the Grand Final.

REMARKABLE ONE-WEEK TURNAROUNDS

1. St George Illawarra—2000

The Saints had been Grand Finalists the previous season, but their disastrous 2000 campaign hit a new low when they were humiliated 50-4 by last-placed battlers North Queensland in Round 13. With a rejigged line-up, the Dragons bounced back in emphatic fashion seven days later, decimating the Auckland Warriors 54-0 in Wollongong. Amos Roberts scored a premiership-debut-record 22 points and Nathan Blacklock bagged a hat-trick as the Dragons completed a 100-point turnaround.

2. Canterbury—1935
Canterbury's debut season in 1935 is chiefly remembered for the Bulldogs being on the end of the two heaviest defeats in premiership history, but the fledgling club also staged one of the biggest turnarounds of all time. After being crushed 91-6 by St George and then 87-7 by Easts a week later, Canterbury scored its maiden victory by trouncing battlers University 21-2—a seven-day turnaround of 99 points.

3. Manly—2004
Rebuilding Manly conceded its highest-ever score in Round 22 of 2004, letting 13 tries through in a 72-12 defeat to defending premiers Penrith. Rookie coach Des Hasler rang the changes and his Sea Eagles responded with a 48-10 demolition of top-eight hopefuls Newcastle—a turnaround of 98 points. Teenage fullback Brett Stewart scored two tries and mercurial five-eighth Andrew Walker kicked eight from eight.

4. Brisbane—2005
Brisbane travelled to Melbourne in Round 4 of 2005 only to let in 10 tries in a then club-record 50-4 defeat. The Broncos returned to form in the familiar surroundings of Suncorp Stadium, however, blitzing eventual minor premiers Parramatta to the tune of 54-14 eight days later—an 86-point turnaround. They led the Eels 42-0 at halftime before easing off in the second stanza.

5. North Sydney—1998
Brisbane racked up the highest score conceded in North Sydney's history in Round 7 of 1998, running in 11 tries in a 60-6 thumping despite having four players backing up from a Test match two days earlier. Coach Peter Louis stuck solid with his line-up, however, and the Bears responded with a 32-8 defeat of bitter rivals and perennial heavyweights Manly the following weekend.

6. New Zealand Warriors—2013
The Warriors' dreadful start to their first campaign under coach Matt Elliott culminated in an insipid club-record loss to Penrith, Elliott's former club, in Round 10. The Panthers, coached by former Warriors mentor Ivan Cleary, ran up a 62-6 scoreline, with former Warriors Isaac John and Lewis Brown scoring five tries between them. But following a weeklong media hailstorm at their expense, the Warriors carved out a convincing 28-12 victory over fifth-placed Newcastle in Auckland, sparking a giant-killing run of seven wins in eight matches.

7. Canberra—2007
The Raiders performed an 88-point turnaround in seven days in 2007—a rare highlight in a disappointing campaign for the Green Machine. Canberra was swamped 58-16 by fellow also-rans St George Illawarra in Round 17, but recovered

to decimate the Titans—who were desperately clinging to eighth spot—by a 56-10 scoreline a week later.

8. Parramatta—2013
There were few positives to draw from Parramatta's 2013 wooden-spoon season, but the woeful Eels' ability to bounce back from a frightful beating with a win was noteworthy. Five days after a 50-0 rout at the hands of the Sydney Roosters, the Eels rolled eventual finalists Cronulla 13-6. Melbourne inflicted the second-biggest loss in Parramatta's history—a 64-4 destruction—late in the season, but the blue-and-golds defeated St George Illawarra 26-22 the following weekend.

9. Western Suburbs—1944
Western Suburbs was obliterated 64-2 at Pratten Park by Balmain late in the 1944 season, conceding 14 tries in the second-biggest defeat in the club's history. But a week later the Magpies upset Norths, who were still in finals contention, by 12-11 at North Sydney Oval.

10. Canberra—1982
The Raiders were cannon fodder for most sides during their 1982 debut season, most notably going down 54-3 to defending premiers Parramatta in Round 7—a defeat that remains the second biggest in Canberra's history. But the ragtag Raiders hit back to score their maiden win in first grade by eclipsing Newtown—the Eels' Grand Final opponents seven months earlier—12-11 at Seiffert Oval seven days later. Celebrations of the milestone were short-lived as the Raiders crashed to a 45-0 loss to fellow newcomers Illawarra in the next round.

GREATEST CLUBMEN

1. Darren Lockyer—355 games, Brisbane Broncos (1995-2011)
The game's most capped top-grader and arguably the most decorated player in the history of the code, Darren Lockyer never played a game against the Brisbane Broncos. A four-time premiership winner, he debuted off the bench as an 18-year-old midway through 1995 and went on to win the club's Rookie of the Year honour. Assuming the captaincy in 2005, Lockyer led the Broncos for seven years before retiring at the end of the 2011 season. He is the club's greatest point-scorer and a four-time winner of the Broncos' Player of the Year gong.

2. Steve Menzies—349 games, Manly Sea Eagles/Northern Eagles (1993-2008)

Though he technically played for two clubs, Steve Menzies spent his entire 16-year NRL career at Brookvale. The second-greatest try-scorer in premiership history, Menzies is the grandson of foundation Manly centre Mackie Campbell and was a Manly junior. Debuting in 1994 at the age of 20, he won the Dally M Rookie of the Year. He represented NSW and Australia before retiring after the 2008 premiership decider, where he scored a try in the 40-0 drubbing. A club legend, he returned to play with Manly in 2014 in the inaugural version of the Auckland Nines.

3. Nathan Hindmarsh—330 games, Parramatta Eels (1998-2012)

A Parramatta stalwart who stuck with the Eels through good times and dark days, Nathan Hindmarsh made his premiership debut in Parkes against Adelaide in 1998. A workaholic backrower, he was the greatest tackling forward of the first 15 years of the NRL era. Renowned for his massive heart, Hindmarsh was arguably the most popular in the game for the latter part of his career. The two-time Grand Finalist retired after the 2012 wooden-spoon season, finishing with a famous penalty goal.

4. Andrew Ettingshausen—328 games, Cronulla Sharks (1983-2000)

A Cronulla junior, the great Sharks tryscoring three-quarter Andrew Ettingshausen debuted in 1983 at fullback under the stewardship of Terry Fearnley. He spent 18 seasons (a premiership record for consecutive years at one club) at the Sharks but played in just one Grand Final—the losing 1997 Super League decider. A speedster with a great swerve, Ettingshausen complemented his vast array of attacking skills by being a reliable defender. A back injury in 2000 brought the curtain down on a fine career a year after he became the first player to bring up 300 games for one club.

5. Jason Croker—318 games, Canberra Raiders (1991-2006)

Canberra's longest-serving player, Crookwell junior Jason Croker debuted in 1991 during the Raiders' glory era and played on until 2006. One of the most versatile players in premiership history, he played every position bar halfback and hooker for the Raiders. Croker missed Canberra's 1991 Grand Final loss but was central to the 1994 premiership success. A NSW and Australian representative, the tough utility was presented with the keys to Canberra after his final game for the Raiders in '06.

6. Hazem El Masri—317 games, Canterbury Bulldogs (1996-2009)

The greatest point-scorer in premiership history, Hazem El Masri was not only a Canterbury legend but an inspiration to people from non-traditional Rugby League backgrounds. A devout Muslim born in Lebanon, El Masri was a Belmore Boys High student who progressed through the grades to debut in first grade in 1996. Though he didn't kick until the 2001 season, he became the greatest point-scorer the premiership has known in 2009 and only the seventh player to score 150 tries. His last home game attracted a crowd in excess of 40,000 people.

7. Luke Ricketson—301 games, Sydney Roosters (1991-2005)
The son of great Easts clubman Doug Ricketson, who spent four seasons as a Tricolours first grader, Luke Ricketson debuted in 1991 as an 18-year-old, starting a decorated career that would see him win a premiership and represent NSW and Australia. A hardworking lock, Ricketson began his career as an outside back. He captained the club in his farewell 2005 season and retired after 301 games with the Roosters.

8. Geoff Toovey—286 games, Manly Sea Eagles/Northern Eagles (1988-2001)
An out-and-out Manly icon, Geoff Toovey spent 14 seasons playing for both the Sea Eagles and the Northern Eagles before being appointed Manly coach in 2012. Small in stature but huge in heart, the courageous halfback-cum-hooker was a NSW and Australian rep for a decade and famously played the 1996 Grand Final with a fractured eye socket. Toovey was appointed skipper of Manly in 1993 and was captain until he retired in 2001. He coached the club to the Grand Final in 2013, his second year in charge.

9. Greg Florimo—285 games, North Sydney Bears (1986-98)
Red-headed star Greg Florimo helped usher in North Sydney's last great era. Since the Bears' exclusion from the premiership, he has fought for a Central Coast team bearing the club's history, name and colours to enter the NRL. A North Sydney junior, Florimo played 13 seasons with the Bears, racking up 285 games—then a record for most appearances with one club. The local hero called Bears fans on to North Sydney Oval after a famous win over rivals Manly.

10. Corey Parker—277 games, Brisbane Broncos (2001-13)
One of the game's most durable players, underrated lock Corey Parker debuted in 2001 and was still going strong in 2014. An all-round player who kicks goals, leads the tackle count and often makes more metres than any teammate, Parker was appointed co-captain of the club in 2014. A Queensland and Australian rep, he has twice won the Broncos' Player of the Year gong and is a two-time recipient of the *Rugby League Week* Player of the Year award.

Chapter 5

THE PLAYERS

BEST PLAYERS

1. Andrew Johns
The Team of the Century halfback and the eighth player to be named an Immortal, Andrew Johns could do what no other player could. The Newcastle No.7 had no weaknesses in his game: his in-play kicking was revolutionary, his passing game was sublime, his defence was as good as any halfback, his goalkicking gave him the mantle of one-time top point-scorer in premiership history, and his running was devastating. Johns won two premierships with the Knights and starred for NSW and Australia in 23 Origins and 26 Tests. He won a host of individual awards, including two Golden Boots, three Dally Ms, a Clive Churchill Medal, three *Rugby League Week* Player of the Year gongs and four State of Origin man-of-the-match awards.

2. Clive Churchill
'The Little Master', Clive Churchill, breathed life into Australian Rugby League post-World War II and changed the fortunes of both South Sydney and Australia. A sublime talent from Newcastle, Churchill's decorated career saw him named as an inaugural Immortal and the Team of the Century fullback. He featured in five successful premiership campaigns with his beloved Bunnies during the 1950s—

coaching them to a further four in the late 1960s and early 1970s—and played in an incredible 99 consecutive representative matches, including captaining Australia in the famous third Test of the 1950 Ashes series, which saw the urn return to the country for the first time in 30 years. Churchill was named as the greatest player ever by *Rugby League Week* in 1992 and *The Daily Telegraph* in 2000.

3. Wally Lewis

'The King', Wally Lewis, is a revered figure in Queensland Rugby League and the greatest five-eighth the game has known. A polarising figure who was as loathed in NSW as he was beloved in Queensland, Lewis was respected everywhere as the best player in the game in the 1980s. He made his mark during the infant days of Origin, winning an incredible eight man-of-the-match awards for the Maroons—twice the number of any other player. Lewis's tenacious and skilful play translated to the Test arena, where he captained Australia in 24 Tests. He skippered Australia to three Ashes series wins as well as a World Cup triumph. While he only entered the NSWRL premiership at the backend of his career, he won three titles in the BRL. Lewis was named as the five-eighth in the Team of the Century.

4. Dave Brown

The most phenomenal point-scorer in premiership history, Eastern Suburbs centre Dave Brown created many records that still remain. Though he played just 94 premiership matches (scoring 93 tries), the mercurial Brown was the star of maybe the greatest side in League history—the Eastern Suburbs outfit of the mid-1930s. The freakish talent's 38 tries in the '35 season has never been approached, while his 45 points in a single game against Canterbury remains a premiership record. His 285 points on the 1933-34 Kangaroo Tour also stands as a record. Brown ascended to the Test captaincy at the age of just 22 and was named in the NSW Team of the Century in 2008, though he was a notable omission from the ARL team.

5. Johnny Raper

A devastating cover defender and one of the great ball-playing forwards, Johnny Raper is almost unanimously recognised as the greatest lock forward to play the game. A member of the great St George team that won 11 straight titles—Raper winning eight in a row—the Team of the Century lock was also the cornerstone of the Australian team that won back the ascendancy from Great Britain in the 1960s. Raper's crowning moment came in the 1963 'Swinton Massacre' Ashes Test, where he set up nine of Australia's 12 tries; he toured with the Kangaroos three times, captaining Australia on his last trip. Raper won three *Sun Herald* Player of the Year awards and two EE Christensen Player of the Year honours, and was named as an original Immortal. Legendary caller Frank Hyde rated Raper the greatest player he had seen.

6. Darren Lockyer
Rugby League's most durable great, Darren Lockyer achieved all there was to achieve in Rugby League. The premiership's most capped player, Lockyer won four premierships with Brisbane, skippering the last, and has played more matches for Queensland (36) and Australia (59) than any other player. Australia's most successful skipper, he has also scored more tries in the green-and-gold than any other player. Lockyer is the finest clutch player in League history, his late game heroics becoming the stuff of legend. The two-time Golden Boot winner incredibly won the prestigious award in two different positions. He was named at fullback in the QRL Team of the Century in 2008 despite making an incredibly successful shift to five-eighth four years earlier.

7. Reg Gasnier
A graceful and gliding centre, Reg Gasnier's career was cut short by injury—but not before he left an indelible mark on the game. An outstanding tryscoring centre who crossed for 127 tries in 125 premiership games with the great St George team of the 1950s and '60s, Gasnier won six titles with the indomitable Dragons. Tremendously balanced, with scintillating pace and an innate understanding of how to position his supports, he was a delight to watch. 'Puff, the Magic Dragon' toured three times with the Kangaroos and became Australia's youngest Ashes captain in 1962 at the age of just 23. Gasnier was named in the Australian Team of the Century in 2008 and was an inaugural Immortal.

8. Dally Messenger
Rugby League's first superstar, the awe-inspiring centre Dally Messenger, has not faded into history, remaining potentially the game's most revered figure over a century after he signed on with the professional code. A supreme attacking player and unrivalled kicker, Messenger drew crowds in hordes to see his amazing talents. He skippered Eastern Suburbs to three premierships and was the star of the 1908-09 Kangaroo Tour, but statistics do not do justice to his freakish ability to do almost anything on a Rugby League field. Known as 'The Master', the Dally M Medal was named in his honour and was included as a reserve in the ARL Team of the Century in 2008.

9. Harold Horder
Dubbed 'The Wonder Winger' for his amazing deeds, Harold Horder was regarded as one of the code's first champions. Scoring a remarkable 152 tries in just 136 premiership games with South Sydney and North Sydney, He signalled his greatness on debut with a marvellous solo try that rates among the greatest in Rugby League history. Horder won four premierships at club level and scored a near-unbelievable 23 tries in just nine interstate appearances, while he crossed 11 times in 13 Tests.

Horder was a shock omission from the ARL Team of the Century but is regarded by many as the greatest winger in premiership history.

10. Frank Burge
The greatest tryscoring forward in the history of the game, Glebe forward Frank 'Chunky' Burge crossed for 146 tries in 154 games, including a premiership-record eight in one match. A giant both figuratively and metaphorically, Burge debuted aged 16, with his career spanning 17 seasons. Though he never won a premiership, he was regarded as unstoppable, crossing for an incredible 33 tries in 23 games on the 1921-22 Kangaroo Tour. He was named on the bench in the ARL Team of the Century and as a prop in the NSW Team of the Century, despite being primarily regarded as a backrower.

11. Graeme Langlands
One of the game's most popular players, St George champion Graeme Langlands was rated second by *The Daily Telegraph* in the game's top 100 players in 2000. 'Changa' won titles in his first four seasons with St George as a great fullback/centre during its record-breaking title run; he played on until 1976, touring three times with the Kangaroos and winning two World Cups. Such was his stature in the game that the SCG crowd chanted 'Changa' as he was chaired from the field after spearheading the 1974 Ashes triumph as captain. Langlands was selected on the bench in the ARL Team of the Century and was named as an Immortal in 1999.

12. Cameron Smith
The finest hooker in Rugby League history, Melbourne Storm legend Cameron Smith won three Grand Finals and played in four deciders with the Storm while captaining Australia to a World Cup win and starring in all eight of Queensland's incredible successive series wins. A flawless player who consistently played at the highest level, Smith became one of the game's most respected leaders and has often been touted as a future Immortal. He has been awarded the Golden Boot and Dally M Medal and has cemented the importance of the hooker in modern Rugby League.

13. Arthur Beetson
A maligned player during the early part of his career, Arthur Beetson went on to be recognised as the greatest prop in Australian history. A giant of a man, he was a deft ball-player and the most phenomenal offload merchant the game has seen. Remarkably, much of the prodigious young talent's success came in the second half of his career, when he led Eastern Suburbs to consecutive titles, became the first Indigenous Australian to captain a national sporting team and set the tone for State

of Origin at the age of 35 with a courageous display for Queensland in the first-ever Origin encounter. Beetson was named in the Team of the Century and as the code's seventh Immortal.

14. Bob Fulton
An inaugural Immortal, brilliant centre/five-eighth Bob Fulton enjoyed a long career with Manly before finishing with Eastern Suburbs. He won three premierships with Manly as a player, with his finest performance coming in 1973 when his cleverness proved the difference in a brutal decider. Renowned for his speed and evasion, Fulton was the top try-scorer on the 1973 and '78 Kangaroo Tours. He was named on the bench in the ARL Team of the Century.

15. Billy Slater
The greatest testament to Melbourne fullback Billy Slater's astonishing talents came from Joyce Churchill, widow of the great Clive, who said that no player reminded her more of her husband than Slater. A former jockey, the diminutive Slater was possessed with blinding speed and daring courage that lit up the game. A fabulous try-scorer who had crossed for 158 for the Storm heading into the 2014 season, he has scored some of the game's most memorable tries. Slater won the 2008 Golden Boot, the 2009 Clive Churchill Medal and the 2011 Dally M Medal, and has starred in the No.1 for Queensland and Australia.

16. Ken Irvine
The only player in premiership history to score 200 tries, dashing North Sydney and Manly winger Ken Irvine crossed for 212—a record tally that has never been neared. One of the fastest players to play the game (he was once matched with a racehorse in a battle at Wentworth Park), Irvine went on to become one of the greatest wingers in Rugby League history, named in the ARL Team of the Century. The Bears' finest-ever player, he scored 33 tries in 33 Tests and finished his career with back-to-back premierships at Manly.

17. Duncan Thompson
A transcendent Queensland halfback in the immediate aftermath of World War I, Duncan Thompson was blessed with a brain for Rugby League like few others. Fast, brilliant and creative, Thompson was the finest halfback Rugby League knew in its first eight decades. He was central to North Sydney's only two premierships and starred for Queensland during its domination of NSW in the 1920s, as well as being the star of the all-conquering Toowoomba Clydesdales. An attacking genius, Thompson added a beautiful element to the tough game.

18. Mal Meninga

A force of nature with a fearful combination of size and speed, Mal Meninga was a dominant centre who thrived at the game's highest echelons for 15 seasons. He debuted for Queensland as a 19-year-old and thrived in the Origin format. He is the only player to make four Kangaroo Tours and captain two, while his premiership career with Canberra netted him three titles, all as skipper, including a fairytale farewell in 1994. A colossus, Meninga was named as a centre in the ARL Team of the Century.

19. Johnathan Thurston

A fiery, competitive, supremely gifted half, Johnathan Thurston dominated at rep level for a decade. The only player to turn out in all 24 matches of Queensland's eight-straight series wins from 2006 to 2013—breaking the record for consecutive Origin appearances, he sits second in the history of the format with four man-of-the-match awards. His exploits at Test level have been equally brilliant, and he became Australia's great Test point-scorer at the 2013 World Cup. A Golden Boot winner and two-time Dally M Player of the Year, Cowboys linchpin Thurston was named in the Indigenous Team of the Century.

20. Allan Langer

A four-time premiership winner as captain of the Brisbane Broncos despite being short in stature, Allan Langer was the game's grandest figure of the 1990s. A halfback who seemingly had the ball on a string, with a sensational short kicking game and a beautiful ability to find a hole, Langer did it all. He was Queensland's most capped player on his retirement and starred for Australia, winning a host of individual accolades including a Rothmans Medal, a Dally M Medal and a Clive Churchill Medal. Langer is the only halfback to have scored 100 premiership tries.

BEST INDIVIDUAL SEASONS

1. Dave Brown—1935

Eastern Suburbs pointscoring champion Dave Brown had an incredible year in 1935, breaking a number of records that still stand. He crossed for 38 tries in a season and scored 45 points in a match, and smashed the premiership record for points in a season with 244. Though he missed the final through injury, he was instrumental in Eastern Suburbs' title win. He became the Australian Test captain at the age of just 22.

2. Clive Churchill—1950

'The Little Master' enjoyed a spectacular 1950, with the highlight being his hand in Australia's Ashes triumph as captain—the first time Australia had claimed the Ashes in 30 years. He was scintillating in NSW's interstate series triumph and had a magnificent year in the premiership, playing a key role in South Sydney's title. Churchill was duly awarded EE Christensen's Player of the Year award after a sublime season.

3. Wally Lewis—1984

Wally Lewis swept all before him in 1984 in a season that netted him the inaugural Golden Boot award for best player in the world. Lewis was the best on the paddock in Wynnum Manly's 42-8 Grand Final win and the star of Combined Brisbane's Panasonic Cup win over Eastern Suburbs. His State of Origin legend was in full swing, with two man-of-the-match awards in the 2-1 series triumph. At Test level, he captained Australia to an Ashes clean sweep, with a man-of-the-match showing in the series opener. It was a magnificent year from a special player.

4. Darren Lockyer—2006

Darren Lockyer won it all in 2006, captaining Brisbane to an unlikely premiership triumph, Queensland to an Origin series win and Australia to a famous Tri-Nations win; he claimed the Golden Boot along the way. Lockyer was Brisbane's best in its 15-8 Grand Final win over Melbourne, and amazingly scored the winning try in both the Origin decider and the Tri-Nations final. His 2006 season elevated him from great player to all-time champion.

5. Bob Fulton—1973

Manly sensation Bob Fulton could not put a foot wrong in a fairytale 1973 season. He was in red-hot form all year, with his two-try effort in the violent Grand Final the difference in the Sea Eagles' 10-7 win. He carried that form on to the Kangaroo Tour, where he played in all five Tests in the successful series against Great Britain and France, and scored 20 tries in 14 appearances. EE Christensen awarded him the Player of the Year.

6. Allan Langer—1992

Inspirational halfback Allan Langer enjoyed a truly remarkable 1992, playing a key hand in Brisbane's inaugural premiership triumph, Australia's Ashes success and a memorable Origin victory during a tight series loss. The Rothmans Medal winner and third in the Dally M, Langer carried his outstanding form into the Grand Final against St George, winning the Clive Churchill Medal after a dominant two-try display. He was Australia's best in the hard-fought 2-1 defeat of Great Britain during the Ashes series, and was again outstanding in the World Cup final win over the same opponents. Langer's clutch field goal in the second Origin clash gave Queensland a memorable 5-4 victory to boot, in a stellar season.

7. Joe Jorgenson—1946

Strike Balmain centre Joe Jorgensen dominated at all levels of the game in 1946. In the premiership, he scored a second-half double in the Grand Final against St George to lift Balmain to a 13-12 win and the club's ninth title. On the rep scene, he starred for City and NSW and was appointed Australian Test captain for the first post-war Ashes series.

8. Johnny Raper—1963

Immortal Johnny Raper dominated the 1963 season both at home and abroad. He had a magnificent domestic season in driving St George to another premiership victory and winning the *Sun Herald* Player of the Year, while his performance in the Ashes win on English soil was sublime. His hand in nine of Australia's 12 tries at Swinton is considered the greatest individual Test performance of all time.

9. Billy Smith—1966

A shift to halfback in 1966 from the centres was a natural fit for St George's Billy Smith. He was magnificent throughout the year, guiding the Saints to their 11th straight premiership and being awarded the Harry Sunderland Medal as Australia's best during the '66 Ashes campaign. Smith won the EE Christensen Player of the Year-*Sun Herald* Best and Fairest double.

10. Tom Gorman—1926

Champion Queensland centre Tom Gorman enjoyed success on all fronts during an unforgettable 1926 season. He skippered Past Brothers to the BRL premiership and Brisbane to a famous Bulimba Cup win, and was superb in the 3-2 interstate series win, scoring in two of the three victories.

GREATEST CAPTAINS

1. Arthur Beetson

Regarded early in his career as talented but enigmatic, Arthur Beetson became one of the great club, state and Test captains. He was first appointed to the top job in 1974 by Jack Gibson, and his leadership was instrumental to Eastern Suburbs winning premierships in 1974-75. Appointed Australian captain in 1975 (the first Indigenous Australian to captain a national sporting team), he led Australia to wins in the 1975 World Series and 1977 World Cup. He famously stood down from a Test in '77 after being overlooked due to interstate politics. Beetson's most famous moment as a skipper came in 1980, when he led Queensland in the inaugural State of Origin match. His pre-match address and on-field leadership have since become ingrained in the lore of Origin.

2. Ken Kearney

The architect behind St George's first six titles in its famous run of 11, tenacious hooker Ken Kearney was captain-coach for four, skipper for five and non-playing coach for another after succumbing to injury. Appointed captain-coach of the Saints in 1954 and despite a tempestuous relationship with referees, he skippered the club until injury forced his retirement in 1961. A rugged competitor, Kearney also skippered Australia in the 3-0 series win against New Zealand in 1956 and on the 1956-57 Kangaroo Tour.

3. Darren Lockyer

Darren Lockyer enjoyed his first taste of captaincy in 2001 as a 24-year-old for Brisbane and Queensland following an injury to Gorden Tallis. He would go on to become Australia's most prolific skipper, also captaining Brisbane to the 2006 premiership. Lockyer's 38 Tests at the helm is a record (11 ahead of second-placed Clive Churchill) and his 22 Origins as captain is second only to Lewis, with Lockyer at the helm for six of the Maroons' first seven wins in their incredible streak.

4. John Sattler

A captain who led by example, John Sattler's courage as leader in the 1970 Grand Final, when he played with a broken jaw, has defined Rugby League toughness. A surprising choice by coach Clive Churchill to captain Souths in 1967, Sattler led the Rabbitohs to four premierships and five Grand Finals in a decorated run as Bunnies skipper. While he played just four Tests for Australia, such was his reputation as a leader that the first three of those were as captain.

5. Cameron Smith

The skipper of the Melbourne Storm through an era of dominance, Cameron Smith emerged as a leader aged just 22 in 2006; in the near-decade following, he led the side to three premierships and five Grand Finals. Calm and thoughtful, Smith did few things wrong and set a culture that likened winning to breathing. He succeeded Darren Lockyer as skipper of both Queensland and Australia, continuing Queensland's irrepressible undefeated run while guiding Australia to the 2013 World Cup.

6. Mal Meninga

While Mal Meninga did not taste the captaincy until the latter years of his career, he achieved significantly as a leader at all levels of the game. Taking over the Raiders' captaincy midway through the '89 season, he led the club to its maiden premiership and was skipper in its only three title triumphs. Succeeding Wally Lewis as the Australian captain in 1990 and as Queensland's captain in '92, Meninga led Australia on two successful Kangaroo Tours (the first player to do so) but failed to win an Origin series as skipper.

7. Steve Edge

A quality hooker with St George and Parramatta, Steve Edge was a natural leader who was handed the captaincy reins as a 24-year-old and led two clubs to four premierships. In his first year as the Dragons' leader, he skippered them to their first premiership since their golden run of 11 straight. Moving to Parramatta, Jack Gibson appointed him as skipper ahead of bigger-name stars—a testament to his leadership and one that paid dividends when Edge captained the club to its first three premierships. He remains the only player to captain two clubs to Grand Final glory.

8. Wally Lewis

Marked as a leader from a young age, Wally Lewis was appointed Queensland captain at just 21, a post he held with distinction for the next 10 seasons. A ferocious competitor, he set the tone for a Queensland culture that has lasted well beyond his retirement. Lewis won seven series as Queensland captain and achieved as much success at Test level, winning 21 of 24 Tests as captain, including a sweep of the 1986 Kangaroo Tour and the 1988 World Cup final. He captain-coached Wynnum Manly to a BRL premiership in 1986 and was the Broncos' foundation skipper.

9. Norm Provan

St George's captain over the back half of its famous run of 11 straight titles, Norm 'Sticks' Provan is a giant of St George, both figuratively and literally. An imposing second-rower, he played in the Dragons' team that won the first 10 of 11 premierships, captain-coaching the team from 1962 to '65.

10. Brad Fittler

An occasional captain at Penrith when still only a baby in football terms, Brad Fittler went on to become a fine leader at club, state and Test level. Appointed permanent skipper of the Sydney Roosters in 1997, he retired with the most first grade games as captain at 216 (a record since broken by Nathan Cayless) and steered the Tricolours to a title in 2002 among four Grand Finals as skipper. At state level he captained NSW more times than anyone bar Danny Buderus, leading the Blues to three series wins.

He skippered Australia in 25 Tests, winning two World Cups and enjoying Ashes series success on his farewell Kangaroo Tour in 2001.

YOUNG CAPTAINS

1. Dave Brown
Legendary centre Dave Brown was a Rugby League prodigy, installed as Easts' club captain in 1932 at the preposterously young age of 19. He skippered NSW for the first time in 1934 a couple of months after turning 21, and became the youngest Australian Test captain in history the following season at 22 years and 177 days. Brown also led the Tricolours to premiership success in 1935, although injury ruled him out of the final.

2. Wally Lewis
Veteran prop Arthur Beetson was slated to captain Queensland again in the one-off Origin clash in 1981, but injury restricted the 36-year-old to the role of non-playing coach. The Maroons selectors went from one extreme to the other and installed 21-year-old five-eighth Wally Lewis as skipper. Lewis led his state to a come-from-behind 22-15 victory and captained it in 30 of his 31 Origin appearances—a record likely to stand the test of time. He was installed as Test skipper at the age of 24.

3. Laurie Daley
Bradley Clyde was touted as the next NSW skipper after touring Papua New Guinea in 1991 as Australian vice-captain at just 21 years of age. But when the Canberra lock declined the role, Blues selectors opted for a player just three months his senior—Raiders five-eighth Laurie Daley. The 22-year-old captained NSW to three straight series successes from 1992 to 1994, and led Australia in one Test in '93, aged 23.

4. Reg Gasnier
Brilliant St George centre Reg Gasnier became the youngest captain in Anglo-Australian Test history in 1962, aged 23 years and 28 days. He was replaced by Keith Barnes after the 31-12 first Test loss, but later skippered the 1967-68 Kangaroos.

5. Bob Fulton
Destined for greatness from an early age, Bob Fulton captain-coached City Firsts against Country Firsts and skippered Manly in a Grand Final loss to Souths in 1967 at the tender age of 20. Ironically, the Sea Eagles legend starred in the 1972-73

Grand Finals under Fred Jones' captaincy. He captained Manly to a premiership as a 28-year-old in '76 and was 30 by the time he skippered Australia in a Test match.

6. Nathan Cayless

With the likes of Jim Dymock making himself unavailable for the Parramatta captaincy in 2000, coach Brian Smith made the surprise call to pitch 21-year-old New Zealand Test prop Nathan Cayless into the role at the start of the year. The consistent front-rower was a Kiwi Test skipper and losing Grand Final captain at 23 in 2001, and eventually became the first player in history to captain one club in 200 first grade matches.

7. Brad Fittler

A self-confessed larrikin, Brad Fittler was forced to mature at a rapid rate after the Super League War broke out in 1995 when he was catapulted into the dual roles of NSW and Australian Test captain only a few months after his 23rd birthday. But 'Freddy', who had been a stand-in skipper for Penrith aged just 20 in 1992, led the green-and-golds to a 3-0 whitewash of New Zealand and a World Cup triumph in '95. He went on to become one of the great captains.

8. Neville Smith

Former Queensland forward Neville Smith joined St George in 1939 and, despite being just 22 years of age, was given the captain-coach duties in his first season at the club. He debuted for NSW in 1940 before captain-coaching the Saints to their maiden premiership the following season.

9. Phil Gould

In just his second first grade start, 20-year-old backrower Phil Gould was made captain of Penrith following the retirement of long-serving skipper Mick Stephenson early in 1978. Gould did not hang on to the role, but the promotion was an early indication of the football nous that saw him become one of the great coaches after his 104-game first grade career with Penrith, Newtown, Canterbury and Souths wrapped up. He became the youngest non-playing coach to win a premiership in 1988, guiding the Bulldogs to a title at his first attempt.

10. Cameron Smith

At the age of 22, Queensland hooker Cameron Smith was made part of Melbourne's novel five-man captaincy rotation in 2006. The youngest of the leadership group, Smith, who turned 23 during the season, was given the honour of leading the Storm into the Grand Final—a 15-8 loss to Brisbane. He was made sole skipper of the club during 2007 and led the Storm to a premiership that year, while he captained Australia and Queensland for the first time as a 24-year-old in the injury absence of Darren Lockyer.

BEST INDIGENOUS PLAYERS

1. Arthur Beetson
Australia's first Indigenous captain in any sport, champion ball-playing forward Arthur Beetson is one of the game's greats. Named an Immortal in 2003, Beetson was named in the ARL Team of the Century, the Queensland Team of the Century and the Indigenous Team of the Century five seasons later in the game's Centenary year. Big-framed and full of heart, he was renowned as a creative forward whose offload was unrivalled. Beetson joined Balmain from Queensland but found most success with Eastern Suburbs, where he skippered the great 1974 and '75 teams to titles. At 35 he was inspirational in establishing State of Origin, leading from the front as Queensland captain in the inaugural game. A Kabi Kabi man, Beetson was a strong advocate for the rights of Indigenous Australians.

2. Johnathan Thurston
Unquestionably the top half in the game from 2005, Johnathan Thurston won a premiership as a reserve with Canterbury in 2004 before shifting to North Queensland in '05 and setting in motion a stunning club and rep career. Thurston won the Dally M Medal in 2005 and '07, won the Golden Boot in 2011, represented Queensland in 27 straight Origins (a record) from 2005 to 2013 (encapsulating eight straight Origin series wins) and played 30 Tests for Australia, losing just once. A phenomenal point-scorer and great clutch kicker, Thurston was equally adept running and passing. He is Australia's greatest-ever Test point-scorer and broke the record for most points at a World Cup in 2013, which was previously held by fellow Indigenous star Eric Simms. Thurston is a Gunggarri man and has become an Indigenous ambassador.

3. Eric Simms
One of the game's great kickers, South Sydney champion Eric Simms was so proficient at potting field goals that he forced down their value from two points to one. Simms, who once slotted five field goals in a match, was deadly accurate in all forms of kicking. His kicking extended to shooting for goal: he scored an incredible 1841 first grade points and at one time held the premiership record. Simms' 265 points in 1969 broke Dave Brown's long-standing single-season mark. He became the fourth Aboriginal man to represent Australia in 1968, playing eight Tests at the 1968 and '70 World Cups.

4. Laurie Daley

A champion centre/five-eighth who won a premiership with the Canberra Raiders aged just 19, Laurie Daley went on to win two more titles with the Green Machine while becoming the NSW and Australian captain. The 1995 Dally M Medal winner was a reliable match-winner and much-lauded leader during the troubling Super League War, which cost him the chance of playing more rep footy than his 23 Origins and 21 Tests. While injuries late in his career forced an early retirement, Daley stands tall as one of the best—if not the best—player of the 1990s. He coached the Indigenous All Stars in their first three clashes.

5. Greg Inglis

One of the most exciting athletes ever to play the game, Greg Inglis set Rugby League fields alight with his rare combination of size, speed and skill that made him one of the most feared players in the code from 2006. Capable of playing anywhere in the backline, Inglis won a Clive Churchill Medal at five-eighth with Melbourne, played in the centres and on the wing with Queensland and Australia, and starred at fullback with South Sydney at club level. Awarded the Golden Boot in 2009, he became the greatest try-scorer in Origin history in the opening game of 2012 when he scored his 13th four-pointer for Queensland. Inglis is a Dunghutti man from Kempsey in NSW.

6. Gorden Tallis

A feisty and aggressive forward who became known as 'The Raging Bull', Gorden Tallis captained Queensland and Australia. A controversial player throughout most of his career, he enjoyed a wildly successful time at the Broncos, where he won three premierships and picked up the 1998 Clive Churchill Medal. He spent a decade in Queensland colours and six years wearing the green-and-gold. In his autobiography Tallis plays down his Indigenous background, saying his Torres Strait Islander heritage is not something he has ever concerned himself with.

7. Steve Renouf

A brilliant centre with the Brisbane Broncos, Steve Renouf was one of the most accomplished try-scorers of the 1990s, scoring 142 tries in 183 games. He topped 10 tries for eight straight seasons and scored four tries in a match an incredible five times, with Ken Irvine the only post-war player to achieve the feat on more occasions. 'The Pearl' scored a try in Brisbane's inaugural Grand Final triumph and a hat-trick in the '97 Super League decider. His try on debut in the 1992 World Cup final was the only four-pointer of the 10-6 win, and the first of 11 tries in 10 Tests. Beautiful on his feet with incredible speed, Renouf was an out-and-out star.

8. Lionel Morgan
The first Indigenous player to represent Australia, dashing winger Lionel Morgan was a schoolboy star who spent his career playing with Wynnum Manly in Queensland. He scored two tries in three Tests and crossed for nine in 12 interstate matches for the Maroons. His selection for the 1960 World Cup made him the first Indigenous Australian to represent Australia in any sport. Morgan was named on the wing in the Indigenous Team of the Century.

9. George Green
Regarded as the first Indigenous Australian to play top-grade Rugby League, utility forward George Green was a stalwart of Eastern Suburbs and North Sydney during the code's early years. He played in Rugby League's first 15 seasons, winning a premiership with Eastern Suburbs in 1911 and playing in North Sydney's two premierships a decade later in 1921-22. Green was a smart player with good skills, and his wholehearted performances made him a popular star of the era.

10. Cliff Lyons
One of Rugby League's most enduring players, Cliff Lyons forged an incredible career, predominantly with Manly, throughout the 1980s and '90s that netted two premierships (and the Churchill Medal in '87) and saw him play for NSW and Australia. The 1990 Kangaroo Tour hero and two-time Dally M medallist was one of the most creative five-eighths ever to play the game, with his ball-playing thrilling Manly fans for the better part of 15 years. Retiring from the NRL in 1999 aged 37, Lyons continued to play senior football until he was well past 40.

GREATEST FAMILIES

1. The Pearce family
The only family members to be named in Australia's 100 Greatest Players list in 2008, Sandy and Joe Pearce were giants in the early years of the code. Sandy, a foundation player, played 14 seasons for Eastern Suburbs and Australia, while his son Joe also played 14 seasons with Easts. When Joe was selected for Australia in 1932, the Pearces became the first father-son combo to represent Australia. The wider Pearce family excelled in other sports, including rowing and cycling.

2. The Burge brothers

A famous set of four brothers who predominantly played for Glebe, the Burges were a talented bunch who were some of the game's early drawcards. Two of them, Frank and Peter, were dual internationals. Frank, the most talented of the foursome, was a prolific tryscoring forward who holds the record for most tries in a game and was named in the Team of the Century. Peter, the eldest, moved to Souths in 1910 after representing the Wallabies, then joined Glebe and toured with the 1911-12 Kangaroos. Alby captained Glebe to the 1911 final and skippered the club for much of the next decade, and Laidley had a seven-year career with the 'Dirty Reds'.

3. The Mortimer family

With five Mortimers reaching the heights of first grade and two playing for Australia, the Mortimer clan has left an indelible mark on Rugby League. Brothers Steve, Peter and Chris played in four Grand Finals together for Canterbury and were staples of the blue and white for over a decade. Talented halfback Steve was a feature of rep sides, captaining NSW to its first series victory, and was named in the 100 Greatest Players in 2008. Chris was a hard-nosed utility who played one Test for Australia and finished his career at Penrith; Peter was a speedy winger who was Canterbury's only try-scorer in the 1985 Grand Final triumph; and youngest brother Glen played 26 games for Cronulla during the 1980s. A second generation of Mortimers reached the top grade in 2009 when Daniel, son of Peter, debuted for Parramatta and played in the decider in his first season. He shifted to the Roosters in 2012 and played in the Grand Final triumph a year later.

4. The Walters brothers

An exceptionally talented trio of brothers, Steve and twins Kevin and Kerrod Walters all represented Australia in the 1990s. Regarded as one of the great hookers (and a three-time Dally M Hooker of the Year), oldest brother Steve debuted for Canberra in 1986 and spent 11 seasons at the club during a glory period that netted three premierships before he rounded out his career with North Queensland and Newcastle. His representative ambitions were stymied early on by younger brother Kerrod, a fellow hooker with the Brisbane Broncos (and two-time Dally M Hooker of the Year) who spent three seasons as Queensland and Australia's first-choice rake before being usurped by his brother. Kerrod spent nine years with Brisbane before a two-season stint with the ill-fated Adelaide Rams. Kevin, a zippy and intelligent half/centre, won a Grand Final with Canberra before winning another five with the Broncos (the last as captain), and played 20 Origins and 11 Tests.

5. The Morris family

Two generations of the Morris family have represented Australia. Father Steve was a speedy halfback-cum-winger, while his sons Brett and Josh have both excelled as outside backs in the NRL era. A 12-year premiership player, Steve played his only Test in 1978 from Dapto before joining St George, where he played eight years before moving to Easts and retiring in 1990 after scoring 121 tries in 247 games. Brett has followed in his father's footsteps, scoring 98 tries in 151 games for St George Illawarra heading into the 2014 season, while Josh has 86 tries in 155 outings, predominantly for Canterbury. The brothers debuted for Australia in 2009.

6. The Rogers family

One of the all-time greats, Steve Rogers, produced decorated dual international Mat. Named in 2008 among the Top 100 Players, Steve is widely regarded as Cronulla's greatest star, playing 202 games and scoring 1253 points for the club. Mat debuted for the Sharks in 1995 and scored 1112 points for the club (the father-son pair sit first and second) before defecting to Rugby Union and playing for the Wallabies. Both father and son represented Australia in Rugby League—Steve 24 times, Mat 11 times—while Steve won the Rothmans and Dally M medals. Mat returned to Rugby League in 2007 to play five seasons with the Gold Coast Titans. Steve and Mat hold the individual distinction of playing for different states in State of Origin.

7. The Hughes family

With two generations of three brothers, the Hughes family is maybe the most prolific in NRL history. Brothers Garry, Graeme and Mark were stars for Canterbury in the 1970s into the 1980s, helping the Bulldogs gain the moniker 'The Family Club'; Steven, Glenn and Corey, sons of Garry, turned out for Canterbury from 1992 to 2008. Graeme played one match for NSW. In total, the six played 924 first grade games for Canterbury with at least one representative in seven Grand Finals.

8. The Burgess brothers

A quartet of hulking brothers from Dewsbury in England, the Burgess foursome equalled a century-old record in 2013 when they played together against the Wests Tigers in August 2013. A decorated international, Sam joined South Sydney in 2010 after debuting for England two seasons earlier and was a crowd favourite before announcing his defection to English Rugby Union in 2014. Luke, a tough prop, followed a year later while George won the Dally M Rookie of the Year in 2013, the same year twin Thomas debuted. Sam, George and Thomas were selected for England at the 2013 World Cup; oldest brother Luke was a controversial omission.

9. The Norman brothers

A set of four brothers who played predominantly for Annandale, the Norman brothers held the record for most brothers to play together in first grade for 103 years before their mark was equalled by the Burgess brothers of Souths. Outstanding centre Ray was the pick of the Normans, playing two Tests for Australia and representing NSW. Youngest brother Rex toured with the 1921-22 Kangaroos but did not play a Test. Roy and Bernard also played with Annandale in the early years of the premiership but did not reach the representative heights of their brothers.

10. The Gartner family

With four generations playing top-grade Rugby League, the Gartners' involvement in the premiership spanned from Joe Gartner's debut in 1931 until Daniel Gartner's retirement in 2000. Family patriarch Joe played 11 seasons with Newtown and Canterbury, including in the latter's first premiership side. His three sons—Clive, Jim and Ray—played 296 matches for the Berries between 1953 and '68. Jim's son Russel, a talented three-quarter, played 237 games for Manly, Eastern Suburbs and Balmain, becoming the family's first representative in 1977 when he won selection for NSW and Australia. Russel's nephew and Clive's son Daniel played eight seasons with Manly and the Northern Eagles, and a single Test for Australia in 1996.

AGELESS STARS

1. Billy Wilson

The only player in premiership history to play beyond his 40th birthday, 'Captain Blood' spent 20 years in the premiership playing for the great St George team and then North Sydney. Debuting in 1948 as a 20-year-old, Wilson won six premierships with the incomparable St George team of the 1950s and '60s, making his international debut at 32 in 1959 and playing for Australia until he turned 36; he captained his country in 1963. Wilson finished his career with five seasons at North Sydney. He retired after the 1966 season but played three games in 1967 after his 40th birthday when Norths, whom he was coaching, were crippled by a serious run of injuries.

2. Tedda Courtney

One of the greats of Rugby League's early days, Tedda Courtney played in the game's first season of 1908 and continued until 1924, forging a 17-year career predominantly with Western Suburbs. A durable prop, he played 11 Tests for Australia until 1914. His last game was two months short of his 40th birthday and he held the mark as the oldest premiership player for nearly 50 years until Billy Wilson eclipsed it. Incredibly, Courtney played alongside his son of the same name for Wests in '24.

3. Steve Menzies
The modern game's foremost ageless wonder, who played two decades in the NRL and Super League, Steve Menzies is the longest-lasting and most durable player of the modern era. A prodigy who debuted in 1993 as a 19-year-old, Menzies spent 16 seasons with Manly and the Northern Eagles, winning two premierships and playing in five Grand Finals—the last of which was his final game for the club at 34. Menzies scored a try in that decider triumph, a game in which he equalled Terry Lamb's premiership games record. Incredibly, he then played another five seasons in Super League, accumulating an amazing 518 appearances in NRL, Super League and rep footy. He turned out for Manly at the inaugural Auckland Nines at the age of 40.

4. Roy Kirkaldy
Nicknamed 'The Prince of Hookers', Roy Kirkaldy joined Canterbury in 1938 as a 28-year-old and played a decade for the Berries, winning two premierships and playing 172 games. Part of the famed front-row triumvirate with Eddie Burns and Henry Porter, Kirkaldy retired as the second-oldest premiership player (he is now third on the list). He played in the 1947 Grand Final at the age of 37.

5. Henry Porter
A Canterbury front-rower who debuted with Newtown in 1933 as a 22-year-old, Henry Porter moved to Canterbury in 1936 and played on until 1948, a month after his 38th birthday. Part of the famed front-row with Eddie Burns and Roy Kirkaldy, Porter won a premiership with the Berries at 32 and played in the 1947 Grand Final at 37. He was considered unlucky not to be selected for Australia in 1946.

6. Sandy Pearce
Australia's oldest international, Sandy Pearce is regarded by many as the greatest hooker the game has produced. Debuting in the premiership's first season in 1908 as a 24-year-old, he played on until the 1921 season, touring with the Kangaroos at the end of that year. Pearce was the only player to tour with both the 1908-09 and 1921-22 Kangaroos sides. Named in the NSW Team of the Century, he won three premierships with Eastern Suburbs. Pearce died in 1930, just eight years after his final game.

7. Ken Kearney
One of the most important figures in Australian Rugby League history, Ken Kearney made his Wallabies debut at 23 and defected to English Rugby League a year later, joining glamour club Leeds. He did not make his premiership debut until 1952, when

he was 27. Yet in the decade that followed, he would play 31 Tests for Australia and make 33 appearances for NSW, while leading St George to the first six of its record 11 straight titles as skipper, captain-coach and then non-playing coach. Kearney retired in 1961 aged 37, finally giving in to a knee injury.

8. Bob Craig

A dual international who won a gold medal with the Wallabies at the 1908 Olympic Games, Bob Craig was a giant in Rugby League's formative days. He did not play his first game of premiership Rugby League until he was 29, but enjoyed a 10-year career with Balmain that lasted until 1919, just short of his 38th birthday. He debuted for Australia in 1910 and played international Rugby League until he was 32. Craig won premierships with Balmain in four of his last five seasons.

9. Cliff Lyons

One of the great five-eighths of the 1980s and '90s—an era abundant with outstanding No.6s—Cliff Lyons did not debut until he was 23, spending a season with North Sydney and then moving to Manly, where he would see out his career. A wizard with the ball, Lyons made 332 first grade appearances in a 15-year career that saw him represent NSW and Australia six times each. He made his Test debut at 29 and was named Dally M Player of the Year and *Rugby League Week* Player of the Year at 32. The ball-playing wizard played his final game two months short of his 38th birthday. Lyons continued playing Grade A football with Hornsby and Narraweena well into his 40s.

10. Darren Smith

An outstanding centre/backrower whose NRL career spanned 16 years, Darren Smith played premiership football until just shy of his 37th birthday. Debuting with Canterbury in 1990, he enjoyed two stints each with the Bulldogs and the Broncos, scoring 115 tries and winning premierships with Brisbane in 1997 and '98. He famously was recalled to the Australian team at 34 when playing for St Helens in England in 2003. Smith started in 16 games in his farewell 2005 season.

PRODIGIES

1. Brad Fittler

An Australian Schoolboy rep from McCarthy Catholic School in 1988-89, Penrith junior Brad Fittler made a stunning first grade debut for the Panthers late in '89 while still a 17-year-old. He was sensationally pitched into the starting five-eighth role during that season's finals before setting records in 1990 as the youngest Origin player (18 years and 114 days) and Kangaroo tourist (18 years and 225 days), as well as scoring a try in a Grand Final. Fittler remains the only player to represent Australia at schoolboy and senior level in consecutive years. The brilliant five-eighth, centre or lock was a Test captain at 23 and carved out one of the great careers before retiring in 2004.

2. Frank Burge

Frank Burge made his first grade Rugby Union debut for South Sydney at just 15 in 1910 before joining his brothers Peter and Alby at Glebe Rugby League club in 1911 and breaking into the top grade aged 16 years and 258 days—a mark bettered by just two players since. He featured in a trial for the 1911-12 Kangaroo Tour squad and performed well, but his tender years counted against him and he missed selection. Nevertheless, 'Chunky' scored three tries on debut for NSW as a 17-year-old in 1912 and made his Test debut at the next available opportunity, against the touring England side in 1914 while he was still a teenager. Burge became the greatest tryscoring forward the game has known and was named as a reserve in Australia's Team of the Century in 2008.

3. Dave Brown

Christian Brothers Waverley product Dave Brown joined Eastern Suburbs as a 16-year-old in 1930, making his first grade debut shortly after his 17th birthday that season. The devastating centre was barely 18 when he debuted for NSW in 1931, and he was named as Easts' club captain at just 19 in '32 before smashing all manner of pointscoring records on the 1933-34 Kangaroo Tour and subsequently at premiership level. Brown became Australia's youngest Test captain in 1935 (22 years and 174 days); his status as one of the code's greatest players remains intact.

4. Laurie Daley

Laurie Daley starred in Junee Diesels' Group 9 premiership victory as a 16-year-old in 1986, attracting the interest of Canberra. He made his first grade debut for the Raiders aged 17 in '87, scoring two tries in his initial start in the top flight and sitting as an unused replacement on the Canberra bench in the Grand Final. The freakishly talented centre/five-eighth became a first grade regular in 1988 and was still just 19 when he debuted for NSW and featured in the Raiders' Grand Final triumph in '89. Daley broke into the Test side the following season, captained the Blues at 22 in 1992 and was one of the decade's dominant players.

5. Ray Stehr

Ray Stehr overcame a blood clot in his spine that threatened to leave him crippled as a child to become the youngest player in premiership history. The Randwick High

School product was just 15 when he played a trial for Eastern Suburbs in 1928, and made his full-fledged first grade debut the following season at 16 years and 85 days. Stehr represented NSW at 18 in 1931 and made the first of two Kangaroo Tours in 1933. One of the most feared enforcers and greatest props the game has produced, he won five premierships in a 17-season career with Easts.

6. Will Hopoate
Earmarked for the game's heights from an early age, Will Hopoate—son of controversial former international John—was signed by Manly to an unprecedented $300,000 three-season deal as a 16-year-old in 2008. The 2007-08 Australian Schoolboys rep made his NRL debut for the Sea Eagles a month after turning 18 in 2010, and became the fourth-youngest Origin player of all time the following season at 19 years and 35 days; the veteran of 15 first grade games scored a brilliant try on debut. But after playing an integral role in Manly's 2011 Grand Final triumph, the gifted centre, wing or fullback embarked on a two-year Mormon mission. He was still just 21 when he returned to the code with Parramatta in 2014.

7. Peter Sterling
All-time great halfback Peter Sterling's vision and class was apparent from his early high-school days, and he was tipped to become a first grade star accordingly. Named the Amco Player of the Series after steering Fairfield Patrician Brothers to victory in the schoolboy competition in 1978, the 18-year-old five-eighth made his first grade debut in Parramatta's minor semi replay loss to Manly later that year—as a fullback. Moving to the No.7 spot, Sterling flourished after the arrival of Jack Gibson as Parramatta coach in 1981. He made his NSW debut aged 20 that season before guiding the Eels to a maiden Grand Final victory, and broke into the Australian Test side the following year.

8. Tim Brasher
An Australian Schoolboys star in 1988, Tim Brasher was still a high-school student when he was called into Balmain's side early the following season—a month after his 18th birthday. He showed maturity well beyond his years as a centre to score nine tries in 20 rookie-season games, culminating in a Grand Final appearance at the end of the year in the Tigers' extra-time loss to Canberra. Brasher was still just 21 when he made his debuts for NSW and Australia in 1992, eventually making 21 Origin and 14 Test appearances as one of the 1990s' finest fullbacks.

9. Adam Ritson
Burly prop Adam Ritson became the fourth-youngest player in premiership history at 16 years and 303 days when he was blooded by Cronulla coach Arthur Beetson

in 1993—the same season he represented Australian Schoolboys from De La Salle College. But despite being singled out for punishment by the competition's hard-heads, Ritson lived up to his billing as one of the most exciting front-row prospects in years, representing City Origin at the age of 18 in '95. The 19-year-old tyro joined Parramatta the following season after signing with the ARL, but his 40-game career ended abruptly when a routine scan following a high shot by Canberra's John Lomax revealed a cyst on his brain. Ritson underwent a series of lifesaving operations but was forced to retire from Rugby League while still a teenager.

10. Greg Alexander
Following in Peter Sterling's footsteps by leading Fairfield Patrician Brothers to victory in the 1983 Commonwealth Bank Cup and taking out the Player of the Series award, Greg Alexander debuted for Penrith shortly after turning 19 and was named Dally M Rookie of the Year in '84. The former Australian Schoolboys rep created history by winning the Dally M Medal the following season after spearheading the long-suffering Panthers' maiden finals appearance. A supremely gifted halfback or fullback, 'Brandy' went on to make two Kangaroo Tours before captaining Penrith to its first title in 1991.

BEST ROOKIE SEASONS

1. Israel Folau
Israel Folau scored a try on NRL debut for Melbourne in the opening round of 2007, two weeks before his 18th birthday. The tall, robust three-quarter bagged doubles in his next three outings and notched a hat-trick later in the year against the Bulldogs, finishing atop the competition's regular season tryscoring table with a club-record 21 touchdowns. After collecting a premiership ring as a centre in the Storm's 34-8 Grand Final thrashing of Manly, the Dally M Rookie of the Year was selected in the Junior Kangaroos side. But an injury to Justin Hodges saw Folau called into Australia's Test side and become the youngest Australian Test representative in history at 18 years and 194 days. He crossed for two tries on debut in a 58-0 demolition of New Zealand.

2. Reg Gasnier
Immortal centre Reg Gasnier enjoyed a meteoric rise during his 1959 rookie season, debuting for St George shortly before he turned 20 and scoring four tries in a match against Wests in his fifth appearance, after which he was chosen for NSW. The prodigious talent was called up to make his Test debut after just one further first grade

game; he played all three Tests against New Zealand, scoring a hat-trick in the second Test and a double in the third. Gasnier's semi-final double against the Magpies helped the Saints into the Grand Final and took his season tally to 13, but he was ruled out of the decider by injury. That disappointment was tempered by his selection in the Kangaroo Tour squad, where he starred with 20 tries in 19 games. Gasnier played in all six Tests against Great Britain and France, scoring another hat-trick in the first Ashes encounter.

3. Larry Corowa

Snapped up by Balmain after scoring five tries for Monaro against Great Britain in 1977, Queanbeyan Kangaroos winger Larry Corowa produced a magnificent debut season in the premiership. The 20-year-old Indigenous flyer—labelled 'The Black Flash'—topped the '78 competition with 24 tries, eight clear of his nearest rival, despite the Tigers' ninth-placed finish. He scored four tries against Newtown in just his second appearance and had three more hat-tricks to his name before the end of the year. Corowa crossed on debut for NSW and was picked in the Kangaroo Tour squad at the end of the season, although he made just seven minor match appearances (crossing for six tries) and would have to wait until the following year to make his Test debut.

4. Daly Cherry-Evans

Daly Cherry-Evans slotted into the Manly No.7 jumper with astounding poise and confidence in 2011. The 22-year-old half played all 27 games as the Sea Eagles finished second in the minor premiership and surged to Grand Final glory. He finished equal 15th in the Dally M Medal and was a runaway Rookie of the Year winner before he scored a vital try just before halftime of Manly's 24-10 decider victory over the Warriors. Cherry-Evans leapfrogged the likes of NSW halfback Mitchell Pearce for a place in the Kangaroos' Four Nations squad and scored a try on Test debut, coming off the bench against Wales in his only appearance at the tournament before being named RLIF Halfback of the Year.

5. Steve Rogers

Cronulla's 18-year-old centre Steve Rogers packed a career's worth of experiences into his 1973 rookie season. A fresh-faced star as the Sharks reached their maiden finals series, Rogers top-scored for the club with 119 points. He scored a try in the preliminary final victory over Newtown and slotted two goals in the 10-7 Grand Final loss to Manly, regarded as the most violent decider on record. Rogers played two interstate games for NSW mid-season—scoring a try in each game—and was selected in the Kangaroo Tour squad at the end of the year. Although he did not play any Tests, he made six minor match appearances and turned 19 while abroad.

6. Ian Schubert

Wauchope product Ian Schubert earned instant acclaim as a dashing, long-haired teenage winger/fullback for dominant Eastern Suburbs in 1975. The 18-year-old debuted on the wing for City Firsts during the season and starred as the Roosters pieced together a premiership-record 19-game winning streak. He turned 19 on the eve of the finals and stepped into the fullback role for the injured Russell Fairfax, scoring a try—his 12th touchdown of the year—in Easts' 38-0 Grand Final destruction of St George. He was subsequently selected in Australia's World Series squad, playing all four matches and crossing for seven tries, including hat-tricks against Wales and England.

7. Jim Leis

The inaugural Dally M Rookie of the Year in 1980, Wests lock Jim Leis achieved a string of representative honours during his debut season. The 20-year-old scored an incredible four tries against Penrith in his second first grade appearance, and came off the bench for NSW in a residence-selected interstate match before winning selection in Australia's squad to tour New Zealand. Although he did not play any Tests on tour, the tyro was chosen at lock in the Blues side for the historic one-off State of Origin match at Lang Park with Ray Price unavailable. He also collected the Dally M Lock of the Year gong and finished the season with eight tries as the Magpies reached the preliminary final.

8. Jarryd Hayne

Jarryd Hayne was a standout Dally M Rookie of the Year in 2006 as an 18-year-old winger for Parramatta, scoring an incredible 17 tries in just 16 games. He was immediately promoted to first grade by caretaker coach Jason Taylor in Round 11 after Brian Smith quit the club, and impressed right away with his speed, balance and freakish skills. Hayne scored 11 tries in a seven-game burst—including a four-try haul against Newcastle—to help lift the Eels from second last to an eventual finals berth. The blockbusting flyer was chosen in Australia's Tri-Nations squad at the end of the season, although he was not called upon for a Test debut.

9. Steve Martin

Wagga half Steve Martin came from relative obscurity to steer Manly to a premiership in 1978. The 21-year-old made a tryscoring debut for NSW at five-eighth during his first year in the premiership before crossing for a late season hat-trick against Norths. Injury to Johnny Gibbs saw Martin step into the No.7 role during the finals; he handled the pressure with aplomb as the Sea Eagles survived two replays to secure the title in extraordinary circumstances. Martin was subsequently picked in the Kangaroo Tour squad and played 11 games, including a Test debut against France at centre.

10. David Williams
A former lower-grade backrower at Parramatta, David Williams became an instant cult hero on the wing for Manly in 2008. The bearded flyer was dubbed 'The Wolfman' and scored 14 tries in 20 rookie-season games—including a four-pointer in the Sea Eagles' Grand Final hammering of Melbourne. Pipped for Dally M Rookie honours by Chris Sandow, Williams' hard running and innate finishing ability saw him chosen as the bolter in Australia's squad for the Centenary World Cup. He scored a hat-trick on Test debut against Papua New Guinea before earning a call-up for the final and crossing again in the Kangaroos' shock loss to New Zealand.

FORWARD PACK ENFORCERS

1. Frank Farrell
A hardened Newtown prop forward whose reputation as a no-nonsense inner-city cop arguably exceeded his on-field standing, Frank 'Bumper' Farrell may have upheld the law off the field but had little respect for it on the paddock. Renowned for stiff arms and an anything-goes attitude, he was famously accused of biting off an opponent's ear. None other than Clive Churchill called him the most feared player in the game.

2. Billy Wilson
A thoroughly tough and courageous player, Billy 'Bluey' Wilson survived an incredible two decades in the top grade, testament itself to his toughness. During his time he was as rugged as they came. Few messed with Wilson, who had mastered the stiff-arm tackle and had a mean left hook, which he used to knock out Wests forward Jim Cody in the 1962 Grand Final in an incident that saw him sent off in his last game for St George. He played on often with serious injury—three times with a broken arm—and garnered the nickname 'Captain Blood' for how often he wore the claret. Wilson stood tall for his toughness during the game's hardest era.

3. Noel Kelly
Perhaps the most sent-off player in premiership history, Noel 'Ned' Kelly was so tough his autobiography was titled *Hard Man*. Kelly was very much a believer in getting in first, and few opponents got the upper hand over the Team of the Century hooker. Kelly was consistently in trouble for knocking opponents out cold; his reputation grew to such an extent that once he was sent off in a Kangaroo Tour match he wasn't playing in, and on another occasion he was dismissed twice. Kelly would undertake any tactic to win—something he did frequently.

4. John Sattler

John Sattler's name is rightly etched in the game's fabric as a symbol of toughness and courage after he played most of the 1970 Grand Final with a shattered jaw. Sattler copped it that day but was not averse to dishing it out—the fiery South Sydney prop and captain was a demon when crossing the white line. He often found himself suspended, but his fearlessness inspired a young Rabbitohs team through its last great era.

5. Vince Karalius

Known as 'The Wild Bull of the Pampas', Vince Karalius is revered to this day as the toughest Englishman of them all. Johnny Raper called him a "monster", and those who played against him were adamant that his first intention was to hurt his opposition—something Karalius himself acknowledged. He could dish it out and he could take it, famously starring in the '58 'Battle of Brisbane' with a near-broken back. No English player terrified Australians more.

6. Herb Narvo

An accomplished boxer who was at one time the Australian heavyweight champion, Newcastle, Newtown and St George forward Herb Narvo was a hard-hitting, tough-as-nails scything tackler whom opponents rarely sought out in a brawl. He was the leader of the Newtown pack for many years and starred with his rugged performances on the 1937-38 Kangaroo Tour.

7. Kevin Ryan

A testament to Kevin Ryan's hardness as a player is his nickname, 'Kandos'—the one-time cement capital of Australia. Ryan, simply, was as hard as cement. A giant of a man, he was a brutal tackler but rarely relied on violence. Ruthless and as determined as any player to strap on a boot, he was the toughest to play the game according to fellow tough nut John Sattler. Few one-on-one tacklers did as much damage.

8. Malcolm Reilly

One of the greatest British players to grace Australia's shores, Malcolm Reilly was also one of the most controversial. If there was one word to describe his style it was "uncompromising". He would happily deliver a head-high shot, a knee or an elbow if it helped his side. In the 1973 decider—the toughest and bloodiest of them all—he caused havoc and played on for part of the match after being kneed in the back and pelvis by Cronulla hooker Ron Turner; his clash with Souths' George Piggins earlier that year remains one of the most notorious stoushes in the game's history.

9. Ray Stehr

An aggressive and sizable prop with Eastern Suburbs during the 1930s and '40s, Ray Stehr developed a reputation as a player capable of dishing out plenty of rough stuff. He was playing first grade from the age of 16 and lasted 17 seasons, with his taste for violence well and truly in vogue in England. He was regularly at war with his British counterparts and famously became the only man to be sent off twice in an Ashes series as he staged an ongoing battle with Jack Arkwright.

10. John 'Dallas' Donnelly

A fearless and rampaging giant from Western Suburbs, John 'Dallas' Donnelly was the heart of 'The Fibros' side that pushed its way to heavyweight status in the late 1970s. He thrived under the psychological coaching of Roy Masters, who tapped into Donnelly's never-ending passion. Donnelly refused attention for fractured cheekbones and busted ribs but inflicted just as much damage, copping a long suspension for kneeing, among other acts of violence and intimidation. He gave no inch and asked none in return.

BACKLINE ENFORCERS

1. Peter Dimond

Powerhouse three-quarter Peter Dimond was as renowned for his penchant for the rough stuff as any of the era's toughest forwards. The Dapto winger joined Wests in 1958 and, despite being sent off in a fiery NSW v Great Britain clash that season, the 19-year-old played all three subsequent Ashes Tests. A veteran of 10 Tests—encompassing the 1963-64 Kangaroo Tour—he scored a record 84 tries in 163 games for the Magpies, including three Grand Finals. The bulldozing back was infamously marched in a City-Country match in 1967 for ironing out popular footballing priest and Newcastle winger Father John Cootes.

2. Tom Raudonikis

One of the great halfbacks, Tommy Raudonikis played with the ferocity of a front-row firebrand. The veteran of 29 Tests for Australia and two Kangaroo Tours (1973 and 1978) typified the wild Western Suburbs spirit during the 1970s as he racked up over 200 games for the club. The terrier-like Raudonikis was hell-bent on playing over the top of his opposing No.7 every time he took the field, regularly employing roughhouse tactics to get the job done (he was sent off during the 1978 Ashes series). He drew criticism and a fine from the NSWRL after revealing himself as 'The Phantom Biter' who took a chunk out of rival Manly half John Gibbs in a 1976 clash, but remained one of the competition's finest competitors and captained Newtown to a gallant 20-11 loss in the 1981 Grand Final. A unique and much-loved Rugby League character, Raudonikis imparted his old-world wisdom during a long and eventful coaching career that included stints with Ipswich, Wests and the NSW Origin side.

3. Brian Clay

St George five-eighth Brian 'Poppa' Clay ranks among the most feared and effective defenders of the post-World War II era. After partnering Dick Poole in the centres in Newtown's 1954-55 Grand Final defeats to Souths, he became an integral figure in the Dragons' world-record sequence of premierships at pivot, featuring in eight Grand Final wins (1957-61 and 1964-66). Clay missed the 1962 Grand Final with injury, and played in the club's reserve grade premiership victory in 1963 as he recovered from a broken arm. As an astute playmaking five-eighth, his bone-shattering defence was his trademark. The bald-headed hitman featured in Australia's 1957 World Cup triumph before playing five Tests on the 1959-60 Kangaroo Tour.

4. Johnny Graves

A brilliant attacking winger and one of the most potent try-scorers of all time, Newcastle product and South Sydney great Johnny 'Whacka' Graves was equally renowned for his aggressive and wild temperament on and off the field. He was always at full throttle with the ball in hand and was just as uncompromising in defence, infamously sending Huddersfield's Australian star Johnny Hunter off on a stretcher with a stiff-arm tackle on the 1948-49 Kangaroo Tour. A handful for club officials as much as opposition defenders, 'Whacka' scored an extraordinary 79 tries in 77 games for the Rabbitohs—including four in the 1951 Grand Final thrashing of Manly.

5. Chris Mortimer

Chris Mortimer was a cast-iron presence in the centres alongside his brothers Steve and Peter in three Grand Final victories for the Bulldogs during the 1980s before featuring at five-eighth and in the backrow in the twilight of his career at Penrith. 'Louie' toured with the 1986 Kangaroos and made nine Origin appearances for the Blues. A robust runner and punishing defender, his toughness was illustrated when he famously pulled out two steel pins from a broken thumb to participate in the Panthers' 1989 finals campaign. The 258-game veteran retired after the club's 1990 Grand Final loss as one of the most respected players of his era.

6. Jarrod McCracken

A fearsome competitor in the centres for Canterbury and later as a backrower at Parramatta, Kiwi firebrand Jarrod McCracken was no stranger to the judiciary during a decade-long premiership career. He burst on to the first grade and representative scenes with Canterbury and New Zealand in 1991, but was sent off with Peter Jackson for fighting in the second Test against Australia and slapped with an eight-match ban for biting near the end of the season. The ruthless defender and renowned pugilist was suspended for attacking the head of an opponent in 1993 before he switched to Parramatta in 1996, and spent a five-match stretch on the sidelines for a dangerous throw in '98. Installed as Wests Tigers' inaugural captain, the 22-Test veteran's career ended in 2000 when he was on the receiving end of a spear tackle by Melbourne duo Stephen Kearney and Marcus Bai.

7. Steve Matai

Adored by Manly fans and loathed by opposition supporters in equal quantities, 10-Test Kiwi centre Steve Matai has become established as one of the NRL's most renowned hitmen. The two-time Grand Final winner's aggressive approach frequently attracts the attention of the judiciary—he was sent off in a 2007 Test against Australia for a savage high tackle on Mark Gasnier, and incurred a seven-match suspension for another reckless high tackle at club level in 2010. A ferocious defender who appears to play through serious injury on a weekly basis, Matai's attacking class has netted 67 tries in 177 games and created scores more for his wingers.

8. John Hopoate

Few players have longer judiciary rap sheets than notorious Manly winger John Hopoate, and his sheet is easily the most bizarre. An Origin and Test debutant in an award-winning 1995 rookie year, Hopoate was swiftly labelled as an aggressive, niggly player with an uncontainable penchant for trash-talking and eagerness for putting up his dukes. After joining Wests Tigers, he infamously was found to have inserted his finger into the backsides of several opposition players in 2001, which attracted a 12-match contrary conduct ban. The Northern Eagles threw Hopoate a lifeline after he was sacked by the Tigers, and although his form was outstanding for the joint venture and later for Manly, he eventually courted trouble again. His 2004 season ended prematurely due to a nine-match ban for making threatening and derogatory remarks to an official, and his NRL career was extinguished two matches into his '05 comeback with a 17-match suspension for a sickening elbow to the head of Cronulla forward Keith Galloway.

9. Mal Meninga

Centre colossus Mal Meninga's size and status meant he was rarely messed with during a 17-season career in the limelight. A devastating ball-runner with deft skills, he was a pointscoring machine with Brisbane Souths, Canberra, Queensland and Australia, but also intelligent and punishing in defence. His toughness and courage were personified by his ability to fight back from four broken-arm injuries in 1987-88—he recovered to captain the Raiders to three premierships and become the first player to tour four times with the Kangaroos and captain two squads to Britain and France. The Origin legend thrived in the rugged and hostile interstate arena, controversially leaving former Test teammate and NSW danger-man Michael O'Connor with a badly broken nose in the 1991 decider.

10. Billy Smith
Brilliant, tough and impetuous, Billy Smith rates as one of the finest halfbacks of all time. He made 26 Test appearances and won four Grand Finals among 234 appearances for St George during the 1960s and '70s, mixing dazzling attack with a keenness to mix it up off the ball. Vice-captain of Australia's 1970 World Cup campaign, Smith played a resolute role in the infamously brutal 12-7 final victory over Great Britain at Leeds before being sent off in the closing stages with British centre Syd Hynes.

COURAGEOUS PERFORMANCES

1. John Sattler plays with a broken jaw
Etched deep in Rugby League lore, John Sattler's courage to play most of the 1970 Grand Final with a smashed jaw is held up as the personification of toughness and heroism in the game. A tough front-rower and natural leader, Sattler had skippered the Rabbitohs to their fourth Grand Final in as many years. Just six minutes into the decider, Manly enforcer John Bucknall felled him with a vicious punch that broke his jaw and dislodged a number of teeth. Sattler was in excruciating pain but battled on, refusing to go off or even acknowledge the damage. Although he stayed on the field afterwards to collect the trophy for Souths, the damage was revealed soon after when he was hospitalised for two weeks and had his jaw wired for three months. It was as tough and courageous an act as Rugby League has ever seen.

2. Allan Prescott and the Battle of Brisbane
The second 'Battle of Brisbane' became known as 'Prescott's Test' for the courage shown by the Great Britain skipper to guide his team to a series-levelling victory in 1958. The tough prop refused to leave the field despite suffering a savage compound fracture to his arm. He said he would play until he dropped, refusing even a painkilling injection. Great Britain had lost star five-eighth Dave Bolton to injury earlier in the match and, with no subs, Prescott refused to leave his team short two players. Britain won the deciding Test two weeks later and Prescott never played another international for his country.

3. Clive Churchill kicks Souths to victory with a broken arm

Souths staged an incredible comeback during the back half of the 1955 season, overcoming a dreadful start to their premiership defence to win their final 11 games and claim their fifth title in six years. That run nearly came to an end in the second-last game of the year when Souths trailed Manly late. Champion fullback Clive Churchill broke his arm early in the match, but with minutes remaining put Les 'Chicka' Cowie over to level the scores at 7-all. With his arm wrapped in a cardboard textbook cover, Churchill slotted the sideline conversion to keep the Rabbitohs in it. The injury ruled him out of the finals series but kept Souths' dream alive as they completed the 'Miracle of '55'.

4. England and the Rorke's Drift Test

A historic Test win that is still revered a century on, England held on with 10 men to defeat Australia 14-6 and wrap up the 1914 Ashes series in Australia. Losing winger Frank Williams, centre Billy Hall and forward Douglas Clark to injury, Harold Wagstaff's great English team battled most of the second half with just 10 players in the third and deciding Ashes Test at the SCG. Against an Australian team that contained eight players named among the country's greatest 100 in 2008, England held on grimly with an Albert Johnson try sealing the win. The match was named in honour of a famous English battle during the Anglo-Zulu War, when 150 British soldiers held off over 4000 Zulu warriors in 1879.

5. Arthur Patton survives a broken leg

Legendary Balmain speedster Arthur Patton, the club's all-time leading try-scorer, didn't score in his final game—but it stands as his finest hour. St George led the 1948 final 2-0 just before halftime when Patton suffered a horrific broken leg. With no substitutes allowed at the time, he had his leg heavily strapped and returned to play out the encounter, which was won by Balmain 13-12. Patton was lauded for his courage but didn't play in the Grand Final loss a week later—or ever again.

6. Jason Croker plays through a ruptured ACL

In one of the most spirited and gutsy showings ever, Canberra veteran Jason Croker played through a host of serious injuries to guide the Raiders to a famous victory. A run of casualties left Canberra without a bench five minutes after halftime in a clash with the Sydney Roosters. The Raiders trailed 10-22 but surged home to win 32-22. It was later revealed that Croker, who had hurt both his ankle and his shoulder earlier in the match, had played the final quarter of the match with a ruptured ACL; it ended his season. He was subsequently awarded the John Sattler Award for Rugby League courage.

7. Trevor Gillmeister risks death
Proud Queenslander Trevor Gillmeister risked death to lead the Maroons to a historic clean sweep of the Super League-ravaged '95 series. With Super League-aligned players disregarded, the Maroons were long odds to beat the Blues but, led by coach Paul Vautin and skipper Gillmeister, they wrapped up the series in two games. In the lead-up to the third game, Gillmeister was hospitalised with a blood disorder and placed on a drip. He was told he would risk his life if he took the paddock, but did it anyway, discharging himself from hospital in an act of defiant courage to lead Queensland to an extraordinary whitewash.

8. Battered Queensland outlasts Blues
In a match that has gone into State of Origin—and Rugby League—lore, a 12-man Queensland team held on to defeat NSW 16-12 in the second game of the '89 series, which sealed the result for the Maroons. Queensland had suffered a brutal injury toll, with Allan Langer (broken leg), Paul Vautin (fractured elbow) and Mal Meninga (fractured cheekbone) all forced from the field before halftime. A shoulder injury then forced Michael Hancock from the field, leaving Queensland with no reserves for most of the second half. Tony Currie and Trevor Gillmeister played on through concussions, Sam Backo battled on with an ankle injury and Bob Lindner played on one leg until the final five minutes, when he eventually succumbed and was stretchered off. It is regarded as one of the great Origin wins.

9. Locky's last play
In what was a long and decorated Rugby League career, Darren Lockyer's most courageous play was his last. In the elimination final clash with St George Illawarra in 2011, he became the victim of friendly fire when fullback Gerard Beale's knee collided with Lockyer's face as Beale attempted to collect a bomb. The collision left the inspirational skipper with a fractured cheekbone. When the Dragons scored two minutes from time, the match was sent into golden point. Playing through obvious pain, Lockyer calmly slotted the decisive field goal under immense pressure in what would be his final premiership play. He battled to play in the preliminary final against Manly but pulled out of the side late in the week.

10. Joey goes from punctured lung to Grand Final hero
Newcastle's progression into its first Grand Final was tempered by the news that champion halfback Andrew Johns could miss the decider after puncturing his lung thanks to a misplaced injection on a rib injury in the preliminary final. Johns was hospitalised during Grand Final week and risked death by playing, according to Australian team doctor Nathan Gibbs. He played but was in such discomfort that at one stage he attempted to leave the field. Johns battled on to become the Knights'

Grand Final hero, his blindside charge in the final minute sending Darren Albert over and giving Newcastle its first premiership.

12-MONTH TURNAROUNDS FOR THE BETTER

1. Todd Carney—2009-10
Sacked by Canberra after a string of off-field atrocities, precocious half Carney was deregistered by the NRL for 2009. His UK work visa was denied, which prevented him from taking up a Super League contract with Huddersfield, and he was also banned from his hometown of Goulburn for alcohol-related mayhem. He eventually spent the season playing for the Atherton Roosters in North Queensland and working in the local pub. The Sydney Roosters offered him a lifeline for 2010, however, and he produced a Dally M Medal-winning season to inspire the previous year's wooden spooners to the Grand Final. Carney also scored 255 points for the Tricolours, made his Test debut for Australia and was named the RLIF Player of the Year.

2. Gary Freeman—1991-92
Two-time Grand Final halfback Freeman was the highest-profile victim of incoming Balmain coach Alan Jones' politics, dumped from the Tigers side in 1991 for former Jones Rugby Union protégé Brian Smith and forced to captain New Zealand against Australia from reserve grade. Freeman played just eight first grade games for the Tigers that season, but linked with Easts the following season and won the Dally M Player of the Year award after a stellar campaign. Spearheading dual wins over Balmain for the Roosters in '92, he re-established himself as one of the premiership's dominant players despite Easts' late season fade to miss the finals.

3. John Simon—1996-97
Former NSW halfback Simon was a prized acquisition from Illawarra for the big-spending Roosters in 1996. Expected to partner another recruit in the halves in Brad Fittler, Simon was kept in the background by Adrian Lam; he made 12 of his 15 appearances off the bench and was not used during the finals, and was left out of the Country Origin side for the first time since making his rep debut in 1992. He reignited his career at Parramatta in '97, winning a Blues recall after a five-season absence and playing his only Test for Australia against Rest of the World. The dexterous No.7 finished second to Fittler in the Provan-Summons Medal—the ARL's official Player of the Year award—as he steered the Eels to their first finals series in 11 years.

4. Preston Campbell—2002-03

The career of livewire half Preston Campbell hit the skids after he won the 2001 Dally M Medal, with Cronulla's signing of high-profile No.7 Brett Kimmorley leaving Campbell in no-man's-land. Upset at the Sharks' pursuit of Kimmorley, Campbell was shunted around the team sheet by incoming coach Chris Anderson from hooker to wing and fullback, then back to the bench and eventually out of the side. Years later, Campbell revealed he slipped into a desperate battle with depression and attempted to take his own life after seemingly being thrown on the scrapheap. But he was offered the chance to resurrect his career by his previous Sharks coach, John Lang, at Penrith, and was magnificent throughout the Panthers' unlikely charge to the minor premiership and Grand Final success. The diminutive playmaker starred at five-eighth, scoring 13 tries and 164 points as one of the club's key contributors; he was consistently brilliant during a further eight seasons for Penrith and Gold Coast.

5. Manu Vatuvei—2007-08

Warriors winger Manu Vatuvei was known as much for his butter-fingered performances as he was for his blockbusting runs and tryscoring feats early in his career. His unreliable handling peaked with a notorious, error-strewn performance in a 30-6 loss to Parramatta in 2007—Vatuvei made six mistakes, three of which led directly to Eels tries. He was dropped for a week and, despite finishing the regular season solidly, was ruled out of the finals by injury and New Zealand's post-season Test schedule. Vatuvei was an obvious target for opposition kickers, but the giant winger responded superbly in a breakthrough '08 season. He scored 16 tries in just 17 games, including a demon-exorcising final-round hat-trick against the Eels to propel the Warriors into the finals. Vatuvei then scored a try and set up a spectacular match-winner in the club's qualifying final boilover against Melbourne. After scoring four tries in a pool victory over England, he played a key role in the Kiwis' World Cup final triumph over Australia. He scooped the Dally M and RLIF Winger of the Year awards, but perhaps the greatest honour bestowed upon him was being named one of the top five players of the season in David Middleton's *Official Rugby League Annual*—just the second time in 22 years a winger had been selected.

6. Jarryd Hayne—2008-09

Hayne was a recent Test debutant and one of the NRL's brightest talents as the 2008 season approached, but he endured a tumultuous year that began with being part of a group that was shot at outside a Kings Cross nightclub in March. A dangerous throw suspension ruled him out of game two of NSW's Origin campaign, while he scored a career-low six tries for flailing Parramatta. He was then left out of Australia's World Cup squad at the end of the year, instead opposing the Kangaroos in the semi-final as Fiji's star player. After a failed stint at five-eighth early in '09, Hayne switched permanently to fullback and carried the Eels from 14th after 18 rounds to an unlikely finals berth. He produced one of the most incredible form streaks by any individual in premiership history, winning six straight man-of-the-match awards to win the Dally M Medal and *Rugby League Week* Player of the Year award before spearheading Parramatta's surge to the Grand Final. Hayne was recalled to the Australian side on the wing and was named the RLIF Player of the Year as he helped the Kangaroos to Four Nations success.

7. James Maloney—2012-13
Denied a compassionate release to return to Sydney by the Warriors at the start of 2012, James Maloney then had a dismal campaign that mirrored that of the club he had piloted to the previous year's Grand Final. The tenacious five-eighth was benched for his last appearance for the Warriors—but his belated move to the Sydney Roosters proved worth the wait. Besides becoming a darling of *The Footy Show*, Maloney debuted for City Origin and NSW—holding his own in a tight series loss to Queensland—and was magnificent throughout the season for the Roosters, starring in the Grand Final defeat of Manly and topping the premiership with 252 points.

8. Cliff Lyons—1993-94
Not for the first or last time in his career, ball-playing mastermind Cliff Lyons was seemingly on the scrapheap at Manly in 1993. Relegated to the bench for much of the season, the enigmatic Lyons featured at five-eighth in the Sea Eagles' finals exit against Brisbane only because of an injury to Geoff Toovey. Kiwi prodigy Gene Ngamu was tipped to permanently take Lyons' five-eighth spot at the club in '94, but the wily veteran had other ideas. He was named Player of the Tournament as Manly took out the World Sevens, and then produced his mesmerising best on a weekly basis in the premiership to win his second Dally M Medal. Reconfirmed as one of the most valuable players in the competition, Lyons featured in the ensuing three Grand Finals for Manly before eventually hanging up the boots in 1999.

9. Michael Jennings—2012-13
Brilliant tryscoring centre Michael Jennings was a regular off-field bad boy during his time at Penrith, but his errant behaviour peaked during 2012. He was dropped to NSW Cup duty with Wentworthville following further transgressions and a form slump, but was nonetheless plucked out of the lower grades to play for the Blues in the Origin series opener; unfortunately his sin-binning for a wild punch contributed to an 18-10 loss. Despite playing all three matches of the series and winning back a spot in first grade, persistent rumours that Jennings was on the outer with Panthers general manager Phil Gould came to fruition when he was let go by the club in the off-season.

He was snapped up by the Sydney Roosters for 2013, scored a career-high 20 tries—including a spectacular effort in the Tricolours' Grand Final victory—and kept his nose clean off the paddock. Jennings won a Kangaroos recall for the World Cup after a four-year absence in the wake of his best and most consistent NRL season.

10. Darren Lockyer—2005-06

For the first time in his charmed career, the pressure of responsibility and expectation appeared to weigh heavily on Brisbane, Queensland and Australian captain Darren Lockyer in 2005. The Broncos suffered yet another late season fade-out after opening up a huge lead in the minor premiership, eventually finishing third and slipping out the back door of the finals. Meanwhile, the Maroons lost their third straight series convincingly after winning the opening game, and Lockyer missed the Tri-Nations final loss to New Zealand—Australia's first defeat in a series or tournament for 27 years—through injury. Several critics called for him to step down from his representative posts and make a return to fullback, but the cool-headed No.6 instead produced one of the most extraordinary individual seasons ever in 2006. After scoring the winning try in Queensland's euphoric Origin decider victory, he led from the front as the Broncos captured the premiership—including a dominant Grand Final display—and again crossed for the match-winner in the Kangaroos' extra-time defeat of the Kiwis in the Tri-Nations final. Lockyer was awarded his second Golden Boot after a season of unparalleled success.

12-MONTH TURNAROUNDS FOR THE WORSE

1. Wally Lewis—1989-90

'The King' continued to bask in his long-held 'world's best' tag in 1989, leading Queensland to a third straight series victory—highlighted by two big wins and a man-of-the-match performance in the injury-ravaged Maroons' heroic game-two win, featuring Lewis's iconic solo try. He skippered Australia on a successful mid-season tour of New Zealand and, although his Brisbane side fell short in its bid to reach the finals, his status as the most influential player in the game was assured. But Broncos coach Wayne Bennett dropped a bombshell by stripping Lewis of the club captaincy ahead of the 1990 season, which the peerless five-eighth later described as the low point of his career. Shifted to lock at club level to accommodate Kevin Walters, Lewis was ruled out of the opening Origin clash with a hamstring injury—just the second time he had missed an Origin game—and the Maroons went on to lose the series after he returned. A broken arm then sidelined him for three months. Despite making a comeback off the bench in Brisbane's heavy preliminary final defeat to Canberra, Lewis was controversially ruled unfit to captain the Kangaroos to Britain and France for an unprecedented second time by the Australian team doctor. To cap his *annus horribilus*, he was virtually forced to leave the Broncos due to a significantly reduced offer, and joined the lowly Gold Coast at the end of the year.

2. Mark Geyer—1991-92
Penrith enforcer Mark Geyer was simultaneously regarded as the most feared and most dynamic forward in the game after an action-packed '91 season laced with achievement. He countered an infamous performance in NSW's game-two win at the SFS (for which he was suspended for five weeks) by starring in Australia's subsequent Test series defeat of New Zealand. The towering second-rower was outstanding later in the year as the Panthers secured their maiden title. But the 24-year-old's stocks nosedived in 1992: a pre-season suspension for a positive marijuana test saw him miss the early rounds and relinquish his representative spots, while the tragic death of teammate and close friend Ben Alexander in June sent him into a downward spiral. Geyer did not play again in '92 and joined Balmain for a similarly rocky stint after a bust-up with Penrith coach Phil Gould.

3. Ben Barba—2012-13
Ben Barba was the undisputed star of the 2012 NRL season. In just his second year as a fullback, he swept to a Dally M Medal win by a six-point margin and scored 22 tries to top the competition for the second straight season, spearheading minor premier Canterbury's drive to the Grand Final. He was considered unlucky to miss out on call-ups to the Queensland and Australian sides, but the fleet-footed No.1 was seemingly established as one of the game's best players. After a disruptive off-season, however, he was stood down by the Bulldogs and entered a rehabilitation facility to treat his problems with alcohol and gambling; a widely publicised relationship breakdown was at the heart of his issues. He returned to the field a month into the season, but struggled to regain his brilliant form of the previous year and battled injury throughout the latter stages of the season as the Bulldogs lost ground on their 2012 achievements. Domestic violence reports in the media continued to haunt Barba, who was granted a release to join Brisbane at the end of a tumultuous season.

4. Jack Elsegood—1993-94
Jack Elsegood was a runaway Rookie of the Year winner in 1993, scoring 12 tries on the wing for Manly to be pencilled into virtually every pundit's squad for the Kangaroo Tour squad to be chosen 12 months down the track. But a pre-season shoulder injury and a head-high tackle early in the season by Souths halfback Craig Field appeared to rattle his

confidence. Elsegood was a shadow of the player who had lit up the Sea Eagles' flank in his debut season and was eventually dropped to reserve grade later in the '94 season.

5. Paul Vautin—1989-90

Manly skipper Paul 'Fatty' Vautin's status as one of the game's most respected players was confirmed by his selection as Australia's vice-captain for the tour of New Zealand in 1989, where he played all three Tests of the series clean sweep. He also captained St Helens in the Challenge Cup final loss to Wigan at Wembley and featured in Queensland's 3-0 drubbing of NSW in a hectic year. But in the wake of the Sea Eagles' dismal campaign, Vautin reluctantly left the club after receiving a reduced offer to re-sign. He joined Easts and captained Queensland in the 1990 series opener after Wally Lewis pulled out injured, but the 22-game veteran was dumped following the Maroons' 8-0 loss. Compounding the Roosters' diabolical results on the field, Vautin's loss of form saw him spend time in reserve grade, capping a lamentable fall from grace for the popular backrower.

6. Les Boyd—1982-83

Australian Test regular Les Boyd was at his best in 1982, featuring prominently as Manly captured the minor premiership and scoring a try in the Grand Final loss to Parramatta. He featured in the mid-season Test series defeat of New Zealand before being one of the standouts on his second Kangaroo Tour, playing all five Tests for the unbeaten 'Invincibles'. But Boyd, who sailed close to the wind throughout a colourful career, was rubbed out of the game for 12 months after being cited for a savage elbow that smashed Queensland prop Daryl Brohman's jaw in the opening State of Origin encounter in 1983. He played just three more first grade games in Australia and was suspended for 15 months after an eye-gouging incident in '84.

7. Todd Carney—2010-11

Resurrecting his career at the Sydney Roosters in spectacular fashion with a Dally M Medal win and an Australian Test debut in 2010, Todd Carney found himself at yet another crossroads after finding off-field trouble again the following season. Early-season injuries stymied his quest to claim the NSW No.6 jumper, while a string of minor alcohol-related transgressions saw him released by the club that had thrown him a lifeline less than two years earlier.

8. Benji Marshall—2012-13

Although well short of his stellar form for Wests Tigers and New Zealand of the previous two seasons, Benji Marshall remained one of the NRL's most influential playmakers in 2012. He finished equal 12th in the Dally M Medal despite the

Tigers' subpar campaign, and captained the Kiwis in two Tests against Australia. But Marshall's four-season reign as skipper of his country ended when Simon Mannering was announced as his replacement in the 2013 pre-season, while injury ruled him out of the clash with the Kangaroos early in the year. His stocks plummeted at club level as the Tigers languished near the foot of the ladder, and he was relegated to the bench for a mid-season match against Souths in the wake of several ordinary performances. The steady flow of criticism became a raging torrent after he signed a deal to switch to Rugby Union with the Auckland Blues; his decision to announce the move via a video on the Blues' website—decked out in an Auckland jersey—just hours after another dismal Tigers loss exacerbated the ill feeling. Little fanfare greeted Marshall's passing of the 200-game milestone or his exit from the code—a sad end to the 11-season tenure of one of the modern era's great entertainers and a genuine Wests Tigers great.

9. Solomon Haumono—1997-98
Former Manly wrecking ball Solomon Haumono produced some of the standalone highlights of Super League's sole season after joining Canterbury, including an astonishing 40-metre individual try against Cronulla and a memorable bone-rattling hit on Brisbane's wing powerhouse Michael Hancock. After playing in NSW's Tri-Series thrashing of Queensland, Haumono was a bolter in Super League Australia's side that defeated New Zealand on Anzac Day. But he fell off the map in '98, infamously going AWOL midway through the season to chase his model girlfriend, Gabrielle 'The Pleasure Machine' Richens, to England. Haumono did not play for the Bulldogs again, eventually resurfacing for an unremarkable stint with Balmain the following season.

10. Chris Anderson—1983-84
In 1983, Canterbury great Chris Anderson captained the Bulldogs to the preliminary final and scored a club-record 19 tries, while he also became the first player to bag an Origin hat-trick in NSW's decider loss. But the veteran winger fell out of favour under incoming coach Warren Ryan in 1984. Relieved of the captaincy halfway through the year, Anderson could not force his way back into the first grade line-up after a spell on the sideline with a broken arm, and missed the Bulldogs' Grand Final victory—an unbefitting end to the Australian club career of one of Canterbury's finest servants.

INDIVIDUAL RIVALRIES

1. Peter Sterling and Steve Mortimer
A rivalry between two of the finest halfbacks who ever played the game, the competition between Peter Sterling and Steve Mortimer was also a battle in style. Sterling, the great puppet-master, and Mortimer, a superb individualist, grappled for premierships and rep jerseys for a decade. Both won four titles each and Sterling often held a slight edge on Mortimer in rep selection, though Mortimer captained NSW to its first series win. An award-winning regular, Sterling's individual accolades also outstripped Mortimer's.

2. Wally Lewis and Brett Kenny
Two of the great five-eighths, Brett Kenny and Wally Lewis, were rep football staples throughout the 1980s as the duo battled for the Australian No.6 jumper. Lewis held the upper hand on most occasions, with Queensland dominating Origin throughout the 1980s and Lewis usually winning Australian selection. But Kenny came out on top during the '82 Kangaroo Tour, where he played five of six Tests at pivot before playing centre outside Lewis in the Australian team for the remainder of his Test career. Remarkably, Kenny held an 8-4 win record over Lewis when directly opposing him at Origin level.

3. Allan Langer and Ricky Stuart
Allan Langer and Ricky Stuart could not have been more different halfbacks, but the pair constantly traded blows throughout a thrilling battle for the top No.7 slot during the early 1990s. At club level, Stuart won three premierships to Langer's two between 1989 and 1995, but Langer kept Stuart from ever representing Australia on home soil. Stuart usurped Langer for the Test halfback job on back-to-back Kangaroo Tours and steered NSW to four Origin series wins in five years opposite the Queensland linchpin, but Langer is regarded historically as the superior player.

4. Noel Kelly and Ian Walsh
Two of the finest hookers Rugby League has seen, Noel Kelly and Ian Walsh were contrasting players for the two powerhouses of the early 1960s who often fought it out for rep jerseys. Walsh had the upper hand on the 1959-60 Kangaroo Tour, but Kelly wrestled away the Australian spot soon after. Walsh's Saints rolled Kelly's Wests in consecutive Grand Finals, though, and Walsh remained the top hooker

until his retirement, with Kelly shifted to prop at Test level. Kelly was named hooker in the ARL Team of the Century, a controversial decision to the many who believed Walsh deserved the nod.

5. Paul Harragon and Mark Carroll

NSW teammates and behemoth props Paul Harragon and Mark Carroll built an intense, explosive rivalry that was marked by flying fists and fearless runs. It started when Carroll moved to Manly and the duo famously clashed in '95 in a battle that saw Newcastle enforcer Harragon knocked out and then sin-binned. The two met in the 1997 Grand Final and came to blows on numerous occasions.

6. Ray Stehr and Jack Arkwright

Australian prop Ray Stehr and British counterpart Jack Arkwright staged a furious battle over the course of the 1936 Ashes series. Both were rugged firebrands with a penchant for the rough stuff: Stehr was sent off in the opening Test of the series, while the two were both marched in the decider after Arkwright flattened Stehr in back play.

7. Ben Elias and Mario Fenech

During a feud built on seemingly legitimate hatred, Ben Elias and Mario Fenech staged some brutal battles against each other as they battled to become the top rake in NSW. Both from migrant families, they had plenty in common but could not stand each other. Souths captain Fenech was sent off after being accused of gouging Balmain's Elias in a 1986 finals match. Elias was a regular NSW hooker but Fenech won the job in '89 before the Tigers No.9 took top spot back again in 1990.

8. Wendell Sailor and Adam MacDougall

In one of Rugby League's most famous modern rivalries, powerhouse wingers Wendell Sailor and Adam MacDougall battled it out at club and state level for over a decade. The two quality players, who both represented Australia, liked to talk up their own abilities off the field. Their most famous clash came when Sailor returned to League in 2009. He scored an early double but MacDougall scored the match-winner and let Sailor know about it.

9. Chris McKivat and Arthur Halloway

Fighting over the mantle of best halfback in the early days of the premiership, Glebe's Chris McKivat and Balmain/Easts linchpin Arthur Halloway were two of the stars during Rugby League's infancy. McKivat had the early upper hand after defecting from Rugby Union, but after Halloway helped Easts to consecutive titles he assumed the belt before McKivat retired in 1914. Both were named in the ARL's 100 Greatest Players.

10. Andrew Johns and Brett Kimmorley

For most of his career, Brett Kimmorley's ambitions were stunted by Immortal Andrew Johns. Coming through the grades at the Knights, Kimmorley was forced to leave his hometown club after being stuck behind Johns in the pecking order. He briefly assumed the upper hand in 1999-2000 when he won a premiership with the Storm and held the Blues No.7 jersey, but Johns quickly returned to dominance in 2001 and never lost his spot as top dog.

INDIVIDUAL STREAKS

1. Clive Churchill—99 consecutive rep games

Considered by many to be the game's greatest-ever player, Clive Churchill played an incredible 99 straight rep games for City, Sydney, NSW and Australia. He toured five times with Australia (making three Kangaroo Tours) and skippered the Aussies when they reclaimed the Ashes in 1950 for the first time in 30 years, and represented NSW more than any other player. His rep career lasted from 1948 until 1957, when he was controversially overlooked for Sydney.

2. Norm Provan—10 consecutive Grand Finals

One of St George's finest sons, towering second-rower Norm Provan was the centrepiece of the Saints' incredible run of 11 straight titles, playing in the first 10. He started in the second-row of all 10 Grand Final wins and captain-coached the final four. Provan scored a double in '57 and crossed for tries in '59 and '60.

3. Luke Douglas—200 (and counting) consecutive games

The most durable player in premiership history, Luke Douglas debuted for Cronulla in the opening game of the 2006 season and had not missed a single game by 2014. In the final game of the '13 season for the Gold Coast, he equalled Jason Taylor's long-standing consecutive games record of 194; he surpassed it in the 2014 opener before extending the mark past 200 games. Douglas returned a week after doing his MCL in 2011—a testament to his toughness.

4. Johnathan Thurston—27 consecutive Origin games

A sublime playmaker who was almost overlooked for a first grade career because of his thin, wiry frame, Johnathan Thurston became one of the game's finest halves. His physique certainly was no reflection of his toughness or durability—he played in 27 straight Origins from his debut in 2005. Thurston's consecutive-games streak surpassed Maroons backrow ironman Gary Larson's run of 24. Eight of Thurston's nine series were victorious, and he won four man-of-the-match awards.

5. Johnny King—Tries in six straight Grand Finals
One of the incredible records to come out of St George's incomparable run of 11 straight titles is Johnny King's feat of six straight Grand Finals posting a try. The dashing Saints flyer set a record that will almost certainly never be broken with tries in every decider from 1960 through '65. He scored the only try in the '61 and '64 deciders, as well as one of the most controversial Grand Final tries in history in 1963.

6. Billy Wilson—20 seasons
'Captain Blood' Billy Wilson was a hard-headed prop forward with St George and North Sydney whose durability and toughness allowed him to spend two decades playing first grade in the premiership. His first grade run was only interrupted by captain-coach stints in Picton (1950-51) and Wagga (1957). Debuting in 1948, Wilson did not retire until 1967 at the age of 40. He won six titles with the Saints and represented NSW and Australia. To put that in perspective, the second-last survivor from that '48 season was South Sydney's Bernie Purcell, who retired in 1960.

7. Wayne Bennett—28 straight seasons as a head coach
Regarded as perhaps the greatest coach in Rugby League history, Wayne Bennett has coached 28 consecutive seasons of first grade since he started with Canberra in 1987. Over that period he has won seven premierships and coached in eight Grand Finals, missing the finals just five times. Bennett has coached the full regular season in each year since '87 and has been a head coach for more than a quarter of the premiership's existence.

8. Terry Lamb—20 straight Kangaroo Tour appearances
Canterbury five-eighth Terry Lamb had the unique distinction of playing every game on the 1986 Kangaroo Tour, the only player to appear in every match on the long trip through Britain and France. Despite touring with Immortal five-eighth Wally Lewis, Lamb played in all tour matches as well as the Tests. He came off the bench in all five Tests against Britain and France, scoring 19 tries and booted 20 goals on the undefeated tour.

9. Ray Price—Five straight Dally M positional awards
Ray Price's five straight Dally M Lock of the Year awards stand as the most consecutive positional awards since they came into being in 1980. The Parramatta lock won the award from '82 until his retirement in '86. Kevin Hastings' Halfback of the Year wins in the award's first three years, Brad Fittler's three straight positional gongs in the 1990s, Terry Lamb's three straight Five-eighth of the Year gongs, Shane Webcke's Prop of the Year three-peat in the early 2000s and Cameron Smith's three straight Hooker of the Year awards from 2011 to 2013 are as close as any other player has come.

10. Hazem El Masri—35 consecutive goals
Canterbury great Hazem El Masri set the premiership record and tied the world mark for most consecutive goals when he booted 35 straight in 2003. El Masri's streak amazingly came over just five games; it surpassed Daryl Halligan's former mark of 30 and tied Henry Paul's world record of 35. His run came to an end after the fulltime siren at Brookvale Oval when he faded a sideline shot. Astonishingly, Batley halfback Barry Eaton broke El Masri's joint world record that same weekend, landing his 36th straight and extending the mark by another two goals.

IRONMEN

1. Luke Douglas
Playing his 195th game in succession in the opening round of 2014, hardworking Titans prop Luke Douglas claimed ownership of the all-time premiership record for most consecutive first grade appearances. Despite toiling at the NRL's front-row coalface, he has not missed a match for Cronulla or Gold Coast since making his debut at the start of 2006. He courageously defied an MCL knee injury sustained in 2011, initially predicted to keep him out for six weeks, to take his place in the Sharks' line-up just five days later and keep the run going.

2. Steve Menzies
A tireless backrower and a tryscoring freak, Steve 'Beaver' Menzies left Manly at the end of 2008 having equalled Terry Lamb's premiership record of 349 first grade appearances in the club's Grand Final triumph (Lamb's total was extended to 350 several years later following new research). The mark has been bettered only by Darren Lockyer since, but while the pair of legendary five-eighths hung up the boots after finishing with their Australian clubs, Menzies went on to play another five seasons and 128 games for Super League sides Bradford and Catalans, giving him an incredible 477 top-line club appearances. Just months after retiring, the 40-year-old Menzies turned out for the Sea Eagles at the inaugural Auckland Nines. He also played more than 20 first grade games in an unprecedented 12 straight seasons (1994-2005)—a feat since equalled by Andrew Ryan and Brent Kite.

3. Darren Lockyer
Along with establishing a legacy as one of the greatest players of all time, Lockyer smashed records for most appearances at first grade, Origin and Test level. In his final season he surpassed Terry Lamb's first grade mark, finishing with 355 appearances

for Brisbane from 1995 to 2011, and extended the Origin record to 36 matches after overtaking former Queensland teammate Allan Langer. Meanwhile, Lockyer's international career, which spanned a record 14 seasons, garnered 59 Test appearances for Australia, 13 clear of Mal Meninga. The talismanic fullback/five-eighth also holds the records for most Tests as captain (38) and most Test tries (35).

4. Terry Lamb
Revered Wests and Canterbury five-eighth Terry Lamb became just the second player in history to reach the 300-game milestone in first grade in 1994; he passed record-holder Geoff Gerard and extended the mark to 349 appearances by the end of '96. Recent research has revealed that Lamb's total was in fact a suitably dignified 350 games, which has been passed only by Darren Lockyer since. Lamb's durability and versatility earned him a unique distinction on the 1986 Kangaroo Tour when he created history by playing all 20 of Australia's games in Britain and France.

5. Andrew Ryan and Brent Kite
Along with Steve Menzies, industrious rival NRL forwards Andrew Ryan and Brent Kite share a record of durability unmatched in premiership history. Former Parramatta and Canterbury backrower Ryan, and St George Illawarra and Manly prop Kite, who were teammates in seven Origins for NSW and five Tests for Australia, both played in at least 20 first grade matches in 12 consecutive NRL seasons. Ryan featured in 22 or more matches for the Eels and Bulldogs from 2000 to 2011 for a total of 291 appearances before hanging up the boots. Kite has featured in at least 21 games per season for the Dragons and Sea Eagles from 2002 to 2013 to rack up 288 appearances, and could take sole ownership of the marvellous record with his new club Penrith in 2014. The feat takes on added significance due to the fact that the unassuming engine-room mainstays started their runs in their respective rookie seasons.

6. Roy Fisher
The original first grade ironman, Parramatta prop Roy Fisher's record of 143 consecutive first grade games, starting in 1954, stretched over nine seasons and stood for 36 years. In a cruel irony, the resilient front-rower's run came to end in 1962 and he missed the Eels' maiden finals appearance later that year. Fisher joined North Sydney the following season. His record of 170 straight games in all grades was broken by Illawarra's Michael Bolt in the late 1980s.

7. Michael Bolt
An honest worker at hooker during Illawarra's first nine seasons, the durable Bolt is one of the most celebrated clubmen in the Steelers' history. Although not always able to command a first grade spot during the 1980s, he played 187 consecutive

matches in all grades in the scarlet-and-white, bettering Roy Fisher's premiership record by 17. Bolt retired in 1990 with 210 grade appearances, including a club-record 167 in first grade.

8. Jason Taylor
Wests, Norths and Northern Eagles pointscoring machine Jason taylor broke Roy Fisher's long-standing premiership record for consecutive appearances in 1998 and extended it by 51 games, eventually playing 194 games in a row from 1993 to 2000. Although the more cynical Rugby League pundits point to his tackle-shy tendencies and reluctance to run the ball as key factors in the halfback's record-breaking run, Taylor's durability cannot be questioned. Ironically, his streak came to end when he was dropped for poor form at the Northern Eagles, and not because of injury. His record was beaten by Luke Douglas in the opening round of 2014.

9. Matt Ballin
One of the NRL's busiest defenders and hardest-working hookers, Matt Ballin has not missed a match for Manly since the beginning of the 2008 season. The ultra-consistent Kingaroy product, who has won two Grand Finals with the Sea Eagles and represented Queensland in one Origin match, headed into 2014 with an unbroken run of 159 appearances to his credit—the fourth-longest streak in premiership history.

10. Hazem El Masri
Prolific tryscoring winger and goalkicker extraordinaire Hazem El Masri had Jason Taylor's all-time consecutive matches record in his sights before he was cut down with a season-ending knee injury midway through 2005. The Bulldogs sharpshooter had played 174 straight games since early 1999. El Masri missed just four games in the remaining four seasons of his career, finishing with a club-record 317 first grade appearances—the ninth-highest total of all time and the fifth-highest total for one club.

TEXTBOOK DEFENDERS

1. Nathan Hindmarsh
Parramatta legend Nathan Hindmarsh was a workhorse defender who became the greatest tackler of the NRL era, consistently finishing in the top three throughout his career. In 2007 he set the record for most tackles in a single game with an incredible 75 against Melbourne, and became the first player to record

10,000 tackles since statistics have been kept. Relentless and ultra-competitive, Hindmarsh set new frontiers for defensive ethos.

2. Kevin Ryan
Nicknamed 'Kandos' because of his cement-hard tackling, Kevin Ryan was renowned for his self-acknowledged "controlled aggression". Few players hit as hard or as fiercely as Ryan, who is one of the greatest one-on-one defenders to have played the game. With a body like granite, he wrought fears in opponents who knew they would feel the impact of one of the toughest but fairest players of his era.

3. Johnny Raper
The greatest lock in Rugby League history, Johnny Raper built a reputation as the greatest cover defender the game has known, chopping down opponents with precision timing. A fitness fanatic who was one of the few players of his era to lift weights, Raper was also extremely strong front-on. Such was his standing that there has been no more decorated forward to play the game.

4. Ron Coote
Maybe the finest post-war player not to be named an Immortal, Ron Coote played in nine Grand Finals with South Sydney and Eastern Suburbs and was a regular for NSW and Australia. A scything cover defender like Johnny Raper, Coote's size made him a feared tackler. An eminently fair player, he lived by the motto that "opponents can't run without legs".

5. David Gillespie
The man known as 'Cement' was the most feared defender of the 1980s and '90s. David Gillespie hit as hard and as sweetly as any player to pull on a boot. Often supported by hefty shoulder pads. His incredible technique and fearlessness frequently left ball-carriers splayed on the turf. Gillespie played in five Grand Finals and represented NSW and Australia in a career built on his near-perfect defence.

6. Trevor Gillmeister
Known as 'The Axe' for his perfect form in chopping down opposition ball-carriers, Trevor Gillmeister built his career on his devastating defence. The unfashionable but forever trying Gillmeister's punishing tackling was perfect for State of Origin football, where he made 22 appearances over a decade, including skippering the famous 1995 series win to earn a sole Test appearance.

7. Barry 'Bunny' Reilly
An unyielding defender who, like Trevor Gillmeister, was also known as 'The Axe', Barry 'Bunny' Reilly was revered for his scything defence. A popular Eastern Suburbs

backrower throughout the 1960s and '70s, Reilly became a favourite of coach Jack Gibson for the amount of defensive work he got through and his ability to change games with his heavy hitting.

8. Nigel Plum

Hardly a high-profile player during his career with the Sydney Roosters, Canberra and Penrith, Nigel Plum was consistently voted the NRL's hardest hitter in the annual *Rugby League Week* players' poll. Plum learnt his craft tackling sheep on his family farm in the Riverina before making a habit of rattling the bones of opposition backs and forwards alike.

9. Dallas Johnson

Melbourne and North Queensland lock Dallas Johnson had few attacking chops but was a mule in defence and the backbone of four Storm Grand Final appearances. Tough with a heavy hit despite his small frame, Johnson was a human missile who threw himself around with reckless abandon. He hit so hard that testing found the impact of a tackle from him had an incredible 10Gs of force—akin to being hit by a 200kg wrecking ball.

10. Brian Clay

An uncompromising defender who loved to hit opponents in the ribs and drive up, Brian 'Poppa' Clay was small but a dreaded defender. Hardly a likely-looking type, the bald-headed Clay was a star during St George's famous era of dominance, with his bone-crushing defence at the forefront of his game.

LATE BLOOMERS

1. John Ferguson

Brilliant winger John Ferguson was finally lured to the Sydney premiership by Newtown in 1981 as a 26-year-old. After a star turn in Wigan's victory in the fabled '85 Wembley final, Ferguson—then with Easts—made his NSW and Australian debuts just shy of his 31st birthday. 'Chicka' joined Canberra the following season and topped the competition's tryscoring in 1988 before making his last Origin appearance in '89. Unlucky not to play more Test football, he scored a career-defining try to send the '89 Grand Final into extra-time, and retired in 1990 at the age of 36 with another premiership medal.

2. Bryan Fletcher

Backrower Bryan Fletcher was not graded by the Roosters until 1997—he made his first grade debut later that season as a 23-year-old—but the laidback forward's rise was rapid after his delayed start to top-flight football. He became recognised as one of the game's most skilful and dynamic forwards the following season, and made his Test and Origin debuts in '99. Fletcher starred in the Roosters' 2002 premiership triumph before joining Souths and finished with 14 appearances for NSW and 13 Tests for Australia to his name.

3. Matt King

A former lower-grader with North Sydney and Cronulla, Matt King quit Rugby League in 2002, citing disinterest. But after working in several menial jobs and having a rethink, the tall three-quarter joined Brisbane Norths—a feeder club for Melbourne—and made a belated NRL debut for the Storm on his 23rd birthday late in the '03 season. Less than two years later King was an Origin hero, scoring a hat-trick in NSW's 2005 decider victory and winning a Test call-up. The afro-haired cult hero played nine matches for the Blues and represented Australia 10 times before starring in the Storm's 2007 Grand Final success. A prolific try-scorer in four subsequent seasons at Warrington, he returned to the NRL as a 31-year-old for two injury-plagued seasons at Souths.

4. Brenton Lawrence

Born in Mackay and raised in Adelaide, Brenton Lawrence was an Australian Schoolboys rep in 2002 but was unable to force his way into first grade during five seasons with Canberra. The mobile prop finally made his NRL debut for the Gold Coast at the age of 26 in 2011, playing 18 games across two seasons for the club—but his career took off in 2013 after he became a low-profile acquisition for Manly. The 28-year-old played 27 games as the Sea Eagles bravely marched to the Grand Final. Lawrence was touted as a potential World Cup bolter for Australia, and while a Test call-up didn't eventuate, he was in the Queensland Origin frame as the 2014 series approached.

5. William Kennedy

Indigenous centre William 'Bubba' Kennedy became a mature-aged sensation when he debuted for the Tigers in 1996. The 27-year-old "rookie" had been spotted by Wayne Pearce via a video, and scored eight tries as one of '96's most impressive newcomers. He represented Country Origin the following season—scoring a try in a 17-4 defeat of City—and crossed 12 times for battling Balmain. Kennedy returned to the bush at the end of '98, becoming a Group 10 legend and winning premierships with three clubs; he was still starring for the Bathurst Panthers in 2013 at the age of 45.

6. Steve Bell

Emerald product Steve Bell made his NRL debut for Melbourne in 2001 as a 24-year-old after spending several seasons with feeder club Brisbane Norths. He was an outstanding success, racking up double-figure season-try tallies in all but one of his eight seasons at Melbourne and Manly. The elusive centre earned a maiden Queensland Origin call-up in 2006 just prior to his 29th birthday, and departed for Super League two years later after scoring a try in the Sea Eagles' 40-0 Grand Final demolition of the Storm—his 94th try in 172 first grade games.

7. Paul Rauhihi

Graded by the Warriors as a 22-year-old, giant prop Paul Rauhihi did not make his first grade debut until 1999 with Newcastle, a week before his 26th birthday. He cracked the New Zealand Test side three years later while playing for the Bulldogs, and was named Dally M Prop of the Year at the age of 31 after helping the Cowboys to a maiden finals series in 2004. Rauhihi starred in the Cowboys' run to the '05 Grand Final and made the last of 16 Test appearances that season before joining Warrington; he finally retired at the end of 2009 aged 36.

8. Ben Cross

Rugged Wagga-born prop Ben Cross made his first grade debut for Canberra in 2003 at the age of 24, but only managed 21 games in his first three seasons. However, his career embarked on an upwards trajectory after he joined Melbourne, where he featured in the Storm's 2006-07 Grand Finals. Cross won a NSW call-up as a 29-year-old from Newcastle in '08 and endured an injury-hampered run but finished with the Knights after a strong 2010 campaign. He was still playing for Widnes three years later at 34.

9. Jeremy Smith

Christchurch-born Runaway Bay junior Jeremy Smith failed to break into first grade with the Northern Eagles, but earned an NRL debut for Melbourne in 2004 aged 24 after starring for feeder club Brisbane Norths. The aggressive backrower played in three straight Grand Finals (2006-08) for the Storm, broke into the New Zealand Test side as a 27-year-old in 2007, and won another premiership after his 30th birthday with St George Illawarra in 2010. Smith made the last of his 22 Test appearances in 2012 from Cronulla before linking with his former Dragons mentor, Wayne Bennett, at Newcastle.

10. Fuifui Moimoi

Bullocking front-rower Fuifui Moimoi was 24 when he made a belated NRL debut for Parramatta in 2004, but it took several seasons for him to cement a regular spot.

He earned a New Zealand Test call-up in 2007 before truly arriving as a top-class prop two years later. The 30-year-old scored a memorable try in the Eels' 2009 Grand Final loss to Melbourne and was subsequently named RLIF Prop of the Year. One of the struggling blue-and-golds' few consistent contributors in recent seasons, Moimoi represented Tonga at the 2013 World Cup at the age of 34.

GOALKICKERS

1. Daryl Halligan
The first player in premiership history to break the 2000-point barrier, Kiwi winger Daryl Halligan set new standards for goalkicking excellence during the 1990s. The Rugby Union convert landed 855 goals for Norths and Canterbury at 79.31 per cent, topping 100 goals in a season twice and kicking a then Bulldogs club-record 10 goals in a match three times. He broke Mick Cronin's long-standing consecutive goals record with 30 in a row in 1998—the year of his famous preliminary final conversion against Parramatta. Halligan improved as his career wore on, kicking at over 85 per cent in his last three seasons, and is also credited with 60 goals in 20 Tests for New Zealand.

2. Hazem El Masri
Hazem El Masri was handed the daunting task of succeeding Daryl Halligan as the Bulldogs' goalkicker in 2001, but arguably exceeded his long-time teammate's achievements with the boot. The elusive winger slotted a club-record 11 from 11 against Souths in 2003, kicked over 100 goals in four seasons (including a premiership-record 129 in 2003, which he extended by 10 goals the following season) and finished his career with 891 goals at 81.97 per cent in becoming the highest point-scorer of all time. Forging a unique style—keeping the ball relatively low with a strong draw—El Masri landed a then world-record-equalling 35 straight goals in '03.

3. Matthew Ridge
Former All Black Matthew Ridge's radar-like precision after joining Manly in 1990 changed Australian clubs' perception of the importance of possessing a quality goalkicker—and sent talent scouts scouring New Zealand's Rugby Union ranks for more like him. The fullback kicked 580 first grade goals for Manly and Auckland at 80.22 per cent, including a career-high 106 goals in both of the 1994 and '95 seasons, and landed 11 goals in a match for the Sea Eagles on two occasions. Ridge also kicked a Kiwis-record 71 goals in 25 Test appearances.

4. Michael Cronin
The last of the great front-on goalkickers, Parramatta legend Michael Cronin held all-time records for most goals in a career (865) and a season (123 in '82) for 16 and 26 years respectively. Although his misses in the Eels' 1977 Grand Final draw and '84 Grand Final loss were crucial, 'The Crow' landed 15 goals in deciders and was regarded as the code's premier marksman throughout his career. The pointscoring phenomenon still holds the record for most Test goals for Australia with 141 in 33 appearances—including 10 in one Ashes Test in 1979. His mark of 26 consecutive goals, set in 1978, stood for two decades.

5. Eric Simms
South Sydney fullback Eric Simms kicked a then record 803 goals from 1965 to 1975, including 112 in 1969 (another unprecedented total), and landed 16 goals in six Grand Final appearances. The front-on sharpshooter booted 39 goals in eight Tests (all World Cup matches), starring with 25 successful kicks in just four matches as Australia claimed the 1968 World Cup crown.

6. Keith Barnes
Nicknamed 'Golden Boots', Balmain great Keith Barnes kicked a then premiership record 742 goals in 194 games from 1955 to 1968. Barnes, from the front-on school of goalkicking, landed a club-record 90 goals in 1956. His greatest days with the boot included a haul of 11 in 1960, two massive penalty goals to sink premiers St George 19-15 that same season, and seven second-half goals against Manly in '66 to inspire a 22-17 victory after the Tigers had trailed 2-15 at halftime. Barnes' tally of 59 goals in 17 Tests includes 10 in a match against France in 1960; he booted 101 goals as captain of the 1959-60 Kangaroo Tour squad.

7. Johnathan Thurston
The phenomenal right-to-left arc that North Queensland superstar Johnathan Thurston achieves off the tee marks him as one of game's most unique goalkickers, but he is also one of the best ever: to the end of 2013, he had kicked 538 goals for the Cowboys at 79.36 per cent. His success rate from the sideline is extraordinary. The brilliant half landed 68 goals for Queensland—one short of Mal Meninga's Origin record—from 2005 to 2013 at the magnificent success rate of 80.95 per cent, while his 135 goals in 30 Tests is just six shy of Mick Cronin's all-time record.

8. Jason Taylor
Scheming halfback Jason Taylor holds the premiership record for most goals, with 942 in 276 games from 1990 to 2001, kicking at a career success rate of 75.24 per cent. He landed a North Sydney club-record 108 goals in 1996 and '98, and booted a career-

high 116 goals for Parramatta in 2001 (his final season before retiring), including a club-record-equalling 11 from 11 in a match against Wests Tigers.

9. Ryan Girdler
Dynamic centre Ryan Girdler was an inconsistent goalkicker early in his career with Illawarra and Penrith, travelling along with a percentage in the mid-60s. But his performances for the Panthers during the 1997 Super League season marked him as one of the best in the game: he kicked 76 goals from 82 attempts—an unheard-of season success rate of 92.68 per cent. Girdler set several representative records in 2000, including an Origin-record 10 goals from as many attempts in NSW's game-three thrashing of Queensland, and a world-record 17 goals in Australia's World Cup rout of Russia. He finished an admirable career with 624 first grade goals and kicked at over 80 per cent during his farewell 2004 campaign.

10. Andrew Johns
Second in premiership history with 917 career goals for Newcastle at 74.25 per cent, Andrew 'Joey' Johns was a magnificent clutch goalkicker. He booted a club-record 110 goals in 2001 and followed that up with 102 in '02, and slotted a Knights-best 11 in a match in 2006 and nine or more in a match on five other occasions. Johns kicked 38 goals for NSW at Origin level and 89 in 30 appearances for Australia, including a then Test-record 12 against Fiji in 1996.

GOALKICKING FORWARDS

1. Craig Fitzgibbon
One of the hardest-working backrower/props of the modern era, Craig Fitzgibbon still had enough energy in store to rack up the most points by a forward in premiership history (1604) and kick 718 goals—the ninth-most of all time—at an outstanding 77 per cent. A classic around-the-corner kicker, the bald-headed Fitzgibbon landed 56 goals in 20 finals matches, including five in the Roosters' 2002 Grand Final victory. The Tricolours great also slotted 39 goals in 18 Tests for Australia and 20 goals in 11 Origins for NSW, and booted 11 in Australia's non-Test drubbing of Wales in 2003.

2. Arthur Oxford
Regarded as potentially the game's best goalkicker of the 1920s, Arthur Oxford held a long-standing premiership record of 23 consecutive goals. He kicked 378 goals in

165 games for Souths and Easts from 1915 to 1929. Equally at home at hooker, prop or second-row, Oxford landed a career-high 49 goals in leading the premiership's pointscoring in 1923, and slotted 10 in a match against University in 1920. The durable forward also goaled seven times in five Tests for Australia, and kicked 18 goals in eight interstate matches for NSW.

3. Cameron Smith
The consummate all-rounder, Melbourne's talismanic hooker Cameron Smith ranks among the best goalkickers of the NRL era. He was set to become the highest-ever pointscoring forward and push his way into the overall top 10 in 2014, heading into the season with 684 goals at 72 per cent. He kicked a career-high 10 goals in a match on two occasions in 2013. At rep level, the cool-headed left-footer has also landed 30 Test goals and 16 Origin goals.

4. Harry Bath
Former Brisbane Souths and Balmain forward Harry Bath crafted his legend as one of the all-time greats in a decade with Warrington, kicking over 700 goals on the English club scene. Returning to Australia with St George, he landed 240 goals in 60 games—including 108 in 1959, a premiership record for a forward. His best efforts included a Grand Final-record eight in the '57 decider, nine goals in a match on four occasions, and a career-high 11 goals against Parramatta in '59.

5. Bernie Purcell
South Sydney backrower Bernie Purcell was the first player in premiership history to kick 500 first grade goals; he held the record as the highest pointscoring forward of all time for 40 years after his retirement. Purcell, who began his career with a season at Wests, kicked seven goals in the Rabbitohs' 1951 Grand Final thrashing of Manly, while his goalkicking was also a vital component of decider victories in 1954-55. He played his only Test against Great Britain in 1950 before touring with the 1956-57 Kangaroos.

6. Wayne Bartrim
Gold Coast and Dragons lock/hooker Wayne Bartrim was one of the great clutch goalkickers, booting 489 goals in 232 games (1991-2001) at 70 per cent. He kicked a towering sideline conversion to give St George a 16-14 finals win over Canberra in 1996, and nailed an after-the-bell goal from out wide to clinch the St George Illawarra joint venture's maiden win (also against the Raiders) in '99. A niggly competitor, Bartrim's lone goal on Origin debut saw Queensland home 2-0 in the 1995 series opener; he finished with 11 goals in nine appearances for the Maroons.

7. George Taylforth
Canterbury and Cronulla second-rower George Taylforth was renowned as one of the finest long-range goalkickers of his era, landing 314 in a 120-game career spanning 1965-72. He set club records (since surpassed) for points in a season for the Berries (204 in 1967, including 99 goals) and Sharks (202 in 1970, including 95 goals). Taylforth landed four goals in Canterbury's '67 Grand Final loss to Souths, and slotted nine in a match on three occasions.

8. Corey Parker
Emerging as a burly prop before becoming one of the hardest-working and most dynamic backrowers in the NRL, Brisbane stalwart Corey Parker counted superb goalkicking ability as a string on his broad bow. Parker had kicked a Broncos-record 418 goals at 74 per cent to the end of 2013. He broke a club record by kicking 10 goals against Penrith in 2008, slotted nine against the same opponent the following season, and nailed eight from eight in a finals defeat of Newcastle in '06.

9. David Furner
Canberra backrower David Furner was far from the most consistent kicker—as his career strike rate of 65 per cent attests—but he could certainly knock over a bagful of goals on his good days. Furner broke Bernie Purcell's long-standing forward pointscoring record to set a new mark of 1218—including 511 goals. He set a club record in 1993 with 10 in a match against Parramatta before kicking a career-high 86 goals in the Raiders' '94 premiership season. On the '94 Kangaroo Tour, he netted 24 goals in nine appearances.

10. Henry Tatana
Rugged prop Henry Tatana kicked 23 goals in nine Tests for New Zealand—including six in the Kiwis' shock 24-3 win over Australia in 1971—before joining Canterbury. He booted 265 goals in 90 games for Canterbury and St George, including a career-high 81 for the Berries in '73, and kicked the Dragons into the 1975 Grand Final, slotting four goals in an 8-5 major semi upset of runaway minor premiers Easts.

LEFT-FOOTED GOALKICKERS

1. Ken Wilson
A prolific point-scorer in a 13-year career with Newtown and Penrith, left-footer Ken Wilson racked up 1261 points in first grade. He became the 11th player in premiership

history to top 1000 points, and finished second in scoring in 1980. Wilson famously featured in the only 0-0 and 1-0 premiership games.

2. Luke Burt
The highest-scoring left-footed kicker in premiership history, Parramatta great Luke Burt booted 646 goals for the Eels in a 14-year career that began in 1999 and ended in 2012. His career tally of 1793 points is eighth in premiership history. He finished top three in the NRL's scoring in 2005, 2008 and 2009.

3. Cameron Smith
Melbourne, Queensland and Australian skipper Cameron Smith was the Storm's kicker for the better part of a decade but only occasionally kicked in rep football, deferring to Johnathan Thurston. With 1508 points heading into the 2014 season, southpaw Smith was poised to join the top 10 point-scorers ever, and was already the ninth-highest accumulator of goals in first grade history.

4. Jamie Soward
Enigmatic pivot Jamie Soward was a prolific point-scorer in the lower grades before he debuted for the Sydney Roosters in 2005. A shift to St George Illawarra in 2007 saw him take up kicking duties and score 398 goals for the club. Soward finished second in the NRL's pointscoring in 2009 and left the Dragons as the club's greatest-ever scorer.

5. Len Killeen
An outstanding goalkicking three-quarter with St Helens, South African-born Len Killeen spent five seasons at Balmain and one at Penrith, where he amassed 700 points. His 207 points in 1969 was a Balmain club record (and second in the premiership), and he kicked two goals in the Tigers' last Grand Final win that year.

6. Luke Covell
A favourite of the Cronulla faithful, winger Luke Covell scored 1090 points in an eight-year career that started with the Wests Tigers. Covell finished top four in scoring each year from 2005 to 2008 and led the NRL in 2008. Cronulla fans famously stretched their arms out and moved their fingers whenever Covell attempted a shot at goal.

7. Jarrod Croker
A head-geared Canberra centre, Jarrod Croker scored 690 points in his first five years to become the club's fourth-highest scorer. Kicking at a career strike rate of just under 80 per cent, he led the premiership in 2012. His most famous effort off the tee was a missed equalising penalty shot from in front of the sticks in the 2010 finals loss to the Wests Tigers.

8. Mat Rogers
Dual international and son of Cronulla great Steve, Mat Rogers trails only his father on the Sharks' all-time pointscoring list. In a 12-year NRL career, including a stint with the Gold Coast, Rogers scored 1360 points (all-time 22nd) and finished second in the NRL in 2000. He famously kicked all of Queensland's points in his Origin debut, a 9-8 win in 1999.

9. Darren Lockyer
Rarely regarded as a terrific goalkicker, the premiership's most capped player Darren Lockyer, kicked 376 career goals and scored 1191 points to lead Brisbane's all-time tally. He scored a further 82 points for Queensland and 204 for Australia (all-time fifth). Lockyer's 272 points in 1998 was second in the NRL and, at the time, fourth in history.

10. Josh Hannay
A tough centre for North Queensland, Josh Hannay retired as the Cowboys' top pointscorer and their record-holder for most points in a game and a season. He finished behind just Hazem El Masri on the top point-scorers table in both 2003 and 2004.

GREATEST FIELD-GOAL EXPONENTS

1. Eric Simms
The player most responsible for the halving of the field goal's value from two points to one, Souths fullback Eric Simms piloted a whopping 86 field goals over during his career—the most in premiership history. He also set all-time records for most field goals in a season (29 in 1968) and a match (five against Penrith in 1969), and slotted four in the 1970 Grand Final victory over Manly. The Indigenous pointscoring machine also kicked eight field goals in nine Test appearances.

2. Neil Baker
Canterbury, Souths and Penrith utility back Neil Baker was the field-goal king of the 1980s, slotting 45 (a record for one-point field goals) in a nine-season career. He kicked an unbelievable 20 for the Rabbitohs in 1986—by far the most during the one-point era—and landed three field goals in a match on two occasions.

3. Tony Melrose
Former Wallaby Tony Melrose's Rugby Union background helped him become one of the premiership's most potent field-goal merchants of the 1980s, steering 30 between

the posts in 179 games for Parramatta, Souths, Manly and Easts. The versatile back's career-high eight for the Rabbitohs in '83 included two in a match in consecutive wins over Newtown and Canberra. In '87, he landed two in the Roosters' 12-all draw with Balmain—one off each foot—and backed up the following week to kick a booming 40-metre match-winner in the final minute of a 15-14 defeat of Penrith.

4. Darren Lockyer

Brisbane champion Darren Lockyer kicked a relatively modest 21 field goals in 355 first grade games, but many of them were match-winning efforts. A brilliant clutch performer, he slotted a match-sealing field goal in the Broncos' 15-8 win over Melbourne in the 2006 Grand Final; nailed an incredible 40-metre field goal to sink the Gold Coast in golden point in '07, bouncing the ball off each upright before it dropped over; and knocked over a high-pressure one-pointer despite the discomfort of a fractured cheekbone in Brisbane's golden point semi-final defeat of St George Illawarra in 2011, which proved to be his final act for the club. Lockyer also kicked an angled 46-metre attempt over for Queensland during the 2010 Origin series.

5. Terry Lamb

All-time great five-eighth Terry Lamb kicked 44 field goals in 17 seasons for Wests and Canterbury—a shade behind Neil Baker for most in the one-point era—including a career-high 10 in 1986. Lamb potted a vital field goal in the 17-4 upset of Manly in the 1995 Grand Final, but it was an ill-timed one-pointer against Newcastle in 1992 that unfortunately ranks as the most memorable of his career. The Bulldogs skipper, believing the scores were locked 10-all, snapped a late field goal in his side's 12-11 loss.

6. Phil Hawthorne

Rugby Union convert Phil Hawthorne kicked 55 field goals in the last three seasons of the two-point era, including 25 in 1970. The St George five-eighth slotted four in a match once and three in a match on four occasions. He landed two field goals in Australia's 37-15 win in the first Ashes Test of 1970 before captaining his country in the deciding third-Test loss. Hawthorne has the distinction of kicking the first-ever one-point field goal—in a reserve grade game against Balmain in '71—but booted just one field goal in first grade that season.

7. Barry Glasgow

Barry Glasgow's Rugby League fame stems almost solely from his field-goal aptitude: he slotted 44 in three seasons for Western Suburbs, including 29 in 1969 to equal Eric Simms' record set a year earlier. The rule change decreasing the value of field goals to one point had a dramatic effect on Glasgow's imprint on the game: he kicked a solitary one-point field goal in four seasons for Norths.

8. Andrew Johns
Australian Team of the Century halfback Andrew 'Joey' Johns was the game's great all-rounder, counting exceptional field-goal kicking among his vast array of talents. He landed 22 field goals in 249 games for Newcastle, and slotted an Origin-record four one-pointers in 23 games for NSW.

9. Bob Fulton
Immortal Bob 'Bozo' Fulton kicked 58 field goals during his glittering career at Manly and Easts, and is second only to Eric Simms in premiership history. His career-high total of 19 in 1970—the last season of two-point field goals—included three in the Sea Eagles' preliminary final win over St George and two in the ensuing Grand Final loss to Souths.

10. Jason Taylor
A sweet striker of the ball, points-hungry halfback Jason Taylor slotted 35 field goals in 276 games for Wests, Norths, Northern Eagles and Parramatta. His career-high seven for Norths in 1994 included memorable match-winners against Brisbane in a regular season clash and during the finals. In 1997 he kicked three in the Bears' extra-time finals loss to the Roosters, and in 1993 he potted a key field goal in a 7-0 win on debut for City Origin.

POINTSCORING FEATS

1. Dave Brown—Most points in a game
Arguably the most incredible record in Rugby League, Dave Brown's 45 points against Canterbury came in his famous 1935 season, when he racked up an unbelievable 244 points in just 15 matches. Against the Berries—in their debut season—Brown scored five tries and booted 15 goals. Astonishingly, when the two teams met later in the season, he scored 38 points through six tries and 10 goals—a record that eight decades later is still tied for second on the all-time list.

2. Hazem El Masri—Most career points
A legendary goalkicker with Canterbury, Hazem El Masri became the fourth player to surpass 2000 career points in 2007, and in the opening round of the 2009 season— his final year in the NRL—became the premiership's greatest-ever point-scorer. El Masri retired at year's end with 2418 points from 159 tries and 891 goals, kicked at just under 82 per cent. Incredibly, he did not become Canterbury's first-choice kicker until 2001, the sixth year of his career.

3. Hazem El Masri—Most points in a season
The premiership's greatest scorer achieved the greatest scoring season in history when he scored 342 in Canterbury's premiership season of 2004. Hazem El Masri topped the pointscoring tally six times throughout his career but had his finest season in '04 when he scored 16 tries and booted 139 goals. He racked up four hauls of 20-plus points, including 22 in the preliminary final win against Penrith.

4. Craig Fitzgibbon—Most points by a forward
The premiership has seen its share of great pointscoring forwards, with Cameron Smith, David Furner, Wayne Bartrim and Bernie Purcell all scoring in excess of 1000 points. The man with the most points by a forward, though, is raw-boned backrower Craig Fitzgibbon, who scored 1604 (all-time equal 10th). A great goalkicker, he booted 718 career goals to go with 51 tries.

5. Mick Cronin—Most points in a calendar year
Parramatta great Mick Cronin ate points for breakfast in 1978, posting the all-time mark for a calendar year with 547 in just 52 matches. The goalkicking centre scored 282 points in the premiership (then a record) and booted 26 consecutive goals (then a record), and led the scoring tally on the Kangaroo Tour and interstate series that year.

6. Mal Meninga—Most State of Origin points
One of State of Origin's most revered figures, Mal Meninga has scored more Origin points than any other player: 161. He scored five tries and kicked 69 goals in a decorated 32-game career that spanned the first 15 seasons of the format, with his greatest haul 16 points in the series-opening 36-6 hammering of 1989.

7. Johnathan Thurston—Most Test-match points
Playing in his 30th Test in the 2013 World Cup final, Johnathan Thurston surpassed Mick Cronin to become the greatest point-scorer in Test history, booting seven goals against New Zealand in the 34-2 romp to lift his tally to 318.

8. Ryan Girdler—Most points in a Test/Most points in an Origin
Veteran Penrith centre Ryan Girdler smashed the world record for points in a Test when he scored 46 in Australia's 110-4 win over Russia in Hull at the 2000 World Cup. Girdler scored three tries and kicked 17-from-19 in the demolition job. He also holds the mark for the most points in an Origin match, posting 32 in the game-three blowout of 2000 with three tries and 10 goals.

9. Tom Kirk—First player to 1000 career points
Journeyman fullback Tom Kirk became the first player to score 1000 premiership points, achieving the honour in the League's 40th season. Debuting with Canterbury

in 1936, he shifted to Newtown in 1940 and scored 680 points in 98 games for the Bluebags. He broke the record in 1947 in his one-year stay with North Sydney. Kirk topped the premiership's scoring five times.

10. Daryl Halligan—First player to 2000 career points

Considered the greatest clutch kicker of all time, North Sydney and Canterbury winger Daryl Halligan became the first player in premiership history to surpass 2000 career points, breaking the 2000-point barrier in his final season. 'Chook' bettered 200 points five times and kicked many big goals in his career, including the leveller from the sideline in Canterbury's famous preliminary final comeback in 1998.

TRYSCORING FEATS

1. Ken Irvine—Most premiership tries

A lightning-quick winger with North Sydney and then Manly, Ken Irvine is the only player in premiership history to break the 200-try barrier. He finished his extraordinary 16-year tryscoring career with 212 touchdowns, scoring at least 13 tries in the 14 years he played near-full seasons. Irvine is tied with Frank Burge for most career hat-tricks on 16.

2. Dave Brown—Most tries in a season

In what is possibly the most amazing premiership record, magical Eastern Suburbs centre Dave Brown scored a stunning 38 tries in just 15 games. He scored six tries twice, five tries once, four tries three times and two doubles to boot, crossing in all bar two of the games he played in. Brown incredibly scored 14 tries in a 14-day period.

3. Frank Burge—Most tries in a game

In the most incredible single-game tryscoring performance in history, legendary Glebe tryscoring forward Frank Burge crossed eight times against University in 1920 in a 41-0 flogging that also saw him kick four goals. He surpassed his own record of six in a match, scored against North Sydney four seasons earlier. To put the record in perspective, just one other player has scored seven tries in a game, only five others have scored six in a game and no player since 1950 has scored more than five in a match.

4. Greg Inglis—Most State of Origin tries

Big and strong, Greg Inglis debuted for Queensland as a 19-year-old in 2006 and scored 15 tries in his first 21 Origin appearances. He scored doubles in his first two Origin outings and passed Dale Shearer's 20-year record of 12 in the opening game of the 2012 season at just 25 years of age.

5. Darren Lockyer—Most Test tries for Australia
Broncos champion and most capped premiership player Darren Lockyer has scored more tries in Tests than any other player, with 35 tries in 59 appearances. In a decorated 14-year international career that saw him captain Australia a record 38 times, he scored in his first Test as a starter and in his final Test.

6. Steve Menzies—Scored a try in the most games
One of the great tryscoring forwards, Manly great Steve Menzies sits second on the all-time tryscoring list with 180 in 349 top-grade games, but is atop the list of tries in the most games. He crossed for tries in 140 premiership matches—one more than record tryscoring winger Ken Irvine and 10 ahead of Cronulla whiz Andrew Ettingshausen.

7. Matt Sing—70 tries for two clubs
The only player in premiership history to score 70 tries for two separate clubs, Matt Sing achieved the feat with the Sydney Roosters and North Queensland Cowboys after playing his first three seasons at Penrith. A sublime finisher, he scored 72 tries in 135 games for the Tricolours before going better at the Cowboys, where he crossed 73 times in 104 outings.

8. Johnny Graves—Most tries in a Grand Final
Affectionately known as 'Whacka', Maitland-bred winger Johnny Graves is the only man to have scored four tries in a premiership decider. After a stellar 1951 season that saw him top the tryscoring tally, Graves scored four tries in the 42-14 demolition of Manly at the SCG. It is a record that has not been matched, with a hat-trick achieved in a Grand Final only a handful of times.

9. Johnny King—Tries in six consecutive Grand Finals
A speedy winger from St George, Johnny King scored 143 tries in 191 games—the club's all-time leading mark. His most impressive tryscoring feat, however, was his ability to cross when it mattered: he scored a try in six consecutive premiership wins. He scored in every Grand Final between 1960 and '65 and was the sole try-scorer in '61 and '64.

10. Don Manson—Most tries on premiership debut
South Sydney winger Don Manson had a field day on debut, scoring five tries in a 63-0 rout of University in the opening round of the 1937 season. He didn't recapture that initial form though, scoring just 19 more tries in his three-season career that included an appearance for NSW in 1938.

THE PLAYERS

TRYSCORING DROUGHTS

1. Bryce Gibbs
Bustling young prop Bryce Gibbs scored a try in each of his first three NRL seasons, culminating in a memorable four-pointer in Wests Tigers' 2005 Grand Final victory. But Gibbs, who was controversially let go by the Tigers at the end of 2011 and joined Cronulla, then went on an eight-year tryscoring hiatus. His drought garnered a fair bit of media attention, and was finally broken when he dotted down in the Sharks' final-round defeat of Canberra in 2013—his 142nd appearance since the '05 decider.

2. Jason Lowrie
Jason Lowrie became just as well known for his inability to find the stripe as for his aggressive, no-nonsense front-row performances. Try-less in his first seven seasons of first grade with Easts and Balmain after debuting for the Roosters in 1993, he amazingly scored tries in back-to-back New Zealand Test wins over Australia and Tonga in the '99 post-season. Lowrie collected his maiden first grade try in his 139th game, Wests Tigers' mid-season win over the Northern Eagles in 2000.

3. Shaun Berrigan
During his mid-career stint in the centres, Brisbane's valuable utility Shaun Berrigan was leading the NRL's tryscoring race in 2005 with 19 tries in just 16 games—including a streak of crossing in eight consecutive games. But the four-pointers dried up dramatically, with Berrigan failing to post a try in his last eight appearances in '05 and first six games of 2006. He moved to hooker with spectacular results later that season, including a two-try performance in the Broncos' preliminary final comeback defeat of the Bulldogs.

4. Martin Bella
After scoring his maiden try in his first season at North Sydney in 1986, elite prop Martin Bella was forced to wait five years and 105 games for his next 'meat pie', finally scoring again for Manly against Illawarra in 1991. One of the best hard-yards men in the business, Bella also went try-less in his nine Tests for Australia and 21 Origin appearances for Queensland.

5. Matt Bowen
North Queensland's ubiquitous fullback led the NRL with 21 touchdowns in 25 games in 2005, but Matt Bowen's burgeoning tryscoring talents deserted him the following season. After scoring the match-winner early in '06 against Newcastle,

he suffered through a 16-match try-less run. But this proved merely an aberration, with Bowen crossing for 22 tries in 2007 to top the competition once again.

6. Clive Churchill
Fullbacks of yesteryear were not the prolific try-scorers that their modern-day No.1 counterparts have become. Clive Churchill, regarded by many as the greatest fullback and player in the game's history, did not record a try in 37 Test appearances for Australia—18 Tests more than the next try-less international, hooker Kevin Schubert. Incredibly, the brilliant Churchill also did not cross for his first try for Souths until his fifth season in first grade, and endured a two-year try drought towards the end of his career.

7. Brent Todd
New Zealand Test veteran Brent Todd played in four Grand Finals in five seasons with Canberra—but never scored a try in the lime-green jumper. The rugged front-rower, who scored his maiden Test try in his 18th appearance for the Kiwis in 1991, finally crossed the stripe in first grade after joining the struggling Gold Coast in 1992, celebrating his 100th first grade appearance with a long-awaited four-pointer.

8. Michael Jennings
One of the NRL era's most potent try-scorers—91 in 148 games to the end of 2013—Michael Jennings produced the paltry return of just one try in 15 games for Penrith in 2011. The centre's previous lowest in four seasons was 12. Jennings also recorded an 11-game try drought (his previous longest try-less streak was five games), but proved he was back to his prolific best by notching a career-high 20 touchdowns for the Roosters in 2013.

9. Martin Lang
After scoring his first NRL try in 1998, kamikaze hit-up merchant Martin Lang went through an 81-game try drought with Cronulla. He belatedly grabbed a four-pointer in the Sharks' semi-final thrashing of the Bulldogs in 2001, but that was to be his last: he failed to score in his remaining 68 first grade appearances after joining Penrith. Lang's nine-season career incurred seven Mad Monday nude runs.

10. Matt Parsons
Towering South Sydney and Newcastle prop Matt Parsons endured a scoresheet hiatus of over four years. He dotted down in the Rabbitohs one-point win over St George Illawarra in Round 5 of 1999, and did not cross again until the Knights' Round 6 defeat of Cronulla in 2003—with 95 try-less appearances in between.

UNLIKELY TRYSCORING CHAMPS

1. Nathan Merritt
Although Nathan Merritt is recognised as one of the modern era's most prolific finishers, even his most ardent supporters could not have predicted the success he would find in 2006 at battling South Sydney. The Rabbitohs junior had just returned from an indifferent two-season stint at Cronulla that netted just eight tries in 18 games, but, despite Souths' meagre tally of three wins in 2006, he bagged 22 tries in 24 games to become the first player from a team finishing last to top the tryscoring table.

2. Stan Gorton
St George winger Stan Gorton debuted for powerful St George in 1966 but did not cement a first grade spot until 1968—when he streeted the competition with 22 tries, eight clear of Manly's Les Hanigan. Gorton grabbed four tries against Norths and a double in a finals defeat of Easts, but his next-best season total following that breakthrough year was four tries in 1971, his last year of first grade.

3. Steve Linnane
St George's Steve Linnane was a standout for the Dally M Rookie of the Year award in 1985, leading the competition with 17 tries in 26 matches as the Dragons qualified for the Grand Final. But the tenacious halfback's tryscoring form proved to be a once-off—he scored just eight tries in the remaining 91 games of his first grade career with St George and Newcastle.

4. Jack Gray-Spence
Jack Gray-Spence topped the premiership in his debut season, 1933, with 11 tries. But the real surprise comes from the fact that Gray-Spence played for struggling University, who finished third last. His total, which included tries in eight of University's 13 matches, is a record for the hapless 'Students', who finished with the wooden spoon in 10 of their 18 seasons (1920-37).

5. Terry Hill
Terry Hill was one of the game's leading centres of the 1990s but was not a noted try-poacher heading into the 1997 ARL season—his best season total to that point had been nine tries for Manly in 1995. But he found the stripe with incredible regularity for the heavyweight Sea Eagles in 1997, scoring 22 tries in 23 games—including two hat-tricks and a haul of four tries—to top the premiership. He finished an admirable career with 89 tries from 246 appearances.

6. Matthew Ryan

Across the divide in the 1997 Super League premiership, a centre more renowned for creating scoring opportunities for his wingers than scoring himself was leading the try charts. Canterbury's Matthew Ryan, who had boasted a previous career-best effort of six tries in 17 games, dotted down 17 times in 19 appearances to lead the rebel competition. He retired in 1999 with modest tryscoring figures of 37 in 104 games.

7. Amos Roberts

Amos Roberts' career had stalled at St George Illawarra in 2003, but he was signed by defending premiers Penrith for the following season with modest winger's career figures of 29 tries in 65 appearances. He was a sensation for the Panthers, however, heading the 2004 NRL's tryscoring stakes with 23 in as many games, including a haul of four against the Warriors. Roberts went on to become one of the decade's most potent try-scorers with the Roosters, finishing his post-Dragons premiership career with 77 tries from 112 games.

8. Charles Cahill

Newtown lock Charles 'Chicka' Cahill is one of the few forwards in premiership history to lead the season tryscoring, heading the field with 13 in 1945. Cahill, whose next-best total in a seven-season career was just five tries, bagged a hat-trick against Balmain and crossed in six straight regular season games for the high-flying Bluebags. Another backrower, Easts' Dick Dunn, was one of three players tied for second on 12 tries.

9. Garry Schofield

Brilliant Great Britain centre Garry Schofield did not take the field with Balmain until Round 9 of 1986, but his sizzling form saw him equal Manly wizard Phil Blake on 13 tries at the top of the competition by the end of the year. Schofield crossed for three tries in a vital final-round defeat of Souths before terrorising the Rabbitohs again in the minor semi with another hat-trick.

10. Noa Nadruku

Former Fiji Rugby Union international Noa Nadruku was snapped up by Canberra after starring for his home country in the 1993 World Sevens. The unknown 25-year-old enjoyed a remarkable debut season in the professional code, scoring a club-record 22 tries in just 21 games—five clear of his nearest premiership rival. Nadruku crossed for three hat-tricks during '93, including the Raiders' losing minor semi effort against Brisbane. He led the competition again in 1996 with 21 touchdowns in as many games.

THE PLAYERS

SPEEDSTERS

1. Ken Irvine
The premiership's greatest try-scorer with an incredible 212 in just 236 games, Ken Irvine equalled the world professional 100-yard sprint time of 9.3 seconds and ran a sizzling 10.2 for the 100 metres (the record was 10.1 seconds at 1960, to put his speed in perspective). He won the 1961 Dubbo Gift off scratch and many believe could have won an Olympic medal had he focused on sprinting. Such was his speed that he was paired with a racehorse in a match race (won, incidentally, by 'Gill' the horse).

2. Michal Cleary
South Sydney speedster Michael Cleary has the honour of winning a Commonwealth Games medal and beating the great Ken Irvine in a match race. The Rugby Union convert, who joined South Sydney in 1962 and who would score 93 tries in 153 games with the Rabbitohs and Eastern Suburbs, kept his amateur status to compete in the '62 Commonwealth Games in Perth, where he won bronze over 100 yards. That same year he defeated Irvine in a £2000 sprint at Wentworth Park. In 1966 Cleary won the Australian professional 130m sprint.

3. Johnny Bliss
One of Rugby League's true speedsters in the 1940s, Johnny Bliss received nearly as much renown for his beach-sprinting exploits as he did for his dashing Rugby League displays. Nicknamed 'Blistering' for his incredible speed, he played 10 first grade seasons with Balmain, North Sydney and Manly, where he scored 78 tries in 121 games. While he represented Australia in Rugby League, Bliss is best remembered for winning 12 straight national beach sprint titles from 1939 to 1951. In 1947, in full football gear, he ran 11.1 seconds over 110 yards and 9.9 seconds over 100 yards—world-class speed.

4. Shane Whereat
A professional sprinter before joining Eastern Suburbs, Shane Whereat set Rugby League fields alight in the 1990s when he was given space. Whereat was signed by the Roosters after winning the 1993 Botany Bay Gift but scored just 12 tries in 35 games over the ensuing four seasons. In a League sprint early in his career, he ran a ripping 10.5 seconds. A move to Parramatta in 1997 saw him discover his best football: he scored 25 tries in 38 appearances.

5. Martin Offiah
One of Great Britain's elite tryscoring wingers throughout the 1980s and 1990s, Martin Offiah crossed for 478 tries in 462 games for Great Britain, English clubs Widnes, Wigan, London Broncos and Salford, and Sydney premiership teams Eastern Suburbs and St George. He famously won a race at Wentworth Park against John Ferguson and Dale Shearer on the Lions' 1988 tour but lost to Lee Oudenryn in 1992 in a match race that saw Oudenryn heavily backed. Offiah's speed was near unstoppable at the height of his decorated career.

6. Arthur Patton
Nicknamed the 'Port Kembla Flyer', Arthur Patton placed in a Stawell Gift and was considered the fastest pre-war player in premiership history. Patton, who spent 12 seasons with Balmain, where he scored 95 tries in 117 games, ran third in the time-honoured Stawell Gift and won the Deniliquin and Benalla Gifts early in his career. He is Balmain's greatest try-scorer, captained the side to the 1944 premiership and played in the victories of 1946 and '47, the latter with a broken leg.

7. Ian Moir
A decorated international and South Sydney premiership player who scored a ridiculous 119 tries in 138 matches, Ian Moir was unbeaten in match races when in football gear throughout his career and was widely regarded as the fastest player of the 1950s. Moir was a beach-sprint champion who won the Canberra Gift in his first season in the top grade. Seven years into his career he won the NSWRL 110-yard sprint, running 11.1 seconds in full football attire. In 1988 he won the NSW Veterans 100m Championship, running 12.7 seconds at 56 years of age.

8. Marika Korobiete
One of the modern day's fastest players, the Fijian flyer burst on to the scene in 2012 with a four-try second-half haul in just his second top-grade experience. When just 17 years of age, Korobiete clocked an incredibly sharp 10.75 over 100 metres. A legitimate flyer, he makes speedy players look slow.

9. Kevin Gordon
Voted by his peers in 2010 as the fastest in the game, Gold Coast Titans flyer Kevin Gordon has proven himself an electric blitz on the paddock. With 50 tries in 94 games heading into the 2014 season, he has become a fan favourite with the Gold Coast faithful. He made his mark in athletics as a junior before focusing on Rugby League.

10. Lee Oudenryn
A genuine flyer, Lee Oudenryn's most famous moment in the top grade came when he won a match race against British speedster Martin Offiah. Oudenryn and Offiah

squared off at Parramatta Stadium in 1992 during the Lions' tour of Australia, running 11 seconds. While rumours remain that the British team had backed Oudenryn heavily and that Offiah may not have run to his best, the four-club veteran was one of League's fastest in the 1990s.

PREMATURE RETIREMENTS

1. Reg Gasnier
An inaugural Immortal and one of the finest centres to play the game, St George champion Reg Gasnier was forced to retire at the age of 27 after a series of knee injuries. He scored 127 premiership tries in just nine seasons with the Saints and was Australia's most capped international, but a knee injury on the 1967-68 Kangaroo Tour saw him quit the game at a young age.

2. Andrew Johns
One of the game's finest players and the eighth to be named an Immortal, Andrew Johns endured some nasty injuries towards the backend of his career. However, it was a neck injury sustained at training after just two games of the 2007 season that forced the great No.7 to retire at 32. When told he risked spinal injuries if he continued to play, Johns immediately retired.

3. Anthony Mundine
Probably Rugby League's most controversial and outspoken figure, Anthony 'The Man' Mundine quit the game aged just 25 to pursue a boxing career. He won a Super League premiership with Brisbane and played in a further two Grand Finals with the Dragons, but became disillusioned with the game after, he claimed, racism stopped him from gaining higher rep honours. Mundine won multiple world titles in his equally controversial boxing career.

4. Geoff Starling
Geoff Starling, a highly gifted centre with Balmain who debuted for Australia at just 18, retired at just 21 due to a serious disease. A red-haired centre with plenty of speed, he went to the 1972 World Cup and toured with the 1973 Kangaroos, but was forced to retire soon after his return following a debilitating illness that was later found to be Addison's disease. He attempted a comeback in 1976 but did not reach first grade.

5. Adam Ritson
The career of one of the most promising prop forwards during the mid-1990s and a major ARL coup during the Super League War, Adam Ritson, ended in 1996 after a high tackle from Raider John Lomax led to a cyst being found on the hulking 19-year-old's brain. After three years with the Sharks, his signing with the ARL led to him shifting to Parramatta but he lasted just 11 games with the Eels after signing a mammoth deal. Ritson had 14 operations to remove the cyst.

6. Greg Brentnall
An outstanding fullback/centre with Canterbury who won a premiership with the club in 1980, Greg Brentnall was forced into retirement at just 26 after the 1983 season when a series of knee injuries derailed his career. He toured with the 1982 Invincibles and was a Test and Origin regular when he gave the game away.

7. Bobby Lulham
The career of Bobby Fulham, a flyer with Balmain during the 1940s and '50s, ended when he was just 26 amid a poisoning controversy that gripped Sydney. Lulham won a premiership with Balmain in his first year and scored an amazing 28 tries before going on the 1948-49 Kangaroo Tour, where he played three Tests. In 1953 he was famously poisoned by his mother-in-law, with whom he was having an affair, and never played football again.

8. Taniela Tuiaki
A crushing ankle injury curtailed the career of Taniela Tuiaki, a bulldozing winger with the Wests Tigers, at just 27. Tuiaki scored 21 tries in 22 games during his final season with the Tigers, winning the Dally M Winger of the Year, but a cruel ankle injury in Round 24, 2009 ended a career that was just nearing its potential. He attempted numerous comebacks but gave up his NRL dream in 2011.

9. Simon Bonetti
A talented hooker with the Sydney Roosters, Simon Bonetti shocked the Rugby League world after winning the 2002 Grand Final by retiring to run the family farm near Griffith. He debuted in 1997 and played in two deciders for the Tricolours before calling it quits to run his 4000-acre property.

10. Ben Ikin
A silky-skilled centre/five-eighth who became the youngest Origin player in the concept's history when plucked from obscurity in 1995, Ben Ikin went on to play 17 Origins and two Tests. A serious knee injury impacted his speed, though, and he retired after the 2004 campaign aged just 27.

OUT OF RETIREMENT

1. Allan Langer
Few players have made a more spectacular return from retirement than Broncos half Allan Langer. The diminutive playmaker made a shock decision to retire early in the 1999 season after a lacklustre start to the year. He soon moved to Warrington in Super League before being flown back for the Origin decider in 2001 in one of the concept's most treasured moments. The 35-year-old made a fulltime comeback with the Broncos and played another Origin series in 2002, receiving a more deserving farewell than his inglorious exit four seasons earlier.

2. Ken Thornett
'The Mayor of Parramatta', Ken Thornett, rates as one of the club's finest players—and among the finest custodians the game has known—due to his decorated career in the 1960s. He retired to take up farming after the 1968 season but after the Eels' shocking 4-18 season in 1970, he returned at the age of 33 to help his former club. Thornett took up the captaincy and the club returned to the finals before he called it quits for good at the end of the '71 season.

3. Larry Corowa
A sensation when he joined Balmain aged just 20 in 1978, Larry Corowa scored 24 tries and toured with the Kangaroos. His career petered out, though, and at 26 he quit the Tigers for a successful country football career. 'The Black Flash' retired from bush footy in 1987 and made a stunning premiership return in 1991 for Wally Lewis' Gold Coast Seagulls. He played two games, scoring a try in his comeback match against South Sydney.

4. Billy Wilson
One of Rugby League's greatest warriors, Billy 'Captain Blood' Wilson retired in 1966 after a career spanning 19 seasons with St George and North Sydney that included winning six premierships with the Dragons. He took up the coaching job at the Bears in 1967 but a glut of injuries saw him come out of retirement aged 40 to play three games.

5. Terry Lamb
Canterbury legend Terry Lamb finished his brilliant career in fairytale fashion in 1995, skippering the Bulldogs to premiership success. The defection of Dean Pay, Jason Smith, Jarrod McCracken and Jim Dymock to Parramatta, though, left

Canterbury short on troops and Lamb offered his services for the '96 season. He played 21 games and retired as the most capped player in premiership history with 349 (since passed by Darren Lockyer in 2011) and second in tries with 164.

6. Cliff Lyons
Ageless Manly pivot Cliff Lyons was one of the competition's premier five-eighths from the mid-1980s to the mid-1990s but retired after the end of the 1998 season aged 37. Manly had a shocking start to the '99 season, though, and Lyons came back for one more campaign, playing 20 games to surpass 300 apppearances for the Sea Eagles. He continued to play A-grade football well into his 40s and retired as Manly's oldest-ever player.

7. Kevin Schubert
A veteran of 19 Tests and a two-time Kangaroo tourist, Manly hooker Kevin Schubert retired after the 1954 season at the age of just 27. After a year out of the game, he returned for Manly's 1956 campaign; the Sea Eagles finished just sixth and he quit the game again.

8. Stacey Jones
One of New Zealand Rugby League's finest, Stacey Jones stunned the Warriors faithful with an unexpected comeback in 2009 aged 32. He had left the NRL after the 2005 season to play with French club Catalans, and played two seasons in Super League before hanging up the boots in 2008. His comeback in 2009 with the Warriors was a mixed one, with some match-winning hands, but after falling foul of the critics, he retired from premiership football at the end of the season.

9. Darren Smith
A durable centre/backrower who enjoyed multiple stints with both Canterbury and Brisbane, Darren Smith was plucked from Brisbane Easts in 2004 to join the Broncos for a second stint at the club at the age of 35. He surprisingly played 16 games the following season at the ripe old age of 36 before hanging the boots up for good.

10. Tonie Carroll
Brisbane enforcer Tonie Carroll called it quits after the 2008 season to pursue a real-estate career, but his time away from the field did not last long—the burly lock returned midway through the 2009 season to alleviate a Broncos form crisis. He kept his spot in the team through to the preliminary final loss to Melbourne before giving the game away for good.

SHOCK EXITS

1. Sonny Bill Williams
The player Canterbury had hoped to build their team around when he signed a five-year deal in 2007, Sonny Bill Williams, walked out on the Bulldogs midway through the 2008 season. Williams, who had linked with controversial manager Khoder Nasser, fled to France without telling anybody at the Bulldogs to take up a Rugby Union career. He was forced to pay the Bulldogs compensation of $750,000 and could not play in the NRL until 2013. He returned that year with the Roosters, playing a key role in their premiership triumph.

2. Allan Langer
One of Brisbane's favourite sons, Allan Langer, shocked the Broncos and the Rugby League world when he announced his immediate retirement midway through the 1999 season after the Broncos had won just one game in the first eight rounds. Langer came out of retirement soon after to resume his career with Super League club Warrington, and made a stunning return to the Queensland side in 2001. He enjoyed a farewell season with the Broncos in 2002.

3. Dennis Tutty
Dennis Tutty became a Rugby League martyr in the late 1960s after his attempted move from Balmain to Penrith was thwarted by the Tigers, who would not release the talented backrower. He sat out the better part of three years before the courts ruled against the Tigers and the NSWRL in a landmark restraint-of-trade decision. Tutty's shock exit paved the way for free agency in Rugby League.

4. Solomon Haumono
A blockbusting forward who left Manly for Canterbury at the height of the Super League War, Solomon Haumono shocked the Rugby League world when he fled Belmore for England in pursuit of his girlfriend, Gabrielle Richens. Haumono and 'The Pleasure Machine' were involved in a highly publicised affair when he left Australia without telling the Bulldogs or his family halfway through the 1998 season. He returned, but was never again selected in first grade before he shifted to Balmain in 1999.

5. Jamie Lyon
A highly talented centre who had risen to prominence as the most promising Parramatta outside back in 15 years, Jamie Lyon sensationally walked out on the Eels early in the 2004 season following a dispute with coach Brian Smith. He returned

to his home town of Wee Waa and played local football before joining St Helens in England, where he starred. Lyon returned to the NRL in 2007 with Manly and won two premierships.

6. Jim Dymock, Jason Smith, Dean Pay and Jarrod McCracken
Canterbury's four highest-paid players in 1995, Jim Dymock, Jason Smith, Dean Pay and Jarrod McCracken, walked out on the Bulldogs and their Super League contracts to defect to Parramatta and the ARL. Taking Canterbury to court to force their release, the foursome eventually won their freedom late in the '95 season after claiming unfair inducement. Incredibly, Dymock, Pay and Smith played in the Bulldogs' Grand Final win that season before shifting to the Eels in 1996.

7. Bob Fulton
Manly's greatest player, Bob Fulton, shocked the Sea Eagles by defecting to Eastern Suburbs. He announced his move to Easts after captaining the Sea Eagles to the 1976 premiership, his third title with the club. A future Immortal, Fulton signed a three-year deal with the Roosters but retired midway through '79 with a chronic knee injury. He returned to the Sea Eagles as coach and led them to five Grand Finals.

8. Les Boyd
An aggressive front-rower who thrived under Roy Masters' coaching at Western Suburbs, Les Boyd moved to Manly on a huge contract in 1980. His departure shocked the Magpies faithful, who had long positioned Boyd as one of the faces of the 'Fibros' in the class war with the 'Silvertail' Sea Eagles. He continued his rep career at Manly but soon earned the ire of judiciary chairman Jim Comans, who essentially ended his Australian career.

9. Doug Laughton
A skilful British backrower who had played 14 Tests for the Lions before joining Canterbury in 1974, Doug Laughton lasted less than a season before sensationally walking out on the club. Appointed skipper at the start of the season, Laughton was sacked as captain midway through the year and boarded a plane back to the UK soon after, missing the Berries' Grand Final appearance.

10. Ken Irvine
North Sydney champion Ken Irvine seemed destined to be a one-club player before a falling-out with coach Roy Francis in 1970 saw the Bears skipper walk out on the club he had served so brilliantly for 13 years. He joined rivals Manly and spent three years with the Sea Eagles, winning two premierships and scoring 41 tries before retiring after the '73 triumph.

UNFULFILLED POTENTIAL

1. Karl Filiga
In the biggest signing bust in premiership history, Cronulla reportedly forked out $600,000 to sign schoolboy prodigy Karl Filiga from Canterbury in 2007 but he played just one first grade game for the Sharks in 2008 before he was released from his deal. Chest and foot injuries and the weight of expectation combined to see Filiga fail to live up to his billing as one of Rugby League's most exciting prospects.

2. Tony Williams
A massive-framed winger with Parramatta, Tony Williams was signed by Manly coach Des Hasler in 2009. Hasler undertook the immense task of shifting Williams to the second-row while re-teaching him how to run. It paid significant dividends in 2011 when Williams proved devastating off the bench, winning a premiership and earning rep honours, but Williams' move to Canterbury to reunite with Hasler in 2013 proved a disaster when Williams failed to rediscover his 2011 form.

3. Matthew Rodwell
A skilful halfback who was tipped to play for Australia after winning Dally M Rookie of the Year and Norwich Rising Star honours in 1992, Matthew Rodwell instead spent his 12-year career as a journeyman, with stints at Newcastle, the Western Reds, St George, St George Illawarra and Penrith. Forced out of the Knights by the emergence of the Johns boys, he never settled anywhere and subsequently couldn't recapture the magic of his brilliant debut year.

4. Ewan McGrady
Canterbury utility Ewan McGrady enjoyed a spectacular first two years with the Bulldogs, winning the Rothmans Medal in 1991 after a dominating season that set the Rugby League world alight. McGrady's form went south soon after his magical '91 campaign, and he played just 25 more first grade games with the Bulldogs and Western Suburbs before returning to Moree, disappearing as quickly as he had arrived.

5. John Hopoate
One of Rugby League's most controversial figures, John Hopoate was also one of the most talented outside backs of his generation. But a long rap sheet of both on- and off-field misdemeanours meant he played just one Origin and two Tests early in his career. A tarnished reputation and a refusal to mend his ways meant Hopoate did not leave the lasting impact on the game his skills suggested he should have.

6. David Woods
David Woods, a brilliant centre with great football smarts and a fine combination of strength and speed, had a shocking run with injuries—cruelling what would surely have been a long representative career. He played 160 first grade games over 13 seasons but a shocking series of leg injuries at the most inopportune times limited his rep career to two appearances for Country.

7. Jason Martin
A scintillating debut season with North Sydney had long-haired halfback Jason Martin in the mix for a Kangaroo Tour berth in 1990, but despite his popularity he failed to live up to his potential in six subsequent seasons with the Bears, Knights and Cowboys. Martin struggled to make an impact and lost his No.7 jumper to Mark Soden before he was predominantly used off the bench at Newcastle and North Queensland.

8. Jacin Sinclair
A schoolboy prodigy who debuted with Balmain in 1991 aged just 19, centre Jacin Sinclair played 80 premiership games in a nine-year career with the Tigers, Rabbitohs and Roosters but never reached the heights the early hype suggested he would. Sinclair, a volatile and rash player, was connected to a match-fixing allegation while at Souths in 1994. He sadly committed suicide in 2010 aged just 38.

9. Paul Hauff
A revelation after his outstanding debut year in 1990, lanky Broncos fullback Paul Hauff seemed destined for a long, decorated career. He played in all three Origins for Queensland in 1991 and made his Test debut immediately afterwards, but injuries ensured he never played more than six games over the next five years. He retired in 1996 aged 26, having played just 30 games since his 21st birthday.

10. Brett Papworth
Brett Papworth was a highly touted Rugby Union convert who had played 15 Tests for the Wallabies, but injuries cruelled his Rugby League career. He played just seven first grade games in four years with Eastern Suburbs before retiring at 28.

ENTERTAINERS

1. Dally Messenger
The game's biggest drawcard in its infant years, Dally Messenger remains revered a century on for his incredible exploits. Ingrained with a penchant for entertainment, Messenger thrilled with both hand and foot. He was renowned for scoring incredibly unusual tries, such as diving over an opponent or throwing the ball over the opponent's head and regathering, and could boot goals from well beyond halfway.

2. Andrew Johns
The most amazing footballer of his generation and granted with Immortal status five years after his retirement, Andrew Johns seemed capable of nearly anything on the football field. His in-play kicking was revolutionary, his clutch goalkicking nearly always on the mark and his passing otherworldly. No footballer has captured the imagination more in the last century than 'Joey'.

3. Graeme Langlands
Long-serving Saints fullback and a future Immortal, Graeme Langlands is one of the most popular players ever to play the game. A try he scored in 1964 when catching the ball over the sideline while balancing on his toes and then running diagonally across the field to score 50 metres out remains a legendary moment in the history of the code, as was the shocking no-try call against him in the 1972 World Cup that came about because the referee could not believe Langlands' speed or athleticism. When he played his last Test, the entire SCG broke out into a chant of "Changa! Changa!"

4. Billy Slater
A pocket rocket who is one of the greatest fullbacks Rugby League has known, Billy Slater could cause fans to gasp at his sheer brilliance like few others. A sensational talent with great vision, he scored some of the most sublime tries ever. His chip-and-chase for Queensland in 2004 remains one of the great Origin tries.

5. Wally Lewis
An Immortal and a player with unrivalled charisma, Wally Lewis was one of the great personalities the game has known. A natural leader, he was a fiery competitor with deft skills who could turn a game on his own hand. Lewis could rile a crowd—either to cheer him or boo him—like no other player.

6. Ken Irvine

Rugby League's greatest try-scorer, Ken Irvine, was a legitimate speedster who had an addiction to scoring tries. His 212 remains a premiership record, and he has scored more tries for NSW than any other man. In the name of entertainment, he even ran a race against a horse.

7. Harold Horder

Nicknamed 'The Wonder Winger' and one of Rugby League's greatest attacking forces, Harold Horder was so revered in the early days of the code that he was often regarded as equal or superior to Dally Messenger. He was capable of scoring from anywhere on the paddock.

8. Nathan Blacklock

A tryscoring freak who was the last man to lead the premiership in tries for three consecutive years, Nathan Blacklock was blessed with blinding speed and a set of skills that allowed him to do almost anything on the field. The entertainment didn't end once he crossed the line, either, with Blacklock becoming famous for his backflips after scoring. His 0.85 tries per game leads all players since 1980.

9. Jarryd Hayne

A superstar fullback blessed with the stride of a 100-metre sprinter and a freakish, rarely seen athleticism, Jarryd Hayne could tear open a game anywhere on the field. His sublime skills carried Parramatta to the 2009 Grand Final, and he scored one of Origin's most memorable tries on debut when he tiptoed along the sideline and kicked ahead.

10. Phil Blake

One of the great individual performers, Phil Blake seemed capable of anything on a football field. Renowned for his chip-and-chase tries, he had speed to burn and an innate understanding of how a defence could be broken down. Blake scored 138 tries in a nomadic career where he was largely overlooked for rep honours but remained a fan favourite for his magical abilities.

ENIGMAS

1. Krisnan Inu

The enigma's enigma Krisnan Inu has the rare capacity to produce the astonishingly brilliant and the frustratingly inept in equal quantities—often within the same

80-minute period. A rookie sensation with Parramatta in 2007, the outside back's freakish skill was countered by an at times lackadaisical and seemingly disinterested attitude. Dropped by the Warriors after an error-riddled fullback display against Melbourne in 2012, the "rocks or diamonds" Inu confounded all and sundry with a series of match-winning outings after joining Canterbury mid-season to become the second player in history to lose Grand Finals with three different clubs. His follow-up season was marred by suspension and characteristically inconsistent form.

2. Andrew Walker

Andrew Walker was a prodigiously talented five-eighth or fullback capable of turning the course of a match with a searing break, brilliant pass or pinpoint kick. But he was also prone to going to pieces after a glaring error—the archetypal confidence player. Regarded as one of the premiership's finest individualists during the second half of the 1990s, the elusive ball-player represented Australia in one Test in '96, but his inconsistency and dubious big-match temperament prevented a NSW Origin call-up. The Indigenous star switched to Rugby Union in 2000 and became the inaugural League-first dual international.

3. Feleti Mateo

An enormously gifted ball-playing backrower capable of playing five-eighth, Feleti Mateo's most dependable quality is his inconsistency, which has held him back from rising above City Origin representation (2008 and 2012-13). Contributing strongly to the enigmatic reputation of his two NRL clubs—Parramatta and the Warriors—Mateo has few rivals in the domain of offloading and sleight of hand, but harnessing those skills for the appropriate situation has been a continual struggle. He is without doubt among the most devastating attacking forwards of recent years, capable of tearing opposition defences apart on his own, but often goes into his shell when the chips are down.

4. Ted Goodwin

'Lord Ted' was one of the most charismatic, dazzling attacking players of the 1970s, but also one of the most unpredictable and erratic. He debuted for NSW and Australia as a 19-year-old in 1972, his first season with St George, and went on to play two Grand Finals with the club; his kick-and-chase try in the historic drawn decider against Parramatta in '77 has passed into folklore, and he kicked six goals and a field goal in the emphatic replay victory. A game-changing performer—for better or worse—at fullback, centre or wing, Goodwin regularly clashed with Dragons officials and failed to produce his customary magic in late career stints with Newtown and Wests.

5. Manu Vatuvei
Few wingers in the game's history have simultaneously possessed the ability to win and lose a match as emphatically as Warriors freight train Manu Vatuvei. 'The Beast' is responsible for some of most notoriously mistake-riddled individual displays of the modern era—most notably against Parramatta in '07 and in the qualifying loss to Brisbane in '11—but invariably follows up his lamentable performances with an out-and-out blinder. Relentlessly targeted in defence due to his shaky handling and the fact that he has the turning circle of a combine harvester, Vatuvei's lapses are contradicted by his remarkable aerial skills at the other end and ability to score down the narrowest of corridors. His 118 tries in 171 games for the Warriors stamps him as one of the most potent try-scorers of the NRL era, and he has crossed 17 times in 24 Tests for New Zealand.

6. David Taylor
David Taylor's 188cm and 120kg-plus frame, remarkable turn of speed and outstanding ball skills should render him among modern-day Rugby League's ultimate players. But the prop/second-row goliath's penchant for going missing in games and his questionable work rate and fitness have instead pegged him as one of the game's great unfulfilled talents during stints with Brisbane, Souths and Gold Coast. A devastating ball-runner with the passing game of the code's most dexterous five-eighths, the fickle Taylor has still managed one Test appearance for Australia (2010) and six Origins for Queensland (2010-12), but inconsistency and poor attitude have resulted in him being one of the few regulars to be dropped from the Maroons' squad during their recent reign.

7. Dale Shearer
Adept at any position in the backline, Dale 'Rowdy' Shearer was among the game's truly brilliant match-winners of the 1980s and '90s, but also one of its most erratic stars. He was blessed with blinding speed and wonderful hands, debuting for Queensland as a 19-year-old in '85, starring on the following season's Kangaroo Tour and winning a Grand Final with Manly in '87. Shearer struggled for first grade form post-Manly—he was frustratingly inconsistent and regularly absent at five clubs from 1990 to 1998—but was nevertheless a representative staple. He held the Origin tryscoring record for two decades.

8. Benji Marshall
Ball-playing magician Benji Marshall was undoubtedly one of the most unique talents Rugby League has ever witnessed. The Wests Tigers linchpin was an unstoppable attacking force on his day, but was prone to the odd howler of a performance where everything he tried would backfire. Unfortunately, his 2013 season produced much more of the latter and he eventually quit to play Rugby Union amid a barrage of

criticism—a finish unbefitting of one of the modern era's great entertainers and dominant playmakers. The Tigers' fortunes hung on Marshall's form—his peerless bag of tricks was laced throughout the 2005 premiership success, and he emerged from a horror injury run to produce career-best seasons in 2010-11, culminating in the club's only other finals appearances. He single-handedly won the 2010 Four Nations final for New Zealand with one of the great performances in Test history, but barely fired a shot on the international stage thereafter and was dumped as skipper two years later.

9. Ewan McGrady
Painfully shy but naturally gifted half/fullback Ewan McGrady was finally coaxed to leave Moree by Canterbury. He was an instant sensation, scoring 13 tries in 16 games in 1990 before winning the Rothmans Medal the following season. 'Panda' crossed 14 times in 23 games and created many more opportunities for his teammates, frequently unleashing his searing pace off the mark and his breathtaking ball skills. But the Indigenous playmaker's effortless brilliance deserted him in subsequent seasons; he gradually faded out of the Bulldogs' first grade picture and failed to reignite his career with Wests.

10. Olsen Filipaina
One of the New Zealand's greatest-ever Test players, making 27 appearances from 1977 to 1986, centre/five-eighth Olsen Filipaina's eight-season Sydney career was plagued by inconsistency. A bulldozing runner with tree-trunk thighs and a classy ball-player, the goalkicking Samoan powerhouse rarely produced his best on a regular basis in 105 first grade games with Balmain, Easts and Norths. Joining the Roosters in '85, his form was so poor he was dropped from first grade. However, he was famously plucked from reserve grade to produce a career-defining series performance for the Kiwis in which he outplayed incomparable Australian five-eighth and captain Wally Lewis in three straight Tests. The series included two last-minute losses and an emphatic dead-rubber victory for the Kiwis. But those dominant displays failed to reignite his premiership career, which petered out with the Bears.

MALIGNED PLAYERS

1. Braith Anasta
A long-serving five-eighth who won a premiership with Canterbury and represented Australia early in his career, Braith Anasta was voted the most overrated player in the game by his peers on numerous occasions during his career. Criticised for his stature in

the game as well as for lacking toughness, he paid little heed in a career that closed in on 300 games with the Bulldogs, Roosters and Tigers. Anasta's good looks and media presence only spurred the critics.

2. Jamie Soward

Jamie Soward was a flighty player with immense skill whose dislike of Rugby League's physicality and abrasive personality saw him fall from the mantle of most popular player in the game to one of the most chastised. The diminutive five-eighth won the Provan-Summons Award in 2009 as the most popular player in the NRL, but his refusal to run the ball and his inconsistent form saw fans turn on him. Soward was controversially dumped by the Dragons midway through 2013 but landed with Penrith a year later.

3. Paul Carige

The first grade career of Paul Carige, an outside back with Illawarra and Parramatta who played just three first grade seasons, ended after his infamous performance in the 1998 preliminary final with the Eels against Canterbury. He was listed among Rugby League's most maligned players, having a stinker as Parramatta blew an 18-2 lead with 11 minutes to play to lose 32-20 in extra-time. Carige spilled the ball, put in a poor kick, caught a ball while standing out and butchered an in-goal pick-up in one of the great finals chokes. After a torrent of criticism from the Eels faithful, he quit the game following a year in England.

4. Benji Marshall

A sensitive showman with a streak of brilliance in his play, Benji Marshall was beloved and belittled. He was a sublime talent whose flick pass to Pat Richards in the 2005 decider ranks as one of the great Grand Final plays, but his inability to bring further success to the Tigers frustrated the faithful. His apparent politicking and love of the spotlight only spurred knockers, while his defection to Rugby Union coupled with a shocking final season saw him depart the game on less than friendly terms.

5. Brett Finch

A lippy half who was beloved by teammates but given short shrift by fans, journeyman Brett Finch could annoy as well as inspire. His Canberra career is best remembered for an unsuccessful gamble when he attempted to find touch from a 20-metre tap but the resultant penalty gifted Newcastle a late victory. He left the Roosters and Eels on less than favourable terms and, despite his heroics in kicking a match-winning drop goal for NSW, seemed to rub fans the wrong way. A quality late career move to the Storm saw him win a premiership, and he came to be viewed as an old-school throwback.

6. Eric Grothe jnr

The son of champion 1980s Parramatta winger Eric Grothe, Eric junior had all the physical tools to be a star in Rugby League but his heart was rarely in the game. This didn't sit well with the fans and most of his coaches. Grothe famously didn't show up to a NSW camp and seemed more intent on kick-starting his music career than learning the nuances of Rugby League. He retired in 2010 and then made a shock comeback with Cronulla in 2014.

7. Jason Ryles

A hulking prop forward who spent the majority of his career with St George Illawarra before late stints with the Sydney Roosters and Melbourne, Jason Ryles was a rep regular from 2001 to 2005. The latter did little to sate frustrated Dragons fans, who struggled with Ryles' penchant for silly penalties and brain-snaps deep in his own half. The lumbering Ryles' ability to offload was often more a curse than a blessing.

8. Ben Roberts

A skilled half with a low football IQ, Ben Roberts frustrated fans at both Canterbury and Parramatta. He was prone to brain explosions that left both supporters and teammates flabbergasted. The New Zealand international famously grubbered to himself on the first tackle after Canterbury won a scrum in golden point against Souths, costing the Bulldogs the match, and he was prone to acts of madness at any point.

9. John Hopoate

Perhaps Rugby League's most controversial figure of the NRL era, John Hopoate had undoubted ability that was unquestionably overshadowed by his provocative style. A bullocking winger whose rep calling was limited by a string of suspensions and scandals, Hopoate was widely lambasted for his on-field behaviour, which stymied a promising career.

10. Arthur Beetson

One of the game's greats, Arthur Beetson spent much of his early career with Balmain being chastised for not reaching his potential due to his poor training and questionable diet. The outstanding ball-playing backrower quit the Tigers after 1970 and found career-best form at Eastern Suburbs, where he led the club to two premierships, and then skippered Queensland in the first Origin clash at the age of 35. Bestowed Immortal status, his position as a maligned player was well and truly overcome in the second half of his career.

UNLIKELY HEROES

1. Dick Dunn
Goalkicking lock Dick Dunn became a finals hero for Easts in 1945 just a year after he had been unwanted by the club. A centre in the Tricolours' 1940 premiership victory, his career appeared to be on the scrapheap at the end of '44. The local junior stayed and fought for his spot, however, and scored a try and booted five goals in the minor premiers' semi-final defeat of Wests before playing the game of his life in the premiership decider. Dunn scored three tries and five goals for a 19-point haul to help subdue Balmain 22-18. He kicked a crucial penalty to edge Easts in front with eight minutes remaining before sealing the result with a late try in a career-defining display.

2. Paul Osborne
A late replacement in Canberra's side for the suspended John Lomax, ball-playing prop Paul Osborne became a Grand Final hero for the ages with a brilliant cameo. He played just 10 regular season games in 1994, stuck behind Kiwi Test front-rowers Lomax and Quentin Pongia, and was set to take up a deal in England before the Australian season finished. But he delayed his departure to provide depth for the Raiders' finals campaign, receiving his opportunity on the biggest stage of all. Sensational Osborne offloads produced two tries for David Furner and Ken Nagas in the opening 16 minutes as Canberra hammered Canterbury 36-12 in a one-sided Grand Final. Osborne retired after the match (aged just 28), benefiting from his new-found popularity in the capital by embarking on a career in ACT politics.

3. Craig Smith
Winger Craig Smith was the unwitting, unconscious hero of Melbourne's Grand Final victory over St George Illawarra in 1999. A first grade regular in the club's debut 1998 season, Smith was out of favour the following year and spent the entire regular season turning out for feeder club Brisbane Norths before he received a shock call-up to first grade during the finals series. He booted three goals and produced a crucial try-saving tackle on Anthony Mundine as the Storm clawed back from a 14-point halftime deficit in the decider. He was then awarded a premiership-winning penalty try after being tackled high by Jamie Ainscough as he was about to score in the dying minutes. Sadly, Smith retired after the match aged just 26, disillusioned with the game after a difficult year.

4. Brett Finch

Brett Finch was an 11th-hour inclusion for NSW in the 2006 series opener after Craig Gower was injured at training a day before the match. Blues legend Andrew Johns turned down an invitation to rescind his rep retirement, and myriad other options were considered for the key role before selectors opted for Finch. But the Roosters half experienced a dream game in his first Origin appearance since his debut match in 2004. He backed up a long movement to score the opening try of the match in the first half before booting a 35-metre field goal with less than two minutes on the clock to break a 16-all deadlock. Finch's kick was later honoured with the inaugural Peter Frilingos Memorial Award at the Dally Ms for Headline Moment of the Year.

5. Steve Jackson

Hardworking Canberra prop Steve Jackson became ensconced in Grand Final folklore with one of the most memorable solo tries ever scored in a decider. He sat on the bench for most of the 1989 Canberra-Balmain epic, but grabbed his moment of glory in extra-time after the Raiders had edged in front 15-14. Making just his fifth first grade appearance of the season, Jackson accepted an offload from captain Mal Meninga and embarked on a bumping, weaving run from the 20-metre line, leaving defenders strewn in his wake and carrying three over the line to seal the Raiders' maiden premiership 19-14. He subsequently played nine Origins for Queensland from Wests and Gold Coast, but is chiefly remembered for his phenomenal try in the greatest decider of all time.

6. Adam Mogg

Adam Mogg, a former Queensland Cup star who earned only moderate plaudits at Parramatta and Canberra, was the shock choice to replace injured winger Greg Inglis on the Maroons' flank for their must-win second game of the 2006 series. The gangly three-quarter produced a dream debut, scoring a memorable double in Queensland's 30-6 victory at Suncorp Stadium to keep the series alive. Retained for the decider, he scored the opening try in spectacular fashion, planting the ball in the corner while falling backwards in mid-air after latching on to a cross-field kick. Queensland went on to win the dramatic decider 16-14, with Mogg one of the heroes.

7. Ron Roberts

St George winger Ron Roberts' name is synonymous with the series-winning try he scored for Australia in 1950 to break a 30-year Ashes drought. A bulldozing winger who scored 51 tries in 51 first grade games for the Dragons, Roberts was notorious for his poor ball-handling skills. But the 190cm winger, who had not played in the opening two Tests of the series, latched on to the one that mattered in the deciding Test against Great Britain on an SCG quagmire. With the match deadlocked at 2-all inside the final quarter, he accepted a pass from centre Keith Middleton and sprinted 40 metres to score in the corner. Lost in the euphoria of the 5-2 victory was the fact that Roberts dropped the ball with the line open minutes later—his place in Test folklore was already assured.

8. Scott Sattler

Workhorse Penrith backrower Scott Sattler spent much of his career in the shadow of his father, famed South Sydney enforcer John, who is revered for playing through the 1970 Grand Final with a broken jaw. But Scott also played himself into Grand Final folklore as a 31-year-old in 2003. The decider against the Roosters was evenly poised at 6-all when, in the 55th minute, Roosters winger Todd Byrne streaked away down the touchline. The veteran Sattler, not renowned for his speed, hared across the sodden field to cut Byrne down and bundle him into touch in one of Rugby League's most famous cover tackles. The momentum swung Penrith's way and the underdogs went on to win the premiership 18-6, with Sattler lauded as the hero in his final game as a Panther.

9. Michael Robertson

In a team of backline superstars, underrated winger Michael Robertson was the standout in Manly's record 40-0 Grand Final rout of Melbourne in 2008. Electrifying fullback Brett Stewart, rookie winger David Williams and rep veteran Jamie Lyon had attracted most of the plaudits during the season, but Robertson outshone the trio to become just the second player in 47 years to score a hat-trick of tries in a decider. The ultra-consistent flyer also set up departing Manly great Steve Menzies for a late try, capping an excellent performance that was unlucky not to be rewarded with the Churchill Medal and World Cup selection for Australia.

10. Chris Hicks

Underrated winger Chris Hicks was a reluctant goalkicker for Penrith, boasting a career strike rate of only 55 per cent heading into a 2000 clash with Parramatta. He had landed just two from seven a fortnight earlier against the Knights; consequently, Hicks' confidence was ebbing low when he was called upon to kick a 40-metre penalty with the scores locked 14-all in the shadows of fulltime. But he stepped up and nailed the kick, becoming the archetypal reluctant hero. Incredibly, he reprised his match-winning role with the boot two weeks later in a phenomenal comeback against the Tigers. Penrith fought back from a 23-point deficit midway through the second half, with Hicks landing a pressure conversion from the sideline to seal a remarkable 32-31 triumph.

UNIQUE NAMES

1. Dragan Durdevic
Mona Vale-born forward Dragan Durdevic, of Serbian heritage, made his first grade debut for Manly in 1997, playing two games for the Sea Eagles and a further nine for the Northern Eagles. While his first grade career was brief, his name ensured he stood out on any team sheet. Durdevic later played for French club Villeneuve.

2. Bronko Djura
Boasting an equine name and an outstanding blond mullet, Bronko Djura was destined for cult-hero status. He was a fine all-round sportsman, representing Australian Schoolboys at Rugby League and cricket. A highly regarded wicket-keeper, he famously kept future Test great Ian Healy out of the national side but found senior sporting success on the football fields of Sydney. The goalkicking fullback or five-eighth progressed from the Newtown juniors to play 96 games for Souths, St George and Wests from 1984 to 1991. Djura featured in three finals campaigns with the Rabbitohs and remains one of the most oft-recalled curiosities of the era by fans—surely, in part, thanks to his moniker.

3. Anthony Xuereb
Just one player in the history of the premiership has carried a surname starting with the letter X—Penrith and Wests fullback Anthony Xuereb. The name is of Maltese origin. The St Mary's junior debuted for the Panthers in 1991, playing 13 games and coming off the bench in the club's major semi defeat of Norths to secure a Grand Final berth. He was an unused replacement in the subsequent decider victory before featuring in the World Club Challenge final loss to Wigan at Anfield in Liverpool. Xuereb played a career-high 16 games in 1993, crossing for five tries, before finishing his premiership career with the Magpies in 1994. He later represented Malta at international level.

4. Ziggy Niszczot
Smashing the record for most Zs for a Rugby League player, Ziggy Niszczot's quirky name, handlebar moustache and robust wing-play for South Sydney set him on an inevitable path to cult-hero territory. The Newcastle product spent five seasons with the Rabbitohs, playing 114 games and captaining the club to the 1984 finals, and represented NSW in two Origins in 1982, scoring two tries on debut. His surname, of Central European origin, was a commentator's nightmare on the surface but was simply pronounced (perhaps erroneously) "NIS-cot".

5. John Ribot de Bresac

Better known simply as John Ribot (pronounced "ree-BO") during his days as a blockbusting winger for Wests, Manly, Queensland and Australia in the 1980s and as a prominent administrator with the QRL, Brisbane, Melbourne and Super League, Ribot's full surname was in fact Ribot de Bresac, which he went by when he first came on to the scene as a lock with Newtown. The protracted family name has French origins.

6. Fuifui Moimoi

Born in Mataika, Tonga, Fuifui Moimoi was already assured of cult-figure status due to his full-throttle approach to life as an NRL front-rower, but the double repetition of his name sealed the deal. He played 12 Tests for New Zealand from 2007 to 2011 and was magnificent in Parramatta's charge to the 2009 Grand Final, scoring a memorable try in the Eels' gallant decider loss to Melbourne.

7. Kylie Leuluai

Although he was undeniably christened with a female name, rival players would be foolhardy to sledge Auckland-born prop Kylie Leuluai. An imposing 110kg powerhouse, he is part of the famous Leuluai Rugby League family, counting Kiwi centre great James as an uncle and long-serving Test half Thomas as a cousin. Kylie played 78 games for Balmain, Wests Tigers, Sydney Roosters, Parramatta and Manly before playing over 200 games and celebrating in five Super League Grand Final wins with Leeds (2007-09 and '11-12)—he should be so lucky.

8. Steele Retchless

Sporting a name perhaps better suited to a WWE professional wrestler, Steele Retchless was the genuine article—and a handy prop/second-rower during a decade-long career in Australia and England. Retchless was destined to command more attention for his name than his industrious forward play, but he nevertheless played 233 games at the top level with Brisbane (1995-96), South Queensland (1997) and London (1998-2004).

9. Setaimata Sa

The record for the shortest surname in premiership history belongs to former Sydney Roosters centre/backrower Setaimata Sa. Born in Samoa, he debuted for the Roosters as an 18-year-old in 2006 and played 66 games for the club. Sa represented New Zealand in three Tests and was part of the Kiwis' victorious 2008 World Cup squad, although he was not required for the final. He spent three seasons with Super League club Catalans before switching to Rugby Union with London Irish, and made his Test debut for Samoa before having played a first-class game in the 15-a-side code.

10. Double-barrelled Kiwi Roosters

The Sydney Roosters' premiership-winning side of 2013 contained five players with either hyphenated surnames or two-pronged first names—and in a further coincidence, they were all New Zealanders. Sonny Bill Williams, Frank-Paul Nuuausala, Jared Waerea-Hargreaves, Roger Tuivasa-Sheck and Shaun Kenny-Dowall all played key roles in the Tricolours' surge to the title. Williams, Nuuausala, Waerea-Hargreaves and Tuivasa-Sheck went on to star in the Kiwis' subsequent World Cup campaign, while Kenny-Dowall was ruled out of the tournament after courageously playing out the Grand Final with a broken jaw. The initialisms SBW, RTS and SKD have become some of the most recognisable in the game.

SMITHS

1. Cameron Smith
One of the most decorated players in the history of the code, Cameron Smith has achieved everything there is to achieve in Rugby League. He has captained Melbourne to three Grand Final wins, Australia to a World Cup victory and Queensland to numerous State of Origin series wins. Throw in individual accolades like the Golden Boot and the Dally M Medal and the hooker's greatness becomes apparent.

2. Billy Smith
A St George great, tenacious halfback Billy Smith has won more premierships than any other Smith except Melbourne's Cameron, playing in three of the Saints' titles during their record run of 11 straight. A decorated international, he was renowned for his never-say-die attitude and his willingness to play through injury.

3. Darren and Jason Smith
The most talented pair of Smith brothers, Darren and Jason both won premierships and played Origin and Test footy. Older brother Darren won two titles with Brisbane and played 22 Origins and seven Tests, while Jason spent 18 years in the top grade, winning a premiership with Canterbury and playing 16 Origins and 15 Tests. Popular callers Roy and HG referred to them as 'Cheese and Chives' and 'Salt and Vinegar' alluding to the popular potato-chip manufacturer.

4. The Craig Smiths
The premiership has had three Craig Smiths, with two featuring in the 1999 Grand Final. The Melbourne winger played just two seasons of first grade with the Storm

after debuting for Norths, but was the unwitting hero of the decider when he was tackled high when attempting to catch a bomb that led to the decisive penalty try. The tough St George Illawarra prop was against him that day; though he represented New Zealand 12 times, he was more renowned for being a regular attendant at the judiciary. North Queensland also had a Craig Smith during that 1999 seasons.

5. The Jeremy Smiths
From 2006 to 2008, the NRL incredibly had two Kiwi Jeremy Smiths. One was a hard-headed backrower who won premierships with Melbourne and St George Illawarra, with his team generally winning. The other was a vanilla halfback who was in and out of first grade for three seasons; his lasting infamy was pushing referee Sean Hampstead in a famous 8-1 Parramatta loss in 2006. The two met twice in 2007, and debuted for New Zealand together that year. They were not the first Jeremy Smiths in the NRL—a winger by the same name played five games for South Queensland in the mid-1990s.

6. Tyran Smith
One of Rugby League's great journeymen, lock Tyran Smith spent 13 seasons in the top grade, playing for South Sydney, North Queensland, Hunter, Auckland, Balmain, the Wests Tigers and Canberra. He played in just three finals in his nomadic career, all with the Raiders.

7. Jimmy Smith
Today a popular media identity, Jimmy Smith did the rounds in the 1990s, playing five seasons with Eastern Suburbs before a year with Wests and two with South Sydney. The tough forward managed just 10 tries in his 120-game career.

8. Brian Smith
A Rugby Union convert who had played six Tests for the Wallabies when he signed with Balmain in 1991, Brian Smith was a favourite of controversial coach Alan Jones. He played just 43 first grade games and, despite an appearance for City, never really made his mark in the 13-man code.

9. Athol Smith
A fine Western Suburbs and Balmain forward from 1935 to 1944, Athol Smith played in two Balmain premierships. He starred in the 1939 hammering of South Sydney, where he scored a try, while also playing in the 1944 triumph over Newtown. Smith scored 42 tries in a fine career.

10. Greg Smith
The least talented—and most incredible—Smith to play in the premiership, Newcastle winger Greg Smith claimed to be a former NFL player with the Philadelphia Eagles.

Though the year was 1999 and the internet did exist, Warren Ryan still played him. Smith could not catch or tackle and the Bulldogs buried him into infamy among an aerial bombardment.

HEART-THROBS

1. Andrew Ettingshausen
A good-looking outside back with Cronulla, League bosses successfully used Andrew Ettingshausen to woo women to the game during the "Simply the Best" era. Known as "the male model of Rugby League", Ettingshausen successfully sued the Australian magazine *HQ* in 1991 after it published a fully nude image of the star centre without his permission.

2. Nick Youngquest
A journeyman winger who played 37 NRL games with four clubs, Nick Youngquest quit Rugby League at 29 to become an international model. He earned up to $10,000 a day living as a model in New York City, a far cry from crossing over for a try at Shark Park.

3. Matt Cooper
A perennial winner of the Sexiest Man in League competition throughout the 2000s, St George Illawarra centre Matt Cooper overcame a rat's tail in his hair to become a female favourite. Away from the football field, he took up modelling with great success.

4. Jack Elsegood
The grandson of grizzled Newtown hardman Frank 'Bumper' Farrell, Jack Elsegood played 149 games for Manly and the Sydney Roosters in a nice career before quitting to take up ute racing. Such were his looks that he was chosen as an ex-player to compete in the Sexiest Man in League competition eight years after his retirement.

5. Greg Cox
A zippy halfback with Balmain, Cronulla and Western Suburbs, blond-haired Greg Cox was compared favourably to Robert Redford by female fans of the game.

6. Gary Connolly
A favourite among English fans of the game, Gary Connolly joined Canterbury in 1993 and was an instant hit on and off the field. A classy attacking player, he was a darling of female fans with his blond hair and chiselled jaw.

7. Russell Fairfax
Very popular throughout the 1970s thanks to his long hair and rebellious attitude, Russell Fairfax starred at fullback for Eastern Suburbs in its great 1974-75 teams. He was banned from Eastern Suburbs Leagues Club for refusing to cut off his long locks.

8. Stephen Knight
Named in *Rugby League Week*'s sexiest team in 1977, Wests, Balmain and Manly winger Stephen Knight was often a favourite with the ladies. His pretty-boy looks did nothing to impact his toughness—he was once sent off for fighting with John 'Dallas' Donnelly.

9. John Williams
John Williams was a fair winger who played 98 games for Parramatta, Sydney Roosters, North Queensland and Cronulla. The affection female fans had for him far outweighed his abilities on the field. The brother of David 'Wolfman' Williams scored 45 career tries.

10. Luke Ricketson
A baby-faced star throughout a 15-year career with the Sydney Roosters that saw him play for NSW and Australia, Luke Ricketson was always regarded as a heart-throb. That status was confirmed after his retirement when he married socialite and media personality Kate Waterhouse.

BEST HAIR

1. Fuifui Moimoi
Rugby League's greatest hair chameleon, Parramatta prop Fuifui Moimoi only added to his status as one of the game's cult heroes with a head of hair that would change style weekly. Moimoi toyed with braids, an afro, tipped, a flat-top, big and wild, and extensions. He rarely had the same hairstyle week-to-week in an impressive career that lasted over a decade.

2. Russell Fairfax
A long-haired pin-up of the 1970s, Russell Fairfax was an immediate hit in Rugby League with Easts after he defected from Rugby Union. With his long, golden hair, Fairfax was a favourite of the game's female supporters but not the board of the Eastern Suburbs Leagues Club, who refused him access to the club despite him starring for the football team.

3. Willie Mason
Behemoth forward Willie Mason burst on to the Rugby League scene in 2000 with a huge frame and an even bigger afro hairstyle. His huge head of hair quickly became a marketing tool for the Bulldogs, who frequently sold replica wigs to fans at games. Mason shaved his afro off midway through his tenure with Canterbury.

4. Kevin Hardwick and Kerry Hemsley
Two fearless forwards with Balmain during the 1980s, Kevin Hardwick and Kerry Hemsley were both hard to miss with their huge mullets. Hemsley sported an incredible long mullet that defied belief even in an era before they were worn ironically, while Hardwick was known for his curly version.

5. Matt Petersen
Known throughout his career as 'Sideshow Bob' after *The Simpsons* character of the same name, Parramatta and Gold Coast winger Matt Petersen became a cult hero in the 2000s with his big, curly puff of hair.

6. Daly Cherry-Evans
With a haircut dubbed "horrendous" by Newcastle great Matthew Johns, Manly halfback Daly Cherry-Evans briefly rocked an off-centre mohawk during the 2013 season. Compared to Travis Bickle of *Taxi Driver* fame, Cherry-Evans received the haircut from teammate Jamie Buhrer.

7. Carl Webb
Revered for having various ridiculous haircuts throughout the early part of his career, the Queensland blockbuster went through a phase where he was known as 'Crazy Carl'. This was no better highlighted than when he shaved various things into his hair, including a 'Q' for Queensland.

8. Steve Matai
An aggressive Manly enforcer, Steve Matai donned cornrows for much of his career. He occasionally confused media types when he presented in an afro rather than his buttoned-down braided rows, which were most famously worn by NBA star Allen Iverson.

9. Dave Brown
Bald from a young age, pointscoring whiz Dave Brown lost his hair after contracting a virus while swimming. 'The Bradman of League' at first wore a hairpiece before embracing his naked dome, and his bald head and leather headgear became trademarks throughout his outstanding career.

10. Tony Puletua and Joe Galuvao
Known affectionately as 'The Hair Bears', Penrith duo Tony Puletua and Joe Galuvao were the wild-haired backrowers at Penrith from 2002 to 2005. The duo, with their big shocks of black hair, were central to the Panthers' 2003 premiership triumph.

BEARDS

1. Noel Cleal
A bruising outside-back-cum-second-rower, Noel 'Crusher' Cleal sported one of Rugby League's most iconic beards. Looking like a bushranger—along with his brother Les, who sported a similar style of facial hair—Cleal was fast and strong and a representative player for most of his career. He continued to wear his beard into the late 1980s even when facial hair became unfashionable.

2. David Williams
A wildly popular player who regularly used his facial hair to stand out, David 'Wolfman' Williams played for both NSW and Australia and won a premiership with Manly, but is best known for his liberal facial hair. Williams' nickname came directly from his wild beard, which he seemingly fashioned after *Teen Wolf*. He at times dyed it pink for matters of charity and, seemingly, for attention.

3. Geoff Robinson
A fearless forward with Canterbury who was known across the Rugby League world as 'The Wildman', Geoff Robinson became synonymous with his long dark hair and wild beard that made him look more like Charles Manson than Prince Charles. His look made him a cult hero in a Canterbury team on the rise in the late 1970s and early 1980s.

4. Kirk Reynoldson
Nicknamed 'The Bushranger' after his wild Ned Kelly-like facial hair, Kirk Reynoldson had a sandy beard that was possibly more famous than Reynoldson himself. A worker with Melbourne, Newcastle and St George Illawarra, he became a cult hero after liberating his facial hair. It didn't save him from Brian Smith's wrath when the Knights coach controversially forced Reynoldson's exit from Newcastle.

5. Brad Meyers
A prop forward who reached the peak of Australian selection during his first, non-bearded stint in the top grade, Brad Meyers returned to the NRL after a two-year hiatus in Britain

with an enormous red beard that made him a favourite among the Titans faithful. Whether he kept his hair long or short, Meyers' beard remained a flowing river of red rolling hair.

6. Sisa Waqa
A Fijian winger with the Melbourne Storm, Sisa Waqa sports one of Rugby League's unique beards. A flyer who played in the 2012 Grand Final triumph, he is renowned for wearing a "bike-strap" beard around his cheeks and chin without the need for a moustache. It lacks depth or size but gets maximum points for creativity.

7. Geoff Gerard
At one time Rugby League's most capped player, tireless prop forward Geoff Gerard spent the majority of his 16-year career with Parramatta, Manly and Penrith bearded. Be it short and neatly trimmed or a little rough but still maintained like a young Chuck Norris, Gerard wore a beard both when a beard was cool and when a beard was passé.

8. Ruben Wiki
While New Zealand legend Ruben Wiki seemed to don a beard for much of the latter part of his career, his beard was no more notable than many before or after it. Wiki's love of the beard is best seen through the Warriors' dedication to him in his final year, when all of his teammates donned a beard to pay homage to their departing fuzzy-faced leader.

9. George Peponis
A dogged Canterbury hooker who became an Australian Test skipper, Dr George Peponis was of Greek heritage and it showed in his neatly cropped but thick black beard. Dr George took the short boxed beard on as his identity and, while the good doctor's facial hair has greyed over time, he has maintained the beard.

10. Ziggy Niszczot
A husky South Sydney winger who played for NSW in 1982, Ziggy Niszczot had probably Rugby League's worst goatee to go along with its most unusual name. While he oscillated between goatee and moustache, the former stands tall for making him look like the greatest carnie ever to play top-grade football.

MOUSTACHES

1. J.J. Giltinan
James Joseph Giltinan was one of the founding fathers of Australian Rugby League, and sported a glorious, stately moustache that was popular among his contemporaries

in the first decade of the 20th century. Giltinan was the NSWRL's foundation secretary before being personally bankrupted by the 1908-09 Kangaroo Tour. Moustaches wouldn't be as popular again for another 70 years.

2. Wally Lewis

Wally Lewis played in the inaugural State of Origin match clean-shaven and employed the full-beard look intermittently in the early years of his Test career, but the enduring image of 'The King' is of his sandy standalone moustache bristling as he snarled at opponents and inspired Queensland and Australia to countless victories—more than compensating for his balding pate.

3. Graham Murray

Graham Murray possessed one of the strongest moustaches of the late 1970s as a clever ball-playing halfback for Parramatta and Souths before he crafted one of the great coach moustaches in Rugby League history. Thick, lustrous and fatherly, Murray's 'tache was surely one of the great unsung factors behind the Illawarra Steelers' unprecedented success during the early 1990s. He had lamentably shaved it off by the middle part of the decade, but wore a perpetual five o'clock shadow on his upper lip while taking the Roosters and Cowboys to Grand Finals in the 2000s. The much-loved 'Muz' tragically passed away in 2013, aged 58.

4. Rod Reddy

St George enforcer Rod 'Rocket' Reddy's carefree moustache and bushy mane epitomised the wild, hot-blooded spirit of premiership football in the late 1970s. Ray Price's sandy beard was no match for Reddy's powerful handlebar in the '77 Grand Final replay, as the Dragons backrower battered his Parramatta counterpart from pillar to post in a 22-0 shutout. Reddy used that performance—and his confidence-instilling moustache—as a springboard to making 17 Test appearances, including two Kangaroo Tours.

5. Peter McWhirter

Peter McWhirter was Valleys' five-eighth when they won the 1979 BRL premiership (with a young Wally Lewis playing lock) and wore the No.6 in three interstate matches for Queensland, boasting a moustache that would have done Frank Zappa proud. But his moustache was so thick during the 1980s as the Diehards' coach that it cast a half-moon shadow over the bottom part of his face—an intimidating characteristic when combined with his steely gaze on the sidelines of Brisbane's suburban grounds.

6. Sam Backo

During the late 1980s, husky Canberra prop Sam Backo took the battle for the best moustache in Australian sport to Hawthorn midfielder Robert DiPierdomenico, cultivating a magnificent horseshoe number. He may have come up short to 'Dipper', but Backo—who enjoyed a short but spectacular rep career with Queensland and Australia—undoubtedly possessed the Winfield Cup's best moustache.

7. Terry Lamb

Terry Lamb entered first grade with Western Suburbs in 1980 sporting a questionable Amish-style, sans-moustache beard. But he soon combined his status as one of the premiership's most valuable players at Canterbury with being among its most stylish, pairing a sensible mullet with a light-brown slug that became his trademark throughout the decade—encompassing two Grand Final wins and a memorable Kangaroo Tour. Lamb followed the trends and did away with the moustache in 1992; fortunately, the move did not have Samson-like consequences and he went on to lead the Bulldogs to an unlikely Grand Final triumph in '95.

8. Greg Bird

Greg Bird's remarkable inability to grow a proper moustache is matched only by his admirable determination to persevere with it, despite trailing most 16-year-olds in the upper-lip hair-growing stakes. Bird's 'tache is patchy and lacking volume, and it is unclear whether the massive gap at the centre of it is due to a follicular abnormality, a failing attempt to grow a traditional Fu Manchu, or the niggly Test backrower's wicked sense of humour. Whatever the reason, it ranks among the most popular and recognisable moustaches in the current game.

9. Cliff Lyons

Manly maestro Cliff Lyons' fuzzy, dark mop-mullet combo and thick, ever-present moustache saw him bear a striking resemblance to Lionel Richie. And Lyons was possibly as entertaining as the *Dancing on the Ceiling* pop megastar, mesmerising audiences with his ball-playing trickery in 309 games from 1985 to 1999, without ever giving a thought to taking the clippers to his upper lip. He was one of the last genuine Rugby League moustache icons.

10. Martin Bella

Burly, balding prop Martin Bella's no-nonsense moustache suited his gruff exterior and outspoken nature. A two-time Kangaroo tourist from Norths (1986) and Manly (1990) and an institution in the Queensland front-row, Bella's decision to ditch his mo at the start of '94 can be blamed for his play-the-ball gaffe in his last Origin appearance and his costly knock-on at the kick-off of Canterbury's Grand Final loss to Canberra.

REDHEADS

1. Wally Prigg
One of the all-time great locks and finest players of the pre-World War II era, Newcastle legend Wally Prigg's trademark was the curly red hair protruding from his leather headgear. Prigg was the first player to make three Kangaroo Tours; he was named captain on his last voyage in 1937-38—becoming the first NSW Country-based Australian Test skipper—and finished with 19 Test appearances. The revered Prigg, who made 34 interstate appearances, was named as a reserve in the NSW Team of the Century in 2008—the only player who did not feature in the Sydney premiership to win selection.

2. Paul Vautin
No player in the history of Rugby League—or Australian sport for that matter—has been as famous for having red hair as Manly, Queensland and Australian backrower Paul 'Fatty' Vautin. But he was also one of the most wholehearted forwards and popular players of the 1980s. An Origin legend with 22 appearances for the Maroons (including two as captain) from 1982 to 1990, Vautin played 13 Tests for Australia and skippered the Sea Eagles to Grand Final glory in 1987 before finishing his career with Easts. The ginger hair of the self-deprecating host of TV's ever-popular *Footy Show* has provided plenty of fodder for jokes—particularly during the lookalikes segment.

3. Geoff Starling
Gifted Balmain centre Geoff Starling, who holds the distinction of being the youngest player to represent Australia, had a glorious shock of auburn hair. He was just 18 years and 178 days old when he played a tour match in New Zealand in 1971, and went on to feature in 11 Tests in 1972-73. But a mystery illness—later diagnosed as Addison's disease—struck him down in '74 and tragically cut his career short.

4. Brett Dallas
Probably the fastest red-headed player of all time, diminutive Canterbury and Norths winger Brett Dallas appeared to leave a trail of flames when he hit full stride. He was a freckly 17-year-old rookie with the Bulldogs in 1992 and became Queensland's youngest Origin representative the following season at 18 years and 225 days (a record later broken by Ben Ikin). Dallas finished with 10 interstate appearances, scoring nine tries in just six Tests for Australia. The flyer netted 64 tries in 119 first grade games before embarking on a fruitful seven-season tenure at Wigan that garnered over a century of touchdowns.

5. Alan Tongue

A Canberra great and one of the best players to miss out on playing Origin football for NSW, Alan Tongue flew the flag proudly for redheads with a luminous mop of orange locks. The hardworking and skilful Tongue, best suited to the backrow or hooker, was extremely versatile in 220 games for the Raiders, was named Dally M Captain and Lock of the Year in 2008, and represented Country Origin in '09.

6. Brad Meyers

Rangy 'ranga' backrower Brad Meyers broke into the Queensland and Australia forward packs in 2001 as a 21-year-old, his first full season of first grade with the Broncos. The representative opportunities dried up and his career appeared to fizzle out, but after a successful stint with English club Bradford he returned to Australia with the fledgling Gold Coast Titans. He co-opted a flowing, flaming bushranger-style beard into his look to become a cult figure with the club, briefly igniting calls for an Origin recall before he retired in 2011 with 175 NRL games to his credit.

7. Keith Galloway

A 17-year-old NRL debutant with Cronulla, Keith 'The Towering Inferno' Galloway developed into one of the code's most intimidating props with Wests Tigers, cracking the NSW Origin side and playing five Tests for Australia in 2011. A rugged and no-frills prop from the old school, Galloway has been hampered by injuries since his representative breakthroughs but remains a popular figure for the Tigers—particularly with Channel Nine personality Phil Gould.

8. Joel Monaghan

Although his NRL career ended following an infamous 'Mad Monday' prank at the end of 2010, Joel Monaghan was one of Australia's most damaging red-headed outside backs. The tall, robust centre/winger scored 92 tries in 173 games for Canberra and the Roosters, represented NSW in three Origins and scored four tries in five Tests for Australia at the 2008 World Cup. He resurrected his career at Warrington after his Raiders sacking, scoring an incredible 90 tries in just 87 games for the Wolves from 2011 to 2013.

9. Michael Neil

Dubbed 'Ginger Meggs' due to his curly red mop, Mick Neil was a wiry, creative and courageous five-eighth in 12 seasons of first grade. He began his career at Wests with his rusty-headed brothers Alan and Craig, but found his greatest success at Balmain. Neil played in the Tigers' 1988-89 Grand Final losses, and is destined to be remembered for being ankle-tapped by Mal Meninga just metres from the try-line in the heartbreaking defeat to Canberra in the latter decider. The diminutive and gritty half helped Illawarra to its first finals series in 1992 before finishing his 166-game career back at Balmain in '94.

10. Lance Thompson
Lance Thompson's head glowed like lava, but his unwaveringly industrious backrow performances for St George, St George Illawarra and Cronulla were equally eye-catching. A 17-year-old first grade debutant in 1995 with the Dragons, he played 239 first grade games and represented City Origin five times—an equal record for a player who did not progress to State of Origin level.

DALLY M AWARDS DOMINATORS

1. Andrew Johns
Andrew 'Joey' Johns is the only three-time Dally M Medal winner, emerging victorious in 1998-99 and 2002. He also claimed Halfback of the Year honours four times (including 1995, when he finished equal second in the overall award) and was named Representative Player of the Year in 2005. Johns was denied another Dally M Medal by suspension in 2001, and finished second to Johnathan Thurston by a point in '05—despite playing just 16 games for the last-placed Knights—after scoring 23 of a possible 33 points in the last 11 weeks of the season. He took out the people's choice Provan-Summons Award five years straight from 1998 to 2002.

2. Terry Lamb
Terry Lamb won his only Dally M Medal while playing for last-placed Wests in 1983, but he finished second on three occasions (1984, '87 and '92) and third in 1986 during his time at Canterbury. He also won the prestigious, now-defunct Players' Player of the Year award in 1984, '86 and '95, while his seven Five-eighth of the Year gongs is a record for any position.

3. Johnathan Thurston
A dual Dally M Medal winner who carried off the honour in 2005 and '07, 'JT' has been a perennial contender throughout his career. He finished second in 2009 and '13, fourth in 2011-12 and fifth in 2006, and has collected three Halfback and two Five-eighth of the Year gongs.

4. Brad Fittler
Although Brad Fittler rarely contended for the top honour, he is the only player to win awards as player of the year in three different positions. 'Freddy' was named Centre of

the Year in 1992-93, Lock of the Year in 1994 and Five-eighth of the Year in 1998-99 and 2002. He finished third in the Dally M Medal in 1999 and seventh in '02.

5. Ray Price
Parramatta's champion lock Ray Price won the Dally M Medal in 1982, starting a run of five consecutive Lock of the Year honours—a record for consecutive positional gongs—in the last five seasons of a decorated career. He finished second in the '83 Dally M Medal count, and was named Representative Player of the Year in '81 and Captain of the Year in '86.

6. Cameron Smith
Hooker of the Year a record five times (2006, '08 and '11-13), Cameron Smith won the Dally M Medal in 2006 with a whopping 34 points. He also finished equal second in 2008, third in '07 and equal fifth in 2012-13—all despite playing alongside votes-hungry Melbourne teammates Billy Slater and Cooper Cronk. Smith claimed Representative Player of the Year honours in 2007 and '11, and the Captain of the Year gong in 2011.

7. Michael Potter
Michael Potter is the only player to win Dally M Medals with two different clubs, prevailing in 1984 with Canterbury—in his first full season of first grade—and in 1991 after joining St George. He also claimed his third Fullback of the Year gong in 1992, and was named Captain of the Year in 1993.

8. Darren Lockyer
Brisbane legend Darren Lockyer is the only player to win three awards in two different positions, carrying off the Fullback of the Year award in 1998 and 2001-02, and the Five-eighth of the Year gong in 2004 and 2006-07. He recorded several top-10 finishes in the Dally M Medal, was named Representative Player of the Year in 2001 and '06, and collected the Provan-Summons Award in '04.

9. Peter Sterling
Serial award-winner Peter Sterling became the first player to win consecutive Dally M Medals in 1986-87. The Parramatta magician also finished third in the 1981 count and collected four Halfback of the Year gongs (1983-84 and '86-87).

10. Allan Langer
Allan Langer won the 1996 Dally M Medal but featured prominently in previous awards nights. The Brisbane champion finished third in 1988, '92 and '94, was named Halfback of the Year in 1988 and '94, and took out the Players' Player gong in 1991-92. He also carried off the Representative Player of the Year award in 1998.

11. Nathan Hindmarsh
Parramatta workhorse Nathan Hindmarsh won five Dally M Second-rower of the Year awards (2000-01 and '04-06) and would have won another in 2002, but was ruled ineligible for being suspended twice. He also won five Provan-Summons Awards (2005-08 and '11), and finished second in the '06 Dally M Medal count and fifth in '02 and '04.

12. Greg Alexander
Penrith prodigy Greg Alexander won the Dally M Rookie of the Year honour in 1984 and claimed the Dally M Medal the following season—a feat unmatched in the award's history. He also won further Halfback of the Year awards in 1989 and '91, finishing third in the Dally M Medal count in each of those seasons.

13. Cliff Lyons
Manly's ball-playing wizard Cliff Lyons was a two-time Dally M Medal winner, taking out the award in 1990 and '94; he finished equal second in 1995.

14. Cooper Cronk
After several years in contention for the game's highest individual honour, Cooper Cronk finally won the Dally M Medal in 2013. Halfback of the Year in 2006 and '11-13, the Melbourne No.7 finished third in 2011-12 and equal sixth in '10.

15. Billy Slater
Billy Slater was denied the Dally M Medal in 2008 by a one-match suspension, instead finishing equal second, but he belatedly won the award in 2011. Fullback of the Year in each of those seasons, he also recorded four other top-10 finishes and was named Representative Player of the Year in 2010.

16. Gavin Miller
Cronulla's ball-playing backrower Gavin Miller collected a plethora of individual honours in the late 1980s, including the Dally M Medal in 1988-89. He was also named Players' Player in '88.

17. Ricky Stuart
Halfback of the Year and second in the Dally M Medal in 1990, Canberra architect Ricky Stuart claimed a rare Dally M Medal-Players' Player double (and another Halfback of the Year gong) in 1993.

18. Kevin Hastings
Regarded as one of the finest players not to represent Australia, Kevin Hastings was also desperately unlucky to miss out on a Dally M Medal. The gritty Roosters No.7 finished second in each of the first three years the award was run (1980-82) and claimed three straight Halfback of the Year honours.

19. Jarryd Hayne
Dally M Rookie of the Year in 2006, Jarryd Hayne was named Winger of the Year the following season before charging to a memorable Dally M Medal and Fullback of the Year victory in '09 when he picked up maximum points in six straight matches as the Parramatta juggernaut's spearhead.

20. Robbie Farah
One of the unluckiest players in Dally M awards history, Robbie Farah finished second in 2007 and '10—getting the Hooker of the Year nod in each of those seasons—and equal fourth in 2009.

BEST SEVENS PLAYERS

1. Cliff Lyons
A master of sleight of hand and setting up his supports, Cliff Lyons could also hold his own in open space and predictably excelled at Sevens football. The five-eighth starred in Manly's 1990 Nissan Sevens win as the tournament's top point-scorer, and spearheaded the Sea Eagles' consecutive triumphs in the 1994-95 World Sevens editions, taking out Player of the Tournament honours in '94. Lyons led the Aboriginal Dream Team in the 1996 tournament.

2. Phil Blake
Sevens football was custom-made for Phil Blake, one of the premiership's fastest and most individually brilliant players. He owned the inaugural Nissan Sevens in 1988, setting never-bettered records for most points in a tournament (62) and a match (26, from three tries and seven goals in the final) as Souths took home the title. He was the top try-scorer at the '94 tournament, with eight, as his St George side finished runners-up to Manly.

3. Terry Hill
Terry Hill was a long-time Sevens dominator, beginning with his naming as Player of the Tournament in 1993 despite Western Suburbs going down in the third-tier Plate final. He was shaded for the honour by Manly teammate Cliff Lyons in '94, but made history by winning it again as the Sea Eagles claimed back-to-back crowns in '95. Hill was also the top try-scorer at the 1997 edition, with seven.

4. Wes Patten
Tiny Indigenous halfback Wes Patten was an unpredictable Sevens dynamo—elusive, skilful and quick off the mark. He was the top try-scorer at the 1995 tournament, with

eight, as his Sydney Tigers took out the second-tier Trophy final. Patten was superb again in '96 as the Tigers reached the Cup semi-finals.

5. Martin Offiah
Wigan accepted an invitation to play in the 1992 tournament—the first edition of the 'World' Sevens—and duly won it, with wing flyer Martin Offiah the undisputed star. The flamboyant Offiah scored an unprecedented 10 tries on a wet weekend at the SFS, including a record-equalling four in the Cup final defeat of Brisbane. He was an obvious choice as Player of the Tournament.

6. Andrew Johns
Andrew Johns' vast array of attacking tricks often saw him play 13-a-side football as if it were Sevens, and he was one of the abbreviated form's dominant players. He was named Player of the Tournament as Newcastle emphatically won the 1996 World Sevens, starring with 18 points in the Knights' 48-18 thrashing of Norths in the Cup final.

7. Nathan Hindmarsh
Parramatta won the 2003 World Sevens—the first time in six years the event had been staged—and Nathan Hindmarsh emulated Newcastle backrower Marc Glanville's effort of 12 years earlier by being named Player of the Tournament on the back of relentless workhorse displays. The tireless Hindmarsh was magnificent in the energy-sapping early-season competition.

8. Noa Nadruku
Former Fiji Rugby Union international Noa Nadruku famously picked up a contract with the Canberra Raiders after starring for his country at the Rugby League World Sevens in 1993. Elusive, strong and fast, the winger was a crowd favourite and scored a record-equalling four tries in Fiji's Plate final defeat of Wests. He then joined the Raiders and topped the premiership's tryscoring table in his first season.

9. Matthew Johns
Although shaded by his younger brother for Player of the Tournament honours in 1996, Matthew Johns was an equally impressive Sevens exponent. Boasting great footwork, brilliant ball-playing ability and tremendous ad-lib attacking skills, he was a devastating Sevens force when paired up with 'Joey'.

10. Marc Glanville
Proving that Sevens football is not just for flashy playmakers and speedy wingers, Marc Glanville was named Player of the Tournament as Newcastle took out the 1991 Nissan Sevens. The non-stop lock's work ethic and underrated ball skills came to the fore as the Knights—pigeonholed as a dour, forward-oriented team in 13-a-side—emerged as surprise victors.

Chapter 6

THE POSITIONS

GREATEST FULLBACKS

1. Clive Churchill
An original Immortal and considered by many to be the greatest ever Rugby League player, South Sydney fullback Clive Churchill stands above all challengers as the game's greatest custodian. Arriving from Newcastle in 1947, he forged a career that saw him become known as 'The Little Master'. Dominant at every aspect of fullback play, Churchill won five premierships (playing in three deciders) with the Rabbitohs and started in an incredible 99 consecutive rep matches for Sydney, NSW and Australia. Among the highlights of a decorated Test career that saw him represent 37 times, he captained Australia to its first Ashes series win for 30 years in 1950 and held the record for most Tests as Australian captain. At club level, his brilliance was matched by his courage, seen when he kicked a match-winning conversion from the sideline with a broken arm in 1955. The beloved Churchill was named fullback in the ARL Team of the Century as well as the NSW and CRL versions, and was Ernie Christensen's Player of the Year three times.

2. Billy Slater
The most decorated fullback of the NRL era, the speedy and incredibly skilful Billy Slater was rated by none other than Joyce Churchill—widow of the great Immortal—

as "up there with Clive"; she compared their styles by saying Slater does "much the same thing". A Dally M Medal and Golden Boot winner, Slater played in five Grand Finals for Melbourne, winning three premierships as well as the Clive Churchill Medal (in 2009). The freakish talent debuted for Queensland in 2004 but became the undisputed Maroons and Australian first-choice fullback in 2008. To the beginning of the 2014 season he had started more Origins in the No.1 for Queensland than any other player, and he has played more Tests for Australia at fullback than all bar Churchill and Darren Lockyer. Slater won the Dally M Fullback of the Year award in 2008 and '11 and is widely regarded as one of the game's best players of the modern era.

3. Graeme Langlands

Named Rugby League's fifth Immortal in 1999, Graeme 'Changa' Langlands delighted fans across the world during a stellar career with St George, NSW and Australia. Playing in four consecutive premierships with the Saints in his first four years in Sydney, he made his international debut in 1963 and went on to play 45 Tests. He is a veteran of three World Cups and three Kangaroo Tours, including the famous '63-64 tour, and the '68 and '75 World Cup wins. Capable of the freakish and the sublime, Langlands' popularity was no better shown than after the final Test of the '74 Ashes series, when he was chaired off to chants of "Changa! Changa!" He claimed the fullback spot in 'The Masters' 1970-85 team and was named on the bench in the ARL Team of the Century and in the centres in the NSW and CRL honorary teams, all behind Churchill. He was rated fifth in the *Rugby League Week* Top 100 of all time in 1992.

4. Darren Lockyer

A scintillating fullback for the first half of his career, Darren Lockyer played his last eight years at five-eighth but remains widely recognised as one of the code's finest custodians. Debuting off the bench in 1995, he retired in 2011 as the most capped player in premiership history, Australia and Queensland's most capped player, and Australia's most capped captain. A two-time Golden Boot winner (one while playing fullback), Lockyer was named fullback in the QRL Team of the Century while also filling the No.1 position in the 25-year Origin anniversary *Rugby League Week* team. Spending his entire career with Brisbane, he won four titles with the Broncos—three while at fullback—and won the Clive Churchill Medal as a fullback in 2000. Lockyer won three Dally M Fullback of the Year awards and played more Tests at fullback for Australia than all bar Churchill before switching to five-eighth.

5. Charles Fraser

Australia's youngest representative for nearly a century after being selected to tour with the 1911-12 Kangaroos at 18, Charles 'Chook' Fraser was once rated as "the next Messenger" due to his skilful use of the ball and incredible natural ability. A superb playmaker who enjoyed a 17-year career with Balmain, Fraser won six premierships and two City Cups with the Watersiders. His Test career spanned 11 Tests and 12 years; he made two Kangaroo Tours, deputising as captain on the 1921-22 Tour where he sadly suffered ligament damage in the final Test. Also adept at five-eighth and centre, he is a member of the Rugby League Hall of Fame and is ranked 52nd in the 1992 *Rugby League Week* list of 100 greatest players, also making top 100 lists in 2000 and '08.

6. Graham Eadie

Known affectionately as 'The Wombat', Graham Eadie was one of the most dynamic fullbacks the game has known as well as one of the great points accumulators. Spending his entire premiership career with Manly, the powerful Eadie played in six Grand Finals, winning four titles with the Sea Eagles during the 1970s. He was best afield in the 1978 decider. An outstanding goalkicker, he retired in 1983 as the game's greatest point-scorer. Eadie, the Rothmans Medal winner in 1974, won four Ashes series and two World Cups with Australia among 20 Tests. He was named in the Top 100 players in 2008.

7. Howard Hallett

A beloved star with South Sydney during the code's infant years, Howard Hallett rates as the first great fullback Rugby League in Australia knew. Born in Victoria and raised on Australian Rules, Hallett brought his long and forceful kicking game to Souths when he switched codes. He debuted in the top grade in 1909 and played 15 seasons with the Rabbitohs, winning three premierships and three City Cups. Hallett shifted to fullback on the famous 1911-12 Kangaroo Tour, playing six Tests—including the famous 'Rorke's Drift Test'. Though his rep career was stymied by World War I and the emergence of 'Chook' Fraser, 'The Rock of Gibraltar' was named the 40th greatest player of all time by *Rugby League Week* in 1992 and in top 100 lists in 2000 and 2008.

8. Les Johns

A sandy-haired superstar with Canterbury, Les Johns overcame a career interrupted by injury to rank as one of the great custodians. Coming to prominence in the 1960s— an era of great fullbacks that featured Langlands, Thornett and Keith Barnes—Johns managed 14 Tests and 16 appearances for NSW and was named the fullback of the decade in 2006. He toured with the famous 1963-64 Kangaroos who became the first Australian team to win the Ashes on British soil in 52 years, but his greatest season came four years later when he starred for a Canterbury team that ended St George's run of 11 straight titles. That season he won EE Christensen's Player of the Year award and played all six Tests on the 1967-68 Kangaroo Tour. A dynamic runner, Johns' career came to a premature end and he retired at 29 when his knees gave out. He was named in all three Top 100 greatest player lists.

9. Ken Thornett

A Rugby Union convert, Ken Thornett was a star for the perennially terrible Parramatta. Switching to Rugby League in 1962, he quickly became known as 'The Mayor of Parramatta' after leading the club to its first finals series in his debut year after six straight wooden spoons. He debuted for Australia a season later and played 12 Tests, including all six on the successful 1963-64 Kangaroo Tour, forcing future Immortal Graeme Langlands to the centres. A remarkable runner with incredibly safe hands, Thornett has a grandstand named in his honour at Parramatta Stadium. He won the 1965 EE Christensen Player of the Year and was selected in all three Top 100 lists in 1992, 2000 and 2008.

10. Frank McMillan

A champion fullback who spent 14 of his 15 premiership seasons with Western Suburbs, Frank McMillan was regarded as one of the game's finest pre-war custodians. Great Rugby League writer Tom Goodman declared that McMillan revolutionised fullback play by pushing himself into the front-line in attack. A veteran of nine Tests, McMillan captain-coached the 1933-34 Kangaroos five years after making his debut. He was named in the 100 Greatest Players in 2008 (as well as by *Rugby League Week* and *The Daily Telegraph*) and played more games at fullback for NSW in pre-Origin interstate matches than all bar Clive Churchill, with 20. A brilliant long-range kicker, McMillan led Wests to their first two premierships.

GREATEST WINGERS

1. Harold Horder

The 'Wonder Winger' of Australian Rugby League's early years, Harold Horder's strike rate of 152 tries in just 136 first grade games from 1912 to 1924 dwarfs all of the game's great try-poachers. Horder succeeded Dally Messenger as the code's premier superstar, featuring in two title triumphs each for Souths (1914 and '18) and Norths (1921-22), including in 1921 as captain with the latter. World War I restricted his representative career, but he managed 11 tries in 13 Tests and an unbelievable 23 tries in just nine games for NSW, as well as 35 tries in 25 games on the 1921-22 Kangaroo Tour. Lightning quick with mesmerising footwork and a deceptive swerve, Horder set an unattainable benchmark for wingers of future generations to strive for. He was controversially overlooked for the Australia and NSW Teams of the Century in favour of Brian Bevan and Messenger respectively.

2. Ken Irvine

Ken Irvine's premiership record of 212 tries in 236 games for Norths and Manly, along with astonishing representative returns of 33 tries in 33 Tests and 29 tries in 25 games for NSW, marks the blisteringly quick winger as the most prolific accumulator of tries in Australian Rugby League history. North Sydney's greatest-ever player, Irvine topped the competition's tryscoring in 1959, '65 and '69-70 despite the Bears' perennial also-ran status. He joined Manly as a 31-year-old and won Grand Finals with the club in 1972-73—the final two seasons of one of the code's most decorated careers. A brilliantly balanced ball-runner who also dabbled with goalkicking, Irvine starred on three Kangaroo Tours and scored less than 13 tries in a season only once from 1959 to 1973—in an injury-wrecked '68 campaign. Exceedingly popular on and off the field, 'Mongo' was named as a winger in Australia's and NSW's Teams of the Century in 2008.

3. Brian Bevan

Brian Bevan played only seven games for Eastern Suburbs but became one of the most legendary figures in Rugby League history during two decades in English club football. His spindly, balding and frail-looking appearance was certainly deceptive as he carved out a legacy as the most prolific try-scorer the game has seen after joining Warrington in 1946. His speed, elusiveness, skill and cunning netted an astounding 834 tries at club and representative level, while he won two Challenge Cups and savoured two Championship triumphs with the Wire before finishing his career at Blackpool Borough. Bevan crossed 26 times in 16 appearances for Other Nationalities. 'The Galloping Ghost' was named in Australia's Team of the Century in 2008—the only player selected who did not represent Australia at Test level.

4. Brian Carlson

A backline genius in multiple positions, Brian Carlson played most of his representative football on the wing. The creative, skilful, naturally brilliant and adventurous Carlson's nomadic club career encompassed stints in Newcastle, Wollongong, country Queensland and North Sydney, but he was virtually an automatic Test selection throughout the 1950s. He scored 16 tries in 23 Test appearances—including 13 in 15 Tests on the flank—and eight tries in 10 games for NSW, all as a winger. As a 19-year-old, Carlson topped the 1952-53 Kangaroo Tour tryscoring with 29; he also toured with the 1959-60 squad, and starred at fullback in Australia's historic 1957 World Cup success.

5. Benny Wearing

Souths legend Benny Wearing's constant snubbing by the Test selectors is one of the game's enduring mysteries, but there is no doubt he was the greatest winger—and one of the best players—of the late 1920s and early 1930s. The 'people's champion' scored a club-record 144 tries in 172 games, and featured in seven premiership triumphs

(1925-29 and 1931-32) with the Rabbitohs. He crossed for 10 tries in 13 interstate games for NSW and scored two tries in his only Test—a dead-rubber victory to give Australia its only win of the 1928 Ashes series—but was inexplicably overlooked for future international duty.

6. Eric Grothe

An unstoppable force on the Parramatta flank, Eric Grothe combined size, power and explosive speed to become possibly the finest winger since Ken Irvine— and probably the most terrifying of all time to oppose. Grothe was a key member of the Eels' four premiership-winning sides of the 1980s, scoring blockbusting tries in the 1982 and '83 Grand Finals, and finished with 78 tries for the club in 152 games— those figures would have been much higher but for a succession of knee injuries later in his career. He scored in each of his eight Test appearances (for a total of 10 Test tries) and was at his devastating best on the 1982 Kangaroo Tour, scoring 21 tries in 14 games and leaving British audiences gobsmacked. Grothe also represented NSW in nine Origins, scoring twice on debut. He was a unique player and his opposition-scattering charges were a glowing feature of the defence-oriented early '80s.

7. Cec Blinkhorn

Overshadowed by clubmate Harold Horder during his career, Cec Blinkhorn was a brilliant winger in his own right, crossing for 86 tries in 108 games for North Sydney and South Sydney. He was a star of Norths' 1921-22 premiership successes, scoring a then club-record 20 tries in the latter season, and enjoyed a brief but sparkling period in the representative spotlight. Blinkhorn scored a Kangaroo-Tour-record 39 tries in 29 games on the 1921-22 voyage before playing the last of his four Tests for Australia against the touring England side in 1924. He also finished a stellar first grade career in '24 with Souths, retiring after the club's final loss to Balmain. Kept out of the North Sydney Team of the Century by Horder and Ken Irvine, Blinkhorn assuredly ranks in the top echelon of the club's best-ever players.

8. Eddie Lumsden

St George powerhouse Eddie Lumsden played in nine Grand Final victories during the club's unprecedented reign, second only to Norm Provan. The ex-Manly winger's stunning tally of 136 tries in 158 games for the Saints featured a record eight Grand Final tries, including a hat-trick against the Sea Eagles in 1959. One of the most fearsome presences on the flank in premiership history, the giant flyer topped the competition's tryscoring table in 1958 and '62. He played 15 Tests for Australia and toured with the 1959-60 Kangaroos, while he crossed for 14 tries in 16 interstate appearances for NSW. The Kurri Kurri product was named in the Newcastle district and NSW Country Teams of the Century.

9. Johnny King

A prolific try-scorer and dazzling winger in general play, Johnny King played in the last seven of St George's run of 11 straight Grand Final victories. He set a record unlikely to be repeated by scoring tries in six consecutive deciders, and finished a glittering career with a club-record 143 tries in 191 appearances. The competition's top try-scorer in 1961 and '65, he waited until 1966 to make his debut for Australia, but eventually racked up eight tries in 15 Tests and starred on the 1967-68 Kangaroo Tour. The popular King achieved double-figure try tallies in nine of his 12 first grade seasons, and was named as one Australia's 100 Greatest Players in 2008.

10. Kerry Boustead

Diminutive, elusive and speedy winger Kerry Boustead burst into the consciousness of the Rugby League public as an 18-year-old in 1978 and was regarded as possibly the best in his position for the next seven seasons. The Innisfail flyer starred on debut for Queensland and Australia in '78 before playing all five Tests on the Kangaroo Tour at the end of the year. He moved to Sydney the following season, where he played in losing Grand Finals for Easts ('80) and Manly ('83). Boustead finished with 15 tries in 25 Tests and was a key member of the 'Invincibles' Kangaroo Tour side in '82, while he scored five tries in six matches as an early Queensland Origin star. Injuries plagued his career at Manly and, later, Norths, but he retired in 1990 with 70 tries in 178 first grade games.

GREATEST CENTRES

1. Dave Brown

His nickname, 'The Bradman of League', says it all. Dave Brown was a brilliant attacking centre who starred for the great Eastern Suburbs teams of the 1930s and still holds many of Rugby League's pointscoring records. A gifted footballer rated among the greatest ever to play the game, Brown debuted for NSW as an 18-year-old and was appointed captain a year later; his Australian debut came on the 1933-34 Kangaroo Tour, where he broke the record for most points on a Kangaroo Tour with 285. He became Australia's youngest Test captain on the tour of New Zealand two years later. Brown won four premierships with Easts and along the way scored 45 points in a match (still a record), 38 tries in a season (still a record) and 244 points in a season, which was the most in the first six decades of the premiership. Selfless and technically adept, he was named in Australia's 100 Greatest Players in 2008.

2. Reg Gasnier
A phenomenal talent who was a graceful mover and a deadly attacking weapon, Reg Gasnier is rated by many as the greatest of the famous St George team of the 1950s and '60s. Named an Immortal in 1981, he was also named as a centre in the Team of the Century in 2008. Fast, balanced, strong and smart, Gasnier was revered as the world's best player for much of his career, winning EE Christensen's Player of the Year award three times. 'Puff, the Magic Dragon' won six titles with the Saints in a sublime career that netted him 127 tries in 125 games. His record at Test level is just as impressive, with his 28 tries third on the all-time list. He made three Kangaroo Tours, captain-coaching the '67-68 squad. A series of knee injuries led to his retirement at just 28.

3. Dally Messenger
The man who made Rugby League a success, Herbert 'Dally' Messenger was the unquestioned superstar of the game's infant years and the player who gave the new code legitimacy. Capable of amazing deeds, Messenger was an unparalleled Rugby Union draw when he made the call to sign with the League. While he played just six seasons in the premiership, he is still revered today for the contribution he made to the game, with its highest individual award named in his honour and his naming as a reserve in the Team of the Century. Brilliance was expected wherever he went and he rarely let down expectations, with strong running, incredible intuition and unrivalled kicking. He held the premiership record for season scoring for 24 years but was regarded equally highly for his mesmerising tryscoring.

4. Mal Meninga
The only man to make four Kangaroo Tours and the only player to lead two, behemoth centre Mal Meninga was one of the most feared players across a stunning career that lasted 17 years. A three-time premiership-winning captain with Canberra, an Ashes and World Cup-winning skipper with Australia and Origin's greatest-ever scorer with Queensland, Meninga combined size, strength and speed like few before him. 'Big Mal' was a fine goalkicker and devastating runner who won the Golden Boot award in 1990 and was named in the centres in the Australian and Queensland Teams of the Century.

5. Steve Rogers
One of the most naturally gifted footballers ever to strap on a boot, Steve Rogers stands as one of the great centres to play the game. A three-time Kangaroo tourist, Rogers was recognised as one of the top players in the game for most of his career. Debuting with Cronulla in 1973 and spending all bar two seasons with the club, he never won a premiership but dazzled with 82 tries and 1253 points for the Sharks. At Test level he played 24 times, winning three Ashes series. Presented with both the

Rothmans Medal and the Dally M, he was named as a reserve in the NSW Team of the Century and among the 100 greatest players ever.

6. Mick Cronin

A decorated centre who spent his entire premiership career with Parramatta, gentleman Mick Cronin was a pointscoring machine. Strong and robust, he achieved all there was to achieve in Rugby League. At club level, he played in Parramatta's only four premierships and turned out in seven Grand Finals for the Eels. Cronin's career points tally of 1971 was a record for nearly 20 years: his 183 points for NSW in interstate and Origin matches remains a record, and his Test career lasted 33 matches with his 309 career points only passed at the 2013 World Cup by Johnathan Thurston. In 1978 he set the record for most points in a calendar year (547)—a record that remains. Cronin was named the Rothmans Medal winner in 1977 and '78 and Dally M Centre of the Year three times, as well as in the CRL Team of the Century and as a starting centre in 'The Masters' 1970-85 team.

7. Tom Gorman

A champion Queensland centre who was named in the QRL Team of the Century, Tom Gorman was one of the finest players to come out of the Sunshine State. Playing 10 successive seasons of interstate football, Gorman was part of six Queensland series wins—a huge achievement given that the Maroons won just 12 times in the first 72 seasons. His finest hour came as captain on the 1929-30 Kangaroo Tour, where he starred in the 31-8 thrashing of the Lions with an injured leg.

8. Jim Craig

An outstanding athlete who was known as 'Mr Versatile', Jim Craig won the premiership in each of his first five seasons with Balmain before taking Queensland to its first interstate series win, captaining Australia and leading Western Suburbs to its first title. Pioneering Rugby League all-rounder 'Latchem' Robinson called him "the greatest all-round player Australia has produced". Craig was named as a reserve in the QRL Team of the Century and as one of the 100 Greatest Players in 2008.

9. Greg Inglis

Capable of playing anywhere in the backline, Greg Inglis spent most of his top-grade career in the centres. An outstanding athlete, he was a star for Melbourne and South Sydney while excelling at rep level for Queensland and Australia. The greatest State of Origin try-scorer of all time, he has scored 10 of his 15 Origin four-pointers in the centres. Inglis won the Golden Boot in 2009 when spending most of the season in the centres. His 18 Test tries while playing as a centre ranks as all-time third to the start of 2014.

10. Harry Wells
A tough and uncompromising centre who descended from a long line of boxers, Western Suburbs centre Harry Wells was a NSW and Australian regular during the 1950s. Though he debuted with South Sydney and spent most of his career playing in Wollongong, Wells was recognised as a Magpie through and through. He played on two Kangaroo Tours and in three World Cups and was ranked in the 100 greatest players ever in 2008. His strong running was a feature of his excellent all-round game.

GREATEST FIVE-EIGHTHS

1. Wally Lewis
Wally Lewis dominated the 1980s and is regarded by many as the greatest player the game has seen, reflected by his selection as five-eighth in Australia's Team of the Century. Tenacious, abrasive, an inspirational leader and a master ball-player, 'The King' was the ultimate competitor and regularly carried teams on his back at club and rep level. Lewis owned the first decade of State of Origin, playing 31 matches (30 as captain) and winning eight man-of-the-match awards in leading the Maroons to victory in seven of the first 10 three-match series; his legacy continues to loom large over the code's showpiece event. He captained Australia in 24 of his 34 Tests, encompassing the unbeaten 1986 Kangaroo Tour and World Cup success in '88. Also a 'Roo tourist in '82, Lewis was controversially prevented from leading the squad in '90 by injury. His NSWRL club career with Brisbane and Gold Coast provided more setbacks than highlights, but he won BRL premierships with Valleys in 1978 and Wynnum Manly in 1984 and '86—the latter as captain-coach. Boasting peerless vision and control, brilliant kicking and passing attributes, ferocious defence and the ability to bust a tackle, Lewis was the complete No.6.

2. Bob Fulton
A reserve in Australia's Team of the Century, Wollongong product Bob Fulton was named at five-eighth in the NSW and CRL Teams of the Century. He was a dazzling attacking force in the centres at club and rep level, but his playmaking class, magnificent skill and devastating footwork were best utilised at pivot. The ultimate professional, 'Bozo' played in five Grand Finals for Manly and was the linchpin of the club's premiership successes in 1972-73 and '76—the latter as captain—before joining Easts. He scored 147 tries in 263 first grade games but was even more potent for state and country, crossing 14 times in 17 games for NSW and notching 25 tries in 35 Tests.

A No.6 in 17 of his Test outings, Fulton was one of the brightest young talents of the late 1960s and possibly the player of the 1970s, captaining the 1978 Kangaroos in the twilight of his playing career before going on to become one of the great coaches.

3. Darren Lockyer

The incumbent Test captain and already established as one of the great fullbacks at the end of 2003, Lockyer switched to his junior position of five-eighth for the benefit of his club Brisbane—and duly became one of the finest No.6s in history over the last eight seasons of a glorious career. The appearance record-holder for first grade games (355), Origins (36) and Tests (59), Lockyer played 166 games for Brisbane, 20 for Queensland and 34 for Australia at five-eighth. But his greatness transcends mere numbers—he was idolised for his calm leadership, coolheaded match-winning ability and all-round class and silky skills. Lockyer famously captained the Broncos, Maroons and Kangaroos to glory in an amazing 2006 campaign—earning his second Golden Boot—and went on to lead Queensland to a further four Origin series wins and become the highest try-scorer in Test history.

4. Vic Hey

Vic Hey is one of the most influential figures in Australian Rugby League history, and his status as the game's best-ever five-eighth went unchallenged until the emergence of Bob Fulton and Wally Lewis several decades later. He toured with the 1933-34 Kangaroos as a 20-year-old after just one season of first grade with Western Suburbs, and returned to spearhead the previous season's wooden spooners' drive to a premiership triumph in 1934. Hey played the last of his six Tests from Toowoomba before a stellar tenure at Leeds and a stint as Parramatta's foundation captain-coach. Stocky and powerful, he was a punishing defender and a dazzling ball-runner who possessed tremendous hands—the hallmark of all the great five-eighths.

5. Brad Fittler

Schoolboy prodigy Brad Fittler developed into one of the modern era's great leaders and dominant match-winners, and although he was a devastating centre and valuable at lock, his vision and ball-playing class were best suited to five-eighth. 'Freddy', whose top-line career ran from 1989 to 2004, played 202 of his 336 first grade games, 15 of his NSW record 31 Origins and 16 of his 38 Tests in the No.6 jumper; he was named Five-eighth of the Year three times among six Dally M positional awards. A legend at Penrith and the Sydney Roosters, Fittler was the complete package. He was a powerful ball-runner with a superb all-round kicking game and majestic passing ability, and possessed a devastating step off either foot that left countless defenders grasping at air.

6. Laurie Daley

Canberra icon Laurie Daley combined game-breaking flashes of individual brilliance and an intense competitive streak to become one of the 1990s' dominant players. Predominantly a centre early in his career and often used there at rep level to accommodate Brad Fittler at five-eighth, Daley wore the No.6 in 12 of 21 Test appearances, 14 of 23 Origins and 173 of 244 games for the Raiders. He starred in three Grand Final wins for Canberra and became one of the great representative captains. Fiercely determined and a strong defender, Daley was blessed with exquisite hands. His devastating running game and playmaking instincts saw him inherit Wally Lewis' title as the game's dominant five-eighth early in his career.

7. Brett Kenny

Brett Kenny's breathtaking natural ability carried him to the loftiest of Rugby League's heights. The Parramatta champion was fast and elusive and possessed extraordinary anticipation and wonderful hands. His 110 tries in 265 games for the Eels included doubles in three consecutive Grand Finals (1981-83); he also starred in the club's last premiership success in 1986. Regularly used as a centre at rep level, Kenny still played five of his 17 Tests and 12 of his 17 Origins at five-eighth. He unseated Wally Lewis for the Australian No.6 on the 1982 Kangaroo Tour before starring on another trip to Britain and France in '86, while his record directly opposing Lewis for NSW was eight wins and four losses.

8. Eric Weissel

One of the two greatest NSW Country players never to play in the Sydney premiership (the other is Newcastle's Wally Prigg), Riverina legend Eric Weissel was widely described as the complete five-eighth. He played 18 seasons with Riverina clubs and dominated the famed Maher Cup competition. Weissel's international career consisted of eight Tests against England in three hard-fought Ashes series; he earned an incredible plaudit from revered England halfback and captain Jonty Parkin, who proclaimed Weissel the best player he ever saw. A fine goalkicker, he top-scored with 127 points on the 1929-30 Kangaroo Tour, while his brilliant long run on an injured ankle to set up a try for halfback Hec Gee during the 1932 series has passed into Ashes folklore. Cootamundra-born Weissel also captained Country Firsts to upset wins over City Firsts in 1928 and '30.

9. Ernie Norman

Overshadowed historically by his 1930s rival Vic Hey, Ernie Norman played 12 Test matches (nine at five-eighth and three at centre) after debuting as a 19-year-old, and toured with the 1937-38 Kangaroos as the only specialist pivot after missing the trip four years earlier with injury. Norman's legacy is closely intertwined with

Eastern Suburbs' brilliant 1935-37 premiership-winning combination: he was the key link in one of the most devastating backlines of all time. The stocky Norman was regarded as one of the great defenders, tremendously courageous, a slick ball-handler and a clever running pivot.

10. Terry Lamb

A star for a Wests side in decline before he became a Canterbury legend, Terry Lamb built his game on peerless support play (which netted 164 tries in a then record 350 first grade games), deft playmaking ability and an unyielding tenacity in everything he did on the football field. Dally M Player of the Year in '83 for Wests and the Rothmans medallist in '84 for Canterbury, Lamb won seven Dally M Five-eighth of the Year gongs—a record for any position. He won Grand Finals with the Bulldogs in 1984 and '88 before assuming the captaincy in the early 1990s and leading the club to an unlikely premiership in 1995 in the twilight of his career. The presence of Wally Lewis and Brett Kenny limited Lamb's rep opportunities, but his utility value saw him come off the bench in all eight of his Test appearances and achieve the unique feat of playing every game on the 1986 Kangaroo Tour (scoring a team-high 19 tries); he also played eight Origins for NSW.

GREATEST HALFBACKS

1. Andrew Johns

Arguably the greatest player in Rugby League history, Andrew 'Joey' Johns was a rare talent who redefined the boundaries of how a halfback could play. Brilliant at every aspect of his craft, Johns' kicking game was revolutionary, his passing game precise and his ability to thrive in the clutch exemplary. There has been no more complete player in the history of the code. Johns signalled his greatness in an outstanding starting debut that saw him score 23 points. He spent his entire career with Newcastle, winning titles in 1997 and 2001, and his 23 Origins and 26 Tests were as exceptional as they were memorable. Johns played in Australia's 1995 and 2000 World Cup wins and orchestrated many NSW victories, including a remarkable performance in his comeback Origin in 2005 that helped lift the Blues to a series win. Johns won four man-of-the-match awards during his decorated Origin career, as well as myriad awards in a spectacular career, including two Golden Boot awards, three Dally Ms, three *Rugby League Week* Player of the Year awards and a Clive Churchill Medal. He was named the halfback in Australia's Team of the Century.

2. Duncan Thompson

One of the most revered halfbacks the code has known, Duncan Thompson spent just five years in the premiership but stood for the first half of the code's existence as the game's greatest playmaker. 'The Downs Fox' led North Sydney to its only two premierships in 1921-22, orchestrating a champion backline that included Harold Horder and Cec Blinkhorn. His Sydney career ended in bitterness when he walked out after an unjust suspension, but he then starred for the great Toowoomba side of 1924 that defeated every team in Australia. Thompson was integral to Queensland's domination of NSW in the 1920s. He was ranked 10th in 1992 by *Rugby League Week* in a list of the game's greats and was named on the bench in the QRL Team of the Century.

3. Johnathan Thurston

Taking over the mantle from Andrew Johns as the best halfback in the game, Johnathan Thurston has ranked as one of the game's top halves for a decade while sweeping many records aside. Easily identifiable in his headgear, he won a premiership off the bench with Canterbury in 2004 before a stunning move to North Queensland saw him win the Dally M Medal and take the Cowboys to the decider. Thurston went on to win the honour again in 2007, and was named the Golden Boot winner in 2011 and '13. The greatest playmaker of his generation, Thurston had won five Dally M positional awards to the start of the 2014 season. A Queensland regular since 2005 and an Australian starter since 2006, he is the Kangaroos' and Maroons' greatest point-scorer. He has won four Origin man-of-the-match awards and was Australia's best in the 2013 World Cup final.

4. Peter Sterling

A beautifully skilled halfback who won four premierships with Parramatta during a stellar career predominantly in the 1980s, Peter Sterling was the Eels' on-field general and iconic playmaker. With almost unparalleled vision and a celebrated calmness under pressure, he won a host of awards across a spectacular career. In 1984 Sterling was named the *Rugby League Week* Player of the Year and in '86 he won the Dally M Medal and inaugural Clive Churchill Medal. In 1987 he won everything there was to win in a spectacular individual season for a declining Parramatta: the Golden Boot, the Rothmans Medal, the Dally M Medal and the *Rugby League Week* Player of the Year. He backed up that Rothmans Medal win with a second in 1990. Sterling's rep career was equally as impressive: he was Australia's top choice half on the undefeated Kangaroo Tours of 1982 and '86, while his four Origin man-of-the-match awards remains a record (tied with Andrew Johns) for NSW. The four-time premiership winner was named in the ARL's Top 100 players in 2008.

5. Keith Holman

Australia's most capped halfback and a beloved figure, Keith 'Yappy' Holman was one of the finest players over a career that spanned 1949-61. A gritty and wholehearted competitor whose drive accentuated his fine skill set, Holman was the most decorated individual player of the 1950s, winning four *Sun Herald* Best and Fairest awards along with three EE Christensen Player of the Year awards. He never won a premiership with Western Suburbs but played in two losing Grand Finals with the traditional strugglers. His Australian record stands tall to this day: he toured with the 1952-53 and 1956-57 Kangaroos and played in the 1954 and '57 World Cups, and featured in the famous third Test of the 1950 series that saw Australia reclaim the Ashes for the first time in 30 years.

6. Allan Langer

A diminutive playmaker who was selected from obscurity to represent Queensland as a 20-year-old before going on to become the state's greatest halfback, Allan Langer achieved all there was to achieve in Rugby League. One of the game's peerless No.7s, Langer had a brilliant short kicking game and deft passing game to go with the leadership and organisational skills of a general. His club career with Brisbane netted four premierships as captain and a host of awards, including the 1992 Clive Churchill Medal, the 1992 Rothmans Medal, the 1996 Dally M Medal and the 1996 *Rugby League Week* Player of the Year gong, as well as three Dally M positional awards. Langer represented Queensland in an astonishing 34 Origins (a record only surpassed by Darren Lockyer), winning four man-of-the-match awards and making the most incredible comeback in the format's history in the 2001 decider. His Australian career consisted of 24 Tests, including the 1990 and '94 Kangaroo Tours. He was named as the QRL Team of the Century halfback and in the code's 100 greatest in '08.

7. Billy Smith

A tenacious halfback who was as graceful with the ball as he was ferocious in defence, St George great Billy Smith's 15-year career spanned the tail-end of the Dragons' run of 11 titles to their next premiership in '77. Though Smith didn't play in the decider in his final year, he won four premierships in his first four years (three starting in the centres) before leading the club into the 1970s with fellow great Graeme Langlands. His rep career flourished in the 1960s, when he was twice named Australia's best player during an Ashes series, and he played in the 1968 and '70 World Cup teams. Smith was named as the halfback in the 'Masters' team named in 1985 to celebrate 15 years of *Rugby League Week*, while EE Christensen named him the best player of 1966. He was named in the ARL's 100 Greatest Players

8. Arthur Halloway
The finest halfback of the first decade of the code's existence in Australia with Chris McKivat, Arthur 'Pony' Halloway played top-grade football for 13 years, representing Australia for nearly that entire span while winning seven premierships with Eastern Suburbs and Balmain. An opportunistic halfback who was highly regarded for both his defence and his smarts, Halloway played over 100 rep games during a decorated career where he rose to the standing of Australian Test skipper. He was named in the game's Top 100 players in 2008.

9. Chris McKivat
A dual international whose decision to cross to Rugby League in 1910 was one of the seminal moments of the code's formation in Australia, Chris McKivat enjoyed five excellent years with Glebe, NSW and Australia. A shrewd, thinking man's halfback who was as yappy as he was dependable, McKivat was an immediate hit in the professional code, playing for NSW and making his Test debut in his first year before skippering the successful 1911-12 Kangaroos, who were unbeaten in three Tests. His leadership was critical to the tour's success. McKivat was named in the ARL's 100 Greatest and is a member of the Rugby League Hall of Fame.

10. Steve Mortimer
A brilliant individual No.7 and outstanding cover defender, Steve Mortimer was a tenacious halfback with Canterbury, NSW and Australia who won four premierships with the Bulldogs. Debuting in 1976 after being recruited from Wagga, he went on to become one of Canterbury's greatest in his 13-year career. A strong personality who was ultra-competitive and very much an individualist, Mortimer occasionally rubbed his coaches the wrong way but was a special talent and reached the pinnacle of Rugby League. At club level he started in three Grand Final wins and made a cameo off the bench in a fourth, his final game. He starred in the '85 decider and became NSW's first victorious captain earlier that year. Mortimer toured with the '82 Kangaroos and played nine Tests; he was named in the ARL's 100 Greatest Players in 2008.

LOCKS

1. Johnny Raper
An Immortal and generally accepted as the greatest lock in Rugby League history, Johnny Raper was central to St George's great premiership run and helped Australia take the upper hand against England. Though he debuted with Newtown, outstanding

cover defender and beautiful ball-player Raper became synonymous with the Saints. The star lock was named as EE Christensen's Player of the Year in 1960 and '64 and was retrospectively awarded the Clive Churchill Medal for his outstanding performance in the '66 decider. It was at rep level, though, where he shone brightest. Raper made three Kangaroo Tours and captained Australia to World Cup success in 1968, with his finest performance coming in the 50-12 'Swinton Massacre' decimation of England on the 1963-64 tour, where he had a hand in seven of Australia's 12 tries. Raper won eight premierships with the Dragons and was named an inaugural Immortal; he was rated by Frank Hyde as the greatest player ever. He was named as the lock in the ARL and NSW Teams of the Century.

2. Frank Burge

Glebe lock Frank 'Chunky' Burge is the greatest tryscoring forward in the code's history, and a giant of the game in Rugby League's formative years. From a famous sporting family, Burge was the most skilled of the lot and with his giant frame and incredible vision was near impossible to stop. A powerful, long-striding runner, he scored 146 tries in 164 games after debuting at just 16. His record of eight tries in a single game remains a premiership record. He debuted for NSW at 17 and Australia at 19, playing 13 Tests—a number stymied by World War I—and touring with the successful 1921-22 Kangaroos. Burge was named as a reserve in the Team of the Century and in the code's 100 Greatest Players in 2008.

3. Ron Coote

Known as 'The Prince of Locks', Ron Coote was, if anything, a winner. A scything defender who was equally adept with the ball in his hands, Coote played in nine Grand Finals during his 15-season first grade career with South Sydney and Eastern Suburbs, winning five titles. He was perhaps South Sydney's best player during its run of four titles in five years from 1967 to 1971, and was an effective member of the great Eastern Suburbs outfits that won premierships in 1974-75. Coote also played in three World Cup triumphs, skippering Australia to glory in the 1970 tournament. He won an incredible four EE Christensen Player of the Year awards, and was named in the second-row of the ARL Team of the Century and NSW Team of the Century, as well as being among the ARL's 100 Greatest Players.

4. Wally Prigg

Considered one of the great running locks Rugby League has known, Wally Prigg never played a single premiership match but toured three times with the Kangaroos. He spent his entire career playing in the Newcastle competition, where he primarily turned out for Centrals, resisting the temptation to shift to a Sydney club. His refusal to move to Sydney hardly stymied his rep career, though, with Prigg touring with the '29-30, '33-34 and '37-38 Kangaroo Tours—the latter as captain—and playing 19 Tests. His 34 NSW appearances remains a record and he led Country Firsts to two famous victories. A testament to Prigg's greatness was his selection in both the NSW (reserve) and CRL (lock) Teams of the Century in 2008.

5. Brad Clyde

A tireless worker and underrated ball-carrier, Bradley Clyde starred in a Canberra team filled with internationals and all-time greats, but injuries kept him from reaching his full potential. Bursting on to the scene in 1988 aged just 18, Clyde won the Clive Churchill Medal after a stellar performance during the Raiders' 1989 premiership triumph and again two years later on a losing Canberra team, becoming the only man in Grand Final history to win the award twice. He debuted for Australia in 1989 but missed the 1990 Grand Final and Kangaroo Tour because of a knee injury. Though he played 12 Origins and 19 Tests—including the 1992 World Cup final—Clyde's representative career was sadly stymied by persistent injuries and the Super League War. He won a second premiership in 1994 and played in all four Tests on the subsequent Kangaroo Tour, but never again played for Australia or NSW despite his career extending until 2000; he played his final two years with Canterbury. Clyde has been named as one of the code's 100 greatest players and in NSW's 25 best Origin players.

6. Ray Price

A dual international who starred during Parramatta's glory period of the 1980s, Ray Price was known as 'Mr Perpetual Motion' for his relentless work ethic. A rabid defender, he helped turn the Eels around, playing in eight Grand Finals during his 11-year stint with the club and winning four titles—the last in 1986 as retiring captain. Though the Eels didn't win the title in 1979, Price was the best player in the premiership, winning the Rothmans Medal and *Rugby League Week*'s Player of the Year award. He went on to win the Dally M Medal in 1982 and a second *RLW* Player of the Year award in 1985, while he won the Dally M Lock of the Year award from 1982 to 1986. Price played for Australia 22 times, touring with the 1978 and '82 Kangaroos. He is honoured by a statue outside Parramatta Stadium.

7. Wayne Pearce

A skilful and tenacious lock forward who spent his entire career with the Balmain Tigers, Wayne 'Junior' Pearce was credited with bringing a new professionalism to players' diet and preparation in the 1980s. The ultra-competitive Pearce gained a major edge through his focus on nutrition and his abstinence from alcohol. Smart and determined, he was regarded among the top handful of locks throughout his 11-year first grade career, during which he played 19 Tests and 15 Origins. Pearce won the

1985 Rothmans Medal and was twice named Dally M Lock of the Year. He took Balmain to its last two Grand Finals but was destined never to win a premiership. One of Balmain's favourite sons, Pearce was named in the Top 100 players in 2008.

8. Andy Norval
Described by teammate Dick Dunn as the greatest player he had ever seen, Andy Norval was a champion lock forward during Eastern Suburbs' era of dominance in the 1930s. He won four premierships with the Tricolours and was a rangy type known for his hard-hitting defence. Norval played just three Tests for Australia, touring with the 1937-38 Kangaroos, but his rep career was stymied by World War II. He was named in the 100 Greatest Players of all time in 2008.

9. Paul Gallen
A relentless lock who stood as the top forward in the game in the early part of the 2010s, Cronulla forward Paul Gallen has set a new standard for work ethic, regularly topping average metres in the premiership by a significant distance. Though he has regularly run afoul of officials for his ultra-competitive approach, Gallen was appointed NSW captain in 2011 and was a standout for the Blues in his 16 showings to 2014. He has played 30 Tests, including the 2013 World Cup final win, and has twice won both the Harry Sunderland Medal as Australia's best in a series, and the Dally M Lock of the Year award. He was named *Rugby League Week*'s Player of the Year in 2010.

10. Billy Cann
A brilliant utility forward who sailed to Great Britain on the first two Kangaroo Tours, Billy Cann rates as one of the game's greats of the early days. The prototype of the modern ball-playing lock forward, he was a pioneer in not only establishing the code in Australia but in changing the way locks played. Cann spent his entire career with South Sydney, winning three premierships, and played eight Tests for Australia and nine matches for NSW. He was named in the ARL's 100 Greatest Players in 2008.

GREATEST SECOND-ROWERS

1. Norm Provan
Norm Provan's phenomenal Grand Final record alone is an obvious sign of the towering second-rower's influence. 'Sticks' featured in 10 consecutive premiership victories for the mighty St George side, beginning with the 1956 Grand Final that started the club's world-record run and culminating in a triumphant exit from the

game after the pulsating 1965 decider against Souths—his fourth straight triumph as captain-coach. Provan's imposing physical presence, powerful ball-running and tough defence were his on-field trademarks. His 18-Test tenure began in the 1954 Ashes triumph on home soil before he toured with the 1956-57 Kangaroos, featuring in the World Cup-winning campaign in 1957; he grappled with the British forwards again in 1958. Provan's selection as a second-rower in the ARL Team of the Century in 2008 secured his rightful place as one of Australia's greatest forwards, and he gained plenty of support to become the game's eighth Immortal—an honour that instead went to Andrew Johns.

2. George Treweek

When *Rugby League Week* assembled a panel of experts to select a "best-ever" team in 1982 to mark 75 years of Rugby League in Australia, South Sydney great George Treweek was chosen in the second-row alongside Norm Provan; many fine judges who were fortunate enough to see the tall, destructive ball-runner attest that he was the greatest second-row forward the game has seen. An integral part of the Souths dynasty that dominated the late 1920s and early 1930s, Treweek shared in seven premierships, captaining the side in 1933. He played seven Tests against England in the 1928 home Ashes series and on the 1929-30 Kangaroo Tour, but business commitments curtailed his representative career thereafter.

3. Harry Bath

Referred to as "the greatest forward never to play for Australia" for more than half a century, it is doubtful whether any player has been as revered or achieved more success without starring in the rigours of Test football than 'The Old Fox'. The Brisbane Souths junior won premierships in all five of his seasons in Sydney—with Balmain in 1946-47 and St George in 1957-59—but achieved legendary status in Britain with Warrington during the meat of his career. Rugged and tough, he developed into an outstanding ball-playing forward in the midfield, with the experience and guile he garnered on the fields of England providing yet another facet to the unstoppable Saints machine's armoury. A prolific point-scorer on the British club scene, Bath set a Sydney premiership record for most points in a season by a forward (225), and his eight goals in the 1957 decider remains a Grand Final record.

4. Herb Narvo

Herb Narvo led a nomadic Rugby League existence but left a legacy as one of the toughest forwards Australia has produced and as one of the foremost players of the 1930s and '40s. He toured with the 1937-38 Kangaroos after just one season with Newtown, starring in four Tests. World War II curbed his rep career, but after several seasons back in his native Newcastle he returned to Newtown and helped the club win its last premiership in 1943. In 1946—a year after he won the Australian heavyweight boxing title—he captain-coached St George to a Grand Final. A punishing defender and a fearsome ball-runner, Narvo was a genuine enforcer but a scrupulously clean and fair player. He was named as a second-rower in the Newtown, Newcastle district and NSW Country Teams of the Century in 2008.

5. Vic Armbruster

A product of the NSW north coast, Vic Armbruster played one game for his state of birth in 1922 but became a Queensland legend after being lured to Toowoomba by the great Duncan Thompson. A vital component of Toowoomba's fabled 'Galloping Clydesdales' side of the mid-1920s, he played eight Tests for Australia—all against England—and starred on the 1929-30 Kangaroo Tour when he formed one of the great international second-row combinations with George Treweek. A rugged, intimidating presence and a vigorous attacking forward, Armbruster eventually played 26 games for Queensland and was regarded as the northerners' answer to the legendary Frank Burge.

6. Brian Davies

The calibre of players ahead of whom Brian Davies was chosen to partner Arthur Beetson in the second-row of the Queensland Team of the Century in 2008 is a clear indication of his standing in his home state, which he represented 31 times, and Australian Rugby League in general. Equally at home at prop, Davies made 17 of his 33 Test appearances—encompassing the 1952-53 and '56-57 Kangaroo Tours—in the second-row. Tough, resourceful and a fine ball-player, Davies played for 17 seasons (1948-64) in first grade with Brisbane Brothers and Canterbury. He captained Australia in the 1958 Ashes series at home, but his legacy as one of the great forwards was confirmed by his brilliant performances in Britain.

7. Bob McCarthy

South Sydney great Bob McCarthy was a revolutionary figure who was utilised as a devastating wide-running second-row forward to combat the changes the limited-tackle rules made to the game. His combination of speed, power and size saw him become one of the game's most dangerous attacking weapons of the 1960s and '70s. Playing in five Grand Finals for the Rabbitohs, McCarthy won premierships in 1967 and 1970-71, scoring a famous intercept try in the '67 decider. He was a shock omission from the subsequent Kangaroo Tour squad, but went on to play 15 Tests and captain Australia in the series-saving second Test victory against Great Britain on the 1973 Kangaroo Tour. The powerhouse backrower became the first forward since the legendary Frank Burge to score 100 career tries in making a record 211 appearances for Souths and in two seasons at Canterbury.

8. Sid 'Joe' Pearce

The son of legendary pioneering hooker Sid 'Sandy' Pearce, 'Joe' Pearce carved out a brilliant career of his own, becoming one of the great pre-World War II forwards. Part of Easts' dominant pack who powered the club to premierships in 1935-37 and '40, he played 31 games for NSW and 13 Tests for Australia, touring with the 1933-34 Kangaroos after captaining the Tricolours to the '33 finals. A broken leg prevented a second tour four years later, but the powerful, rugged and skilful forward's status as one of the great second-rowers has never been in doubt.

9. Kel O'Shea

One of the unluckiest omissions from the Queensland Team of the Century in 2008, Kel O'Shea made 20 Test appearances from Ayr Colts and Sydney's Western Suburbs, while he represented Queensland eight times and played seven games for NSW. The tall, imposing backrow forward cut his representative career short for financial reasons, but was a key part of the big-spending Magpies' rise to heavyweight status in the late 1950s and early '60s, playing in three Grand Final losses to St George.

10. Gorden Tallis

Among the most destructive ball-running forwards in Rugby League history, the intimidation factor Gorden Tallis brought to the table in attack and defence rendered him one of the game's top players of the late 1990s and early 2000s. He started out as an impact player at St George but became a vital cog of Brisbane's premiership-winning sides of 1997-98 and 2000. An Origin icon, Tallis skippered Queensland in 10 of his 17 appearances, and scored nine tries in 13 Tests for Australia. The aggressive game-breaker fought back from a serious neck injury at the height of his career to finish with 66 tries in 214 first grade games.

GREATEST PROPS

1. Arthur Beetson

A master ball-player and debatably the greatest attacking forward Rugby League has produced, Arthur Beetson's vast list of achievements in the game is matched only by his phenomenal natural ability and magnetic personality. The burly forward battled criticisms of being lazy for much of his career and garnered a reputation as a hothead (he missed Balmain's 1969 Grand Final win through suspension), but he quashed those jibes after being handed the captaincy at Easts and magnificently leading the Roosters to emphatic premiership victories in 1974-75. Inconceivably skilful and fast for a big man, Beetson was a cornerstone of much of Australia's success during the 1970s, while his role as the 35-year-old skipper of Queensland's inaugural State of Origin side in 1980 provided a glorious addendum to his colossal legacy. Named as the seventh Immortal in 2003, Beetson was honoured with selection at prop in the ARL Team of the Century, and in the second-row in the Queensland Team of the Century in 2008.

2. Duncan Hall

The inimitably tough and skilful front-row enforcer Duncan Hall was one of five Queenslanders picked in the ARL's Team of the Century in 2008—but the only one to not feature in the NSWRL premiership. His outstanding performances in 23 Tests for Australia swayed the judges to include him. Hall's nomadic career featured stints in Rockhampton, Home Hill, Toowoomba and Brisbane (with Valleys and Wests). He proved a frequent thorn in the side of British Test teams, clashing with some of the great forwards in home Ashes series triumphs in 1950 and 1954, and on the 1952-53 Kangaroo Tour. Never taking a backward step in the face of provocation or intimidation, Hall was a tremendous scrummager and an expert of tight forward play, but also a prolific try-scorer for a prop, crossing for nine Test tries. His selection in the Australian and Queensland Teams of the Century was due recognition for the outstanding front-row forward of one of the game's toughest eras.

3. Glenn Lazarus

Glenn Lazarus was the dominant front-rower of the 1990s and the prototype for the modern-day prop: big, mobile and a rock-solid defender, with a liberal dash of skill to top it off. The only player to win Grand Finals with three clubs, Lazarus was the engine-room cornerstone of Canberra's, Brisbane's and Melbourne's inaugural premiership successes. He was equally dominant at representative level, starring on the 1990 and 1994 Kangaroo Tours and laying the forward platform for NSW Origin series victories in 1990, 1992-94 and 1996. He was named as a prop in the NSW Team of the Century in 2008.

4. Shane Webcke

Brisbane great Shane Webcke challenged Glenn Lazarus's mantle as the finest prop of the modern era and was unanimously regarded as the best in his position for the majority of his magnificent career. A durable and courageous front-row powerhouse, Webcke played 21 consecutive Origin matches for Queensland and represented Australia in 25 Tests; his ability to defy serious injury to continue playing was awe-inspiring. The three-time Dally M Prop of the Year was the pack anchor of the Broncos' 1997-98, 2000 and 2006 premiership successes, and retired in triumph after the '06 Grand Final, his 254th first grade appearance.

5. Ray Stehr

Easts stalwart Ray Stehr's status as one of the most colourful characters Rugby League has produced is matched only by his standing among the code's greatest forwards of all time. The youngest first grade player in history at 16 years and 85 days, his career spanned 17 seasons (1929-45) and encompassed premiership victories with the Tricolours in 1935-37, '40 and '45—the latter two as captain. An unrelenting front-row warrior and a brutal enforcer, Stehr pushed the rules to their limit—he was sent off twice during the 1936 Ashes series—but represented Australia in 11 Tests and on two Kangaroo Tours. He established records for most first grade games (184) and appearances for NSW (30).

6. Roy Bull

A reserve in the NSW Team of the Century named in 2008, Manly stalwart Roy Bull was one of the code's most respected players of the late 1940s and '50s. He was a dominant scrummager who excelled in the trenches during a tough era, playing 25 Tests for Australia and making two Kangaroo Tours. Although he was not the most mobile of forwards, Bull was super-fit and unwaveringly hardworking on the field. His 177 games for Manly encompassed three Grand Final defeats, and he captain-coached the club in 1953.

7. Mick Madsen

Voted on by some of the most experienced and respected judges in the game, the best-ever Australian line-up named in a 1982 *Rugby League Week* promotion contained Peter 'Mick' Madsen alongside Duncan Hall at prop. While he was a surprise choice, Madsen's credentials are watertight: he played a then record 36 games for Queensland (1928-37) and nine Tests for Australia, embarked on two Kangaroo Tours, and was regarded as one of the toughest and most courageous players of the era. The powerful Toowoomba front-rower was named in the Queensland Team of the Century in 2008.

8. Petero Civoniceva

A relentless, hard-hitting front-row workhorse, Fiji-born Petero Civoniceva achieved all-time records for most Tests (45) and Origins (33) for a forward—testament to his supreme durability and the quality and consistency of his play. The tall, raw-boned prop featured in Brisbane's 1998 and 2006 Grand Final victories before an admirable four-season stint as captain of a young Penrith outfit. He finished his career with the Broncos in 2012, becoming the first career front-rower to play 300 first grade games. Civoniceva won the Harry Sunderland Medal in 2006 and was named Queensland's Players' Player in '08 and '11.

9. Herb Steinohrt

Herb Steinohrt remains one of the most revered figures in Queensland Rugby League history. He was the rugged front-row leader of the dominant Toowoomba and Queensland combinations of the 1920s, finishing his career with 34 interstate appearances from 1925 to 1933. Steinohrt played nine Tests, featuring in the 1928 Ashes series and on the 1929-30 Kangaroo Tour before captaining Australia against England in the 1932 home series. Equally valuable in the second-row, the universally respected Steinohrt was named as a reserve in the Queensland Team of the Century in 2008.

10. Noel Kelly

Noel 'Ned' Kelly was a controversial choice as hooker in the Australia and Queensland Teams of the Century—he played much of his career as a prop—but the selection was a expression of his stellar career in the front-row: a place had to be found for the colourful enforcer. Famous for his unmatched records for send-offs and broken noses, Kelly became the first front-rower to make three Kangaroo Tours—in 1959-60 from Ipswich, and 1963-64 and '67-68 from Sydney's Western Suburbs. He made 12 of his 28 Test appearances as a prop, and featured in three Grand Final defeats for the Magpies. A brutal, take-no-prisoners customer, Kelly ranks as one of the most popular characters of Australian Rugby League's golden era.

HOOKERS

1. Cameron Smith

The most accomplished hooker ever to play the game, Cameron Smith enjoyed incredible success at club, state and international level. An almost faultless player—a tireless defender, underrated playmaker, brilliant leader and reliable goalkicker—Smith proved himself a natural winner throughout his career. At Melbourne, he has won three premierships and played in four Grand Finals. He has played in all eight of Queensland's consecutive series wins, succeeding Darren Lockyer as skipper of the Maroons. He also assumed the Test captaincy from Lockyer and led his country to the 2013 World Cup victory, while he has lost just three of his 40 internationals to the start of the 2014 season. No hooker has received the individual accolades of Smith, either. The winner of the Golden Boot in 2007 and the Dally M Medal in 2006, he has also received five Dally M Hooker of the Year awards and two Wally Lewis Medals. Touted as a future Immortal, Smith ranks as one of the all-time great players.

2. Ian Walsh

Australia's third-most capped hooker behind Cameron Smith and Ken Kearney, Ian 'Abdul' Walsh had the honour of captaining the first Australian team to win the Ashes in England in 50 years in 1963-64. After debuting for Australia from Eugowra in 1959 on that year's Kangaroo Tour, he signed with St George in 1962 and won five premierships with the Saints, including captain-coaching the '66 team. Physical and respected, Walsh was a natural leader who was desperately unlucky to be overlooked by selectors for the Australian Team of the Century. He was named in the CRL Team of the Century and in the game's Top 100 players in 2008, and as EE Christensen's Player of the Year in 1963.

3. Steve Walters

Though he was stuck behind his brother Kerrod in the representative pecking order during the early part of his career, Steve Walters revolutionised the hooking role in the 1990s with his outstanding attacking play. A three-time premiership winner with Canberra and a three-time Dally M Hooker of the Year, 'Boxhead' Walters was the game's best hooker from 1991 to 1994 before injuries stymied his career. A sublime playmaker from dummy-half and a rugged defender, he won man-of-the-match honours in the deciding Ashes Test in 1994. He was named in the Top 100 Players in 2008.

4. Sid Pearce

Known as 'The Prince of Hookers', Sid 'Sandy' Pearce debuted in the premiership's first season and was playing Test football 14 years later at the age of 38. He rates as one of the code's earliest stars and most accomplished footballers, remains Australia's oldest Test player and stands as one of its most durable. The champion rake, who was a fine scrummager and tough tackler, won three premierships with Eastern Suburbs and made the 1908-09 and 1921-22 Kangaroo Tours. He was named in the NSW Team of the Century and in the ARL's 100 Greatest Players.

5. Noel Kelly

A tough and aggressive hooker/prop who was a controversial selection as the Team of the Century hooker in 2008, Noel 'Ned' Kelly never took a backward step during a decade-long career with Australia and a nine-season spell with Western Suburbs that netted three Grand Final appearances. The first front-rower to go on three Kangaroo Tours, he was also named in the QRL Team of the Century. A fiery forward whose aggression often overshadowed his smarts and skill, Kelly often battled with Ian Walsh for the Australian hooking role during the 1960s and regularly played alongside him at prop. He played in all six Tests of the famous '63-64 Kangaroo Tour sweep.

6. Ken Kearney

The driving force behind St George's incredible success in the 1950s and into the 1960s, Ken Kearney was a tenacious competitor and visionary who brought a professional training regime into Australian football. A dual international and Australia's second-most capped hooker, he captained St George's five titles between 1956 and 1960 and coached the team to victory in 1961. A firm believer in brutal defence, 'Killer' was uncompromising and tough. He toured with two Kangaroo squads and two World Cup teams. Kearney finished the 1957 season with a broken jaw but played through it, a sign of his toughness—one of the many qualities that saw him named in the ARL's Top 100 players in 2008.

7. Danny Buderus

A champion hooker who played 257 games spanning 17 seasons with Newcastle, Danny Buderus ruled the roost as the game's No.1 hooker through the early part of the 2000s. A tireless worker and a skilled dummy-half, Buderus won a premiership with Newcastle in '01 and played 21 consecutive Origins and 24 Tests. He became the first hooker in the code's history to win the Dally M Medal in 2004, and is the longest-serving skipper in NSW Origin history (15 games). Only three hookers have played more Test football than Buderus.

8. Dan Dempsey

A champion hooker who played his entire career in Queensland, Dan Dempsey made two Kangaroo Tours and played 11 Tests in a stellar career. He was a star in the great Toowoomba sides of the mid-1920s who beat all before them. Though never a hooker at club level, he was a regular rake on the rep stage, where he became the first forward to play in four Ashes series. A Queensland regular for nearly a decade, Dempsey was renowned for his scything tackling and courageous play. He was named in the ARL's 100 Greatest Players in 2008.

9. Kevin Schubert

An outstanding rake who was Australia's starting hooker when the Kangaroos reclaimed the Ashes for the first time in 30 years in 1950, Kevin Schubert twice toured England and France and was Australia's top rake from 1948 through 1952. He was a tough and skilful 19-Test hooker who spent his premiership career with Manly, turning out in the 1951 Grand Final. Schubert was named in *Rugby League Week*'s Top 100 in 1992 and *The Daily Telegraph*'s Top 100 in 2000, but missed the ARL list in 2008.

10. Elwyn Walters

A gritty and resolute hooker who won five premierships with the all-time-great South Sydney team of the late 1960s and the Eastern Suburbs team of the mid-1970s, Elwyn

Walters also enjoyed a six-year international career that saw him win 20 Test caps. He made two Kangaroo Tours and two World Cups during a stellar Test career and was a NSW regular for the same period. Rugged and determined, Walters was a fearless runner and a ruthless defender.

GREATEST UTILITIES

1. Jimmy Craig

One of the greatest of all pre-World War II players, Jimmy Craig was aptly dubbed 'Mr Versatile'. In seven Test appearances from 1921 to 1928 he made starts at centre, halfback and fullback, while in 20 interstate matches—18 for Queensland and two for NSW—he featured at halfback, five-eighth, centre and fullback. In a brilliant 16-season club career at Balmain, University, Ipswich and Western Suburbs, Craig often played wing and lock; he even played at hooker for Wests in the days when packing down in the front-row was reserved for the fearless. A true Rugby League legend, Craig retired after captain-coaching Wests to their maiden premiership, playing halfback in the 1930 Grand Final.

2. Shaun Berrigan

Brisbane stalwart Shaun Berrigan began his NRL career as a versatile centre/five-eighth, coming off the bench in the 2000 Grand Final victory. As a five-eighth in 2002, he formed a halves partnership with Allan Langer in the Broncos and Queensland line-ups before assuming the No.7 jumper in both sides the following season, after Langer retired. Berrigan made his Test debut off the bench in 2004 but was transformed into a centre at club level and featured in that position throughout Australia's Four Nations campaign. He scored 19 tries for Brisbane and represented the Maroons as a centre in 2005, but his switch to hooker late in '06 was crucial to the Broncos' premiership triumph; he won the Clive Churchill Medal wearing the No.9 in the Grand Final. Berrigan became the first-choice bench utility for Queensland and Australia, ultimately playing six of his 14 Tests and six of his 15 Origins as an interchange. After three seasons with Hull, he featured at centre, hooker, halfback and off the bench for the Warriors and Canberra.

3. Des Hasler

After debuting for Penrith, Des Hasler became a tenacious halfback at Manly, breaking into the NSW and Australian sides in the No.7 in 1985. But his remarkable utility value saw him start nine of his 12 Tests and six of his 12 Origins on the bench.

Hasler was Manly's 1987 Grand Final-winning halfback but moved to lock—while also filling in regularly at centre—to accommodate the rise of Geoff Toovey (Hasler also played one game at fullback in '88). He was named Dally M Lock of the Year in 1991 before he returned to the halves for most of '93. Following a year in England, the super-fit veteran returned to the Sea Eagles reinvented as a hooker and played two Grand Finals, including the '96 victory over St George. He finished his career with one season at Wests, flitting between lock, hooker, halfback and the bench. Fittingly, his biography, written by noted author Tom Keneally, was entitled *The Utility Player*.

4. Craig Wing

Craig Wing emerged as a teenage attacking livewire at Souths in the late 1990s, where he starred at five-eighth, halfback, lock, fullback and centre in two seasons before the Rabbitohs' expulsion from the NRL. He joined the Sydney Roosters in 2000 and was a fullback, half or bench specialist for the next two seasons before featuring in the No.7 in the Tricolours' 2002 premiership triumph. Wing's move to hooker—his best-known position—in 2003 was a rousing success, turning him into an automatic interchange selection in the NSW and Australian line-ups. He played 10 of his 16 Tests (2002-05) off the bench, making starts at five-eighth and hooker, and played all three Ashes Tests in '03 at centre for the injury-hit Kangaroos. Wing came off the bench in all 12 of his Origin appearances (2003-06 and '09). Returning to Souths in 2008, he played predominantly at five-eighth and lock.

5. Kurt Gidley

Simultaneously regarded as one of the NRL's best fullbacks and halfbacks in the late 2000s, Newcastle stalwart Kurt Gidley became an interchange staple for NSW and Australia. He filled in at fullback and centre early in his career before becoming Andrew Johns' halves partner—or a No.7 replacement during 'Joey's' regular injury breaks—and then settling at fullback in 2007 after Jarrod Mullen emerged. He made his Origin and Test debuts as an interchange in '07, used as injury cover and a dynamic dummy-half option; to date he has come off the bench in 11 of 12 appearances for Australia and seven of his 12 matches for the Blues. Gidley created history during the 2010 Origin series by becoming the first player to captain a side starting on the bench after being displaced from the fullback spot. A long-serving skipper for the Knights before a string of injury-interrupted seasons, he switched regularly between fullback, halfback and hooker as the club's injury- and form-related needs dictated.

6. Luke Lewis

A potent tryscoring three-quarter who later became one of the NRL's best backrowers via a stint in the halves, Luke Lewis's utility journey ranks as one of Rugby League's most remarkable. He scored 18 tries as a robust, swift centre/winger in Penrith's

2003 premiership triumph, winning Kangaroo Tour selection that year (although he controversially did not play any Tests) and making appearances at wing and centre for NSW in his debut Origin series in '04. He fell off the rep radar in subsequent seasons, but his impressive efforts at halfback in 2008 and five-eighth and lock early in '09 piqued the interest of Blues selectors again. Lewis also made his Test debut that season and has been a Kangaroos and NSW regular in the second-row or on the bench since, making 15 Test and 14 Origin appearances to the end of 2013. Dally M and RLIF Lock of the Year in 2010, he has maintained his reputation as one of the game's top backrowers since joining Cronulla in 2013 and remains an excellent backline option when required. In a 2011 Four Nations Test against England, Lewis started in the second-row but switched to the wing after an injury-enforced reshuffle, and scored a try.

7. Jason Croker

Canberra's longest-serving player with 318 appearances, Jason Croker was also one of the club's most valuable and versatile. He emerged as a teenaged winger in 1991, but earned his NSW spurs two years later on the back of outstanding form at lock. Croker filled in extensively at five-eighth for the injured Laurie Daley during the Raiders' '94 premiership season before featuring in the second-row in the Grand Final. The prolific try-scorer replaced retired great Mal Meninga at centre the following season but eventually returned to the backrow and gained selection in Australia's 2000 World Cup squad after winning Dally M Lock of the Year honours. He played five matches at the tournament—four off the bench and one as a winger. The veteran spent the latter seasons of his career interchanging between lock, second-row, five-eighth and centre for the Raiders.

8. John Plath

John Plath's bench specialist role for Brisbane throughout the 1990s was a forerunner to the likes of Shaun Berrigan, Craig Wing and Kurt Gidley becoming such important members of representative sides in the 2000s. With no way past Allan Langer for a regular first grade spot, the halfback forged a permanent interchange role and ultimately started 99 of his 149 games for the Broncos—including four Grand Final victories—on the bench. A niggly, tenacious competitor, Plath was the solution for any in-game contingency and made starts at halfback, five-eighth, centre, hooker and lock.

9. Lance Hohaia

'The Huntly Hurricane' was a 19-year-old rookie sensation for the Warriors at five-eighth in 2002, eventually coming off the bench in that season's Grand Final before making his New Zealand Test debut in the No.6 at the end of the year. He played in the halves and at centre in subsequent seasons at club level before a stint at hooker in 2005 that saw him earn a Test recall as a dummy-half after a three-year absence. Hohaia was outstanding after being pitched into the

Warriors' fullback role in 2008 when Wade McKinnon was struck down by injury, and eventually made the last 16 of his 26 Test appearances in that position—including the '08 World Cup and '10 Four Nations final triumphs over Australia. Regularly returning to centre or five-eighth when McKinnon was intermittently available, Hohaia fulfilled a valuable bench utility role during 2011 after Kevin Locke emerged; he started at hooker throughout the finals series, including the Grand Final loss to Manly—his last game for the club.

10. Chris Flannery
Sunshine Coast product Chris Flannery played every position bar prop and hooker—most to a high standard—during seven seasons with the Sydney Roosters. Best suited to the backrow, Flannery featured predominantly at wing and fullback in 2001 before playing an outstanding 'Mr Fix-it' role during the Tricolours' '02 premiership season. Rarely featuring in the same position—or even in the pack and backline—two weeks in a row, he played two finals matches in the No.1 before scoring a try off the bench in the Grand Final defeat of the Warriors. Used more as a backrower in subsequent campaigns, Flannery was an interchange again in the 2003-04 Grand Final losses, regularly slotting in at five-eighth and centre. In 10 Origin appearances for Queensland he came off the bench six times, started at lock three times and stood in at five-eighth for injured skipper Darren Lockyer in one match.

GREATEST BENCH-WARMERS

1. Danny Williams
The most capped benchman in premiership history, Danny Williams started 155 of his 210 games from the pine. A fiery backrower for North Sydney and then Melbourne, Williams had his NRL career ended by an 18-match suspension following a king hit on Mark O'Neill. A move to Super League club London saw him come off the bench in 31 of 42 outings.

2. Richie Fa'aoso
A well-travelled, aggressive prop forward who played with Penrith, the Sydney Roosters, Parramatta, Newcastle, Melbourne and Manly, Richie Fa'aoso came off the bench in 130 of his 163 top-grade games. He started the 2012 Grand Final with Melbourne as an interchange, but a broken neck he sustained in the 2013 preliminary final cost him a spot in that season's decider after he switched to Manly. The neck injury brought about his premature retirement.

3. Ashton Sims
A heavily maligned front-rower with St George Illawarra, Brisbane and then North Queensland, Ashton Sims had started 124 of his 203 first grade matches as a substitute up to the beginning of the 2014 season. Surprisingly, in 13 finals appearances, he has started seven times while coming off the pine just six.

4. Frank Puletua
A tough prop forward who spent most of his career with Penrith, the shaven-headed Frank Puletua started off the bench in 116 of 178 top-grade games. After debuting in 1998, he did not start a game until the 2001 season. Puletua crossed for just one try in his 116 games as an interchange player.

5. George Rose
A cult hero with Manly before shifting to Melbourne in 2014, 'Gorgeous' George Rose debuted with the Sydney Roosters and played 115 of his 133 top-grade games with the Roosters and Sea Eagles as a bench-warmer. Rotund and with plenty of personality, he was often used as an impact player. Rose started the 2011 and 2013 Grand Finals from the bench.

6. Dean Widders
A talented utility with deft skills, Dean Widders was a favourite at the Roosters, Parramatta and South Sydney, where he started as a sub in 114 of his 159 first grade appearances. A three-season stint with Castleford saw him play 33 of 60 games off the bench, while his only rep appearance—with Country in 2006—was as an interchange player.

7. Matthew Bell
Nondescript Penrith and Wests Tigers forward Matthew Bell was an oft-used bench-warmer, starting 113 of his 142 first grade games off the interchange bench. He started more than five games only twice in a season in his eight-year career. His single career try came off the bench against Canterbury in 2008.

8. Craig Wing
An outstanding utility who was typically afforded a starting position at club level, South Sydney and Sydney Roosters star Craig Wing was regularly used as an impact interchange at rep level. All 12 of his State of Origin appearances came off the bench while 10 of his 16 games for Australia came off the pine. Only 60 of his 256 club games were as an interchange player.

9. Chris Armit
An up-and-down prop for Parramatta, Canterbury and Penrith, Chris Armit started 106 of his 160 first grade games as a benchman. An honest type with few bells and whistles about his game, he was often seen as the reliable third or fourth prop in the rotation.

10. John Plath
One of Rugby League's first 'Super Subs', John Plath was a sharp-thinking utility who spent the majority of his career as a bench player in Brisbane's great teams of the 1990s. Debuting in 1990, he played in four Broncos Grand Final wins off the bench. He started as a substitute in 99 of his 149 first grade appearances.

BEST POSITIONAL SWITCHES

1. Darren Lockyer—Fullback to five-eighth
The world's best fullback when he made an unexpected shift to five-eighth in 2004, Darren Lockyer became the world's greatest No.6. The premiership's appearance record-holder and the most capped Queensland and Australian player of all time, Lockyer spent seven years wearing the Broncos, Maroons and Kangaroos No.1 jerseys. At fullback he won three premierships, the 2000 Clive Churchill Medal and three Dally M Fullback of the Year gongs. A controversial move to pivot in 2004 was a raging success, with Lockyer guiding the Broncos to another title, breaking records with Queensland and Australia, and picking up three more Dally M positional awards. Such was his adeptness at both positions that Lockyer won Golden Boots playing both fullback and five-eighth.

2. Brad Fittler—Centre to five-eighth via lock
A prodigious talent who debuted as a 17-year-old, Brad Fittler won Dally M positional gongs at centre, lock and five-eighth during a stellar 16-year career that saw him win titles at both Penrith and the Sydney Roosters while captaining both NSW and Australia. Though playing a touch of five-eighth in the early part of his career, he spent his first five years primarily at centre and the next three as a lock before finishing at No.6. With Laurie Daley on the rep scene, Fittler switched between five-eighth and lock throughout the 1990s.

3. Billy Smith—Centre to halfback

One of the greatest players to don the red and white of St George, revered halfback Billy Smith started his premiership career as a centre. Renowned tough nut Smith played in the centres in St George's 1963, '64 and '65 Grand Final teams before moving to the halfback slot previously occupied by George Evans in 1966. The move was destined to be a success after Smith debuted for NSW and Australia at halfback in 1964; he won Ernie Christensen's Player of the Year gong in 1966. He was named in Australia's Top 100 Players in 2008.

4. Greg Inglis—Centre to fullback via five-eighth

One of the great athletes in the modern game, Greg Inglis played predominantly at centre in club and rep football and won a Clive Churchill Medal at five-eighth before a permanent shift to fullback at South Sydney took his career to the next level. A star of the game from his debut in 2005, Inglis broke into the Queensland and Australian sides a year later. Billy Slater's grip on the mantle of the game's best No.1 meant Inglis was kept from the Storm, Maroons and Kangaroos fullback position, but Michael Maguire's decision to move him at Souths was central to the Bunnies making back-to-back preliminary finals. Inglis won a Golden Boot playing predominantly centre in 2009 and was named Dally M Fullback of the Year in 2013. He has played one Origin and one Test at fullback in Slater's absence.

5. Geoff Toovey—Halfback to hooker

A tough-as-nails Manly icon, the diminutive and blond-haired Geoff Toovey enjoyed stellar careers at both halfback and hooker at all levels of the game. Debuting in 1988 as a half, he wore the Australian No.7 jersey on nine occasions from 1991 to 1995—including the '95 World Cup final, where he played predominantly at dummy-half while hooker Andrew Johns dominated first-receiver duties—and started in the halves for Manly in three straight deciders from 1995 to 1997. He reprised his combination with Johns for NSW in 1996-97 before wearing the No.9 in eight of his last nine Origins. Toovey moved to hooker permanently in 1999 for the last three years of his club career, winning Dally M Hooker of the Year in '99.

6. Steve Morris—Halfback to wing

An outstanding halfback who debuted for Australia from Dapto in 1978, Steve Morris spent over four seasons as a No.7 for St George before Dragons coach Roy Masters successfully moved the diminutive speedster to the wing in 1983. Though a second Test appearance proved elusive, Morris won Dally M Winger of the Year honours in 1984 and '87 and twice represented NSW in Origin football on the flank. His 122 tries for St George and Easts was 26th in premiership history at the start of the 2014 season.

7. Craig Gower—Hooker to halfback

Though he debuted for Penrith at halfback, the Panthers legend spent most of his first six seasons in the top grade at hooker before a permanent shift to the halves for the second half of his Rugby League career. Making his Australian debut at hooker in 1999, Gower played five of his first six Tests at No.9 before his remaining 12 were played in the halves or off the bench. He won the Dally M Hooker of the Year in 2000 and started at halfback for NSW in 2004 and '06.

8. Noel Cleal—Wing/centre to second-row

Behemoth country three-quarter Noel 'Crusher' Cleal spent the better part of his first four years in the premiership in the centres—and debuted for NSW Firsts as an outside back in 1981—before a successful switch to the second-row in 1983 reaped representative rewards and higher accolades. Shifted by coach Bob Fulton during his first year with Manly, the bearded Cleal won the Dally M Second-rower of the Year in 1984 and '86, while all of his 12 Origins and eight Tests came in the second-row or off the bench.

9. Luke Lewis—Wing to lock/second-row

One of the game's finest utilities, Luke Lewis began his career primarily as an outside back before becoming one of Australia's top backrowers. A fine three-quarter with Penrith, he was selected for the 2003 Kangaroo Tour and played three Origins for NSW in '04 as a winger/centre. He moved into the halves for Penrith in 2008 before shifting to lock forward in 2009. Lewis was recalled to the NSW and Australia line-ups in '09 and was a regular in both sides through to the start of the 2014 season, winning the Dally M and RLIF Lock of the Year gong in 2010.

10. Brian Clay—Lock to five-eighth

One of the great figures of the St George team of the 1950s, Brian 'Poppa' Clay started his career with Newtown at centre, playing there in the 1954 and '55 deciders before being signed to the Saints as a lock in 1957. He played at lock in the '57 decider before shifting to five-eighth in 1958 following the emergence of the great Johnny Raper. Clay wore the No.6 jersey in Grand Finals in 1958-61 and 1964-66. His eight Tests included five at five-eighth and three at lock.

Chapter 7

ALL SHAPES AND SIZES

BIGGEST PLAYERS

I. Mark Tookey
To the long soundtrack of "Toooooks" every time he hit the ball up, sizable prop Mark Tookey was a cult hero during stints with South Queensland, Parramatta and New Zealand. He played 125 games, the same (in kilograms) as his listed weight—although that certainly ballooned as his career went on.

2. Jarrad Hickey
A fringe first grade Canterbury prop from 2006 to 2010, Jarrad Hickey was a giant at near 198cm and 130kg. Never a superstar, he had a smart offload and got through plenty of work. Nicknamed 'Oaf' by his teammates.

3. Sam Kasiano
A behemoth front-rower who once claimed to regularly consume seven kebabs in a sitting, the Canterbury prop has remarkable skill for a man his size. Known as 'Dogzilla' because of his immense frame that gets to 135kg and 196cm, Kasiano resembles a professional wrestler more than a professional footballer—though he did win the Dally M Prop of the Year in 2012 and has played six Tests for New Zealand.

4. Dave Taylor
So big that he is known as 'Coal Train', Dave Taylor has been a frustrating player who has the physical tools to be the best in the game but rarely puts it together. A giant at 190cm and 125kg, Taylor has preferred to let his deft passing and kicking do the talking rather than his massive frame. He has represented Queensland six times and Australia once.

5. George Rose
A fan favourite over the course of a decade-long career with the Sydney Roosters, Manly and Melbourne, George Rose was a throwback to a different era when legitimately plump and overweight front-row types were commonplace. He was renowned for his coloured underwear, which was seen more often than would be expected. Known universally in Rugby League as 'Gorgeous George'.

6. Darryl Brohman
Known as 'The Big Marn' because of his hefty girth, Darryl Brohman was a cult figure in a 114-game premiership career with Penrith and Canterbury that saw him twice represent Queensland. A talented ball-playing type with deft skills and some form as a goalkicker, Brohman personified the notion of a halfback in a prop's body.

7. Jamal Idris
Labelled by commentator Phil Gould as "the world's biggest human", Jamal Idris stands at 199cm and weighs in at around the 117kg mark, an incredible size for an outside back. Idris made his mark early in his career with appearances for NSW and Australia, but was widely lambasted for being overweight after a move to the Gold Coast.

8. Sam Backo
An old-school prop with a hefty belly, Sam Backo was one of the dominant front-rowers of the late 1980s. He played 135 games for Canberra and Brisbane, and was a Queensland and Australian representative for three years from 1988 to 1990. He is the only forward to score a try in all three Tests of an Ashes series, achieving the feat on home soil in '88.

9. Billy Weepu
Weighing in at 130kg, the brother of All Black Piri Weepu played 13 games for Manly between 1994 and 1997 as a rugged prop. Big Billy struggled to hold down a first grade berth, though, as his size proved more hindrance than help. Punted by the Sea Eagles, Weepu later worked as a sound technician for *60 Minutes* in New Zealand.

10. Arthur Beetson
An Immortal and all-time Rugby League great, 'Big Artie' joined Balmain in 1965 weighing well under 90kg, but retired at Parramatta tipping the scales at more than 110kg. A peerless ball-playing backrower and prop, he was named in the Team of the Century and is arguably the greatest forward ever to play the game.

TALLEST PLAYERS

1. Phil Mann
Phil 'Spider' Mann, a veteran of 51 first grade games for Parramatta from 1974 to 1981, is arguably Rugby League's most oft-recalled beanpole. The gangly fullback's extra-slim frame accentuated his vertigo-inducing height, which was believed to be beyond the two-metre mark—or over six foot and seven inches in imperial measurement. Mann scored 19 tries for the Eels and featured in the club's 1975 and '77 finals campaigns. He was a late inclusion at fullback for the historic drawn Grand Final against St George in '77.

2. Matt Parsons
South Sydney and Newcastle prop Matt Parsons is quite possibly the tallest player of the modern era, clicking the stadiometer up to 201cm. While his unrivalled height was an obvious talking point, Parsons was a quality front-rower—hard with a dash of skill. Among 164 first grade appearances, he won a Grand Final with the Knights in 2001 and represented Country Origin the following season. With Andrew Johns sidelined, the respected Parsons skippered Newcastle in a finals match in '02.

3. Paul McNicholas
A rugged prop who played 71 first grade games for Souths, Cronulla and North Queensland from 1996 to 2003, the 200cm Paul McNicholas is the type of man-giant that would make you do a double-take in the street. An honest toiler, he represented Ireland and finished his professional career at Hull FC.

4. Paul Hauff
At a shade under 200cm, the mantis-like Paul Hauff immediately evoked comparisons with Parramatta stringbean Phil 'Spider' Mann after debuting for Brisbane in 1990. The fullback enjoyed a meteoric rise, starring in Queensland's heart-stopping Origin series win in '91 and playing in one Test for Australia. Hauff was fast with a loping running style and a massive step, but his career was routinely thwarted by injuries and

he did not participate in the Broncos' Grand Final successes, retiring in 1996 aged just 26. In a freakish coincidence, he played 51 games and scored 19 tries in first grade—the exact same numbers racked up by Eels custodian Mann.

5. Dane Tilse

The tallest timber among a massive front-row rotation at Canberra, the 200cm Dane Tilse developed into a rugged and durable competitor with the Raiders after being sacked by Newcastle at the beginning of 2005 and deregistered by the NRL over an alcohol-fuelled incident. The man-mountain had racked up 171 appearances for the Green Machine by the end of 2013.

6. Peter Shiels

Standing at 197cm (thereby being narrowly denied the moniker 'Two-metre Peter') and aptly nicknamed 'Stretch', Peter Shiels was the tallest second-rower running around in the 1990s when he made 120 first grade appearances for Penrith, Western Suburbs, Western Reds and Newcastle. Shiels was gangly but willing, improving with age and playing in five finals matches for the Knights. He spent the 2001-02 seasons with St Helens, winning a Challenge Cup final and Super League Grand Final before retiring.

7. Garrick Morgan

An absolute pine tree of a Wallabies lock, Garrick Morgan was rated among the best Rugby Union forwards in the world when he became a high-profile acquisition for the fledgling South Queensland Crushers in 1995. The two-metre 25-year-old's code switch garnered just two first grade appearances at prop, however, and he returned to Union and the Australian Test side the following season.

8. David Klemmer

Thankfully, Canterbury tyro David Klemmer graduated to the NRL ranks in 2013—watching the 199cm prop terrorising opposing teenagers in the NYC was enough to make even the most sadistic of Rugby League viewers wince. Klemmer was just 19 when he debuted in the opening round of the season, but he was somehow still not tall enough to avoid a kick to the face from airborne Melbourne fullback Billy Slater. Injury wrecked his rookie season after just four first grade appearances.

9. Dane Laurie

While enforcer Dane Laurie was a fearsome sight in the pack for Wests Tigers and Penrith at 198cm, his career has failed to reach similar heights. The giant front-rower made 20 appearances for the Tigers (2008-09) and three for the Panthers (2010) but has been plagued by off-field issues. The dreadlocked monster was selected in the inaugural Indigenous All Stars team in 2010 but withdrew injured.

10. George Treweek

Science boffins hypothesise that the average human height for males has increased by up to 10cm over the past 100 years. Accordingly, pre-World War II Rugby League players are unlikely to win any "tallest player ever" contests. But at 194cm (six feet four inches), legendary South Sydney second-rower George Treweek was a bona fide giant of his era in both stature and ability. Work commitments restricted the genial but devastating Treweek—who was described as "all arms and legs"—to seven Tests for Australia, but he featured in six Rabbitohs premierships from 1926 to 1932 and rates among the greatest forwards in the history of the game.

SMALLEST PLAYERS

1. George McGowan

George McGowan is regarded as the smallest first grade player in history, reportedly tipping the scales at just 47.6kg during his career. He played 73 games for Easts (1915), Souths (1916-18) and Wests (1919-22).

2. Arthur Justice

Historians have recorded St George hooker Arthur 'Snowy' Justice as the lightest player to feature at international level. A fierce competitor, the tiny rake played five Tests against England in 1928 and on the 1929-30 Kangaroo Tour despite weighing in at only 63.4kg. Justice played 111 games for the Saints and represented NSW in 18 interstate games, and later made a major contribution to his club as a coach and administrator.

3. John Kolc

The shortest player to represent Australia, Parramatta halfback John Kolc scored a try in his only international appearance—a 13-12 win over Great Britain in the 1977 World Cup. He ticked the stadiometer over at just 160cm but still managed 112 games for the Eels, including Grand Final appearances in 1976-77.

4. Mark Shulman

Pocket-sized St George halfback Mark Shulman was quite possibly the shortest player in first grade history at just 155cm. A long-time understudy to the great Billy Smith, Shulman played 58 games for the Dragons from 1971 to 1978. He turned out in the historic drawn Grand Final against Parramatta in '77, but missed the club's replay victory through injury.

5. Dennis Ward

Halfback Dennis Ward was a measly 55kg when he was graded by Canterbury, and had only added 6kg by the time he debuted in first grade in 1964. After joining Manly, he made the first of four Test appearances in 1969 at a welterweight-esque 65.2kg. Ward left Sydney after helping the Sea Eagles to their maiden title in '72; he toured with the Kangaroos the following season from Newcastle Wests.

6. Allan Langer

Providing proof that there is still room for the little men in modern Rugby League, the 165cm Allan Langer became one of the greatest halfbacks of all time and was perhaps the dominant player of the 1990s. Queensland coach Wayne Bennett and several senior players famously held reservations over the blond Ipswich No.7's ability to handle the rigours of Origin football when he was selected to debut in 1987, but his brilliant and courageous performances saw him thrive at representative level for 16 seasons. The impish Langer was purportedly under the 70kg mark when he debuted for Australia in 1988.

7. Geoff Toovey

Regularly described as pound-for-pound one of the toughest and most courageous players in the game's history, Manly halfback Geoff Toovey didn't just tackle players who were 40-plus kilos heavier than him—he routinely smashed them. The tenacious, brave livewire weighed around the 70kg mark (less when his top-grade career began in 1988) and was just 168cm tall. An inspirational leader, he played 286 first grade games, 15 Origins for NSW and 10 Tests for Australia, and skippered Manly to a premiership in 1996.

8. Preston Campbell

One of the most courageous small men of the NRL era, Indigenous utility back Preston Campbell was just 167cm tall and weighed around 70kg during his remarkable 267-game first grade career. The three-time Country Origin rep was a Dally M Medal-winning halfback at Cronulla in 2001 and won a Grand Final as a five-eighth with Penrith before playing predominantly at fullback in five seasons for the Gold Coast Titans.

9. James Sandy

Miniature Redcliffe halfback James Sandy became a Challenge Cup hero during an off-season stint at Castleford. The 162cm Indigenous livewire, a popular star of the BRL throughout the 1980s, was used as a winger by Cas during the 1985-86 English winter, and scored a memorable individual try to help the club to a 15-14 Wembley final triumph over Hull KR.

10. Steve Topper

Just 163cm tall with a wiry physique, Steve Topper played seven games for South Sydney in 1979 at halfback and hooker. His tiny size was seen as a factor behind the Rabbitohs cutting him from their import list prior to the following season, but the Cronulla junior joined Wests Wollongong and represented City Firsts, playing opposite Tom Raudonikis in a 55-2 loss. Topper was the Illawarra Steelers' foundation halfback and made 25 first grade appearances during their first three seasons.

Chapter 8

SELECTIONS

LEFT-FIELD FIRST GRADE SELECTIONS

1. Greg Smith
In Australian Rugby League's favourite curiosity of the modern era, it is doubtful whether more words have been written about the rise to first grade and subsequent debut of a player who appeared in just one game. African-American Greg Smith was signed by Newcastle in 1999 on the falsified pretence of having previously played for NFL franchise the Philadelphia Eagles. He was, however, fast and athletic—and the Knights' incoming coach, Warren Ryan, who had coached Smith in the USA team at the '97 World Sevens, could not wait to get him on to the wing in the top grade. Smith had spent 1998 with Western Suburbs in the Metropolitan Cup, but it has passed into folklore that his defensive ineptitude and Teflon-like handling allowed Canterbury to turn a 16-point deficit with 18 minutes remaining into a 28-26 Round 3 victory over Smith and the shell-shocked Knights. He was unsurprisingly dropped by Ryan and released by the club midway through the season, by which stage his pro-football ruse had been uncovered.

2. Sam Thaiday
Brisbane's premiership defence descended into injury-ravaged chaos during the second half of 2007, most notably with the loss of five-eighth and captain Darren

Lockyer with seven rounds remaining. Lock hitman Tonie Carroll and young backrower Greg Eastwood were used in the pivot role as the Broncos limped towards the finals, but master coach Wayne Bennett was forced to come up with another alternative when Carroll broke down ahead of their qualifying final showdown with minor premiers Melbourne. He opted for burly representative second-rower Sam Thaiday in the No.6—and the eighth-placed Broncos were duly buried 40-0 by the rampant Storm.

3. Larry Corowa

Electrifying winger Larry 'The Black Flash' Corowa scored 64 tries in 98 games for Balmain from 1978 to 1983 and represented Australia in the '79 Ashes series. He returned to Tweed Heads in the mid-1980s and had long disappeared from the consciousness of the Rugby League public when he was named as a shock inclusion at fullback for the struggling Gold Coast in 1991, fulfilling a promise he had made to Seagulls captain Wally Lewis. In his first top-grade match in eight years, the 34-year-old scored a try in a 34-18 loss to Souths; he completed his fascinating comeback with an interchange appearance against Penrith a week later.

4. Brad Fittler

Schoolboy prodigy Brad Fittler dazzled when he came off the bench for heavyweights Penrith in the last two regular season matches of 1989. But crusty coach Ron Willey stunned everyone by pitching the 17-year-old into the starting five-eighth role for the finals, leaving cast-iron veteran Chris Mortimer—a NSW Origin No.6 earlier in the season—on the bench. Fittler performed admirably as the Panthers sank to back-to-back losses, scoring a try against Balmain, but Willey's outlandish selection policy was not appreciated by the club's management and he was punted as coach at the end of the year. History would show that Fittler was selected as the Blues' five-eighth in an Origin decider opposite Wally Lewis at just 19, and went on to become one of the best ever to play the position.

5. Palmer Wapau

A Redcliffe cult hero equally suited to prop, second-row or five-eighth, 108kg Torres Strait Islander Palmer Wapau was the shock choice to replace underperforming bench behemoth David Taylor in 2009 by Brisbane coach Ivan Henjak. A part-time groundsman, the 26-year-old Wapau—previously described by Matt Bowen as "the best footballer not to play NRL"—ultimately made five appearances for the Broncos in '09.

6. Billy Wilson

Front-row tough guy Billy Wilson played 11 Tests for Australia and featured in six premiership triumphs for the famous St George side of the 1950s and '60s, joining Norths in 1963 after a tenure with the Dragons spanning 15 seasons. 'Captain Blood' retired in 1966 and took over as the Bears' non-playing coach the following season, but was forced to pull on the boots for three games in '67 as injuries decimated his first grade squad. Wilson thus remains the only player to appear in first grade at the age of 40, and the only player with a first grade career spanning 20 seasons.

7. Sonny Bill Williams

Controversial code-swapper Sonny Bill Williams made a spectacular return to the NRL in 2013 as an industrious, destructive and brilliantly skilled second-row force with the Roosters. But with NSW Origin commitments claiming both of the Tricolours' first-choice halves, the 194cm and 108kg Kiwi became quite possibly the biggest starting halfback in premiership history after a late line-up reshuffle for their clash with Canterbury. 'SBW' produced his second man-of-the-match showing against his former club in the space of nine weeks, displaying ample ball-playing class to spearhead the Roosters' short-handed 20-18 win.

8. Jordan Rankin

With the Gold Coast's halves stocks taking an injury-inflicted battering late in 2008 and the club's finals hopes dwindling, coach John Cartwright called up the youngest first grade player in 72 years to come off the bench against Newcastle. At just 16 years and 238 days, promising schoolboy Jordan Rankin became the third-youngest player in premiership history—and the youngest since prop Jack Arnold debuted for Wests in 1936. Rankin performed creditably in the 20-point loss but did not receive another NRL chance until 2011 (he was still just 19), and had made only 17 appearances as a half or fullback by the end of 2013.

9. Phil Blake

Any player with a turn of pace and half-decent ball skills is considered a potential hooker these days, but the phenomenon of selecting livewire backline specialists in the front-row was still in its infancy when Auckland coach John Monie pitched tryscoring freak Phil Blake into the dummy-half role in 1996. Experienced in every position in the backline, the 32-year-old journeyman wore the Warriors' No.9 in five games and—true to form—still managed a couple of tries.

10. Alex Glenn

Brisbane reached the preliminary final stage in 2009 after despatching minor premiers St George Illawarra in week two, but the club's campaign was thrown into disarray after halfback Peter Wallace suffered a serious ankle injury late in the win over the Dragons. First-year coach Ivan Henjak mulled over the options, eventually settling on rookie Alex Glenn—a second-rower or centre—to wear the No.7 against the mighty Melbourne Storm. In a late reshuffle, captain Darren Lockyer moved to halfback and lock Tonie Carroll, who had come out of retirement mid-season, shifted to five-eighth. The Broncos were trounced 40-12, a loss that was reminiscent of their heavy finals defeat at the hands of the Storm with a makeshift halves pairing two years earlier.

ONE-GAME WONDERS—FIRST GRADE

1. John Rheinberger (Eastern Suburbs)
Eastern Suburbs centre John Rheinberger's only top-grade start was, incredibly, the 1975 Grand Final rout of St George. Rheinberger replaced the injured Mark Harris after being plucked from obscurity by coach Jack Gibson. The three-quarter didn't play top grade again despite having a fine game in the 38-0 win, injuring himself during the following pre-season.

2. Richard Clarke (Newcastle)
A toiling front-row forward who got his only start against Balmain representing the Newcastle Knights in 1989, Richard Clarke scored a try in the 20-12 win but it wasn't enough to earn another top-grade spot. Clarke did play a Test for France in 1993— a 48-6 loss to Great Britain.

3. Dane Chisholm (Melbourne)
Another who played just one top-grade game yet represented France, journeyman Dane Chisholm tasted first grade with Melbourne in 2011. Chisholm, whose father Rick and uncle Wayne played premiership football, played on the wing in the Storm's 20-12 loss to Canberra as a late inclusion. He played three end-of-season Tests for France, scoring three tries against Scotland, but has yet to get another shot at first grade football.

4. Adrian Bubb (Newcastle)
Talented Under-23s prop Adrian Bubb received his only top-grade cap in Newcastle's debut season of 1988. Bubb turned in a fearless showing, crunching Balmain centre Scott Gale, before leaving the paddock with a broken nose. Bubb was told by coach Allan McMahon to smash any Tiger he could, and he followed those instructions to a tee.

5. Jeremy Robinson (Canberra)
An honest five-eighth who got the call-up to top grade in 1996, Jeremy Robinson proved the difference in a solid debut. With Canberra losing a number of stars to Origin, he was called into replace Laurie Daley and successfully landed his only shot at goal in a thrilling 16-14 win over Illawarra.

6. Steve Meredith (Sydney Roosters)
A highly rated junior who was an Australian Schoolboys and NSW Under-19 rep, Sydney Roosters prop Steve Meredith carried high hopes. He enjoyed plenty of success in taking the Roosters to two Premier League deciders, but a season-ending knee injury in his first grade debut brought his promising career to a halt.

7. Greg Smith (Newcastle)
The most infamous one-gamer in premiership history, American Greg Smith endured one of the most horrific top-grade outings as the Bulldogs peppered him with bomb after bomb. Smith had been touted as a former Philadelphia Eagles NFL player but it was later revealed he had fabricated the entire story.

8. Scott Lacaze (Brisbane)
One of the famous 'Baby Broncos' who famously toppled the Wests Tigers in 2002, Scott Lacaze's only top-grade showing was in that famous win. He came off the bench in a team bereft of stars captained by Shane Walker, and celebrated in the shock 28-14 victory at Campbelltown.

9. Alwyn Simpson (Brisbane)
A speedy winger who was graded by Canberra, Alwyn Simpson played his only first grade game on the flank of Brisbane's 40-0 qualifying final loss to Melbourne in 2007. Simpson received precious few opportunities in the rout but went on to enjoy a nice career with Redcliffe in the Queensland Cup.

10. Karl Filiga (Cronulla)
Signed from Canterbury in 2007 on a huge $600,000 contract despite never having played a top-grade game, Sharks recruit Karl Filiga made just one appearance before quitting the club in 2009. He came off the bench and played 11 minutes in a 24-22 win over Penrith in 2008, but a series of knee injuries stymied a promising career.

GRAND FINAL BOLTERS

1. John Rheinberger—Eastern Suburbs, 1975
John Rheinberger was drafted into Eastern Suburbs' line-up for the 1975 Grand Final after Test centre Mark Harris suffered a broken leg in the preliminary final. The unknown 21-year-old played his part in the record-breaking 38-0 defeat of St George in just his second first grade appearance and his maiden start. With a shoulder injury

stunting his progress the following season, Rheinberger never featured in the top flight again but went on to become an indoor cricket star.

2. Peter Boulton—Balmain, 1969

Balmain's 1969 Grand Final boilover defeat of South Sydney was achieved with a hooker making his first start in the top grade. John Crawford replaced Norm Miller at dummy-half in the Tigers' side for the preliminary final showdown against Manly, and Peter Boulton made his debut off the bench. The Grafton product was elevated to the starting side for the Grand Final and produced a fine display opposite Test rake Elwyn Walters as the Tigers downed raging-hot favourites the Rabbitohs 11-2. Boulton represented NSW Colts against Great Britain in 1970 and went on to play 95 first grade games during a lean period for the Tigers, departing at the end of 1975.

3. Greg Norgard—South Sydney, 1967

Young centre/five-eighth Greg Norgard arrived at Souths from Newcastle in 1967, making five first grade appearances during the regular season before featuring in the club's reserve grade Grand Final loss. He sat on the bench for the first grade Grand Final as Souths' reserve back, entering the fray after winger Michael Cleary left the field injured. Following a backline reshuffle, Norgard slotted in at pivot and helped the Rabbitohs to a gripping 12-10 win over Canterbury. He stayed at the club for a further five seasons but made just 21 appearances in the top grade, including only one further finals match—again as a replacement, in the 1968 major semi loss to Manly.

4. Matthew Callinan—Canterbury, 1985

Young fullback/winger Matthew Callinan made his first grade debut off the bench for defending premiers Canterbury in the penultimate round of the 1985 regular season. After starting the finals series in reserve grade, he scored the Bulldogs' only try as a replacement in their major semi loss to St George three weeks later and crossed for a memorable double on the wing as they routed archrivals Parramatta 26-0 in the preliminary final. Callinan featured on the flank in the club's dour 7-6 Grand Final defeat of the Dragons—just his fifth appearance in the top flight. He began 1986 as a first-choice winger and scored an early-season hat-trick against Penrith, but was replaced by Peter Mortimer after six rounds and never played first grade again.

5. Russell Aitken—Melbourne, 2008

A fringe NRL player after he had debuted as an 18-year-old for Cronulla in 2003, Russell Aitken was thrust into the hot seat following Melbourne skipper Cameron Smith's controversial suspension during the 2008 finals series. The versatile Aitken had made seven appearances at five-eighth, hooker and centre during the regular season before he was handed the No.9 jumper for the preliminary final clash with his former club. Melbourne swept aside the Sharks 28-0, with Aitken performing adequately at dummy-half, but the Storm missed Smith's influence as they crashed to a record 40-0 loss to Manly in the Grand Final. The decider was Aitken's 17th and last first grade appearance; he was released by Melbourne during the off-season and had subsequent stints in France with AS Carcassonne, in England with Gateshead, and in the Illawarra competition with Helensburgh.

6. Steve Halliwell—Parramatta, 1982

England-born Steve Halliwell, whose father, Frank, played for Wigan, immigrated to Australia as an infant and represented Australia in Rugby Union at schoolboy level. He played a solitary game for St George in 1981 before linking with Parramatta the following season. His initial appearance for the Eels was as a replacement in the 33-0 preliminary final drubbing of Easts, and he retained a bench spot for their Grand Final victory over Manly a week later—his third first grade game. He scored two tries off the bench against Newtown in the opening round of 1983, but that was to be his last appearance for Parramatta. Returning to England, Halliwell enjoyed stints with Leigh and St Helens before playing two games for the fledgling Gold Coast-Tweed Giants in '88 to take his first grade total in Australia to a modest six.

7. Nigel Gaffey—Canberra, 1990

Backrower Nigel Gaffey made his first grade debut for Canberra in 1989 with a solitary appearance off the bench, then forced his way back into the Raiders' squad in round 18 of 1990. The 20-year-old capitalised on Test lock Bradley Clyde's season-ending injury to forge a starting spot on the eve of the finals, receiving a premiership winner's medal in just his ninth top-grade game courtesy of Canberra's 18-14 defeat of Penrith in the Grand Final. The versatile Gaffey represented Country Origin in 1993 and retired in 2000 with 177 appearances to his credit following stints with Eastern Suburbs, South Queensland and Penrith.

8. Chris Guider—St George, 1985

Chris Guider created history in 1985 as St George qualified for Grand Finals in all three grades, despite his slipping down the pecking order to third-string hooker at the club. The pint-sized rake played 15 first grade games in '84, but Phil Ritchie and Tony Townsend were preferred the following season. Nevertheless, Guider helped the Dragons' Under-23s to victory in their Grand Final and came off the bench in the reserve grade side's decider success. He was then used as a replacement as the Saints went down 7-6 to Canterbury in the first grade Grand Final—just his second appearance in the top flight that season, and only the 17th of his career. Guider captained the club during a disappointing '86 campaign before quitting the game to dedicate his time to the Church of Scientology, a faith he later publicly renounced (in 2011). His achievement in playing Grand Finals in all three grades on the same day is unique in the code's history.

9. John Plath—Brisbane, 1992
Uber-utility John Plath featured in four Grand Final victories for Brisbane, but his first grade career was only just gathering momentum when he came off the bench in the club's inaugural triumph. After making just three appearances in 1990-91, the specialist half secured an interchange spot in the closing rounds of '92 and took the field during the Broncos' 28-8 defeat of St George in the decider—his 10th game in the top grade. He came off the bench in subsequent Grand Final wins in 1993 and '97-98 among 149 appearances for the club.

10. Daniel Abraham—Newcastle, 2001
Hardworking Newcastle backrower Daniel Abraham collected a premiership ring in just his 14th first grade appearance. The Macquarie United junior debuted for the Knights as a 19-year-old in 2000 but was unable to forge a permanent first grade position. He played just three NRL games in the first six months of the 2001 season but featured in the Knights' last three regular season matches and came off the bench in the preliminary final defeat of Cronulla to snag an interchange spot for the Grand Final showdown with Parramatta, playing his role in Newcastle's 30-24 upset victory. A fine goalkicker, Abraham made 100 first grade appearances during an injury-plagued tenure with Newcastle and represented Country Origin in 2003-04; he ended his NRL career with a season for North Queensland in 2008.

ORIGIN BOLTERS

1. Ben Ikin
Ben Ikin had made just four first grade appearances with the lowly Gold Coast Seagulls when he was called into Queensland's Super League-depleted squad for the 1995 series opener. The centre/five-eighth became the youngest player in Origin history at 18 years and 83 days. Famously mistaken for an autograph-hunting schoolboy by coach Paul Vautin at the team hotel, Ikin made a fine contribution off the bench to the Maroons' extraordinary 3-0 series triumph, and went on to represent his state 17 times.

2. Phil Duke
Moree Boomerangs star Phil Duke became the first player to represent NSW in Origin from a country club after he received a call-up for the 1982 decider—he was

the Blues' fifth winger selected in the series despite having played in Country Firsts' 47-3 loss to a star-studded City Firsts outfit. The Indigenous flyer scored a dubious first-half try in his only Origin outing before an infamous in-goal mix-up with NSW fullback Phil Sigsworth resulted in a series-winning try to Wally Lewis and sealed Duke's place in the Rugby League hall of infamy.

3. Rex Wright
North Newcastle hooker Rex Wright holds the distinction of being the last country-based player to represent the Blues, ousting the likes of Royce Simmons, Ray Brown and Michael Bolt to wear the NSW No.12 in the 1984 series opener after starring in Country Seconds' upset of City Seconds. Wright topped the tackle and run counts for the Blues, but was replaced by Simmons ahead of game two following Queensland's emphatic 29-12 victory.

4. Jacob Lillyman
Cowboys second-rower Jacob Lillyman earned his first Queensland call-up for the must-win game-two encounter in 2006 despite boasting just 19 NRL appearances, including only one hit-out in the previous 10 weeks due to injury. After a sound debut he was kept out of the decider by injury, but he went on to make a further five Origin appearances in 2007-08 and '11 from the Cowboys and Warriors.

5. Willie Carne
Roma winger Willie Carne's first grade career with the Broncos was just six games old when he was drafted into the Queensland line-up for the 1990 game-three dead-rubber, replacing Norths' Les Kiss. He repaid the Maroons selectors' foresight by becoming arguably the world's best winger in the ensuing seasons and representing Queensland a further 11 times.

6. Adam Mogg
Adam Mogg was a Queensland Cup star with Redcliffe and had developed into a handy outside back for Canberra, but he would have been on very few pundits' radar as a contender to help alleviate Queensland's backline injury crisis during the 2006 series. He was called up to replaced injured teenage sensation Greg Inglis for the must-win game two and his selection was greeted by "Adam who?" headlines. However, he sealed a place in Origin folklore with a brilliant double on debut and another spectacular try in the Maroons' decider triumph.

7. Brad Izzard
Penrith rookie Brad Izzard had just turned 20 and had only 12 first grade appearances under his belt when he was selected on the NSW bench for the 1982 series opener. He crossed for a match-sealing try on debut as the Blues recorded their first Origin win,

then scored a sensational 50-metre individual try in the game-two loss after being promoted to starting centre. Izzard's outing in the dour decider loss was his last for NSW until 1991—an Origin-record gap between appearances of almost nine years.

8. Chris Beattie
Arguably the least heralded of Queensland's 10 debutants selected for the crucial 2001 series opener, Chris Beattie was picked despite boasting just 18 NRL appearances for Cronulla and spending two weeks on the sideline earlier that season on a biting charge. The 24-year-old Ipswich product enjoyed a sound debut in the game-one victory before being dropped in the wake of the Maroons' comprehensive game-two loss. He made one further Origin appearance, as the suspended Petero Civoniceva's replacement in Queensland's gripping 26-18 game two win in 2002.

9. Jamie Buhrer
A veteran of 37 NRL games and a Grand Final victory with Manly, the versatile Jamie Buhrer was a controversial selection as NSW's bench utility for the 2012 series opener, with regular interchange specialist Kurt Gidley on the injured list. Buhrer was afforded just seven minutes at dummy-half in the Blues' 18-10 loss in Melbourne and has not been sighted at Origin level since.

10. Terry Cook
An honest toiler in the centres or in the backrow during four seasons at the Gold Coast, Terry Cook joined the South Queensland Crushers in 1995 and was selected on the bench in Queensland's ragtag squad after the embargo on Super League-aligned players robbed the Maroons of most of their stars. Cook's contribution to the famous 3-0 boilover is often overlooked, but the 29-year-old was superb throughout the series and memorably set up Adrian Lam for a crucial try in game two.

ONE-GAME WONDERS—STATE OF ORIGIN

1. Arthur Beetson
One of Origin's most revered figures, Immortal Arthur Beetson, set the tone for Rugby League's most intense rivalry when he captained Queensland in the inaugural 1980 encounter as a 35-year-old. He turned in one of his finest performances, setting up two tries with brilliant offloads while smashing anything in blue. Beetson started Origin's first brawl by thumping Graeme Wynn, while his swinging arm on fellow Parramatta Eel Mick Cronin set aside fears that club teammates would take it easy on each other.

2. David Peachey

Long-striding Cronulla fullback David Peachey astonishingly played just a single Origin encounter despite winning back-to-back Dally M Fullback of the Year gongs in 1999-2000. A shock omission from the NSW team in 1999, he was a late call-up for the injured Robbie Ross in the 2000 opener and was magnificent, scoring the match-winner after setting up the equaliser nine minutes from time. Injury ruled Peachey out for the remainder of the series, though, and cruelled his chances over the next two seasons.

3. Hazem El Masri

Record-pointscoring Canterbury winger Hazem El Masri made a belated Origin debut in 2007 at 31 years of age and five years after playing his solitary Test. El Masri was a late call-up for the 2007 dead-rubber, replacing the injured Jamie Lyon, and was superb, scoring a try and booting three sideline goals in the 18-4 win. Despite being named in the Team of the 2000s, he was not selected again with Jarryd Hayne, Anthony Quinn, Steve Turner, James McManus and David Williams all preferred during the following two years.

4. Tom Raudonikis

A NSW Origin legend and one with unparalleled Blue passion, Tom Raudonikis rated among his state's best during the first State of Origin match. The tenacious Raudonikis, who captained NSW in the inaugural clash, was reliable in defence and scored the Blues' only second-half try in the 20-10 defeat. He would go on to coach NSW to a series victory in 1997.

5. Brett Rodwell

A tough and burly centre from the Illawarra Steelers, Brett Rodwell made his only Origin appearance from the bench during the 1995 series. He scored a superb bustling try in the 20-12 loss at the MCG but cruelly had his season ended in the same movement, with his knee giving way during the play.

6. Rod Reddy

Among Queensland's best in the inaugural Origin encounter of 1980, Rod Reddy was one of the highest-profile stars to return to the Maroon jersey under the new format. The experienced Reddy—a Test player and two-time premiership winner—carted the ball up 19 times, menacing the Blues all game in a 20-10 boilover.

7. Ricky Walford

A great tryscoring winger who played primarily with St George, Ricky Walford made his one Origin appearance in the opening game of the 1990 series. Walford was instrumental in setting up NSW's only try in the 8-0 victory. He was selected for the second encounter but was a late withdrawal through injury and was never again named on the NSW wing.

8. John Hopoate

A notorious figure on and off the field, John Hopoate made his Origin debut in 1995—his first full season of first grade—but inconsistent form and a long list of misdemeanours prevented him from ever again donning the blue of NSW. Hopoate was famously involved in the game-two brawl, squaring off with Manly teammate Danny Moore, but was outplayed by opposite Brett Dallas and dumped for David Hall in the dead-rubber series finale.

9. Phil Blake

Arguably the greatest tryscoring half in the history of the premiership, Phil Blake set the competition alight during the 1980s while at Manly and South Sydney. He won the Dally M Rookie of the Year in 1982 but made just a single Origin appearance for NSW seven years later, coming off the bench in the 36-16 game-three defeat. Blake spent another eight seasons in first grade but was never recalled.

10. Phil Duke

One of Origin's most infamous figures, Phil Duke was plucked from the Moree Boomerangs to play his only interstate encounter for the Blues in the 1982 decider. He scored a questionable try but is best remembered for his in-goal mix-up and fumble with fullback Phil Sigsworth that led to a Wally Lewis try and a 10-5 Queensland win.

BEST NOT TO PLAY ORIGIN

1. Darren Britt

Despite playing nine Tests between 1998 and 2000, hulking Orange-born prop Darren Britt was overlooked time and time again by Origin selectors. Playing with Canterbury over the latter stages of his career, he was a fine offloader and a tenacious defender. The likes of Paul Harragon, Glenn Lazarus, Mark Carroll, Jason Stevens, Robbie Kearns and Rodney Howe all got the nod ahead of Britt when it came to NSW selection.

2. Nathan Blacklock

Dragons flyer Nathan Blacklock was one of the grandest and most exciting wingers ever to play the game, and it remains a tragedy to this day that he never pulled on the blue jersey of NSW. The last player to top premiership tryscoring three years in a row, he scored an amazing 96 tries in four seasons from 1998 to 2001 and won three Dally M Winger of the Year gongs on the way, but was passed over for the likes of Jason Moodie, Matt Geyer and Jamie Ainscough. Blacklock played two Tests for Australia.

3. Luke Patten
An ultra-reliable fullback and one of Canterbury's favourite sons, Luke Patten played 282 games predominantly for the Bulldogs, but in an era of fine custodians he was consistently overlooked. A three-time Country Origin rep and a premiership winner, he was stuck behind the likes of Anthony Minichiello, Brett Stewart, Brett Hodgson and Mark Hughes.

4. Lance Thompson
A passionate and committed backrower who never gave anything short of his best, Lance Thompson was touted for Origin selection a number of times during his 14-year career but never received the tap on the shoulder. He played five times for City and was often rated among the Dragons' best in the early part of his career, but the likes of Nathan Hindmarsh, Andrew Ryan, Ben Kennedy and Bryan Fletcher prevented his elevation to Origin rep status.

5. Preston Campbell
Preston Campbell was the shock winner of the 2001 Dally M Medal, but his size and versatility counted against him with NSW selectors. One of the toughest players the code has known, the tiny halfback-cum-fullback played 14 seasons in the NRL and won a title with Penrith but was constantly overlooked for higher rep honours, playing for Country just three times.

6. Matt Orford
The 2008 Dally M Medal winner, Matt Orford, is one of just four eligible Dally M winners not to play State of Origin football. The short and stocky halfback was called into the NSW side in 2004 for the second game, but a calf injury ruled him out and he was destined never to represent his state. Orford captained Manly to a premiership in 2008.

7. Colin van der Voort
A tireless lock with Penrith whose body sadly didn't allow him to win the rep honours he deserved, Colin van der Voort was selected on the bench for the series opener in 1991 but a knee injury ruled him out and he was never selected again. He played twice for City Origin, won a premiership with Penrith in 1991 and was touted for selection on the 1990 Kangaroo Tour before injury again took hold.

8. Chris Lawrence
Chris Lawrence is a scintillating Wests Tigers outside back who played six Tests across 2010-11, but injuries and inopportune form lapses have kept him out of the Blues' Origin picture. Mark Gasnier, Michael Jennings, Josh Morris and Beau Scott are some of the names to have played centre for NSW since Lawrence has been touted.

9. Danny Lee
A relentless worker who regularly topped tackle counts before they became trendy, Danny Lee grafted out a fine 11-year career with Cronulla. He won the Dally M Prop of the Year award in 1995, but his Super League allegiances ruled him ineligible for Origin as backrowers Adam Muir and David Fairleigh were both selected as back-up starters to Paul Harragon and Mark Carroll. Lee represented Country in 1996 and played a single match for the Super League NSW outfit in 1997.

10. Alan Tongue
Tamworth-born Alan Tongue, a hardworking lock and inspirational captain for Canberra who played 220 games for the Raiders, was regularly overlooked for representative honours. The 2008 Dally M Lock of the Year award and a Country call-up in 2009 garnered a push for Tongue's inclusion but his size counted against him, with the likes of Trent Waterhouse, Luke O'Donnell and Ben Creagh preferred.

INTERNATIONAL BOLTERS

1. Geoff Starling
Teenage centre Geoff Starling was picked for Australia's short tour of New Zealand in 1971 after he had made only a handful of first grade appearances for Balmain. He played both minor matches across the Tasman, becoming Australia's youngest-ever representative at 18 years and 178 days. Starling made the first of 11 Test appearances the following season and toured with the 1973 Kangaroos, but a mystery illness—later diagnosed as Addison's disease—halted his progress soon after and prematurely ended his career.

2. Brad Godden
Brad Godden had made just four first grade appearances prior to 1992, but his stellar performances at fullback in Newcastle's charge to a maiden finals series caught the attention of the national selectors and the 23-year-old contentiously ousted Grand Final custodians Michael Potter and Julian O'Neill for a place in Australia's World Cup final tour squad at the end of the year. He played in warm-up matches against Huddersfield and Sheffield, but Tim Brasher was preferred in the No.1 for the showdown with Great Britain and Godden never featured in representative football again.

3. Jim Lisle
Rugby Union convert Jim Lisle's ascension to dual international status was preposterously fast. A hamstring injury delayed the four-Test Wallaby's start with

South Sydney in 1962, but after just one match for his new club he was selected to debut for NSW and subsequently received a call-up to play five-eighth in the dead-rubber third Ashes Test. Lisle's League career was chequered by injury, but he toured with the 1963-64 Kangaroos, made the last of six Test appearances and captained Souths to a Grand Final in '65, and won a premiership with the Rabbitohs in '67.

4. Kerry Boustead
Innisfail winger Kerry Boustead became just the second 18-year-old to play Test football for Australia in 1978, coming from nowhere to claim a spot on the flank for the series against New Zealand after starring in Queensland's interstate series loss. Debuting aged 18 years and 316 days, the diminutive flyer scored four tries in the three Tests against the Kiwis before carving out a career as one of the greatest-ever wingers. He finished with 15 tries in 25 Test appearances.

5. Brad Fittler
Penrith prodigy Brad 'Freddy' Fittler became the first player to graduate to full international honours a year after representing Australian Schoolboys. The centre/five-eighth's outstanding finals performances saw him oust the likes of Rookie of the Year Jason Martin for a spot in the 1990 Kangaroo Tour squad and became the youngest-ever Australian player to tour Britain and France at 18 years and 229 days. Fittler scored eight tries in eight minor tour matches before making the first of 40 Test appearances the following season against Papua New Guinea while he was still a teenager.

6. Krisnan Inu
Even the most scrupulous of New Zealand Rugby League fans would have been puzzled when the Kiwi line-up for the 2007 trans-Tasman Test was announced. The player named in the perpetually troublesome fullback spot was Parramatta's Krisnan Inu, a veteran of one NRL match—as a centre. The unknown 20-year-old was nevertheless outstanding on debut, arguably the Kiwis' best in a disappointing 30-6 loss in Brisbane, and he went on to become one of the season's standout rookies after cementing a permanent role in the Eels' backline.

7. Steve Morris
'Slippery' Steve Morris became the last player to represent Australia in Test football from a NSW country club when he was selected to play halfback against New Zealand in 1978. The 21-year-old Dapto whippet had only recently debuted for NSW before he featured in the 24-2 first Test defeat of the Kiwis, but he was replaced by Queenslander Greg Oliphant for the second encounter and was left out of the Kangaroo Tour squad at the end of the year. Morris won a premiership with St George in '79 and later made a successful transition to the wing, but he did not rise above NSW Origin status during the remainder of his career.

8. Braith Anasta

Bulldogs five-eighth Braith Anasta became the first player to represent the Junior Kangaroos and the senior Australian Test side in the same season. He skippered the Junior Kangaroos midway through 2001 before claiming Dally M Rookie of the Year honours and winning selection in the Kangaroo Tour squad at year's end. The 19-year-old came off the bench in all four Tests against Papua New Guinea and Great Britain. Although he was a NSW regular and one of the NRL's most prominent playmakers, Anasta never represented his country again.

9. Trent Waterhouse

Premiership success often yields a Test bolter, and Penrith's surprise capture of the 2003 title catapulted backrower Trent Waterhouse into the representative limelight. Virtually unknown at the start of the year and a veteran of just 30 NRL matches (including only five starts), Waterhouse was selected in the Kangaroo Tour squad at the end of '03. The 22-year-old came off the bench in all three Tests of the injury-hit Australian side's remarkable Ashes whitewash of Great Britain, beginning an international career that stretched to 2009 and garnered 11 Test appearances.

10. Israel Folau

At the end of a spectacular debut NRL season in 1997 that included a Grand Final victory with Melbourne and a club-record 21 tries, Israel Folau was selected in the Junior Kangaroos side to take on the Junior Kiwis at the end of the season. But when Justin Hodges pulled out of the senior Kangaroos side with injury, the rookie was promoted from the curtain-raiser to the Test arena, becoming the youngest player in Australian Test history at 18 years and 194 days. Folau scored two tries in the record 58-0 drubbing of New Zealand in Wellington.

ONE-GAME WONDERS—TESTS

1. Benny Wearing

In one of representative Rugby League's great mysteries and injustices, Benny Wearing, one of the greatest wingers in Rugby League history (he scored 144 tries in 172 games from 1921-33 for the dominant South Sydney club), was selected for just one Test match. After having scored nine tries in 13 interstate appearances for NSW, Wearing was belatedly called into the side for the dead-rubber third Test against the 1928 Lions after Australia had gone down in the first two encounters.

He scored two tries and kicked three goals in Australia's 21-14 success, but despite his match-winning turn, was left out of the 1929-30 Kangaroo Tour squad and never represented his country again.

2. Bernie Purcell

Souths' goalkicking second-rower Bernie Purcell made his only Test appearance in arguably Australia's most famous victory. He replaced Fred de Belin for the feverishly anticipated third Test against Great Britain in 1950, with Australia claiming a historic 5-2 victory on an SCG quagmire to reclaim the Ashes for the first time in three decades. Purcell was a key part of four Rabbitohs premierships and represented NSW in 1951 and '56, but did not receive an international recall until he was named in the 1956-57 Kangaroo Tour squad. He played seven matches on tour but was not picked for any of the six Tests against Great Britain and France. Purcell's 1152 points was a premiership record for a forward that stood for 40 years after his retirement in 1960.

3. Allan McKean

With esteemed international fullbacks Graeme Langlands and Eric Simms on the injured list, and Queenslander Ray Laird (a fellow one-Test wonder) dropped after Australia's heavy second-Test defeat, Allan McKean was called up for the 1970 Ashes decider at the SCG. The steady Easts custodian was selected for his goalkicking prowess and lived up to his billing by slotting seven goals—but it was not enough to prevent a 21-17 loss to the Lions, who scored four tries to Australia's one. McKean, who never represented NSW, left the Roosters in 1973 with a then club-record 903 points and finished his career back at junior club St George.

4. Hazem El Masri

Elusive winger and goalkicker extraordinaire Hazem El Masri was selected for his one and only Test at the end of 2002, with incumbent Lote Tuqiri not considered due to an impending switch to Rugby Union. The Bulldogs flyer landed four goals as Australia overturned an eight-point halftime deficit to run out 32-24 victors over New Zealand in Wellington. El Masri had to wait five years to play his sole Origin match for NSW, and despite his ultra-consistent wing play and peerless form off the tee for the Bulldogs, he was never again selected for Australia. He retired in 2009 with a premiership-record 2418 points to his credit and was named on the flank in the NRL's Team of the 2000s.

5. Matt Bowen

One of the great entertainers and finest fullbacks of the modern era, Cowboys legend Matt Bowen—a veteran of 10 Origin matches for Queensland—represented Australia in just one Test, against France in 2004. 'Mango' played his part for the Kangaroos, who were given an almighty fright by the lowly French before running out 52-30 winners in Toulouse. The gifted custodian was repeatedly overlooked by the national selectors in subsequent seasons, which often provoked public outcry. Anthony Minichiello, Karmichael Hunt, Brett Stewart and Billy Slater were preferred in the green-and-gold No.1 while Bowen continued to star at NRL level.

6. Peter Provan
Although he lived in the shadow of his older brother Norm 'Sticks' Provan, Peter was a fine backrower in his own right, playing alongside his sibling in St George's 1958-59 Grand Final wins before joining Balmain in '61. He played his only Test in the opening encounter with New Zealand in 1963, featuring in the second-row alongside Ken Day in a 7-3 win at a muddy SCG; he was replaced by stalwart Brian Hambly for the remaining Tests. Provan played in two losing Grand Finals with Balmain against St George, but retired on a glorious high after captaining the Tigers in their famous upset of Souths in the '69 decider.

7. Brett Stewart
Quicksilver fullback Brett Stewart's tryscoring feats and electric ball-running for Manly resulted in a NSW call-up in 2007 and, with incumbent Karmichael Hunt ruled out of the post-season Test against New Zealand, he ousted the likes of Matt Bowen and Billy Slater to make his Kangaroos debut. Stewart scored a try in Australia's record 58-0 thrashing of the Kiwis in Wellington, but is yet to add to his Test tally despite being one of the NRL's elite players. He was ruled out of the 2008 World Cup squad with a shoulder complaint, and further injuries and the presence of Slater have conspired to keep the dual premiership-winning No.1 out of the national side.

8. Col Maxwell
Wests centre Col Maxwell was an unwitting player in the biggest selection controversy in the game's history when he was chosen as captain-coach of the 1948-49 Kangaroo Tour squad despite not having played for Australia and struggling for form at club level. He was infamously picked at the expense of incumbent Len Smith, who was farcically overlooked altogether in an apparently politically motivated move by the selectors. Maxwell's tour was hampered by injuries and he played just one of the five Tests abroad, leading Australia to a 16-7 loss to Great Britain in the second Ashes encounter. He left Wests to return to Newcastle at the end of the following season, and is the only Kangaroo Tour skipper since 1921-22 to play fewer than nine Tests in his career.

9. Alf Blair
Revered South Sydney captain and highly regarded five-eighth Alf 'Smacker' Blair played just one Test for Australia—although he was selected for two. A late call-up for the first Test against Great Britain in Brisbane in 1920 prompted a frantic dash

from Sydney by Blair and Balmain centre Jack Robinson, but they were thwarted by floods and he missed the match. Not considered for the 1921-22 Kangaroo Tour, Blair finally made his international debut in the first Ashes Test against the 1924 Lions; he was replaced by Ipswich pivot Johnny Hunt in the wake of the 16-3 loss. Blair retired in 1930 after 167 games in 14 seasons at Souths, having skippered the club to four premierships, including one as captain-coach.

10. Norm Pope

Valleys fullback Norm Pope represented Queensland in 10 interstate matches from 1953 to 1956, kicking 35 goals. The Balmain junior was called into the Australian side for the third Test against New Zealand in '56 after second-Test custodian Gordon 'Punchy' Clifford was ruled out and the great Clive Churchill broke his arm in a club match. Pope kicked five goals in Australia's whitewash-sealing 31-14 victory at the SCG. While it was his last international appearance, he skippered Valleys to a BRL premiership the following season.

CONTROVERSIAL INTERNATIONAL OMISSIONS

1. Len Smith

Newtown centre Len Smith was the victim of the greatest selection injustice in the game's history. He captain-coached Australia's series victory over New Zealand during 1948, but was inexplicably left out of the Kangaroo Tour squad at the end of the season. For many years, the prevailing school of thought among experts and historians was that the selectors' decision was religiously motivated—Smith was Catholic while the majority of the panel were Masons. But it is now believed that former Balmain player and coach Norm 'Latchem' Robinson, who was one of the selectors, wanted the Kangaroos coaching post. Smith's Newtown club attempted to seek reasoning for his exclusion from the NSWRL but was denied, despite ARL chairman Harry 'Jersey' Flegg maintaining that the board was as dumbfounded as the public. Robinson was ultimately overlooked for the coaching position. Wests centre Col Maxwell was the shock replacement as captain-coach of the squad despite his having been a non-playing reserve in the Test series earlier in the season and struggling for form at club level—a bizarre selection that none of the proposed reasons for Smith's omission can explain. The injustice led to Smith's retirement from the game at the end of the season and left a blot on the careers of the conspirators. He was named as 1948's Player of the Year but severed his ties with the code and politely declined NSWRL general manager John Quayle's offer to begin the healing process in 1990.

2. Benny Wearing

South Sydney legend Benny Wearing was one of the greatest wingers of all time but made just one Test appearance. A shock omission from the Australian line-up for the first two Tests of the 1928 series against the touring England side, he was called up to debut in the third Test and inspired Australia to its only win of the series by scoring two tries and three goals in a 21-14 result. But despite producing one of the great Test performances, Wearing was inexplicably left out of the 1929-30 Kangaroo Tour squad. The prolific try-scorer instead remained at home and helped the Rabbitohs to their fifth straight premiership triumph.

3. Bob McCarthy and Bob Fulton

The 1967-68 Kangaroo Tour squad announcement was controversial not only because of reports that several players had been told they were already in the squad well before it was made public. There was also widespread disbelief at the omission of young superstars Bob Fulton and Bob McCarthy. Manly centre/five-eighth Fulton was quickly gaining a reputation as one of the premiership's outstanding players in 1967 and made his debut for NSW, while McCarthy was thought to be a certainty even before his decisive long-range intercept try in Souths' Grand Final defeat of Canterbury. Fulton was eventually selected in the 1968 World Cup squad and later captained Australia on his way to being named as an Immortal. McCarthy had to wait until 1969 to make his international debut, but also skippered his country and is recognised as one of the greatest backrowers of all time.

4. Arthur Beetson

Despite leading NSW to two victories over Queensland in 1977, future Immortal forward Arthur Beetson was inexplicably left out of Australia's subsequent midyear tour squad to New Zealand by the national selectors. The disbelieving ARL took the extraordinary step of refusing to accept the team without Beetson and demanded the selectors add him to the tour party. Upon hearing of the furore, Beetson pulled out of the squad and Queenslander Greg Veivers led the Australian side across the Tasman. Beetson regained his green-and-gold jersey at the end of the season and guided Australia to victory in the World Series tournament—the incomparable prop's last international football campaign.

5. Luke Lewis

In one of the most bizarre selections in Australia's Test history, 34-year-old centre/backrower Darren Smith became the first England-based player to represent Australia. The 2003 Kangaroos encountered several injury problems during the end-of-year Ashes series in England, but despite having a fit Luke Lewis in the squad for the dead-rubber third Test, coach Chris Anderson drafted in his former

Canterbury charge Smith, who had spent the season with Super League club St Helens. The selection caused much consternation back in Australia, but Smith nonetheless made his first international appearance since 1999 and became the third-oldest Australian Test player of all time in the 18-12 win over Great Britain. Lewis eventually made his Test debut six years later during the 2009 Four Nations tournament.

6. Darcy Henry

Forbes five-eighth Darcy Henry made his debut for Australia in the first Test against France in 1955. Unlucky to be dropped for the second encounter, which Australia lost, he was recalled as a centre for the decider as a controversial replacement for Harry Wells. But when the side ran out on to the SCG, debutant Dick Poole—wearing the No.14—was in Henry's place. His mystery absence was finally resolved by Henry's widow after his death in 2004: captain Clive Churchill had told Henry in the changing rooms that he would have him switch places with selected pivot Graham Laird once the team took the field. After hearing of Churchill's plans, irate coach Vic Hey had told the Australian selectors, who then came into the changing rooms and dumped Henry from the team. Henry played one more Test against New Zealand in 1956.

7. Paul Vautin and Kevin Hastings

Few could question the selection of the 1982 Kangaroo Tour squad after it became the first team to go through Britain and France unbeaten, but the omissions of Manly backrower Paul Vautin and Easts halfback Kevin Hastings were controversial before the squad departed. Vautin had starred for Queensland in his first Origin series, made his Test debut against New Zealand and helped the Sea Eagles to a Grand Final. Hastings had won the *Rugby League Week* Player of the Year award and finished second in the Dally M Medal for the third straight season, but was overlooked for Maroons No.7 Mark Murray.

8. Ken Nagas

Canberra's long-striding winger Ken Nagas was arguably the unluckiest omission from the 1994 Kangaroo Tour squad after he had made his Origin debut for NSW and scored two slashing tries in the Raiders' Grand Final victory. Instead, the third specialist winger spot went to fellow greenhorn Wendell Sailor. Nagas's international representation was restricted to five Tests for Super League Australia in 1997.

9. Matt Bowen

One of the great attacking players of the modern era, superlative North Queensland fullback Matt Bowen was accustomed to representative rejection, making eight of his 10 Origin appearances for Queensland off the bench and playing just one Test for Australia—against minnows France in 2004. Admittedly, he starred in an era swarming with sensational No.1s, but he was favoured to win the fullback spot for the post-season Test against the Kiwis in 2007 when regular Kangaroos Anthony Minichiello and Karmichael Hunt were unavailable through injury. Manly's Grand Final fullback Brett Stewart was chosen to debut instead, despite Bowen's sizzling form that saw him top the NRL's tryscoring table for the second time and poll fourth in the Dally M Medal count.

10. Alan McIndoe
Flying Queensland winger Alan McIndoe became Illawarra's first international when he played in Australia's win over Rest of the World in 1988. But after joining Penrith, he was a baffling exclusion from the squad to tour New Zealand in '89 following his stellar campaign in the Maroons' 3-0 Origin whitewash. McIndoe and Michael Hagan (a game-three replacement for injured halfback Allan Langer) were the only available members of Queensland's starting line-ups during the Origin series who did not make the 20-man Australian squad.

BEST NOT TO REPRESENT AUSTRALIA

1. Brian Bevan
Named in Australia's Team of the Century, Waverley-born winger Brian Bevan became a legend in English Rugby League, scoring an incredible 834 tries in an exceptional 20-year career. After managing just seven games in two seasons with Eastern Suburbs during World War II, he moved to England and became the code's greatest try-scorer. Bevan's career in England prevented him from ever donning the green-and-gold.

2. Harry Bath
Often called the greatest player never to represent Australia, skilled backrower Harry Bath won five premierships in his five seasons of top-flight Australian Rugby League while also winning two championships and a Challenge Cup with Warrington. A talented ball-player, 'The Old Fox' was prevented from an Australian call-up in 1946 due to injury, and a move to England in 1947 scuppered his national ambitions.

3. Kevin Hastings
A supremely talented halfback with Eastern Suburbs in the 1970s and '80s, Kevin Hastings was an unfortunate victim of circumstance who emerged in an era of great halfbacks such as Peter Sterling, Steve Mortimer and Tommy Raudonikis. Despite winning the Rothmans Medal in 1982 and three consecutive *Rugby League Week* Player of the Year and Dally M Halfback of the Year awards from 1980 to 1982,

Hastings was stuck so far down the queue that his rep career consisted of a lone Origin appearance off the bench in 1983.

4. Frank Rule

A champion centre with the great North Sydney premiership teams of the early 1920s, Frank Rule was selected to tour with the 1921-22 Kangaroos but withdrew because of business commitments. Champion hurdler Rule was selected with three-quarter partners Harold Horder, Cec Blinkhorn and Herman Peters for the tour. Despite playing on until 1927, he was never again picked to don the green-and-gold of Australia.

5. Paul Langmack

The most capped player in premiership history not to play a Test for Australia, Paul Langmack toured with the 1986 Kangaroos and played 10 tour matches but was not called into the Test team. A wonderful servant at Canterbury and Western Suburbs, he was an exceptional lock forward who had the misfortune of being stuck behind the likes of Wayne Pearce, Paul Vautin, Bob Lindner and Brad Clyde.

6. Phil Blake

One of the great entertainers—and journeymen—of the 1980s and '90s, utility Phil Blake hardly received the representative career he was due. The Dally M Rookie of the Year in 1982, he scored 27 tries in his second season but his off-the-cuff play and defensive woes did not wash with rep selectors, who gave him just one NSW appearance off the bench.

7. Ray Preston

Few players have had the tryscoring success of Ray Preston—109 tries in 113 premiership appearances—without representing Australia. A professional athlete, Preston had one of the great tryscoring seasons in 1954, crossing for 34 tries (the second most in premiership history). Stuck behind greats such as Brian Carlson and Noel Pidding, he played a sole game for NSW in 1949 before appearing for 'Rest of Australia' against Australia in '54.

8. Ashley Harrison

Honest journeyman backrower Ashley Harrison holds the distinction of playing the most State of Origin matches without ever getting a call-up for Australia. Capable of playing in the halves and with a great work ethic, he played in six of Queensland's record series-winning run from 2008 until 2013 and finished with 15 Origin appearances.

9. Tom Kirk
The first player to score 1000 premiership points, goalkicking fullback Tom Kirk, never rose above NSW selection. No doubt hampered by the lack of international football during World War II, he played just four matches for NSW. Kirk led the premiership in points in five of his 11 seasons.

10. Arthur Patton
A lightning-quick winger with Balmain during its last great era of the 1940s, Arthur Patton scored 95 tries in 114 games for the Tigers but was never chosen for higher honours. The greatest try-scorer in Balmain's history suffered a series of broken legs that stymied his representative career and left him with just one NSW cap.

SNUBBED AFTER EARLY REPRESENTATIVE REWARDS

1. Braith Anasta
Bulldogs five-eighth Braith Anasta created history by becoming the first player to represent the Junior Kangaroos and the Australian Test side in the same season. The 19-year-old capped a brilliant 2001 debut season that included Dally M Rookie of the Year honours by winning selection for the shortened Kangaroo Tour, coming off the bench in all four Tests against Papua New Guinea and Great Britain. But despite making 10 Origin appearances for NSW over the next seven seasons and remaining one of the NRL's foremost match-winners, Anasta was never again selected to play for his country. The likes of Trent Barrett, Darren Lockyer and non-specialists Shaun Timmins, Craig Wing, Michael Crocker, Craig Gower and Greg Bird wore the Australian No.6 instead.

2. Paul Langmack
Canterbury's backrow prodigy was only 21 but had already played in three Grand Finals when he was selected as Wayne Pearce's lock understudy for the 1986 Kangaroo Tour. Langmack played 10 matches in Britain and France (no Tests) and represented NSW four times in 1987-88. But despite being a leader and creative hub for Canterbury and, later, Wests over the next decade, he never again played for Australia, NSW or even City Origin, bringing his major representative career to an end at the tender age of 23.

3. Steve Morris
Steve Morris was the last player to represent Australia from country NSW, plucked from Dapto in the Illawarra competition to play halfback in one Test against New Zealand in

1978. But he missed the Kangaroo Tour squad at the end of the year, and after joining St George and winning a Grand Final in '79, still found himself behind Tom Raudonikis, Steve Mortimer, Peter Sterling, Steve Martin and Mark Murray in the No.7s queue. 'Slippery' shifted permanently to the wing in 1983, representing NSW in two Origins and winning two Dally M Winger of the Year gongs, but was thwarted by Eric Grothe, Ross Conlon, Kerry Boustead, John Ribot, John Ferguson, Michael O'Connor and Dale Shearer in his bid for another green-and-gold jumper in his adopted position.

4. Andrew Gee

Former Australian Schoolboys rep Andrew Gee made his Queensland Origin debut in 1990 after just 22 first grade games for Brisbane. He was selected for Australia's historic tour of Papua New Guinea the following season but was injured in his only appearance, against Islands Zone. Despite celebrating in four Grand Final triumphs and tallying 17 appearances for the Maroons in an Origin career that stretched to 2003, Broncos great Gee did not receive another opportunity at international level. He holds the dubious distinction of having played the most Origin matches without playing a Test for Australia.

5. Michael Potter

Canterbury fullback Michael Potter came off the bench in one Origin match for NSW in 1984 with just 18 first grade games under his belt. But after claiming the Dally M Medal and winning a Grand Final the day before his 21st birthday that year, injuries—and the presence of Garry Jack and Gary Belcher—conspired to keep him out of representative calculations. Potter returned to top form in the early 1990s with St George, but could not win the approval of state and national selectors despite collecting a second Dally M Medal in 1991 and Fullback of the Year honours in 1991-92 and starring for Country Origin from 1990-92. He was a controversial omission from Australia's World Cup squad in '92, with Greg Alexander, Andrew Ettingshausen and Tim Brasher—none of whom were regular No.1s for their clubs—preferred as NSW's fullback options.

6. Jarrod Mullen

Thrust into the Newcastle No.7 hot seat following Andrew Johns' injury-enforced retirement early in 2007, Jarrod Mullen was then selected at halfback for NSW for the subsequent Origin series opener. The veteran of 31 NRL games mixed the good with the bad on debut in a 25-18 loss at Suncorp Stadium, but injury ruled him out of the return clash. Mullen, a linchpin for the Knights at five-eighth or halfback, has been on the cusp of an Origin recall since, but despite NSW's record series-winning drought, he still has just one sky-blue jumper in his wardrobe. Selectors have unsuccessfully tried 11 different players at No.6 and No.7 since his solitary Origin outing.

7. John Hopoate
Blockbusting winger John Hopoate had only just established himself on the Manly flank when he was selected to debut for NSW in 1995—the 21-year-old boasted a total of 20 first grade appearances. The volatile youngster was dropped after the Blues' series-sealing loss but won a place in Australia's World Cup squad after finishing the year with 21 tries for the Sea Eagles. His Test debut is best remembered for a terrible error that led to a try in the tournament-opening loss to England, and his only other appearance at the World Cup was a three-try effort against minnows South Africa. Hopoate was never again called upon by NSW or Australia, although he came close to an Origin recall in the early 2000s after making an excellent comeback from his infamous finger-poking exploits.

8. David Stagg
A tireless backrower with the versatility to slot into the backline (he was a centre in Brisbane's 2006 Grand Final victory), David Stagg was granted just one opportunity at Origin level. The 22-year-old, a veteran of 42 NRL games, was picked in Queensland's second-row for the '06 series opener but felt the selectors' axe in the wake of the 17-16 loss. He continued to produce the goods at club level, winning the Dally M Lock of the Year award in 2009 after joining the Bulldogs, but was constantly overlooked for a Maroons recall.

9. David Williams
At the end of a spectacular 2008 rookie season that netted 14 tries and a Grand Final triumph with Manly, instant cult hero David Williams was selected in Australia's World Cup squad and scored a hat-trick on debut against Papua New Guinea, crossing again in the shock final loss to New Zealand. He played two matches in the following season's Origin series for NSW, scoring a try in each outing but also making a spate of glaring errors. Although he has consistently been one of the NRL's most reliable try-scorers (65 in 93 games), Williams fell out of favour with the selectors, with a 2012 appearance for City Origin his only notable representative assignment since '09.

10. Jamal Idris
Giant dreadlocked sensation Jamal Idris quickly scaled the representative heights after winning the 2009 Dally M Rookie of the Year award. The 19-year-old Canterbury centre was picked on the NSW bench for the opening match of the 2010 series, but was unceremoniously dumped despite scoring a try and making a solid contribution in the Blues' disappointing loss. He maintained his club form to win a Test call-up for the early-season clash with the Kiwis in 2011 and scored another debut try off the bench, but Idris, who embarked on a mixed two-season stint with the Gold Coast before abruptly joining Penrith in the 2014 pre-season, has since been ignored by state and national selectors. The hapless Blues used seven different centres from 2010 to 2013.

ELIGIBILITY CONTROVERSIES

1. Greg Inglis
Kempsey-born Bowraville junior Greg Inglis made himself available for Queensland after breaking into first grade with Melbourne on the basis of having attended high school in Brisbane, but an earlier appearance for Hunter Sports High in Newcastle technically made him NSW-eligible. Inglis went on to become Origin's greatest try-scorer as a key member of the Maroons' juggernaut, featuring in eight straight series wins from his debut in 2006. His case set the platform for the vigorous interstate eligibility debate that continues to bubble away.

2. James Tamou
James Tamou was born in Palmerston North, in the North Island of New Zealand, before moving to Sydney with his family as a 13-year-old. He made his NRL debut for North Queensland in 2009 after coming through the Roosters' junior ranks, and the towering prop's talent was recognised by the Kiwi selectors when they named him in the train-on squad for the 2011 Four Nations. Although Tamou missed the touring squad, he signed a letter of intent to play for New Zealand early the following season. But just weeks out from the 2012 trans-Tasman Test—after coercing from Blues captain Paul Gallen—Tamou made himself available for NSW and Australia. The former New Zealand Maori rep was duly selected for the Kangaroos, with his selection dominating the build-up for the Auckland-hosted Test. He quickly became an automatic selection for his adopted state and country, featuring in the 2013 World Cup final rout of the Kiwis, and remains an unpopular figure in his homeland.

3. Adrian Lam
Rabaul-born Adrian Lam moved to Brisbane at the age of seven and played for Wests Panthers before making his Test debut for Papua New Guinea at the end of an impressive 1994 rookie season with Eastern Suburbs Roosters. But with Queensland's ranks ravaged by the embargo on Super League players ahead of the '95 Origin series, Lam was given special dispensation to play halfback for the Maroons—and starred in their 3-0 boilover success. He went on to play 14 Origins (eight as captain) while concurrently representing the Kumuls in 11 Tests and captaining Rest of the World against Australia in 1997.

4. Ken Nagas
Bundaberg-bred winger/fullback Ken Nagas moved to Kyogle in northern NSW as a teenager and subsequently played his first senior football in the region, which technically qualified him for the Blues. The Canberra flyer was selected to debut for NSW in 1994 despite admitting he had always been a Queensland supporter. Nagas's father explained that he hoped young Ken would win the man-of-the-match award—but he would still be barracking for the Maroons. Nagas ultimately played only two Origins for the Blues but later admitted he regretted making himself available to play against his native state.

5. Nathan Fien
Mt Isa product Nathan Fien played one Origin match for Queensland in 2001 during his five-season stay at North Queensland, before linking with the Warriors in 2005. He was controversially picked in the Kiwis' Test squad for the '06 Tri-Nations on the basis of having a New Zealand-born grandmother. But after playing in the first two matches of the tournament, it was discovered it was in fact Fien's *great*-grandmother who had been born in New Zealand. The utility was released from the squad and the Kiwis had the points from their win over Great Britain stripped. Fien qualified for New Zealand selection on residential grounds two years later, however, and featured in the Kiwis' '08 World Cup and '10 Four Nations final victories among 20 Test appearances, leaving the 'Grandma-gate' debacle behind him.

6. Rangi Chase
Castleford half Rangi Chase represented New Zealand Maori and the Super League 'Exiles' against England in 2010 and '11 respectively, but was lining up alongside his former international opponents at the end of the latter season. Born in Dannevirke in the central North Island of New Zealand, the former Wests Tigers and St George Illawarra playmaker qualified for England selection through residency after spending three seasons at Castleford. Despite criticism of his selection by former British greats, he played eight Tests for England during the 2011 Four Nations and 2013 World Cup campaigns.

7. Josh Papalii
Born in Auckland, Josh Papalii moved to Woodridge in Queensland at the age of six and played his junior football for Logan Brothers. He represented Queensland Under-18s in 2010 but opted to turn out for the Junior Kiwis in 2011 at the end of his NRL rookie season with Canberra. He switched camps after a breakout 2012 campaign with the Raiders, however, pledging his allegiances to Queensland and Australia—with the persuasive powers of Origin coach Mal Meninga playing a key role. Papalii duly made his debuts for the Maroons and Kangaroos in 2013, featuring in the World Cup final defeat of his native New Zealand.

8. Israel Folau

Born in Sydney and a junior of the Minto Cobras in the city's west, Israel Folau followed a similarly tenuous path to Queensland representation as his Melbourne clubmate Greg Inglis, with a couple of years in Goodna, near Ipswich, enough to get the boom three-quarter into a Maroon jumper. Folau's and Inglis's dubious eligibility claims were lumped together by detractors south of the border, but Folau nevertheless scored seven tries in eight Origins before defecting to the AFL and, later, Rugby Union.

9. Tonie Carroll

Brisbane centre/lock Tonie Carroll made eight Origin appearances for Queensland in the 1998-2000 series. But after signing a deal to join Super League club Leeds at the end of 2000, Christchurch-born Carroll made himself available for New Zealand's World Cup campaign. He scored four tries in the Kiwis' five matches at the tournament, including a touchdown in the 40-12 final loss to an Australian side that contained five of his former Maroons teammates. After two seasons with Leeds, Carroll returned to the Broncos in 2003 and represented Queensland 10 more times, while also making his Kangaroos debut in '04 and making seven Test appearances in the green-and-gold.

10. Andrew Ryan

A proud Dubbo boy who played his first graded football over the age of 16 during an eight-month stint at Emu Plains, Parramatta backrower Andrew Ryan had a compelling case for representing Country Origin and City Origin. And so it transpired in 2002, when both camps selected him in their respective sides for the City-Country clash at Wagga Wagga. A bizarre impasse unfolded before sanity prevailed and City relented, allowing the tyro to debut for Country. Ryan eventually represented Country Origin six times during a wonderful career that included 11 Tests, 12 Origins and a Grand Final victory as captain of the Bulldogs.

Chapter 9

INJURIES

INJURY-PRONE PLAYERS

1. David Woods
A naturally gifted centre who could have been anything, David Woods was the most notoriously injury-prone player of the 1990s. He was a teenage debutant for Parramatta in 1989 and a first-choice proposition for the Eels and Panthers for the ensuing 13 seasons, but made just 160 first grade appearances. Ravaged by various leg complaints, he never played more than 19 games in a year, and made 14 or fewer appearances in nine of his seasons at the top level. Woods never played a finals match in his career, but represented Country Origin in 1995-96.

2. Brett Papworth
A brilliant Rugby Union centre who played 16 Tests for the Wallabies from 1985 to 1987, Brett Papworth was a highly anticipated signing for Eastern Suburbs in '88. But a broken arm ended his maiden Rugby League campaign in Round 3, shoulder problems kept him out of the entire following season, a badly broken jaw finished him for 1990 in the opening round, and a season-ending knee injury in '91 eventually convinced him to retire from the code after just seven first grade appearances.

3. James Pickering
Burly, skilful Fiji international James Pickering was regarded by some judges as potentially the best prop in the game and was consequently a hyped signing for Canterbury in 1995 after he spearheaded Workington Town's charge back to Britain's first division. But the Auckland junior's first season with the Bulldogs ended at his fifth appearance and he was plagued by broken-arm and knee injuries in 1996 and '97, cut down after just one and three games respectively. The bustling ball-player made 14 appearances after joining the Roosters in '98 but was injured again three weeks out from the finals. His return to the Bulldogs in 2000 (after a season at Castleford) was thwarted by another injury in the opening round, forcing him to retire.

4. Micheal Pattison
A brilliant five-eighth prospect at Parramatta, Mick Pattison had a career that was dogged by unusual injuries. He was ruled out of the Eels' 1979 finals campaign after being hospitalised by a knee infection, and was later forced to pull out of the NSW Origin side in '81 with an inner-ear infection after he joined Souths. On the verge of Blues selection again the following season, he broke both collarbones in a freak tackle playing for City Firsts. A return to Parramatta garnered just four first grade appearances in 1983-84, while his outstanding two-season stint with struggling Illawarra ended in '86 with his retirement at the age of 27 due to a chronic back injury.

5. Justin Hodges
A season-ending knee reconstruction suffered during the Origin series opener in 2003 started gun Roosters centre Justin Hodges' serious injury woes. Returning to Brisbane in 2005, he made 20 appearances in a season just once in nine seasons as injuries consistently halted his progress. Hodges became an automatic Queensland selection but played in just nine of a possible 18 Origins from 2006 to 2011. Hamstring complaints were his most regular ailment, but he missed all of 2010 with a snapped Achilles tendon. He snapped the other Achilles towards the end of 2013 and was sidelined for the first month of the following season.

6. Chase and Kyle Stanley
Sydney-born brothers Chase and Kyle Stanley were naturally gifted footballers, but unfortunately they shared genetics that saw them in the injury ward more than almost any other players in the NRL. After making his New Zealand Test debut as an 18-year-old at the end of his 2007 rookie season at St George Illawarra, three-quarter Chase made just 41 appearances in the ensuing five seasons with the Saints and Melbourne after frequently breaking down. Fellow teenage Dragons debutant Kyle, an extremely versatile and potentially more talented player than his older sibling, was

restricted to 37 NRL games from 2010 to 2013 after undergoing a painstaking four knee reconstructions, the last of which ruled him out for the entire '13 campaign.

7. Luke Davico
Rugged Canberra prop Luke Davico's frequent and ill-timed injuries stymied his representative aspirations and ensured he was a regular absentee from club football. He missed the first half of the 1996 and '99 seasons, while a pectoral injury ended his year after just three games in 2002. His 11-season tenure at Canberra was ended by another pectoral tear near the end of 2004, and he reinjured the area in a pre-season match for Wigan in '05. Davico eventually returned home without playing an official match in the cherry-and-white jumper. Linking with Newcastle and remaining relatively injury-free during 2006, he retired after one game (ironically against Canberra) in '07 after the pectoral went again.

8. Brent Tate
Brent Tate's fortitude in fighting back from multiple devastating injuries ranks as one of the more inspiring triumph-over-adversity tales of the modern era. The young Test three-quarter suffered a career-threatening neck injury late in 2003 that has seen him take the field in a trademark brace ever since. A short-term casualty-ward regular from 2004 to 2006, his career with Brisbane was cut short courtesy of a season-ending knee injury suffered in an Origin match in '07. Joining the Warriors, Tate was brought down by another serious knee injury just three games into the 2009 season, and he required a third reconstruction after reinjuring the joint in the 2010 Four Nations final. He recovered to take the field for the Cowboys midway through 2011 and capped his courageous journey by reclaiming representative wing spots in ensuing seasons.

9. Adam MacDougall
Blockbusting Newcastle three-quarter Adam MacDougall's long line of injuries began in 2002, when he suffered a season-ending knee injury in his first match back from groin surgery. 'Mad Dog' played just 116 games in the last 10 seasons of a long career that had earlier reaped 11 Test and 11 Origin appearances. South Sydney received just 31 games out of him during a three-season stint, and he managed no more than 16 games in each of his last four campaigns after rejoining the Knights. MacDougall's first grade career spanned 17 seasons and ultimately garnered 92 tries from 195 appearances.

10. Jerome Ropati
A quality centre who counts appearances at fullback, five-eighth and hooker among his 10 Tests for New Zealand, Jerome Ropati has endured a horrific injury run in recent seasons. The key Warriors back battled various difficulties throughout 2007, playing

just 12 games before being ruled out of the finals with a shoulder injury. An ACL knee reconstruction in 2011, a dislocated patella in '12 and a succession of leg injuries in '13 caused the popular clubman to miss the Warriors' 2011 Grand Final and restricted him to 15 games in three years. A broken jaw interrupted his promising 2014 comeback.

WORST INJURIES

1. John Farragher—Neck
A Penrith prop forward from the country NSW town of Gilgandra, John Farragher was left a quadriplegic after breaking his neck in a clash with Newtown in 1978. He never walked again after the collapse of the scrum at Henson Park.

2. Bill McRitchie—Ear
Bill McRitchie, a St George prop who spent four years in first grade during the 1940s, had his career ended after part of his ear was bitten off in a clash with Newtown in 1945. He spent 22 weeks in hospital and did not play again. His assailant was never found, though Frank 'Bumper' Farrell was accused of the atrocity.

3. Jharal Yow Yeh—Ankle
After perhaps the worst leg break in the history of the game, Broncos and Australian winger Jharal Yow Yeh missed most of 2012 and all of 2013 due to a horrific compound fracture during a clash with South Sydney in Perth that threatened not only his career but his leg. Doctors considered amputating the leg and Yow Yeh endured 10 surgeries before announcing his retirement early in 2014.

4. John Sattler—Jaw
In perhaps the most famous Rugby League injury of all, Souths captain John Sattler had his jaw smashed by Manly's John Bucknall in the 1970 Grand Final. Sattler played most of the match and led the Bunnies to a famous victory after having his teammates hold him up. He played with blood streaming from his mouth in the enduring image of Rugby League toughness.

5. Richie Barnett—Face
A head clash with Australian winger Wendell Sailor ended Richie Barnett's premiership career in 2000, with the Sydney Roosters and Kiwis winger suffering five facial fractures as a result. Barnett said he clearly remembers his face "imploding" before he was bedridden for two months. He miraculously fought back to captain New Zealand at the year-ending World Cup before joining London in '01.

6. Taniela Tuiaki—Ankle

Giant Wests Tigers winger Taniela Tuiaki was in the latter stages of a career-best 2009 season, during which he scored 21 tries in 22 games, when a shocking ankle injury brought his career to a premature end. Named the Dally M Winger of the Year in '09, Tuiaki battled valiantly for three years but was unable to return to Rugby League and did not play again after the injury could not be healed.

7. Ross Conlon—Hip

Ross Conlon, a brilliant goalkicking centre with Canterbury, had his 1983 season ended in the finals defeat to Parramatta when he suffered a vicious dislocated hip. He bounced back in 1984 to represent NSW and Australia, but those who witnessed the dislocation remain scarred.

8. Tony Caine—Knee

Promising Cronulla hooker Tony Caine's career was derailed by a shattering knee injury that forced the NRL to change its rules regarding kickers. On debut, Caine had his leg ripped apart by Warriors skipper Steve Price, who was attempting a charge down. Caine needed surgery on his anterior, lateral and posterior ligaments as well as his calf. Players can no longer attack the legs of kickers following the horrific injury.

9. Danny Peacock—Hip

Like Ross Conlon before him, Danny Peacock suffered a horrific hip dislocation playing fullback for the Gold Coast against St George. He lay splayed on the turf slamming the ground in agony after suffering the dislocation, but managed to return eight weeks later.

10. Lee Pomfret—Jaw

Lithe Illawarra winger Lee Pomfret was left with a broken jaw, fractured cheekbone and shattered nose after Western Suburbs forward Bob Cooper unleashed on the unsuspecting Pomfret during an all-in brawl in 1982. Cooper was suspended for 15 months while Pomfret missed the remainder of the '82 season.

BIZARRE INJURIES

1. David Kidwell

A prized recruit for big-spending Souths in 2007, David Kidwell had played just four games as co-captain for the club when he had to undergo a knee reconstruction after injuring himself tripping over his two-year-old daughter at a family barbecue. He made a return off the bench five months later in the Rabbitohs' qualifying final loss to Manly.

2. John Simon
Illawarra linchpin John Simon's 1993 season ended prematurely when he suffered a nasty foot gash in an after-match shower accident. The former NSW halfback's freak mishap cruelled the Steelers' tenuous finals bid, and they lost three of their remaining five games to finish out of the running.

3. Matt Keating
Struggling Parramatta's woes were compounded during 2011 when Matt Keating was sidelined after a mishap with the family pet. The workmanlike hooker had to have surgery for a compound fracture of the index finger after it was bitten by his pet bulldog in what he described as a "playful accident". Keating was out of action for six weeks.

4. Bradley Clyde and Robbie Kearns
An attempt to move away from the traditional, boozy Origin camps had disastrous ramifications for coach Wayne Pearce and a pair of NSW forwards in 1999. Pearce took the Blues on a horseriding trek in the Blue Mountains, during which Bradley Clyde and Robbie Kearns were thrown from their mounts. Clyde, who was making an Origin return after an absence of five years, injured his shoulder and missed the entire series, while Kearns was knocked unconscious, broke his collarbone and missed two months of football. Nik Kosef also had an unpleasant excursion, suffering swollen, weeping eyes thanks to an allergic reaction.

5. Jamie Ainscough
Former Test and Origin three-quarter Jamie Ainscough's career was effectively ended by an incident in a 2002 match between his Wigan side and Super League rivals St Helens. Ainscough left the field to have an arm wound stitched up after making a tackle on Saints centre Martin Gleeson, but the wound became badly infected—weeks later, an X-ray revealed that part of Gleeson's tooth was embedded in there. The infection was so severe that there were fears Ainscough may have to have the arm amputated, but while that did not eventuate, ongoing problems with the limb forced his early retirement midway through '03.

6. Stephen Kearney and Jason Donnelly
New Zealand's disappointing tour of Great Britain and France in 1993 hit its lowest ebb on the French leg of the trip when a hotel balcony collapsed in Carcassonne, injuring young stars Stephen Kearney and Jason Donnelly. Wests backrower Kearney,

who had been a shock choice as captain for the third Test against Great Britain, suffered bruising to the brain and was hospitalised for a week; he recovered to carve out a decorated Test and premiership career. St George winger Donnelly broke his ankle in the incident and did not represent the Kiwis again.

7. Allan Langer

In the lead-up to the 1993 Grand Final, Brisbane halfback and captain Allan Langer was at the Doomben racecourse when his head struck a bookmaker's stand while he was rushing out of the betting ring. 'Alfie' suffered a cut above the eye, swelling and severe headaches, and also exacerbated the effects of a virus that laid the No.7 genius low virtually until kick-off. Langer recovered sufficiently to lead the Broncos to a second successive title.

8. Les Heidke

Revered Queensland forward Les 'Monty' Heidke, son of pioneering great Bill, made his Test debut in 1932 but was ruled out the 1933-34 Kangaroo Tour after he was bitten on the leg by a redback spider. Supporters paid for Heidke to accompany the squad, but he was forced to pull the pin in Fremantle fearing amputation after blood-poisoning set in. Heidke later toured as a player with the 1937-38 'Roos.

9. Ken Nagas

Long-striding fullback/winger Ken Nagas did not take the field for Canberra in 1998 until the halfway mark of the season because he was sidelined by a knee injury suffered while clowning around on the team bus during the pre-season. Nagas had been one of the stars of the previous '97 Super League season, but the mishap was the beginning of a wretched injury run for the popular flyer, who eventually retired in 2002.

10. David Gillespie

While working on a garbage truck in 1986, 22-year-old Canterbury enforcer David Gillespie lost half an index finger after it became jammed between the truck and a telephone pole. The accident—which occurred with one round of the regular season remaining—cost Gillespie a Grand Final appearance and an almost-certain Kangaroo Tour berth. But he bounced back to win premierships with the Bulldogs and Manly and enjoyed a long representative career as the code's undisputed No.1 hitman.

11. Greg Florimo

Future North Sydney great Greg Florimo made his first grade debut for the club as an 18-year-old in 1986. The precocious centre showed his tender years by having to line up for his first game in the big time wearing headgear to cover up injuries suffered while skateboarding.

12. Jack Wighton
Brilliant Canberra rookie Jack Wighton's debut season in the NRL was severely interrupted by a backyard accident. The 19-year-old outside back had eight first grade games under his belt in 2012 when he injured his toe while jumping on a trampoline with his six-year-old brother in his hometown of Orange, leaving Raiders coach David Furner unimpressed. Expected to miss the rest of the season, Wighton returned four months later in the club's semi-final exit at the hands of Souths.

13. David Taylor
Queensland behemoth David Taylor sent a scare into the Maroons camp just days out from the second Origin clash in 2012 when he suffered head injuries after falling out of bed. The enigmatic 122kg forward trained the following day with his head heavily bandaged and eventually took the field in the Sydney loss.

14. Tim Brasher
Veteran fullback Tim Brasher's long and illustrious career began to wind down when he fell while trying to clean a ceiling fan during the 2001 pre-season. He suffered a knee injury that required a reconstruction and ruled him out of the entire NRL season with North Queensland. Brasher retired after making just three appearances for the Cowboys in '02.

15. Ben Czislowski
Prop Ben Czislowski played nine NRL games for Brisbane and the Bulldogs from 2004 to 2006, but was the victim of a bizarre injury after he returned to play in the Queensland Cup. Three months after a head clash with an opponent, Czislowski developed an eye infection and severe pain; scans revealed a tooth lodged in his head.

16. John Gillam
Oldham winger John Gillam booked a lengthy stint on the sidelines at the beginning of 2012 when he suffered a shocking compound fracture of the big toe, caused by jumping out of bed after having a nightmare.

17. David Liddiard
A former Dally M Rookie of the Year and premiership winner at Parramatta in 1983, Indigenous winger David Liddiard was forced to withdraw from a match for Manly during the early 1990s after he pulled a back muscle while brushing his teeth.

18. Greg Eastwood
Canterbury's ball-playing lock Greg Eastwood was forced to carry an ankle injury into a 2011 match after he stepped on his son's toy car while getting out of bed.

19. Mark Murray

Queensland Origin stalwart Mark 'Muppet' Murray's career came to a premature end in unfortunate circumstances when he was forced to undergo surgery and retire after a piece of glass went in his eye at a Leagues club in Brisbane in 1987.

20. Luke Lewis

Short in-goals and little space between the field of play and the fence have long been a feature of Rugby League in Britain. These spatial constraints had terrible consequences for Kangaroos backrower Luke Lewis at the 2013 World Cup, when he crashed into the advertising hoardings after chasing a kick late in the pool win over Fiji at St Helens' Langtree Park. Lewis was knocked out in the collision and suffered a serious shoulder injury that ruled him out for the remainder of the tournament.

Chapter 10

RECRUITMENT

BEST RECRUITS

1. Johnny Raper—St George
The greatest lock forward in the history of the game, St George legend Johnny Raper debuted with Newtown and spent two seasons with the Bluebags before shifting to the Saints. He debuted for Sydney Colts while at Newtown as a prodigious 18-year-old but was astonishingly released by Newtown after just two seasons to don the Red V. Raper went on to win eight Grand Finals with the Dragons, represent NSW 24 times and Australia on 39 occasions, and be named at lock in the Team of the Century.

2. Terry Lamb—Canterbury
A Canterbury legend who won three premierships with the Bulldogs and played 262 games for the blue-and-whites, Terry Lamb debuted for Western Suburbs in 1980 and spent his first four seasons with the Magpies before being recruited by Peter Moore. A Canterbury junior, he was seemingly lost to the Bulldogs because they couldn't promise him a top-grade spot. Lamb made his NSW debut and won a Dally M Medal at the Magpies before going on to a decorated career at five-eighth with the Bulldogs.

3. Brian Clay—St George
A rock-solid and reliable five-eighth, Brian 'Poppa' Clay was a Newtown junior who spent three years with the Bluebags before making a highly successful transition to the great St George team. Clay had played in two premiership deciders with Newtown before settling in with the Dragons, where he turned out in eight Grand Final wins during his stellar 11-year career. He played eight Tests for Australia and was named in the 100 Greatest Players in 2008.

4. Arthur Beetson—Eastern Suburbs
Arthur Beetson's career was at the crossroads when he left Balmain after the 1970 season to join Eastern Suburbs. The career of the superb ball-playing forward, who had played for Australia but was hindered by discipline and attitude issues, was rejuvenated at the Roosters. Under the astute coaching of Jack Gibson, Beetson was appointed skipper of the great Eastern Suburbs teams that won titles in 1974-75; he went on to become the first Indigenous Australian to captain a national sporting team and be named an Immortal.

5. Brad Fittler—Sydney City
A local prodigy who became the youngest Origin player in history when he debuted as an 18-year-old in 1990, Brad Fittler played in the Panthers' first premiership and captained Australia to the 1995 World Cup before he followed ex-Penrith coach Phil Gould to the Sydney Roosters at the height of the Super League War. A key ARL signing, Fittler had little choice but to find a new club after the Panthers aligned with News Limited. The Roosters, who had not made the finals for eight years before Fittler's arrival, never missed the finals in his nine-year career at Bondi, winning a premiership in '02 and playing in four Grand Finals. Fittler was named in the ARL's Top 100 players in 2008.

6. Jamie Lyon—Manly
Jamie Lyon, a highly talented centre from Parramatta who made his Australian debut as a 19-year-old, had a nasty falling-out with coach Brian Smith that saw him quit the Eels and return to his native Wee Waa. Lyon eventually signed with St Helens in the Super League, and won the Man of Steel award in his first year, before joining Manly in 2007. His signing saw the Sea Eagles reach four Grand Finals, winning premierships in 2008 and 2011, with Lyon—captain of the latter title triumph—a three-time Dally M Centre of the Year and the key component of the most dangerous edge in the NRL.

7. Greg Inglis—South Sydney
One of the most naturally brilliant footballers Rugby League has seen, Greg Inglis was forced out of the club with which he had won two premierships by Melbourne

Storm's salary-cap dramas of 2010. After initially agreeing to terms with Brisbane, Inglis signed with South Sydney and was the club's star as it reached back-to-back preliminary finals in 2012-13 for the first time in more than four decades.

8. John Ferguson—Canberra

A lightning-quick winger who didn't make his premiership debut until he was 26, John 'Chicka' Ferguson enjoyed five successful seasons at Newtown and Eastern Suburbs before a spectacular five years with the Canberra Raiders saw him score 50 tries in 94 games and play in the club's first two premierships. Ferguson scored the critical try in the 1989 decider to send the match to extra-time, and also crossed in the 1990 triumph.

9. Cliff Lyons—Manly

A star player who had incredible longevity, Cliff Lyons spent a year with North Sydney before Manly recruited the exciting pivot at the end of his rookie season with the Bears. Lyons went on to play 309 games over 14 seasons for the Sea Eagles, becoming one of their most enduring and successful stars. He played in the '87 and '96 premiership wins and won the Clive Churchill Medal in '87.

10. Ron Coote—Eastern Suburbs

A star backrower who won four premiership with South Sydney and played 18 Tests for Australia, Ron Coote made a highly publicised and successful move to rivals Eastern Suburbs in 1972. It was one of the great signing coups, with Coote skippering the club during his first two years (including a Grand Final in '72) before it won premierships in 1974-75. Ernie Christensen twice named him the top player in the premiership after his move to the Tricolours.

WORST RECRUITS

1. Matt Orford—Canberra

A Dally M medallist and premiership-winning captain with Manly, Matt Orford was signed by Canberra in 2011 for three seasons after a modest year at Bradford—despite being on the verge of 33 years old. It was a disastrous move for both club and player. Seen as an ideal substitute for injured linchpin Terry Campese, Orford played just six games for the Raiders, all of them losses. He infamously knocked on at the back of a scrum in the last minute of a match against the Titans, allowing them to level the scores and subsequently win the match in extra-time. So incensed were the club's fans about the high-profile halfback's woeful form that one of them lost the plot and vandalised his car in the Canberra Stadium carpark after the Raiders' 49-12 loss to the Wests Tigers. Orford was then sidelined by a groin injury and released from the final two years of his contract at the end of the season.

2. Adam Blair—Wests Tigers
The Wests Tigers lured dynamic Melbourne forward and New Zealand Test vice-captain Adam Blair to the club on ridiculous money in 2012, sacrificing long-serving crowd favourite Bryce Gibbs and emerging impact forward Andrew Fifita. Two seasons of drastic underperformance has rendered the Whangarei product one of the most maligned players in the game and cost him his Kiwis spot. The fallout surrounding Blair's ill-fated acquisition contributed to coach Tim Sheens' demise, while Fifita was regarded as one of the world's best forwards by the end of 2013; three more Tigers stalwarts quit the ailing club to join Fifita and Gibbs at Cronulla in short time.

3. Tony Williams—Canterbury
Manly coach Des Hasler developed Tony Williams into one of the NRL's most damaging forwards, with Williams earning a Kangaroos call-up after playing a key role in the Sea Eagles' 2011 premiership triumph. His follow-up season was marred by suspension, but he nevertheless debuted for NSW and was eagerly recruited by Canterbury to reunite with Hasler. 'T-Rex' played 23 games for the Bulldogs in 2013 but offered none of his trademark wrecking-ball impact; he was chastised by the media and fans alike for his reluctance to charge on to the ball in the manner that had made him a star at Manly.

4. Mark McGaw—Penrith
Long-serving Cronulla, NSW and Australia centre Mark McGaw left the struggling Sharks at the end of 1992 and was viewed as tremendous backline acquisition for Penrith. But 'Sparkles' was a shadow of the player who had become a representative regular. He made 16 uninspiring appearances for the Panthers in '93 before seeking a release from the club, and wound up his career with a modest two-season stint at Souths before becoming the character 'Hammer' on television's *Gladiators*.

5. Bob O'Reilly—Penrith
Bob 'The Bear' O'Reilly was one of the game's premier props during the first half of the 1970s, representing Australia 16 times despite his Parramatta side's also-ran status. He was signed in a rich deal by Penrith in 1976 but became yet another high-priced flop for the struggling Panthers, losing all semblance of his ferocious form in two dismal seasons at the club. O'Reilly resurrected his career and his reputation as one of the game's finest ball-playing forwards at Easts before returning to the Eels and playing a key role in their maiden premiership success.

6. Ted Goodwin—Newtown

One of the great entertainers of the 1970s—starring in St George's '77 premiership win—'Lord Ted' Goodwin parted company with the Dragons at the end of 1978. The former Test star joined Newtown, but the move was an unequivocal flop. He spent just one season with the Jets, playing only six games in the top flight and spending most of the year languishing in the lower grades. The enigmatic utility back salvaged his reputation somewhat with Wests from 1980 to 1982.

7. Mark Geyer—Balmain

Mark Geyer was regarded as the most destructive forward in the world in 1991, but his career went off the rails the following season after a recreational drug suspension and the death of his teammate and close friend Ben Alexander. He attempted to pick up the pieces at Balmain in 1993 but lasted just one ordinary season that incorporated 13 first grade appearances. Geyer was also kicked out of the City Origin side by former Panthers mentor Phil Gould for missing a team medical. The tempestuous second-rower was sacked by the Tigers the following January for repeatedly skipping training without explanation, and instead spent '94 with Central Coast club Umina Bunnies; he resurfaced with the Western Reds.

8. Paul Green—North Queensland

Ex-Cronulla linchpin Paul Green was viewed as the marquee halfback capable of turning the struggling Cowboys into a premiership force—but after the former Rothmans medallist and Super League international relocated to Townsville in 1999, he was benched for much of the second half of the season, with coach Tim Sheens preferring the halves pairing of Noel Goldthorpe and teenaged sensation Scott Prince. Struggling for form the following season, Green was sacked by the club in June for allegedly negotiating with rival clubs. His subsequent stints with the Roosters, Parramatta and Brisbane were ravaged by injuries, but he made a successful transition into coaching—ironically receiving his first NRL head coach opportunity with the Cowboys in 2014.

9. Bob Lindner—Parramatta and Gold Coast

Although Bob Lindner was a representative star for almost a decade, he gained his reputation as an underperforming mercenary in the late 1980s during stints with the Eels and Giants. As the much-hyped replacement for Parramatta's retired legend Ray Price in '87, the dynamic lock rarely produced his best form in two seasons in the blue and gold before joining the Gold Coast. He played just 10 games for the battling Giants in an injury-hampered '89 season, then controversially returned to Sydney to link with Wests. The Queensland and Australia backrow stalwart provided better value to the Magpies, and later enjoyed the best of his eight seasons in the NSWRL with Illawarra in '93.

10. Carl Webb—Parramatta
Parramatta made a string of diabolical purchases for the 2011-12 seasons—Chris Walker, Paul Whatuira, Willie Tonga, Chris Sandow and Ben Roberts all spring readily to mind—but possibly the most disappointing of them all was former North Queensland enforcer Carl Webb. The 12-match Queensland Origin rep, who played his only Test for Australia in 2008, was expected to add starch to the Eels' pack in 2011 but made just six first grade appearances in an injury-ravaged year. The 30-year-old announced his retirement with a month of the regular season remaining.

ONE-SEASON STINTS

1. Frank Burge (St George, 1927)
The greatest tryscoring forward of all time, the legendary Frank Burge was lured to St George as captain-coach in 1927 after 16 seasons with Glebe. The Saints had struggled since their 1921 inception and finished with the wooden spoon in '26. But the revered Burge, 33, guided the club to a second-placed finish and an eventual 20-11 final loss to the dominant South Sydney club, while also maintaining his prolific tryscoring form with nine touchdowns. 'Chunky' Burge retired as a player at the end of the season but remained as coach for three more years, taking St George to the finals in each.

2. Herb Narvo (St George, 1946)
After a dismal seventh-place finish in 1945, St George enlisted Kangaroos, Newcastle and Newtown great Herb Narvo as captain-coach. The Dragons finished as minor premiers and won the club championship under the 34-year-old forward enforcer's leadership before going down 13-12 to Balmain in the challenge Grand Final. Narvo famously backed up to skipper the Saints a day after losing the Australian heavyweight boxing championship in a bout with Jack Johnson. The much-admired hardman left to captain-coach Cootamundra in 1947.

3. Amos Roberts (Penrith, 2004)
A highly rated fullback/wing prospect after scoring a premiership-record 22 points on debut for St George Illawarra in 2000, Amos Roberts' progress stalled in subsequent seasons amid fierce competition for backline spots. But he reinvigorated his career via a one-year stay with defending champs Penrith in 2004. Roberts topped the NRL with 23 tries in as many appearances, including a haul of four against the Warriors, and equalled the then club record with 28 points in a match (two tries, 10 goals)

against Manly. The Indigenous flyer also scored a try on debut for City Origin and was named Dally M Winger of the Year. He joined the Sydney Roosters for a fruitful stint the following season.

4. John Elias (Brisbane Souths, 1985)

After struggling to get his top-grade career going at Newtown and South Sydney, rugged and skilful forward John Elias—already a well-known off-field rogue—embarked on a sea change with Brisbane Rugby League heavyweights Souths in 1985. He thrived under the coaching of Wayne Bennett, and was named man-of-the-match for his marvellous display in the Magpies' Grand Final defeat of a star-studded Wynnum Manly side that featured the likes of Wally Lewis and Gene Miles. Elias honoured his decision to sign with Canterbury for the '86 season, but has since admitted he wished he had stayed in Brisbane, with the remainder of his career a succession of mid-season club switches and strife off the paddock.

5. Ellery Hanley (Balmain, 1988)

Great Britain captain Ellery Hanley linked with Balmain after his commitments with the 1988 Lions Tour ended, making his first Australian premiership appearance with three rounds of the season remaining and the Tigers' finals hopes on tenterhooks. The brilliant centre spearheaded the club's remarkable charge to the Grand Final, scoring a try in the fifth-place playoff victory over Penrith, bagging a double in the minor preliminary semi upset of Manly four days later, and crossing in subsequent sudden-death defeats of Canberra and Cronulla. A groggy Hanley was helped off the SFS in the Grand Final after a controversial tackle by Canterbury five-eighth Terry Lamb, taking Balmain's fairytale victory chances with him. He then spent half a season with Wests in '89, and finished his career with another stint for the Tigers in 1996-97.

6. Brett Mullins (Sydney Roosters, 2002)

Brett Mullins was a 1994 Kangaroo Tour star and scored 105 tries in 183 games for Canberra, but the last seasons of his tenure with the Raiders were plagued by indifferent form and ill-discipline, and his brief stint with Leeds in 2001 was a disaster. The 30-year-old was thrown a lifeline for a 2002 swansong by ex-Canberra teammate Ricky Stuart, who was approaching his rookie season as an NRL coach with the Sydney Roosters. Mullins was outstanding on the wing and in a handful of games at fullback, scoring 17 tries in 26 appearances and celebrating in the Tricolours' Grand Final triumph before he hung up the boots.

7. Sean Hoppe (North Sydney, 1994)

A rookie star and Kiwi Test debutant from Canberra in 1992, young winger Sean Hoppe was shown the door by the club at the end of '93 when it was revealed he had signed with the Auckland Warriors for their '95 premiership entry. He was without a club for '94 before he was snapped up by North Sydney as a ready-made replacement for New Zealand teammate Daryl Halligan, who sought a release to link with Canterbury. Hoppe enjoyed a stellar campaign on the flank for the high-flying Bears, scoring 15 tries in 25 games—the most by a Norths player since the great Ken Irvine in 1970. He departed after the Bears' preliminary final loss to his former club Canberra, and went on to score 19 tries and collect Dally M Winger of the Year honours in the Warriors' debut campaign.

8. Dean Bell (Auckland, 1995)
New Zealand Test great Dean Bell's three seasons with Easts were punctuated by injuries and suspension before he became a legendary figure as captain of the all-conquering Wigan combination. He joined former Wigan coach John Monie in Auckland in 1995, becoming the Warriors' inaugural skipper at the age of 32. A revered Rugby League identity in his homeland, the tough centre played 19 games in the club's debut season—leading the Warriors to within an ace of a finals appearance—before winding up his career with Leeds in '96.

9. Jonathan Davies (Canterbury, 1991)
Welsh Rugby Union and Great Britain Rugby League superstar Jonathan Davies arrived at Canterbury nine weeks into the 1991 season and scored 100 points in 14 appearances. A brilliant performer at fullback, he switched to centre late in the year and his 18-point haul (two tries, five goals) rescued the Bulldogs from a 16-0 deficit against Cronulla in the final round, spearheading a 26-16 comeback win and a fifth-place playoff berth. He returned to the British competition at the end of the year, but later enjoyed a nine-game stint at North Queensland in '95.

10. Bob Lindner (Illawarra, 1993)
A brilliant representative performer for Queensland and Australia for a decade, Bob Lindner was derided as a mercenary during his stints with Parramatta, Gold Coast and Wests, which were hampered by frequent injuries and inconsistent form. But he produced his finest first grade season after opting to finish his premiership career with Illawarra in 1993, where he played a career-high 20 games and collected Dally M Lock of the Year honours. He also enjoyed a wonderful Origin farewell and became just the second Australian Test player from the Steelers before joining English club Oldham.

SUCCESSFUL MID-SEASON TRANSFERS

1. Krisnan Inu—Warriors to Canterbury (2012)
Regarded as one of the NRL's most talented and frustrating enigmas, Krisnan Inu was granted a release by the Warriors in May 2012—just seven months after helping the club to a Grand Final. He had been dropped from first grade following an error-strewn Anzac Day display against Melbourne. Most were sceptical when Des Hasler brought the utility back to Canterbury as a replacement for injured wingers Steve Turner and Bryson Goodwin, but Inu produced his best season since his 2007 rookie year. He scored two tries on club debut and was a vital part of the Bulldogs' charge to the minor premiership and Grand Final, scoring 148 points (including nine tries) in just 16 games. He barely put a foot wrong, scoring or setting up numerous freakish tries and slotting match-winning field goals before earning a New Zealand Test recall after a four-year absence. True to form, however, Inu slipped back into his inconsistent ways during a suspension-marred 2013 campaign.

2. Rod Silva—Sydney City to Bulldogs (1995)
Despite winning back-to-back minor premierships in 1993-94, the Bulldogs had struggled to settle on a permanent fullback. That changed when elusive, big-stepping Easts custodian Rod Silva, who had been dumped to reserve grade by Roosters coach Phil Gould after signing with Super League, joined the club halfway through '95 and quickly found a home at Belmore. Silva starred in 16 straight matches as the besieged Bulldogs stormed to an unlikely premiership triumph, setting up a vital try for Terry Lamb in the preliminary final and scoring a match-sealing four-pointer in the Grand Final upset of Manly. He became the first player in history to win a premiership after switching clubs mid-season.

3. Brett Finch—Parramatta to Melbourne (2009)
After two seasons as Parramatta's dominant half, former NSW Origin hero Brett Finch was granted a release just four weeks into the 2009 season in the wake of the Eels' dismal start. He was playing for Melbourne within three weeks and proving an excellent foil at five-eighth for star No.7 Cooper Cronk while allowing Greg Inglis to revert to the centres. Finch, who had lost two previous Grand Finals with the Sydney Roosters, played 20 games for the Storm and celebrated their victory in the decider—ironically, against his former Parramatta teammates.

4. Mark Gasnier—French Rugby to St George Illawarra (2010)

Brilliant St George Illawarra centre Mark Gasnier stunned the Australian Rugby League fraternity in 2008 by forgoing a certain World Cup campaign to take up a Rugby Union deal in France. But after two seasons with Stade Francais, he rejected overtures from the Melbourne Rebels and the ARU and rejoined the Dragons midway through 2010. He played his first game in Round 17 and was eased back into the table-topping Dragons' side off the bench by coach Wayne Bennett. After returning to his favoured centre spot, the 29-year-old scored the opening try of the Saints' Grand Final victory over the Sydney Roosters—their long-awaited first as a joint venture. Gasnier won a NSW recall in 2011 and announced his surprise retirement at the end of that season.

5. Graham Appo—Canberra to Adelaide (1998)

Utility back Graham Appo was dumped by the Raiders early in '98 for disciplinary breaches, but proved an extraordinarily valuable pick-up for struggling expansion club Adelaide. Featuring at fullback, wing and centre after making his first appearance in Round 9, he scored 12 tries and 116 points—both club records—in just 14 games, and chalked up record 24-point hauls in consecutive weeks against Gold Coast and Balmain. After the Rams folded, Appo embarked on modest stints with Sydney City and North Queensland.

6. Nathan Fien—Warriors to St George Illawarra (2009)

Deemed surplus to requirements after four and a half seasons and 105 games for the Warriors, half/hooker Nathan Fien was snapped up by Wayne Bennett—who had worked with the utility in the Queensland Origin and New Zealand Test teams—and the ladder-leading Dragons. Fien cemented a bench role with the Saints and played in their '09 finals campaign while the Warriors languished near the foot of the ladder. He fought back from a broken leg suffered in the opening round of 2010 to score a try in the Dragons' Grand Final victory, and finally retired in 2013 after 276 NRL appearances.

7. Sam Perrett—Sydney Roosters to Canterbury (2012)

The Roosters reluctantly released New Zealand Test winger Sam Perrett after 16 rounds of the 2012 NRL season, allowing him to join fellow Kiwi Krisnan Inu in alleviating the Bulldogs' three-quarters injury crisis. The ever-reliable Perrett slotted seamlessly on to the Canterbury flank, featuring in the minor premiers' last 12 games and bagging a double in the preliminary final defeat of Souths before scoring the Bulldogs' only try in the Grand Final loss to Melbourne.

8. Clint Newton—Newcastle to Melbourne (2007)

Incoming Newcastle coach Brian Smith ruffled plenty of feathers in 2007, most notably by advising energetic backrower Clint Newton that his services would not be required beyond the end of the season. The 100-game veteran, who had debuted for Country Origin the previous season, quit the club midyear and was playing for Melbourne within a fortnight. He secured a second-row spot in the Storm pack and scored a try in a 44-0 defeat of his former club in just his fifth match, and crossed again in Melbourne's victory over Manly in the Grand Final to become only the second player after Rod Silva to win a title following a mid-season change of clubs. The USA international joined Hull KR at the end of the year but eventually returned to Newcastle in 2014 via Penrith.

9. Richie Fa'aoso—Newcastle to Melburne (2012)

Journeyman prop Richie Fa'aoso settled in Newcastle for several seasons, racking up 99 games for the Knights before falling out of favour with new coach Wayne Bennett during 2012. He opted to take up a short-term deal with Melbourne—his fifth NRL club—before the 30 June transfer cut-off. Fa'aoso found tough competition for forward spots at the Storm, making just two regular season appearances, but an injury to Jason Ryles opened up a bench spot and he featured throughout the club's finals campaign—including the Grand Final victory over the Bulldogs. The hard-hitting front-rower joined Manly in 2013 but a neck injury suffered in the preliminary final robbed him of another Grand Final appearance and forced him into retirement.

10. Chris Walker—South Sydney to Sydney Roosters (2003)

A brilliant but erratic attacking three-quarter with a penchant for off-field trouble, Chris Walker was a prized 2003 acquisition for the lowly Rabbitohs, who lured the 23-year-old from Brisbane. The Queensland Origin star walked out on Souths after just five appearances and was eventually picked up in June by defending premiers the Roosters, where he found a home on the right wing. Walker scored 10 tries in just 14 games (including a double in the preliminary final win over the Bulldogs) but endured Grand Final defeat at the hands of Penrith. He was a try-scorer in another decider loss a year later, but his subsequent seasons with the Roosters, Melbourne, Gold Coast, Catalans and Parramatta were plagued by injuries.

CONTRACT WRANGLES AND BACKFLIPS

1. Dennis Tutty

Balmain backrower Dennis Tutty played a Test for Australia in 1967, but his lasting legacy to Rugby League is as the player who stood up to the NSWRL and achieved greater equality for his peers. He attempted to join Penrith for the 1969 season, but the

Tigers refused to place him on the transfer list. At great personal and financial cost, Tutty chose to sit out two seasons of football while fighting for his right to change clubs—missing out on Balmain's famous '69 Grand Final victory. Eventually winning a court case to overturn the League's archaic transfer system, he joined the Panthers in 1971, but ironically finished his career back at Balmain in '76.

2. Terry Hill
Teenage centre Terry Hill became the highest-profile case study of the controversial player draft's short lifespan. After starring in his 1990 rookie campaign with Souths, Hill was set to join Western Suburbs the following season until Eastern Suburbs swooped in and snapped up the exciting three-quarter in the draft, as the club was within its rights to do. Hill initially refused to play for the Roosters, but after a drawn-out stand-off he lined up for his first game in the Tricolours in Round 6 of '91 and ended up scoring eight tries in 13 appearances. The draft was later declared a restraint of trade, and Hill gained a release to belatedly link with the Magpies at the end of the year.

3. Ruben Wiki
Auckland product and former Junior Kiwis star Ruben Wiki was viewed as an exciting signing for the Warriors' 1995 premiership entry, having cut his teeth in the all-star Canberra backline. But after playing a key role in the Raiders' 1994 title success, scoring 15 tries in 25 games as Mal Meninga's centre partner, Wiki backed out of his contract with the Warriors to remain in the Australian capital. A bitter and protracted dispute between the clubs played out over the summer, and it appeared Wiki would sit out the '95 season until the Warriors reluctantly eased off in their pursuit of the 22-year-old. He returned home a decade later and finished his career in 2008 after four strong seasons for the Warriors.

4. Tim Moltzen
Wests Tigers utility back Tim Moltzen briefly became the NRL's most maligned player in 2011 after he reneged on a three-year contract he had signed with St George Illawarra. The Dragons trumpeted Moltzen's acquisition mid-season, but at the end of the year the Tigers' hierarchy stated that he had never been formally released from his contract with the joint venture. Moltzen wanted to stay put, and after much deliberation between the clubs and the NRL, the Saints announced in November that they would not be seeking registration of his contract.

5. Greg Inglis
Superstar centre Greg Inglis was the highest-profile player forced to move on from Melbourne in the wake of the club's 2010 salary cap scandal. He announced he would

be joining Brisbane, although the signing of a contract was delayed due to the Storm's refusal to release him, reportedly because of legal fees he owed the club. Inglis skipped the Broncos' first pre-season training session in early November, citing bad weather in Sydney as the reason, before missing the club's deadline to sign a contract despite multiple assurances from the Queensland gun. The livid Broncos pulled their deal from the table and Inglis signed a rich contract with South Sydney a week later.

6. Jim Serdaris
Former Souths hooker Jim Serdaris resurrected his career in Canterbury's surge to the 1993 minor premiership, but became entangled in a contract dispute after signing an agreement to link with battling Western Suburbs for '94. Attempting to renege on the deal, he penned a two-year contract with the Bulldogs—but the Magpies held their ground and he eventually honoured his agreement with the club. While Wests continued to struggle, Serdaris flourished and made the Kangaroo Tour squad at the end of 1994. He joined Manly two years later.

7. Olsen Filipaina
A tug-of-war over New Zealand Test five-eighth Olsen Filipaina at the end of 1984 strained the long-standing friendship of Arthur Beetson and Jack Gibson, coaches of Eastern Suburbs and Cronulla respectively. The Sharks disputed the enigmatic Balmain back's signing with Easts for '85 on a one-year contract, claiming they had a handshake agreement with Filipaina and his manager for a two-season deal. The feud eventually dissipated and Filipaina linked with the Roosters, but the move was a dismal failure—he played just eight games for the club and represented the Kiwis from reserve grade before later joining North Sydney.

8. Luke Lewis
Versatile Penrith star Luke Lewis signed a rich deal with South Sydney during 2008, but the Panthers exercised their right under the NRL's rules to make a counteroffer to their charge prior to Round 13. They matched the Rabbitohs' big money (after reportedly offering him only half that amount before he signed with Souths) and signed Lewis to a four-year extension a fortnight before the deadline, with Lewis citing a family illness as the primary reason for backing out of the Souths deal. The Test stalwart eventually sought a release from Penrith in 2012 to join Cronulla.

9. Henry Paul
The Auckland Warriors pegged Henry Paul as a special talent when he was a junior, signing the teenaged fullback a couple of years before their 1995 entry to the premiership. But after he starred as captain on the Junior Kiwis' '93 tour of Great Britain, Paul became one of the game's hottest properties during an off-season stint

with Wakefield Trinity. His immediate earning potential skyrocketed and he backed out of his deal with the Warriors, who eventually relented when his proposed club, Wigan, agreed to waive the massive transfer fee they had slapped on Auckland's front-row recruit Andy Platt. Paul became one of the British game's dominant players over the next decade and played 24 Tests for the Kiwis, but never tested his talents in the Australian premiership.

10. Josh Papalii

Burgeoning Canberra backrower Josh Papalii signed a healthy three-year deal at the beginning of 2013 to join struggling Parramatta at the end of the season. But the deal had wriggle room, with the Raiders having until the halfway point of the season to make a counteroffer, and Papalii got cold feet about his impending move to Sydney. The 20-year-old signed a three-season extension with the Raiders on the eve of the 2013 campaign, incensing Parramatta fans, officials and coach Ricky Stuart. He went on to debut for Queensland and Australia that season and, in an ironic twist, played under Stuart in 2014 after the coach controversially quit the Eels to take over at Canberra.

Chapter 11

THE BAD AND THE UGLY

BLUNDERS

1. Martin Kennedy

Trailing 0-22 during the first half of an early season 2010 clash with Canterbury, the Sydney Roosters finally got on the board just before the half-hour mark. But any prospects of a miracle comeback were dashed by front-row tyro Martin Kennedy from the ensuing kick-off. Roosters halfback Mitchell Pearce collected the ball on his own line and popped a regulation pass to his charging prop, but the young Queenslander tripped and the ball ricocheted off his head. Bulldogs pivot Ben Roberts scooped up the loose ball and shifted it to centre Josh Morris, who evaded three defenders—including Kennedy—to dot down for the third of his four tries in the 60-14 walloping.

2. Max Mannix

Speedy winger Max Mannix played 24 games for Canterbury and Illawarra, but his name is synonymous with one unfortunate gaffe. Canterbury was leading fellow contender St George 8-4 in a 1984 clash when Mick Potter sliced through. The Bulldogs fullback's pass found Mannix—playing in his second first grade game—who set off on a thrilling 60-metre run to the try-line, outpacing the cover defence. But as Mannix dived and stretched out his arms to score, the ball flew out of his hands.

Luckily for the rookie the Bulldogs clung to their four-point lead, but footage of the incident is routinely wheeled out when memorable clangers are mentioned.

3. Glen Fisiiahi
Glen Fisiiahi was a quicksilver fullback star for the Warriors' dominant National Youth Competition side before he broke into first grade, and he produced maybe the most replayed moment in Under-20s history—for all the wrong reasons. 'The Flying Fish' scooped up a loose ball in a match against Souths and raced 80 metres in trademark fashion before slowing up for a salute to the heavens as he crossed the try-line. His casual approach allowed Rabbitohs backrower Hayden O'Donnell to hare through and crunch the speedster, who dropped the ball and became a blooper-reel standard in perpetuity.

4. Terry Lamb
Canterbury legend Terry Lamb kicked the most poorly timed field goal of all time late in a 1992 clash with Newcastle. He struck the ball sweetly from 40 metres out and it went straight down the middle—but the only problem was that the Bulldogs were two points behind at the time. A sheepish Lamb admitted after the match he thought the scores were tied. His miscalculation allowed the Knights to hang on for a 12-11 win.

5. Andrew Gee
Brisbane prop Andrew Gee cost the Broncos at least one competition point on a technicality in a 1996 match against Sydney City. He took a 20-metre tap inside the final minute of a classic Monday night encounter with the scores locked at 10-all, but incorrectly brought his foot up to meet the ball in his hands (instead of executing a mandatory tap with the ball on the ground) and drew a penalty in front of the posts. Roosters centre Ivan Cleary slotted the simple goal after the fulltime siren to secure a 12-10 victory over the shattered Broncos. The rule regarding tap restarts has since been amended—but this is scant consolation for the unfortunate rep forward.

6. Luke Phillips
Valuable Sydney Roosters custodian Luke Phillips produced one of the most lamentable howlers ever witnessed in an NRL finals match. With his side trailing Parramatta 8-10 just after halftime in the 2000 qualifying final, Phillips spilled a deep kick by the Eels. Instead of cleaning up the scraps, he ran past the ball in exasperation, expecting a scrum to be packed; Eels centre David Vaealiki played to the whistle and toed the ball through to score an easy try, setting the underdogs on a path to a 32-8 boilover. Phillips bounced back to play a brilliant hand in the Roosters' Grand Final loss to Brisbane three weeks later, and won a premiership with the club in 2002.

7. Adam O'Neill

The son of former Test cricketer Norm O'Neill, South Sydney winger Adam quickly gained a reputation as a fiery customer. His short fuse did not stop him from representing City Firsts and the President's XIII in 1988, but it cost the Rabbitohs a competition point later that season. With Souths tied 12-all with Cronulla at the SFS in the dying minutes, O'Neill was being held on his own 20-metre line when he reacted wildly to the tackle of Sharks prop Craig Dimond. O'Neill was penalised and Cronulla winger Sean Watson calmly slotted the match-winning penalty goal after the siren.

8. Krisnan Inu

Erratic utility back Krisnan Inu channelled his Warriors clubmate Glen Fisiiahi in a 2011 home game against Souths. Inu looked set to complete a long-range intercept try, but shifted down to first gear as he neared the try-line, unaware of teenage flyer James Roberts' valiant chase. Roberts cut Inu down a metre short of the line, and the enigmatic Kiwi was ruled to have been used as an obstruction when Kevin Locke dived over from dummy-half at the ensuing play-the-ball. Inu atoned for his blunder by scoring the winning try in a tense 12-6 result.

9. Nathan Merritt

After retrieving a kick in his own in-goal in the 2010 season opener against the Roosters, mercurial South Sydney winger Nathan Merritt broke through the first line of defence and set sail for the try-line with only open pasture in front of him. Few players in the NRL would have been capable of reining in the Rabbitohs flyer and the closest chaser was determined backrower Nate Myles. Nevertheless, Merritt looked up at the giant screen to check his progress and the ball popped out of his grasp, denying him a 101-metre try. He still managed to score both of Souths' tries in the 36-10 loss, but his howler was replayed countless times in the days the followed.

10. Russell Richardson

With Cronulla comfortably leading the Hunter Mariners during a 1997 Super League fixture, Sharks centre sensation Russell Richardson looked set to put the icing on the win with a length-of-the-field runaway try. But after he had done all the hard work, his lackadaisical attitude to planting the football resulted in the youngster dropping it over the line without a Mariner in sight, sealing his place in the Rugby League botched tries hall of infamy.

BAD BOYS

1. Les Boyd
A hardened prop forward renowned for getting white-line fever, Les Boyd was driven from the game after smashing the jaw of Darryl Brohman and eye-gouging Billy Johnstone. Talented and skilful, Boyd was volatile on the paddock. Always willing to gain an edge wherever he could, he continually flouted the rules and was sent off in an Ashes Test for kicking. A gentleman off the field, Boyd was one of the most feared Rugby League players of all time.

2. John Hopoate
A talented Manly winger whose game was built on aggression, John Hopoate was the most suspended player of the NRL era. Outed for such infamous grubby acts as sticking his finger into the anuses of opponents, his career was ended when he aimed a vicious elbow at the head of Cronulla prop Keith Galloway, for which he was suspended for 17 weeks. He also received a nine-game suspension for threatening a touch judge. Hopoate spent 45 weeks on the sideline through suspensions.

3. Paul Gallen
NSW captain and decorated international Paul Gallen has been one of the top forwards of the NRL era but has developed a reputation as a bad boy with numerous suspensions for questionable acts. Among these was his famous raking of Anthony Laffranchi's face in an attempt to dislodge his stitches. Gallen has also received suspensions for fighting, high tackles, headbutting and even racist remarks.

4. Danny Williams
There have been few more vicious acts on a Rugby League field in the history of the code than Danny Williams' king hit on Wests Tigers forward Mark O'Neill. Williams was sent off and suspended for 18 weeks for the act of thuggery, showing no remorse at his hearing and claiming to suffer from amnesia. Williams never again played in the NRL. He missed a total of 29 games through suspension.

5. Luke O'Donnell
The career of Luke O'Donnell, a judiciary regular during stints with the Wests Tigers, North Queensland and the Sydney Roosters, was constantly stymied by lengthy suspensions. Sin-binned on his debut, he received an 11-week suspension in 2003 for a vicious swinging arm that broke Michael Monaghan's jaw. In 2008, he was banned for seven weeks after a game of madness that saw him charged twice for

striking and once for abusing an official. Playing Origin in 2010, he was banned for three weeks following a spear tackle and headbutt. O'Donnell was sent off twice in his career and suspended for a total of 32 weeks.

6. Steve Matai
An aggressive and skilled centre from Manly, Steve Matai has built a reputation as a hothead who will happily breach any rule to gain an edge. He was famously sent off in a trans-Tasman Test for a nasty high shot on Mark Gasnier, and was rubbed out for seven weeks for a late shot on Michael Ennis in the last round of the 2010 season. Matai has been suspended an incredible 11 times for a total of 19 weeks.

7. Mark Geyer
Today a popular media figure, in his playing days Mark Geyer was a feared antagonist who often earned the ire of referees and the judiciary, missing 34 weeks over the course of his career with Penrith, Balmain and the Western Reds. Famous Geyer incidents include his Origin hell storm, where he was involved in numerous incidents, including an attempted elbow to Paul Hauff and a swinging arm on Steve Walters, and a 10-week suspension during the 1997 Super League season for a high shot and gouging in the same game.

8. Noel Kelly
One of Rugby League's most renowned hardmen—his 1996 autobiography is actually entitled *Hard Man: A Life in Football*—Noel Kelly was known for operating under the "retaliate first" principle. A Western Suburbs legend who was named in the Australian Team of the Century, Kelly became the most sent-off player in Rugby League history. Such was his reputation that he was once sent off when he wasn't even playing. On another occasion he refused to go and the French referee allowed him to stay on.

9. Mal Reilly
Maybe the most feared footballer ever to lace a boot, British legend Mal Reilly was one of the most destructive players the game has known. Sent off on numerous occasions during his time with Manly, Reilly was widely loathed by Australian fans during his time here. His first play for the Sea Eagles was an elbow to the head of Bob McCarthy, and he later had a vicious fight with George Piggins at Brookvale Oval. He was menacing in the 1973 Grand Final, injured and attempting to wreak as much havoc as he could before being forced from the paddock.

10. Quentin Pongia
Suspended for a grand total of 40 weeks, the journeyman forward—who spent most of his career at Canberra—earned more time on the sidelines than any player bar John Hopoate. A rugged and ruthless forward, New Zealander Quentin Pongia constantly

found trouble with his aggressive tackling style. He was famously sent off for a high tackle in a 1993 Test against Great Britain, and was sent off with teammate John Lomax in a clash with St George, for which he was suspended for six weeks.

OFF-FIELD MENACES

1. Craig Field
Former South Sydney, Manly, Balmain and Wests Tigers halfback Craig Field was rarely far from trouble during his career, and has found plenty after retiring. In 2009, he was charged with staging a robbery of a pub he worked at, and in 2012 he was charged with murder following an incident that resulted in the death of a 50-year-old man.

2. John Elias
A Rugby League journeyman who played for six premiership clubs, John Elias regularly found himself in the headlines and in trouble with the law. He was jailed for nine months in 1995 for drug supply and gun possession and spent another four years in prison from 2004 for shooting a former business partner in the leg. He was also mixed up in match-fixing scandals in 1994 and 2010.

3. Julian O'Neill
One of Rugby League's most infamous bad boys, Julian O'Neill built a lengthy rap sheet during his tumultuous career. His list of off-field atrocities include defecating in Souths teammate Jeremy Schloss's shoe, urinating under a table at Jupiters Casino, a string of drink-driving offences, and a bizarre incident in which he attempted to set fire to a 13-year-old who was wearing a dolphin outfit.

4. Barney Dalton
A winger with Eastern Suburbs from 1910 to 1915, who played in the 1911 final win, Barney Dalton turned to crime during his Rugby League career. He was a standover man for Kate Leigh's razor gang until he was shot dead in 1929, aged just 38.

5. Todd Carney
The career of Todd Carney—a recidivist whose talent could not save him at the Canberra Raiders—was redeemed with a Dally M-winning season for the Roosters in 2010 and a more mature approach with Cronulla. He eventually had his contract torn up after numerous alcohol-related incidents while in Canberra, and was banned from his hometown of Goulburn.

6. Willie Mason
Willie Mason is a larger-than-life character whose career is littered with a string of well-publicised off-field incidents. Included in his file are some ill-advised public remarks, verbally abusing a female reporter, public urination, drink-driving and testing positive to a recreational drug.

7. Reni Maitua
Canterbury, Cronulla and Parramatta backrower Reni Maitua has endured a controversial career that at one stage saw him rubbed out for two years for testing positive to a performance-enhancing drug. He also has a drink-driving rap on his sheet, as well as charges of assaulting an off-duty police officer in 2002 and a taxi driver in 2013.

8. Darrell Trindall
A superb talent, Darrell 'Tricky' Trindall also had an ability to find strife off the paddock. The former South Sydney and Canterbury half—who knocked his Rabbitohs teammate Justin Doyle's tooth out with a king hit on an end-of-season trip to Bali in '98—was charged with numerous assaults throughout and after his career, including one instance of assaulting a police officer.

9. Chris Walker
A journeyman outside back who played with six premiership clubs, Chris Walker seemed to perennially find himself in strife off the paddock. In 2004 he was arrested after a drunken altercation in Brisbane that saw him kicked out of the Queensland Origin camp; he faced further alcohol-related dramas in 2007, which garnered a suspension from his club, Gold Coast.

10. Phil Franks
Involved in the death of former Balmain player George Piper following an incident outside a nightclub in 1968, Phil Franks has since found himself battling bankruptcy and local councils due to some controversial business moves. Franks played 20 games for Penrith, Norths and Wests in the early 1970s.

VIOLENT MATCHES

1. 1954: NSW v Great Britain
The only senior match in Australian Rugby League history to be abandoned, the 1954 clash between NSW and Great Britain stands tall as the most violent game

ever played on Australian soil. It was always destined to be that way when Britain picked a side of fringe forwards out of position in what was their final trial before the third and deciding Test. Great Britain was trying to do nothing more than rough up potential Australian players, but Clive Churchill described the game as "a filthy brawl of back-lane thuggery, the most disgraceful match I ever played". The clash saw one violent act after another, with punching and kicking the primary orders of the day. With 17 minutes remaining, referee Aub Oxford abandoned the match and announced his immediate retirement.

2. 1932: Australia v England
The first 'Battle of Brisbane' was one of the bloodiest Rugby League matches ever played down under. After England had beaten Australia in the opening Test of the series in Sydney, Australia desperately needed to start well in Brisbane. They did just that, but violence soon took hold. Giant England prop Joe Thompson was knocked out cold in a scrum and his teammates retaliated in kind. England centres Stanley Brogden and Arthur Atkins continually bashed debutant Ernie Norman, halfback Hec Gee needed his lip stitched, and Frank O'Connor's head was opened up by a boot to the skull. Australia was forced to play the last 10 minutes with 10 men after Dan Dempsey broke his arm. Eric Weissel ran 75 metres on a broken ankle after a huge defensive stand to set up the match-sealing try for Gee in the 15-6 win.

3. 1928: St George v Balmain
The famous 'Earl Park Riot' started with an act of on-field violence and descended into mass civil disobedience. The fiery affair between St George and Balmain ended soon after popular local George 'Bluey' Carstairs was kicked in the head by Balmain prop Tony Russell. Fans were incensed and starting demanding Russell's head, ripping off fence palings and attacking the burly Tiger. They rioted long into the night, with one fan seen on the ground with an axe. Ironically, Russell ended up in the same ambulance as Carstairs and the two went at it again until they were broken up by ambulance officers.

4. 1973: Manly v Cronulla
The 1973 Grand Final was described in the papers the following day as being as "tough and dirty as any bar-room brawl". It was a fight where a game of Rugby League occasionally broke out. Cronulla, looking to intimidate the talented Sea Eagles, laid a late shot on Mal Reilly, who seriously injured his hip. Knowing he would not survive, Reilly attempted to create carnage and brawls broke out so continually that referee Keith Page issued two mass warnings. Manly won the decider 10-7. The match was labelled by John Raper as "the most disgusting game of Rugby League I've ever seen".

5. 1945: Newtown v St George

A more violent incident has not been seen on a Rugby League field than what was witnessed at Henson Park in 1945, when an unknown assailant bit off the ear of St George's Bill McRitchie. Newtown captain Frank 'Bumper' Farrell was the man accused, but after a lengthy hearing he was acquitted in a close vote. McRitchie spent nearly six months in hospital and never again played premiership football.

6. 1981: Newtown v Manly

Probably the most violent final in premiership history, the Newtown-Manly preliminary final clash in 1981 is best remembered for the wild brawl kicked off by niggling Jets halfback Tommy Raudonikis and finished by Newtown enforcer Steve Bowden. Bowden walloped Sea Eagles hardman Mark Broadhurst and scuffles broke out across the park. Just as the fighting died down, Bowden headbutted Broadhurst and tensions flared again. Bowden and Manly forward Terry Randall were sent off; Bowden was suspended and missed out on the Grand Final loss to Parramatta.

7. 1966: Australia v Great Britain

Lang Park Tests between Australia and Great Britain have historically been violent, and the 1966 clash was no different. After Great Britain won the series opener in an attacking affair, the Brisbane encounter was a violent scrap ultimately won 6-4 by Australia. British prop Brian Edgar flattened debutant John Wittenberg early, Australian centre Graeme Langlands clotheslined England halfback Tommy Bishop, Noel Kelly and Cliff Watson had a running war all day, and a spectator even ran on to the field and took a swing at England fullback Arthur Keegan. The most violent incident occurred late in the game when Englishman Bill Ramsey kicked Mick Veivers in the head, leading to 33 stitches and Ramsey's dismissal.

8. 1991: NSW v Queensland

On a rain-soaked SFS, the second game of the '91 interstate series turned into one of League's most violent thanks primarily to NSW firebrand Mark Geyer. Claiming to have been given a "green light" by selectors, Geyer went on a rampage. On the stroke of halftime, his swinging arm collected Maroons hooker Steve Walters around the head, sparking a brawl and a famous push-and-shove with Wally Lewis heading up the tunnel. Geyer didn't tone down his play in the second stanza, elbowing lanky Queensland fullback Paul Hauff in the head and sparking another brawl. A Michael O'Connor conversion ultimately won NSW the game, and Geyer was suspended for five weeks.

9. 1981: Manly v Western Suburbs

The 'Fibros v Silvertails' feud was at its zenith in the opening round of the 1981 season, with a history of violence and antagonism between Western Suburbs and

Manly having been built from 1978 when Roy Masters joined the Magpies as head coach and used socio-economic psychology to motivate his club. The feud began in a pre-season trial in Melbourne in '78 and continued through finals matches and the Sea Eagles' poaching of key Wests players in 1980. The Round 1 clash in '81 was a spiteful affair that saw eight players sent to the judiciary and John 'Dallas' Donnelly suspended for 14 weeks for kneeing an opponent in the head.

10. 1984: NSW v Queensland

The second game of the 1984 Origin series started with a brawl and rolled on as one for much of the contest. Attempting to strong-arm Queensland after the opening-game loss, the Blues started an all-in on the second tackle of the game when they brazenly thumped Maroons youngster Gene Miles. The scrimmage lasted for more than a minute, with Chris Close losing his jumper and Peter Tunks and Ray Price dishing out vicious blows to the Queenslanders. In sodden conditions, the tight contest caused high tensions among both outfits and led to plenty of niggle and fire for the rest of the clash—which incidentally was won by the Maroons.

LONGEST SUSPENSIONS

1. Bob Cooper—15 months

A rough-and-ready backrower with Western Suburbs, Bob Cooper effectively had his career ended after a wild brawl in a clash against Illawarra in 1982. Having been dumped to reserve grade earlier in the year, Cooper felt he needed to make an impact to keep his first grade spot after being recalled for the Steelers clash. After he broke Illawarra winger Lee Pomfret's jaw with a vicious punch and seriously injured two others Cooper was handed a record 15-month suspension by judiciary chairman Jim Comans, who said, "Acts such as these must be obliterated from the game and I'll begin by obliterating you." Cooper made a brief return in 1984 with Norths.

2. Les Boyd—15 months

Just three games back after a 12-month suspension for breaking the jaw of Darryl Brohman, Les Boyd's premiership career was ended at the judiciary by Jim Comans, who gave him a record-equalling 15-month ban. Boyd was found guilty of eye-gouging Canterbury hooker Billy Johnstone in a 16-6 loss to the Bulldogs. He continued his career in England, where he played four seasons with Warrington.

3. Les Boyd—12 months
The perennially suspended Les Boyd received his second-longest ban after a violent elbow to the jaw of Darryl Brohman during a 1983 State of Origin encounter at Lang Park. In what appeared to be a premeditated and deliberate act of thuggery, Boyd cocked his elbow and shattered Brohman's jaw. Judiciary enforcer Jim Comans took a dim view of the act, outing Boyd for 12 months, and Brohman later sued Boyd over the incident.

4. Bill Maizey—12 months
Balmain forward Bill Maizey was handed a record 12-month suspension after breaking the jaw of Eastern Suburbs hooker George Clamback in the final game of the 1927 season. A promising prop forward, Maizey had represented NSW in his debut season a year prior, but after unloading on Clamback, he was suspended for the entire 1928 season and never again played premiership Rugby League.

5. Steve Kneen—12 months
Cronulla hardman Steve Kneen received a 12-month suspension in 1982 for an incident in reserve grade as he was attempting a comeback from a 15-game suspension. The 1978 Kangaroo tourist hit an opponent high and never played premiership football again.

6. Steve Linnane—20 weeks
St George halfback Steve Linnane copped a 20-week suspension in 1987 over a vicious eye-gouge on Penrith youngster Greg Alexander. Alexander's Penrith teammate Mark Geyer said Linnane had "attempted to rip Alexander's eye out" in one of League's ugliest incidents. Linnane played a further three seasons with the Dragons before moving to Newcastle.

7. Danny Williams—18 weeks
Melbourne backrower Danny Williams incurred the longest suspension of the NRL era after a vicious king hit on Wests Tiger Mark O'Neill. Williams claimed to have suffered post-traumatic amnesia after punching O'Neill in the back of the head in the spiteful 2004 encounter. When the NRL judiciary handed down the record 18-game ban, Williams refused to apologise; he never again played in the NRL.

8. John Hopoate—17 weeks
The oft-suspended Manly winger John Hopoate regularly flouted the laws of the game and found himself sidelined for 17 weeks in 2005 after he left young Cronulla forward Keith Galloway unconscious following a launched, cocked elbow to the prop's head. Hopoate claimed he was attempting a shoulder charge but his defence didn't move the judiciary, who ended his Rugby League career with the lengthy ban. Manly immediately tore up Hopoate's contract.

9. Steve Kneen—15 weeks
Sharks enforcer Steve Kneen was one of the first players to fall victim to Jim Comans' attempt to clean up Rugby League. Kneen was outed for 15 weeks in 1981 for a head-high tackle off the ball. He returned at the back end of the season but received a longer ban in 1982.

10. John Donnelly—14 weeks
Renowned Wests larrikin John 'Dallas' Donnelly was a regular at Phillip Street headquarters throughout his career. In 1981, he earned the ire of Jim Comans and company as one of eight players to front the panel after a violent clash with Manly in the opening round of the year. Donnelly was charged with kneeing an opponent in the head and was sidelined for 14 weeks.

BITING INCIDENTS

1. Frank Farrell
In one of the most infamous and unsavoury incidents in the game's history, St George forward Bill McRitichie had his ear almost completely severed in a scrum against Newtown during a 1945 first grade encounter. Bluebags prop Frank 'Bumper' Farrell, the most feared hardman of the era, was accused of biting McRitchie's ear but was narrowly cleared by the NSWRL due to a lack of evidence. McRitchie spent 22 painful weeks recuperating in hospital, while the larger-than-life policeman 'Bumper' cagily maintained his innocence until his death—including claiming he had left his false teeth in the dressing room that day and therefore could not have been the culprit.

2. James Graham
British prop James Graham chewed his way into the Grand Final hall of infamy at the end of a stellar maiden campaign at Canterbury. An in-goal melee followed Bulldogs winger Sam Perrett's first-half try in the 2012 decider against Melbourne, in which Graham came to grips with Billy Slater and inexplicably latched on to the superstar Storm fullback's ear with his teeth. Remarkably, Graham escaped on-field sanction for his Mike Tyson-esque act, but the NRL judiciary compounded the blue-and-whites' 14-4 loss by slapping the overzealous front-rower with a 12-match suspension.

3. Graeme Wynn
Towering St George second-rower Graeme Wynn created history in 1982 by becoming the first player to be suspended for biting by the NSWRL judiciary. The

charge arose from a complaint laid by Parramatta's Ray Price—a teammate of Wynn's on Australia's tour of New Zealand two years earlier—who claimed his rival had chomped on his arm. "The act of biting an opposing player shows a total indifference to normal human behaviour," said hard-nosed judiciary chairman Jim Comans before handing down a 12-match suspension. The devastated Wynn played another decade of first grade with Saints and Wests, but his career never fully recovered from the half-season ban.

4. Tom Raudonikis
Rugby League Week outed Tom Raudonikis as 'The Phantom Biter' in 1976, when it featured the hyper-aggressive Western Suburbs legend on its cover with a mask and vampire teeth superimposed—and an accompanying first-person admission. This followed the revelation that rival Manly halfback Johnny Gibbs had been bitten on the nose. Raudonikis was handed a $200 fine by the NSWRL for bringing the game into disrepute, which *RLW* gladly paid on the Test No.7's behalf.

5. Jarrod McCracken
Jarrod McCracken had already proved himself a firebrand during his rookie first grade season at Canterbury when he was sent off (along with Australian five-eighth Peter Jackson) for fighting in just his second Test appearance for New Zealand midway through 1991. But a far more severe punishment awaited the 21-year-old centre after he was cited and found guilty of biting Souths winger Ross Harrington on the chest during the Bulldogs' 40-2 late season win. McCracken copped an eight-match stint on the sidelines, which ruled him out until Round 4 of 1992.

6. Brad Morrin
Rugged Bulldogs forward Brad Morrin was handed an eight-game ban after chowing down on Parramatta centre Timana Tahu's arm in a match late in the 2007 season. The remorseful 25-year-old was rubbed out of the club's finals campaign but returned to play a further three seasons at Canterbury. Morrin consequently picked up the nickname 'The Nibbler' from fans on the club's online forum.

7. Grant Izzard
Versatile Grant Izzard's first grade career came to an abrupt end when he was found guilty of biting tempestuous South Sydney halfback Craig Field. The Illawarra interchange—a former clubmate of older brother and Penrith great Brad, and partnered on the Steelers' bench this day by another brother, Craig—was outed for six matches in the wake of his side's 24-12 win in Round 16 of 1993. The suspension ruled Izzard out for the remainder of the season, and he was released by Illawarra at the end of the year.

8. Anthony Watts
A string of off-field disciplinary issues ended the NRL career of aggressive former Cronulla and North Queensland utility Anthony Watts, while injury cruelled his Super League stint at Widnes. He subsequently became involved with notorious bikie gang 'The Finks' after relocating to the Gold Coast. Watts attracted worldwide media attention in 2013 while he was playing for Tugun Seahawks in the Gold Coast Rugby League competition and was accused of biting an opponent's penis during a match against Bilambil Jets. Watts vigorously denied the charge but was nevertheless banned for eight games—and attracted headlines of John Hopoate proportions around the globe.

9. William Zillman
Gold Coast fullback William Zillman was slugged with a four-match suspension in 2009 after South Sydney winger Jamie Simpson made an on-field complaint regarding an alleged bite on his arm. Zillman vehemently denied the charge but was found guilty by the NRL judiciary, who subsequently rejected the Titans' appeal bid.

10. Peter Ryan
Brisbane's hitman backrower Peter Ryan's rapid progress was momentarily halted during 1994 when he was cited and suspended for three weeks after being found guilty of biting Souths five-eighth Jason Bell. Ryan's ban soured the Broncos' comprehensive 40-10 victory. He was the fourth player from the club to have fallen foul of the judiciary during a difficult title defence.

GOUGING INCIDENTS

1. Steve Linnane
The career of St George half Linnane—Dally M Rookie of the Year and a Grand Final No.7 in 1985—went into a tailspin when he was found guilty of gouging Penrith rival Greg Alexander in a late season match in 1987. Cited on two counts of gouging and one of attacking the face of an opponent, Linnane vehemently refuted the ugly charges. But according to some reports he had almost ripped Alexander's eye out of his head, and the diminutive Saint was suspended for a whopping 20 weeks. Linnane's career never fully recovered. No player has received a longer suspension for an on-field incident since.

2. Les Boyd
After Round 18 of 1984, Manly's forward-pack wildman Les Boyd—in just his third match back from a 12-month suspension for breaking Daryl Brohman's jaw with a

savage elbow in an Origin match the previous season—was hauled before the judiciary for the umpteenth time in his career, this time for gouging Canterbury hooker Billy Johnstone. The reprehensible actions of Boyd, who was one of the most talented forwards of his era, incurred an astounding 15-month suspension, and effectively ended his professional career in Australia.

3. Gary Freeman

Livewire Balmain halfback Gary Freeman was controversially slammed with a 12-week suspension for eye-gouging in the wake of a spiteful match against Newcastle early in 1989. Freeman, whose two tries effectively sealed the Tigers' 22-20 win, was found guilty of gouging Knights prop Mark Sargent despite the Kiwi No.7's vigorous denials. During the same match Newcastle's other prop, Peter Johnston, was sent off for gouging; he was later exonerated by the judiciary.

4. George Piggins and Mal Reilly

Legendary tough guys George Piggins and Mal Reilly resorted to eye-gouging during one of the most infamous and brutal one-on-one confrontations in premiership history. Souths hooker Piggins reacted to having his face stomped on by Manly's British backrow enforcer Reilly in a 1973 clash at the SCG, prompting a back-and-forth eruption of punches and vicious headbutts before the brawl stepped up another notch when gouging was added to the mix. Piggins recalled years later that he copped Reilly's finger in his eye as they grappled on the ground—and the Rabbitohs rake responded in kind: "I went straight for one of his eyes, and I'll swear I had it out in my hand. Ray Branighan, an ex-teammate with Souths who had joined Manly, ran in at exactly that moment and pushed me, and Reilly's right eye popped back in." With the match played in the days before video reviews, the pair escaped censure.

5. Darren Maroon

South Sydney prop Darren Maroon was cited after a typically fiery Charity Shield clash with St George during the 1988 pre-season, with Test forward Wally Fullerton-Smith—who was sent off for a headbutt in the match—claiming the Rabbitohs tyro had eye-gouged him. Maroon was outed for 12 matches.

6. Mark Geyer

A judiciary staple throughout his wild and tumultuous career, Mark Geyer was rubbed out for 10 weeks during 1997 on reckless high tackle and eye-gouging charges emanating from Perth Reds' narrow win over Adelaide. The Reds captain denied the accusation of gouging Rams fullback Chris Quinn, but his plea fell on deaf ears and he was forced to endure yet another long stint on the sidelines.

7. Matthew Ridge

Auckland captain Matthew Ridge was a valuable but volatile fullback whose 1999 NRL season was marred by a hefty suspension for multiple charges emanating from a match against Canberra. Ridge kicked the Warriors to a 32-30 win via a late penalty goal, but was forced to front the judiciary for tripping, a Grade 1 high tackle and—the most serious charge—a Grade 5 contrary conduct citing for contact with the fingers to the eyes. The veteran was pinched on the latter charge for dragging his hands across the face of young Raiders winger Lesley Vainikolo, and was suspended for a total of eight weeks. (He was exonerated on the tripping charge.)

8. Ryan Cross

Sydney Roosters centre Ryan Cross missed a significant chunk of the 2005 season after being found guilty of eye-gouging Parramatta backrower Glenn Morrison. In a hero-to-villain performance that was eerily similar to Gary Freeman's 16 years earlier, Cross scored both of the Roosters' tries to spearhead a 12-8 victory that turned sour after the judiciary ignored Cross' not-guilty plea and handed down a six-week suspension.

9. Mario Fenech

Aggressive, passionate South Sydney hooker and captain Mario Fenech's hot-head reputation was largely built on his infamous send-off in a finals loss to Balmain in 1986. Lining up against bitter rival Ben Elias, Fenech was marched by referee Kevin Roberts for gouging in a scrum just after halftime. The Tigers used their one-man advantage to turn the 8-all scoreline into an emphatic 36-11 victory, while Fenech was handed a four-match suspension in the aftermath and left out of the Kangaroo Tour squad in favour of Elias.

10. Paul Gallen

A couple of years before he garnered a reputation as the game's most inspirational forward, Cronulla lock Paul Gallen was in the headlines for a string of unsavoury on-field incidents. The grubbiest of these was in an early season encounter with Gold Coast in 2008, when he was cited for raking at a wound on the face of Titans forward Anthony Laffranchi, who was forced off to the blood bin. Gallen was outed for three weeks on a contrary conduct charge (unnecessary face contact) but escaped censure after Josh Graham accused him of grabbing his testicles in the same match. Ironically, Laffranchi made his NSW debut alongside Gallen less than two months later.

SPITTING INCIDENTS

1. Wally Lewis and Jim Cowell
In 1989, Brisbane superstar Wally Lewis and comparatively unheralded Gold Coast forward Jim Cowell were involved in possibly the most sensational of all Rugby League spitting incidents. After Cowell had allegedly remarked on Lewis' receding hairline, Lewis spat at his opponent and declared he would be back in reserve grade the following week. Cowell retaliated by spitting at 'The King'. Lewis was fined $2000 and Cowell $1000 by the NSWRL, but neither player was suspended.

2. Jamie Corcoran
Balmain's Jamie Corcoran, in just his third appearance for the Tigers after joining the club in 1993, became the first player ever to be suspended by the NSWRL judiciary for spitting. The former Canterbury utility back was cited for gobbing at Canberra's Test hooker Steve Walters, and was later outed for two matches and fined $2500. Corcoran returned to first grade and finished with a career-high 18 appearances in '93 before embarking on a modest two-season stint with Souths.

3. Matthew Ridge
Brilliant but tempestuous fullback Matthew Ridge was at the centre of spitting allegations after a controversial afternoon at Belmore Oval. The Auckland skipper was accused of letting fly at Canterbury fans in the crowd after he had been sin-binned in a highly publicised incident, but he was subsequently cleared due to a lack of evidence. The Warriors carved out a remarkable 20-6 win despite having prop Jerry Seuseu sent off.

4. Shayne Dunley
Manly interchange dummy-half Shayne Dunley, ironically a bench regular for the Eels just two years earlier, was charged with spitting at Parramatta hooker PJ Marsh by the video review committee in 2005. The NRL judiciary found Dunley guilty and suspended him for four matches, but he successfully appealed the ban during a second hearing that lasted almost two hours. The Sea Eagles' legal team convinced the panel that a case of reflux—causing excess saliva to build up in the throat—was the reason for Dunley's spit, and that he'd had no intention of directing it at Marsh.

5. Wade McKinnon
Fiery Warriors fullback Wade McKinnon was no stranger to trouble with referees, having been suspended in 2007 for pushing whistle-blower Jason Robinson in 2007. The star No.1 received another black mark against his name when he was charged

with spitting towards touch judge Brett Suttor during a victory over Penrith in the penultimate round of 2008. The Warriors stood behind McKinnon, who defended the charge—to no avail, as he was outed for three weeks. The Warriors won their way through to the preliminary final despite the absence of their attacking dynamo, and McKinnon made his return in the season-ending loss to Manly.

6. John Donnelly
One of the great characters and true rogues of a volatile era in Rugby League's history, Wests enforcer John Donnelly frequently made his way to the judiciary—on a variety of violent charges. But after receiving a five-match suspension during 1979, an irritated Donnelly took out his frustrations on the media throng that followed him from the hearing. The irrepressible 'Dallas' began to cross the street but then turned around and spat towards a trailing cameraman. The unsavoury footage was aired in subsequent news broadcasts.

7. Glenn Hall
North Queensland forward Glenn Hall was at the centre of a spitting allegation in a 2011 match against Penrith. Panthers halfback Luke Walsh informed the referees of an incident with Hall but declined to make an official complaint during or after the game. Video footage failed to show any evidence of Hall spitting, and he was not charged.

8. Matt Hilder
Newcastle hooker Matt Hilder was charged with spitting on the same weekend as Wade McKinnon in 2008, following a complaint made by Melbourne and former Knights winger Anthony Quinn. Quinn was seen wiping his face at the end of the Knights' dramatic 17-16 win, but Hilder—who became a key figure in Newcastle's ultimately futile finals bid following a season-ending injury to Danny Buderus—maintained his innocence and was subsequently exonerated.

9. Blake Ferguson
Gifted Canberra three-quarter Blake Ferguson's spectacular downward spiral was one of the stories of 2013, but his ignominious streak of off-field atrocities had begun during the previous off-season. He attended the Foreshore Festival in November 2012 with Raiders teammates but was escorted from the VIP area by security staff for spitting on fellow patrons. He was punished internally by the Raiders at the time, and his career unravelled the following season when—among other indiscretions—he was dumped from the NSW Origin side after being charged with sexual assault.

10. Jorge Taufua
Blockbusting Manly winger Jorge Taufua undid some of the goodwill garnered by his stellar 2012 rookie season when he was arrested and charged with spitting at police

during an ill-fated off-season night out on the Gold Coast. A remorseful Taufua pleaded guilty when he fronted court the following August, and was subsequently stood down by the Sea Eagles for the final two rounds of the regular season. The tyro returned to first grade during the finals and scored the opening try of Manly's Grand Final loss to the Sydney Roosters—his 20th touchdown of the season.

UNLUCKY SEND-OFFS

1. Trent Waterhouse
Backrower Trent Waterhouse became the first NSW player to be sent off in an Origin match in the dying stages of the explosive 2009 dead rubber at Suncorp Stadium. Rival props Brett White and Steve Price went toe-to-toe, with White landing the knockout punch as Waterhouse simultaneously arrived on the scene to tackle Price. Waterhouse was marched as Price lay unconscious on the turf, but he was exonerated by the judiciary on the subsequent contrary conduct charge.

2. Bill Cann and Henry Knight
Australian forward Bill Cann and New Zealand rival Henry Knight were sent off in the third Test at Sydney's Wentworth Park in 1909—on the mild charge of "shaping up to each other". The pair were marched by referee Charlie Hutchison despite no punches being thrown, and were cheered by the crowd as they shook hands and left the field in one of Rugby League's more quaint anecdotes.

3. Wade McKinnon
Combative Warriors fullback Wade McKinnon was dismissed after an innocuous incident two minutes from fulltime in a 2007 clash with Wests Tigers. He was shocked when referee Paul Simpkins pointed to the sheds after McKinnon had made a regulation tackle; he was charged with kneeing Tigers winger Taniela Tuiaki in the head. Tuiaki was equally baffled, and McKinnon was cleared of any wrongdoing by the match review panel after video evidence showed there had been no indiscretion.

4. Duncan Thompson
A highly controversial send-off and suspension ended the Sydney career of one of the code's greatest players, North Sydney halfback Duncan Thompson. He was contentiously dismissed for "indiscriminate kicking" in the defending premiers' encounter with Glebe late in 1923 before being suspended for the remainder of the season. The brilliant Thompson, who was regarded as one of the game's cleanest

and most honourable players, vehemently denied the charge. Shattered, he returned to Queensland and added to his enormous legacy with the all-conquering Toowoomba combination.

5. Mario Fenech
Fiery Souths captain Mario Fenech was sent off twice during the 1987 season—and was cleared by the judiciary on both occasions. After being sin-binned earlier in the Rabbitohs' Round 3 clash with Balmain, a heavily concussed Fenech was marched during the second half on a repeated infringements charge. In Round 19, the skipper was dismissed for alleged headbutting in Souths' tight win over Parramatta, but he was again found not guilty by the judiciary.

6. Martin Martin
New Zealand's last-gasp 16-15 first Test win over France's brilliant 1951 tourists was marred by a series of violent incidents, but the only player to be sent off—French hooker Martin Martin—was reportedly the victim of mistaken identity. Martin was accused of throwing a handful of the Carlaw Park mud in the face of referee Jim Griffin and was promptly dismissed, but both he and skipper Puig-Aubert vigorously denied the rake was the perpetrator. Team manager Antoine Blain had to take to the field and forcibly remove Martin, but he joined the players in their assertion Griffin had got the wrong man; several Kiwi players also backed the claims that another French forward was the culprit.

7. Gary Freeman
New Zealand veteran Gary Freeman endured a gruelling Auckland homecoming as Parramatta captain against the Warriors in 1996. The niggly halfback, incessantly roasted by the crowd, was sin-binned and then sent off for giving away a succession of penalties during the second half. A furious Freeman headed to the dressing rooms to the strains of *Hit the Road, Jack* blasting over the Ericsson Stadium PA, but he was cleared by the judiciary on the vague "misconduct" charge.

8. Phil Sigsworth
In 1986, Canterbury fullback Phil Sigsworth became the first player to be sent off in a Grand Final for 24 years—and he remains the last unfortunate player to be marched in a decider. Chasing through on a kick near Parramatta's line with 13 minutes of the tense Grand Final remaining, Sigsworth hung an arm out and caught Eels five-eighth Brett Kenny high. Referee Mick Stone immediately dismissed the hapless Bulldogs custodian despite having disciplined more serious incidents earlier in the match with a mere penalty. Canterbury lost the try-less classic 4-2, consigning Sigsworth to the dubious honour of being the first player to lose a Grand Final with three different clubs.

9. Clive Churchill

Australian Test captain Clive Churchill was sent off in South Sydney's big win over St George on Anzac Day 1953 for the seemingly tame offence of "cheeking". The incomparable fullback, who had been knocked out by a Billy Wilson high shot during the first half, was reported by touch judge Fred Erikson for a stoush with Saints winger Ross Kite early in the second stanza. Churchill gave Erikson a spray as he ran back into position—and was reported again. Referee Aub Oxford, best known as the referee who abandoned the violent NSW v Great Britain international and announced his immediate retirement the following season, sent Churchill from the field. Churchill escaped with a caution at the judiciary after contending he could not remember the incident following his heavy hit in the first half.

10. Derek Turner

Australian prop Dud Beattie duped Great Britain rival Derek Turner into getting sent off in a famous Ashes incident in 1962. After suffering a dislocated shoulder during the second half of the third Test at the SCG—and with no replacements allowed for injured players in those days—Beattie deliberately set out to take a British forward off the field with him. The Ipswich great goaded veteran lock Turner into fighting him—Turner obliged, and the pair were dismissed by referee Darcy Lawler. Australia snatched a famous 18-17 dead-rubber victory after a late sideline conversion by Ken Irvine, with Beattie's crafty gamesmanship playing a key role.

Chapter 12

CONVERTS

BEST CONVERTS—UNION TO LEAGUE

1. Dally Messenger
Rugby League's first superstar and the man credited with giving the code the kick-start it needed, Dally Messenger was the 15-man game's undisputed top player before he defected to the professional game in 1908. A freakish wing/centre with unmatched athleticism and skill for his era, Messenger represented the Wallabies twice in 1907 before joining the trailblazing New Zealand 'All Golds'—considered the first League team to tour—as a guest player. He played the first five seasons of the NSWRL premiership with Eastern Suburbs, winning three titles, and seven Tests for Australia, scoring 44 points. The Dally M Medal is named in his honour.

2. Ray Price
The son of former North Sydney player Kevin, Ray Price rose to prominence as an uncompromising breakaway/No.8 in the amateur code, making eight Test appearances between 1974 and '76. He signed with the Parramatta Eels for the '76 season and went on to become one of the greats of the club. In his 259-game career with the Eels, Price played in the club's only four premierships and won the Rothmans Medal (1979) and Dally M Medal (1982). Parramatta made the Grand Final in his

first two seasons at the club and in seven of his 11 years. Price represented NSW 15 times and Australia on 22 occasions in one of the great Rugby League careers.

3. Michael O'Connor

One of the most coveted Rugby Union talents in Australia when he defected to Rugby League, Michael O'Connor forged a tremendous career in the professional code and is regarded as one of the finest of Australia's dual internationals. After playing 12 Tests for the Wallabies as a speedy wing/centre, O'Connor was poached by St George in 1983 and had an immediate impact, scoring a try on debut. He really made his mark in his third season in the game, leading the Dragons to the Grand Final and debuting for NSW and Australia. While he enjoyed a fine club career that included a premiership with Manly and 981 career points, it was on the rep stage that he shone brightest. Playing 19 Origins for NSW and 18 Tests for Australia, O'Connor still holds the record for most tries and points as a Blue.

4. Kevin Ryan

A behemoth of a man, Kevin Ryan debuted for the Wallabies on the 1957-58 tour of the UK and played on a further tour of New Zealand from Brisbane before switching states and codes, joining St George in 1960. Playing in both the backrow and front row with the Saints, Ryan's seven seasons saw him win seven titles. He played the role of enforcer and was nicknamed 'Kandos'—after the NSW cement-producing town—for his hardness. He joined Canterbury in 1967 as captain-coach and led the team that ended St George's 11-season premiership run with a 12-11 win against his old club in the preliminary final. The 1963-64 Kangaroo played two Tests for Australia and later served as a politician in the NSW Legislative Assembly.

5. Arthur Summons

The man immortalised on the NRL premiership statue with Norm Provan actually played 10 Tests for the Wallabies before reaching the peaks of Rugby League. A diminutive five-eighth/halfback, Arthur Summons played just four seasons in the Sydney premiership with Western Suburbs, but he left a permanent mark on the game, guiding Wests to three straight Grand Finals—and being photographed muddy and bloody after the last of these, a heartbreaking and controversial 8-3 defeat to St George in 1963. Summons played nine Tests for Australia, leading his country to five wins from five matches as skipper and captain-coaching the 1963-64 Kangaroos.

6. Dick Thornett

One of only five Australians to represent in three sports, Dick Thornett was part of Australia's water polo team at the 1960 Olympic Games before playing 11 Tests in just two seasons of Rugby Union. In 1963 he joined Parramatta, where his brother Ken was the popular fullback, and made a significant contribution in his nine-year, 148-game career as a ball-playing lock with tremendous skill. Thornett played 14 Tests for Australia and scored a try in the famous 'Swinton Massacre' 50-12 win over Great Britain.

7. Ken Kearney
A tough-as-nails hooker, Ken Kearney played seven Tests for the Wallabies in the shadows of World War II before he switched to Rugby League with English club Leeds in 1948. He returned to Australia in 1952 and signed with St George, where he was immediately selected for Australia in his first premiership season. Kearney would represent Australia 31 times in a distinguished Test career that included three Test series and a Kangaroo Tour as captain-coach. He is regarded as one of the most important Dragons signings ever, with his commitment to professionalism and his unquestioned leadership central to the rise of the Saints in the mid-1950s. Kearney led St George to five straight premierships and coached it to its sixth after a chronic knee injury forced his playing retirement.

8. Chris McKivat
The Wallabies captain at the hour of Rugby League's birth in Australia, Chris McKivat led Australia to the gold medal at the 1908 Olympics before he turned professional in 1910 with Glebe. Although he was 30 at the time of his defection, McKivat was one of the great stars in League's infant days. He played five seasons with Glebe, taking it to runners-up in two straight seasons, and skippered Australia to an undefeated Ashes victory on the fabled 1911-12 Kangaroo Tour. After retiring in 1914, he coached Norths to their only two premierships in 1921-22.

9. Russell Fairfax
A flamboyant five-eighth in the 15-man code, Russell Fairfax joined Eastern Suburbs in 1974 after an eight-Test Wallaby career and was an immediate sensation in Rugby League. Playing for an Eastern Suburbs team that is regarded as one of the greatest ever, Fairfax won premierships in his first two seasons (although a broken leg kept him out of the '75 Grand Final) and became a crowd favourite with his long hair. Though he never represented Australia in an injury-interrupted career, his flair and popularity made him one of the great Rugby Union converts.

10. Ricky Stuart
Born into a stringent Rugby League family, Ricky Stuart played Rugby Union at school and was selected for the 1987 tour of Argentina before returning to the 13-man code in 1988, where he would go on to become one of the great modern-day halfbacks. Joining his hometown team at Canberra, Stuart would play a central role in guiding

the Raiders to three titles and four Grand Finals between 1989 and 1994 while helping NSW regain the Origin shield for the first time in four seasons. Though he never played a Test in Australia, he wore the green and gold nine times on two successful Kangaroo campaigns. Stuart won the Dally M and Rothmans medals in 1993. He finished his playing career with Canterbury in 2000 before taking up coaching.

WORST CONVERTS—UNION TO LEAGUE

1. Garrick Morgan
Regarded as the best Rugby Union lock in the world in the mid-1990s after a 16-Test career with the Wallabies, Garrick Morgan was hyped as expansion club South Queensland's big-name signing in 1995. The two-metre-tall Morgan managed just two first grade games as a front-rower in an inglorious Rugby League career before the Crushers released him. He returned to Union and played a further eight Tests for the Wallabies.

2. Tony D'Arcy
A lumbering prop who played 10 Tests for the Wallabies, Penrith signed Tony D'Arcy to a huge contract in 1983. He couldn't manage a game in the top flight for the 11th-placed Panthers, who used 41 first graders. Ross Gigg, a centre at Penrith during '83, said teammate Ken Wilson quipped that "his backyard tap would run faster than D'Arcy", who finished up in third grade before retiring.

3. Kent Lambert
Another famous Penrith Rugby Union convert, 11-Test All Black prop Kent Lambert had built a fearsome reputation in the amateur code before he was lured to the Panthers in 1978 under coach Don Parish. Lambert played a single game against the Dragons before a knee injury ended his uninspiring Rugby League career.

4. John Gallagher
Regarded as the premier fullback in world Rugby Union in the 1980s, John Gallagher played 18 Tests for the All Blacks between 1987 and '89, keeping talented understudy Matthew Ridge out of the Test team. His defection to League in 1990 proved a disaster, though, with his five seasons with English clubs Leeds and London marred by suspect defence and a failure to grasp the tactical nuances of the new code.

5. John Kirwan

Auckland superstar John Kirwan was knighted for his long contribution to New Zealand Rugby Union, which saw him score 35 tries in 63 Tests for the All Blacks. Regarded as one of the best wingers in the world, Kirwan played a starring role in New Zealand's 1987 World Cup win and has been included in many greatest All Blacks lists. He switched to Rugby League in 1995 at the age of 30, signing with new club the Auckland Warriors. He played 35 matches and scored 13 tries but failed to make a significant impact after converting.

6. Brian Smith

A protégé of Wallabies coach Alan Jones, Brian Smith followed the now-radio personality to Rugby League in 1991 after a Union career that saw him play six Tests for Australia and a further nine for Ireland. His League career was not nearly as successful: he played 37 games in the halves over three seasons for a terrible Jones-led Balmain side and his career came to an end following the '94 season with Easts, where he played just six top-grade games.

7. Mark Carter

A flanker in New Zealand's failed 1991 Rugby Union World Cup campaign, Mark Carter joined the Auckland Warriors for their second season in 1996, hyped as a major signing. He didn't adapt to the speed or defensive aspect of League and returned to Union after just one year and eight first grade appearances, winning back his All Black jersey and celebrating a Super 12 title with the Auckland Blues.

8. Matt Burke

The son of Australian Rugby League international Peter, Matt Burke debuted for the Wallabies as a 20-year-old in 1984 and regularly played as David Campese's wing partner. He represented Australia 23 times and had a stellar World Cup in 1987 before he defected to League. After a promising start at Manly, Burke managed just 11 tries in 52 games across three clubs and five seasons, failing to adapt to the speed and intensity of the professional code as he languished in the lower grades with Easts and Balmain.

9. Jim Hindmarsh

Another failed Penrith Rugby Union convert, Jim Hindmarsh—uncle of Parramatta legend Nathan—joined the Panthers in 1977 after winning nine caps for the Wallabies as a goalkicking fullback. He continued to kick goals for the Panthers but made little impact in a two-season spell that ended his footballing career.

10. Peter Swanson
Penrith's foray into Rugby Union converts started in 1973 when an expedition to South Africa uncovered centre Peter Swanson and prop Keith Howie. Swanson scored six tries in two seasons while Howie only saw first grade in '74, the last year the two found themselves at the club.

BEST CONVERTS—LEAGUE TO UNION

1. Brad Thorn
Undoubtedly the most remarkable code-hopper ever, Dunedin-born Brad Thorn debuted for the Broncos in 1994, winning three Grand Finals and playing eight Origins for Queensland and three Tests for Australia as a big, formidable second-rower before switching codes in 2001 to chase his boyhood dream of representing the All Blacks. Thorn joined the Canterbury Crusaders and won a national call-up in his first season, but stunned everyone by declining his selection because he felt he had not yet earned it. He sat out the '02 season, but returned to make his All Blacks debut during 2003 and featured in that year's World Cup. He was used in the loose forwards initially, but lock gradually emerged as his best position. After playing in the Crusaders' 2003-04 Super 12 final losses, he returned to League and immediately won an Origin recall for the '05 series; he starred in the Broncos' '06 premiership success and brought up 200 appearances for the club the following season. Aged 33, Thorn embarked on another 15-a-side stint from 2008, celebrating a Super 14 title with the Crusaders and winning back a place in the All Blacks' pack. He retired from international football after playing in New Zealand's belated World Cup final success in 2011—his 59th Test appearance—before taking up short contracts in Japan and Ireland. Thorn played for the Otago Highlanders in the 2013 Super 15 competition, bringing his professional career span to an extraordinary 20 seasons.

2. Sonny Bill Williams
Sonny Bill Williams stamped himself as one of the NRL's most dynamic and unique talents after he debuted in 2004, winning a rookie-year premiership with the Bulldogs and breaking into the New Zealand Test side. Injuries restricted the devastating backrower to seven Test appearances in his first five seasons, and he became one of the most polarising figures in the code's history after walking out on the Bulldogs in 2008—just half a season into a five-year deal—and joining French Rugby Union side Toulon. Used exclusively in the backline in Union, 'SBW' spent two seasons with Toulon before pursuing an All Black jumper by joining the Canterbury Crusaders in

2010. Although a regular starting spot proved elusive, he scored six tries in 19 Test appearances (seven as a replacement), playing on the wing or in the centres. He came off the bench in the All Blacks' gripping 2011 World Cup final win. Williams became renowned for his ability to pop brilliant offloads in the midfield, but debatably his greatest legacy to Rugby Union was starring at second five-eighth as the Waikato Chiefs surged to a maiden Super Rugby title in 2012. The hype surrounding his return to the NRL with the Sydney Roosters was matched only by his extraordinary performances: he inspired the Roosters to the 2013 premiership and the Kiwis to the World Cup final. Williams surprised most pundits by signing on for another season with the Roosters before confirming he would be returning to the Chiefs in 2015 with a view to playing in another World Cup and making the New Zealand Sevens side for the Olympics Games a year later.

3. Mat Rogers

Wiry goalkicking winger Mat Rogers scored 1112 points (including 75 tries) in seven seasons with Cronulla, accumulated 168 points in 11 Tests for Australia, and played five Origin matches for Queensland. Frustrated by an unfulfilled desire to play in the centres or at five-eighth, Rogers switched to Union in 2002 with the NSW Waratahs. He displayed remarkable versatility in 45 Tests for the Wallabies across five seasons, featuring in every position from fly-half to fullback and wearing the No.15 in Australia's extra-time World Cup final loss to England in 2003. Lauded as an outstanding convert success, Rogers returned to the NRL with the fledgling Gold Coast Titans in 2007 and played 77 games for the club at centre, five-eighth and fullback.

4. Lote Tuqiri

Long-striding Fiji-born winger Lote Tuqiri was only 23 when he switched codes at the end of 2002, but he already had a premiership with Brisbane, five Tests for Australia and six Origins for Queensland to his credit. He spent seven seasons with the NSW Waratahs and was virtually an automatic selection for the Wallabies during that period, scoring 30 tries in 67 Test appearances, encompassing two World Cups. His ARU contract was terminated in 2009 for an undisclosed off-field incident, but he made a superb NRL return with the Wests Tigers the following season, scoring 18 tries and winning a Test recall during the Kangaroos' Four Nations campaign. Tuqiri's subsequent three seasons were ravaged by injury, but after a short stint with Irish Rugby Union club Leinster at the end of 2013 and, despite turning 34, he was snapped up by South Sydney for the 2014 season.

5. Israel Folau

A gifted tryscoring phenomenon in four Rugby League seasons for Melbourne, Brisbane, Queensland and Australia, Israel Folau made a shock switch to the AFL with the fledgling Greater Western Sydney Giants at the end of 2010. The high-profile move was a dismal on-field failure, with Folau struggling to get to grips with the new code; he was granted a release by the Giants at the end of 2012. Folau looked certain to return to Rugby League with Parramatta, but shunned the Eels to sign with the NSW Waratahs and the ARU. Folau was an immediate sensation, firstly on the wing and then at fullback. His outstanding 2013 Super Rugby season for the Waratahs garnered a Wallabies call-up and, after he scored a magnificent double on Test debut against the British Lions, he went on to score 10 tries in 15 Tests—equalling Lote Tuqiri's record for most tries in a season for Australia.

6. Berrick Barnes

Berrick Barnes was being groomed as a long-term halves partner for Darren Lockyer at the Broncos, having impressed in nine rookie-year appearances in 2005 as a 19-year-old before being lured to Rugby Union by the Queensland Reds. Barnes made his Wallabies debut at the 2007 World Cup and racked up 200 points in 51 Tests over seven seasons, making appearances at fly-half, in the midfield and at fullback. The level-headed playmaker featured in another World Cup in 2011 during his four seasons with the NSW Waratahs, but took up a rich deal in Japanese Rugby at the end of 2013.

7. Jason Robinson

Dazzling winger Jason Robinson became an all-time great at Wigan during the 1990s and made 19 Test appearances for Great Britain and England. Robinson, who spent an off-season with Rugby Union powerhouse Bath in 1996, switched codes permanently with the Sale Sharks in 2000 and became one of the finest English players of the modern era. Brilliant at fullback, wing or centre, he made 51 Test appearances for England and scored 28 tries—including a five-pointer in the dramatic extra-time victory over Australia in the 2003 World Cup final. Robinson also toured Australia (2001) and New Zealand (2005) with the esteemed British Lions combination.

8. Andrew Walker

Andrew Walker was a brilliant match-winner for the Roosters during the mid to late 1990s—making a solitary Test appearance against Papua New Guinea in 1996—but was also an unmistakably enigmatic talent at fullback or five-eighth. A Randwick Rugby Union prodigy before starring in League, he returned to the 15-a-side code in 2000, playing in the ACT Brumbies' Super 12 final loss in his first season and kicking 21 points as the franchise claimed a historic maiden final win a year later. A fullback for the Brumbies, Walker was predominantly selected on the wing in seven Tests for the Wallabies in 2000-01. He returned to the NRL with Manly in 2004 after a string of disciplinary breaches, but a fine season for the Sea Eagles was sullied by a two-year ban for cocaine use. The veteran enjoyed an impressive stint with the Queensland Reds in 2007-08 before coming back to League again with Brisbane Easts and, later, Ipswich club the Goodna Eagles.

9. Wendell Sailor

Widely regarded as Rugby League's best winger from 1995 until his switch to Rugby Union at the end of 2001, Broncos great Wendell Sailor won three Grand Finals, scored 17 tries in 16 Tests for Australia and represented Queensland in 14 Origins. He joined the Queensland Reds in 2002 and walked straight into the Wallabies Test line-up. Although an oft-maligned figure during his five seasons in Union, Sailor made 37 Test appearances and scored 13 tries. After spending the '06 Super Rugby season with the NSW Waratahs, he was slapped with a two-year ban for cocaine use, but made an impressive two-season return to the NRL with St George Illawarra.

10. Clinton Schifcofske

A brilliantly elusive fullback for South Queensland, Parramatta and Canberra, Clinton Schifcofske's 1604 points placed him in the top 10 in premiership history. After playing in Queensland's dynasty-starting decider victory (the last of his two Origin appearances) and winning the Dally M Fullback of the Year award in 2006, Schifcofske accepted a deal with the Queensland Reds Super Rugby franchise. He transferred to Union his superb broken-field running and remarkable ability to beat the first defender, and starred at fullback for the Reds while injured Test great Chris Latham was sidelined with injury. Unlucky not to represent the Wallabies—the likes of Julian Huxley and Adam Ashley-Cooper were preferred in the No.15—Schifcofske instead played for Australia A in the 2007 Pacific Nations Cup. After a stint with Irish club Ulster, he returned to the 13-a-side game with doomed Wales-based Super League club the Celtic Crusaders.

WORST CONVERTS—LEAGUE TO UNION

1. Willie Carne

The world's best Rugby League winger during the early 1990s, Roma-product Willie Carne won two Grand Finals with Brisbane among 134 appearances for 72 tries, played 12 Origins for Queensland, and scored 10 tries in as many Test appearances. His career stalled after he was the victim of several nasty high shots in 1994-95, and he switched to Rugby Union's Queensland Reds following a forgettable '96 campaign for the Broncos, becoming the first high-profile League star to switch after Rugby Union turned professional. After a tentative start in the 15-a-side game, the 28-year-old was ultimately unable to force his way into the Super 12 franchise's line-up and retired from professional sport altogether in 1997.

2. Nathan Blacklock

One of Rugby League's greatest-ever try-scorers, Nathan Blacklock embarked on perhaps the shortest code switch of all time in 2003. The Indigenous winger topped the NRL's tryscoring charts in three straight seasons (1999-2001), and although he was chosen in the 2001 Kangaroo Tour squad, playing one Test against each of Papua New Guinea and Great Britain, his constant and inexplicable snubbing by NSW selectors reportedly contributed to his shock departure from St George Illawarra midway through 2002. Blacklock linked with the NSW Waratahs in 2003 (playing alongside another new League recruit in Lote Tuqiri), but made just five Super Rugby appearances. He was subsequently dropped from the Waratahs' reserve side for disciplinary reasons during the first season of a two-year deal, and was back playing for the Dragons by June. Blacklock finished his NRL career in '04 with the remarkable record of 121 tries in only 142 games before joining Super League club Hull FC.

3. Timana Tahu

Gifted three-quarter Timana Tahu ranked among the NRL's most prolific try-scorers when he made a shock switch to Rugby Union at the end of 2007, leaving behind a record of 102 tries in just 143 games for Newcastle (including a four-pointer in the Knights' 2001 Grand Final win) and Parramatta. He also crossed eight times in 12 Origins for NSW, and bagged five tries in five Tests for Australia. Joining the NSW Waratahs on a big-money deal in conjunction with the ARU, Tahu was fast-tracked into the Wallabies' squad in his first season, making four Test appearances against New Zealand, South Africa and Italy. He was tried at wing, centre and second five-eighth, but failed to settle in the new code and abruptly returned to the NRL at the end of 2009—just two years into his four-season Union contract. Tahu's Rugby League comeback included an immediate Origin recall but has been hampered by injury problems and racism controversies—in which the Aboriginal and Maori star has been on both sides.

4. Luke Rooney

Tall winger Luke Rooney famously scored two tries in Penrith's 2003 Grand Final upset of the Roosters, using that triumph as a springboard to participating in back-to-back NSW Origin series victories and scoring six tries in six Tests for Australia in 2004-05. After a 140-game career for the Panthers that netted 65 tries, Rooney accepted an offer from French Rugby Union powerhouse Toulon. But his 15-a-side foray was consistently thwarted by injuries and he played just 22 games in two seasons with Toulon (alongside Sonny Bill Williams) before taking a deal with Super Rugby newcomers the Melbourne Rebels for 2011. A stint with New Zealand provincial side Hawkes Bay was also cut short by injury, and he played only two games for the Rebels before rejoining Toulon.

5. Jarrod Saffy

South African-born Jarrod Saffy represented the Australian Schoolboys, Under-21s and Sevens sides in Rugby Union but earned his full professional stripes after joining Wests Tigers in the NRL. A big, aggressive forward, Saffy made his first grade debut as a 21-year-old in 2006 and went on to make 61 appearances for the Tigers and Dragons across five seasons, culminating in a premiership ring as part of St George Illawarra's 2010 Grand Final side. He was a highly anticipated signing for Super Rugby franchise the Melbourne Rebels' inaugural 2011 campaign, but failed to live up to the 15-a-side promise he displayed as a junior. The openside flanker played 35 games in three seasons for the Rebels before signing with French club US Bressane.

6. Michael Witt

Clever Toowoomba-born five-eighth Michael Witt toiled away for a regular first grade chance with Parramatta and Manly before finding a niche at the New Zealand Warriors. Witt was a key driving force in the Warriors' 2007-08 finals campaigns and proved himself one of the NRL's genuine sharpshooters off the kicking tee. But the 25-year-old slipped down the halves pecking order during the 2009 pre-season and made the surprise move of signing with the Otago Rugby Union. He played for the Taieri Eels in the Dunedin club competition and made the Otago provincial squad, but struggled to get off the bench. Witt resumed his 13-a-side career with doomed Super League side Celtic Crusaders in 2010 before linking with London and returning to the NRL with St George Illawarra in 2014.

7. Lesley Vainikolo

Lesley Vainikolo was a wing powerhouse in four seasons at Canberra before scoring an incredible 143 tries in 148 games for Super League heavyweights Bradford and featuring in two Grand Final victories. He also crossed for 14 tries in 14 Tests for New Zealand. Vainikolo was a hyped acquisition for Rugby Union club Gloucester in 2007 and was given an armchair ride into the England squad after just nine games in his new code, qualifying on residential grounds. The giant winger featured in each match of England's Six Nations campaign but failed to make the anticipated impact and was left out of subsequent training squads and touring sides. Vainikolo joined French club La Rochelle in 2012.

8. Lenny Beckett

Former Australian Schoolboys winger Lenny Beckett—brother of long-serving Penrith flyer Robbie—enjoyed an impressive start to his NRL career, scoring 12 tries for heavyweights Newcastle in 2000. After two subsequent seasons for the Northern Eagles, he joined Super Rugby franchise the ACT Brumbies. A reserve in the Brumbies' final-winning side in '04, Beckett became a regular starter the following season. He then faded off the map, however, failing to earn a Super Rugby contract for 2006 and instead turning out for club side Sydney University.

9. Tasesa Lavea

An outstanding schoolboy Rugby Union prospect in Auckland, Tasesa Lavea joined the Melbourne Storm and was named Dally M Rookie of the Year in 2000. The goalkicking five-eighth made his Test debut for the Kiwis at that season's World Cup, but returned to Union after playing just five games for the Northern Eagles in 2002. Lavea was a regular in the No.10 jumper for the Auckland and Counties provincial sides, but struggled to hold down a position during Super Rugby stints with the Auckland Blues and Waikato Chiefs. He later played with Clermont in France and English club Sale and played Test football for Samoa in 2010-11.

10. Denan Kemp

Wing speedster Denan Kemp suffered a stunning fall from grace after a breakout 19-try season for Brisbane in 2008, with a brief Rugby Union stint failing to turn around his flagging fortunes. A prized signing for the Warriors, Kemp left Auckland midway through 2009 after a dramatic form slump, only to have his return to the Broncos thwarted by injury. Kemp signed a contract with the ARU in 2011 to play for the Australian Sevens side, and played for Southern Districts in Sydney's Shute Shield competition without making a notable impact. A return to Rugby League and subsequent seasons with St George Illawarra and Brisbane did not garner a first grade recall.

RUGBY LEAGUE AND AFL

1. Karmichael Hunt

The Rugby League world was stunned in 2009 when Brisbane, Queensland and Australian fullback Karmichael Hunt announced that he had signed with the AFL's new franchise the Gold Coast Suns. The 125-game veteran, who represented the Maroons 10 times and the Kangaroos in 11 matches had a stint with French Rugby Union side Biarritz before joining the Suns. After a disappointing first season in

2011 he proved his credentials as a cross-code star, culminating in an after-the-siren goal to down Richmond. Despite continuing speculation that he will return to the NRL, he is currently in his fourth year with the Suns.

2. Barry Spring

The first AFL-Rugby League cross-code convert is hardly a household name but was an instant success, winning premierships in both pursuits. A Queensland Australian Rules legend, Barry Spring was a prolific goalkicker for Mayne in the QAFL. At the age of 26 he switched to Norths Devils, where legendary coach Bob Bax hoped to channel his honed drop-kicking in Rugby League. Under the four-tackle rule and with field goals worth two points, Spring was an instant star. He kicked five field goals in a game against Valleys at fullback and played every game as Norths went on to win the 1969 premiership. He returned to Australian Football in 1972.

3. Israel Folau

Attempting to replicate the battle plan launched in Queensland with the signing of Karmichael Hunt, the AFL made a huge offer to League sensation Israel Folau. The youngest Australian Test player of all time had scored 73 tries in 91 NRL games and played for Australia eight times in four seasons before he defected to the AFL in 2010. Folau was widely criticised for his inability to grasp his new code in 2011 when Greater Western Sydney played in the New England Australian Football League, but he made his AFL debut in the Giants' first premiership match in 2012 and played 13 games before being released from his contract during the off-season to play Rugby Union.

4. Ray Smith

A talented junior Aussie Rules player from Queensland who also represented his state in Under-19s Rugby Union, Ray Smith actually made his top-level debut in Rugby League in the BRL in 1970 with Brisbane club Valleys (who won the premiership). A move to Victoria saw him sign with VFL club Essendon, where he played five seasons and 77 games for the Bombers before finishing his career with Melbourne following a mid-season move in 1975. Smith retired after the 1976 season, having become the first Queensland-born footballer to play 100 VFL games.

5. Adrian Barich

Canberra-born Adrian Barich was a talented multi-code junior sportsman who first came to prominence with the Perth Football Club in the WAFL in 1984. He was signed to the West Coast Eagles for their inaugural '86 season. A talented and tough midfielder, Barich played 47 games and kicked 69 goals for the club, but is most renowned for a moving letter he wrote to the team after he was overlooked for selection in the club's first Grand Final in 1992. He made a surprise move to the Western Reds in 1995, but played just one trial for the club before moving into the Perth sports media.

6. Greg Brentnall

Born smack on the fabled 'Barassi Line' in Wagga—one of the few places in Australia that has equal affection for Rugby League and Australian Rules—Greg Brentnall grew up adept at both codes. He was pursued by a number of VFL clubs before signing on with Rugby League team Canterbury, where he debuted in 1977. He played a starring role in the 1980 Grand Final, setting up the most famous of Grand Final tries by bombing on halfway for Steve Gearin. Brentnall played 13 Tests for Australia—including as fullback for the 1982 Kangaroo 'Invincibles'—and won the Rothmans Medal in 1982. A knee injury forced his retirement aged just 26.

7. Bob Cooper

Western Suburbs hardman Bob Cooper was one of the most feared players in the game, and among the key figures of Roy Masters' Western Suburbs 'Fibros' outfit. A moustachioed warrior who would not take a backward step, Cooper's Rugby League career was effectively ended by judiciary chairman Jim Comans, who outed the Magpies backrower for a record 15 months for his role in a vicious brawl in 1982 that left Steelers Lee Pomfret with a broken jaw and Greg Cook with a smashed nose. During his sidelining, Cooper played Australian Rules for Sydney first-division club St George. He made a Rugby League comeback with North Sydney but it lasted just four games.

8. Fabian Francis

Popular Brisbane Bears and Port Adelaide Power midfielder Fabian Francis grew up in Darwin playing both Australian Football and Rugby League. After one season with Melbourne in 1991, Francis quit the AFL to return to Darwin and play Rugby League, where he won a premiership with the Litchfield Bears. He returned to the AFL in 1993 with the Brisbane Bears before playing a key role in Port Adelaide's 1996 SANFL win. Francis was a member of Port's inaugural AFL team in 1997 and finished his premiership career with 109 games and 61 goals.

9. Matt Duffie

Melbourne Storm winger Matt Duffie has become known for his soaring catches, a skill he picked up playing AFL in his native New Zealand. While Australian Football was never Duffie's first love—he only took up the game in Rugby League's offseason—the exciting Storm flanker represented New Zealand and starred in the side that won three straight Auckland AFL premierships. He scored a try in his only Rugby League Test for the Kiwis to date, against Australia in 2011.

10. Shaun Johnson
One of the deadliest halfbacks in the game, livewire Warriors No.7 Shaun Johnson very nearly pursued a career in Australian Football. Representing New Zealand at a 2006 international youth tournament, the eight-Test Kiwi star was named player of the tournament and attracted the attention of AFL scouts. He went as far as touring the facilities of the Sydney Swans before deciding to settle on Rugby League in order to stay in his homeland.

RUGBY LEAGUE AND CRICKET

1. Ray Lindwall
One of Australia's greatest fast bowlers, a Test captain and a member of Bradman's famous Invincibles (when he took 27 wickets at 19.62), Ray Lindwall first came to prominence in Rugby League with St George. A talented goalkicking fullback, he debuted with the Dragons at just 19 in 1940 and played in Grand Final losses to Canterbury in '42 and Balmain in '46, quitting to concentrate on cricket after the latter, with 236 points in just 31 games.

2. Herbie Collins
Born in Sydney, Herbie Collins played first-class cricket for South Australia in 1909 before moving back to his hometown in 1911, where he played Rugby League for Eastern Suburbs while pushing for Sheffield Shield selection for NSW. Collins had a fine season with the Tricolours, playing five-eighth inside Dally Messenger in the 11-8 premiership final win over Glebe. After a season with Toombul in Queensland—where he went on to represent the state in the 1912 series—Collins gave up League to concentrate on cricket. He made his Test debut in 1920 and played 19 Tests, serving as captain in 11.

3. Graeme Hughes
One-third of the first generation of famous Hughes brothers that have donned the blue and white of the Bulldogs, Graeme made his first grade debut at just 18 in 1974, and in '75 had the honour of representing NSW in both Rugby League and cricket. Hughes' Rugby League career was eventually cut short by a serious knee injury in 1982, but not before he was a member of the 1979 and '80 Grand Final sides and played a starring role in the Bulldogs' drought-breaking title win in the latter. A stout batsman, Hughes played 20 first-class matches but averaged just 22.37. He is now a well-known Sydney media personality.

4. Verdun Scott

The only man to represent New Zealand in both Rugby League and cricket, Verdun Scott was one of the great Kiwi athletes in the first half of the 20th century. Playing for the Auckland Rugby League team after switching from soccer—having represented Auckland B in the round-ball game—Scott played for the Kiwis in 1939 and was touring Great Britain when World War II broke out and prevented him from earning Test honours. It was on the cricket pitch that Scott achieved greater renown, playing 10 Tests and 80 first class matches as a swashbuckling opening bat. He averaged 28 in a career that spanned 1946-52.

5. Alan Wharton

The only player to play both top-level Rugby League and Test cricket for England, Alan Wharton enjoyed a brief Rugby League career with the Salford City Reds but achieved far greater accolades in the whites. A left-hand bat and right-arm medium bowler, Wharton played 482 first-class matches for Lancashire and Leicestershire from 1946 to 1963, and appeared in his solitary Test in 1949, scoring 13 and 7.

6. Johnny Brown

A tough country halfback with Mount Morgan and then West End in the Ipswich comp, Johnny Brown debuted for Queensland as a 20-year-old in 1963 when filling in for skipper Barry Muir, and was again named in 1965. A move to Norths in the BRL boosted his rep claims and he was Queensland's first-choice No.7 in 1969 and '70, touring with Australia at the end-of-season World Cup in the latter year. He played a solitary Test—a 7-4 win against France—and represented Queensland for the final time in 1971. Brown played six first-class matches for Queensland during his cricket career as a left-hand bat.

7. Les Cody

A multi-skilled sportsman, Les Cody debuted for Eastern Suburbs in 1910 and played 19 games for the Tricolours across two seasons, including the 1911 premiership decider, which they won 11-8 against Glebe. Cody played halfback and was paired in the halves with fellow cricket/League convert Herb Collins. He made his first-class cricket debut in 1912, playing 30 matches for NSW and Victoria in a career interrupted by World War I. Cody never played Test cricket, but represented Australia on tours of North America and New Zealand.

8. Dudley Seddon

A talented three-quarter with Newtown in the 1920s, Dudley Seddon played 59 games across seven seasons with the Bluebags, scoring 20 tries and skippering the club. He won NSW honours in 1921 and '24 and scored a try in the 37-11 win over

Queensland in '21. He gained greater acclaim in cricket, despite playing just six first-class games for NSW in which he averaged 36.10. Seddon was a national selector from 1954 to 1967 with Sir Donald Bradman and Jack Ryder.

9. Rex Norman
Rex Norman was an extremely talented back in the game's infant days, playing 142 games for Annandale, South Sydney and Eastern Suburbs from 1910 to 1924. Part of a famous Rugby League family, Norman toured with the Kangaroos in 1921-22 but did not play in any Tests. He also played one game for NSW in 1921, a year after his seven-game first-class career with the NSW cricket team came to an end.

10. Ward Prentice
A prominent Rugby Union player who represented the Wallabies six times, Ward Prentice was a fine wicketkeeper who made his first-class debut for NSW in 1913. After making a duck he was not selected for NSW again until 1921, when he again fell for a duck. By the time of his second NSW appearance, Prentice had switched to Rugby League; he played five games at five-eighth for Western Suburbs.

RUGBY LEAGUE AND ATHLETICS

1. Michael Cleary
A dual international who scored 93 tries in a decade-long career with Souths and Easts, winger Michael Cleary retained his amateur status in his first season of Rugby League in order to compete at the 1962 Commonwealth Games in Perth. He won a bronze medal in the 100-yard sprint, and recorded a personal best of 9.3 seconds for that distance during his career. Also in 1962, Cleary defeated the great Ken Irvine in a match race at Wentworth for a £2000 collect, while in 1966—a year after playing the last of his eight Tests for Australia—he won the Australian professional 130m sprint.

2. George Smith
A New Zealand Cup-winning jockey and a pioneering Kiwi Rugby Union and Rugby League luminary, George Smith also achieved much acclaim as a sprinter and hurdler. During the first decade of the 20th century, the diminutive winger won the New Zealand 100-yard title five times, the 250 yards once, the 120-yard hurdles four times, and the 440-yard hurdles five times. He also claimed Australasian titles in the 120-yard hurdles (two) and 440-yard hurdles (four). He won the British AAA 120-yard hurdles championship in 1902 and ran the 440-yard hurdles in an unofficial

world-record time of 58.5 seconds. After starring on the famed New Zealand 'All Golds' tour of Britain, 'The Greyhound' played out his career with Oldham.

3. Warren Ryan
One of the most revered coaches in the code's history, Warren Ryan was an elite shot-putter before he embarked on a Rugby League career. He represented Australia at the 1962 Commonwealth Games in Perth, finishing seventh in a field of 16 with a throw of 15.75m. Ryan was graded by St George and made his first grade debut and won a reserve grade Grand Final with the club in 1965. He played 24 games for Cronulla in 1967-68 before representing Country Firsts from Wests Wollongong. Turning his hand to coaching, he went on to win premierships with Canterbury in 1984-85; he also guided Newtown (1981) and Balmain (1988-89) to Grand Finals and took Wests and Newcastle to finals series. He coached 415 first grade games in a career spanning 22 seasons.

4. Wally McArthur
Born in the Northern Territory, groundbreaking Indigenous winger Wally McArthur began playing Rugby League in South Australia and Western Australia before venturing to England and racking up 165 appearances for Rochdale, Blackpool Borough, Salford and Workington. McArthur was an outstanding junior athlete who won the South Australian Under-19s 100- and 220-yard championships, and the national Under-19s title in the 100 yards. It has been proposed by prominent historians that he was left out of Australia's track-and-field team for the 1952 Helsinki Olympics due to his Aboriginal heritage, although this has been a source of conjecture. McArthur became a professional sprinter in 1953 and won his first 10 races—including a victory over Australian champion Frank Banner—but quit to pursue his Rugby League dream.

5. Darren Clark
Among the world's top 400-metre runners of the 1980s, Darren Clark placed fourth at the 1984 Los Angeles and 1988 Seoul Olympics, collected a silver medal at the 1986 Edinburgh Commonwealth Games, and won a gold medal at the 1990 Auckland Commonwealth Games. Controversial Balmain coach Alan Jones recruited Clark for an ambitious Rugby League switch in 1991, but the move was a failure and he languished in reserve grade before returning to athletics, finishing third in the World Indoor Championships at Toronto to in 1993. Clark's personal best of 44.38 seconds at the Seoul Olympics would have been fast enough to win silver at London 2012.

6. Ian Moir
Possibly the finest winger of the 1950s, Ian Moir scored 118 tries in 139 games for Souths and Wests and crossed nine times in 12 Tests for Australia. He also enjoyed

outstanding success as a runner, winning the Canberra Gift early in his first grade career as well as prevailing in a 110-yard sprint race of premiership speedsters in 1958—clocking 11.1 seconds in full football garb, with a young Ken Irvine finishing second. At the age of 56, Moir won the NSW Veterans 100m championship in 1988 in the unmistakably youthful time of 12.7 seconds. He passed away just two years later.

7. Shane Whereat
Undeterred by Darren Clark's failure to make the transition to Rugby League a couple of years earlier, Eastern Suburbs signed professional sprinter Shane Whereat in 1993 after he won the Botany Gift. Whereat, who recorded a personal best for the 100m of 10.05 seconds, was a somewhat erratic winger but enjoyed a respectable seven-season career with the Roosters and Parramatta, scoring 37 tries in 73 games. Uncatchable in open spaces, he scored two tries to help the Eels to an 18-2 lead in the 1998 preliminary final before they were infamously run down by Canterbury in an extra-time classic.

8. Ken Irvine
Ken Irvine bypassed what surely would have been a hugely successful career as a sprinter to become the greatest winger in Australian Rugby League history. He won the 1963 Dubbo Gift in a professional world record of 9.3 seconds for the 100 yards, and boasted a personal best for the 100 metres of 10.2 seconds. In one of the most remarkable careers in the code's narrative, Irvine was the highest try-scorer in premiership history, with 212 in 236 games for Norths and Manly, and crossed for 33 tries in as many Test appearances for Australia.

9. Jack Troy
Promising sprinter—and son of a well-known hurdler of the same name—Jack Troy shelved his athletics career after missing selection in Australia's team for the 1948 London Olympics. He instead harnessed his fleet-footed talents as a flying winger for Newtown, making his first grade debut in '49 and playing two Tests for Australia against Great Britain the following season. He is the last player to score six tries in a first grade match: he achieved the phenomenal haul for the Bluebags against Easts in 1950.

10. Jamal Idris
The son of a champion Nigerian sprinter father and Aboriginal mother, giant centre Jamal Idris—an Origin and Test representative at the age of 20—was touted as an Olympic shot-put and discus prospect as a junior athlete. Idris reached the final of the discus throw at the 2007 IAAF World Youth Championships but chose to channel his energy into Rugby League; he made his NRL debut for the Bulldogs as an 18-year-old in 2008.

RUGBY LEAGUE AND BOXING

1. Herb Narvo
Herb Narvo, a 1937-38 Kangaroo, was one of the greatest of all Australian backrow forwards during a career with Newtown, Newcastle Norths and St George from 1937 to 1949. A pugilist of considerable renown, he won the Australian Heavyweight Championship in his 13th professional fight in 1945, stopping Billy 'Wocko' Britt in just 23 seconds of the first round. He lost the title to Jack Johnson in '46, but displayed his celebrated toughness by backing up to captain the Saints in first grade the next day. Part of the Royal Australian Air Force during World War II, Narvo was a physical training, boxing and paratroop instructor while stationed at Richmond.

2. Anthony Mundine
A brash and brilliant five-eighth for the Dragons and Broncos, Anthony Mundine was one of the finest individual attacking talents of the 1990s—and also one of Rugby League's most controversial and outspoken stars. Mundine walked out on St George Illawarra midway through 2000 to pursue a pro boxing career, to which his motor-mouthed exploits were far better suited. The son of famed Indigenous fighter Tony Mundine, 'The Man' proved to be an excellent boxer in his own right, winning multiple world titles in the super middleweight and middleweight divisions, but his career continued to be plagued by his impetuosity and outlandish statements. Mundine crafted a 46-5 record and had long-running rivalries with prominent Australian fighters Danny Green and Daniel Geale, but key losses hindered his bid to crack the lucrative American market.

3. Billy Johnstone
Cunnamulla-born Billy Johnstone enjoyed a notable boxing career before making his name in Rugby League. He won 21 of 26 fights from 1977 to 1984, challenging for the Australian middleweight and light-middleweight titles. The former Brisbane Souths rake joined Canterbury in 1983, where he won Dally M Hooker of the Year honours in his first season and celebrated in a Bulldogs Grand Final victory in '85. After a season at St George, he became the Gold Coast Giants' foundation skipper in 1988 and finished his 164-game career with the battling club in '90. Johnstone became one of the premiership's most renowned club trainers with Canterbury, North Queensland and Gold Coast, and with the Queensland and Australia representative sides.

4. Sonny Bill Williams

After infamously walking out on the Bulldogs in 2008 to go to French Rugby Union, Sonny Bill Williams began his intermittent professional boxing career by appearing on the undercards of Anthony Mundine fights after 'The Man' and his manager, Khoder Nasser, helped facilitate Williams' release from the NRL club. He had six professional fights in between representing the All Blacks, most of which were criticised for the poor quality of his opponents. He won the vacant NZ Heavyweight Championship against replacement fighter Clarence Tillman III with a first-round TKO, while his next fight—just before he returned to the NRL with the Roosters—was a highly controversial points decision over veteran South African Francois Botha.

5. Solomon Haumono

Tongan enforcer Solomon Haumono was a renowned hitman and destructive ball-runner who struggled for consistency despite playing for Manly in the 1995 Grand Final and representing Super League Australia in '97 from Canterbury. The son of former Australian heavyweight champion Maile Haumono, Solomon followed his close friend and St George Illawarra teammate Anthony Mundine into pro boxing in 2000 and won his first eight heavyweight bouts by knockout before he returned to the NRL to play two seasons at Manly (2003-04) and gain a City Origin guernsey. Haumono hung up the boots and picked up the gloves again in 2007; he had built a 21-2 record (including 19 wins by KO) by the end of 2013.

6. Monty Betham

The son of the professional boxer of the same name who fought the likes of Tony Mundine, Warriors hooker/backrower Monty Betham played 101 NRL games and eight Tests for the Kiwis. He was known as a player who was good with his fists, but someone forgot to tell Broncos utility Casey McGuire, who took a pummelling at the hands of Betham in a 2003 clash. He left the Warriors at the end of '05 and spent a season at Wakefield Trinity before pursuing a career in the ring, where he won five pro fights in the cruiserweight division and took on highly regarded New Zealand heavyweight Shane Cameron in a 'Fight for Life' charity event.

7. Garth Wood

A utility back who played 25 first grade games for Souths and Balmain from 1997 to 2005, Garth Wood—brother of talented 114-game utility Nathan—took a relatively unique path to professional boxing prominence. He was the first winner of the reality television boxing show *The Contender Australia* in 2010, with part of the prize a fight with Anthony Mundine—which he won via a fifth-round knockout in a major boilover. Wood lost a 2011 rematch with Mundine by unanimous points decision and suffered subsequent middleweight title fight defeats to high-profile boxers Sam Soliman and Daniel Geale.

8. Jeff Fenech

A world champion in three weight divisions during the 1980s, Jeff Fenech ranks among Australia's greatest boxers. A handy junior Rugby League player, 'The Marrickville Mauler' maintained close links with several prominent premiership players. He made a high-profile bid to become a professional footballer at the height of his boxing fame, but managed only a handful of reserve grade games for the Parramatta Eels.

9. John Hopoate

One of the most notoriously short-fused, violent and suspended players of the modern era, John Hopoate represented NSW and Australia and won a premiership at Manly in 1996. He turned to boxing after a 17-match suspension for a vicious flying elbow to the head of Cronulla prop Keith Galloway effectively ended his NRL career in 2005. 'Hoppa' made his professional debut on the Anthony Mundine-Danny Green undercard in '06, stopping Frank 'The Big Ship' Faasolo after just 47 seconds. He controversially won the Australian heavyweight title from the Jeff Fenech-trained Bob Mirovic in 2008, and later fought big-name heavyweights Oliver McCall and Shane Cameron, losing to both.

10. Mark Bourneville

Mt Albert product Mark 'Horse' Bourneville boasts the unique distinction of having represented both New Zealand and France at international level, touring Great Britain and France with New Zealand in 1985 (no Tests) and featuring in the second-row for France against the touring Kiwis in 1993. But he gained more widespread fame for his powerhouse performances in the "Fight for Life" charity boxing events held in New Zealand. Bourneville was the talk of the inaugural event in 2001 when he destroyed former All Black and national judo rep Steve McDowell; he scored victories over fellow heavy hitters Va'aiga Tuigamala and Lindsay Raki in subsequent years and trained several prominent sportsmen for 'Fight for Life' bouts.

RUGBY LEAGUE AND OTHER SPORTS

1. Bill Shankland—Golf
Winger Bill Shankland toured with the 1929-30 Kangaroos after playing three first grade seasons with Glebe and Easts; he top-scored with 24 tries in Britain, including three in four Test appearances. Shankland later became one of Warrington's greatest-ever imports, captaining the club in two Challenge Cup and two premiership finals. But he also enjoyed considerable success as a golfer, competing in every British Open from 1937 to 1955. He finished equal third in the 1939 Open and equal sixth in 1951, eventually settling in England and becoming a golf teacher.

> *Probably the most notable Rugby League golfer of recent times, former Test and Origin five-eighth Braith Anasta—who plays off scratch—competed as an amateur at the NSW PGA Championship in 2011, but missed the cut after carding 20-over in the first two rounds. Anasta's new club, Wests Tigers, put the kibosh on him competing at the 2012 event. Balmain stalwart and long-serving rep fullback Tim Brasher has become a prominent golf caddy for Australian professional players in recent years, while also playing off near scratch himself.*

2. George Smith—Horseracing
George Smith holds a treasured place in Rugby League history as one of the two men—the other being Albert Baskerville—most responsible for the pioneering New Zealand 'All Golds' tour of Britain in 1907-08, on which he played all three Tests of the series against England. But Smith also rates as possibly New Zealand's greatest all-round sportsman. He ran away from home as a teenager to work as a stable boy, and as a 20-year-old 49kg jockey rode Impulse to victory in the 1894 New Zealand Cup. A champion sprinter and hurdler at home and overseas, the winger represented New Zealand in Rugby Union from 1897 to 1905—including touring with the famed 1905 'Originals'—before switching codes. He spent several years with English club Oldham following the groundbreaking 'All Golds' tour.

3. Bob Craig—Swimming, water polo and soccer
Dual international Bob Craig is regarded as one of the greatest all-round sportsmen Australia has produced. He won eight consecutive NSW swimming championships from 1899 to 1906, was a member of four Sydney premiership-winning water polo teams, and featured in Balmain's soccer premiership success in 1905 as well as representing NSW in the sport. Craig turned his hand to Rugby Union and played one Test for the Wallabies and was part of Australia's gold-medal-winning side at the 1908 London Olympics. He switched to Rugby League in 1910 and became one of the

finest forwards of his time, representing Australia in seven Tests and featuring in four premiership triumphs during a decade with Balmain.

4. Johnny Bliss—Beach sprint

Flying winger Johnny Bliss played one Test for Australia in 1951, scored six tries in nine games for NSW and crossed 80 times in 125 first grade games for Balmain, Norths and Manly. But he carved out an even greater legacy as a beach sprinter, being regarded in some quarters as the sport's greatest-ever exponent. A representative of the North Narrabeen Surf Club, Bliss won 12 Australian sprint titles in the 1940s and '50s.

Former Wallaby flyhalf Ken Wright, who switched codes and played five seasons at Easts and Souths, was a junior Australian beach sprint champion.

5. Dick Thornett—Water polo

Brilliant Parramatta forward Dick Thornett is part of an elite group to have represented Australia in three sports. He played 11 Union and 14 League Tests for his country, but before his stellar career in the oval-ball codes was part of the Australian water polo team who went to the 1960 Rome Olympics. A product of the Bronte club, Thornett was described as an uncompromising attacker with "a shot so powerful it made most goalkeepers shudder". He was a 1963-64 Kangaroo tourist along with his younger brother and Eels teammate Ken, and was named in the NSW Police Team of the Century in 2008.

Rugged Canberra and Gold Coast prop Brent Todd—a veteran of 28 Tests for the Kiwis—also had a background in water polo, representing New Zealand before his League career took off. Todd married South African-Australian world surfing champion Wendy Botha.

6. Duncan Thompson—Tennis

Widely regarded as one of the greatest of all Rugby League halfbacks for his deeds with Ipswich, North Sydney, NSW, Queensland, Australia and Toowoomba in the 1910s and '20s, Duncan Thompson enjoyed considerable success as a tennis player after retiring from football. He competed in the men's doubles at the 1931 NSW Open and was a Toowoomba champion and Queensland representative player. Thompson also played for the Valley club that won the Brisbane club cricket premiership in 1919-20, had a handicap of three in golf and played bowls for Toowoomba.

7. Dennis Tutty—Rowing

Dennis Tutty was a promising rower before he became a revolutionary Rugby League figure: as a 19-year-old—and with a first grade Grand Final for Balmain already under his belt—he was a member of the NSW crew who won the 1965 King's Cup. Tutty played one Test for Australia in 1967, but his greatest legacy to the game was taking on the NSWRL's transfer system after the Tigers halted his bid to join Penrith.

He sat out two seasons but eventually won a groundbreaking Supreme Court case against the NSWRL, thereby changing the Sydney Rugby League landscape forever. Tutty's brother Ian was a sculler for Australia at the 1960 Rome Olympics.

8. Manfred Moore—Gridiron
African-American running back Manfred Moore was a left-field signing for Newtown in 1977, who created massive, albeit brief interest. After stints with NFL franchises the San Francisco 49ers, Tampa Bay Buccaneers and Oakland Raiders (including a Super Bowl victory with the latter in 1976), Moore ventured to Sydney and scored a sensational try on debut for the Jets when he climbed high to take a bomb against Wests. At the behest of Newtown secretary Frank Farrington, he spiralled a football gridiron-style over the Henson Park grandstand as the teams made their way out for the second half. But his Rugby League odyssey lasted just five games, and he headed back to the States after suffering a nasty head gash against Cronulla. He played one more NFL season with the Minnesota Vikings.

Barnstorming Balmain second-rower Paul Sironen, who went on to make three Kangaroo Tours, took up a gridiron scholarship with the University of Hawaii in 1984 before opting to concentrate on Rugby League, and American Greg Smith made one infamous appearance for Newcastle in 1998 after falsely claiming to be a former Philadelphia Eagles NFL player.

9. Bert Gray—Soccer
A rare soccer convert to Rugby League, Bert Gray had reached Sydney first grade level in the round-ball game before he switched codes. His 13-a-side career with Glebe spanned 16 seasons, during which he represented NSW six times, played four Tests for Australia and toured with the 1921-22 Kangaroos.

Other notable Rugby League players to boast a strong soccer background besides Gray and Bob Craig are St George and Australian Test prop Craig Young, New Zealand Test fullback Matthew Ridge, and erratic Parramatta, Gold Coast and Auckland speedster Lee Oudenryn.

10. Brian Carney—Gaelic football
Cork-born Brian Carney boasted a Gaelic football background, having won a junior championship with the Valleymount GAA club in 1998 before he carved out a brilliant Rugby League and Union career. After stints with Gateshead and Hull, and a fine campaign for Ireland at the 2000 World Cup, Carney became a superstar at Wigan. The powerful winger scored eight tries in 14 Tests for Great Britain (2003-06) and was named Dally M Winger of the Year in 2006 after scoring 16 tries during a charmed one-season stay at Newcastle. But he reneged on a deal to join the Gold Coast Titans for their 2007 debut season, citing homesickness. The 30-year-old joined Irish Rugby Union club Munster and represented Ireland in four Test matches.

Chapter 13

DEBUTS

BEST FIRST GRADE DEBUTS

1. Andrew Johns
Andrew Johns' run-on debut signalled his future greatness, with the champion Newcastle halfback scoring 23 points in a stellar first outing against South Sydney. He scored a double, kicked seven goals and booted a field goal—but more importantly showed the touch and control that would come to be hallmarks of an Immortal career.

2. Kevin Hastings
Debuting as a 19-year-old in 1976 after being given the call-up by supercoach Jack Gibson, Kevin 'Horrie' Hastings was an instant hit. He scored two tries and collected man-of-the-match honours in the last-round clash against Norths, winning a spot in the club's finals campaign. Hastings went on to become a Roosters legend, playing 228 games for the club and winning a host of individual honours along the way.

3. Don Manson
South Sydney winger Don Manson had a remarkable top-grade debut in 1937 when he scored a record five tries in his first outing—the 63-0 rout of Varsity in the opening round of the '37 season. He was that season's top try-scorer and represented NSW in 1938, but spent just three years in first grade.

4. Jordan Atkins
Gold Coast winger Jordan Atkins' career high point came in a remarkable 2008 debut that saw him score four tries in a 36-18 win over North Queensland. Atkins scored some incredible tries and looked destined for a big first grade career, but played just 42 first grade games across five years before moving to the European Super League.

5. Chris Lawrence
Wests Tigers centre Chris Lawrence was a 17-year-old schoolboy when he was named to make his debut at Suncorp Stadium late in the 2006 season. He was not overawed, scoring a scintillating try by standing up international Shaun Berrigan. He then showed great poise in putting Dean Collis over for the match-sealer of a massive 20-6 upset. Lawrence went on to represent Australia aged just 22.

6. Sonny Bill Williams
A teenage phenom, backrower Sonny Bill Williams did not disappoint he was when called on to make his top-grade debut against Parramatta in the opening round of 2004. Picked in the centres, Williams scored a try and decimated the Eels. He made a bust on the second play of the game and looked like a veteran despite being just 19. It was a brilliant start to an extraordinary career.

7. Amos Roberts
Speedy outside back Amos Roberts enjoyed a pointscoring fill-up on debut with a 22-point haul in St George Illawarra's 54-0 thrashing of Auckland in 2000. He scored a try and booted nine goals in his unforgettable debut, which is a premiership-record tally for a first-gamer. Roberts had a nine-year premiership career with the Dragons, Panthers and Roosters.

8. Harold Horder
The man who became a legend at both South Sydney and North Sydney, Harold 'The Wonder Winger' Horder showed signs of his greatness with a mighty length-of-the-field try on first grade debut for Souths in 1911. He ran 90 metres, beating every Glebe player in a swerving, spectacular try that remains among the greatest the code has seen.

9. Luke Brooks
Wests Tigers halfback Luke Brooks enjoyed such a remarkable debut that he elicited comparisons to Immortal Andrew Johns after just 80 minutes. He debuted on the hallowed turf of the SCG against St George Illawarra late in the 2013 season and was anointed a future international after a poised showing that netted a try, multiple try assists and man-of-the-match honours.

10. Billy Slater
Champion Melbourne fullback Billy Slater's debut came in the opening round of the 2003 season—Craig Bellamy's first as head coach—and remains one of the highlights of his decorated career. Cronulla led the Storm 22-0 at Shark Park but Slater, playing on the wing, was instrumental in the comeback in the 36-32 win.

UNFORTUNATE FIRST GRADE DEBUTS

1. Greg Smith
Earning an NRL call-up with Newcastle in 1999 under the false pretence of having played gridiron for NFL franchise the Philadelphia Eagles, African-American flyer Greg Smith produced an infamous, error-riddled display against Canterbury. A string of handling errors and poor defensive reads by the fraudulent debutant winger allowed the Bulldogs to recover from a 16-point deficit and pull off a 28-26 victory over the dumbfounded Knights. Smith was swiftly dropped and his ruse was uncovered soon afterwards.

2. Glen Fisiiahi
Warriors National Youth Competition star Glen Fisiiahi was promoted to the first grade flank for the 2011 season-opener against Parramatta—a historic encounter at Eden Park. But the 20-year-old made three glaring handling errors in a 24-18 loss, including a terrible drop of a bomb that gifted a try to the Eels soon after halftime. The youngster's debut garnered a lowly '4' rating from *Rugby League Week*.

3. Peter Wheeler
Peter Wheeler earned his first grade spurs off the bench for Canterbury in a big win over the Western Reds in 1995, but his run-on debut at halfback a fortnight later was less auspicious. The Bulldogs opened up a handy 8-0 lead over fellow heavyweights Brisbane, but Wheeler was sin-binned 10 minutes into the second half for a professional foul. The Broncos scored their first try from the resultant penalty and went on to win 13-8. Wheeler made a total of nine first grade appearances before falling off the radar.

4. Tony Caine
Tony Caine was called up to make his NRL debut off the bench for Cronulla against the Warriors in 2006, but the 19-year-old's season finished courtesy of a severe knee injury sustained while he was making a kick and being charged down by Warriors prop Steve Price. Caine battled back to play a further 15 games for the

Dragons and Sharks, but the troublesome knee continued to hamper the utility and he was forced to give the game away.

5. Alwyn Simpson
In 2007, Brisbane winger Alwyn Simpson became the first player since Parramatta livewire Dennis Moran a decade earlier to make his first grade debut in a finals match. Injury had ravaged the defending premiers during the second half of the season and he was selected on the end of a reshuffled backline to take on Melbourne in the qualifying final. Simpson, who had been formerly contracted to Canberra, experienced a torrid afternoon as his opposing winger, Steve Turner, crossed for three tries in a 40-0 drubbing. The Storm went on to emphatically claim the premiership, while Simpson was destined to slip out of NRL contention, instead plying his trade for the Redcliffe Dolphins.

6. James Tedesco
A highly rated fullback with blistering speed, 19-year-old James Tedesco's NRL debut for Wests Tigers in the opening round of 2012 was eagerly anticipated. But his rookie season was over after just 30 minutes, when he suffered a torn anterior cruciate ligament in his left knee against Cronulla that required a reconstruction. Tedesco returned the following season and made his City Origin debut after just four first grade appearances.

7. Scott Wilson
South Sydney scored a stirring 28-14 upset of defending premiers Manly in Round 8 of 1988, with 17-year-old debutant Scott Wilson making an appearance off the bench, but the Rabbitohs' competition points were stripped after the NSWRL deemed they had breached a rule preventing clubs from fielding players who had played in President's Cup on the same day, which Wilson had done. Through no fault of Wilson, his debut cost Souths the fruits of their victory. He eventually made 109 appearances for six clubs during a nomadic and tumultuous career.

8. Ken Jackson
The thrill of taking part in a courageous victory on debut was somewhat doused for young Gold Coast fullback Ken Jackson. The Seagulls downed emerging powerhouse Illawarra 18-8 despite having Test prop Brent Todd sent off during the first half. But the short-handed Seagulls inadvertently used an illegal fifth interchange player—the 22-year-old Jackson—and their competition points were stripped a few days later. Jackson went on to make 12 first grade appearances for the struggling club.

9. Adrian Toole

Blooded by North Sydney as a replacement in three first grade games in 1985-86, Adrian Toole's run-on debut against Canterbury in the opening round of '87 was one to forget—although the young front-rower couldn't have remembered it if he wanted to as he was concussed by a swinging arm from Bulldogs enforcer Peter Kelly after 20 minutes. Remaining on the paddock, Toole was crunched in another tackle involving Kelly and had to be assisted from the field, sick and bloodied. "I looked like the Elephant Man," Toole remarked about his appearance the following day. He later became a cult hero in 130 games for the Bears.

10. Steve Meredith

Former Australian Schoolboy Steve Meredith achieved outstanding lower grade success with the Roosters before he earned the call-up to make his NRL debut in 2006. But he lasted just 13 minutes against Brisbane before suffering a season-ending knee injury in a 24-6 loss. Meredith, a Samoan international, recovered to play at NSW Cup level but never received another first grade chance.

BEST ORIGIN DEBUTS

1. Michael O'Connor (NSW)

Former Wallaby Michael O'Connor won his initial NSW call-up for the 1985 series opener in his third season at St George. On a wet and muddy night at Lang Park, the brilliant centre raced in for the only two tries of the match and added five goals to hold a monopoly on the Blues' scoresheet in an emphatic 18-2 victory. His 18-point haul remained an Origin record for 15 years, and he went on to set NSW marks for most appearances, tries and points—of which the latter two still stand—in a decorated representative career.

2. Brett Hodgson (NSW)

Lightweight fullback Brett Hodgson racked up extraordinary numbers in his first Origin appearance—a stunning 32-4 series-opening victory for an underdog Blues side featuring eight debutants in 2002. The Parramatta custodian made an incredible five line breaks and 384 metres from 23 runs, including a bust to put Andrew Johns over for a first-half try, and a 90-metre run to score from a scrum win that completed the rout. Unfortunately for the courageous Hodgson, his six-match Origin career is predominantly remembered for the time he was rag-dolled by Gorden Tallis in the '02 decider and the wayward pass he threw in '06 that cost NSW the series.

3. Les Davidson (NSW)
A 1986 Kangaroo, Les Davidson produced a man-of-the-match performance on debut in the following season's Origin series opener. The Souths enforcer made 32 tackles and 18 hit-ups and scored a barnstorming first-half try in NSW's heart-stopping 20-16 success at Lang Park. He made just four further appearances for the Blues, but remains the only player—other than inaugural man-of-the-match Chris Close—to have been named best on ground on Origin debut.

4. Allan Langer (Queensland)
Pint-sized halfback Allan Langer's maiden Origin call-up for game one of the '87 series was questioned in several quarters, including among some of his experienced Queensland teammates. But the Ipswich No.7 silenced the doubters with an inspirational display, quashing misgivings over his suspect defence with several ultra-committed scything efforts among 19 tackles; he also made a line break and was a constant threat in attack. Despite the Maroons' last-minute loss, Langer had arrived. He went on to become one of the contest's most iconic players in 34 appearances.

5. Peter Wallace (NSW)
Brisbane halfback Peter Wallace became the sixth player to be selected in the NSW No.7 in the space of eight matches when he was picked to debut in the 2008 series opener. The Blues started as rank outsiders, but Wallace steered them to a convincing 18-10 boilover, having a hand in three of his side's four tries and dictating terms with a brilliant kicking game that prevented the star-studded Maroons from getting into the contest. Wallace, who made the last of his four Origin appearances in 2009, was desperately unlucky to miss out on man-of-the-match honours on debut.

6. Adam Mogg (Queensland)
One of the biggest selection bolters in Origin history, Adam Mogg, replaced Greg Inglis on the wing for game two of the 2006 series as injuries decimated Queensland's backline stocks. The relatively unknown Mogg began a charmed debut by barrelling NSW centre Mark Gasnier into touch in the lead-up to the Maroons' first try, and then scored two superb second-half tries—outfoxing Gasnier to dive over in the corner and complete his double—as his side kept the series alive with a memorable 30-6 thrashing. Mogg scored another spectacular try in Queensland's dramatic decider triumph to seal his place in Origin folklore.

7. Mark O'Meley (NSW)
Less than three weeks after his 20th birthday, aggressive Northern Eagles prop Mark O'Meley was called into the NSW side for the must-win game-two clash in

2001 after Queensland had steamrolled the Blues 34-16 in the series opener. The bald-headed tyro produced an explosive representative debut, making 19 hit-ups for a game-high 222 metres as NSW powered to a 26-8 win. The icing on O'Meley's dream introduction to Origin football was stepping past Shane Webcke, the game's No.1 front-rower, and charging into open territory before sending captain Brad Fittler away for the match-sealing try. O'Meley finished with 10 appearances for the Blues.

8. Mat Rogers (Queensland)
Cronulla winger Mat Rogers made the most of a long-awaited opportunity at Origin level by scoring all of Queensland's points in a gripping 9-8 victory in the 1999 series opener. He landed four penalty goals from as many attempts—despite a first-half stint on the sideline with an injured knee—and was narrowly denied a diving try in the corner by the video referee before he snapped a 74th-minute field goal to snatch a 1-0 series lead for the Maroons. The wiry flyer played four subsequent Origin matches before switching to Rugby Union.

9. John Doyle (Queensland)
Cowboys hooker John Doyle was perhaps the least heralded of Queensland's 10 debutants for game one of the 2001 series, but he had a monumental impact in the stunning 34-16 upset. Selected in the No.9, Doyle started on the bench but ripped up the NSW defence after entering the fray in the second half. He made a brilliant break out of dummy-half and linked with Darren Lockyer before backing up the fullback to score the opening try of the second stanza. He was at it again four minutes later, throwing an audacious dummy to again slice through from acting half and set up clubmate John Buttigieg for a try. Doyle capped a dazzling attacking display by starting another long-range movement that led to Chris Walker's four-pointer. He featured in the '01 decider triumph but was dropped after the Maroons' heavy defeat in the following season's series opener.

10. Anthony Minichiello (NSW)
Anthony Minichiello was just 11 games into his tenure as Roosters fullback when he was selected in the NSW No.1 jumper and chosen to debut in game one of the 2003 series. He made an immediate impact at the recently reopened Suncorp Stadium, combining twice with Andrew Johns to notch a first-half double, and his general play at the back was outstanding. Minichiello recorded 20 runs for 227 metres in the Blues' hard-fought 25-12 victory. His stellar representative career was interrupted by a horror run of injuries, but he nevertheless made 11 Origin appearances across nine seasons.

WORST ORIGIN DEBUTS

1. Justin Hodges (Queensland)
In a performance unrivalled among Origin shockers, Queensland winger Justin Hodges endured a horrific debut in the second game of the 2002 series when he twice attempted to pass in his own in-goal, both of which led to Blues tries. Hodges was immediately hooked by Wayne Bennett and dropped for the decider despite the Maroons' 26-18 win, but he went on to play 18 games over 12 seasons as one of their finest centres.

2. Phil Duke (NSW)
One of Origin's most infamous selections, Moree winger Phil Duke was a bolter for the 1982 decider. He scored a dubious try when he stepped out and fumbled the ball, but is most remembered for his in-goal mix-up with fullback Phil Sigsworth that allowed Wally Lewis to fall on the ball and score the decisive try. Duke never again played Origin and only tried his hand in the premiership five seasons later with Wests.

3. Nathan Merritt (NSW)
A prolific try-scorer with South Sydney, Nathan Merritt received a long-awaited NSW call-up at the age of 30 for the second game of the 2013 series. He played on the opposite side to that on which he would traditionally play, but made two awful defensive reads that led to two Darius Boyd tries, and was out-jumped by Greg Inglis for another Maroons try. Merritt was overlooked for the returning Jarryd Hayne in the decider.

4. David Williams (NSW)
Popular Manly winger David 'Wolfman' Williams endured a torrid Origin debut in the second game of the 2009 series. He scored a powerhouse try but made the madcap decision to kick on the first tackle with a desperate NSW in good field position, and was beaten twice by Willie Tonga in the 24-14 loss. Williams survived the axe for game three but has not played for NSW since.

5. Todd Carney (NSW)
Following a fabled redemption story when he returned to the NRL and won a Dally M Medal and a NSW jersey after being thrown out of the League, Todd Carney's upward ascension did not continue in his first Origin outing. He had a miserable debut in which he made three key handling errors, missed a simple penalty shot and ran the

ball just four times in the 18-10 loss. The five-eighth saw out the rest of the series but was replaced by James Maloney in 2013.

6. Steve Turner (NSW)
A favourite of NSW coach Craig Bellamy, reliable Melbourne winger Steve Turner replaced the suspended Jarryd Hayne in the second game of the 2008 series. The Blues were smoked 30-0 and Turner had an unhappy defensive night, with Greg Inglis laying a massive fend on him and opposite Darius Boyd scoring a double. Turner was dropped and never again turned out for the Blues.

7. Jamie Buhrer (NSW)
The most left field of left-field selections, Jamie Buhrer was an unexpected bench choice by Ricky Stuart for the opening game of the 2012 series. The utility played just seven uninspiring minutes of the 18-10 loss in Melbourne before he was replaced by Manly clubmate Anthony Watmough for the second encounter.

8. Mark Geyer (NSW)
Firebrand second-rower Mark Geyer debuted in the dead-rubber third game of the 1989 series and had a less than auspicious first game. In a 36-16 hammering, coach Jack Gibson hooked Geyer after 50 minutes. He was not selected in 1990 but famously made a lasting impact on the '91 series when he feuded violently with the Queensland side and was suspended for five matches.

9. John Hopoate (NSW)
Controversial winger John Hopoate got the call-up for his Origin debut in the second game of the 1995 series but endured an unhappy game. His lasting legacy from the match was his involvement in an all-in brawl, where he squared off with Manly teammate Danny Moore. Hopoate made a host of errors before being dropped for the third game, and never played Origin again.

10. Steve Menzies (NSW)
Manly legend Steve Menzies was widely criticised after his State of Origin debut in 1995. He topped the NSW tackle count in the 2-0 loss in the series opener, but the prolific try-scorer's failure to make an impact with the ball in hand contributed to the Blues' limp attack. He was dropped to the bench for the second game, but went on to play 20 Origins for NSW.

BEST TEST DEBUTS

1. Don Adams
Maitland winger Don 'Bandy' Adams was Australia's saviour in the opening Test of the 1956 series with New Zealand. The stocky winger—who was rated the fastest player over 20 yards in the game at the time—scored two tries, including the match-winner when the scores were locked at 9-all, to make a fantastic start to his five-Test career.

2. Andrew Johns
Gifted halfback Andrew Johns enjoyed a feast of points on debut, tallying a world-record-equalling 30 when Australia tackled South Africa during the 1995 World Cup. Johns scored two tries and booted 11 goals against the minnows as Australia marched towards World Cup glory. It was the start of a spectacular Test career for the future Immortal.

3. Lionel Cooper
Speedster Lionel Cooper was one of 13 debutants for Australia in the first post-war Test in 1946 and enjoyed a marvellous—and heroic—first outing. With Australia trailing 5-8 late in the match, he made a spectacular 70-metre run, with a smart change of pace fooling the cover defence and allowing him to score the equaliser in a classic Test that ultimately finished 8-all.

4. Bobby Bugden
St George halfback Bobby Bugden played just two Tests, both in 1960 against France, with Queenslander Barry Muir often preferred at scrum half. The 1959-60 Kangaroo made the most of his opportunity, though, with a clever hat-trick on debut in the second Test of the '60 series. Australia won 56-6, with Bugden's first try after the halftime siren extremely controversial.

5. Bernie Purcell
Goalkicking South Sydney backrower Bernie Purcell played just one Test during his illustrious career, but it was the most famous in Australian Rugby League history. Purcell debuted in Australia's famous drought-breaking series win over Great Britain in 1950 on a mud-soaked SCG, where Ron Roberts' try in the third Test brought the Ashes home to Australia for the first time in 30 years.

6. Brad Mackay

Athletic St George lock Brad Mackay enjoyed a fairytale Test debut in 1990. Named to play his first Test against France in the NSW Central West centre of Parkes, he scored three tries in sopping-wet conditions in an emphatic 34-2 victory.

7. Benny Wearing

South Sydney star—and maybe the most popular player in the premiership throughout the 1920s—Benny Wearing made his belated debut in the dead-rubber third Test against Great Britain in 1928. He scored two tries and booted three goals in the 21-14 victory, but remarkably never played for Australia again.

8. John Muggleton

Versatile Parramatta utility John Muggleton was a surprise selection for the 1982 series against New Zealand and became an unlikely hero in the series opener. Coming off the bench, he charged on to a Craig Young pass to score the winning try in the final minute of the match. It was the only try in Australia's 11-8 win and Muggleton's only try in his three-Test career.

9. Israel Folau

Code-hopper Israel Folau capped a spectacular debut year in 2007 by becoming Australia's youngest Test player at just 18. He did not disappoint, with a two-try performance in a 58-0 drubbing of New Zealand. The Melbourne three-quarter started on the wing and was marvellous.

10. Norm Provan

St George legend Norm 'Sticks' Provan made an immediate impact in the first game of his Test career, starring in the 37-12 thrashing of Great Britain during the 1954 Ashes series at the SCG. Provan scored a try and had a hand in a number of others in a dominant debut alongside outstanding second-row partner Kel O'Shea.

WORST TEST DEBUTS

1. Darren Lockyer

Darren Lockyer, the record holder for most Test appearances and one of Rugby League's all-time greats, made the most notorious debut in the history of international football. Selected on the bench for the 1998 Anzac Test, he replaced injured fullback Robbie O'Davis during the first half with Australia ahead 12-2 and was caught behind his goal-line just before halftime, and the Kiwis posted their first try from the resultant dropout. But it got much worse for Lockyer after the break, when he made two errors that led directly to New Zealand tries as the underdogs rallied to a 22-16 victory. Ironically, Lockyer had made a stellar debut for Super League Australia at the end of the previous season, scoring two tries.

2. Brendan Tuuta

Western Suburbs backrower Brendan Tuuta was dubbed 'The Baby-faced Assassin' after a wild debut for New Zealand in the first Test of the 1989 home series against Australia. The 24-year-old Chatham Islands product's international introduction was marked by reckless tackling and the blatant kneeing of Australian vice-captain Paul Vautin. Pilloried by the media in Australia and in his homeland, the skilful and hardworking Tuuta somehow escaped censure over several unsavoury incidents but never fully shed the stigma of his hot-headed Test debut despite making a further 15 appearances for the Kiwis and enjoying a decade-long professional career in Australia and England.

3. Paul Hauff

Paul Hauff claimed the Australian fullback berth for the first Test against New Zealand after a brilliant Origin series for Queensland. But the 21-year-old, a veteran of just 25 games for the Broncos, experienced a tough debut in a shock 24-8 loss to the Kiwis in Melbourne. His ordinary night culminated in a fumble of a Gary Freeman kick to gift the Kiwis' fourth try to Tawera Nikau. The gangly custodian never played another rep match, and the remainder of his career was frequently interrupted by injuries.

4. Noel Pidding

St George's Noel Pidding was selected to debut as Australia's fullback for the opening Test against New Zealand in 1948—the first trans-Tasman series in 11 years. The green-and-golds led 13-5 at halftime, and Pidding made a long break early in the second half. But instead of passing to unmarked winger Pat McMahon, he went himself and was brought down as a match-sealing try went begging. The Kiwis clawed back to claim a 21-19 upset. Pidding was dropped after his crucial mistake, beginning the Test career of Clive Churchill, but went on to play a further 18 Tests as a winger.

5. John Hopoate

After scoring 21 tries for Manly, John Hopoate ousted several strong wing contenders to make his debut for Australia in the opening match of the 1995 World Cup against England at Wembley. But a vital error bringing the ball off his own line gifted a try to opposing winger Jason Robinson with 11 minutes to go, helping England to a 20-16 win. Hopoate scored three tries in a subsequent pool match against South Africa, but was left out of the tournament's big matches and never again represented Australia.

6. Gene Ngamu

Five-eighth Gene Ngamu was chosen to make his Test debut for New Zealand against Great Britain at Wembley in 1993 at the tender age of 19. But the youngster, opposing seasoned international Garry Schofield, was one of several Kiwis to endure a torrid afternoon at the hallowed venue as they were thumped 17-0. He was dropped for the remaining Tests on tour, but reclaimed his spot in '94 and was a Kiwis regular for several seasons. The Auckland Warriors pivot eventually made 22 Test appearances, scoring 11 tries.

7. Ray Laird

Mackay fullback Ray Laird was the surprise choice to replace injured captain Graeme Langlands in the No.1 jumper for the second Test of the 1970 Ashes series. The debutant was peppered with high balls by the Great Britain side, one of which he allowed to bounce for Lions five-eighth Roger Millward to score the opening try. The 18-game Queensland rep was dropped for the decider in the wake of Australia's 28-7 SCG loss and did not play another Test.

8. Wendell Sailor

Exciting young Brisbane winger Wendell Sailor was a bolter in the 1994 Kangaroo Tour squad, and his tremendous form in the early club matches garnered a spot on the flank for the opening Test at Wembley. But after being closely marked by Great Britain and making little impact as the Kangaroos went down 8-4 to the 12-man hosts, Sailor was dropped in favour of Rod Wishart for the remaining Tests. He went on to score 17 tries in 16 Test appearances.

9. Dennis Manteit

Queensland forward Dennis Manteit was selected in the 1967-68 Kangaroo Tour squad and made his Test debut in the first Ashes encounter at Headingley. But the front-rower was sent off, leaving the tourists short-handed as they went down 16-11. Dropped for the second Test, Manteit was recalled for the decider, which Australia won 11-3 at Manchester.

10. Luke Covell

An unlikely New Zealand representative, Goondiwindi-born Cronulla winger Luke Covell was selected to make his Test debut for the Kiwis against Australia at the end of 2007. But the unlucky Covell was forced from the field after just six minutes in Wellington when he suffered a dislocated elbow. His exit set the tone for a terrible day for the Kiwis, who were crushed by a record 58-0 scoreline, and he did not play another Test match.

Chapter 14

THE BIG PLAYS

GREATEST PREMIERSHIP TRIES

1. Ian Schubert: 1982—Eastern Suburbs v Manly
In an amazing team effort that saw the ball go from one corner of the field to the other through 16 pairs of hands, Ian Schubert finished what champion caller Ray Warren at the time called, "The greatest try I've ever seen." Easts showed tremendous handling throughout the incredible play, which featured a beautiful one-two between Ian Barkley and Kerry Boustead, a fabulous pirouette from halfback Kevin Hastings, a pop ball from Barkley (touching it for the fourth time), a scything run and dummy from Dave Brown (who eventually threw a short ball to Les Cleal), a tough catch from Rocky Laurie and Schubert's eventual finish. It capped a 40-2 belting of the Sea Eagles at the Sydney Sports Ground.

2. Harold Horder: 1912—South Sydney v Glebe
The most highly regarded try from the code's infant days in Australia, Harold Horder's magnificent three-pointer came during his debut for Souths. As a zippy 18-year-old 'The Wonder Winger' bamboozled the Glebe defence in a spiralling 90-metre run in which he collected a missed penalty shot and took off straight down the middle of the park, swerving and stepping past defenders before making his way to the corner. It is

said Horder beat every Glebe player on the park, with winger Mick Muggivan around his ankles when he dived over. There has been no greater solo try in premiership history.

3. Josh Morris: 2012—Canterbury v Melbourne

Ben Barba enjoyed a magical season in 2012, and there was probably no bigger high than the try he set up for Josh Morris in his home town of Mackay against Melbourne. Barba collected a kick deep in the corner of his own in-goal and looked sure to be tackled before astonishingly stepping past two shocked defenders. He then flew past Cooper Cronk, avoiding the horde of cover defenders, before chipping off his right foot with the cover on top of him. The kick sat up perfectly for Josh Morris, who finished under the sticks. It was incredible Rugby League.

4. Steve Gearin: 1980—Canterbury v Eastern Suburbs

Rugby League's most memorable Grand Final try, Steve Gearin's tremendous catch sealed Canterbury's first premiership in 38 years in 1980. Inside its own half Canterbury shifted the ball to its left, with international Greg Brentnall steaming on to a Graeme Hughes short ball. The Wagga-born Brentnall burst through the Easts defence before launching a towering bomb 40 metres from the Roosters line. Canterbury winger Gearin came flying through and outjumped the shocked Eastern Suburbs defenders to score a magical try.

5. Ty Williams: 2005—North Queensland v Manly

North Queensland winger Ty Williams was one of the most potent wingers in the game between 2001 and 2005, and he tore Manly apart late in the '05 season with a hat-trick at Brookvale Oval, including a length-of-the-field ripper. Williams took a pass flat-footed, millimetres from his own dead-ball line, and sprinted into space, burning the staggered Sea Eagles defence. Speedster Brett Stewart got to Williams 25 metres out but the Cowboys winger fended and then palmed off again, rolling out of the tackle before laying a fend on Steve Menzies coming across, and then finishing out wide in a spectacular individual effort.

6. Jack Dougherty: 1954—South Sydney v Newtown

In a play that is revered as one of the great tries of the game's first 50 years, South Sydney five-eighth Jack Dougherty finished off a length-of-the-field try that has gone down in Rugby League lore. With the scores locked at 5-all early in the 1954 semi with Newtown, Clive Churchill picked up the ball in his own in-goal. With Brian 'Poppa' Clay closing in on him, Churchill ducked behind the posts before grabbing a hold of the upright and swinging back the other way. He then charged up the left wing, dummying to Ian Moir and splitting Dick Poole and Kevin Considine. He made it to halfway before firing a long pass to lock Les 'Chicka' Cowie, who hit Moir and then found Dougherty, who finished under the sticks.

7. Ted Goodwin: 1977—St George v Parramatta
The flamboyant 'Lord' Ted Goodwin scored one of the great individual Grand Final tries in the drawn '77 decider. Playing fullback, he collected a pass from a standing Rod Reddy near halfway, charging on to the ball and through the Parramatta defence. With only lanky Eels custodian Phil Mann between Goodwin and the try-line, the Dragons No.1 chipped ahead. He and Mann chased desperately, with an exaggerated lunge from Goodwin seeing the Dragons score. He knocked himself out in the play but etched himself into Grand Final lore with the tremendous try.

8. Brett Mullins: 1995—Canberra v Brisbane
Few players in premiership history have more long-range or solo tries to their name than Brett Mullins. The Raiders fullback was one of the most exciting players during the mid-1990s and scored a plethora of contenders for greatest try ever, but his double chip against Brisbane was the most memorable. He chipped from dummy-half with Julian O'Neill standing deep, kicked again when the fullback approached and then outsprinted the Broncos cover for a miracle try.

9. Eric Grothe: 1983—Parramatta v Canterbury
Parramatta winger Eric 'Guru' Grothe was known for his blockbusting style, and there was no bigger show of force and dominance than his try against rivals Canterbury in the 1983 finals series. The giant Eels flanker collected a pass from Steve Ella on his own 40-metre line and preceded to steamroll the Canterbury side. He fended off five Canterbury defenders, who were left splayed on the SCG turf after Grothe's bustling show of strength and power.

10. Ben Barba: 2011—Canterbury v Newcastle
Freakish try-scorer Ben Barba scored possibly the most freakish try of his career with a disbelieving finish in a clash with Newcastle in 2011. Bulldogs centre Josh Morris made a bust down the left-edge and threw it to winger Jonathan Wright, who ran 30 metres before chipping. Speedster Barba sprinted through and dived with the ball already beyond the dead-ball line. He somehow managed to pull it in and plant it down millimetres inside the dead-ball line for one of the great tries.

GREATEST INTERCEPT TRIES

1. Bob McCarthy
The most famous intercept try of all time, Bob McCarthy's effort was the pivotal moment of the 1967 Grand Final and has passed into Rugby League folklore. The big, fast South Sydney second-rower was lurking in the backline when he plucked Canterbury hooker Col Brown's floating pass out of the air and raced 75 yards to give the Rabbitohs a two-point halftime lead. Souths eventually edged out the Berries 12-10.

2. Shaun Kenny-Dowall
Sydney Roosters centre Shaun Kenny-Dowall ended one of the greatest matches in Rugby League history with a 100th-minute intercept try. The Roosters' pulsating 2010 qualifying final against the Tigers went into golden point extra-time but neither side could find the decisive score until Kenny-Dowall pounced on a long ball from Tigers backrower Liam Fulton. He set sail for the corner on the opposite side of the ground, outlasting Lote Tuqiri in a thrilling 65-metre chase to snatch a 19-15 victory.

3. Matt Bowen
The opening match of the 2005 Origin series was locked at 20-all at the end of 80 minutes after an extraordinary NSW comeback and a late field goal by Johnathan Thurston. Queensland took a 1-0 lead in the series when interchange back Matt Bowen snaffled an all-or-nothing long pass from Blues halfback Brett Kimmorley in the fourth minute of golden point, racing 40 metres unopposed to finish the epic contest. Kimmorley was subsequently dropped for game two.

4. Michael Cleary
Although not as famous as Bob McCarthy's effort the previous season, Souths winger Michael Cleary's long-range intercept try was equally crucial to the outcome of the 1968 Grand Final. The flying Rabbitohs winger grabbed a misdirected pass from Manly fullback Bob Batty during the first half and scorched 85 yards to score his side's only try of the match. Souths withstood a Sea Eagles fightback to claim their second straight premiership 13-9.

5. Craig Fitzgibbon
The tense 2002 semi-final between the Sydney Roosters and Newcastle was delicately poised at 6-all in the 57th minute when the game was busted open by an unlikely source. The Roosters' workhorse backrower Craig Fitzgibbon intercepted a Danny Buderus pass and strode 90 metres for a memorable try, crashing over in the corner

despite Matthew Gidley's valiant chase and cover tackle. The floodgates opened and the Roosters progressed with a 38-12 win.

6. Paul Loughlin
Great Britain came desperately close to snatching the Ashes in 1990 after centre Paul Loughlin's brilliant intercept try in the second Test at Old Trafford. Australia—down 1-0 in the series—led 10-6 during the second half when Ricky Stuart fired a pass towards an overlap, but a flat-footed Loughlin showed superb fingertip control to snatch it out of the air and scooted 50 metres to score. Paul Eastwood missed the relatively simple conversion to leave the scores tied, and in injury time Stuart engineered a famous long-range try for Mal Meninga to steal the win.

7. Jason Williams
Shell-shocked Canterbury had fallen 14-0 behind against Canberra in the 1994 Grand Final when winger Jason Williams provided the Bulldogs with some desperately needed respite. The Kiwi flyer reeled in a Laurie Daley cut-out pass and outpaced Brett Mullins and Jason Croker on an 80-metre sprint to the try-line. Williams' try against the run of play was not a turning point, however, with the Raiders going on with the job to carve out a 36-12 victory.

8. Tommy Ryan
Powerhouse St George winger Tommy Ryan scored an 80-yard intercept try in the 1957 Grand Final from a wayward pass by Manly forward Rex Mossop, crossing in the corner despite a gallant cover tackle by fullback Ron Willey. The touchdown broke a 4-all deadlock and gave Ryan a club-record 26 tries for the season, while the Dragons went on to subdue Manly 20-9 to secure their second of 11 straight premierships.

9. Peter Mortimer
Canterbury winger Peter Mortimer scored one of the great regular season intercept tries against Balmain in a 1985 thriller at Leichhardt Oval. He raced off his own try-line to cut off a long ball from Tigers half Scott Gale before sprinting 90 metres and diving over for a try—just outlasting Gale's valiant chase—to help secure a dramatic 20-18 win for the defending premiers.

10. Eric Grothe snr and Eric Grothe jnr
Parramatta's father-and-son wing monsters Eric Grothe senior and Eric Grothe junior each scored length-of-the-field intercept tries for NSW. The elder Grothe snapped up a fumble by Queensland hooker Greg Conescu in the one-off Origin clash in 1981 and charged 90 metres for a try, helping set up a 15-0 lead before the Blues were run down 22-15. In his only Origin series, Grothe junior defused a dangerous situation in the 2006 decider by snaffling a Johnathan Thurston pass and sprinting 95 metres to

dot down at the other end, locking the scores up 4-all at halftime; the Maroons also prevailed in that match, however, snatching a 16-14 result.

GOLDEN POINT PLAYS

1. Farrell's third a debut match-winner
Souths staged one of great fightbacks of the NRL era in 2010 when they recovered from a 28-12 second-half deficit against Wests Tigers to force extra-time at 30-all, with 19-year-old debutant centre Dylan Farrell scoring two tries. After seven unsuccessful field-goal attempts, the match appeared headed for a draw. But with time ticking inside the final 10 seconds of golden point, Rabbitohs fullback Rhys Wesser made a stunning 25-metre break and floated a speculator to a wide-running Shaune Corrigan. The interchange offloaded inside as he was tackled for Farrell, who crashed over in the corner for his hat-trick and an after-the-siren match-winner.

2. Darren Lockyer sparks 50-metre try
Battling a virus in the lead-up to the match, Darren Lockyer climbed out of his sickbed to inspire a golden point triumph over the Titans late in the 2008 season. With the scores tied at 21-all in the third minute of extra-time, Lockyer shifted the ball to Joel Moon on the last tackle on the halfway line when the Titans rushed up to shut down a field-goal attempt. Moon found space before linking again with Lockyer, who sent burly backrower Greg Eastwood over for a sensational match-winner.

3. Thurston's show-and-go
The 2006 Tri-Nations final between Australia and New Zealand in Sydney was one of the great Test matches, locked 12-all after 80 hard-fought and pulsating minutes. In the seventh minute of golden point extra-time, Kangaroos halfback Johnathan Thurston threw a dummy and shot through an opening 35 metres out from his own line, striding into Kiwi territory before finding his captain, Darren Lockyer, backing up on the inside. Lockyer outlasted the New Zealand cover in a 25-metre sprint to score under the posts and reclaim the Tri-Nations trophy for Australia. The "show-and-go" would become a trademark and regular match-winning play in Thurston's career.

4. SKD's intercept
The epic Sydney Roosters-Wests Tigers qualifying final in 2010 went into golden point at 15-all, and was not decided until Tricolours centre Shaun Kenny-Dowall's all-or-

nothing intercept at the 99-minute mark. Kenny-Dowall plucked Tigers backrower Liam Fulton's pass out of the air 35 metres out from the Roosters' try-line and 15 metres in from the right-hand touchline. He made a beeline for the left-hand corner and outlasted Simon Dwyer and Lote Tuqiri on a thrilling run to claim the win.

5. Broken-face hero
Darren Lockyer's last act as a Brisbane player was maybe his most memorable. Felled by friendly fire inside the last 10 minutes of a tense semi-final against St George Illawarra in 2011, the skipper battled on with what was later revealed to be a fractured cheekbone. The sudden-death match went into golden point courtesy of a late Dragons try, but Lockyer stepped up in the second minute of the added period to take a flat pass from dummy-half and snap a low 27-metre field-goal attempt over the crossbar under heavy defensive pressure. He was mobbed by his teammates as the packed house at Suncorp went berserk, but was forced out of the following week's preliminary final with the facial injury.

6. 'Shrek' under the posts from Roberts magic
The Bulldogs fought back from 0-16 down to force their 2006 clash with the Warriors into extra-time at 18-all. In the first period of golden point, stand-in halfback Ben Roberts—playing in his fourth NRL game—received the ball flat-footed on the last tackle 30 metres out from the Warriors' line. He stepped brilliantly past two defenders and, confronted by the fullback, produced a left-handed flick pass for burly prop Mark O'Meley to dive under the crossbar for the match-winner.

7. Sandow's 49-metre stunner
South Sydney halfback Chris Sandow landed a pressure conversion with four minutes remaining to send the 2011 clash with the Sydney Roosters into golden point, and went on to win the game with one of the great field goals. He kicked a booming 49-metre one-pointer in the 87th minute to seal the come-from-behind victory.

8. Timmins' history-maker
State of Origin's maiden instalment of golden point came in the series-opening encounter of 2004—but the match-winning play came from an unlikely source. After NSW halfback Craig Gower missed several attempts to break the 8-all deadlock, makeshift five-eighth Shaun Timmins stepped up in the third minute of extra-time to hammer a brilliant 37-metre field goal between the posts to snatch victory for the Blues.

9. Locky's field goal hits both uprights
A classic derby between Brisbane and the fledgling Gold Coast in 2007 went into golden point at 18-all, but Broncos talisman Darren Lockyer needed just 50 seconds

of added time to grab victory with a remarkable field goal. He launched from 40 metres out and the ball bounced off both uprights before dropping over the crossbar in front of a rapturous Suncorp Stadium throng.

10. Todd Carney twin long-range efforts
Burgeoning Canberra playmaker Todd Carney produced two stunning golden point field goals during 2006. In Round 12 he nailed a 40-metre attempt in the 87th minute to sink North Queensland, and he proved the match-winner again in Round 23 against Wests Tigers, scraping a low field-goal attempt over the bar from 38 metres out with just 10 seconds remaining.

FIELD GOALS

1. Braith Anasta
Braith Anasta kept the Sydney Roosters' premiership dream alive in 2010 with perhaps the finest field goal in premiership history. In the opening week of the 2010 finals series, the Roosters trailed the Tigers 14-15 in the final 30 seconds when they won a scrum against the head. The first play was a mad scramble that saw the ball sail right and then back to the left as a number of Roosters looked for an opportunity to hit the leveller. On the next play, the Roosters darted down the blind, throwing it around wildly until the ball landed in Anasta's hands as the siren sounded. Anasta, who was 40 metres out and close to the left-hand sideline, fired it off his right boot and hit it sweet and true, sending the game to extra-time. The Roosters won the match 19-15 as they marched towards the Grand Final.

2. Dally Messenger
The game's greatest star in its infant days, Easts star Dally Messenger could do almost anything on the field—including slot magnificent field goals. On one occasion he nailed a 40-metre left-footed field goal because rival Chris McKivat had hold of his right foot. But his most famous field goal came against Glebe in 1911 when, on halfway, he ran towards the sideline before snapping back and drop kicking in the opposite direction to which he was running—landing one of the game's best.

3. Benji Marshall
Wests Tigers pivot Benji Marshall scored one of the great field goals on the stroke of halftime in a clash with the Gold Coast in 2010 when he stepped back and nailed

a towering 52-metre drop goal that hit the crossbar and went over. The kick put the Tigers up 15-2 but later proved decisive, with Marshall's team finishing 15-14 victors.

4. Nathan Merritt
The late afternoon shadows hung over the SCG on a brilliant 2009 heritage-round clash between South Sydney and the Wests Tigers when Nathan Merritt landed one of the NRL era's finest field goals. The great try-scorer, who had never landed a field goal before and hasn't kicked one since, took Souths to an amazing 23-22 win with an incredible drop goal 30 metres out and close to the sideline. He was carried from the field as Souths fans went ballistic.

5. Ken Wilson
A fine field-goal kicker during the 1970s and early 1980s, Ken Wilson holds the distinction of kicking the field goal in the only 1-0 result in premiership history. He slotted the deciding point to roll St George in an epic struggle in 1973.

6. Shaun Timmins
NSW five-eighth Shaun Timmins became a hero in 2004 when his second career field goal booted the Blues to victory in the series opener. In Origin's first golden point game, he hit a brilliant 38-metre match-winner to crush Queensland 9-8. Timmins never again kicked a drop goal.

7. Chris Sandow
One of the NRL era's greatest field-goal exponents, Chris Sandow has struck many marvellous field goals in his career. His most famous—and greatest—came in 2011 against archrivals the Sydney Roosters. With the scores locked at 20-all and the game seven minutes deep into golden point, Sandow hit a 49-metre drop goal that sent the Bunnies faithful into rapture.

8. Andrew Willis
Western Suburbs five-eighth Andrew Willis kicked just one field goal in his career, but it was one of the finest one-pointers in premiership history. In the third-last round of 1996 against North Sydney, with time expiring, he hit a 48-metre shot that proved decisive in sending the Magpies to their last finals series. The kick, which fell over the bar, was a brilliant strike from the handy No.6.

9. Cooper Cronk
Queensland halfback Cooper Cronk slotted the most famous field goal in Maroons State of Origin history when he nailed the match-winner of the 2012 decider. With seven minutes left and the scores locked at 20-all, he struck a beauty from 40 metres out to the left of the uprights that proved the decisive play of a tight Origin series.

10. Eric Simms
The greatest field-goal exponent of all time, Eric Simms landed so many drop goals that the value of a field goal officially dropped from two points to one. Simms' great day with the boot was a five-field-goal effort against Penrith in 1969. The South Sydney great kicked 86 field goals in his career—including four in the 1970 Grand Final—and is regarded as the greatest master of the craft ever.

11. The unlikely heroes: John Muggleton, Mark Carroll and Nathan Cayless
A number of the great field goals have been delivered by unlikely heroes. Parramatta backrower John Muggleton nailed a sweetly hit 42-metre drop goal from dummy-half to defeat St George 21-20 in 1987, while tough Souths prop Mark Carroll potted one from 30 metres out in 1993 in one of the unlikeliest field goals ever kicked. And Eels prop Nathan Cayless kicked a left-footed drop goal to level the scores 23-all in a match against Newcastle in 2008, which Parra went on to win 24-23.

CONVERSIONS

1. Michael O'Connor
Brilliant NSW three-quarter Michael O'Connor kicked Origin's most famous goal in game two of the 1991 series. After missing a similar attempt that would have drawn the series opener, he curled his conversion of Mark McGaw's late try in from the right-hand touchline, defying the immense pressure and driving rain at the SFS. The booming kick gave the Blues a series-levelling 14-12 victory after an epic contest.

2. Clive Churchill
Defending premiers South Sydney's sudden-death run to the 1955 finals was kept alive by a stunning sideline conversion against Manly from incomparable fullback Clive Churchill, who had broken his arm earlier in the match. Lock Les 'Chicka' Cowie's try in the corner levelled the scores at 7-all in the dying moments before Churchill—with his arm wrapped in an exercise-book cover acting as a makeshift splint—courageously stepped up and booted the winning goal. The Rabbitohs battled on without him and claimed another premiership on the back of 11 straight wins. Churchill's heroic goal is regarded as the key moment in Souths' 'Miracle of '55'.

3. Daryl Halligan
Down 18-2 to Parramatta with 11 minutes of the 1998 preliminary final remaining, Canterbury staged an extraordinary comeback via three quick-fire tries. Sharpshooter

Daryl Halligan landed one goal from out wide to bring the Bulldogs back to within six points, but it is his conversion of Willie Talau's late try that has become the subject of countless replays. The winger appeared to hook the kick slightly, but the ball straightened and bisected the goalposts to level the scores. Canterbury went on to win 32-20 in extra-time.

4. Ken Irvine
Part-time goalkicker Ken Irvine slotted possibly international football's most famous goal in the third Test of the 1962 Ashes series. With the series already lost, Australia was desperate for a morale-boosting win at the SCG. The prolific winger's second try in the dying stages pegged the hosts back to 17-16 in arrears of Great Britain, but Irvine admitted to referee Darcy Lawler he was at long odds to kick the sideline conversion. Lawler famously suggested Irvine adjust his positioning of ball, and he nailed the conversion to snatch a classic win.

5. Hazem El Masri
Competition leaders the Bulldogs had staged a phenomenal comeback from 0-19 down to trail defending premiers Newcastle by just one point after a last-minute try in a thrilling 2002 encounter. Contending with a swirling breeze, the sun in his eyes and a baying pro-Knights crowd, Bulldogs winger Hazem El Masri drifted the after-the-bell conversion attempt in from the right-hand touchline to steal a stunning 22-21 triumph.

6. Andrew Johns
Newcastle genius Andrew Johns produced the greatest clutch kick of his career against St George Illawarra in 2003. The Knights had levelled the scores at 30-all via a last-minute try, leaving Johns—who had led NSW to an Origin win just two nights earlier—with an opportunity to win the game. 'Joey' duly landed the conversion from the left-hand touchline after the siren, delighting his teammates and the bumper home crowd.

7. Alan Kempnich
Gold Coast fullback Alan Kempnich's only attempt at goal in first grade was a memorable one. The lowly Seagulls' 1994 clash with Newcastle was Kempnich's second first grade match—and his first in four years. But after regular goalkicker Wayne Bartrim exhausted himself scoring a late, long-range try to tie the game up at 10-all, Kempnich was called upon to win the game. He drilled the sideline conversion attempt to secure one of the club's five wins of '94. Kempnich played just four more first grade games and was not required to kick for goal again, thus finishing his modest premiership career with a flawless record.

8. Tim Brasher
Balmain fullback Tim Brasher, who finished with a career record of 105 goals at a lousy 60 per cent, completed a spectacular Tigers comeback against heavyweights Canberra in 1993 with a towering sideline conversion. The Tigers trailed 12-32 but scored four tries in 10 minutes to pull back to within two points. Graham Lyons' late try in the corner left Brasher with a chance to draw the game, which he did after his shot for goal bounced off an upright and dropped over the crossbar.

9. Matthew Head
St George Illawarra halfback Matthew Head engineered a brilliant score-levelling try for Matt Cooper with three minutes of the pulsating 2005 Anzac Day clash with the Sydney Roosters remaining, producing a chip-and-chase to send the centre over out wide. The left-footed Head then curved the sideline conversion between the sticks to seal a sensational 26-24 victory for the Dragons.

10. Aaron Gorrell
The Origin-weary Broncos were set to record a momentous win over St George Illawarra in 2006 until rookie winger Brett Morris crossed in the last minute to level the scores at 16-all. Left-footed hooker Aaron Gorrell displayed nerves of steel after the bell, defying the 32,914-strong Suncorp Stadium crowd to pilot the conversion over from the left-hand sideline and break Brisbane hearts.

PENALTY GOALS

1. Keith Barnes, 1960 v St George
With potentially the greatest penalty kick in premiership history, Balmain fullback Keith 'Golden Boots' Barnes was chaired off after his match-winning kicking display against heavyweights St George. With the scores locked 15-all and just four minutes remaining, he nailed a penalty goal from 55 out over Saints giant Norm Provan to put Balmain up. Barnes secured the win with a sideline penalty on fulltime before he was hoisted to the shoulders of the Balmain faithful.

2. Eric Simms, 1967 Grand Final v Canterbury
The 1967 Grand Final was an absolute classic between South Sydney and Canterbury that went right down to the final minutes. With the scores locked at 10-all and the clock ticking down, wonderful Rabbitohs goalkicker Eric Simms landed a 40-metre penalty when Ross Kidd was pulled up for a scrum infringement. Simms never looked like missing with his long-range penalty shot.

3. Lin Johnson, 1942 Grand Final v St George

The most famous penalty goal in Canterbury's history, Lin Johnson's decisive kick came from just 10 metres out right in front with minutes remaining, but only just made it over. In what was an SCG quagmire, Berries fullback Johnson slipped and fell as he approached. He got enough of the ball, though, and it snuck over the crossbar to win Canterbury its second premiership 11-9.

4. Greg Alexander, 1990 Major Semi v Canberra

Penrith halfback Greg Alexander's heroics in the 1990 major semi sent the Panthers to their first Grand Final and confirmed his status as the club's finest son. In driving rain and with less than five minutes remaining, he calmly nailed a superb 35-metre penalty close to the sideline to level the scores 12-all. Alexander dominated the extra-time period and the Panthers marched to their first decider.

5. Mark Riddell, 2003 v Brisbane

With one of the great clutch kicks of the NRL era, Mark Riddell stood tall to steal St George Illawarra a thrilling 26-25 win at Suncorp Stadium in 2003. Riddell, who kicked at just 73 per cent over his career, slotted a 41-metre penalty from wide out on the stroke of fulltime to give the Dragons a rare moment of joy in a wretched season.

6. Dally Messenger, 1911 Playoff v South Sydney

For the game's first great hero, Dally Messenger's skill with the boot went a long way to building the legend. One example was when he opened the scoring of the 1911 playoff against Souths, putting Easts on the board with a magnificent booming penalty goal from 5 metres his own side of halfway. The Tricolours went on to win their first title two weeks later.

7. Steve Gearin, 1983 Minor Preliminary Semi v Balmain

One of the most accomplished kickers of the 1980s, St George winger Steve Gearin had his finest hour with the boot in the 1983 finals series. In an epic minor preliminary semi against Balmain, with the scores locked at 14-all in the second period of extra-time, he landed a penalty 35 metres out and just 10 metres in to send the Saints into the minor semi against Canterbury.

8. Andrew Leeds, 1992 v Balmain

Balmain's nemesis during the early 1990s, Andrew Leeds twice slotted penalty goals on the siren to defeat the Tigers. In 1991, he nailed a last-minute penalty when playing for Parramatta to give the Eels a 16-15 win, and then when playing for Penrith one year later he slotted one from halfway that finished the Tigers 14-12.

9. Ben Walker, 2003 v Parramatta

Manly halfback Ben Walker carved himself a piece of NRL history in mid-2003 when he ended the first golden point game with a 35-metre beauty. The penalty kick gave Manly a 36-34 win over Parramatta and kick-started a new era in Rugby League.

10. Nathan Hindmarsh, 2012 v St George Illawarra

There have been better penalty goals, but few have been more popular. In the final play of the last game of his decorated 330-match career, likeable Parramatta backrower Nathan Hindmarsh slotted a penalty from 30 metres out and well to the left of the sticks in a heavy defeat to St George Illawarra. The first and only goal of his career was a wonderful tribute to a true champion.

COSTLY ERRORS

1. Ashton Sims

Clinging to a 14-12 lead in the dying stages of one of the most gripping, drama-charged finals matches in premiership history, Brisbane only had to ruck the ball out of its own territory to seal a momentous victory over Melbourne. Interchange forward Ashton Sims carted the ball over the Broncos' 20-metre line but coughed up possession after a punishing hit by his Storm counterpart Sika Manu. Greg Inglis crossed in the corner two plays later with just 50 seconds on the clock, stealing a 16-14 victory to end Wayne Bennett's 21-season tenure in Brisbane.

2. Neville Glover

A dropped ball in a Grand Final has somewhat unfairly tainted Parramatta winger Neville Glover's career—it is the predominant memory his name evokes, despite the fact that he scored 59 tries in 130 first grade games and represented Australia in 1978. With the Eels in search of their maiden premiership and trailing Manly 10-11 in the 1976 decider, an unmarked Glover spilled a pass with the try-line—and Grand Final hero status—beckoning. Sea Eagles sharpshooter Graham Eadie kicked a fourth penalty two minutes later to clinch a 13-10 win.

3. Brett Hodgson

NSW led 14-10 in the 74th minute of the 2006 decider when courageous Blues fullback Brett Hodgson etched his name into Origin infamy. Jumping into dummy-half on the Blues' 20-metre line, he fired a loose pass that evaded intended recipient Matt King. Queensland skipper Darren Lockyer slipped between King and Mark

Gasnier to snap up the loose ball and fended off Luke Bailey to score under the posts, clinching a 16-14 triumph and breaking the Blues' three-year stranglehold on the Origin crown. It was the beginning of a record eight-series losing streak for the Blues.

4. Jason Bulgarelli

Canberra and the Warriors had struggled for 20 minutes of the second half to break a 16-all deadlock during the 2003 post-season, and with five minutes to go it seemed certain the Raiders were headed for a preliminary final berth. Canberra half Mark McLinden threaded through a grubber and robust centre Jason Bulgarelli only had to claim the bouncing ball, which sat up for him on the Warriors' try-line. But just as finals survival beckoned, the ball rebounded out of Bulgarelli's hands and New Zealand worked the ball to the other end of the park for Stacey Jones to kick the Warriors to a gripping victory with a late field goal.

5. Billy Slater

A brain explosion by Kangaroos fullback Billy Slater was the pivotal moment of their shock loss to New Zealand in the 2008 World Cup final. The Kiwis had fought back to claim an 18-16 lead when Slater cleaned up a kick on the hour-mark near his try-line. With little room to work in, he attempted to get outside Manu Vatuvei, who pushed Slater over the sideline. Slater compounded his miscalculation by flinging a no-look one-handed pass back inside, and Kiwi five-eighth Benji Marshall swooped on the loose ball to dot down in the corner. The try gave New Zealand the impetus to power to a 34-20 boilover as Australia surrendered the World Cup for the first time in 36 years.

6. Martin Bella

Veteran prop Martin Bella set the tone for Canterbury's disastrous Grand Final day in 1994 when he knocked the ball on from Canberra's kick-off—but in fairness to the burly 30-year-old, it should not have been left up to him to claim the kick-off. Nevertheless, Bella made a meal of the loose ball in the in-goal and the Bulldogs were on their heels immediately via a line dropout. The Raiders skipped to an early lead and eventually scored a resounding 36-12 victory.

7. Anthony Mundine

St George Illawarra linchpin Anthony Mundine could have virtually wrapped up the 1999 Grand Final against Melbourne 10 minutes into the second half, but he spilled the ball as he dived over for what should have been a simple try. The Dragons led 14-2 when the five-eighth regathered his own grubber and a desperate tackle by Storm winger Craig Smith forced the ball loose. The Storm scored their first try three minutes later and pipped the Dragons 20-18 after Smith was awarded a late penalty try.

8. Paul Bowman

North Queensland went into the 2005 Grand Final against Wests Tigers as underdogs, but grabbed an early lead via a Matt Bowen try. Origin centre Paul Bowman cost the Cowboys that crucial advantage in the 17th minute, however, with an ill-conceived in-goal pass. He caught a high ball on his own try-line but was forced back by Daniel Fitzhenry and threw a desperate pass that rainbowed over Bowen's head. Young Tigers prop Bryce Gibbs pounced for an easy try, providing the momentum to go on with the job 30-16.

9. Phil Duke and Phil Sigsworth

The dour 1982 State of Origin decider was delicately poised at 5-3 in favour of Queensland midway through the second half when Phil Duke and Phil Sigsworth produced one of the most infamous mix-ups in the code's history. Blues fullback Sigsworth collected a raking Wally Lewis kick in his in-goal but was caught by Maroons forward Paul McCabe and opted to offload to debutant winger Duke. The ball bounced off the unsuspecting Duke's shoulder and Lewis pounced for the decisive try in Queensland's 10-5 victory.

10. Brett Finch

A bold play by 19-year-old Canberra halfback Brett Finch backfired horribly in the final minute of a seesawing clash with Newcastle in the 2001 regular season. With the scores locked 20-all and the Raiders awarded a 20-metre restart, Newcastle junior Finch kicked downfield in an attempt to find touch, which would have given the Raiders a full set in handy position and the opportunity to work for a match-winning field goal. But Finch's kick went out on the full, giving the Knights a penalty directly in front. Andrew Johns knocked over the simple goal after the siren to edge out the Raiders and a forlorn Finch 22-20.

WORST MISSED GOALS

1. Don Fox

The daddy of all goalkicking misses, Don Fox's failed conversion attempt for Wakefield at the end of the 1968 'Watersplash' Challenge Cup final rates near the top of Rugby League's hard-luck stories. The outstanding Great Britain Test forward had already been announced as the Lance Todd Trophy winner as man-of-the-match when Wakefield scored an unbelievable last-gasp try under the posts to trail Leeds 10-11. With time up, Fox was left with the simplest of conversions to win English club football's greatest prize, but he infamously skewed it wide in the quagmire conditions, slumping to the sodden Wembley turf after handing Leeds the Cup.

2. Darren Lockyer

Darren Lockyer's extraordinary farewell season—which included another Origin series victory for Queensland and a semi-final golden point field goal in his last match for the Broncos—was winding down to a fitting conclusion in the 2011 Four Nations final. The legendary skipper scored the Kangaroos' fifth try with a clever kick-and-chase in the dying minutes at Elland Road to round out an emphatic victory over England. He was handed the conversion attempt—which was adjacent to the uprights—after the fulltime siren. But Lockyer, the highest point-scorer in Broncos history, sprayed the seemingly unmissable kick in the final act of one of the great careers. He could only shake his head and offer a wry grin after the gaffe.

3. Mark Levy

The Panthers made the leap from perennial cellar-dwellers to finals contenders in 1984, but were left to rue a lost opportunity against eventual premiers Canterbury that could have earned the club a maiden post-season appearance. Nearing the end of a thrilling Round 20 contest, rookie Greg Alexander pegged Penrith back to 22-20 in arrears with a determined try. Penrith fullback Mark Levy had the chance to draw the match with a conversion attempt slightly to the left of the posts, but he shanked the simple shot into the right-hand upright. The one competition point that went begging would have been enough to put the Panthers into a playoff for fifth spot.

4. Jarrod Croker

In one of premiership football's cruellest missed opportunities, young Canberra centre Jarrod Croker pulled a regulation penalty-goal attempt from less than 30 metres out and almost in front in the 2010 sudden-death semi-final against Wests Tigers. The 77th-minute attempt would have sent the match into golden point, but the Tigers escaped with a 26-24 victory at Canberra Stadium. The 20-year-old Croker was inconsolable.

5. Luke Burt

The Tigers had benefited from another straightforward penalty-goal miss only four weeks earlier, when Parramatta sharpshooter Luke Burt hooked a last-minute attempt from just beyond the 20-metre line and only slightly off-centre. The devastating miss consigned the Eels to a 20-18 loss, effectively ending their finals hopes and bringing the likeable veteran to tears in the dressing room afterwards.

6. Shaun Timmins

A try in the shadows of fulltime by interchange debutant Brendan Hauville drew Illawarra level with heavyweights Norths early in the 1997 ARL season. Left-footed fill-in goalkicker Shaun Timmins had a simple chance to win the North Sydney Oval-hosted match, but he badly hooked the conversion attempt from only a few metres wide of the left-hand upright. Timmins never kicked another first grade goal, but he did land one of the most famous field goals of all time in NSW's golden point win in the 2004 Origin series opener.

7. Johnathan Thurston

Johnathan Thurston had the opportunity to clinch a much-needed win for the floundering Cowboys against Cronulla in Round 16, 2010. The Cowboys had given up an 18-0 lead to let the match head into golden point with the scores tied 19-all at fulltime. Thurston, who earlier in the season had landed his first 25 shots at goal in a row, duffed a simple 30-metre penalty shot from in front during the extra-time period. Cronulla captain Trent Barrett subsequently slotted a field goal, consigning the home side to a heartbreaking loss.

8. Laurie Daley

Canberra superstar Laurie Daley enjoyed a fine Test debut in Australia's 34-2 win over France at Parkes, but he sullied his performance slightly with an appalling conversion attempt from in front: the five-eighth hooked the kick spectacularly and missed the left-hand upright by 10 metres. The green-and-golds used five different kickers for their eight shots on goal, with fullback Gary Belcher's sole attempt the lone success.

9. Joel Caine

The NRL's top point-scorer in 2000, Wests Tigers winger/fullback Joel Caine, produced one of the worst strikes ever seen when he attempted to convert a try against Penrith the following season. The shot—taken from the 20-metre line and 20 metres in from the sideline—barely left the ground and landed just inside the 10-metre mark, becoming *Footy Show* fodder for many years to come, at the expense of the affable Caine.

10. Colin Scott

No one would blame Colin Scott for missing his penalty-goal attempt from out wide in the second match of the 1982 Origin series, but the Queensland fullback's toe-poke strike was perhaps the worst of all time. The ball skewed off the side of his boot and skidded 10 metres along the ground into the waiting arms of NSW halfback Steve Mortimer.

Chapter 15

THE COACHES

GREATEST COACHES

I. Wayne Bennett

Coach of the Queensland Team of the Century and the coach with the most wins in premiership history (87 clear of second-placed Tim Sheens at the start of the 2014 season), Wayne Bennett has won seven premierships and coached in eight Grand Finals as well as mentoring the Maroons to five series victories and Australia to a 12-3-1 international record. Making his start in the BRL (winning a title with Brisbane Souths) before joining Canberra as co-coach in 1987 and leading the Raiders to their first Grand Final, he was appointed as the Broncos' inaugural coach in 1988 and stayed with the club for 21 seasons, winning six premierships and taking the Broncos to the finals in his last 17 years. After leaving the Broncos, Bennett spent three years with St George Illawarra, bringing the club its long-awaited first premiership in 2010. He signed with the Knights in 2012, and guided the club to a preliminary final in his second year. Bennett's win percentage of 62.4 ranks fourth among coaches with 100 games, and he ranks second in premierships won as a coach. His foray into rep football was equally successful: he guided Queensland on three separate occasions, winning series during each tenure, and Australia maintained its dominance with him at the helm.

2. Craig Bellamy

Appointed Melbourne coach in 2003 after serving as an assistant to Wayne Bennett at Brisbane, Craig Bellamy built a premiership force that dominated for close to a decade in spite of the League's ongoing and unfettered pursuit of parity. A solid utility player with the Raiders in 149 games from 1982 to 1992, Bellamy found his true calling as a coach. The Storm have won three Grand Finals and played in five deciders in their 11 seasons under Bellamy, and missed the playoffs just once—when the club was tossed out of the 2010 premiership for salary-cap breaches. Arguably his finest coaching effort came in that ill-fated season, when he got 14 wins out of a team that had no tangible prize to play for. The Storm won the minor premiership the following season and the NRL title in 2012. Bellamy's 67.6 per cent win rate leads all non-playing coaches with 100-plus games, but perhaps the greatest indicator of his ability is the improvement of players who join the Storm and the decline of those who leave. Bellamy's only foray into representative coaching was as NSW coach; he lost three series during Queensland's incredible run through the late 2000s.

3. Jack Gibson

Revered by many as the greatest innovator in the annals of Rugby League coaching, Jack Gibson added professionalism and open thought in his anything-to-win approach to mentoring. Named coach of the Australian Team of the Century, he had seven spells at six clubs, and won five premierships. Gibson started out with Eastern Suburbs in 1967-68, taking a winless wooden-spoon team to back-to-back finals before moving to St George and leading the Dragons to Grand Finals in all three grades in 1971. In his one season with Newtown he claimed the Bluebags' only club championship while guiding them to a pre-season cup win and a preliminary final. Gibson rejoined Easts in 1974, and mentored one of the great Rugby League teams to back-to-back premierships in 1974-75. After an unsuccessful stint at South Sydney, he joined Parramatta in 1981 and became the last coach to win three straight premierships—in the process guiding the Eels to their maiden first grade title after 34 years in the League. Gibson moved to the Sharks after the Eels but even he couldn't weave his magic, declaring that waiting for Cronulla to win a premiership was akin to "leaving the porch light on for Harold Holt". His two-season stint as NSW coach (1989-90) saw the Blues reclaim the shield in the latter year after three straight series losses.

4. Bob Fulton

A Manly legend on the field who was anointed one of Rugby League's inaugural Immortals, Bob Fulton also left his mark as one of the top coaches on the premiership and international scenes. He was appointed captain-coach of Eastern Suburbs in 1979 but a knee injury forced his playing retirement midway through the season; he remained the Roosters' coach, leading them to consecutive minor premierships and the 1980 Grand Final. Fulton returned to Manly in 1983 for the first of two spells as Sea Eagles boss. The club went to the Grand Final in his first year and broke through for a premiership triumph in 1987. Fulton stepped aside after the 1988 season to take up the Australian coaching job, a position he held for seven seasons and two World Cup victories, building a 30-6-1 record. He returned to Manly in 1993 and led the Sea Eagles to three straight deciders (1995-97), winning in 1996 before quitting in the wake of a slow start to the 1999 season. Fulton's 64.4 per cent strike rate ranks second among coaches with 200-plus games, and he is the only coach to win two premierships and two World Cups as both a player and a coach.

5. Phil Gould

A controversial and outspoken figure, Phil Gould won a premiership in his first season as a premiership head coach and soon became respected as NSW's greatest State of Origin mentor. A skilled but unspectacular player with Penrith, Newtown, Canterbury and South Sydney, in 1988 Gould replaced Warren Ryan as Bulldogs coach at just 30 years of age and guided the club to an unlikely premiership. Falling out with club patriarch Peter Moore the year after, Gould moved to Penrith and in his first year took the perennially battling club to a maiden Grand Final; his skilled mentorship and unparalleled motivational speeches then helped the club to its first premiership in 1991. The sad death of Ben Alexander tore the Panthers apart soon after, and Gould left for the Sydney City Roosters, where he reached four finals series—including two preliminary finals—in his five-year stint. It is in the Origin arena, though, that Gould is most renowned: the NSW coach for eight series (1992-96, 2002-04) guided the Blues to six series wins. His only losing Origin series was the infamous 1995 triumph of Paul Vautin's Queensland battlers. A master psychologist and motivator, Gould took his talents to the Nine commentary team upon retirement, also helping to rebuild Penrith as general manager from 2011 onwards.

6. Arthur 'Pony' Halloway

A coaching giant during Rugby League's first four decades, Arthur Halloway made his mark as captain-coach of Balmain during the club's glory period, spanning World War I, and was non-playing coach of four other clubs from 1923 to 1948. A champion halfback with Glebe, Balmain and Eastern Suburbs from the game's first season through to 1920, Halloway captain-coached the 'Watersiders' of Balmain to four premierships in five seasons (1916-17 and 1919-20) before retiring. His first foray into non-playing coaching was a failure, with Newtown struggling in 1923, but four spells with Eastern Suburbs in the 1930s and '40s were a triumph. He led the great Easts teams of 1935-37 to three straight titles as well as a host of records that stand to this day. Halloway left for a disappointing stint with Norths, but returned to the Tricolours in 1945 and steered Easts to another title. His eight premierships as a coach remains a record, while his combined 12 titles as a player and a coach is yet to be neared.

7. Charlie Lynch

One of the great pre-war coaches, Charlie Lynch etched himself into South Sydney folklore with four premierships in his first five seasons at the helm of the Bunnies. A student of the great Ash Hennessy, Lynch was a master attacking technician who brought the most out of a magnificent Rabbitohs outfit that included Benny Wearing, George Treweek, Eddie Root and Frank O'Connor. He joined Souths in 1928 and mentored the club until 1934, and again between 1937 and 1940. During his time Souths won four premierships and finished worse than fourth just twice. Lynch made a shock return with St George in 1947, but had little success.

8. Warren Ryan

A prickly figure who often clashed with the front office and star players of the clubs he worked for, Warren Ryan was the coach of the 1980s and brought success to every team he mentored. An honest but limited lock forward during his playing career, he was one of the game's great thinkers and forged a coaching career that spanned 21 seasons and five clubs. Ryan got his start in 1979 with a Newtown team that had won three straight wooden spoons—and within three years the Jets were in the Grand Final. He moved to Canterbury in 1984 and, on the back of a gritty, defensive style known as 'Wazza Ball', helped the Bulldogs to three straight Grand Finals and titles in 1984 and '85. Internal dramas saw him leave for Balmain in 1988, and he presided over two heartbreaking Grand Final losses in his first two years at the Tigers. Throughout the decade, Ryan's teams played in six of the 10 deciders. A shift to Wests in 1991 saw back-to-back finals appearances for the first time in 12 years. He retired after quitting the Magpies in 1994 but made a shock comeback in 1999 with Newcastle, leading the Knights to consecutive finals series. Ryan sits fourth in games coached and sixth in total wins.

9. Ken Kearney

One of the key drivers behind St George's incredible run of 11 straight premierships, Ken Kearney was short in stature but a giant of the game during the 1950s and early '60s. A former Rugby Union international, Kearney returned to Australia after a spell with Leeds in Britain and brought with him a professionalism in training and preparation that the Australian game had never seen. In his third year with the club he was appointed captain-coach, leading the team to back-to-back prelims. Persistent troubles with referees saw him relegated in 1956, but he was reappointed captain-coach in 1957 and led the

Saints to six straight premierships. St George's policy of only having captain-coaches saw Kearney move on to Parramatta in 1962, where he took the club to its first three finals series in his three years after it had won eight of the last nine wooden spoons. Disappointing results at Wests and Cronulla took little away from Kearney's coaching legacy.

10. Chris Anderson

One of Rugby League's most underrated coaches, Chris Anderson is among Australia's most successful national bosses and one of the few mentors to win premierships at two separate clubs. A Canterbury great as a player, he got his start in coaching in 1986-87, leading Halifax to an unlikely Challenge Cup win as captain-coach. Anderson returned to Australia in 1990 to take the reins at Canterbury, and after a rebuild led the Bulldogs to back-to-back minor premierships in 1993-94. He was instrumental in keeping together a team that was being torn asunder by the Super League War in 1995, giving the Bulldogs the self-belief to win their first title in seven years from sixth place. After two disappointing seasons, he announced he was quitting to become Melbourne's inaugural coach. Thanks primarily to Anderson, the Storm were an immediate on-field success, running third in their debut season before winning the title in just their second year. He took over the Australian job in 1999 and built a 21-3 record that included victory in the 2000 World Cup. A spell at Cronulla ended after two years and an ill-advised comeback at the Roosters didn't last a season.

GREATEST COACHING ACHIEVEMENTS

1. Paul Vautin—The upset of all upsets

Nobody gave Queensland a chance of winning the 1995 State of Origin series. With Super League-aligned players barred from participation, the Maroons had 15 of their squad that had lost the 1994 series unavailable, as well as a new coach who hadn't mentored a single team. Paul Vautin brought a team of youngsters, journeymen and cast-offs together to smoke a star-studded NSW team 3-0 in a boilover that has gone down in Origin folklore.

2. Craig Bellamy—Melbourne thrives playing for nothing

Most teams told they would not be playing for competition points would have folded—but not Craig Bellamy's Melbourne Storm, who in 2010 won an incredible 10 of their last 18 games knowing they would receive nothing for the victories as punishment for severe breaches of the salary cap. The culture Bellamy created at Melbourne would not allow the Storm to throw in the towel despite a lack of tangible rewards.

3. Chris Anderson—Divided, not conquered

Chris Anderson's ability to bring the 1995 Bulldogs team together not only to make the finals but to win the premiership still sends tingles down the spines of the Canterbury faithful. The Bulldogs were stuck mid-table when four of their biggest stars took the club to court in an effort to break their Super League deals and sign with Parramatta. Canterbury was torn apart, but Anderson, a renowned players' coach, bonded the team together and the Bulldogs limped into the finals before embarking on a memorable month of upsets, with defector Jim Dymock winning the Clive Churchill Medal in his final game for the club.

4. Leo Nosworthy—Giant killer

The architect behind the greatest upset in Grand Final history, Leo Nosworthy holds a special place in the hearts of the Balmain faithful. In his first season as a head coach, the former Tigers centre moulded an unfashionable side into one of the great fairytales. Balmain's 11-2 win in the 1969 Grand Final over Souths, where Tigers players continually feigned injury, is still regarded as the greatest Grand Final upset of all time. On the siren, Tigers players chaired their coach around the ground, such was the respect they had for his role in their achievement.

5. Wayne Bennett—A finals regular

No coach has had more success in the history of the premiership than Wayne Bennett, and his incredible run of consecutive finals appearances is testament to his brilliance. From Brisbane's finals appearance in 1992 through to his last season with St George Illawarra in 2011, Bennett's teams made the playoffs for 20 straight seasons.

6. Jack Gibson—Newtown's only club championship

In Newtown's 76-year existence in the premiership, the club won just a single club championship. That came in 1973—Jack Gibson's only season in charge. The Bluebags finished fourth in first grade after making the finals just once in the previous 10 years, and a loss to Cronulla in the preliminary final could not sour one of their finest seasons.

7. Craig Bellamy—The Baby Broncos

Craig Bellamy has enjoyed more victories than most coaches in premiership history, but his most unlikely win was surely with the fabled 'Baby Broncos'. Missing 13 starters, predominantly to Origin selection, Broncos assistant Bellamy managed to get his troops to rally under the leadership of Shane Walker to win 28-14 at Campbelltown over the Wests Tigers.

8. Ken Kearney—Rise of the Eels
Ken Kearney set in motion St George's incredible run of 11 straight premierships as captain-coach, but his ability to drag Parramatta from wooden spooners to contenders is arguably more impressive. The Eels had won 10 wooden spoons—including the six prior to Kearney joining—in their 15-year existence before 'Killer', with minimal recruitment, took them to three straight finals series in his three years in charge.

9. Mal Meninga—Awesome Origin
Before Queensland's incredible run of eight straight Origin series wins, neither the Blues nor the Maroons had won more than three straight series. From 2006 until 2013 Queensland won every series—a generation in football and a lifetime in Origin. Mal Meninga's achievement in the interstate arena is unlikely to ever be matched.

10. Jack Gibson—Hat-trick
The last man to coach three consecutive premierships, Jack Gibson's achievement gets more remarkable with each passing year. Only two coaches—Warren Ryan and Wayne Bennett—have coached back-to-back premierships following Gibson's effort, and no mentor has done it since 1993, two full decades ago.

COACHING COMEBACKS

1. Malcolm Clift (Gold Coast, 1991)
Stability was not commonplace in the entire existence of the Gold Coast Giants/Seagulls/Chargers franchise, and left-field calls were quite often made. So it was in 1991 when the club hired Malcolm Clift as coach. He had coached Canterbury for four years—from 1973 to 1977—but had been out of top-grade coaching for nearly 15 seasons when he was appointed. The Gold Coast won just two games all season, collecting the wooden spoon, and Clift was replaced by Wally Lewis, who in 1992 became the last captain-coach.

2. Peter Sharp (Cronulla, 2013-14)
The Northern Eagles coach who also guided Manly in its last year before the merger and first as a solo entity, Peter Sharp built an uninspiring 46-69-2 record across six seasons before returning to the role of assistant coach. He also spent a three-season stint at Hull as head coach. Sharp was thrust back into top-grade coaching for the opening two games of the 2013 season when the Cronulla assistant replaced Shane Flanagan, who was briefly stood down. Flanagan was again suspended for the 2014 season and Sharp took the reins.

3. Chris Anderson (Sydney Roosters, 2007)
Chris Anderson, a champion coach who led both Canterbury and Melbourne to premierships in the 1990s, had a tumultuous two-season stint at Cronulla that left both parties unhappy when they separated at the end of 2003. The former Australian Test mentor moved to Wales to coach Rugby Union and was a surprise announcement as the Sydney Roosters' coach in 2007 after Wayne Bennett reneged on an apparent deal. Anderson lasted just 16 games. His one-marker ploy was a debacle and it quickly became apparent that the game had passed him by.

4. Don Furner (Canberra Raiders, 1982-87)
A moderately successful coach with Eastern Suburbs from 1970 to 1972, taking the club to the Grand Final in his final year, Don Furner went into the coaching wilderness for a decade before reappearing as the Raiders' inaugural coach. He was in charge of Canberra for five years and co-coach for the last, building the club from newcomers and easybeats into a Grand Final team. Wayne Bennett was originally intended to be his successor, but Bennett's move to Brisbane saw the Raiders replace Furner with Tim Sheens. Furner also coached the Australian team from 1986 to 1988.

5. Harry Bath (St George, 1977-81)
Appointed Balmain coach two seasons after retiring as a player, Harry Bath led the Tigers to four finals series and two Grand Finals in six years from 1961 to 1966, but couldn't get the same from Newtown in a three-season stint that ended in 1971. His Newtown appointment was expected to be his last, but he came out of retirement to coach a young Dragons team in 1977. The Saints won the premiership—and did so again in 1979—and Bath added to his legacy with one of the great comebacks. He retired at the end of the 1981 season.

6. Warren Ryan (Newcastle, 1999-2000)
Without question the coach of the 1980s—his teams played in six of the decade's 10 Grand Finals—Warren Ryan also had success with Western Suburbs in the early 1990s in a four-season stint that garnered two of the club's three finals appearances in its last 17 years of existence. A media career beckoned, however, and Ryan was thought to be done with coaching—until 1999, when he was a shock replacement for Mal Reilly at Newcastle. Though he endured embarrassments such as playing American fraud Greg Smith, the Knights made the finals both seasons Ryan was in charge, laying the groundwork for their 2001 premiership under Michael Hagan.

7. Mark Murray (Melbourne, 2001-02)
A sharp halfback in his playing days, Mark 'Muppet' Murray was appointed Eastern Suburbs coach in 1991 after a messy 1990 season that saw the club finish 14th and use

three coaches. Murray's Roosters failed to make the finals in four years—their sixth in 1992 being his best finish—but he became a surprise choice in 1999 to replace Wayne Bennett as Queensland Origin coach. He parlayed this into the Storm head-coaching job in 2001, replacing Chris Anderson mid-season—but the club's worst finish, in 2002, saw Murray dumped for Craig Bellamy.

8. Charlie Lynch (St George, 1947)
A legend at South Sydney who guided the Bunnies to four titles in a two-stint career that spanned the late 1920s and the entire 1930s, Charlie Lynch made a surprise comeback with St George in 1947. It was an ill-fated move. The Saints, who had played in a Grand Final challenge the year before, went 11-7 and lost a playoff for fourth spot.

9. John Lang (South Sydney, 2010-11)
A premiership-winning coach who sits eighth on the all-time games-coached list, former Test hooker John Lang got his start with Cronulla in 1994 and spent eight years at Shark Park during arguably the club's most successful era. He moved to Penrith in 2002 and spent five years at the Panthers, winning a title in his second season. Lang retired from coaching but was lured back in 2010 by good friend and Souths CEO Shane Richardson to be a replacement for Jason Taylor. The comeback was a failure, with the Bunnies failing to make the finals in either season.

10. Allan Fitzgibbon (Illawarra, 1995)
Illawarra's inaugural coach in 1982-83, Allan Fitzgibbon spent four relatively successful years with the Sharks from 1988 to 1991. His coaching career appeared to be over until he returned for a second stint with the Steelers in '95 following revelations that their coach Graham Murray had signed with Super League and attempted to convince the playing group to join him.

LONG COACHING TENURES

1. Wayne Bennett—Brisbane (526 games, 1988-2008)
Brisbane's inaugural coach was poached from Canberra after just one season with the Raiders, and he built the Broncos into a Rugby League powerhouse. In his 21-season tenure with Brisbane, Wayne Bennett won seven premierships, never lost a Grand Final, and led the Broncos to 17 straight finals series. He won an extraordinary 335 games as the Broncos' boss—far and away the most of any one coach at a single club. Bennett left the Broncos to coach St George Illawarra in 2009.

2. Bob Fulton—Manly (305 games, 1983-88, 1993-99)

A Manly legend on the paddock, Bob Fulton returned to Brookvale in 1983 after finishing his playing career and starting his coaching life at Eastern Suburbs. He coached Manly for spells of six years and seven years, winning premierships in 1987 and 1996 and losing deciders in 1983, 1995 and 1997. Manly won 66.9 per cent of games under Fulton, who quit in 1999 after the Sea Eagles dropped the opening seven games of the year.

3. Craig Bellamy—Melbourne (290 games, 2003-)

Widely regarded as the finest coach of the NRL era, Craig Bellamy built an indomitable empire in a Rugby League outpost. An intense figure with sharp tactical nous, Bellamy guided the Storm to three premierships and five Grand Finals during his first decade in charge of Melbourne, along with four minor premiership titles. The Storm missed the finals only once under Bellamy—when they were thrown out of the NRL in 2010 for salary-cap breaches. The Storm's 14 wins that season are testament to the culture Bellamy built in Melbourne.

4. Charlie Lynch—South Sydney (181 games, 1928-34, 1937-40)

A rarity in the early years of the Australian game, Charlie Lynch coached Souths for 11 seasons from 1928 to 1940, a record that he held until the 1990s. Taking over a Souths team that had won three straight titles, Lynch led the club to four more premierships in the next five years. The beneficiary of a tremendous team, he was nonetheless respected as one of the early coaching innovators. He left after Souths finished second in 1934, but returned three seasons later. In Lynch's final four years, Souths played finals football twice but did not win a further title.

5. Steve Folkes—Canterbury (288 games, 1998-2008)

One of only two men to play and coach in more than 500 games for a club, Steve Folkes bled blue and white from his playing debut in 1978 until his coaching departure at the end of the 2008 season. A son-in-law of club patriarch Peter Moore, he replaced brother-in-law and fellow Moore relation Chris Anderson in 1998 and remained at the helm for 11 seasons, guiding Canterbury to an unforgettable Grand Final berth in 1998. Folkes led the Bulldogs to a title in 2004, but presided over the salary-cap fiasco and the Coffs Harbour allegations before being axed after the wooden-spoon season of 2008.

6. Tim Sheens—Wests Tigers (249 games, 2003-12)

Second on the list of most games coached, Tim Sheens' most successful tenure was at Canberra, but his longest was at Wests Tigers. He took the reins from Terry Lamb in 2003 and guided the Tigers to an unlikely premiership in 2005. Amazingly, it was the only year he led the Tigers to the finals in his first seven years at the helm. They made back-to-back finals in 2010-11, but a disappointing 2012 season and a fallout with star Benji Marshall saw Sheens leave the club in ugly circumstances.

7. Brian Smith—Parramatta (243 games, 1997-2006)
A lightning rod for controversy, Brian Smith coached five premiership clubs—three to Grand Finals—with his most successful stint being at Parramatta. Taking over a club in shambles in 1997, he turned the Eels around, leading them to their most successful period since their glory days of the early 1980s. The Eels made their first Grand Final in 15 years in 2001 and played finals football in seven of nine full seasons under Smith before he quit midway through 2006. He is the only coach to lead a club for more than 200 games without a premiership.

8. Clive Churchill—South Sydney (224 games, 1958, 1967-75)
Regarded by many as the greatest player to ever lace on a boot, Clive Churchill finished his playing career as captain-coach of Souths in 1958 but returned to mentor the club in 1967. Churchill, who as a player had been central to the club's last great run in the early 1950s, coached the Rabbitohs through their most recent period of glory. They made Grand Finals in his first five years at the helm, winning four premierships—the first of which ended St George's run of 11 straight titles—before he resigned midway through a disappointing 1975 season. Sadly, Churchill passed away a decade later aged just 58.

9. Des Hasler—Manly (206 games, 2004-11)
In a surprise choice to replace Peter Sharp as Manly coach, the Sea Eagles turned a masterstroke by signing iconic Manly utility Des Hasler. He immediately turned around the struggling Manly side, which was still rocking from the Northern Eagles debacle. In his second year Manly returned to the finals, and in 2007 it made the first of three Grand Finals under Hasler. Premierships followed in 2008 and 2011, with the coach shockingly departing to Canterbury after the latter triumph. Manly made the finals in seven straight years under Hasler.

10. Norm Robinson—Balmain (143 games, 1930, 1944-47, 1954-56)
A Balmain legend who has a stand named in his honour at Leichhardt Oval, Norm 'Latchem' Robinson led the Tigers to five Grand Finals and three premierships in eight years. After a disappointing year as captain-coach in 1930, he returned in 1944 to take Balmain to its controversial 1944 title. The club made the Grand Final in all four seasons of Robinson's second tenure. His final three-year spell at the Tigers saw a Grand Final appearance in '56. Robinson spent six decades at the Tigers as a player, coach and administrator.

SHORT COACHING TENURES

1. Bob McCarthy—South Sydney (5 games, 1994)
One of the all-time great backrowers and a South Sydney legend, Bob McCarthy had a brief stint as caretaker captain-coach of the Rabbitohs in 1975 before a successful term as coach of Brisbane Souths—including the capture of the 1981 BRL premiership. Three seasons as the Gold Coast's foundation coach brought little success, and McCarthy returned to struggling Souths in 1994 to steer the club to a stunning pre-season Challenge Cup triumph. But his role had already been altered by that stage to accommodate Ken Shine, who was effectively installed as a co-coach, with new football manager Alan Jones pulling the strings behind the scenes. McCarthy stood down after just five weeks of the premiership, citing health reasons (a hip problem). Despite the diplomatic line, media reports claimed the ever-controversial Jones had virtually forced McCarthy's hand, allowing Shine to take sole charge of the first grade side.

2. Harold Johnston—Manly (5 games, 1947)
Harold Johnston, a South Sydney player during the 1930s, was installed as Manly's inaugural coach for its 1947 premiership entry. But after the Sea Eagles opened that debut season with five straight losses—including a humiliating 61-11 defeat at the hands of St George—Johnston was sacked at a special club meeting. Legendary former Test prop Ray Stehr was handed the reins for the rest of the year.

3. Henry Bolewski—Western Suburbs (7 games, 1944)
Bundaberg winger Henry Bolewski enjoyed a first grade career with Glebe spanning 10 seasons, and played a solitary Test for Australia during a return to his native Queensland in 1914. He was installed as coach of Wests, who had collected the previous two wooden spoons, in 1944, but his stint lasted just half a season and he stepped aside after the Magpies' 1-6 start to the year. Halfback Paddy Bugden took over for the remainder of the season.

4. Greg Hawick—North Sydney (15 games, 1985)
An outstanding, versatile player in South Sydney's dominant outfit of the 1950s who played nine Tests for Australia, Greg Hawick finished his premiership career as captain-coach of North Sydney in 1960. He was appointed to take over as coach of the Bears again in 1985 by club secretary Ken McCaffery, a former Australian and Norths teammate. Hawick was a hard-nosed disciplinarian from the old school, and his term

in charge of the Bears was a disaster. He was virtually forced to resign after 15 games following a player revolt against his outdated methods.

5. Laurie Freier—Western Suburbs Magpies (16 games, 1988)
Laurie Freier was an intense and prickly coaching figure who was named Coach of the Year in 1983—his initial first grade season at Easts—before he was sacked after the Roosters' disastrous '84 campaign that netted just five wins and was marked by internal ructions. He resurfaced in 1988 as coach of battlers Wests, where he had won a reserve grade title seven years earlier, but that relationship lasted just 16 games. The club's committee dumped Freier after he guided the Magpies to just two wins, replacing him with lower grade mentor John Bailey.

6. Chris Anderson—Sydney Roosters (16 games, 2007)
A premiership-winning mentor at Canterbury and Melbourne, Chris Anderson made a surprise coaching comeback in 2007 with the Sydney Roosters—his first significant role since leaving Cronulla and stepping down from the Australian Test post in 2003. But 'Opes' endured a torrid year at Bondi, winning just five games in the first four months of the competition. A savage 56-0 beating at the hands of Manly in Round 16 brought matters to a head and Anderson quit two days later citing health reasons—although *Sydney Morning Herald* journalist and former prominent coach Roy Masters claimed he had "jumped before he was pushed". Anderson's departure allowed the inexperienced Brad Fittler to lead the Roosters on a spirited late season charge.

7. Mike Stephenson—Penrith (16 games, 1976)
An ultra-professional and valuable clubman, former Great Britain hooker Mike Stephenson accepted the captain-coach position with Penrith in 1976, his third season at the club. But with dismal results (including a nine-match losing streak), constant interference from the club's committee and the behaviour of tempestuous but brilliant backrow countryman Bill Ashurst weighing heavily upon him, Stephenson handed over the captaincy to Zac Olejarnik and gave the coaching reins to Barry Harris with six rounds of the season remaining. The highly respected Stephenson remained with the Panthers as a player until 1978.

8. Murray Hurst—North Queensland (18 games, 2001-02)
Murray Hurst took the reins at North Queensland when Tim Sheens' tumultuous tenure came to an abrupt end 11 weeks into the 2001 season. Despite guiding the Cowboys to just four wins in the remaining 15 rounds as they finished 13th, the former Tongan national coach was retained for 2002. He was cut loose when that year's campaign began with three heavy defeats, and was replaced by Graham Murray, who steered the long-suffering club to unprecedented success in the ensuing seasons.

9. Steve Martin—South Sydney (18 games, 1998)
Former Australian Test half Steve Martin coached Norths to their best season in 26 years in 1991, but was shown the door just 12 months later after a disappointing '92 campaign. He coached Featherstone Rovers for a season before landing another Australian premiership gig with long-suffering South Sydney in 1998. Dismal results—along with clashes with management and the playing group over team selection policy and the disciplining of troubled star Julian O'Neill—saw Martin stood down by the Rabbitohs after only 18 rounds (and just three wins). Club great Craig Coleman stepped into the role.

10. Brian McClennan—New Zealand Warriors (22 games, 2012)
Brian 'Bluey' McClennan arrived at the Warriors in 2012 with an impressive résumé and a big reputation, replacing Penrith-bound coach Ivan Cleary. He guided the Kiwis to a stunning Tri-Nations triumph in 2005 and Leeds to back-to-back Super League premierships in 2008-09, but he did not see out his first year in charge of the Warriors. After hovering mid-table for most of the season, consecutive losses to Newcastle and Manly after holding 18-point leads in both matches—an unprecedented "feat" in premiership history—sparked a long losing streak for the previous year's Grand Finalists, and McClennan stepped down two weeks before the end of the season.

ILL-FATED VENTURES INTO COACHING

1. Alan Jones—Balmain (1991-93)
Revered for his achievements as coach of the Australian Rugby Union side—including an unprecedented Grand Slam in Britain in 1984, and a Bledisloe Cup success in '86—well-known radio broadcaster Alan Jones was a perplexing choice as Warren Ryan's successor at Balmain in 1991. Grand Finalists in 1988-89 and fifth in '90 under Ryan, the Tigers struggled throughout Jones' tumultuous three-season tenure. He was accused of playing favourites, most notably dropping Kiwi Test halfback Gary Freeman to reserve grade in favour of former Wallaby Brian Smith, and having little knowledge of or interest in Rugby League's defensive structures, preferring to focus on attack. The Tigers went winless in their first eight games under Jones—who coached the club for no fee—and eventually finished 12th. A more respectable 10 wins and 10th-place result in '92 was followed by a disastrous '93 campaign that netted just five victories and saw Balmain finish second-last. The outspoken, ever-controversial Jones unsuccessfully reapplied for the head coach position (which went to club great Wayne Pearce) and was instead appointed football operations manager at South Sydney.

2. Russell Fairfax—Eastern Suburbs (1989-90)

Brilliant Rugby Union convert Russell Fairfax won a premiership with Easts in 1974 and represented NSW before finishing his career with a season at South Sydney in 1981. He went on to coach in the Rabbitohs' lower grades before returning to the Roosters and succeeding former teammate Arthur Beetson as first grade coach in 1989. A poor initial season in charge was somewhat masked by three wins and a draw in the closing four rounds, which lifted Easts to a flattering 11th-place finish. But the cracks at the club became irreparable for Fairfax in 1990, when a club-record 66-4 loss to Canberra started a nine-match winless run that culminated in Fairfax's sacking after Round 14. His coaching career in tatters, Fairfax later found his post-playing niche in the Rugby League media.

3. Bert Holcroft—Eastern Suburbs (1965-66)

British coach Bert Holcroft, a product of Leigh, emigrated to Australia in the 1960s and coached the Past Brothers clubs in Bundaberg and Townsville. His approach to training procedures and diet was years ahead of his time, and his impressive reputation saw him offered the head coach job at Sydney's Eastern Suburbs in 1965—but his premiership tenure was a catastrophe. The Tricolours finished last with just three wins in Holcroft's first season in charge, and then lost all 18 of their matches in an infamous '66 campaign in which they became the last club to go an entire year without a win. (Remarkably, Easts qualified for the finals the following season under Holcroft's replacement, a rising coaching prospect by the name of Jack Gibson.)

4. John Peard—Parramatta (1980), Penrith (1982-83) and NSW (1988)

Eight-Test veteran John 'Bomber' Peard was a shrewd five-eighth in Jack Gibson's premiership-winning Easts juggernaut of 1974-75 and Parramatta's losing Grand Final sides of 1976-77, but his on-field tactical nous did not translate to the role of head coach. The international-laden Eels failed to make the finals for the first time in six years after Peard succeeded Terry Fearnley as coach in 1980, and Gibson took over in '81 to lead the Eels to three straight titles. Peard was long-suffering Penrith's head coach in 1982-83, but recorded just 16 wins in 52 games and the Panthers finished in the bottom-three in each season. His foray into representative coaching was similarly fruitless; he steered NSW to its first 3-0 Origin series loss in 1988. Peard was again succeeded by Gibson, but finally enjoyed some success as an assistant coach to his former mentor during the Blues' drought-breaking 1990 series win.

5. Mark Graham—Auckland Warriors (1999-2000)

All-time great New Zealand and North Sydney second-rower Mark Graham held lower grade and assistant coach positions with the Bears and Cowboys during the 1990s before his close association with Graham Lowe—who was part of a business consortium that purchased the Warriors—helped him secure his first head coach post in first grade in 1999. Several other off-field factors contributed to the club's descent to the brink of collapse by the end of 2000, but Graham's woeful record of just 18 wins in 50 games meant he was no chance of being retained under the new regime. (Daniel Anderson steered the revamped Warriors to their maiden finals series in 2001.)

6. John O'Neill—South Sydney (1977)

Renowned front-row enforcer John 'Lurch' O'Neill played in nine Grand Finals for Souths and Manly, and represented Australia in 10 Tests. But his foray into first grade coaching was less auspicious. Put in charge of the financially stricken Rabbitohs in 1977, O'Neill could only inspire his charges to three wins in 22 games and a second-last finish—although in his defence, the squad he was given to work with had little going for it besides veteran ex-internationals George Piggins and Paul Sait, and blockbusting World Cup winger Terry Fahey. O'Neill did not coach at the top level again.

7. Dennis Tutty—Balmain (1980)

A one-Test second-rower in 1967, Dennis Tutty was best known as the player who, at great personal cost, overturned the League's transfer ban in a landmark court case so that he could leave Balmain for Penrith. Ironically, he later finished his career with a season for the Tigers in 1976 and was installed as Ron Willey's replacement as the club's first grade coach for 1980 after a couple of seasons coaching in the lower grades. But it was an unhappy year for the club, with Tutty's Tigers winning just seven games to finish 10th of 12 teams. Frank Stanton took over as coach in 1981.

8. Wally Lewis—Gold Coast (1992-93)

The dominant player of the 1980s, Gold Coast's Wally Lewis became the last man to captain-coach a premiership club in 1992. After that season's last-place finish, the retired Lewis remained as non-playing coach of the Seagulls in '93, but was at loggerheads with the club's administration throughout another miserable year that garnered just one win and a third straight wooden spoon, and he relinquished the role at the end of the season. Meanwhile, he coached Queensland in the 1993-94 Origin series, but has since admitted he wasn't ready for the role and was talked into it by legendary team manager Dick 'Tossa' Turner. Lewis enjoyed some high points in consecutive 2-1 series defeats, but freely acknowledged he was out of his depth opposite NSW coaching mastermind Phil Gould.

9. Max Krilich—Manly Sea Eagles lower grades (1988-91)
Former Test skipper Max Krilich became a Manly legend after he captained the club to the 1978 premiership and played a then premiership record 334 games in all grades in the maroon and white. He progressed through the coaching ranks in the Sea Eagles' lower grades, guiding the President's Cup and reserve grade sides to finals appearances in 1988 and '89 respectively, and remained in charge of the reserve grade outfit after Graham Lowe took the first grade reins in 1990. However, Krilich's coaching aspirations received a mortal wound when his team infamously failed to win a match during '91. (His replacement, Marty Gurr, fared only slightly better the following season, guiding the Sea Eagles reserves to just three wins and another wooden spoon.)

10. Paul Langmack—South Sydney (2003-04)
A wonderful ball-playing lock for Canterbury and Wests, 1986 Kangaroo Paul Langmack was an outspoken, antagonistic and combative player, but found these to be less effective qualities in the first grade coaching ranks. After fulfilling assistant coach roles at Wests Tigers and Souths, he signed a three-year contract as the Rabbitohs' head coach when Craig Coleman was dumped during the 2003 pre-season. Langmack was always passionate and animated on the sidelines, but brought the club just five wins in 35 matches as the Rabbitohs collected wooden spoons in '03 and '04. He was sacked halfway through the latter season.

COACHING BLOW-UPS

1. Bozo's cement-truck wish
Rugby League's most infamous coaching blow-up came in 1987, when Manly mentor Bob Fulton said he hoped referee Bill Harrigan "would get run over by a cement truck". Fulton delivered the verbal lashing at fulltime of Cronulla's 18-13 defeat of Manly after the Sea Eagles were hammered 13-4 in the penalty count and Des Hasler was sent to the sin bin. Fulton, who later repeated the cement truck comments to the media, was fined $1000 by the League. The feud was reignited in 2010 when commentator Fulton demanded Harrigan's sacking as a video referee after a shocking decision went against the Sea Eagles in a close game with St George Illawarra.

2. Ricky's hotel rant
Australia's shock 2008 World Cup final loss to New Zealand had Ricky Stuart fired up well after the defeat. The following morning, a bitter Stuart launched into a tirade

against referee Ashley Klein when the two crossed paths in the hotel lobby. Stuart was alleged to have "physically and aggressively intimidated" Klein, and to have called the official a "fucking cheat". It is also alleged that fellow official Stuart Cummings was "manhandled" by Stuart when he attempted to intervene. Stuart stood down as Australia's coach within a fortnight of the incident.

3. Gus gets sent off
It is rare for a player to be sent off in the modern game and even more so for a coach to be dismissed. In fact it has happened just once. In a fiery 1994 game between Phil Gould's Penrith and Cronulla, referee Bill Harrigan sent Gould from the sideline for allegedly making "comments" to the touch judge. The bemused, tracksuit-sporting coach sat there in disbelief before retreating down the tunnel. The Sharks won the clash 32-0 and Gould quit the Panthers a week later. He maintains he did nothing wrong.

4. Ian Walsh explodes
In the 22 April 1972 edition of *Rugby League Week*, Parramatta coach Ian Walsh unloaded on his underperforming team in an article entitled "My Team Are Gutless", in which he labelled the Eels a "gutless bunch" and said he was "ashamed to be associated with them". He also said players "bludged money from the club" and that the majority of the team deserved to be fined after an embarrassing loss. Walsh quit the Eels at the end of the season.

5. Des of destruction
Manly coach Des Hasler lived up to his reputation for being an intense and temperamental coach when he ripped a door off its hinges early in the 2010 season. Fuming after his side's 24-20 loss to the Eels, in which the Sea Eagles relinquished a 20-0 lead, Hasler tore the door off Manly's Parramatta Stadium dressing room and it almost hit skipper Jamie Lyon. Channel Nine cameras captured the footage and Manly was billed for the damage, resulting in Hasler threatening to put blankets over all dressing-room cameras.

6. Nathan Brown slaps Trent Barrett
St George Illawarra's Nathan Brown hit the headlines early in the 2003 season when the first-year coach slapped captain Trent Barrett and aggressively grabbed backrower Lance Thompson during a 38-12 loss to Manly. Brown called the pair over to the sideline and then tried to get something out of Barrett by slapping him across the face. Brown was fined $5000 for the incident, which he later said was the biggest regret of his career.

7. Mal lashes out at rats and filth
Six straight Origin series victories for Mal Meninga's Maroons wasn't enough to stop the Queensland boss from launching an unprovoked broadside at NSW powerbrokers

in which he claimed the League was attempting to "destroy a dynasty" with supposed judiciary inconsistencies and personal attacks. In his newspaper column, Meninga hit out at the "rats and filth that tried to poison a monumental team with lies, personal attacks, arrogance and disrespect". He later asserted his vitriol was necessary, and refused to apologise.

8. Gibson gives it to Hollywood
Parramatta coach Jack Gibson and flamboyant referee Greg 'Hollywood' Hartley could hardly tolerate each other and Gibson let the League know with numerous protests over the latter's handling of Eels games. Gibson had had little time for Hartley at previous appointments Easts and Souths, with the feud eventually coming to a head in the final of the 1981 pre-season cup and then exploding after Hartley's handling of the Parramatta-Canterbury game. Gibson labelled it "an outstandingly bad refereeing performance", before stating that "the club hasn't got the players or the ability to contend with [Hartley]." Later in the season Gibson called Hartley "incompetent" and said playing under Hartley was like "carrying a lead bag".

9. Taylor knocked out
A man with a habit of rubbing people the wrong way, Jason Taylor was left seeming petulant and immature after an incident in 2007 with then Parramatta coach Michael Hagan that would lead to his sacking from South Sydney in 2009. According to which version you believe, Souths coach Taylor either punched or kung-fu hit backrower David Fa'alogo at the Rabbitohs' Mad Monday celebrations. Huddersfield-bound Fa'alogo reacted by punching Taylor, who was sacked soon after.

10. Toovey blows his top
After his club's 10-22 loss to South Sydney in 2013, Manly coach Geoff Toovey delivered an epic blow-up by demanding the NRL investigate the officiating in the match, asking "were these the best referees we've got?". The livid Sea Eagles coach called the match "suspicious" and declared he would coach his team to break the rules since officials weren't enforcing the laws of the game. He was fined $10,000 by the NRL.

Chapter 16

REFEREES

GREATEST REFEREES

1. Bill Harrigan

Rugby League's most-capped referee, Bill Harrigan was the game's top—and most controversial—official. After making his debut in 1986, he went on to referee 392 premiership matches, including 45 finals, and 21 Origins and 25 Tests, all records. A policeman during the early stages of his career, he was given the nickname 'Hollywood' in the latter years of his decorated refereeing tenure due to his flamboyance, stubbornness and free-flowing style. Harrigan's first finals series appointment came in 1989 and culminated in a controversial performance in the Grand Final. It was his first of 10 Grand Finals, with him calling the shots from 1989-91, in the 1997 Super League decider, and from 1998 until his retirement after the 2003 Grand Final. He controlled his first Origin in 1991, and then from the reunification of the game in '98 until his retirement he was overlooked for just two Origins. In 2000, Harrigan famously sent off Gorden Tallis for dissent in one of Origin's most heated incidents. He remained prominent in the media following his retirement and had a controversial stint as referees boss.

2. Tom McMahon snr

Rugby League's leading referee in the infant days of the game, Tom McMahon senior, had an often tempestuous relationship with the League. Rising to first grade in the game's first season, he refereed 210 premiership games before retiring in 1926. He officiated deciders in 1911, '22 and '23 (three of only six required in the first 15 years of the premiership), and controlled home Ashes series in 1910, '14, '20 and '24 (refereeing eight of the first 12 Ashes Tests on Australian soil). Between 1917 and 1925 he refereed every City Cup final bar one, and ranks third for most interstate appearances. McMahon was highly regarded for his coolness and strict enforcement of the obstruction rule, but often fell out with the League for his stubborn ways—he sat out much of the 1910 season as protest over small suspensions before being suspended himself for not following League orders in 1916.

3. Darcy Lawler

Although these days he is remembered more for the controversial and suspicious handling of his final game—the 1963 Grand Final—than his decorated career, Darcy Lawler was nonetheless the game's leading official when the Dragons were at their zenith and the code was riding a tidal wave of success. He made his debut in 1944, and was called into his first decider in 1953. It was during the 1950s that he rose to prominence as Australia's No.1 whistleblower, officiating in Ashes series in 1954, '58 and '62, the World Cup in '57, and international tours in '55, '56, '59 and '60—and infuriating numerous touring sides with his unique style of refereeing in the process. His 32 finals remain second on the all-time list, while his eight Grand Finals sits behind only Bill Harrigan. Lawler was the man in the middle for the first six of the Dragons' famous titles in their 11-season stretch, as well as the '63 decider, in which he was alleged to have wagered against Western Suburbs, a charge his family denies.

4. Tom McMahon jnr

Unrelated to McMahon senior, Tom McMahon junior was an outstanding referee in his own right who had the rare distinction of refereeing five Grand Finals and coaching another. He made his premiership debut in 1933 and was appointed to interstate duties that same year, and then went on to make 246 premiership appearances across two decades. By 1935 he had become the leading referee, officiating the premiership final between Eastern Suburbs and South Sydney; he would also referee the 1938, '41, '45 and '50 deciders. He made 17 interstate appearances, though World War II meant he didn't officiate his first Test until 1948. After hanging up his whistle at the end of 1951, he was a surprise choice to coach Western Suburbs, but the move proved to be a masterstroke when Wests won the premiership. He retired from coaching after the 1952 Grand Final.

5. Col Pearce

Behind only Bill Harrigan for premiership games refereed, Col Pearce was a no-nonsense official who was respected across the game. Known for his calm and polite demeanour (and his raised collar), he debuted in first grade in 1947, where he lasted an incredible 22 years. By 1955 he had reached the stature of finals official and called that season's Grand Final, and although he would not officiate in a decider again until Darcy Lawler's retirement in 1964, he would be the man in the middle for five straight between '64 and '68. Pearce was also recognised on the international scene, calling nine Tests, including the 1967 World Cup. He retired after the '68 decider to embark on a prominent media career.

6. Tony Archer

The leading referee across the first decade of the 2000s, the calm and respected Tony Archer ranks as all-time fourth in finals officiated and is one of just three referees to stand in the middle for six straight deciders. A police prosecutor by trade, he debuted in 1999, but really came to prominence in 2005, when he refereed his first final. By 2007 he had risen to the station of leading referee and would control every Grand Final from then until his retirement in 2012—the first two solo and the last four as part of a two-referee platoon. Such was his standing as the undisputed top official that after refereeing his first Origin match in 2008, he controlled 13 of the 15 interstate affairs from then until 2012. He was appointed referees boss for the 2014 season.

7. Jack O'Brien

The 11th most-capped official in premiership history, Jack O'Brien refereed seven Grand Finals, a premiership record before it was surpassed by Darcy Lawler nine years later. O'Brien made his debut in 1940 and, amazingly, was chosen to call the decider that same year, in just his ninth top-grade appearance. After controlling deciders in 1942, '43, '44, '47 and '51, he refereed the first mandatory Grand Final in 1954. Although he never officiated in a Test, he did call interstate matches and French touring teams. O'Brien's seven Grand Finals remains third on the all-time list.

8. Greg Hartley

Maybe the most controversial (and polarising) referee in the history of the premiership, the flamboyant Greg Hartley, known universally as 'Hollywood'—a handle also slapped on top-ranking ref Bill Harrigan a couple of decades later—was christened the leading official in the late 1970s. A former Newtown top-grader whose career ended after three games due to a severe injury, he rose to first grade with the whistle in 1972. He refereed his first final in 1975, and in '78 refereed the Grand Final and replay, despite having been dropped to reserve grade midway through the season and allowing eventual premiers Manly to score a seventh-tackle try in a crucial final. With exaggerated gestures and little tolerance for the notion of a referee being at his best when invisible, Hartley refereed the 1979, '80 and '81 Grand Finals, as well as an Ashes Test in 1979, before retiring to undertake a long radio career in 1982. Never far from the headlines, Hartley was a unique official who divided opinion, putting many offside while simultaneously commanding a great deal of respect.

9. Greg McCallum
A bearded enforcer renowned as a strict disciplinarian during the late 1980s and early 1990s, Greg McCallum stood in stark contrast to more eccentric and controversial referees such as Bill Harrigan and Greg Hartley. He made his premiership debut in 1983 and refereed his first final a year later (a major semi between powerhouses Canterbury and Parramatta), followed by the first of five Origin matches and his first of 13 Tests in 1988. He superseded Harrigan as the top referee in 1992, officiating the next three straight Grand Finals until his retirement after the '94 decider.

10. Lal Deane
A fine official in the days leading up to World War II, Lal Deane refereed an astonishing six deciders in his 11-year premiership career. His ascent was fast—he refereed the 1928 premiership final in just his 22nd first grade appearance after also being called upon to referee two Ashes Tests at the SCG. He refereed every decider between 1928 and '32, as well as the 1936 final, and three straight Ashes series. A former first grade player with Norths, Deane retired in the lead-up to the 1938 season due to injury.

WORST REFEREEING PERFORMANCES

1. Darcy Lawler—1963 Grand Final
Unquestionably the most contentious and controversial refereeing performance in the history of premiership Rugby League, Darcy Lawler's showing in the '63 St George-Wests Grand Final still causes debate today. There were rumours circulating in the lead-up to the game that Lawler had wagered a substantial sum on the Saints, and suspicions were hardly quelled when the Dragons won the penalty count and were the beneficiaries of some contentious calls—the most famous being Johnny King's try after an alleged tackle by Don Parish. Wests players believe Lawler robbed them of the Grand Final to this day.

2. Greg Hartley—1978, Manly v Parramatta

Eccentric whistleblower Greg Hartley went down in infamy during the 1978 semi-final replay between Manly and Parramatta for messing up the tackle count seven times, favouring the Sea Eagles on six occasions. Hartley had been accused of being in Manly's pocket the entire finals series and dived further into the bad books of Parramatta fans when star lock Ray Price was sent off. Price was cleared at the judiciary, but not before the Sea Eagles had won 17-11. Whether or not you believe the rumours, Hartley had Manly eight times in '78 and the Sea Eagles did not lose once.

3. Eddie Ward—1995 Grand Final

Manly might have entered the 1995 Grand Final as the heavy favourite over Canterbury, but a number of contentious officiating calls from Grand Final debutant Eddie Ward would hand the Bulldogs their seventh premiership on a silver platter. The first such call came midway through the opening stanza, when Bulldogs backrower Steve Price scored after a blatant forward pass by Jim Dymock; Canterbury then extended its lead in the second half with a seventh-tackle try to Glen Hughes. Ward capped off his first—and only—Grand Final appearance by disallowing a legitimate Bulldogs try.

4. George Bishop—1952 Grand Final

George Bishop became the central figure of the 1952 Grand Final when, like Darcy Lawler 11 seasons later, he was accused of betting on Western Suburbs to upset South Sydney in the decider. Bishop's most controversial call came early, when he disallowed a try to Souths backrower Ken Macreadie, ruling centre Frank Threlfo had thrown the pass forward; photographic evidence clearly shows the ball travelling backwards. Wests then benefitted from a try to Dev Dines—ironically, off a forward pass. Souths were so incensed at the officiating that skipper Jack Rayner never spoke to Bishop again, despite the two living in the same suburb until their dying days.

5. Ben Cummins—2007 Sydney Roosters v South Sydney

Ben Cummins made one of the most infamous calls of the NRL era when he sent Braith Anasta to the sin bin after he was punched in the face. Souths backrower David Fa'alogo unleashed a vicious right to Anasta's nose after the latter made a seeming legitimate tackle, but it didn't stop Cummins from dismissing the Roosters five-eighth.

6. R Robinson—1929, Australia v Great Britain

The disallowed try to Australian speedster Joe 'Chimpy' Busch in the third Test of the 1929-30 Ashes Series is the most contentious no-try ruling in the history of Anglo-Australian Tests. The score was locked at 0-0 and there were only minutes remaining when, with series was tied at 1-1, halfback Busch took off down the blindside and crashed over in the corner with England lock Frank Butters on his back. Referee Robinson was about to award the try but a touch judge claimed the corner post was dislodged and Robinson reportedly said, "Fair Try Australia, but I am overruled." A fourth Test was played and Australia lost. It would not see the Ashes for another 23 years.

7. David Manson—1996 Grand Final

Queenslander David Manson, the top ARL referee during the Super League War, earned the ire of St George fans—and neutrals everywhere—when an unfathomable decision made during the 1996 Grand Final swung the momentum in the Sea Eagles' favour. A penalty goal by Dragons lock Wayne Bartrim had pegged back the scoreline to 8-2 in favour of Manly when Sea Eagles fullback Matthew Ridge took a short kick-off, regathered and was collared by Saints hooker Nathan Brown. All the Dragons defenders stopped, but Manson inexplicably allowed Ridge to play on and he was pinned close to the line before Steve Menzies scored on the next play. The Sea Eagles went into halftime 14-2 and weren't headed, eventually winning the decider 20-8.

8. Bill Harrigan—2002, Parramatta v Newcastle

Champion referee Bill Harrigan lost the plot during a Friday night affair between Newcastle and Parramatta in 2002, sin-binning three Eels four times in a dramatic 24-18 Knights victory. It was a controversial refereeing performance, with Michael Buettner binned twice and Nathan Hindmarsh and Adam Dykes both marched—but in the aftermath Harrigan, backed by the League, stood by his dramatic officiating.

9. Shayne Hayne—2013 Grand Final

One of the most entertaining Grand Finals of the NRL era was sullied by an ordinary day with the whistle by leading referee Shayne Hayne, who made some incredible blunders, including a key penalty to the Roosters for a late shot on Mitchell Pearce, only matched by a failure to give Manly the same for a worse offence. The Roosters were deserving premiers, but the Sea Eagles got a very rough deal from Hayne.

10. Bill Harrigan—1989 Grand Final

The most dramatic decider in premiership history could have—and perhaps did—swing on many plays: Warren Ryan's substitutions, Benny Elias' field goal, Mal Meninga's ankle-tap on Michael Neil, Wayne Pearce's dropped ball with a try beckoning, and, of course, Bruce McGuire's penalty. The Tigers were well on top when McGuire tapped the ball forward with no marker and ran into an offside Raider; McGuire was penalised for milking—possibly the only time such a penalty was ever awarded—and the Raiders got the ball and field position. The rest, they say, is history.

BIGGEST REFEREEING BLUNDERS

1. Annesley awards bounced-ball match-winner to Broncos
Early in 1990 Brisbane got home 14-12 over Manly on the back of a terrible error by referee Graham Annesley. With 10 minutes remaining at Lang Park, Broncos hooker Kerrod Walters sprinted for the try-line but blatantly bounced the ball in an attempt to slam it down as he was tackled, and the Steeden rocketed two metres into the air. His teammates obviously knew Walters had fumbled (Peter Jackson covered his face with his hands and animatedly threw his head back), but Annesley pointed to the spot for the decisive try and the No.9 could only grin guiltily at his stroke of dumb luck. To his credit, Annesley unreservedly admitted his error post-match, but was nevertheless demoted to reserve grade for the following week.

2. Monsieur Chanfreau baffles Kiwis with penalty try
The poor standard and bias of French referees on Kangaroo Tours is legendary, but audiences Down Under received a first-hand experience in the second Test between New Zealand and France at Palmerston North in 1995. Early in the second half, Kiwi fullback Matthew Ridge tackled Freddie Banquet fractionally late after the French centre had kicked ahead. Despite the fact the ball quickly went into touch and there was ample Kiwi cover to stop any remote possibility of a try, referee Marcel Chanfreau baffled everyone by running to the goalposts and awarding a penalty try. The appalling decision helped France pull off a shock 16-all draw.

3. Sharks awarded seventh-tackle try
Few refereeing blunders have attracted as much backlash as the seventh-tackle try scored by the Sharks in their 2013 qualifying final victory over the Cowboys. North Queensland opened the scoring in just the third minute, but referees Matt Cecchin and Henry Perenara botched a Cronulla tackle count four minutes later and Beau Ryan crossed on the erroneous seventh tackle. The Sharks prevailed 20-18 in a cliff-hanger to end the Cowboys' season—the second campaign in a row in which poor decisions by officials had contributed to their finals exit.

4. Lockyer farcically denied series-winning try
With a 14-12 lead in the pulsating 2002 Origin decider, defending champs Queensland could have taken an ironclad grip on the Origin shield with 11 minutes remaining if not for a mystifying video-referee decision. When Timana Tahu couldn't grasp an Allan Langer kick in the NSW in-goal and instead tipped it into the air,

Darren Lockyer chased through and outleaped opposing fullback Brett Hodgson to claim the ball, before showing remarkable athleticism and composure to reach down and force it inside the dead-ball line. Video referee Chris Ward saw something nobody else did, however, and made the baffling ruling that Lockyer had lost the ball. With five minutes to go NSW snatched the lead with a converted try, but Dane Carlaw's famous last-minute touchdown saw the Maroons retain the crown with an 18-all draw.

5. 'Hand of Foran' try given the green light

A video-referee clanger brought North Queensland's 2012 campaign undone in a tense semi-final loss to Manly. With the Sea Eagles leading 16-12, Daly Cherry-Evans launched a bomb in the 62nd minute; Cowboys skipper Johnathan Thurston and opposing five-eighth Kieran Foran contested the bouncing ball and Manly winger Michael Oldfield dotted down in the aftermath. Despite replays appearing to show Foran's hand knocking the ball forward, a benefit-of-the-doubt try ruling came up on the big screen and the Sea Eagles were propelled to victory. The Cowboys were also seething over a contentious benefit-of-the-doubt try awarded to Sea Eagles winger Jorge Taufua earlier in the match.

6. Video ref gives Whare outrageous try

In the 15th minute of a Round 19 clash with Newcastle in 2013, Penrith centre Dean Whare planted the ball spectacularly in the corner—the only problem was his non-ball-carrying hand had clearly brushed the turf over the sideline. The video referee somehow missed the Kiwi's mit knuckle-deep in the grass outside the field of play, however, and brought up the green light. Fortunately, despite being one of the most ludicrous referred tries ever awarded, it had no bearing on the result, and the Knights prevailed 32-14.

7. Man in the box misses Hodgson knock-on

In the second half of the 2006 Origin decider, video-referee Graeme West made a decision that beggared belief. Blues halfback Craig Gower hoisted a bomb and his fullback Brett Hodgson appeared to almost certainly knock-on in reaching it first; the ball slipped through his grasp and Steve Menzies collected the bouncing pill to send Eric Grothe over. But West bewilderingly ruled no transgression against Hodgson and awarded the 49th-minute try, giving the Blues a handy 14-4 lead. Queensland rallied, however, to pull off a dynasty-starting 16-14 win.

8. Bulldogs' ride to Grand Final upset on forward pass and seventh-tackle try

In 1995 the Bulldogs completed a fairytale finals charge with an emphatic 17-4 Grand Final boilover defeat of Manly—but two of their three tries should not have been awarded. First there was the clear forward pass from Jim Dymock that allowed Steve

Price to crash over for the opening try of the decider, and then, in the 61st minute, with the match delicately poised at 6-4, the Bulldogs went 90 metres in a set from a scrum win, culminating in a try to Glen Hughes on the seventh tackle after referee Eddie Ward had miscounted.

9. Dragons allowed to kick levelling field goal after fulltime
A 2002 encounter between St George Illawarra and Canberra ended with one of the most contentious finishes in premiership history. The Dragons had fought back from a 21-8 halftime deficit to trail by just one point when their hooker, Mark Riddell, was sent off for a high tackle in the 77th minute. The 12-man Saints continued to press for the win, however, and in the dying seconds Brent Kite was held up over the line—but despite the clock showing zero seconds, referee Steven Clark called time-off and awarded the Dragons a rare differential penalty from the scrum, ruling Raiders halfback Brett Finch was offside in charging down opposing No.7 Willie Peters' field-goal attempt. Unable to kick for goal from a differential penalty, the Dragons took a tap and Peters landed a one-pointer to draw the game 21-all. The Raiders were livid and sought to have the result overturned; unsurprisingly, the demand was laughed off by NRL boss David Gallop.

10. Queensland Cup touchie earns unwanted fame
During a 2013 clash between Easts Tigers and Souths Logan Magpies a Queensland Cup touch judge made a howler that was so comically bad it went viral. When a Tigers line dropout bounced awkwardly over the sideline, a Magpies player desperately tried to keep it in the field of play—but took three steps outside before batting it back in. Despite the Magpies player being almost two metres over the sideline, touch judge Marcus Schooth—who was right on the spot—kept his flag down. The Tigers weren't hindered by the error, going on to win 50-6, but the bungle provided substantial fodder for sports programmes and news websites for the ensuing week.

REFEREE HANDLING

1. Steve Roach pats Eddie Ward on the head
In the most famous incident of a player coming into contact with a referee, aggressive Balmain forward Steve Roach patted the bemused referee Eddie Ward on the head after the latter had sent the Tigers prop from the field. Roach, who proceeded to abuse the touch judge on his way off, copped a four-match ban and was fined $5000.

2. Wayne Chisholm flattens Geoff Weekes

In 1991, South Sydney aggressor Wayne Chisholm received a 10-match ban for tackling referee Geoff Weekes in the Round 4 loss to Newcastle. Souths' moustachioed workhorse was deemed to have deliberately tackled Weekes to "obtain an unfair advantage", and was rubbed out for a lengthy stint.

3. Tonie Carroll knocks out Tony De Las Heras

Brisbane defensive ace Tonie Carroll left young referee Tony De Las Heras out cold when the official collided with Carroll's knee. After slipping during a piece of broken play, De Las Heras was attempting to get to his feet at the same time Carroll was trying to hurdle over him. The Bronco's knee connected with the ref's head, and De Las Heras was carted from the paddock.

4. Jeremy Smith pushes Sean Hampstead

The 2006 clash between Parramatta and St George Illawarra was one of the most extraordinary matches of the NRL era, opening with three straight field goals and remaining 2-1 until the last play of the game. In the lead-up scrum to that final play, Parramatta halfback Jeremy Smith pushed referee Sean Hampstead and was suspended for four weeks—although Hampstead later admitted he had contributed to the act of frustration.

5. Matthew Ridge and Nigel Vagana manhandle Paul Simpkins

Auckland Warriors skipper Matthew Ridge had a rocky relationship with referees for much of his career, and this came to a head in his final year. Disputing a field-goal ruling in the 1999 clash with Balmain at Leichhardt Oval, Ridge and young centre Nigel Vagana grabbed referee Paul Simpkins to express their dismay. Both players were suspended for three games, and Ridge was stripped of the Warriors' captaincy soon after.

6. Ricky Stuart fronts up to Ashley Klein

Ricky Stuart's tempestuous relationship with referees came to a head the morning after the 2008 World Cup final, when the Australian coach berated referee Ashley Klein for his handling of the decider and pushed referees boss Stuart Cummings. Stuart was fined and forced to stand down over the incident.

7. Wade McKinnon shoves Jason Robinson

New Zealand Warriors fullback Wade McKinnon received a two-game ban in 2007 for his rough conduct during a clash with South Sydney. While attempting to cover his own line, McKinnon shoved referee Jason Robinson to the side, knocking him down.

8. Gareth Hock's ref history
English forward Gareth Hock has twice been suspended for striking an official. The first incident came in 2008 when he received a five-game ban for grabbing referee Ian Smith; the second in 2013 when, while playing for Widnes, he was slapped with a four-game ban for making deliberate contact with whistleblower George Stokes during a Challenge Cup win over Workington while playing for Widnes.

9. Josh Ailaomai sent for official shoulder charge
In 2011 Newcastle NYC prop Josh Ailaomai was sent off and suspended for eight weeks for deliberately shoulder-charging an official. Referee Jon Stone had no hesitation marching Ailaomai after the 115kg prop dropped the shoulder into him following a penalty.

10. Ian Donnelly downs whistleblower
St George Illawarra Jersey Flegg prop Ian Donnelly was sent off in 2001 after a collision with referee Phil Dorahy. Donnelly, who pushed the official away during a scuffle, was immediately dismissed, but escaped suspension when he argued that he was tangled up with Dorahy and didn't realise who he was pushing.

Chapter 17

THE RULES

BEST RULE CHANGES

1. Play-the-ball rule introduced
With the advent of Rugby League in Australia still more than a year away, the Northern Union introduced the play-the-ball to the code's rulebook in 1906. Previously, a scrum was packed every time a player was held with the ball. The play-the-ball soon became the most distinctive part of Rugby League gameplay and the main feature distinguishing it from Rugby Union.

2. Introduction of the six-tackle rule
Perhaps the most revolutionary rule change of post-war Rugby League was the introduction of a four-tackle rule in 1967, which brought to an end the era of unlimited tackles. This was done to encourage positive, attacking football and make the code more suitable for television audiences, but the understandably controversial modification was bemoaned by a large proportion of purists and those within the game for the ensuing four seasons. Teams struggled to build any pressure or structure with only four tackles to work with, and tackle counts were extended to six in 1971—a happy medium that the vast majority came to accept over time, and a change that would shape modern Rugby League.

3. Replacement of injured players

Before 1963, provisions for replacing injured players were extremely limited, often leaving teams to battle on short-handed. But then a rule was introduced that allowed teams to replace a maximum of two injured players during the first half, including halftime. The rule was amended in 1970 to allow two injured players to be replaced at any time, provided the replacements had played at least half a game in the lower grades earlier that day. The lower grade requirement was scrapped in 1988, with two fresh reserves allowed—a precursor to the many incarnations, both good and bad, of the four-man interchange introduced in 1991.

4. Increase of try value to four points

The Rugby League authorities belatedly increased the value of tries from three points to four in 1983, a decade after Rugby Union made the same change. Although the 1984-86 seasons witnessed three of the four lowest-scoring Grand Finals of all time, the try-value rule change ultimately encouraged more attack-oriented football, with teams gradually forgoing penalty goal attempts to push for a try more often. Fittingly, Manly tryscoring wizard Phil Blake had the honour of scoring the first four-point try—a dazzling, trademark chip-and-chase effort in the opening round of '83.

5. The 20-metre restart rule

The popularity of the bomb as an attacking weapon in the mid-1970s led to it being increasingly used to earn a repeat set of tackles, with a line dropout forced when an opposition player was caught in the in-goal. The Canterbury Bulldogs exploited the tactic with relentless monotony on their way to winning the 1985 premiership, which led to a rule change the following season that gave the opposition side a 20-metre restart if a player caught the ball on the full in his own in-goal.

6. Decrease of field-goal value to one point

The incidence of players shooting for field goals (then worth two points) during the four-tackle era was seen as a blight on the game, with players such as Eric Simms, Phil Hawthorne, Barry Glasgow and Bob Fulton regularly kicking upwards of 20 in a season. The reduction in the value of field goals to one point in 1971 had an immediate impact, with just 22 kicked that year, down from 159 the previous season—Simms landed four and Fulton two in the 1970 Grand Final alone. Canterbury's Terry Reynolds kicked the first one-pointer in first grade, in Round 7 against St George. These days field goals retain an important place in the game as the ultimate deadlock-breaker, rather than a means to accumulate points, as has regularly been the case in Rugby Union, where the scoring play is worth three points.

7. The 40/20 rule
Introduced for the 1997 ARL premiership, the 40/20 rule rewarded players who were able to kick in general play from inside their own 40-metre line and find touch inside the opposition 20-metre line, giving their team a valuable scrum feed deep in enemy territory. Although difficult to execute, this exceedingly popular addition to the rulebook can be a genuine game-turning manoeuvre, while also encouraging wingers and fullbacks to keep the ball in play.

8. Handover rule
Instead of a scrum packing down when a team was caught in possession on the sixth tackle, a handover to restart play was introduced in 1983. The handover rule was extended in 1989 to include instances where a team knocked on, ran into touch or kicked out on the full on the sixth tackle, and further amendments were made ahead of the 2014 NRL season, with a handover to occur when the ball is kicked out on the full on any tackle.

9. Zero tackle
Most of Super League's 1997 rule innovations were ditched when the game reunited under the NRL banner, but one that survived was the zero-tackle rule, albeit in a modified form. During the sole Super League season, whenever a team started their set in general play directly from an opposition knock-on or an opposition kick their first play-the-ball was the 'zero' tackle. The zero tackle was retained in the NRL for opposition knock-ons, but not kicks in general play. In 2014, the NRL announced the first tackle from 20-metre tap restarts would be called the zero tackle, designed to discourage teams from deliberately kicking the ball dead to slow the game down or deny opposition wingers and fullbacks the opportunity to return kicks.

10. The sin bin
Introduced in 1981, the sin bin gave referees the discretion to dismiss players for five- or 10-minute spells (the five-minute option was later repealed) for misconduct not deemed serious enough for an outright send-off—most often fighting, dissent, repeated infringements or professional fouls. Newtown hooker Barry Jensen had the dubious honour of being the first player to be sent to the sin bin.

WORST RULE CHANGES

1. The shoulder-charge ban
The shoulder charge is regarded as one of the highlights of Rugby League, but concerns over concussions and the health of players—as well as the potential to get sued—saw the NRL impose a ban on the tackle late in the 2012 season. The ban was met with outrage by players and fans alike.

2. The McIntyre finals system
Used in the NRL from 1999 until 2011, the McIntyre finals system was a convoluted and unfair playoff system under which teams could be eliminated while watching at home, teams three and four could be eliminated in the opening week, and an opening-week loser from the top of the ladder then had to travel to a lower seeding club's ground for a sudden-death semi. The system was abolished in 2012.

3. Unlimited interchange
Briefly introduced in 1991 (and then again in '96) in a bid to protect player safety, unlimited interchange was a disaster for the little men of the game and ended the era of the 80-minute forward. Unlimited interchange was changed to 12 interchanges in 2001, and then dropped to 10 in '08.

4. The benefit-of-the-doubt interpretation
A crutch that video referees used inconsistently for the better part of a decade, the benefit of the doubt to the attacking team allowed officials to use often tenuous reasons to award a try that generally should not have been given. It was removed in 2013.

5. Striking in the play-the-ball banned
Rugby League lost another means to win the ball back from the attacking team when striking in the play-the-ball was eliminated in 1997, a decade after scrums were effectively castrated. It cleaned up the ruck, but eliminated a lot of the excitement and tipped the advantage even further to the attacking team.

6. Dummy-half running banned
In 1961 the League placed a ban on dummy-half running in an attempt to open up the game. If the dummy-half was caught, a scrum would take place with the non-offending team given the feed. The rule change was overturned two years later.

7. Origin eligibility rules
Lax Origin eligibility rules turned the concept into somewhat of a joke in the 1990s and 2000s, with Papua New Guinea captain Adrian Lam also skippering Queensland; NSW-born-and-bred players like Greg Inglis and Israel Folau becoming stars for the Maroons; and Kiwi-born players like James Tamou representing NSW. The rules were significantly tightened in 2013.

8. Tap penalty banned
Following its introduction in 1954, the tap penalty was again banned in 1959. The abolition of the tap penalty lasted eight years and served to help teams with dominant forward packs, namely St George.

9. Abolition of midweek playoff
After 87 seasons, the midweek playoff to determine finals spots was eliminated in 1995 as the premiership expanded to 20 teams, with finals berths and finals order to be instead determined by for and against. However, as well as adding an extra game to the calendar, the midweek playoff was also a much fairer way of determining finalists.

10. Scoring teams kicks off
In an attempt to stop one-sided scoring—and a thinly veiled effort to imitate the NFL—Super League introduced a rule in 1997 where the scoring team kicked off. The rule, which failed to stop blowout after blowout in the ill-fated World Club Challenge, was never adopted by the NRL.

Chapter 18

AROUND THE WORLD

BRITAIN'S GREATEST PLAYERS

1. Ellery Hanley
Ellery 'The Black Pearl' Hanley was a star at centre, five-eighth and lock during a decorated two-decade career that saw him rise to the role of captain of Great Britain. He made his debut with Bradford Northern as a 17-year-old in 1978, before going on to play with glamour club Wigan and Leeds, and Balmain and Wests in Australia. A three-time Man of Steel winner, Hanley won the Golden Boot in 1988, the same year he came close to winning a premiership with Balmain. He won two championships apiece with Bradford Northern and Wigan, as well as four Challenge Cups with the cherry-and-whites.

2. Harold Wagstaff
Dubbed the 'Prince of Centres', Harold Wagstaff rated as the best English player during the first quarter-century of the code. He played his entire 436-game career with Huddersfield, where he won three championships and three Challenge Cups, and represented England and Great Britain 25 times, debuting against the pioneering 1908-09 Kangaroos aged just 17. A tenacious defender, Wagstaff famously led Britain during the Rorke's Drift Test, where a 10-man Great Britain held off Australia in Sydney.

3. Billy Boston

A Welsh tryscoring wizard who spent most of his career with Wigan, Billy Boston scored an incredible 571 career tries, trailing only the great Australian Brian Bevan. The Rugby Union convert spent 16 seasons with the cherry-and-whites, winning three Challenge Cups and a championship and scoring a double in the '58-59 Cup final. He was later awarded an MBE and had a grandstand named in his honour at Wigan's former home ground, Central Park.

4. Alex Murphy

A yappy halfback who played for St Helens, Leigh and Warrington during his two-decade career, Alex Murphy played 29 Tests and became the first player to captain three different teams to Challenge Cup success, winning a total of five Cups—and taking home the Lance Todd Trophy in the 1971 win—to go with two championships. The high-point of his Test career was the 1960 World Cup triumph, though he twice toured Australia on Ashes campaigns.

5. Gus Risman

Over the course of his incredible 27-year career, which was predominantly spent with Salford and Workington Town, champion centre Gus Risman was a skilful and intelligent player who won four championships and two Challenge Cups, including one with Workington Town as a 41-year-old. After making his debut for Wales at the age of 20, he went on to play 35 Tests for Wales and Great Britain, and appeared in five Ashes campaigns, winning them all. His 4050 career points ranks third all time, and he sits second for career appearances.

6. Roger Millward

A skilful and tough five-eighth with Castleford and then Hull Kingston Rovers, Roger Millward was a prodigious talent who made his Test debut at 18 and enjoyed a 13-year international career. The classy standoff led England into two World Cups, and was simply amazing during the 1970 Ashes series, scoring 20 points in the second Test and playing a match-winning hand in the decider. He had a successful stint with Cronulla in 1976.

7. Neil Fox

The greatest point-scorer in the history of English Rugby League, Neil Fox racked up an incredible 6220 points at club level and a record 228 points for Britain over his 24-year top-grade career. The brilliant goalkicking centre's 20 points in the 1959-60 Challenge Cup final remains a record, and he won the Lance Todd Trophy in 1962. Together with brothers Peter and Don, he was part of one of the famous footballing families.

8. Vince Karalius

A defensive powerhouse and underrated ball-player known as 'The Wild Bull of the Pampas', backrower Vince Karalius was an aggressive enforcer with St Helens, Widnes and Great Britain who was as renowned for standing over an opponent as he was for slipping a one-handed offload. He captained St Helens to a Challenge Cup success, but his finest hour came in national colours during the 'Battle of Brisbane' Test in 1958, when he overcame a seriously injured back to wreak havoc and help his country to a famous win.

9. Malcolm Reilly

One of the great British backrow forwards, very much in the Vince Karalius mould, Malcolm Reilly made his mark in England and Australia as both a player and a coach. Although fiery and temperamental, he was a super-skilful player who won two premierships with Manly and enjoyed many successes at Castleford. Few earned the respect throughout their career that Reilly did.

10. Garry Schofield

Great Britain's most-capped player, the graceful Garry Schofield, excelled at both centre and five-eighth. Named the Golden Boot winner in 1990, he was outstanding for Britain in their close Ashes loss to Australia that year and as Test skipper on the Lions' '92 tour Down Under. He also enjoyed successful stints in the Sydney premiership, and won Britain's Man of Steel Award in 1991. The Hull and Leeds stalwart played a record 46 Tests for Great Britain from 1984-94, scoring 30 tries.

NEW ZEALAND'S GREATEST PLAYERS

1. Stacey Jones

Mercurial halfback Stacey 'The Little General' Jones played 46 Tests for New Zealand (seven as captain), scoring 160 points and 16 tries, second and equal third respectively in the country's history. The 19-year-old unseated Gary Freeman for the No.7 role at the 1995 World Cup after a sensational rookie season with the Auckland Warriors, and was an unwaveringly brilliant and consistent performer for club and country for more than a decade. He played a record 261 games for the Warriors and in 2002 captained the club in its charge to the minor premiership and a Grand Final appearance, claiming that year's Golden Boot along the way. He starred as the Kiwis won the 2005 Tri-Nations, and was equally brilliant as they almost repeated the dose in '06—perhaps only Andrew Johns and Allan

Langer would be regarded as better halfbacks during his era. Jones was named halfback in New Zealand's Team of the Century in 2009.

2. Mark Graham

A bruising and skilful second-rower, Mark Graham was named New Zealand's Player of the Century in 2009 and was regarded by many keen judges as the best in the world in his position during the 1980s. The Otahuhu product played 28 Tests from 1977 to 1988 (18 as captain, including the 18-0 victory over Australia in 1985), which was an era of tremendous progress for New Zealand Rugby League. He won a BRL premiership with Kiwi coach Graham Lowe at Brisbane Norths in 1980, and went on to play 146 games in eight seasons for North Sydney. Graham was one of the premiership's dominant forwards, winning two Dally M Second-rower of the Year gongs and captaining the club for several seasons.

3. Benji Marshall

Benji Marshall was a unique talent and a brilliant match-winner in 11 seasons with Wests Tigers, spearheading the club's 2005 premiership success and playing 201 games, while breaking club records for tries (76) and points (1118). Despite being significantly restricted by injuries early on, the dazzling five-eighth's Test career was equally memorable—he was the linchpin of the Kiwis' watershed World Cup triumph in 2008 and captained his country in the last 16 of his 25 Test appearances. Marshall's tenure as skipper peaked with a magnificent display in New Zealand's Four Nations final upset of Australia in 2010 on his way to being just the third Kiwi to win the Golden Boot.

4. George Menzies

A product of West Coast club Runanga, George Menzies was labelled as the world's best five-eighth in the 1950s. A classy, clever organiser, the diminutive Kiwi played 29 Tests from 1951 to 1961—including three World Cup campaigns, a series victory over Australia in 1952, and further Test victories against the green-and-golds in 1959 and '61—and scored three tries for Rest of the World against Great Britain in 1960. The curly-haired pivot was named five-eighth in New Zealand's Team of the Century in 2009.

5. Ruben Wiki

Otahuhu powerhouse Ruben Wiki rose to prominence as a centre in Canberra's 1994 premiership success, but ultimately played most of his then world-record 55 Tests for New Zealand in the pack. He scored 60 tries in 224 games for the Raiders, eventually gravitating towards the engine-room at club level, and finished his career with four seasons at the Warriors, becoming the first overseas player (and just the 10th player overall) to make 300 first grade appearances. He featured in five Test wins over Australia, and his 18 Tests as captain included the 2005 Tri-Nations final boilover. In 2009, a year after his retirement, he was named as a prop in New Zealand's Team of the Century.

6. Cliff Johnson

Auckland prop Cliff Johnson, who was named captain of the New Zealand Team of the Century in 2009, led the Kiwis in 14 of his 34 Test appearances from 1950 to 1960. The rugged front-rower began his Test career in the Kiwis' series win over the touring Lions, and went on to lead his country to two World Cups and on a tour of Australia. The imposing, highly respected Richmond stalwart also captained Rest of the World in 1960. Johnson's record for most Tests for New Zealand was eclipsed by long-time teammate Jock Butterfield in 1963.

7. Mel Cooke

New Zealand's Team of the Century lock, Mel Cooke, played 22 consecutive Tests for the Kiwis from 1959 to 1964. Representing from Canterbury club Hornby, the former halfback enjoyed Test wins over Australia in 1959, '61 and '63, and toured Great Britain and France with the Kiwis in 1961. A valuable, hardworking loose forward, he captained New Zealand in eight Tests, including an upset home series victory over Great Britain in 1963 and a tour of Australia the following season. Cooke accepted a captain-coach position with Canberra in 1965, and represented Monaro and NSW Country during his time in the ACT.

8. Matthew Ridge

Matthew Ridge might have been overlooked for the NZRL Team of the Century in favour of prolific Auckland goalkicker Des White, but the former All Black's standing in the Australian premiership nevertheless pegs him as one of New Zealand's greatest Rugby League players. He scored 1093 points in seven seasons and 122 games for Manly, and was a key member of the club's 1996 Grand Final triumph. He also broke White's Kiwis pointscoring record with a total of 168 in 25 Test appearances, including 11 as captain, from 1990 to 1998. The courageous and combative Ridge led New Zealand's spirited '95 World Cup campaign, and despite a disappointing three seasons with the Warriors, skippered the Kiwis to a 3-0 whitewash of Great Britain at the end of '96, as well as victories over Super League Australia in '97 and a full Australian Test side in '98.

9. Hugh McGahan

Otahuhu backrower Hugh McGahan played 32 Tests from 1982-90, scoring a then record 16 tries and setting an incredible world record by scoring six tries in a Test against Papua New Guinea in 1983. He went on to captain his country in 15 Tests, including the Kiwis' upset of Australia at Lang Park in 1987 and the tour of Great Britain and France in '89. After captaining Eastern Suburbs to the preliminary final in '87, the rangy 117-game Roosters veteran was named joint winner (with Peter Sterling) of the Golden Boot.

10. Stephen Kearney
A tough second-rower with outstanding ball-playing ability, Stephen Kearney played 46 Test matches for New Zealand from 1993 to 2004. He captained the Kiwis against Great Britain as a 21-year-old in 1993 in just his fifth Test, and led his country in one further Test in '97. A first-choice backrower for virtually his entire career, he played 264 first grade games (a then record for an overseas player) for Western Suburbs, Auckland and Melbourne, including a Grand Final triumph with the Storm in 1999.

FRANCE'S GREATEST PLAYERS

1. Puig-Aubert
Born Robert Aubert Puig, Puig-Aubert is unquestionably France's greatest player and one of the most celebrated figures in international Rugby League history, epitomising the unpredictability, flair, eccentricity and enigmatic nature of the French side during its greatest era. Nicknamed 'Pipette' in reference to his habit of smoking on the field, the diminutive fullback was as laconic as he was charismatic—he often refused to tackle opposing players in protest of his own teammates' defensive failings—but an undeniable genius with the ball and a peerless goalkicker. He became a permanent fixture in the national side in the second half of the 1940s, and then cemented his legend as captain of France's 1951 tour of Australasia when he scored a record 221 points, outplayed opposing fullback and skipper Clive Churchill and kicked 18 goals in the historic 2-1 series win—efforts which earned him his country's prestigious Champion of Champions title, an unprecedented achievement for a footballer of any code. Puig-Aubert also led France to a series victory over the 1952-53 Kangaroos, but missed the '55 tour Down Under; he retired a year later with 46 international appearances to his credit. Puig-Aubert won five French championship finals and four cup finals during a decorated club career with AS Carcassonne and XIII Catalans. He was an original inductee to the international Rugby League Hall of Fame in 1988.

2. Jacques Merquey
Small in stature but big in heart, Jacques Merquey was a dazzling centre/five-eighth who was at the axis of some of France's greatest moments. A four-Test Rugby Union

international, he switched codes in 1950 and won immediate national honours in the professional game. He starred in Les Chanticleers' series success in Australia as a 21-year-old in '51, and returned four years later as captain to lead France to another stunning boilover against the green-and-golds. Merquey also skippered his country against the 1956-57 and '59-60 Kangaroos, and to the '57 World Cup in Australia. He scored 19 tries in 35 internationals, and captained Rest of the World against Australia after the '57 World Cup.

3. Jean Dop

A legendary figure in French Rugby League, brilliant halfback Jean Dop starred against the touring 1948-49 Kangaroos and played an integral role in France's away series triumphs over Australia in 1951 and '55. After wearing the No.7 in the historic '51 success, he played fullback in the '55 campaign in the absence of the great Puig-Aubert. The tempestuous playmaker made the last of his 21 Test appearances in 1957. He was an original inductee to the international Rugby League Hall of Fame in 1988.

4. Max Rousié

The first truly great French Rugby League exponent, Max Rousié, played four Rugby Union Tests in the early 1930s before switching codes and becoming an inspirational leader and brilliantly versatile performer in 15 international appearances. He featured at centre in the fledgling 13-a-side nation's historic 1934-35 European Championship campaign, and led France from five-eighth and centre in the series against the 1938-39 Kangaroos—the first between the countries. The charismatic Rousié also played Tests at fullback and halfback, and signed off on an esteemed international career by guiding his country to victory in the 1938-39 European Championship. He was an original inductee to the international Rugby League Hall of Fame half a century later.

5. Gilbert Benausse

A magnificent five-eighth who also played Tests at halfback and centre, Gilbert Benausse made a record 49 international appearances for France from 1951 to 1964. He arrived on the scene just after his country's momentous 1951 tour of Australia, but was a permanent fixture thereafter—starring in series wins over the 1952-53 Kangaroos and on France's 1955 tour Down Under, on which he kicked six goals in the second Test victory in Brisbane. Among the highest try-scorers and point-scorers in French Rugby League history, the AS Carcassonne stalwart played in two World Cups and racked up 32 points in France's amazing 3-0 whitewash of Great Britain in 1962.

6. Joseph Crespo

A veteran of 27 internationals at halfback, five-eighth, centre, wing and lock, Joseph Crespo was a magnificent performer in France's series triumphs in Australia in 1951 and at home against the 1952-53 Kangaroos. After featuring as a centre in the opening two Tests of the '51 series, he switched to halfback for the deciding third Test at the SCG and scored three tries in the stunning 35-14 upset. He farewelled the international arena after helping France reach the final of the inaugural World Cup in 1954.

7. Ellie Brousse

Half of one of the all-time great second-row pairings with Edouard Ponsinet, Ellie Brousse made his international debut against Wales in 1946. He played one Test against the 1948-49 Kangaroos, but was at his peak on Les Chanticleers' tour Down Under in 1951, starring in the historic series triumph over Australia and scoring a try in the decider. He made the last of his 31 appearances for France in another ground-breaking series result, the 2-1 defeat of the 1952-53 Kangaroos.

8. Claude Mantoulan

Claude Mantoulan played his only Rugby Union Test for France at flyhalf against Ireland in April 1959. By the end of that year he was a Rugby League international and would go on to play 46 times for his country in the professional code— a mainstay for a French side in steep decline. Adept at centre, five-eighth and fullback, the brilliant Mantoulan played against Australia on 13 occasions and represented Rest of the World in 1960.

9. Raymond Contrastin

The greatest try-scorer in France's Test history and an original inductee to the international Rugby League Hall of Fame in 1988, Raymond Contrastin, was one of the great wingers. After debuting against the 1948-49 Kangaroos, he played a vital part in the 1951 series triumph in Australia, crossing for a try in the first Test victory and bagging a double in the deciding third Test. He featured in the defeat of the 1952-53 Kangaroos; scored five tries in four games as France reached the final of the inaugural '54 World Cup; and, after missing the first two games, scored a crucial try in his country's series-winning third Test win in Australia a year later. All told, the flyer dotted down 25 times in 34 internationals.

10. Édouard Ponsinet

Edouard Ponsinet formed a second-row combination with Ellie Brousse that has taken on almost mythical status in international Rugby League folklore. After debuting against New Zealand in 1948, he featured prominently in France's euphoric series victories over Australia abroad (1951) and at home (1952-53), making a total of 18 appearances for Les Tricolores.

PAPUA NEW GUINEA'S GREATEST PLAYERS

1. Adrian Lam
Papua New Guinea's greatest-ever product, Adrian Lam, captained not only Papua New Guinea but the Queensland State of Origin team, and played in Grand Finals in both the NRL and Super League. A fine halfback with deft touch, he signed with Eastern Suburbs in 1994 and forged an outstanding 146-game, seven-year career with the Tricolours. In 1995 he had the unique honour of playing in the Maroons' shock Origin win and for the Kumuls in the World Cup. He represented Queensland 14 times and captained the state in 1997 and from 1999 to 2000, playing in a Grand Final in the last. Lam's relationship with the Roosters was often tempestuous— he threatened to walk out on his contract when John Simon was signed, and the club tried to prevent him playing Origin in '99, claiming he was injured. He rounded out his career with a four-season stint with Wigan. He skippered Papua New Guinea to the 2000 World Cup, and coached them at the '08 and '13 editions.

2. Marcus Bai
A tryscoring wizard whose game relied on his unique combination of speed and strength, Marcus Bai was a cult hero wherever he played. A late bloomer, he debuted for Papua New Guinea aged 23 at the 1995 World Cup, where he scored a try against New Zealand. He signed with Hull but moved to Australia in 1997 and scored five tries in 18 appearances for the Gold Coast. After shifting to new club Melbourne in 1998, he had a career year, scoring 14 tries (including five in the first six games) and winning the Dally M Winger of the Year gong. He scored 70 tries in 144 games for the Storm, winning a premiership with the club in 1999; fans named a stand in his honour and he was named in the club's Team of the Decade in 2007. He rounded out his career with three seasons at Leeds and Bradford, scoring 52 tries in 83 games. Bai scored two tries in 11 international appearances.

3. Stanley Gene
Papua New Guinea's most popular and beloved player, Stanley Gene, was an ageless warrior (his birthdate is not known, but is being researched as a "matter of national importance" by the Papua New Guinea government) who played nearly 350 games in Papua New Guinea and England. A player of rare versatility who has played every position bar wing and fullback, he represented the Kumuls at the 1995, 2000 and 2008 World Cups—he was believed to be more than 40 years old at the last, according to former coach Brian Noble. His English career saw stints with

Hull KR, Hull FC, Huddersfield, Bradford and Halifax, where he scored more than 120 tries. Gene coached the Kumuls to the 2010 Four Nations and remains universally adored in his homeland.

4. Neville Costigan

A journeyman who has spent most of his career under the tutelage of the great Wayne Bennett, Neville Costigan has won a premiership with St George Illawarra, represented Queensland six times in the cauldron of State of Origin, and captained his home country. In a 169-game NRL career with the Broncos, Raiders, Dragons and Knights, the tough utility forward scored 20 tries and built a fearsome reputation as one of the game's true enforcers. All six Origin appearances came during Queensland's unprecedented run of success that began in 2006, and he was one of the Kumuls' best at both the 2008 and 2013 World Cups, captaining Papua New Guinea at the latter tournament.

5. Paul Aiton

One of the most widely respected men in Papua New Guinean Rugby League, Paul Aiton has been a mainstay of top-level football since debuting with Penrith in 2006, two years after his first international appearance. He played 72 games as Luke Priddis' understudy in four seasons with the Panthers, where he was revered for his work rate and his slick dummy-half work. A move to the Sharks lasted two years before he was lured to Super League, where two excellent seasons with Wakefield Trinity saw him snapped up by powerhouse Leeds in 2014. He has played nine Tests for the Kumuls, including captaining Papua New Guinea in the 2010 Four Nations.

6. Bruce Mamando

Hardworking backrower/prop Bruce Mamando forged a premiership career that spanned three clubs and eight years. He debuted off the bench in 1994 for eventual premiers Canberra in his only game of the season, and again played a solitary game off the pine the following year before being called up to represent the Kumuls at the 1995 World Cup. He played 12 games for the Raiders in 1996, including the qualifying final loss to St George, before becoming a cult hero with the Adelaide Rams in 1997. He finished his career with the Cowboys and was a key component of Papua New Guinea's excellent 2000 World Cup showing, where the Kumuls won three games.

7. David Mead

A lightning-quick player with the Gold Coast Titans, David Mead was signed after some fine displays in national colours at the 2008 World Cup and has become one of the club's most reliable players, scoring 51 tries in 89 games to the end of the 2013 season. A genuine speedster rated as one of the quickest in the NRL, his freakish gather and tiptoe-along-the-sideline try against Cronulla was regarded as the 2011 try of the year. He represented the Kumuls at the 2008 and 2013 World Cups, with a poor night with the boot the difference in a 9-8 loss to France in the latter.

8. John Wilshere

A slinky goalkicking outside back, John Wilshere played at the highest levels in both Australia and England, and led the Kumuls to the 2008 World Cup. He moved to England after struggling to lock down a first grade spot in a 15-game NRL career with the Western Reds, Melbourne and St George Illawarra in which he scored four tries. His six-season Super League stint with Warrington, Leigh and Salford was more successful, tallying 46 tries in 114 games. His 480 points for Salford sits second on the club's pointscoring tally in the Super League era, while his 104 points in 16 Kumul appearances is a record.

9. David Westley

A tough prop who played 143 NRL games with Canberra, Parramatta and the Northern Eagles, David Westley was one of the Kumuls' finest players. He was part of the powerhouse Raiders' title-winning side a year after being signed in 1993, and stayed with the Green Machine until 1999. He only played four Tests for the Kumuls, but only two Papua New Guinea-born players have played more premiership games.

10. John Wagambie

The Kumuls' inaugural captain, John Wagambie has been a constant in Papua New Guinean Rugby League. The skilful lock/five-eighth led Papua New Guinea in its first-ever international win, a 37-6 demolition of France at Port Moresby's Lloyd Robson Oval in 1977. A revered figure by the latter stages of his career, he captained the Kumuls in their first two official Tests—a 13-all draw with France in 1981 and a 56-5 loss to New Zealand in '82—before retiring. He later coached Papua New Guinea in three Tests during the 1990s.

GREATEST PACIFIC ISLANDS PLAYERS

(Note: Only players who represented a Pacific Island nation in international Rugby League were considered.)

1. Petero Civoniceva (Fiji)

Born in Suva and the son of a former Fiji Rugby Union international, Petero Civoniceva moved to Redcliffe as an infant. A tremendous ambassador for the game, the genial giant debuted for Brisbane in 1998, winning two Grand Finals with the club and racking up 309 NRL appearances for the Broncos and Penrith. The rugged, unrelenting prop established all-time records for most Test and Origin appearances by a forward (45 and 33 respectively) during 11 seasons in the Australia and Queensland sides. After spending the season with Redcliffe, he captained Fiji in all five of its matches at the 2013 World Cup. He retired after the nation's semi-final loss to a Kangaroos side containing 13 of his former Test teammates.

2. Kevin Iro (Cook Islands)
Nicknamed 'The Beast' while Manu Vatuvei was still in nappies, Kevin Iro was among the most devastating three-quarters of the 1980s and '90s. Although his Australian premiership stints with Manly, Hunter and Auckland were underwhelming, he was a regular Challenge Cup final destroyer with Wigan before starring for Leeds and winning two Super League titles with St Helens late in his career. He scored 16 tries in 34 Test appearances for New Zealand from 1987 to 1998, and captained Cook Islands in its historic World Cup campaign in 2000.

3. Jarryd Hayne (Fiji)
A teenage sensation for Parramatta, Jarryd Hayne made his debuts for NSW and Australia as a 19-year-old in 2007. A form slump the following season saw him instead represent Fiji at the '08 World Cup, but his stellar tournament for the unfancied Batis was a turning point. The fullback won the Dally M Medal and carried the Eels to the Grand Final in '09, earning a Kangaroos recall. A mainstay of the Blues' recent losing run (17 Origin appearances) and something of a one-man band as captain of lowly Parramatta, he starred as a centre in Australia's 2013 World Cup triumph after a three-year absence, taking his tally to 11 tries in 11 Tests.

4. Jim Dymock (Tonga)
A brilliant ball-playing lock or five-eighth, Souths junior Jim Dymock began his first grade career with Wests then joined Canterbury and collected the Clive Churchill Medal in the club's '95 Grand Final success. He represented Tonga at the '94 Pacific Cup and was selected by the island nation for the following year's World Cup but played at lock for the victorious Australian side instead. He represented Australia in six Tests and NSW in six Origins, and won his third Dally M Lock of the Year gong after joining Parramatta, where he finished his 214-game career in 2000.

5. Willie Mason (Tonga)
Auckland-born Newcastle junior Willie Mason broke into NRL football with the Bulldogs in 2000 and represented Tonga in that year's World Cup, scoring two tries in three pool games. The prop/second-rower first became an instant cult hero and, later, a controversial and polarising figure, but was nevertheless one of the dominant forwards of the decade. The Clive Churchill Medal winner in the Bulldogs'

'04 Grand Final win, he played 24 Tests for Australia and 13 Origins for NSW. He moved on to stints of varying success with the Roosters, Cowboys and Knights, racking up his 250th first grade appearance during the 2013 finals.

6. Brent Kite (Tonga)

Brent Kite turned out for Tonga at the 2000 World Cup as a 19-year-old but did not make his NRL debut for St George Illawarra until two years later. The front-rower broke into the NSW side in 2004, but his career really took off after he joined Manly, where he played 14 Tests for Australia and in four Grand Finals for the Sea Eagles—including a Churchill Medal-winning performance in the '08 decider. The veteran of 288 first grade games made a return for Tonga at the 2013 World Cup.

7. Nigel Vagana (Samoa)

The highest non-Australian try-scorer in premiership history—140 tries in 240 games for the Warriors, Bulldogs, Sharks and Rabbitohs—Nigel Vagana ranks among the NRL era's finest centres. He racked up double-figure try tallies from 1998 to 2005, including a Bulldogs club-record 23 in '03. Vagana represented New Zealand in 37 Tests (scoring a Kiwis-record 19 tries) at wing, centre, fullback and five-eighth before captaining Samoa to the 2008 World Cup.

8. Roy Asotasi (Samoa)

A veteran of 217 NRL games, robust prop Roy Asotasi was a key part of the Bulldogs' 2004 premiership triumph and captained rebuilding Souths from 2007 to 2012. He played 24 Tests for New Zealand from 2004 to 2009—including seven as skipper—before representing Samoa against Tonga midway through 2013. Asotasi departed for Super League after the Rabbitohs' preliminary final loss that season, but was a mysterious withdrawal from Samoa's squad on the eve of the World Cup.

9. Lote Tuqiri (Fiji)

Born in Korolevu, Fiji, Lote Tuqiri moved to Brisbane as a teenager and debuted for the Broncos in 1999. He was a try-scorer in the club's Grand Final win the following season before he captained Fiji to the ensuing World Cup at the age of 21, starring with four tries in three pool games. Tuqiri played five Tests for Australia and six Origins for Queensland in 2001-02, but was lured to Rugby Union and represented the Wallabies 67 times. He made a stunning return to the NRL with the Wests Tigers in 2010, scoring 18 tries and playing four post-season Tests for the Kangaroos, but his subsequent seasons for the Tigers were riddled with injury. Tuqiri had scored 83 tries in 151 games ahead of his move to Souths in 2014.

10. Tony Puletua (Samoa)
Tackle-busting second-rower Tony Puletua was a tremendous clubman for Penrith from 1997 to 2008 and was at his peak in the club's '03 premiership season. A veteran of 21 Tests for New Zealand, he later represented Samoa at the 2008 and '13 World Cups. Puletua played 211 games for the Panthers and a further 137 for St Helens, scoring 40 tries for each club.

BEST BRITISH IMPORTS

1. Malcolm Reilly
Brutal and brilliant Castleford lock Mal Reilly's intimidation factor and ball-playing class provided Manly with the edge it needed to break through for belated premiership success. He played 89 games for the Sea Eagles from 1971 to '75, and featured in the club's 1972 and '73 Grand Final victories. Heavy-handed tactics ensured he was always a controversial figure in Sydney, but Reilly's attacking qualities were indisputable. He returned to Australia two decades later as coach of Newcastle to guide the club to its maiden premiership in 1997.

2. Adrian Morley
Former Leeds enforcer Adrian Morley spent the equivalent of an entire NRL season on the sidelines through regular suspensions, but the prop/second-rower's aggression and fearless play on both sides of ball were vital ingredients to the Sydney Roosters' success in the early 2000s. He played 113 games in six seasons for the Tricolours, starring in the '02 premiership triumph and appearing in three straight Grand Finals before a seven-week kneeing suspension in '06 prematurely ended his NRL tenure.

3. Tommy Bishop
Fiery 15-Test veteran Tommy Bishop turned the struggling young Cronulla Sharks into premiership contenders in the early 1970s. The gifted halfback joined the club in 1969 and took over as captain-coach the following season, winning the 1970 *Rugby League Week* Player of the Year award. He gradually led the Sharks up the ladder, culminating in their maiden finals series in '73. Cronulla progressed to the Grand Final, where Bishop was regarded as one of the main instigators of the infamous violence that plagued the match, which Manly won 10-7. He was unable to come to terms with the club for the following season, however, and joined Brisbane Norths after 69 appearances for the Sharks.

4. Sam Burgess

Eager to test himself in the best competition in the world, dynamic Bradford forward Sam Burgess was a marquee acquisition for Souths in 2010. The 21-year-old made an immediate impact, and the bone-rattling defence, tackle-busting runs and all-round game-breaking qualities he displayed in the ensuing four seasons stamped him as one of the NRL's top forwards. Later joined at the club by three of his brothers, he was a key figure in Souths reaching the preliminary final stage in 2012 and '13. The 70-game Rabbitoh subsequently shocked the Rugby League world, however, by announcing 2014 would be his last season in the NRL after signing with the English Rugby Union and gaining an early release from his club.

5. Dave Bolton

Dave Bolton toured Australia twice with the Lions before returning in 1965 to play for Balmain. A wily half and one of the premiership's foremost field goal exponents, he played in the Tigers side that upset Great Britain in '66 and lost the Grand Final to St George later that season. He played a pivotal role in Balmain's monumental Grand Final upset of Souths as a 32-year-old, slotting two field goals and steering the rank outsiders around the park superbly in the 11-2 triumph. He retired at the end of 1970 after 78 appearances, and later had an unsuccessful stint as coach of Parramatta.

6. Ellery Hanley

Ellery 'The Black Pearl' Hanley's performances as a centre in Balmain's miraculous sudden-death run to the 1988 Grand Final hold a treasured place in premiership folklore. The aristocratic Wigan and Great Britain captain scored tries in four straight matches as the Tigers progressed from a fifth-place playoff to the decider, but a groggy exit from the Grand Final courtesy of a controversial Terry Lamb tackle effectively sealed Balmain's fate against Canterbury. Hanley starred during a 13-game stint with battlers Wests the following season before returning to the Tigers as a 35-year-old, proving he had lost some speed but little of his guile in 26 games in 1996 and '97.

7. Dick Huddart

A second-row destroyer for Great Britain on the 1958 and '62 Lions tours of Australia, Dick Huddart was recruited by eight-time premiers St George in 1964. The St Helens via Whitehaven forward was kept out of the Dragons' 1964 and '65 Grand Final victories by injury, before becoming the first Brit to win a Sydney premiership in '66, scoring a try in the 23-4 decider win over Balmain—the last in the club's world-record run of 11 straight titles. An outstanding defender and a dangerous, mobile ball-runner, Huddart stayed with the Saints until 1968, finishing with 78 first grade appearances before joining Newcastle club Macquarie United.

8. John Gray
Prolific pointscoring hooker John Gray, credited with introducing the around-the-corner goalkicking style to Australia, played 138 games and scored 611 points for Norths and Manly—both records for a British player. He joined the Bears in 1975 and was poached three years later by archrivals Manly, where he was often used as a prop due to the presence of Max Krilich and was ruled out of the '78 Grand Final by suspension. The moustachioed rake returned to Norths in 1981 and won the Dally M Hooker of the Year award in '82 after helping the club to its first finals series in 17 years.

9. Gareth Ellis
Veteran Wakefield Trinity and Leeds backrower Gareth Ellis was a magnificent acquisition for the Wests Tigers in 2009—the imposing, tough and mobile forward was named the Tigers' Player of the Year in three straight seasons and was integral to the club's return to the finals in 2010 and '11. He was plagued by injuries in 2012 as the Tigers missed the eight and returned to England at the end of the year after 75 NRL appearances.

10. Gareth Widdop
Classy Halifax-born playmaker Gareth Widdop has played his entire senior career in Australia. He starred at fullback in Melbourne's 2009 NYC premiership win before cementing the first grade five-eighth spot two years later and playing a key role in the Storm's surge to Grand Final glory in 2012. An excellent foil for halfback Cooper Cronk, Widdop made his Test debut for England in 2010. After it was announced that he had signed a four-year contract with St George Illawarra beginning 2014, Widdop's final season with Melbourne was interrupted by a shocking dislocated hip.

WORST BRITISH IMPORTS

1. Doug Laughton (Canterbury)
A highly regarded backrower who toured with the 1970 Lions, Doug Laughton was immediately appointed Canterbury captain for the '74 season, but quit the club and returned to England when he was dumped as skipper after half a season. The Bulldogs went on to reach the Grand Final without him, while Laughton signed with Widnes and played a Test on the '79 Lions Tour after winning the Man of Steel award that year.

2. St John Ellis (South Queensland)

A goalkicking winger who had three caps for Great Britain when he signed with the South Queensland Crushers in 1995, St John Ellis racked up just eight games and a single try for the new club before returning to England to play with Bradford. He died in 2005 after suffering a heart attack during pre-season training with Doncaster.

3. Keith Mason (Melbourne)

A tough prop forward who made his bones with Wakefield Trinity, Keith Mason signed with the Melbourne Storm in 2002 but returned to England after playing just four top-grade games in a season and a half. The Welsh international went on to forge a 250-game career with St Helens, Huddersfield and Castleford.

4. Scott Moore (North Queensland)

An England international brought to North Queensland by former Castleford coach Terry Matterson, Scott Moore was gifted the Cowboys No.9 but ceded it after just a month. The quality rake who had spent time with four English clubs was slow and unable to give quick delivery, and was dropped after four games. He played two more matches later in the season before being released to join the London Broncos.

5. Michael Worrincy (Penrith)

A tall and speedy winger who had been—prematurely—handed the nickname 'Black Pearl', Michael Worrincy joined Penrith in 2011 after six years with Harlequins and Bradford. He spent a season playing for Windsor but was unable to break into a Panthers team that ran 12th and returned to England in 2012 to play lower division football with Leigh.

6. Chris Thorman (Parramatta)

A journeyman halfback in his young career before joining Parramatta in 2004, Chris Thorman scored the fastest hat-trick in English league history two seasons before signing on. But his Australian career was limited to just 11 games, with the goalkicking half in and out of the side all season before being released to join Huddersfield.

7. Jordan Tansey (Sydney Roosters)

A talented utility from Leeds, who scored 21 tries in 53 appearances for the Rhinos, Jordan Tansey was a surprise signing by Brad Fittler's Sydney Roosters in 2009. He debuted off the bench in Round 6 and played seven games (for six losses) before he was released to return to Super League and signed with Hull.

8. Lee Jackson (South Sydney, Newcastle)

A 21-Test veteran who joined the Rabbitohs in 1995, Lee Jackson spent four uninspiring seasons in Australia. He played in the Knights' '97 Grand Final success, but an incompetent performance once led Andrew Johns to yell at coach Malcolm Reilly and demand he take Jackson off the field. Jackson returned to England and played on with Leeds, Hull FC and York.

9. Richie Mathers (Gold Coast)
A highly regarded fullback with Leeds, Richie Mathers joined the Gold Coast Titans in 2007 amid great fanfare and expectation. It went unfulfilled, with him playing just six top-grade games before rupturing his ACL. He was released at the end of the year before floating through four Super League clubs to the start of 2014.

10. Andy Platt and Dennis Betts (Auckland)
The Auckland Warriors forked out big cash for decorated British internationals Andy Platt and Dennis Betts to kick off their first campaign in 1995. Both were paid huge sums and both delivered very little—Prop Platt lasted two years and second-rower Betts three, with neither cutting it in the premiership.

GREATEST KIWI IMPORTS

1. Matthew Ridge
All Blacks fullback understudy Matthew Ridge was recruited by Manly's Kiwi coach Graham Lowe in 1990 and was an instant sensation, initially gaining widespread attention for his outstanding goalkicking and later becoming renowned as a courageous last line general and a fine attacking No.1. He scored 1093 points in seven seasons for the Sea Eagles—including a club-record 257 in 1995, the same year he was named Dally M Fullback of the Year—and signed off with a pivotal performance in the '96 Grand Final win over St George before joining the Super League-aligned Warriors for an injury- and suspension-plagued three-year stint.

2. Benji Marshall
Whakatane product Benji Marshall was scouted by the Wests Tigers after taking up a scholarship with Gold Coast school Keebra Park High. After making his debut for the Tigers as an 18-year-old in 2003, his unique brand of attacking genius marked him as a special talent, and he was the dazzling star of the club's stunning premiership success two years later. Marshall subsequently endured several injury-hampered seasons but recovered to steer the Tigers to finals series in 2010 and '11, winning the Golden Boot in '10 and finishing runner-up in the Dally M Medal in '11. The long-serving Kiwi Test captain endured an acrimonious exit from the NRL in 2013 and eventually switched

to Rugby Union—but he left behind club records for tries (76) and points (1118) in 201 games for the Tigers, as well as a legacy as one of the code's great entertainers.

3. Ruben Wiki
Hailing from Auckland, Ruben Wiki burst on to the premiership scene as a powerhouse centre with Canberra, starring with 15 tries as the Raiders surged to a Grand Final triumph in 1994. He reneged on a contract with the Warriors to remain in the Australian capital, and went on to play 225 games and score 60 tries in the lime-green jumper. He then switched to the pack in the late 1990s and became recognised as one of the NRL's toughest forwards. The New Zealand Test appearances record holder saw out his career with the Warriors after leaving Canberra at the end of 2004, retiring with 312 games—the most ever by a non-Australian.

4. Sonny Bill Williams
Auckland-born Sonny Bill Williams won a rookie-season premiership with the Bulldogs as a teenage centre/backrow sensation in 2004. Rangy, fast, powerful and skilful, he quickly earned superstar status and shaped as the player the Bulldogs would build a team around, but controversially walked out on the club in 2008 just half a season into a five-year deal. After playing Rugby Union in France and winning a World Cup with the All Blacks and a Super XV title with Waikato, Williams returned to the NRL with the Roosters. Arriving under intense scrutiny, the statuesque forward made a monumental impact at the club on and off the field as the Tricolours swept to a premiership, and had scored 39 tries in 97 games heading into his farewell 2014 season.

5. Mark Graham
A supremely tough and skilful player regarded as the world's best second-rower during the 1980s, Mark Graham won a BRL premiership at Brisbane Norths in 1980 under his former Otahuhu coach Graham Lowe. After joining North Sydney the following season, the Kiwi Test great won Dally M Second-rower of the Year honours in his first two years at the club and was a driving force as the Bears reached the 1982 finals, their first post-season appearance in 17 years. He captained Norths for several seasons and was a tower of strength amid the club's largely flagging fortunes before departing at the end of 1988 after 146 first grade appearances.

6. Daryl Halligan
Former Waikato Rugby Union fullback Daryl Halligan was a pointscoring phenomenon in a decade with North Sydney and Canterbury, and an underrated winger in general play despite his famous lack of speed. He topped the premiership's pointscoring in his first four seasons—with Norths from 1991 to '93, and Canterbury in '94—before winning a Grand Final with the Bulldogs in '95. Dally M Winger of

the Year in '94, Halligan became the first player to break the 2000-point barrier in his farewell 2000 season, retiring with then Bulldogs records for points in a match (28), season (270) and career (1490). The rock-steady flankman, who crossed for 80 tries in 230 games at club level, rates in the top bracket of goalkickers in NRL history.

7. Tawera Nikau
An intimidating and creative lock who dominated the British club scene with Castleford, Kiwi Test star Tawera Nikau belatedly headed to Australia in 1995 to link with Cronulla. He was a key member of the Sharks side that finished in the top four in '95, qualified for a preliminary final in '96, and reached the '97 Super League Grand Final. He was named Dally M Lock of the Year after joining fledgling Melbourne in 1998, and was unlucky not to collect the Clive Churchill Medal after a commanding second-half display in the Grand Final defeat of the Dragons the following season. The veteran of 114 first grade games departed at the end of '99 but his impact was reflected in the naming of a grandstand after him at Melbourne's Olympic Park.

8. Kieran Foran
A resilient, intelligent and productive five-eighth, Auckland-born Kieran Foran made his first grade and Test debuts as a 19-year-old in 2009. He was outstanding as Manly surged to premiership glory in 2011, building one of the all-time great club halves combinations with Daly Cherry-Evans in ensuing seasons and playing in another Grand Final in 2013. A courageous defender and clever ball-player, Foran had racked up 100 NRL appearances shortly after turning 23, and had become an automatic Kiwi selection.

9. Stephen Kearney
Wellington backrower Stephen Kearney cut his teeth with Western Suburbs, making 46 first grade appearances from 1992 to 1994. The Kiwi Test regular became a foundation Auckland Warrior and was one of the few consistent players in the underperforming club's formative seasons. He returned to Australia with Melbourne in 1999, playing a pivotal role in the club's premiership success in his first season and later captaining the Storm to the finals in 2003 and '04 before departing for Super League. The rugged ball-playing forward finished with 264 first grade appearances (139 of them for the Storm), a then record for a non-Australian player.

10. Nigel Vagana
The greatest overseas try-scorer in premiership history, Nigel Vagana was a wonderful centre for Sydney clubs the Bulldogs, Cronulla and Souths after beginning his first grade career with the Warriors. He was named Dally M Centre of the Year in his first two seasons with the Bulldogs (2001 and '02), equalling one club record with five tries in a match before breaking another with 23 touchdowns in a season in '02—also first

in the NRL—and following that up with 22 tries the next season. Typically potent in three years at the struggling Sharks, Vagana finished his career with two seasons for the resurgent Rabbitohs, and retired with the imposing record of 140 tries in 240 first grade games.

BEST AUSTRALIAN EXPORTS TO BRITAIN

1. Brian Bevan

The greatest try-scorer Rugby League has known and a member of Australia's Team of the Century, Brian Bevan made his top-grade debut with Easts before playing the majority of his decorated career with Warrington. The only member of the Team of the Century to not represent Australia, Bevan scored an inconceivable 796 tries at all levels, including 740 for Warrington in a 17-year career with The Wire that started in 1946. He was top try-scorer in England five times, broke Warrington's all-time tryscoring record in just four years, scored a hat-trick over 100 times and twice scored seven tries in a match. He won two Challenge Cups and three championships while at Warrington, while he scored 29 tries in 18 Tests for Other Nationalities combinations. He is a member of the British Rugby League Hall of Fame.

2. Albert Rosenfeld

The owner of numerous tryscoring records still standing more than a century later, Sydney-born Albert Rosenfeld set England alight as a dashing winger. Touring with the infamous 1908-09 Kangaroos after debuting with Easts in the first year of premiership football in Sydney, Rosenfeld never left England after falling in love. In a 13-year career with Huddersfield he scored 366 tries in 287 appearances, and his 77 tries in 1911-12 and 80 tries a year later remain the top two marks of all time. He rounded out his career with stints at Wakefield Trinity and Bradford Northern, with the diminutive winger revered as one of the greats of the English game.

3. Vic Hey

Named among Australia's 100 greatest players in 2008, champion five-eighth Vic Hey spent the majority of his well-travelled career in England. Hey debuted with Wests and spent three years there before playing in Queensland prior to a move to England. A veteran of six Tests before joining Leeds in 1937 on a record transfer fee, Hey won two Challenge Cups with the Loiners and was named by the *Yorkshire Evening Post* as one of the 10 greatest Leeds players ever. After rounding out his career with Dewsbury and Hunslet, he returned to Australia to captain-coach Parramatta.

4. Arthur Clues
A devastating second-row forward who left Australia in the great exodus of 1947, Arthur Clues played against the 'Indomitables' before etching himself into Leeds folklore. Crafty and boasting a high work-rate, he was named in Australia's 100 greatest players in 2008 but spent just four years in the premiership before an 11-year English career. He represented Other Nationalities 15 times and was at one time regarded as the best second-rower in Rugby League. A legend around the city of Leeds, Clues was one of Australia's great exports.

5. Harry Bath
Often labelled the greatest forward never to play for Australia, the skilful and sly Harry Bath spent the meat of his career starring in England. Debuting for Balmain and winning two premierships, Bath moved to Barrow and then Warrington, where he became one of the most accomplished footballers of his generation. Bath skippered Warrington to victory in the legendary 1953-54 Challenge Cup replay in front of 102,000 fans, while he still holds the record for the most points in a season for the club. 'The Old Fox' returned to Australia in 1957 and won three premierships with St George.

6. Lionel Cooper
A sensational tryscoring winger who left Australia in 1947 when so many of his compatriots moved to England, Lionel Cooper enjoyed a brilliant nine-year career with Huddersfield after emerging as a star with Easts in 1945-46. He scored an astonishing 432 tries in 333 games, including 10 in a game against Keighley. Cooper won a championship and a Challenge Cup with Huddersfield and rates as one of the top Australian outside backs ever to play in England.

7. Pat Devery
A superstar utility back who won three titles with Balmain in his four-year premiership career that also saw him play three Tests against the famed 'Indomitables', Pat Devery signed with Huddersfield at the end of the 1947 season. He starred in an eight-year career at Fartown, playing in the 1949 championship and two Challenge Cup finals including the 1952-53 win against St Helens, the club's most recent Cup win. He still holds the record for most points in a season for Huddersfield with 332 in 1952-53.

8. Tony Paskins
A goalkicking centre who played Rugby Union for Randwick, Tony Paskins signed with Workington Town in 1948 after being uncovered by the great Gus Risman on Great Britain's 'Indomitables' Tour. Paskins spent eight years with Worky, playing in the club's only premiership and Challenge Cup wins, while he played 12 Tests

for Other Nationalities/British Empire. He returned to Australia in 1955 after a seven-year English career, playing with Easts and Manly.

9. Brett Hodgson
An Origin player and a premiership winner with the Wests Tigers, Brett Hodgson moved to England in the twilight of his career but forged a successful playing finale, spending five years with Huddersfield and Warrington. Hodgson was named Man of Steel in his first year after captaining the Giants to the Challenge Cup final. He moved to Warrington in 2011. Hodgson added to his silverware collection in 2012, winning the Lance Todd Trophy for a courageous performance that netted 14 points in the Wolves' Challenge Cup final win.

10. Jamie Lyon
Defecting to St Helens after controversially quitting Parramatta, skilful centre/five-eighth Jamie Lyon enjoyed a good deal of success in two years in Super League. In his first year with the Saints, he was named the 2005 Man of Steel and a member of the Super League Dream Team. In his second year with the club, Lyon won the premiership-Challenge Cup double and was again named in the Super League Dream Team. He scored 586 points (including 44 tries) in 60 games for the Saints, before returning to the NRL and becoming a legend at Manly.

AUSSIE FLOPS IN BRITAIN

1. Mark Carroll
A veteran of nine Tests and seven Origins, outspoken former Penrith, Souths and Manly enforcer Mark Carroll arrived at the London Broncos in 1998 full of confidence and bravado after three straight Grand Final appearances for the Sea Eagles. After being pilloried for his performances with the underperforming Super League club, he returned to the NRL in '99 to finish his career with the Rabbitohs, citing homesickness.

2. Mario Fenech
Fiery, wholehearted South Sydney hooker and captain Mario Fenech took up an offseason deal with Bradford after missing the 1986 Kangaroo Tour squad. The hot-headed hooker, who was slapped with a four-match ban when he was sent off in Souths' sudden-death semi-final loss, played just two matches for Bradford—as a prop against a Kangaroos midweek side captained by bitter rival Ben Elias, and one further club fixture—before returning home.

3. Brett Mullins
A Canberra veteran with more than 100 tries to his name, Brett Mullins joined former Raiders teammate Bradley Clyde at Leeds in 2001—but fans hoping to witness the form Mullins showed on the fields of Britain as a 1994 Kangaroo tourist were left bitterly disappointed. The long-striding fullback was shunted to the bench before playing a handful of games on the wing, and returned to Australia after making just 12 appearances for the Rhinos. He retired after winning a premiership with the Roosters in '02.

4. Willie Mason
Larger-than-life former NRL and representative star Willie Mason joined Hull KR on a three-season contract in 2011, but was unable to obtain a Tongan passport that would have enabled him to come off the club's overseas quota and was released after playing just six matches. His performances for Rovers were underwhelming, and he had already been in strife with club management for meeting with French Rugby Union side Toulon, where he later spent a similarly unsuccessful stint before resurrecting his career at Newcastle in 2012. He was described by Great Britain legend Garry Schofield as the worst Australian player to feature in Super League.

5. Matt Orford
Halfback Matt Orford arrived at Bradford on a three-year deal at the end of 2009— 12 months after winning the Dally M Medal and captaining Manly to a Grand Final victory. But he made just 14 ordinary appearances for the Bulls before succumbing to a shoulder injury and gaining a release to return to Australia, where his reputation took a further battering during a disastrous stint with Canberra.

6. Bradley Clyde
Regarded as the best lock-forward of the modern era, ex-Canberra and Canterbury champion Bradley Clyde's Super League stint with Leeds in 2001 was a disappointing end to a marvellous career. He was hampered by a recurring achilles tendon injury and was released by the heavyweight Rhinos after only 16 appearances.

7. Craig Coleman
South Sydney linchpin Craig 'Tugger' Coleman was in the top bracket of the premiership's halfbacks when he joined Widnes for an off-season stint at the end of 1986. But after making just three appearances, the cheeky No.7 left the 'Chemics' following a highly publicised dispute with coach Doug Laughton. Coleman was somewhat able to salvage his reputation in Britain thanks to subsequent stints with Hull, Leeds and Salford.

8. Greg Florimo
North Sydney club legend Greg Florimo, a 1994 Kangaroo tourist, returned to Britain in the twilight of an admirable career as a much-hyped signing for heavyweights Wigan. After finishing a disappointing 1999 campaign with the Warriors on the bench, he was released to join lowly Super League rivals Halifax.

9. Steve Stacey
A robust winger in Queensland's 1983 Origin series triumph—in which he scored a memorable try in the decider—Steve Stacey spent a controversial, abbreviated stint at Salford during the 1984-85 offseason. The moustachioed Brisbane Easts flyer left the club abruptly after only a handful of appearances, sparking a bitter public war of words with the Salford hierarchy.

10. Josh Perry
Former Test and Origin prop Josh Perry, a dual premiership-winner at Newcastle and Manly, joined St Helens in 2011 as a highly rated recruit. But the aggressive front-rower's Super League tenure was punctuated by subpar form and injuries, and he was restricted to 44 games in three seasons—including just six in 2013.

AVERAGE IN AUSTRALIA, BRILLIANT IN BRITAIN

1. Michael Withers
Versatile back Michael Withers showed promise in a battling Balmain outfit, playing 40 games from 1995 to '98. After linking with Bradford in '99, he became an instant Super League star, appearing in six Grand Finals for the club, including victories in 2001 (in which he scored three tries and won the Harry Sunderland Trophy as man-of-the-match), '03 and '06. Predominantly a fullback, Withers also featured in the Bulls' 2000 Challenge Cup success and three World Club Challenge triumphs, finishing his eight-year tenure at the club with 117 tries from 184 games.

2. Phil Veivers
Unable to get a start at Brisbane Souths due to the presence of Gary Belcher, Phil Veivers—younger brother of former Test captain Greg—instead became a favourite son at St Helens. After venturing to England with Souths teammate Mal Meninga for the 1984-85 offseason, Veivers stayed on, playing 381 games and scoring 98 tries for the powerful Saints. He featured in Saints' premiership final victory in his initial season and three Challenge Cup final losses at Wembley, sealing a cherished place

in the history-steeped club's folklore on his way to becoming among the most highly rated fullbacks in the British game.

3. Bob Jackson

Prop/second-rower Bob Jackson managed just 10 appearances for lowly Penrith in 1982 and '83. After a season at Fulham, Jackson joined Warrington and became one of the most revered clubmen in the history of 'The Wire'. The strong and skilful forward played 222 games for the club from 1984 to '94; also managing to squeeze in an eight-match stint at Cronulla in '86. The blond, moustachioed Jackson played in Warrington's premiership final win in the 1985-86 season, captained the side in the absence of Les Boyd in its loss in the corresponding match the following year, and featured in the Challenge Cup final loss to Wigan in 1990.

4. Rangi Chase

Young Kiwi half Rangi Chase struggled to make an impact in the NRL, displaying moderate form in 32 games across three seasons for Wests Tigers and St George Illawarra. Deciding to try his luck in Britain, he joined Castleford in 2009 and shot to prominence two years later, winning Super League's Man of Steel Award and the media-voted Albert Goldthorpe Medal in 2011. Qualifying on residential grounds, the former New Zealand Maori representative was controversially picked in England's squad for the 2011 Four Nations tournament; he went on to play eight Tests for his adopted country before being axed from the team ahead of their World Cup semi-final showdown with the Kiwis in 2013.

5. Phil McKenzie

Hooker Phil McKenzie was stuck behind former NSW rake Barry Jensen and then Michael Bolt during Illawarra's formative seasons, making just five first grade appearances for the Steelers in 1982 and '83 and eventually joining Group 6 side Picton. But his value did not go unnoticed in Britain, where he became recognised as one of the game's best hookers with Widnes. He was a key member of the club's championship-premiership doubles in 1988 and '89, and its premiership final win in 1990, and also featured in Widnes' World Club Challenge defeat of almighty Canberra in '89. The British passport holder was picked in Great Britain's extended squad for the 1990 Ashes series, but was overlooked for a Test spot against Australia and had to withdraw from a match against France—his last opportunity to play international football. McKenzie, who turned down overtures from Manly during the Graham Lowe era, finished his career in 1996 after three seasons at Workington Town.

6. Scott Dureau

Taree product Scott Dureau was unable to nail down retired legend Andrew Johns' No.7 jumper at Newcastle, making 42 first grade appearances in four seasons.

Recognition awaited in Super League, however, where he steered Catalans Dragons to the 2011 and '12 finals. The clever half was named in the Super League Dream Team in each season, notching up double-figure try tallies and more than 200 points both years, and he was honoured with the Albert Goldthorpe Medal—a media-voted player of the year award—in 2012. He bravely returned to the field during the second half of 2013 after being sidelined by the discovery of a tumour behind his eye.

7. Justin Murphy

Speedy, diminutive winger Justin Murphy scored an extremely modest 11 tries in 43 games for the Bulldogs and Warriors, with the highlight of his five-season NRL career being an appearance in the latter's 2002 Grand Final loss. He became one of Super League's most potent try-poachers, however, bagging 54 touchdowns in just 66 games for Catalans, including 26 tries in the Perpignan-based club's maiden 2006 Super League season, a four-pointer in its historic Challenge Cup final loss to St Helens at Wembley, and a four-try haul in its first-ever Super League finals match—a 46-8 defeat of Warrington in 2008. His spectacular form saw him named in the 2006 Super League Dream Team, and he represented France in the 2008 World Cup after fulfilling residential requirements.

8. George Carmont

A handy centre for rebuilding Newcastle—playing 83 games from 2004 to '07—without earning widespread acclaim, George Carmont was lauded as one of British giant Wigan's best recruits of the modern era. The late-blooming Kiwi scored 81 tries in 154 games for the Warriors, featuring in the club's 2010 Grand Final victory and 2011 Challenge Cup success. Named in the Super League Dream Team in 2008, '11 and '12, he also scored two tries in Wigan's World Club Challenge loss to St George Illawarra early in 2011 and represented the Exiles against England later that season.

9. Luke Dorn

Maitland-born Luke Dorn was one of the NRL's most promising young halves in the early 2000s, impressing with the Northern Eagles and Manly, but a move to the Sydney Roosters in 2004 garnered just one first grade appearance and he instead featured in the club's Premier League Grand Final win. He linked with London and scored 23 tries in his first Super League campaign, and by the end of 2013 had racked up 139 tries in 218 games (encompassing stints at Salford City and Castleford), compared to just five tries in 38 NRL outings.

10. Dennis Moran

Livewire half or hooker Dennis Moran played 36 games for Parramatta from 1997 to 2000 but was predominantly used off the bench by coach Brian Smith. He went on to become one of Super League's most prolific try-scorers, crossing for 95 tries in 156 games for London and Wigan—including outstanding Super League season totals of 22 (2003) and 24 (2004)—and once scored 13 touchdowns in the space of just five matches during one remarkable stint at fullback for the Broncos in '03.

GREATEST TOURING TEAMS

1. 1982 Kangaroos
Captained by Max Krilich and including champions Wally Lewis, Mal Meninga, Steve Rogers, Ray Price, Peter Sterling and Steve Mortimer, the 1982 Kangaroo side became known as 'The Invincibles' after winning all 22 matches, in which they scored a total of 1005 points and conceded just 120. The Test series was a whitewash: Australia won the first 40-4 on the back of eight separate try-scorers; the second, at Wigan, was won 27-6; the third by a margin of 32-8. The Tests against the French were closer but they could not contain winger Eric Grothe; Meninga scored 166 points on tour, while John Ribot topped the tryscoring with 25. Australia did not concede 10 points after their first match.

2. 1963-64 Kangaroos
The first Australian team to win the Ashes on British soil in a half-century, the 1963-64 Kangaroos contained all-time greats from top to tail, with Immortals Graeme Langlands, Reg Gasnier and Johnny Raper matched alongside record-breaking try-scorer Ken Irvine, fullback greats Ken Thornett and Les Johns and hardened forwards Noel Kelly, Ian Walsh and Kevin Ryan. After a first-up 28-2 win at Wembley, the tourists put on 50 points in the second Test in what became known as 'The Swinton Massacre'—when, led by an inspired Raper, the Australian team ran in 12 tries as records tumbled. Australia lost the dead-rubber but went on to down a strong French side 2-1. Arguably no team has contained more talent.

3. 1946 Lions
Known as 'The Indomitables', the 1946 Lions are the only team to tour Australia undefeated. Led by the great centre Gus Risman and including the likes of Willie Horne, Ken Gee and Tommy McCue, the Lions drew the first Test before comfortably winning the remaining two in the first post-war tour. Risman, a veteran of the '32 and '36 Tours, was the star, while Arthur Basset scored a hat-trick in the second Test in Brisbane (a 14-5 win) and followed that up with a double in the last at the SCG.

4. 1986 Kangaroos

Like their 'Invincible' counterparts four years earlier, 'The Unbeatables' marched through Great Britain and France undefeated, with 20 wins from 20 matches. Led by the great Wally Lewis and including superstars Peter Sterling, Mal Meninga and Brett Kenny, the '86 tourists scored 136 tries and conceded just 16. Michael O'Connor and Gene Miles scored hat-tricks in the 38-16 Test series opener, while Garry Jack scored a double in the 34-4 sealer at Leeds. Australia swept the Ashes with a 24-15 win in Wigan and then belted France in two Tests. Terry Lamb played all 20 matches on tour, becoming the first Kangaroo tourist to achieve the feat.

5. 2013 Australian World Cup team

Stung after losing the 2008 World Cup on home soil, the 2013 Australian World Cup team was determined to atone—and atone it did, with a dominant performance that saw the Aussies concede no tries after a close tournament-opening win against England, racking up an incredible 272 points in six outings. Led by champion hooker Cameron Smith, the team included Billy Slater, Greg Inglis, Paul Gallen and Cooper Cronk. The Australians thrashed New Zealand 34-2 in a scintillating final display.

6. 1958 Lions

Losing just once and retaining the Ashes on Australian soil, the 1958 Lions are lauded as one of the most courageous sides ever to strap on boots. Thrashed in the opening Test at the SCG following internal dissent and a level of complacency, the team etched itself into lore in Brisbane during the second Test, in which captain Allan Prescott played 77 minutes with a broken arm and led a side with just eight fit players to a famous victory. Known as 'The Battle of Brisbane' or 'Prescott's Test', it was a testament to the courage of the side that they left the Queensland capital with a series-levelling win. With a skittling showing from hardman Vince Karalius, Britain prevailed 25-18 before five players were hospitalised. A united Lions side were never challenged in the decider, with a Mick Sullivan hat-trick giving Britain a 40-17 win.

7. 1914 Lions

Led by the 'Prince of Centres' Harold Wagstaff and including one of Britain's most famous victories, the 1914 British Lions have been rightly mythologised as one of the greatest teams to leave British shores. Playing a gruelling schedule that included three Tests in eight days, England and Australia were tied up after the first two before one of the most memorable days in the history of British sport, when a 10-man side ravaged by injury held on for a 14-6 victory over an Australian team that included such greats as Frank Burge, 'Pony' Halloway and Harold Horder. Known as the 'Rorke's

Drift Test', the *Sydney Morning Herald* called it "the most heroic exhibition of pluck and determination ever seen on a football field".

8. 1911-12 Kangaroos

The first Australian team to win the Ashes, the 1911-12 Kangaroos were Australia's greatest team for a half-century. Led by halfback Chris McKivat and featuring the likes of Chook Fraser, 'Pony' Halloway, Tedda Courtney, Viv Farnsworth and Howard Hallett, the 'Australasian' Kangaroos enjoyed far more success than their predecessors three years earlier, losing just five of 35 matches and winning the Ashes 2-0. Farnsworth was the star of the first Test win, scoring a double in the 19-10 triumph. The second Test in Edinburgh finished in a draw, but the Kangaroos trounced Britain 33-8 in the decider. Australia would not win the Ashes on foreign soil for another 50 years.

9. 1951 Les Chanticleers

Setting Australian Rugby League alight with their first tour to the southern hemisphere, the 1951 French side is still regarded as one of the strongest teams to play on Australian soil. Led by the great chain-smoking fullback Puig-Aubert, the flamboyant French won the opening Test of the series at the SCG in front of 60,000 fans. The Australian side, which contained the likes of Churchill, Holman, Hall and Graves, won the second Test in Brisbane, but a hat-trick in the decider to the great halfback Jo Crespo saw Les Chanticleers claim the series. They would go on to defeat New Zealand in a two-Test series.

10. 1970 Lions

The last British team to win the Ashes on Australian soil, the 1970 Lions lost just one of their 24 games on tour. With the likes of famed hardman Mal Reilly, champion pivot Roger Millward, tough prop Cliff Watson and captain Frank Myler, the '70 Lions mixed brilliant attacking play with a stunning brutality. Overcoming a 37-15 loss in the opening Test in Brisbane, they bounced back to win the two remaining Tests at the SCG. All three Tests were brutal affairs; the second was decided on the brilliance of Millward, while the decider saw the Lions score five tries to one but only just hold on after the goalkicking performance of Australian fullback Allan McKean. The Lions finished the tour with a cleansweep of New Zealand.

AROUND THE WORLD

TOUR MATCH UPSETS

1. Northern Division crush '88 Lions
Great Britain's tour of Australia in 1988 was rocked by a humiliating defeat three matches in, when it crashed 36-12 to country representative side Northern Division in Tamworth. Fielding a strong side just six days out from the first Test, the Lions trailed by 10 points at halftime and were held scoreless after the break. Moree halfback Ewan McGrady, who went on to win a Rothmans Medal at Canterbury, was the star for Northern Division with a brilliant double.

2. Referee helps French Colts trounce '78 Kangaroos
Les Espoirs—a French Colts outfit—meted out a 20-5 thrashing to the 1978 Kangaroos in Albi, with the outrageous refereeing of Roland Fielvard proving crucial. Fullback Alain Touchagues booted 10 penalty goals for the locals as the tourists copped an incomprehensible 33-2 caning in the penalty count.

3. Australia goes down to southern men
A South Island representative side staged a major boilover against Australia in 1980, edging the tourists out 12-11 at the Addington Showgrounds in Christchurch. Australia led 11-2, but tries to second-rower Kevin Franklin and winger Paul McCone pushed South Island into the lead. Kiwi Test forwards Tony Coll and Mark Broadhurst were outstanding in the tough win.

4. Oudenryn and Eels upset Offiah and Lions
Parramatta rookie Lee Oudenryn set the tone for the evening when he famously beat Great Britain speed machine Martin Offiah in a goal-line-to-goal-line race before the 1992 Lions' tour match against the Eels. Languishing in 14th in the premiership, the no-name Eels produced their most inspiring performance of the season in front of a bumper home crowd of 18,220. Offiah bagged two tries to overturn Parramatta's halftime lead, but the hosts hit back with tries to Scott Mahon and Stu Galbraith to close out a 22-16 boilover. Wily skipper Brett Kenny was outstanding, laying on three of the Eels' four tries. It was to be the Lions' only non-Test defeat on tour.

5. Auckland foils dominant Australia tourists
The Auckland provincial side exacted Australia's first defeat in a non-Test match in nine years in 1989, snaring a come-from-behind 26-24 win at Carlaw Park. Despite resting captain Wally Lewis and Mal Meninga, the tourists managed to field a strong line-up and led 24-18 after a 10-minute, three-try flurry during the second half. A Francis Leota try levelled the scores in the 70th minute, however, before five-eighth Kelly Shelford slotted a penalty goal to seal the upset. After the match Australian coach Bob Fulton bagged referee Ray Shrimpton over the lopsided penalty count. Australia's only losses in the 25 years since the defeat to Auckland have been in Tests against Great Britain and New Zealand.

6. Toowoomba inflicts Lions' sole defeats on consecutive tours
Despite being whitewashed 3-0 by Australia in the Tests on their 1979 and '84 tours, the Lions were successful in their minor matches—except when they travelled to Toowoomba. Great Britain was upset 19-16 by a Toowoomba representative outfit containing former Test forward Greg Platz and future Test forward Rohan Hancock in '79. Toowoomba again proved the Lions' bogey five years later, with a young line-up featuring future stars Mark Hohn, Dan Stains and Peter Gill scoring an 18-16 victory. The Lions won all of their other non-Test matches on both tours.

7. Widnes the last British club to defeat 'Roos
The Kangaroos' last loss to a British club came against Widnes on the 1978 tour, when they went down 11-10 four days after their victory in the first Test. Although distinctly second-string, the Australian line-up included Mick Cronin, who captained the side, and Ray Price—but a try to Widnes winger Shaun Wright and four goals to the locals' other winger Mick Burke negated touchdowns to Ian Schubert and Bruce Walker. Widnes was captain-coached by Doug Laughton.

8. Kiwis suffer history-making losses in Papua New Guinea
New Zealand bore the brunt of the difficulties of touring Papua New Guinea in 1986, crashing to a controversial 20-26 loss to Southern Zone in Port Moresby. Kiwis coach Graham Lowe was livid over the performance of referee Raymond Hoada, who sent off Mark Elia during the first half, awarded two highly questionable tries to the home side, and disallowed a potentially match-saving try to Gary Freeman on fulltime. New Zealand went on to suffer a historic—and equally contentious—24-22 loss to Papua New Guinea in the second Test.

9. Maoris shake up Britain-bound Kangaroos
The 1937-38 Kangaroos embarked on a short tour of New Zealand before setting sail for Britain, but suffered a 16-5 loss to New Zealand Maori at Carlaw Park in between

the two Test fixtures. Legendary former All Blacks fullback George Nepia kicked four goals, while Rangi Chase and a forward named Brodrick scored the locals' tries. Nepia subsequently inspired New Zealand to a 16-15 second Test win in his only appearance for the Kiwis.

10. Balmain rolls Great Britain in controversial clash

The Lions thrashed the mighty St George side 33-5 in 1962 and were expected to do similar to a Balmain side missing Keith Barnes and Arthur Beetson on their '66 tour Down Under. But the Tigers became the first club side to defeat Great Britain, grinding out a rugged 9-8 win at the SCG. The match had an ugly aftermath, with the Lions' star halfback Tommy Bishop accused of striking touch judge Rowley Morris; The NSWRL judiciary suspended Bishop from playing until he submitted a written apology, but the game's referees were furious with the leniency of Bishop's punishment and threatened a boycott of future matches involving the fiery No.7.

Chapter 19

RUGBY LEAGUE MISCELLANY

BIZARRE MATCHES

1. Final forfeit: South Sydney v Balmain, 1909
South Sydney and Balmain agreed to not play the 1909 final after it was scheduled as a curtain-raiser for a Kangaroos v Wallabies clash. Balmain stood firm and refused to play, but South Sydney showed up, kicked off, picked up the ball and scored a try before being awarded the match—and the premiership—on forfeit.

2. Scoreless draw: Canterbury v Newtown, 1982
The only scoreless draw in the history of the premiership, Canterbury and Newtown played out the dour struggle on a wet day in 1982 at Henson Park. Despite the match containing fine attacking players such as Steve Mortimer, Greg Brentnall, John Ferguson and Phil Sigsworth, neither side troubled the scoreboard attendant.

3. The Earl Park riot: St George v Balmain, 1928
The most infamous match in premiership history, a 21-3 St George win against rivals Balmain at Arncliffe set off a riot that lasted well into the evening. Saints fans were incensed at Balmain prop Tony Russell after he kicked star centre George Carstairs in the head and pandemonium ensued—Russell was attacked by spectators, fans were handcuffed to the goalpost and one spectator was seen swinging an axe.

4. Sin-bin Silliness: Parramatta v Newcastle, 2002
Referee Bill Harrigan lost the plot during the Grand Final rematch in 2002 between the Eels and Knights. Parramatta got under Harrigan's skin, resulting in four Eels being sent to the bin—including Michael Buettner, twice. At one stage Parramatta had just 10 players on the field. The Knights came from behind to win the match and Harrigan was dumped the following week.

5. Winter wonderland: Canberra v Wests Tigers, 2000
The only match played under snow in premiership history came in 2000, when a vicious cold snap left Canberra Stadium white for the Raiders-Wests Tigers clash. Canberra won 24-22 in freezing conditions that had trainers running out warm water and sparked genuine concerns about frostbite.

6. British bashing: NSW v Great Britain, 1954
The only game of big-time football abandoned in Australian history, the NSW-Great Britain clash in 1954 started as a farce and ended in chaotic violence. With a Test following soon after, Britain selected a team of players out of position with the sole aim of pummelling NSW's Australian Test contingent. The match was a rolling brawl and referee Aub Oxford abandoned it with 24 minutes remaining.

7. Wilson's winner: Newtown v St George, 1973
The reduction in the value of the field goal from two points to one meant a 1-0 scoreline became possible from 1971. This has occurred just once—in Round 8 of 1973, with a Ken Wilson field goal giving the Bluebags a 1-0 win over St George.

8. Bumper's ear bite: Newtown v St George, 1945
One of the most infamous matches in premiership history, the Newtown-St George clash in 1945 is remembered as the game St George prop Bill McRitchie had a piece of his ear bitten off. The man accused of the heinous act was Newtown enforcer Frank 'Bumper' Farrell, but the Bluebags skipper was sensationally acquitted. Newtown won the match 23-11 and McRitchie never played again.

9. Belmore walk off: North Sydney v Canterbury, 1970
The opening-round clash of the 1970 season between Norths and Canterbury was a spiteful affair that spilled over into a massive brawl after skipper Ken Irvine was the victim of some late knees. When Bears lock John McDonnell was sent off, Irvine let rip at referee Keith Page and was also sent off. Irvine then ordered the rest of Norths to leave the field in incredible scenes before coach Roy Francis and prop 'Chicka' Norton kept the Bears on the paddock. Norths lost 16-14 and Irvine received a three-week suspension for leading the team off.

10. Field Goal Shootout: St George v Parramatta, 2006
In an age in which field goals have become a rarity, few were expecting the first three scores of a 2006 clash between the Dragons and Eels to be one-pointers. Wet conditions saw scores locked 0-all after 70 minutes before the Eels' John Morris broke the deadlock and Ben Hornby responded with two drop goals to put the Saints up 2-1. Matt Cooper scored the only try of the match on the last play—which also saw Eels halfback Jeremy Smith shove referee Sean Hampstead—for a final score of 8-1.

INCREDIBLE THRASHINGS

1. St George def Canterbury 91-6 (1935)
The biggest rout in premiership history—and a record likely to stand the test of time, having already survived 80 years—St George thrashed newcomers Canterbury 91-6 in Round 5 of 1935. Max Hollingsworth scored four tries, Les Griffin had a personal haul of 36 points, and all 13 Saints starters scored points in the greatest drubbing of them all.

2. Eastern Suburbs def Canterbury 87-7 (1935)
A week after losing by a record 85-point margin, Canterbury went down to Eastern Suburbs 87-7 in what is still the second-largest margin in premiership history. Dave Brown scored a record 45 points through five tries and 15 goals, and Easts ran in an amazing 19 tries.

3. Australia def England 50-12 (1963)
Known as 'The Swinton Massacre', Australia shocked England in the second Test of the 1963-64 series with a 50-12 rout that sealed the Kangaroos' first series win in England in 52 years. Ken Irvine scored a hat-trick, Graeme Langlands posted 20 points, and seven Aussies crossed for tries in one of the Ashes' most devastating wins.

4. Parramatta def Cronulla 74-4 (2003)
Parramatta thumped Cronulla 74-4 in the biggest post-war premiership margin and one of the Sharks' most embarrassing showings. The team that included future internationals Paul Gallen, Greg Bird and Keith Galloway conceded 14 tries, with Jamie Lyon running in five. The Eels missed five shots at goal, while Cronulla—who eventually had captain David Peachey marched for dissent—attempted a field goal late in the match. Incredibly, the scores were locked 0-all after 20 minutes ... in the rain!

5. NSW def Queensland 56-16 (2000)

The Blues became the first team in Origin history to run in 50 points when they humiliated Queensland to the tune of 56-16 in the dead-rubber third game of the 2000 series. It remains the biggest margin in the concept's history, with Ryan Girdler's personal haul of 32 also an Origin record. Queenslanders sight that match as the one that reestablished the steely resolve that has guided them to eight straight series wins.

6. Manly def Melbourne 40-0 (2008)

It was the largest margin in Grand Final history when Manly whacked Melbourne 40-0 to claim its first premiership in 12 years and send club legend Steve Menzies out a winner. The Sea Eagles went into the game as only the barest of favourites but the Storm could not handle missing suspended captain Cameron Smith. Winger Michael Robertson scored a hat-trick for the Eagles, who led 8-0 at the break and ran rampant in the second stanza to break the 38-0 Grand Final record held by Easts for 33 years.

7. Melbourne def St George Illawarra 70-10 (2000)

Defending premiers Melbourne had lost their first four games of the 2000 season and had endured plenty of taunting at the hands of Dragons star Anthony Mundine in the lead-up to the Grand Final rematch in Round 5. But the Storm made Mundine eat his words with a 70-10 belting at the MCG. The Storm had nine individual try-scorers in what is possibly the most shocking result in premiership history.

8. New Zealand def South Sydney 66-0 (2006)

The biggest away win in premiership history, the Warriors belted the Rabbitohs 66-0 at ANZ Stadium midway through 2006. Reserve Lance Hohaia scored a hat-trick, Brent Webb and Jerome Ropati crossed for doubles, and Tony Martin finished with 22 points in the incredible road rout. Souths won just three games that season, while the Warriors also failed to make the playoffs.

9. NSW def Queensland 69-5 (1957)

In what was the biggest thrashing in pre-Origin interstate battles, NSW ran rampant in the dead-rubber third game of the 1957 series, romping home 69-5 at the SCG. Keith Holman and Ian Moir scored hat-tricks, Dick Poole and 'Poppa' Clay bagged doubles, and Greg Hawick kicked 15 goals in the demolition job.

10. Australia def Russia 110-4 (2000)

The greatest margin in World Cup and Test history, Australia thumped minnows Russia 110-4 in front of 3044 fans at The Boulevard in Hull. Australia ran in 19 tries through 11 individual try-scorers, with Ryan Girdler scoring an incredible 46 points from three tries and 17 goals, and Wendell Sailor crossing four times.

TEAM STREAKS

1. St George—11 straight premierships
St George's 11 straight premierships from 1956 to 1966, probably the most amazing accomplishment in Rugby League, is a record that will never be beaten. (It was also a record in any senior football league in the world until surpassed by Latvian soccer team Skon FC.) The Saints won 10 minor premierships on the way to their incredible accomplishment, which led to any number of rule changes. Norm Provan played in 10 of the title wins, and winger Johnny King scored in six straight deciders. Only Parramatta has won three straight premierships since.

2. Queensland—8 straight Origin series
The Maroons' domination of State of Origin started in 2006 and stood unbeaten at eight series heading into the 2014 season. Before '06 the biggest consecutive series-winning streak was just three—achieved by both the Blues and Maroons twice apiece. Queensland has won 17 of the 24 games during its incredible run; half Johnathan Thurston has played in every match and Greg Inglis, Cameron Smith and Nate Myles have appeared in every series.

3. Eastern Suburbs—19 consecutive wins
Eastern Suburbs holds the premiership record for most consecutive wins, coming out victorious in 19 straight matches in the 1975 season to smash the previous record of 16. After opening the season with a win and two losses, the Jack Gibson-coached Tricolours did not lose again until the opening week of the finals, when they were shocked 8-5 by St George. Considered one of the great club sides of all time, the Roosters bounced back to down St George 38-0 in the Grand Final. Only the 2002 Canterbury side's run of 17 has come close to Easts' record since.

4. Eastern Suburbs—35 matches without a loss
The great Eastern Suburbs team of the mid-1930s did not lose a game in 35 consecutive outings. From their 15-2 win over Balmain in Round 9, 1935 to their 21-14 loss to Souths in the second round of the 1938 season, the unbeaten Easts won 31 times and drew four, and collected three straight premierships along the way. Pointscoring records from the '35 season by Easts' Dave Brown still stand 80 years later.

5. University—42 consecutive games lost

Defunct club University holds the inglorious distinction of the longest losing streak in premiership history with 42 straight defeats from Round 2, 1934 to Round 14, 1936. Varsity defeated Norths 4-3 in the opening round of the '34 season and did not taste success again until the final round of the '36 season, when a Harry Ratcliffe double helped them to a 13-11 win over St George. It was University's last win; the club quit the competition after going 0-8 in 1937.

6. Australia—6 consecutive World Cups

After splitting the first six World Cups three apiece with Great Britain, Australia put together six World Cup triumphs on end. The green-and-golds won the 1975, '77, '88, '92, '95 and 2000 versions of international Rugby League's showpiece, a streak that spanned 26 years and included 33 wins, a draw and just four losses.

7. St George—23 consecutive finals series

Almost as incredible as St George's run of premierships was the club's appearance in 23 consecutive finals series. The Saints made the playoffs from 1951 to 1973, encapsulating their title streak of 11 in a row; incredibly, they lost six preliminary finals, won 12 minor premierships and did not win a Grand Final outside of those 11. The Dragons' streak started just after the Korean War and finished 18 months before the end of the Vietnam War. St George finished eighth in 1974.

8. Parramatta—6 consecutive wooden spoons

The hapless Parramatta Eels of the 1950s hold the record for most consecutive wooden spoons, running last from 1956 to 1961. Parramatta had already won three wooden spoons before its streak to give the club nine in its first 15 years of existence. During their streak, in which they had three seasons of 2-16, two of 3-15 and one of 4-13-1, the Eels employed four coaches and failed to beat Manly or Western Suburbs.

9. North Sydney—488 straight games scoring

Despite winning just two premierships in their existence—and being widely regarded as easybeats for much of their time in the big league—the North Sydney Bears hold the record of most consecutive games in which they troubled the scorer. Their run of 488 games on the board lasted for 28 seasons from 1943 to 1970 before eventual premiers South Sydney finished the run in Round 8, 1970, winning 24-0. In second place for pointscoring streaks is Canberra, who scored in 361 straight matches.

10. St George Illawarra—219 Games Scoring a Try

St George Illawarra holds the record for most consecutive premiership games scoring a try, crossing the stripe in 219 straight matches from Round 4, 2000 until Round 18,

2008. The streak, which surpassed previous record-holder Canberra's run of 206 in the 1990s, started after the Bulldogs rolled the Dragons 24-0 in the third round of the 2000 season and ended when Melbourne thumped them 26-0 late in '08.

ICONIC GROUNDS

1. Sydney Cricket Ground
The home of Rugby League from 1913 until 1987, the Sydney Cricket Ground was as renowned for its League fixtures in the winter as its cricket in the summer. The Moore Park venue has played host to more premiership matches (1121), more finals (224), more Grand Finals (53) and more Tests (67) than any other. The SCG regularly hosted the match of the round and was home to many of Rugby League's most historic moments, including Australia's 1950 Ashes win, all of St George's 11 straight premierships, and John Sattler playing on with a broken jaw. The ground continues to be used for special occasions, including hosting the Centenary Test in 2008.

2. North Sydney Oval
Rugby League's most picturesque ground, North Sydney Oval was the home of the Bears from 1910 until their merger with Manly at the end of 1999, and is the third-most-used venue in premiership history. Opened in 1867, North Sydney Oval was renowned for its white picket fence, giant fig tree and rock-hard cricket pitch. The last premiership game was played at the ground in 2005 by South Sydney, but it remains in use for sub-premiership level League. Norths legends Duncan Thompson and Ken Irvine have stands named after them at the gorgeous venue.

3. Lang Park
The home of Rugby League in Brisbane, Lang Park hosted its first game in the 1930s. It became the code's official base from 1955 and maintains that position today as the rebranded Suncorp Stadium. Known as the ground that Rugby League built for the amount of money put into upgrading facilities by the QRL, it has hosted all major events in Queensland Rugby League, including the most Origins (48) and a host of internationals including the 2008 World Cup Final. Its high, steep stands lend an atmosphere of enclosure that has seen the ground become known as 'The Cauldron'. The venue, which has statues of Queensland legends Wally Lewis, Darren Lockyer and Arthur Beetson out the front, continues to play host to some of Rugby League's biggest matches.

4. Leichhardt Oval

Balmain's home ground from 1934 until their merger with the Wests Tigers, Leichhardt Oval was once one of Sydney's top League venues, and remains the part-time home ground of the joint venture to this day. With a giant hill on one side and stands named after Tigers legends Norm 'Latchem' Robinson and Keith Barnes on the other, Leichhardt once hosted interstate matches and was the regular site of midweek night fixtures due to its state-of-the-art lighting (the venue hosted every midweek cup final from 1974 to '86). It is the most popular suburban venue in the competition today and regularly draws large crowds for Sunday afternoon Rugby League.

5. Henson Park

Newtown's home ground from 1936 until the club's demise at the end of the 1983 season (and Eastern Suburbs' home ground in 1987 and '90), Henson Park was one of Sydney's most popular venues. The ground, with a giant hill and old scoreboard, as well as the King George V stand, hosted the only 0-all draw in premiership history and witnessed such memorable moments as American Manfred Moore throwing a ball over the grandstand. Newtown Park remains the home of the Jets' NSW Cup team, with the crowd figure regularly announced as 8972, the club's last official crowd.

6. Redfern Oval

Known as 'The Holy Land' by South Sydney fans, the ground was the home venue for the Rabbitohs from 1948 to 1987, and remains the club's training venue. When a premiership ground, Redfern Oval held more than 20,000 people and played host to many famous moments, including Clive Churchill's sideline conversion with a broken arm. Souths played three games at the ground in 1996 before it was redeveloped into a public space, and still plays an annual 'Return to Redfern' pre-season match.

7. Belmore Sports Ground

Opened in 1920, Belmore Sports Ground was the home to Canterbury from its second season in 1936 until the end of 1998. With the Stewart Stand on one side and the Terry Lamb Family Hill on the other, the ground hosted 602 premiership matches (fifth in competition history), including finals in 1936 and '97. The ground was one of the first in Sydney to get floodlights and had more than 20,000 to its opening—a pre-season night match against Wests, when the ground changed from an oval to a rectangular shape. After redevelopment in the late 2000s, Canterbury returned to training at the venue and hopes to play a premiership match again at its traditional home base.

8. Sydney Sports Ground

One of Sydney's most famous sporting venues, the Sydney Sports Ground hosted 826 premiership matches from 1911 to 1986 before it was knocked down and replaced by the Sydney Football Stadium. The home ground of the Eastern Suburbs Roosters, the Sports Ground ran east-west, meaning the sun was a perennial problem at the venue. The ground hosted 11 premiership deciders between 1929 and '51, including Balmain's famous 13-12 win in 1946. The ground saw the largest individual points haul in premiership history when Dave Brown scored 45 points in Easts' 87-7 win over Canterbury in 1935.

9. Royal Agricultural Ground
Sydney Rugby League's first home ground and the site of the first Rugby League game played in Australia, the Royal Agricultural Ground at Moore Park was a regularly used ground from 1908 to 1930, but hosted just five matches across the next 57 years. The Agricultural Ground, which was surrounded by a brick wall and featured the famous clocktower, hosted six premiership deciders, including the first three premiership finals, but was demolished and repurposed in the 1990s. The venue was the site of the first Ashes Test on Australian soil.

10. Pratten Park
The home of the Western Suburbs Magpies from 1912 to 1966—with Wests playing matches sporadically at the ground until 1985 after moving to Lidcombe Oval—Pratten Park had few conveniences and seemed to represent the battling nature of the club. It was renowned for being an extremely imposing venue for opposition teams.

COINCIDENCES

1. Newtown dominates landmark scorelines
Before being excluded from the premiership at the end of 1983 the Newtown club was part of two pockets of history. The first came in 1973, when the Bluebags defeated St George with a solitary field goal at the SCG, producing the premiership's first-ever—and only—1-0 final score. The scoreline had not been possible until two years earlier, when the value of a field goal was reduced from two points to one. Ken Wilson, the highest point-scorer in the club's history, kicked the historic one-pointer. Wilson also featured at the second historical event nine years later—as captain of Newtown when it participated in the competition's only scoreless draw, in the game against Canterbury at Henson Park. Remarkably, Newtown was victorious in the first of just three 2-0 scorelines in premiership history—against Easts in 1914, and in the maiden 3-0 result, which was against Glebe in 1910, a low-scoring result which has been repeated just five times.

2. Kiwi namesake wingers in succession of crazy coincidences

In Round 4 of 2010 North Queensland unveiled debutant Will Tupou on the wing against the Titans in Townsville. The following day Bill Tupou played his first NRL match for the Warriors against Manly in Auckland. The 19-year-olds were born just 18 days apart in 1990, both in Auckland, but the amazing similarities did not end there—enjoying impressive rookie seasons, both flyers made 12 appearances in 2010 and finished with four tries apiece. Will Tupou struggled to forge a top-grade spot with the Cowboys the following season and eventually switched to Rugby Union; Bill Tupou featured in the Warriors memorable charge to the 2011 Grand Final, but went off the boil and was released to join Canberra midway through '13.

3. ET's handfuls five years apart

Andrew 'ET' Ettingshausen scored a Cronulla club-record five tries in a match on two occasions exactly five years apart—the only times he crossed more than thrice in his 328-game career. On 27 August 1989, he bagged five tries in a 46-14 final-round drubbing of Illawarra, becoming the first player in more than a decade to achieve the feat. He repeated the dose at the expense of South Sydney on 27 August 1994, snaring a five-try haul in a 42-0 success, also in the last round of the season. Both landmark tryscoring performances were at Shark Park.

4. Jeremy Smith squared

Two Kiwis named Jeremy Smith played in the NRL during the 2000s: Jeremy James Smith was a halfback for Parramatta and Souths; Jeremy Jon Smith was a highly rated backrower for Melbourne, St George Illawarra, Cronulla and Newcastle. Remarkably, the pair both made their Test debuts for New Zealand in 2007. It was an inauspicious introduction to international football, however, with the Kiwis subjected to a record 58-0 mauling by Australia. Jeremy James finished with three Test appearances and joined Super League side Salford City in 2009; Jeremy Jon won Grand Finals with Melbourne (2007) and the Dragons ('10), and represented the Kiwis in 22 Tests.

5. Craig Smith squared

Melbourne and St George Illawarra each fielded a player named Craig Smith in the 1999 NRL Grand Final, with goalkicking winger Craig Smith manning the flank for the Storm while Queensland and New Zealand representative Craig Smith packed down in the front row for the Dragons. Melbourne's Craig Smith unwittingly etched his name into Rugby League folklore by being awarded a penalty try that decided the premiership after he was knocked unconscious by Jamie Ainscough as he was about to score. He retired after the Grand Final, while the other Craig Smith left the Dragons at the end of 2001 and went on to enjoy impressive stints at Wigan and Newcastle and play 12 Tests for the Kiwis. The Cowboys also fielded a player named Craig Smith in

1999—he came off the bench in the final round of the season against Norths in his only NRL appearance, four years and one day after the Storm's Craig Smith made his first grade debut for the Bears.

6. Broncos' tryscoring debuts against Cowboys

Brisbane players have enjoyed a remarkable tryscoring strike rate when debuting in Round 1 clashes against North Queensland at Suncorp Stadium. In 2009, wingers Antonio Winterstein and Jharal Yow Yeh notched four-pointers in a 19-18 victory. The following season, Matt Gillett crossed in his maiden first grade outing, and Israel Folau also dotted down on club debut; it was the turn of debutant three-quarters Jack Reed and Dane Gagai in 2011. In previous opening-round derbies between the Queensland clubs, Darius Boyd scored the Broncos' only try on debut in 2006, while Joel Moon scored his first NRL try in his fourth appearance in '07.

7. Struggling Roosters and Sharks notch same scoreline in '09

Enduring similarly disastrous NRL campaigns, the Sydney Roosters and Cronulla produced at least one notable feat in 2009—the cellar dwellers faced off in Rounds 8 and 16 and came up with matching scorelines. The Roosters won 19-12 on both occasions, which is all the more coincidental given field goals were only kicked in 18 per cent of regular season games in '09. Tricolours outside backs Sam Perrett and Shaun Kenny-Dowall bagged tries in both encounters. The battling rival clubs were both inundated with off-field dramas and finished the season with five wins apiece, the Roosters taking out the wooden spoon due to an inferior for-and-against.

8. Randwick Rah Rahs reunited in Roosters v Rabbits reserves

Randwick flyhalf Russell Fairfax played eight Tests for the Wallabies from 1971 to 1973 before switching codes to join Easts in '74. Ken Wright, another 'Galloping Greens' No.10, played nine Tests for the Wallabies from 1975 to 1978 before being lured to the professional code in '79, also by the Roosters. Wright and Fairfax were clubmates in 1979 and '80, playing five-eighth and fullback respectively in the '80 major semi—Fairfax's last game for the Tricolours before being released. Fairfax joined Souths and, remarkably, came head-to-head with Wright in a reserve grade clash in Round 6 of 1981—the former Union stars were opposing five-eighths and captains, with Fairfax's Rabbitohs prevailing 15-13 over Wright's Roosters. Fairfax retired at the end of '81; Wright linked with Souths.

9. 'Johnson & Johnson' fullbacks for City and Country

In a unique occurrence, brothers Lin and Dick Johnson were opposing fullbacks in the annual City Firsts v Country Firsts fixture in 1941. Canterbury custodian Lin was in the City side that beat Newcastle-based Dick's Country outfit 44-21. Lin played 90 first grade games for the Berries and represented NSW in one match in 1940; Dick played 91 first grade games for Newtown, Souths, Wests and Canterbury, and made 11 appearances for his state from 1938 to 1945.

10. Deserters Mason and Williams burn Bulldogs

Polarising Test forward Willie Mason's relationship with the Bulldogs' hierarchy disintegrated at the end of 2007 and he was granted a release to join archrivals the Sydney Roosters. His exit strained his relationship with several ex-clubmates—in particular close buddy Sonny Bill Williams, who publicly slammed Mason. In an ultra-hyped clash early in '08 Mason scored two tries for the Roosters in their 40-12 thrashing of the Bulldogs. Ironically, Williams would later repeat Mason's adding-insult-to-injury feat—after infamously walking out on the Bulldogs a few months after the '08 match, he returned to the NRL in 2013, joined the Roosters … and grabbed a double in a 38-0 early season rout of the Bulldogs.

SCANDALS

1. The Super League War

It was the scandal that tore Rugby League apart. Desperate to win the pay-TV rights to Rugby League in Australia in the early 1990s, Rupert Murdoch's News Limited pressured the ARL to sell the subscription rights as well as rationalise the competition; however, media tycoon Kerry Packer, who owned the free-to-air rights, believed he owned all broadcast rights. In 1994, Super League CEO John Ribot proposed a breakaway competition, which led to open warfare the following season, with eight clubs signing with Super League and 12 remaining loyal to the ARL. Player salaries went through the roof as the competing sides chased the best talent; court action was ongoing for the next three years; Super League signed all international bodies, while Super League-aligned players were banned from ARL representative football in '95 and '96. The split resulted in two separate competitions in 1997 before the warring parties reunited in '98 under the NRL banner. News Limited did not cede ownership of the game until 2012.

2. Kevin Humphreys

The seventh president of the NSWRL, Kevin Humphreys, was an autocratic ruler from his appointment in 1973 to his unsavoury fall in 1983. He was an autocratic ruler with a vision, though, and played a key role in bringing Rugby League to television, the formation of State of Origin, and the cleaning up of the game from cheap thuggery. However, in May of 1983 he was given little choice but to resign after *Four Corners* ran a story entitled 'Big League', which centred on the acquittal of renowned gambler Humphreys on charges of misappropriating $52,519 from Balmain Leagues Club in 1977. The scandal led not only to Humphreys' resignation, but also the jailing of judge Murray Farquhar and the temporary standing-aside of premier Neville Wran.

3. The Storm's salary-cap scandal

Melbourne Storm were the standard-bearers in the latter half of the first decade of the 2000s, playing in four straight Grand Finals and winning deciders in '07 and '09. However, those titles along with three minor premierships and the 2010 season were stripped by the NRL when the Storm were found to have systematically rorted the salary cap under the leadership of CEO Brian Waldron. The club was also fined $1.68 million and forced to dismantle its team to comply with the cap and play the 2010 season for zero competition points. Included in the rort were 'second' contracts guaranteeing money outside of the cap to star players and a boat given to Greg Inglis. The Storm initially accepted the punishment, then pursued court action before withdrawing it.

4. The Bulldogs' salary-cap scandal

The Canterbury Bulldogs were the prohibitive premiership favourites in 2002 when they were deducted 37 premiership points and fined $500,000 for systematic breaches of the salary cap. With three rounds remaining, the Bulldogs had won 17 straight games and had all but wrapped up the minor premiership when the scandal broke following an investigative piece by the *Sydney Morning Herald*. By the end of the week, Canterbury was found guilty of breaching the salary cap by more than $1 million across the 2001-02 seasons. David Gallop immediately issued the severe sanctions, and Bulldogs powerbrokers Bob Hagan and Gary McIntyre were forced to resign in disgrace.

5. Bobby Lulham poisoned

A speedy winger with Balmain who scored an incredible 85 tries in 85 games and played nine games for NSW and three Tests for Australia, Bobby Lulham had his career cut short by a poisoning scandal that gripped Sydney in 1953. The star three-quarter nearly died after being poisoned with thallium by his mother-in-law, who it was later revealed in court had been sexually involved with Lulham. He survived, but was divorced by his wife and never played Rugby League again.

6. The ear-bite incident

Newtown captain Frank 'Bumper' Farrell is widely regarded as one of the toughest, most feared props ever to play top-level Rugby League—and one incident that certainly helped solidify this reputation was the allegation that he bit off Bill McRitchie's ear in a clash between Newtown and St George in 1945. McRitchie spent 22 weeks in hospital and never played top-level Rugby League again after having part of his right ear bitten off. After a seven-month investigation, Farrell was cleared—though he did change his story over the years and no other player was ever charged.

7. Len Smith overlooked

The greatest selection controversy in the history of Australian Rugby League was the omission of NSW and Australian captain Len Smith for the 1948-49 Kangaroo Tour. Smith had led NSW to a 3-1 series win and had captain-coached Australia to a 1-all series draw with New Zealand mid-season, playing 1948 in such good form that he was named Ernie Christensen's Player of the Year. Reasons remain unclear for his shockingly exclusion for the Kangaroo Tour, but most theories centre on sectarianism (Smith was a Catholic while most of the League powerbrokers were masons) and the coaching ambitions of selector Norm 'Latchem' Robinson. Smith quit the game after the selection blunder, and Australia lost the Ashes 3-0.

8. The founding fathers executed

Three of the central figures in the formation of Rugby League in Australia—James Giltinan, Henry Hoyle and cricket great Victor Trumper—were unceremoniously ousted in the lead-up to the game's second season amid charges of financial mismanagement and political secrecy. Giltinan was not even in the country when he was dumped, returning from the famous (and financially disastrous) 1908-09 Kangaroo Tour; Hoyle, president of the League, resigned after being accused of receiving League funds improperly; and Trumper was brought undone when League money was found in a personal bank account. None were accused of dishonesty but all were driven from the game in one of League's darkest and most controversial moments.

9. The 1963 Grand Final

Without question the most controversial in premiership history, the 1963 Grand Final was marred by allegations of corruption against referee Darcy Lawler, a renowned gambler who is alleged to have had a £1200 bet on St George. Western Suburbs prop Jack Gibson, who mixed in betting circles, got wind of the scandal and informed his teammates. The way the mud-soaked game was officiated did little to quell the anger of Western Suburbs players. The Magpies lost the penalty count 18-7 and the most controversial of tries was scored by Saints winger Johnny King—who was tackled, with Lawler allegedly calling held, but scooted away for the match-winner without playing the ball. St George won 8-3 and Lawler never officiated in another game.

10. The Coffs Harbour allegations

NRL was rocked heading into the 2004 season when a 20-year-old woman accused a number of unidentified Canterbury players of gang-raping her on a pre-season trip to Coffs Harbour. While no charges were ever laid, the allegation did significant damage to the Bulldogs brand. Canterbury went on to win the premiership that season, but the club was widely taunted for its involvement and subsequent handling of the scandal, which led to the resignation of CEO Steve Mortimer and the sacking of football manager Garry Hughes.

11. Balmain forfeits 1909 final

One of Rugby League's most enduring controversies took place in the game's second season, when South Sydney reneged on an agreement with Balmain not to play the 1909 final. The two teams were aghast that the premiership decider was to be a curtain-raiser for a fourth 'Kangaroos v Wallabies' match—an "insult" according to the Tigers. Balmain players formed a picket line outside the ground, but Souths kicked off, scored a try against no opposition, and were awarded the title on forfeit. Souths, to this day, deny that an agreement was ever reached with Balmain.

12. John Hopoate's infamous finger poke

Controversial Sea Eagles and Wests Tigers winger John Hopoate's Rugby League career saw him reach the heights of NSW and Australian representation and a premiership with Manly—and the lows of numerous suspensions. The most infamous of these incidents came with the Tigers in 2001, when, in an attempt to unsettle the opposition North Queensland Cowboys, he inserted his finger into the anus of three players. The Tigers immediately sacked Hopoate, who gained worldwide notoriety for the dirty act.

13. Ryan Tandy's rort

Journeyman forward Ryan Tandy found his way to Canterbury midway through the 2010 season and had been at the club less than three months when he became the central figure in an alleged betting rort—an unprecedented plunge on the first scoring play in a clash with the Cowboys to be a North Queensland penalty goal. Tandy made an error during the opening set and then conceded an obvious penalty under the sticks, but the ruse came undone when the Cowboys took a tap and scored a try. Tandy was sacked by Canterbury, banned by the NRL and charged by NSW police.

14. Jets, Magpies kicked out

In 1984 financial difficulties and geographic constraints saw the League kick both Newtown and Western Suburbs out of the premiership in a controversial decision that incensed two passionate fan bases. Western Suburbs immediately filed a court injunction and was given a stay of execution, but the Jets accepted their fate. Both clubs raced to get to Campbelltown to broaden their geographic footprint. Wests, with greater resources, made it first and survived. They continue to exist today as a merged entity with Balmain. Newtown never returned to the premiership and now competes in the NSW Cup.

15. Newtown flops in '44 final

Defending premiers the Newtown Bluebags were the heavy favourites to win the 1944 title after winning the minor premiership and then defeating St George 55-7 in the opening semi-final. But question marks were raised about how hard the Bluebags tried the following week in the final against Balmain, a match described by the *Daily Mirror* as "disgraceful and shocking". In the days before mandatory Grand Finals a win by the minor premiers in the final secured the title while a loss allowed for a Grand Final challenge—a Newtown loss would guarantee a rematch and a second gate. The Bluebags indeed lost the final (with Balmain backed into heavy favouritism) and spent Grand Final week addressing charges that they tanked. Those allegations subsided, however, when the Tigers won the premiership 12-8 the following week. Newtown denied throwing the '44 final, blaming injuries and withdrawals for the loss.

16. Lay-down Tigers

One of the great—and most controversial—Grand Final upsets broke what would have been a run of five straight titles for the great South Sydney team of the late 1960s and early '70s. The Balmain Tigers were huge underdogs heading into the 1969 decider, with Souths losing just four times all season. The two-time defending premiers booked their way into the Grand Final via a 14-13 win over Balmain in the major semi, but the Tigers turned the tables on decider day with an 11-2 win. The Tigers' game-winning plan (which consisted of lying down, feigning injury) was devised by first-year coach Leo Nosworthy and later admitted to by star half Dave Bolton. The tactic succeeded in halting the rhythm of Souths' star-studded backline, who could manage just two points in one of the most famous Grand Finals of all.

17. George Bishop and the '52 Grand Final

The 1952 Grand Final was shrouded in controversy, with South Sydney skipper Jack Rayner adamant that the Rabbitohs were robbed by referee George Bishop following a significant plunge on Western Suburbs. On the back of a great side that contained 'The Little Master' Clive Churchill, Souths had won the premiership in 1950 and '51 and would win from 1953 to 1956, but the money was one way for Wests. Bishop never refereed another game after a 15-4 penalty count in favour of Wests, along with a controversial disallowed try to Bunnies backrower Ken Macreadie and a try to Magpies back George Bain off a blatant forward pass, saw the Magpies win 22-12.

18. Arthur Beetson snubbed

One of the game's all-time greats, an Immortal and a member of the Team of the Century, Arthur Beetson was peerless among forwards throughout the late 1960s and 1970s. After debuting for Australia in 1966 as a 21-year-old, he would eventually play 28 Tests in the green and gold. Following the retirement of Graeme Langlands, Beetson became Australia's first Indigenous sporting captain in 1975, leading the British leg of the World Series before controversially being overlooked for the opening game of the 1977 World Cup against New Zealand. ARL chairman Kevin Humphries refused to accept the selectors' team, but Beetson stood down from the match on principle. He returned for the remainder of the Cup, leading Australia to the '77 title in his final international.

19. Sonny Bill Williams walks

Sonny Bill Williams was the player around whom Canterbury intended on building in the late 2000s, only to have the talented backrower walk out on the club in the first season of a five-year contract. Williams was already a premiership winner and Kiwi international when he penned a five-year deal in 2007 that would keep him at Belmore until the end of the 2012 season, but controversially fled to France in July 2008, quitting the Bulldogs to play Rugby Union. He was forced to pay the Bulldogs $750,000 in compensation and was banned from Rugby League until 2013—at which point he returned to the NRL and won a premiership with the Sydney Roosters.

20. Les Boyd breaks Darryl Brohman's jaw

State of Origin's most infamous moment came in the opening game of the '83 series. New South Wales enforcer and decorated international Les Boyd believed he had been given a green light by Australian selectors to wreak havoc on Queensland and ended up smashing Darryl Brohman's jaw with a vicious cocked elbow. Boyd was suspended for 12 months and never played rep football again. Brohman, who missed a likely Test call-up as a result of the injury and successfully sued Boyd, played just one more Origin three years later before becoming a cult media identity.

RUGBY LEAGUE AND GAMBLING

1. Darcy Lawler and the 1963 Grand Final
The 1963 decider between St George and Western Suburbs is undoubtedly the most controversial Grand Final in premiership history. The Saints had won the previous seven but the Magpies, with their all-star team that included Arthur Summons, Noel Kelly, Peter Dimond and Jack Gibson, were confident of ending the run in '63. It wasn't to be. Gibson, an SP bookmaker and cohort to underground casino operators, told senior Wests players before the match that referee Darcy Lawler had placed £1200 on St George. The game was mired in controversy. Wests were disallowed two tries many considered legitimate, while Johnny King was awarded a try after being tackled and the Saints won 8-3 on a muddy SCG. Lawler, who never refereed again, always denied betting on the match, but Wests players remained adamant they were robbed.

2. Ryan Tandy
A solid if unspectacular forward who had been through four clubs by the time he arrived at Canterbury midway through the 2010 season, Ryan Tandy was at the Bulldogs less than three months when he allegedly took part in an unsuccessful micro-betting rort. In the lead-up to the Canterbury-North Queensland affair in Townsville there was an unprecedented plunge across the country on the first scoring play being a Cowboys penalty goal, the TAB reporting that 95 per cent of first scoring play action was on that option. On the first set of the match Tandy committed a handling error, and on the Cowboys' first set gave away an obvious holding-down penalty under the sticks. However, the plot was foiled when the Cowboys opted to take a tap and scored a try. Player agent Sam Ayoub, lower grader Brad Murray and former journeyman John Elias were all alleged to be part of the scam. Tandy was later arrested and banned from playing Rugby League for life.

3. The 1994 Rothmans Medal plunge
Betting on the Rothmans and Dally M Medals was banned for 15 years after a plunge on David Fairleigh in the 1994 Rothmans Medal embarrassed the League. An honest backrower for North Sydney with plenty of ability, Fairleigh had represented NSW in 1991 and '93 but was overlooked in '94 after what was widely considered no more than a solid year—but after an apparent leak he was backed from 33/1 into even money and duly won the award. The League did not allow official betting on its best player award until the 2010 season.

4. Sean Long and Martin Gleeson

Great Britain internationals Sean Long and Martin Gleeson were both suspended in 2004 for betting against their team, St Helens, to lose by eight-plus in a clash with Bradford. The two Saints stars knew their team would be resting 11 members of the starting side and each wagered £1000, both using accounts in their own name. Bradford won 54-8 and both players were fined £7500, with Gleeson, who played in the match, suspended for four months and Long, who did not, for three. Long returned later that season to win the Lance Todd Trophy in the 32-16 Challenge Cup final win. Five years later Long claimed that more players were involved from both St Helens and Bradford.

5. John Elias

Rugby League journeyman John Elias—who played for six premiership clubs during a colourful 12-season career in the 1980s and '90s—was a central figure to an alleged match-fixing episode in 1994 in a clash between Western Suburbs and South Sydney that involved four players from each side. A connection of convicted Sydney gangster Neddy Smith reportedly gave Elias $25,000 to in turn give to four of his Souths teammates to underperform, while four Wests players were offered the same amount to play out of their skin. Wests won the game—in which Elias came off the bench for the Rabbitohs—though the rort was apparently called off. Channel Seven named Craig Field, Darrell Trindall, Tyran Smith and Jacin Sinclair as the four Souths players but was successfully sued for defamation over the allegations.

6. George Bishop and the 1952 Grand Final

Like the 1963 decider 11 years later, the 1952 Grand Final was shrouded in a betting-related controversy, with South Sydney accusing referee George Bishop of conspiring against the Bunnies and helping Wests to the win. Souths opened $1.50 to win the decider before drifting alarmingly to $2.50, with all the money coming for the Magpies. Souths were on the receiving end of some atrocious decisions and an obscene penalty count—the most controversial call being a disallowed try from a forward pass on backrower Ken Macreadie—and Wests won 22-12. Souths skipper Jack Rayner said he never spoke to Bishop again, despite both living in the same suburb.

7. Eddie Hayson

Controversial Sydney racing identity and brothel owner Eddie Hayson, who had close links to a number of Rugby League players, including Andrew Johns, was implicated in an alleged betting rort at the end of the 2009 season. The match in question was between the Sydney Roosters and North Queensland, and saw the Roosters let a 16-0 lead slip through their fingers to lose 32-16. Hayson was never charged with any wrongdoing.

8. Shaun Leaf

Captain of Championship 1 side Doncaster, Shaun Leaf was suspended for betting against his side in 2011 in a Challenge Cup affair against Super League outfit Wakefield. Leaf placed £200 on Wakefield to cover the 38-point start against Doncaster—which they did, winning 50-10 and providing him with a winning bet. The skipper did not play in the match. He admitted to this bet—and another against Doncaster in Toulouse—to *The Sun* newspaper and was banned for 18 months, but rejoined the club in 2013.

9. Brent Todd

Veteran Kiwi prop Brent Todd was a rugged type who walked a fine line between tough and dirty throughout his seven-season career with Canberra and Gold Coast, during which he won premierships in 1989 and '90 and represented New Zealand in 28 Tests. In 2007, he was sentenced to 12 months home detention in New Zealand after being found guilty of playing a central role in a poker-machine fraud.

10. Andrew Johns

Immortal and Team of the Century halfback Andrew Johns was caught up in one of the most famous racing scandals of the 21st century—the fabled 'More Joyous' inquiry. Johns and bookmaker Tom Waterhouse had engaged in a conversation on the sideline before the Dragons-Roosters Anzac Day match centring on horse More Joyous, trained by Waterhouse's mother Gai. More Joyous failed the next day in the All-Aged Stakes, leading to a fallout between Gai and owner John Singleton relating to information that had been passed to him alleging Tom had told Johns the horse was "off". Waterhouse was cleared of saying any such thing and Johns admitted to exaggerating the claims to brothel owner Eddie Hayson at a Rugby League match at Brookvale Oval.

RUGBY LEAGUE AND DRUGS

1. The 2013 ASADA investigation

Announced as "the blackest day in Australian sport" by a host of Government ministers, sports administrators and ASADA operatives, Rugby League was not spared in ASADA's revelations that Australia's major sporting codes were infiltrated with the use of performance enhancing drugs. Cronulla quickly became the focus, accused of running a systematic doping scheme—coach Shane Flanagan missed the opening two games of the 2013 season and was suspended for all of 2014, and other key staff members were sacked. Canberra winger Sandor Earl became the first player suspended after admitting to using a banned peptide during his time at Penrith.

2. Paul Hayward

A cheeky five-eighth with Newtown in the 1970s, Paul Hayward became the centre of one of the biggest Rugby League stories in the history of the game in 1978 when he was arrested in Bangkok attempting to import 8.4kg of heroin to Australia. He was sentenced to 30 years in prison. He was granted a royal pardon in 1989 and returned home to Australia, but had become a heroin user while in prison and contracted HIV. He died of a heroin overdose in 1992.

3. Peter Jackson

A beloved figure in Rugby League across the late 1980s and early '90s, Peter Jackson was a brilliant five-eighth/centre who played 17 Origins for Queensland and nine Tests for Australia between 1986 and 1992. But the popular clubman with Souths in the BRL, and Canberra, Norths and Brisbane in the Sydney premiership battled depression throughout his life, and in 1997—at the age of 33—was found dead from a heroin overdose in a Sydney hotel room.

4. Robbie O'Davis, Adam MacDougall and Wayne Richards

Knights stars Robbie O'Davis, Wayne Richards and Adam MacDougall all received significant suspensions in 1998 after testing positive for drug use. O'Davis, a Queensland and Australian representative, and Richards received 22-game bans after being found guilty of using performance-enhancing drugs, and MacDougall, who had made his debut that season, was suspended for 11 weeks after being found guilty of having an abnormally high epitestosterone-to-testosterone ratio. Richards was sacked by the Knights and played just one more season with Souths, while O'Davis immediately returned to the Queensland Origin team and MacDougall enjoyed a long career that ended in 2011.

5. Rodney Howe

Melbourne prop Rodney Howe reached Test and Origin honours for the first time in 1998. But the barnstorming prop, who starred in the '98 Origin series, was later barred for the maximum 22 weeks after positive for banned steroid stanozolol. He returned in 1999 and was immediately rushed into the NSW Origin team before helping Melbourne to an inaugural premiership triumph in September.

6. Andrew Johns

An Immortal and the Team of the Century halfback, Andrew 'Joey' Johns is revered as one of the game's greatest. His reputation took a significant blow post-retirement, however, when he was caught leaving a London nightclub in 2007 in possession of an ecstasy tablet, and subsequently admitted he took recreational drugs throughout his career as he battled depression and bipolar disorder. His drug use was a central discussion point when his name was raised as the potential eighth Immortal but enough voters felt his contribution on the field was enough to overcome his admissions off it.

7. Craig Field and Kevin McGuinness
The Wests Tigers faced a difficult second season in 2001, and the drugs crisis that centred on two of their highest-paid stars was just one of the dramas engulfing the club. The scandal revolved around centre Kevin McGuinness, who admitted to taking 11 ecstasy tablets, and halfback Craig Field, who was found guilty of cocaine use—both were suspended by the NRL for six months. McGuiness played two more seasons in the NRL, but Field never played another top-grade match.

8. South Sydney Scandal 1990
After a lightning raid on the battling South Sydney club by the Australian Sports Drug Agency in 1990, the NRL was rocked by revelations that 10 Rabbitohs had tested positive to recreational drugs. Young utility back Scott Wilson—the only player to be publicly named—was immediately sacked by the club for his positive reading for cocaine. Wilson joined Norths, but was stood down for a time after reportedly failing another drug test. Drug use became the biggest hot-button issue in Rugby League that year, exacerbated by reports unnamed players from Brisbane and Easts had tested positive to marijuana.

9. Brad Williams
Brad Williams became the first player in premiership history to admit to using steroids when he revealed to *Rugby League Week* in 1983 that he had gained 20kg after using steroids (which were not yet outlawed) and engaging in an intense weightlifting regimen. The Parramatta winger was being regarded as a potential Australian winger when the story broke but was dropped by coach Jack Gibson the next week and didn't play again for the remainder of the year. Williams spent one more season with the Eels—where he played just one top-grade game—before rounding out his career with a year in Canberra.

10. Andrew Walker
Dual international Andrew Walker's career ended in disgrace when he was suspended for two years for cocaine use. He had burst on to the scene in the 1990s as a supremely talented half with the Dragons and Roosters before defecting to Rugby Union. A return to the NRL with Manly in 2004 lasted just one season before he received the two-year drug ban and immediately announced his retirement from professional football.

RUGBY LEAGUE JAILBIRDS

1. Paul Hayward
Paul Hayward was a tough, wiry five-eighth for Newtown from 1973 to 1978, who played 78 first grade games and toured New Zealand with a Combined Sydney side in 1976. In October 1978, he was arrested in Thailand and convicted—along with Warren Fellows and William Sinclair—for attempting to smuggle 8.4kg of heroin into Australia. Hayward spent the better part of a decade behind bars in the notorious Bangkwang prison, setting a record for time spent in the 'Bangkok Hilton' before receiving a royal pardon in 1989 and returning to Australia. He had contracted HIV while in prison, and died of a heroin overdose in Sydney in May 1992. Hayward's prison plight was exposed in harrowing detail in a controversial, award-winning feature by *Rugby League Week*'s Neil Cadigan in 1984, and Fellows released a best-selling book, *The Damage Done*, about their experiences in 1997.

2. John Elias
One of Rugby League's most renowned off-field rogues, journeyman forward Elias—who played 133 first grade games for six Sydney clubs (1983-94) and won a BRL premiership with Brisbane Souths in 1985—frequently found himself on the wrong side of the law. He was jailed for nine months in 1995 for supplying drugs, gun possession and prohibited articles possession. After coaching stints with the Lebanon national side and in the French domestic competition, Elias was convicted of maliciously shooting his business partner in the leg by a jury in 2004. He was facing up to 25 years in prison, but eventually served just four.

3. Les Mara
Talented five-eighth Les Mara, who made 80 first grade appearances for Balmain, Souths and Newtown from 1975 to 1982 and represented NSW in two interstate matches while with the Tigers, was given a maximum 20-year jail term in 2007 after pleading guilty to being part of a cocaine importing conspiracy involving corrupt airport baggage handlers. He was arrested on the NSW South Coast after an 18-month manhunt encompassing Europe, South America and Canada.

4. Victor Spink
A lower grade centre with Balmain and a backrower in two first grade games for Newtown in 1968, Victor Spink later became a notorious Sydney drug baron and was 'Mr C' in the mid-1990s Jockey Tapes scandal, which was inadvertently uncovered

when the Australian Federal Police were covertly taping him. He was jailed from 1996 to 2002 over one of Australia's largest drug importations—15 tonnes of cannabis resin then worth $225 million.

5. Garry Sullivan
Hardworking Kurri Kurri lock Garry Sullivan, who played 107 games in six seasons at Newtown and featured in seven Tests for Australia from 1970 to 1972, encompassing two World Cups, slipped into a life of crime after his retirement, committing 14 armed robberies that netted more than $3 million from 1985 to '91 before a long stint behind bars.

6. Ricky Montgomery
In 2007 Ricky Montgomery, who played two first grade games at hooker for Souths in 1984 with Mario Fenech sidelined, was convicted of attempting to import 30kg of cocaine into Australia four years earlier. Then, in 2013, he was reportedly involved in a prison punch-up with fellow Rugby League jailbird Les Mara in a Lithgow facility.

7. Danny Wicks
A burly, mobile and dynamic prop/second-rower in 69 games for St George Illawarra and Newcastle from 2006 to '09, Danny Wicks was arrested in December 2009 on drug-possession and supplying charges. In September 2011 he was being found guilty of drug trafficking and sentenced to a maximum of three years in jail, and was released in March 2013 after serving half his sentence. The NRL imposed a ban on Wicks playing Rugby League until October 2014, thwarting his bid to play for Group 2 club Lower Clarence.

8. Chris Nahi
Aggressive backrower Chris Nahi played 46 first grade games for the Gold Coast Chargers, represented Rest of the World and New Zealand Maori, and later turned out for multiple Queensland Cup clubs. Then, in 2005, he fled during a police raid that uncovered 1000 ecstasy tablets and remained on the run for eight days before turning himself in. He was sentenced to three-and-a-half years jail on drug and deprivation of liberty offences the following year. After being released in '08 and playing for Currumbin Eagles in the '08 Gold Coast Grand Final, Nahi was slapped with a two-year ban by the QRL in 2009 for testing positive to ecstasy.

9. Craig Field
A lively and tempestuous halfback for Souths, Manly and Wests Tigers, Craig Field played 183 first grade games from 1990 to 2001—including a Grand Final loss with the Sea Eagles in '97—before a suspension for testing positive to cocaine while at the Tigers ended his NRL career. He was then arrested and charged with murder in

July 2012 following the fatal king-hitting of a man outside a hotel in Kingscliff, but was released on strict bail conditions in December that year. Field has been committed to stand trial in the Supreme Court for murder and causing grievous bodily harm.

10. Whetu Henry
Big Wellington prop Whetu Henry played four Tests for New Zealand in 1977 and '78—two of them alongside his brother, lock Whare. He later spent 18 months in jail after being one of 14 players from Eastern Suburbs convicted of manslaughter in connection with the death of Mongrel Mob gang member Lester Epps in Wellington in 1981.

11. Russell Packer
Beefy prop Russell Packer played 110 games for the Warriors from 2008 to 13, featuring in the club's 2011 Grand Final loss to Manly and representing New Zealand in one Test at the end of that season. After slipping down the pecking order in Auckland, he was snapped up by Newcastle ahead of the 2014 season, but was charged with assaulting a 22-year-old man following a drunken incident in Sydney in November 2013. The Rugby League world was stunned to learn the 24-year-old Packer had been sentenced to two years in jail in January 2014 after pleading guilty to assault occasioning actual bodily harm.

12. Andrew Frew
Andrew Frew was a robust finisher for Parramatta, Manly, Northern Eagles, Huddersfield, Wakefield Trinity, Halifax and St George Illawarra, scoring 59 tries in 115 NRL and Super League games from 1997 to 2004. In 2013, he was convicted of extortion and admitted to blackmailing a 58-year-old postman. Frew, a drug addict, accused the victim of sexually abusing his prostitute girlfriend 20 years earlier, threatening him with physical violence and demanding $100,000. The victim paid $2000 before going to the police, and Frew was sentenced to one year in jail.

13. Joe Kilroy
Flamboyant winger/fullback 'Smokin' Joe Kilroy was a BRL cult figure of the 1980s for Norths and Brothers, finally breaking into the Queensland Origin side for two appearances in '88 as a foundation Brisbane Bronco. The Harley-riding, handlebar-moustachioed Indigenous flyer was jailed in 1989 on marijuana-trafficking charges. He returned to play one last first grade game for the Broncos in 1991.

14. Suaia Matagi
Powerhouse Warriors prop Suaia Matagi spent his teenage years involved with gangs, and in 2006, as a 17-year-old, was sentenced to three years in prison for a violent assault. He found religion and vowed to get his life back on track upon release, playing for

clubs in the Auckland competition, and eventually the Auckland Vulcans, the Warriors' NSW Cup feeder club. In one of 2013's most remarkable stories, the then 25-year-old won an NRL call-up, as well as an army of admirers for his full-throttle performances, and went on to play 11 rookie-season matches and represent Samoa at the World Cup at the end of the year. His rise to first grade came at the expense of Warriors stalwart Russell Packer, who, in a sad irony, was jailed for assault early in '14.

15. Jason Ferris
A goalkicking half who played 123 games for Canberra, North Queensland, Cronulla, Northern Eagles and Manly from 1996 to 2003, Jason Ferris was sentenced to 18 months in prison in 2010 for various driving offences, including stealing $7500 from his former employers at a Gundagai hotel. His sentence was reduced on appeal.

16. Dave Watson
An instinctive attacking player capable of filling any position in the backline, Dave Watson played 15 Tests for New Zealand from 1989 to 1993 while plying his trade with several British clubs. He was jailed in England in 1991 on a drink-driving charge, banned for three months for testing positive to cannabis while playing for Halifax, and received a four-month suspended jail term for assaulting a nightclub owner in 1994, while at Bradford-Northern. Watson went on to spend a season each with Cronulla, Balmain, Gold Coast and South Queensland from 1994 to '97 before returning to England and featuring in Sheffield Eagles' famous upset of Wigan in the '98 Challenge Cup final.

17. Phil Bancroft
A stalwart of the Canterbury and Auckland club scenes, halfback Phil Bancroft played one Test for New Zealand on the Kiwis' 1989 tour of Great Britain and France. After retiring, he was handed a three-year jail sentence for drug dealing.

18. Colin Scott
A BRL stalwart with Easts and Wynnum Manly, Indigenous fullback Colin Scott played 17 Origins for Queensland from 1980 to 1987 and a solitary Test for Australia in 1983, while he was a foundation Brisbane Bronco in '88. He spent several months in a Maryborough prison in 2007 for a spate of driving offences.

19. Ambrose Morgan
Souths junior and renowned off-field scallywag Ambrose Morgan played three first grade games for the Rabbitohs in 1975. The Indigenous prop, who spent a spell in jail on robbery charges, was shot dead in Sydney's Railway Square in August 1975 by a former associate allegedly seeking revenge.

20. John Ryan
John Ryan scored nine tries in six Rugby Union Tests for Australia, but his code switch with the Penrith Panthers was largely disappointing, garnering just 54 games and 14 tries from 1977 to 1980. He was subsequently arrested after committing a series of armed robberies to feed a gambling habit, and died in prison in 1982 aged just 33.

RUGBY LEAGUE AND POLITICS

1. Michael Cleary
One of just five Australians to represent the country in three separate sports, Michael Cleary was an outstanding athlete with true speed as a Rugby Union and Rugby League winger and Commonwealth Games sprinter. After playing six Tests for the Wallabies, he joined South Sydney in 1961 and embarked on a stellar Rugby League career in which he was widely regarded as the fastest player in the premiership throughout the 1960s. After winning his first Test jersey in 1962, he won bronze in the 100-yard sprint at the Commonwealth Games. Cleary scored 88 tries in 144 appearances for the Rabbitohs, winning two premierships with the club, before a farewell season with Eastern Suburbs in '71. Three years after his retirement, he was elected as the Member for Coogee and served for 17 years. He was the Minister for Sport and Racing in the Wran NSW Labor Government.

2. Mal Meninga
Long discussed as a potential Immortal, Mal Meninga is one of the game's finest-ever centres—a premiership-winning captain with Canberra, captain of both Queensland and Australia and the only man to make four Kangaroo Tours. But one of Rugby League's greatest players later embarked on one of politics' shortest careers when he made a bungled and ill-advised foray into ACT politics. Retiring after the '94 premiership triumph, Meninga coached the Raiders from 1997 to 2001. Upon stepping down, he declared his intention to run for the ACT Legislative Assembly as an independent—a campaign that lasted 28 seconds into his first radio interview, where Meninga walked out declaring, "I'm buggered, I'm sorry, I have to resign." In 2006 he was a surprise choice as Queensland coach—but has since etched himself further into state and Rugby League folklore by leading the Maroons to an incredible eight straight series wins.

3. Paul Osborne

A fair prop over a nine-season career with St George and Canberra, Paul Osborne retired after his finest game—a match-winning hand as a late call-up in the Raiders' 1994 Grand Final victory. In a masterful decision from coach Tim Sheens, Osborne, who had not played since Round 15 before being recalled for the suspended John Lomax, set up the first two tries and was unlucky to miss out on the Clive Churchill Medal. He then rode this performance to a seat as an independent in the ACT Legislative Assembly, enduring a controversial six-year political career where he voted against moves to decriminalise abortion and euthanasia, had his political party deregistered, and forced the resignation of Chief Minister Kate Carnell. Since losing his seat in 2001, Osborne served a controversial stint as Parramatta CEO and became a commentator with ABC Grandstand.

4. John Fahey

The former NSW Premier and Federal Finance Minister in the Howard Government, John Fahey, was a fine junior footballer who was graded by Canterbury—he never rose above reserve grade but continued to play in Group 6. He became the Member for Camden in 1984 in the NSW Legislative Assembly and, after serving as a minister in the Greiner Coalition Government, was appointed Premier in 1992 when Greiner was forced to resign. He served as Premier until 1995, when his Government lost in a landslide to Bob Carr. Fahey moved to federal politics in 1996 and was a minister in the Howard Government until resigning in 2001 due to health reasons. He is currently the President of the World Anti-Doping Authority.

5. Ron McAuliffe

Known affectionately as 'The Senator' in Queensland, Ron McAuliffe had a brief career with Brisbane Norths but rose to prominence as the game's supremo north of the Tweed. Elected BRL boss in 1952 and QRL boss in '53, he ran Rugby League in Queensland for more than three decades, stepping down two years before his death in 1988. He was elected on to the ARL board in 1973 and was the man most responsible for establishing State of Origin. Long after his rise to the top administrative post in Queensland Rugby League, McAuliffe was elected as an ALP Senator from Queensland in 1971 and served until 1981, famously accompanying Gough Whitlam on to Lang Park and, after a cacophony of boos and hisses, being told by the then Prime Minister, "I didn't realise you were so unpopular".

6. Glenn Lazarus

The only player to win premierships with three separate clubs, Glenn Lazarus scored an unlikely political victory at the 2013 Federal Election, winning a senate seat for the Palmer United Party. A tough and skilled prop forward dubbed "The Brick With Eyes", he is regarded as one of the finest to play his position after a stellar 254-game career for Canberra, Brisbane and Melbourne, and in 2008 he was named as one of the top 100 players ever to grace a Rugby League field in Australia. At the time of writing Lazarus remains a Senator in the Australian Federal Parliament.

7. Henry Hoyle
One of Rugby League's founding fathers, having chaired the meeting at Bateman's Crystal Hotel that led to the formation of the NSWRFL in 1907, Henry Hoyle had previously served in the NSW Legislative Assembly from 1891 to 1894 as a member of the Protectionist Party. After the 1908-09 Kangaroo Tour led to his dismissal as NSWRFL president, he re-entered politics as the ALP Member for Surry Hills, a position he held from 1910 until his defeat in 1917 after quitting Labor over conscription.

8. Kevin Ryan
Kevin Ryan is regarded as one of the hardest and toughest men to play Rugby League—he was nicknamed 'Kandos' after the cement-producing town—and was also one of the most successful. After representing Australia in Rugby Union, he became a dual international in 1964; he won seven premierships in seven seasons with St George before bringing an end to the Dragons' 11-season reign when joining Canterbury as captain-coach in 1967. In 1973, Ryan unsuccessfully ran for the seat of St George as the ALP candidate, which he eventually won 1976, serving as the Member for the seat until 1984 when he was dumped by the ALP. He also served as Mayor of Hurstville from 1974 until 1979.

9. Graham Annesley
A long-serving premiership referee between 1982 and 1997, Graham Annesley refereed Test, Origin and finals football and was long regarded in the top echelon of the game's officials. He signed with Super League during the split in the mid-1990s and is credited with introducing the video-referee system. After retiring in 1997, he rose through the ranks of the NRL administration before losing by just over 600 votes when he contested the NSW Electorate of Miranda as a Liberal candidate. Recontesting in 2011, Annesley won the seat on a mammoth swing and was immediately appointed the Minister for Sport in the new O'Farrell Government. He quit parliament in 2013 to become the chief executive of the Gold Coast Titans.

10. Mick Veivers
A bruising forward from a fine Queensland sporting family, Mick Veivers was selected for Australia from Souths Brisbane in 1962 and played a total of six Tests, four after he moved south to Manly for a five-season stint, but was kept out of the '68 decider with a knee injury. In 1987 he won the Queensland Electorate of Southport as a National, and served until 2001. He eventually became Sports Minister but was shocked by the nastiness of politics, which he said Rugby League had nothing on.

RUGBY LEAGUE AND MUSIC

1. Tina Turner's anthems
In one of the great marketing coups in the history of Australian sport, the NSWRL acquired American R&B queen-turned-rock-goddess Tina Turner to promote the premiership in the late 1980s and early 1990s. Turner's massive hits *What You Get Is What You See* and *The Best* were used as the game's anthems—complete with flashy videos featuring Turner and a bevy of Rugby League stars—and were incredibly well received, attracting new and wider audiences. The slogan "Simply the Best" became synonymous with the Winfield Cup, and a rerecorded duet of *The Best* by Turner and Jimmy Barnes was subsequently used as the theme song in 1992-93. Turner performed at the 1993 Grand Final, celebrating with the victorious Broncos on the field post-match.

2. Frank Hyde: Player, coach, commentator, crooner
Frank Hyde was an outstanding centre for Newtown, Balmain and North Sydney, and surely would have represented Australia if not for World War II. But it was as a radio commentator that he became entrenched as one of Rugby League's most beloved characters, calling 33 straight Grand Finals. Hyde's dulcet match-calling tones also translated to a wonderful singing voice, and he released three albums during the 1970s: *Frank Hyde Sings*, *Frank Hyde's Party Sing-a-long* and *Frank Hyde Sings for the Good Times*. Best known for his rendition of the Irish classic *Danny Boy*, Hyde released the song as a single (with *Try a Little Kindness* as the B-side) on Parlophone Records in 1973; the song reached No.7 in the Sydney Top 40.

3. Hoodoo Gurus rework a classic
Legendary Australian rockers the Hoodoo Gurus provided the best and most enduring anthem of the NRL era when they reworked their most successful hit—1987's *What's My Scene*—into the rousing *That's My Team*. Ahead of the 2003 season, the NRL approached former Cronulla and NSW Origin backrower Alan Wilson to assist with a new advertising campaign, and Wilson convinced Gurus front-man Dave Faulkner to rewrite the lyrics of *What's My Scene* to embody the passion of Rugby League fans and their anticipation of the new season. The band had been on hiatus since 1998, but reformed to record the new version; band members wore Cronulla and Western Suburbs jumpers in the original promo (Faulkner is a Sharks supporter). It was used as the NRL's theme song until 2007.

4. The Wiggles get behind the Tomahawks

The USA Tomahawks were the surprise packet of the 2013 World Cup, advancing to the knockout stages in their debut at the tournament with victories over Cook Islands and Wales. Australian children's music group The Wiggles, massively popular around the world, decided to honour the Tomahawks' pool-stage heroics with group founder Anthony Fields—a Wests Tigers fanatic—penning a tribute song, *USA Tomahawks Shocked the World*. A clip for the song attracted tens of thousands of views within days, while a line in the song urged "President Obama ... to carve the face of Joseph Paulo on Mt Rushmore" in reference to the Tomahawks' star player.

5. Rookie takes it to the top

Highly marketable with his boyish good looks, flowing locks and surfie style, North Sydney wonderboy Jason Martin apparently had the Rugby League chops to back up the fanfare, winning the Dally M Rookie of the Year award in 1990 and going within a whisker of touring with the Kangaroos. He was also handy with a guitar and could hold a tune, prompting Australian music icon Molly Meldrum—who saw Jason Donovan-esque qualities in the burgeoning footballer—to produce a single by Martin, *Take Us to the Top*. The video featured several Bears teammates posing as a back-up choir for the chorus. But the song was awful, and sales were poor. Martin's career on the field followed the opposite trajectory to that proclaimed by his song, petering out with disappointing stints at Newcastle and North Queensland.

6. The Ipswich Connection

The unbridled popularity of the Brisbane Broncos in south-east Queensland was exploited by the release of many questionable products, including 'Alfie' Langer potato chips. But nothing could compare to the two-song cassette released by The Ipswich Connection, a group made up of Langer and the Walters twins, Kevin and Kerrod. Side A contained *Hey, Hey We're the Broncos*, a tuneless and rather unimaginative reworking of The Monkees' 1967 *(Theme from) The Monkees*. The B-side was *Broncos Rap*, which made Anthony Mundine's 2005 collaboration with *Australian Idol* finalist Joel Turner, *Knock You Out*, sound like a Notorious B.I.G. cut. Predictably, the cassingle sold like hotcakes.

7. Power goes out on Billy Idol

The NRL ramped up its Grand Final entertainment in 2002 by hiring famous British rocker Billy Idol to warm up the crowd pre-match. The singer responsible for huge 1980s MTV hits *White Wedding*, *Dancing With Myself* and *Hot in the City* was revved up for a big performance, screaming "I love my footy!" after arriving at the stage via hovercraft. But the power cut out on the hapless Idol, who was left floundering on stage for several minutes before he pulled the pin altogether.

8. Indie-rock bands pay homage to Rugby League heroes

Hailing from the Sydney suburb of Miranda, indie-rock trio Soap Star Joe named their 2003 EP *Ziggy Niszczot (Never Played Guitar)*. Niszczot had been a popular winger for five seasons at Souths, playing two Origin matches for NSW in 1982 and captaining the Rabbitohs to the '84 finals. The cover of the EP featured a smiling, cherub-like figurine decked out in a South Sydney team uniform and footy boots, holding an oval ball. In early 2014, You Beauty released the concept album *Jersey Flegg*, described as "a pub rock opera about a '90s Rugby League legend who has fallen on tough times". Harry 'Jersey' Flegg was Easts' inaugural captain in 1908 and achieved legendary status as the NSWRL's president from 1929 until his death in 1960; the Jersey Flegg age-group competition was named in his honour.

9. 'What a Game', warbles ageing Welshman

In 2000, Welsh pop megastar Tom Jones became the NRL's first major recording artist to be used in a season promotion since Tina Turner when Salt-N-Pepa's 1993 hit *Whatta Man* was reworked into the Rugby League-centric *What a Game*. The accompanying video featured Jones, then 59, on stage with several leggy dancers, interspersed with shots of on-field action and supporters. The song was terrible and was not used in subsequent campaigns.

10. Bon Jovi comes to 'Our House'

The NRL reverted to big-name, veteran overseas talent for its promotional campaign in 2011, buying the rights to Bon Jovi's *This Is Our House*. Best known as the hair-metal superstars responsible for drunken dancefloor sing-a-long *Living on a Prayer*, the group's frontman John Bon Jovi penned the song—which first appeared as a bonus track on a Greatest Hits compilation—with the intention of it becoming a sports anthem; it was also used by NHL team the New Jersey Devils. Despite sounding dreadful, *This Is Our House* received an overwhelmingly positive reception from the Rugby League public (a microcosm of Bon Jovi's career in general, it could be argued), but the NRL's bid to get the band to perform at the 2011 Grand Final was unsuccessful. The song was used again in 2012 before being replaced by the infinitely more listenable *Something's Got a Hold on Me* by Australian singer Jessica Mauboy.

RUGBY LEAGUE AND MOVIES AND TELEVISION

1. Matt Nable

Backrower Matt Nable played eight first grade games for Manly and Souths from 1991 to 1995 and spent '97 with the London Broncos before turning his hand to acting and screenplay writing. He wrote and starred in the film *The Final Winter*, which depicts the trials and tribulations of a Rugby League player in the early 1980s and also starred Nable's good friend Matthew Johns. Nable went on to feature in the TV series *Underbelly* and *Bikie Wars*, and several films, including 2013's *Riddick*.

2. Wes Patten
Pocket-sized halfback Wes Patten made his first grade debut for Balmain as a 19-year-old in 1993—the same year he guest-starred as Kevin Baker in three episodes of long-running Australian soap *Home and Away*. A child actor in Australian TV movies *Hector's Bunyip* (1986) and *Shadows of the Heart* (1990), he also appeared in six episodes of the TV miniseries *Heartland* (aka *Burned Bridge*, starring Cate Blanchett and Ernie Dingo) in 1994. Patten, who played 91 games for the Tigers, Chargers, Rabbitohs and Dragons, stamped his claim as perhaps Rugby League's most prolific thespian with roles in the 1996 film *Dead Heart* and TV shows *G.P.* and *All Saints*.

3. Sean Garlick
A veteran of 160 games as a resourceful hooker and captain for South Sydney and Sydney City during the 1990s, Sean Garlick earned his big-screen stripes as a teenager and dabbled in acting during and after his Rugby League career. He was a lead in the 1985 thriller *Fortress* and appeared in *Watch the Shadows Dance* two years later. His later credits included guest spots in Australian soaps *Home and Away* and *Heartbreak High* during the first half of the '90s, and a TV comeback in *Rescue Special Ops* in 2010.

4. Ian Roberts
Equally well known for becoming the first Rugby League player to publicly reveal his homosexuality as for being one of the toughest and most talented forwards of the 1980s and '90s, Ian Roberts has carved out an impressive acting career in retirement. The former Souths, Manly and North Queensland enforcer, who played 13 Tests for Australia, graduated from the National Institute of Dramatic Art in 2003 and has chalked up a stack of film and TV credits in Australia and the US. The statuesque Roberts' most notable appearances include roles in feature films *Little Fish* (2005), *Superman Returns* (2006) and *Saltwater* (2012).

5. This Sporting Life
This Sporting Life was the 1963 film adaptation of the acclaimed book of the same name by David Storey, a former professional player in Britain who also wrote the screenplay for the movie. It depicts a fictional Rugby League player in the coalmining town of Wakefield, juxtaposing his prowess and brutality on the field with his romantic failings. The movie starred Richard Harris as the lead character, Frank Machin; William Hartnell gained his big break after playing talent scout 'Dad' Johnson and subsequently became the first eponymous lead in the *Doctor Who* television series. Although it flopped

commercially, *This Sporting Life* was lauded by critics and was rated the No.52 best film in the British Film Institute's greatest British films of all time in 1999.

6. Adam Fogerty

Fearsome front-rower Adam Fogerty, the son of former Great Britain Test forward Terry, found fame on the silver screen during and after his career with Halifax, St Helens and Warrington from 1991 to 1998. His most well-known role was as bare-knuckle boxer 'Gorgeous George' in the 2000 cult classic *Snatch*; he also appeared in a string of other films, and in TV series such as *Coronation Street*, *Emmerdale Farm*, *Hollyoaks* and *Heartbeat*.

7. The First Kangaroos

In 1988, a drama depicting the saga of the pioneering 1908-09 Kangaroo Tour of Britain was released. Entitled *The First Kangaroos*, the cast included British actor Dennis Waterman as ARL founding father James J. Giltinan and Dominic Sweeney as Dally Messenger. Premiership stars Andrew Ettingshausen and Wayne Pearce had minor roles, playing Kangaroos Albert Conlon and Sid 'Sandy' Pearce respectively. *The First Kangaroos* was generally well received; it currently boasts a 7 out of 10 rating on IMDb.

8. Keith Mason

Welsh Test prop Keith Mason, who played four games for the Melbourne Storm in 2002-03 and over 250 top-flight games in Britain, turned his hand to acting after a chance meeting with Mickey Rourke in a London bar after Mason played for Huddersfield in the 2009 Challenge Cup final. Mason scored a role alongside Rourke in the 2014 film *Skin Traffik*.

9. Footy Legends

Footy Legends, a movie released in 2006, stars well-known comedian Anh Do as a Vietnamese-Australian man with an obsession for Rugby League. Filmed and set in Sydney's western suburbs, *Footy Legends* also features cameos from former Test stars Brett Kenny, Bradley Clyde, Cliff Lyons and Rod Wishart. The film grossed over $500,000 at the Australian box office, and Anh Do was later a regular on the short-lived *Matthew Johns Show* on TV.

10. David Williams

Manly cult-hero winger David 'Wolfman' Williams earned rave reviews for his star turn in the short-film *Darkness Comes*, a finalist at the 2013 Tropfest film festival. The film depicts Williams as a desperate man battling his own demons; in something of a prophecy in reverse, it was released just two months after his nightmare performance in the Sea Eagles' Grand Final loss to the Roosters.

ICONIC FASHION ITEMS

1. Graeme Langlands' white boots
White boots—in fact, boots of all colours—are commonplace in the modern game, but in 1975 boots were black, and all black. That was until the '75 decider, when a sponsorship deal with Adidas saw St George fullback and future Immortal Graeme Langlands don a pair of white boots. He would later come to regret the fashion statement, however, when a pain-killing injection led to the worst game of his career—the white boots highlighted every mistake he made in a record Grand Final loss.

2. Dennis Manteit's bowler hat
The most famous story from the 1967-68 Kangaroo Tour came from a night out in the Yorkshire town of Ilkley when a session on the drink led to Australians leaving a "trail of carnage" behind them, with one player parading through town in nothing but a bowler hat. That player was long believed to be the Immortal Johnny Raper, but when chasing an Australian selection job in the 1980s he revealed the culprit to be Brisbane Brothers prop Denis Manteit.

3. Jack Gibson's fur coat
An eccentric and worldly man, coach Jack Gibson was not averse to making a fashion statement. Perhaps his most famous of these was his kangaroo fur coat, which was a regular on the sidelines, including during the 1983 Grand Final. The coat, thought lost on a plane, was actually given to his friend and British prop Harvey Howard.

4. Headgear
Protective headgear has never been overly popular in the guts-and-blood code of Rugby League, but it has been around for a long time and some players, such as legendary pointscoring centre Dave Brown, have made it their own. Brown lost all his hair in his late teens after contracting a virus, and began to don his distinctive headgear after his replacement hairpiece was thrown overboard en route to Britain for the 1933-34 Kangaroo Tour. He was wearing it when he set most of his scoring records, which still stand to this day. Other players renowned for wearing headgear include Jamie Soward, Steve Renouf, Steve Menzies, Johnathan Thurston, Darren Smith and Jonathan Docking.

5. Mal Meninga's armguard
Legendary centre Mal Meninga was one of the most fearsome players in the game throughout his career, but was kept sidelined in the late 1980s with a series of broken

arms—the first (and worst) of which occurred when his arm collided with a goalpost. To counter his failing arm over the latter part of his career he wore a huge padded arm guard that went from wrist to elbow—and used it to great effect, too, with many defenders feeling its impact.

6. Ewan McGrady's suit
A shy player from the small country town of Moree, Ewan McGrady struggled to adapt to Sydney life. After a blistering and brilliant year for the Bulldogs in 1991, he won the coveted Rothmans Medal. When he was nowhere to be seen on the presentation night, Bulldogs CEO Peter Moore and skipper Terry Lamb desperately tried to locate him, and eventually found him getting his hair cut. A police escort got McGrady there in time, looking very uncomfortable in a dinner suit with red tie and cummerbund that did not stand the test of time.

7. St George players' thigh pads
During the early 1990s, bulky gridiron-esque thigh-pad shorts, which were worn under regular footy shorts, briefly came into vogue. St George players were the foremost purveyors of the dubious fad, but the white-on-white pads and shorts failed to add any aesthetic pizazz to their dour, forward-oriented style of play. Tony Priddle, Michael Potter, Michael Beattie, Ian Herron and Jason Donnelly were the main perpetrators in this crime against Rugby League fashion.

8. Eye black
One of the fads of the 1980s, pushed by great coach and Americanophile Jack Gibson, was to smear black grease under the eyes to stop glare during night matches. It was used primarily in State of Origin matches, with the likes of Wayne Pearce and Peter Sterling donning it, but was out of fashion by the early 1990s and has never made a return.

9. Tape around the head
Electrical tape around the head has become something of a fashion statement for some burly front-rowers and forwards with long hair, with some using it to keep hair out of the eyes, others to keep their ears out of danger. A few notable types to regularly don the electrical tape include hard-running kamikazes Paul Sironen, Nathan Long, Martin Lang and Kerry Hemsley.

10. Socks down
The vast majority of players prefer to wear their socks pulled up, often held in place with tape, but a special few prefer the socks bunched around the ankles. In 2009, radio station Triple M named their 'Socks Down' team: Garry Jack, Ross Conlon, Steve Matai, Nigel Vagana, Jarryd Hayne, Olsen Filipana, Gary Freeman, Ellery Hanley, Geoff Robinson, Gavin Miller, Sam Backo, Max Krillich, Craig Salvatori.

ABOUT THE AUTHORS

NICK TEDESCHI

Nick Tedeschi is a lifelong Rugby League fan who has covered the game for nearly a decade. He is the author of the annual *Punters Guide to the NRL Season*, is a regular contributor to *The Guardian*, serves as Head of Editorial at William Hill Australia and authors the popular weekly column *From The Couch* at MakingTheNut.com. He believes that there is nothing greater in the world than The Greatest Game of All.

WILL EVANS

Will Evans was born in Southport, Queensland, in 1981, and was brought up in Tutukaka and Queenstown in New Zealand, where his obsession with the great game of Rugby League began. He is the author of the books *A Short History of Rugby League in Australia* and *A History of State of Origin*, and writes for *Rugby League Review* magazine, and The New Daily, Commentary Box Sports and Betfair websites.

ACKNOWLEDGMENTS

There have been many people who have helped with this book and we would like to thank them all, from those who edited the book and answered questions to those who assisted with their support and love.

The team at Slattery Media, as always, have been spectacular. This wasn't our first dance and it was as enjoyable as ever. Geoff Slattery and his team of superstars—Nancy Ianni, Bronwyn Wilkie, Courtney Nicholls—have all been such a treat to work with. We couldn't have done this without you guys.

To all those who answered our questions, both interesting and ridiculous, thanks—Ian Heads was a fantastic source; Ben Ikin as helpful as ever; and cheers to Rohan Kendall, Cliff Bingham, Nathan Boss, Chris Parkinson and the rest of the Fantasy Football League who continually helped when thrown a list topic.

And lastly, thank you to our wonderful partners, who have been in our corner and tolerated a lot as we buried ourselves in Rugby League history. To Louise Marshall and Ruth Evans our eternal gratitude for being so supportive and so loving.

ALSO BY WILL EVANS

*A History of State of Origin: The Complete
Reference to Rugby League's Greatest Rivalry—
New South Wales v Queensland Since 1980*

A Short History of Rugby League in Australia

ALSO BY NICK TEDESCHI

*Chasing Greatness: Words of Wisdom from
Rugby League Fans* (compiler)

The Rugby League Almanac 2012 (co-editor)

The Punters Guide to the 2012 NRL Season

The Punters Guide to the 2013 NRL Season

The Punters Guide to the 2014 NRL Season